Rebels and Lovers

Shakespeare's Young Heroes and Heroines

Rebels and Lovers

Shakespeare's Young Heroes and Heroines

A NEW APPROACH TO ACTING AND TEACHING

Alice Griffin

Professor of English

Director of Graduate Studies in English

Herbert H. Lehman College

The City University of New York

New York ● New York University Press ● *1976*

Copyright © 1976 by New York University

Library of Congress Catalog Card Number: 75-27102

ISBN (cloth): 0-8147-2959-2

ISBN (paper): 0-8147-2960-6

Library of Congress Cataloging in Publication Data

Griffin, Alice Sylvia Venezky, 1924-
  Rebels and lovers.

  Includes the texts of Shakespeare's King Henry IV,
part 1, A Midsummer Night's Dream, Romeo and Juliet, and
Hamlet.
  Includes bibliographical references.
  1. Shakespeare, William, 1564-1616—Criticism and
interpretation—Addresses, essays, lectures. 2. Youth
in literature. I. Shakespeare, William, 1564-1616.
Selected works. 1976. II. Title.
PR2759.G7   822.3'3   75-27102
ISBN 0-8147-2959-2
ISBN 0-8147-2960-6 pbk.

Manufactured in the United States of America

For Angela and Tony

CONTENTS

Introduction: Rebels and Lovers ix

Foreword: A New Approach to Acting and Reading xvii

A Midsummer Night's Dream
 Introduction 1
 Text and Glossary 13
 Textual Notes 78

Romeo and Juliet
 Introduction 79
 Text and Glossary 91
 Textual Notes 186

King Henry The Fourth Part I
 Introduction 187
 Text and Glossary 199
 Textual Notes 289

Hamlet
 Introduction 291
 Text and Glossary 303
 Textual Notes 425

INTRODUCTION

Rebels and Lovers
Shakespeare's Young Heroes and Heroines

> And then the lover,
> Sighing like furnace, with a woeful ballad
> Made to his mistress' eyebrow. Then a soldier,
> Full of strange oaths, and bearded like the pard,
> Jealous in honour, sudden and quick in quarrel,
> Seeking the bubble reputation
> Even in the cannon's mouth.
>
> *As You Like It* (II, vii, 147-153)

The Age of Youth in Shakespeare's plays is as distinct from the other ages of man as Jaques depicts it in *As You Like It*. Shakespeare's youth occupy a world of their own, withdrawn from the bustle of daily life associated with the school of the preceding age of childhood or the court of the subsequent age of maturity. In this world of youth, the chief inhabitant is occupied almost entirely with himself or herself, with seeking fulfillment through a goal which may be marriage or a career and "reputation."

The youth in Shakespeare's plays are young men and women from about thirteen (Juliet's age) to nineteen, pursuing a loved one with intent of marriage or pursuing a course of action with intent of achieving public recognition and approval. By the age of twenty, an Elizabethan was expected to be mature. Fifteen or sixteen was the average age for matriculation at Oxford, although some entered at thirteen. At a time when the life expectancy was so much shorter than at present, early maturity was taken for granted. Shakespeare married at eighteen and at twenty-one was the father of three children. He died a sick, old man (to judge from the shaky signature on his will a month before) on his fifty-second birthday.

As Shakespeare's young heroes and heroines share a common age group, so do they find themselves in similar situations. All of them have at least one parent who insists on maintaining the dominant hand in planning the future of the teen-aged child. Almost all of the rebellion on the part of the young lovers is against parents or other figures of authority who wish to thwart their child's marriage to a partner of his or her own choice. Lacking the power of their elders, the youth generally resort to secrecy and sometimes deception in their rebellions.

In *A Midsummer Night's Dream*, Hermia's father is determined that she will marry Demetrius, although she and Lysander are in love. They lament the obstacles placed in love's way by family and by circumstance:

> The course of true love never did run smooth;
> But either it was different in blood . . . .
> Or else misgraffed in respect of years . . . .
> Or else it stood upon the choice of friends [family] . . . .
> Or if there were a sympathy in choice,
> War, death, or sickness did lay siege to it . . . (I, i, 134-42)

Even though the penalty may be death not to accede to her parent's wishes, Hermia runs off with Lysander under cover of night. The pattern is similar in other comedies. Anne Page in *The Merry Wives of Windsor* rejects her parent's choice of marriage partners and with the help of ruse and disguise, elopes with Fenton. When the King of Bohemia objects to the union of his son Florizel with Perdita in *The Winter's Tale*, they elope to Sicilia, seeking refuge at the court of Leontes and posing as Bohemian emissaries of good will. In *The Merchant of Venice*, Shylock's daughter Jessica not only marries outside her faith against her father's wishes, but also steals his money and jewelry to finance her honeymoon. Some of the heroines, like Celia and Rosalind in *As You Like It*, make their own marriage arrangements without consulting their fathers; Miranda in *The Tempest* ignores a parental injunction and offers her beloved Ferdinand assistance in the arduous task set for him by Prospero. Yet despite their rebellion against parents, their secrecy, and their deception, these young lovers in the comedies win the marriage partners they have chosen, and seem destined to live happily ever after, in the tradition of comedy's original definition—a play that ends happily for those with whom we are in sympathy. All except Jessica are forgiven by their parents.

The less happy side of youthful rebellion is depicted by Shakespeare in the tragedies. Romeo and Juliet marry in secret, after Juliet deceives her mother and father to hide her love for the son of their family enemy. But fate, coincidence, and their own impetuosity defeat their hopes, as Juliet fears will happen:

> It is too rash, too unadvised, too sudden,
> Too like the lightning which doth cease to be,
> Ere one can say, 'It lightens.' (II, ii, 118-20)

Even though the only union they can attain is in death, Romeo and Juliet achieve positive good by their deaths—the ending of the families' feud. Arthur Brooke's poem of "Romeus and Juliet," which Shakespeare used as his source for the play, states that the lovers' sad fate is a punishment for rebelling against their parents and a warning to other young people who might do likewise. Shakespeare, however, chooses to omit this "moral" from his play. At the end, the Prince says that the parents' feud of hatred is being punished by the deaths of their children: "See what a scourge is laid upon your hate,/ That heaven finds means to kill your joys with love" (V, iii, 292-3).

Desdemona is another tragic figure who marries despite parental objection. Although Othello is middle-aged ("declined into the vale of years"), she is pictured as being quite young ("tender"), probably in her teens, and being actively courted by Venetian youths, "wealthy, curled darlings of our nation." Among them is Roderigo, whom Iago is duping of money supposedly for jewels to win Desdemona's favor. Throughout Othello's courtship and their elopement, she has deceived her father Brabantio, who is outraged when Iago breaks the news in the opening scene. Brabantio's bitter parting words to Othello will be recalled to the Moor later by Iago when he falsely accuses Desdemona of infidelity: "Look to her, Moor, if thou hast eyes to see:/ She has deceived her father, and may thee" (I, iii, 292-3).

Because of her youth and inexperience, Desdemona reacts overemotionally to the shocking charge of adultery. The more rational Emilia, who is obviously older and experienced in the ways of the world, correctly diagnoses Othello's puzzling behavior as jealousy and the cause as false rumor, spread by "some cogging, cozening" rogue. Someone with Emilia's toughness would have demanded the name of her supposed lover. But Desdemona is dazed and dream-like, "half asleep" as Othello berates her for falseness, having struck her in front of the Venetian envoys. It is not until just before Othello kills Desdemona that she asks for facts.

Emotionalism, generally to an excessive degree, is a characteristic all Shakespeare's young lovers would be expected to display. Sometimes their behavior is as extreme as that of the traditional courtly lover, including sleeplessness, suffering, weeping, and pouring the heart out in verse. Above all, the foremost image in thought and speech is the beloved, with whom the lover desires union on the physical, mental, and spiritual levels. The pattern is as true of all the lovers as it is of Romeo and Juliet. Beatrice and Benedick in *Much Ado About Nothing* may depart from the traditional mold and ridicule the conventional behavior of the courtly lover, but once each learns of the other's love, they are as moonstruck as any sonneteer. In *As You Like It*, Rosalind likewise satirizes the lover's emotional extremes, but in her moments alone with Celia, Rosalind is, quite humanly, as woeful as Corin is over Phoebe.

Although his young heroes and heroines are highly emotional, Shakespeare is careful to differentiate between the emotion of true love and that of infatuation, or "fancy," as it is described in song in *The Merchant of Venice:*

> Tell me where is fancy bred,
> Or in the heart, or in the head,
> How begot, how nourishèd?
> Reply, reply.
> It is engendered in the eyes,
> With gazing fed, and fancy dies,
> In the cradle where it lies:
>
> (III, ii, 63-9)

Infatuation or fancy in Shakespeare's plays is an excessive, brief attachment based purely on looks, as suggested by the application of the magic juice to the eyelids of Titania, Lysander and Demetrius that causes them to "dote." True love, on the other hand, does not depend on appearance, as Hermia points out: "Love looks not with the eyes, but with the mind" (I, i, 234). Desdemona speaks of her love for Othello in the same way when her father asks how she could marry a man Brabantio considers ugly: "I saw Othello's visage in his mind" (I, iii, 252), that is, his mind (and character), not his looks, are important to her.

Like good looks, infatuation is short lived. Orsino, infatuated with Olivia when we meet him in the opening of *Twelfth Night*, by the end of the play is planning to marry Viola (who has loved him throughout). The fact that Olivia does not return his love is another characteristic of infatuation or "fancy"—it is one-sided. Rosaline's disdain for Romeo is an indication that his feeling for her is infatuation, not love. Demetrius in *A Midsummer Night's Dream* originally loved Helena, then became infatuated with Hermia, and later (with the help of flower juice) returns to his earlier "natural taste" after "doting" on Hermia (IV, i, 167-73).

In the comedies the young heroes and heroines who are truly in love and destined for each other are united in the end of the play; often their marriage is celebrated in the closing scene with songs and dances, expressing the hope for children and a long, happy life together.

Hal in the *Henry IV - Henry V* trilogy, Cordelia in *King Lear*, and Hamlet are in the same age group as the characters mentioned above, and like them are either about to be married (Hal, Cordelia) or in love, a situation that could lead to marriage (Hamlet and Ophelia) but does not. While their relationship to love and marriage indicates their age, they are not primarily occupied with love, nor is their rebellion against obstacles to love. Hal and Cordelia are rebelling against conventions to which they feel they cannot conform. Hamlet's rebellion is against evil itself which only he recognizes, because it is posing as good.

The character of Prince Hal in *Henry IV Part I* and *Part II* is Shakespeare's fullest-length character study of a young man as he progresses from carefree youth to a position of highest responsibility. Shakespeare followed the histories of his day in depicting Hal, who was to become the "star of England," as a wild youth who suddenly reforms. However, Shakespeare makes the reformation believable by depicting Hal's behavior in the taverns and the robbery as his personal rebellion against the way his father believes the prince should prepare for the kingship. King Henry IV feels that Hal should remain at court and occupy a seat on the king's advisory council, a position Hal forfeits, because of his absences, to his younger brother. One reason Hal rebels against this type of training for himself is that he has inherited his father's talent for gauging public opinion. In the first scene in which we meet Hal, after jesting with Falstaff and the others, he tells us in soliloquy that his seemingly irresponsible behavior will lead the people to expect nothing from him, so that when he does become a good king, he will win more public approval and support than if they had impossibly high expectations of him:

My reformation, glitt'ring o'er my fault,
Shall show more goodly, and attract more eyes
Than that which hath no foil to set it off.

(I, ii, 193-5)

It is a good strategy, because Hal will need all the public support he can muster. Henry IV's claim to the crown is shaky; the uprising of the Percies (who originally put Henry on the throne), Glendower, and Mortimer threatens overthrow and division of England into three countries with themselves as rulers.

Having inherited as well his father's instinct for governing, Hal realizes that it is important to know his subjects in every station in life, not just those in the nobility. Henry IV confesses that he "stole all courtesy from heaven," went among the ordinary people, and won their hearts and loyalty away from the reigning King Richard II. Not needing to assume or "steal" courtesy, Hal is courteous by nature to everyone in all walks of life. He emerges from the vat room in the tavern and tells Poins that the young apprentices who draw the wine call him "the king of courtesy," and vow that when he is king, he will "command all the good lads in Eastcheap" (II, iv, 10-13). This incident helps convince us that Hal's way of training for the future is right for him. A minor reference in *Henry V* reminds us that Hal never loses his sympathy for the ordinary people, nor they their affection for him. When he is king, in his St. Crispin's Day speech, he describes himself and all the soldiers, not just the nobility, as a "band of brothers" and paints a picture only someone once familiar with tavern life could envision: the veterans of this battle in future years will celebrate the anniversary of the victory by standing their friends to rounds of drinks (IV, iii, 40 ff.).

For Hal, then, his rebellion is really a learning process on his own terms. The ideal education for a prince was the subject of many essays, sermons, poems, and pageants in Shakespeare's day. Counter to all the prevailing recommendations, Hal's ideas are unconventional, but they work for him. Hal proves successful; he defeats Hotspur, whose political rebellion is a parallel to Hal's personal rebellion. While Hal's affects only himself and proves beneficial, Hotspur's would destroy England. A self-centered youth, a "Mars in swaddling clothes," Hotspur lives for personal honor through fame on the field of battle. Like the soldier in Jaques' Ages of Man, Hotspur's behavior is excessive, "seeking the bubble reputation even in the cannon's mouth." But Hal recognizes the narrowness of such a point of view. In a gesture unheard of in the code of battle honor, which assigned the victor all the glory previously won by the vanquished, Hal magnanimously allows Falstaff to claim the victory over Hotspur. Because Hal has inner self-confidence, he can give away the outward glory.

Like Hal, Cordelia in *King Lear* rebels against established convention. All of the courtiers, especially her two sisters, flatter her father's vanity in the play's opening scene. She alone refuses. She will not make a flowery speech of love to gain the largest third of the kingdom Lear is dividing among his daughters. Rather than approve of Lear's misconception that material reward can buy love, she stands by her principles and utters the one word "nothing," when Lear asks what she can say to expatiate upon her love for him. Denunciation and disowning are her reward, which she accepts rather than compromise her beliefs. Later in the play, after Lear has suffered greatly, he realizes that she was right; the child instructing the parent is one of the many inversions in this tragedy.

Just as Hamlet is the most complete youth Shakespeare draws, so is his rebellion more complex than those observed so far. With the support of a single friend, Horatio, Hamlet fights alone against an entire kingdom. In the opening scenes, Hamlet reveals the same emotional extremes shared by other members of his age group. He is bitter against his mother because he feels she has betrayed his beloved dead father by marrying Claudius, whom Hamlet instinctively mistrusts. "O my prophetic soul," he utters to the ghost on hearing that the former King Hamlet has been murdered by his brother Claudius. After his encounter with the ghost, Hamlet's personal rebellion against his mother broadens to include political rebellion against the usurpation of the kingdom by a murderer. Like other youthful rebels, Hamlet lacks power and must employ deception against the corrupt authority of Claudius. Polonius and Ophelia believe Hamlet's assumed madness when he decides to "put an antic disposition on," but this does not deceive Claudius, an old hand at practicing deception, to which he owes his power and his position. Having murdered his own brother, assumed his crown, and married his wife, Claudius now sits smiling at the court and posing as a "loving father" to Hamlet and an able administrator for the country. Only Hamlet is undeceived. He knows that "one may smile, and smile, and be a villain."

Hamlet's mission is to carry out his personal and political duty of revenge by destroying Claudius, an act which will restore the kingdom of Denmark to honest rule. In order to achieve this defeat of an arch-pretender, Hamlet must learn to distinguish the "seeming" from the "being," the deception from the truth. Only by so doing can he prove the ghost, whose appearance is that of Hamlet's dead father, to be "honest," and Claudius, whose appearance is that of a good king and kind father, to be dishonest and guilty of murder. Developing this ability to make the right choice, to look behind the appearance for the reality, is also one of the primary concerns of Shakespeare's other youthful heroes and heroines, who must test appearances, advice, and platitudes, and as here, recognize falsehood disguised as truth.

Hamlet's rebellion is successful. Although he uses deception only as a tool against Claudius, and fails with his "antic disposition," the play *The Murder of Gonzago* fares better. Through it, he proves the ghost's honesty and Claudius' guilt. By defeating Claudius, Hamlet delivers the kingdom of Denmark from an evil ruler to a young man of action and achievement, as Hamlet might have been under other circumstances—Prince Fortinbras. But Hamlet and six others die too. In part, these deaths are due to two deceptions in which Hamlet fails to distinguish between actuality and "actions that a man might play." He does not kill Claudius when he seems to be praying because Hamlet believes the king is doing so, and Hamlet does not examine the swords to be used in the fencing match and spot the unbated (untipped) one, which Laertes will use to kill him.

Just before the fencing match, as Hamlet speaks with Horatio, he says that even though Claudius has "thrown out his angle" for Hamlet's life, he believes there will be enough time to defeat the king; Hamlet will accept whatever comes. Just as Providence guides the fall of a sparrow, says Hamlet, what matters is to be prepared: "the readiness is all." This rational acceptance suggests a new note of maturity. Hamlet is no longer undecided about his course of action. He has made his choice.

Hamlet has just returned from a voyage which he is describing as the final scene opens, and which may be, as in other plays, symbolic of the journey to maturity which we all make in life. So too when Romeo travels to Mantua, Hal to Shrewsbury, and the lovers through the woods of Athens, they acquire a new-found maturity. Their physical journey, then, represents an emotional and intellectual one as well. They arrive at the point of decision and base their decisions not on what someone else tells them to do, but on what they think is right for themselves. As in life itself, choosing what is right for oneself does not guarantee a happy ending—some of the young people end happily and others end tragically. But in their worlds they have lived vitally; in their quests they have used all their resources of mind and body and spirit, and whether or not they have succeeded by the world's standards, they are better in their own eyes and in ours for having made their journeys.

FOREWORD

This edition has two aims: to bring together four plays proved to be successful in introducing Shakespeare to the student reader and for that purpose, to provide the best possible text, glossary, and commentary. The texts themselves are at the same time the newest and the oldest, for they closely follow the four original good Quartos of these plays, the first authentic printed versions, published during Shakespeare's lifetime and based either on his own manuscript copy (which seems virtually certain in the case of *Hamlet* and *Romeo and Juliet*) or on the playhouse "fair copy" made from his manuscript.

Keeping in mind that Shakespeare wrote for the speaking voices of actors, his lines to be heard by the ear rather than seen by the eye, this editor believes that the original punctuation of the Quartos is a good guide to the interpretation of these lines. Compatible and contemporary with the poetry, this original punctuation indicates tone, stress, rhythm, and units of thought, and amplifies meanings. Modern investigation confirms that the Elizabethan typesetters set whatever they saw before them in manuscript—letters, words, punctuation marks, even Shakespeare's "false starts," where he begins a passage but changes the wording, with both versions being printed (See p. 186, V, iii, 102, 108). Even though proofreading was haphazard compared to modern practice, and errors were inevitable, we should not discard a punctuation system that is at least reliable and at best sensitive and helpful, in favor of a later system superimposed on the text only to conform with current grammatical rules.

Although modern textual scholars like R. B. McKerrow (*Prolegomena for the Oxford Shakespeare*) stress that except where there is obvious error, the punctuation should remain unaltered from the original, no classroom edition has yet appeared with the original punctuation restored. Instead we are using editions based either upon the Globe text, which is over a hundred years old and reflects in its heavy punctuation the histrionic stage delivery of the nineteenth century, or upon texts on which a modern grammatical punctuation system has been superimposed, for which there is no scholarly or artistic justification.

At the same time, classroom teaching is increasingly using oral interpretation, dramatization, and improvisation; hearing Shakespeare's lines spoken is an important adjunct to a study of the text. Fifteen years of classroom experimentation with the four texts printed here, working with students and with teachers of secondary-school and junior-college English, convinces this editor that the original system of punctuation employed by these texts is not only practicable but superior to those alien systems imposed upon Shakespear's plays. The original punctuation is an important key to the interpretation of the text, by defining blocks of thought as well as by indicating tempo and cadence.

We praise the flow of Shakespeare's lines, yet all of the punctuation systems of the last three centuries, substituted for the original, fragment his text into short sentences, destroying the flow and breaking down the thought. For instance, when Hamlet in his soliloquy mentions his plan to use the actors' play to trap his uncle into revealing his guilt, the Quarto punctuates the passage as follows:

> I'll have these players
> Play something like the murder of my father
> Before mine uncle, I'll observe his looks,
> I'll tent him to the quick, if a' do blench
> I know my course.   (II, ii, 569-73)

Yet one of the newest American editions makes four sentences of the passage. In the recording of the soliloquy by Sir John Gielgud, he instinctively reads it as the Quarto punctuates, briefly pausing at the commas and building up the tension to the full stop (and completion of the thought) at the word "course."

It was Sir John who first suggested to me in Stratford, England, that the Shakespearean actor should train himself to convey a large section of thought by sustaining it vocally throughout the passage until the stop which ends that thought. Good lungs, he said, are the first requisite for the Shakespearean actor. Five years later, at another Stratford, in Ontario, Canada, discussing existing texts of the plays with Dr. Tyrone Guthrie, I mentioned Sir John's idea. Agreeing, Dr. Guthrie, whose brilliant direction of the Shakespeare plays there launched the Ontario festival full-blown as a major contribution to modern Shakespearean production, added that the units of thought were more clearly defined in the original printed Quarto texts, which he felt could be more helpful than most theatre people realized. Why not use a text with the original punctuation, which had the advantage of being contemporary with the poetry? From that suggestion grew this volume.

The first noticeable effect of reading the lines with the original punctuation is that the tempo is faster; this old approach is also a "new" trend in modern Shakespearean production. (Compare Sir John's pace with the slow, studied approach of older recordings.) The pace is good because the punctuation is light—there is less of it. This means also that timing and stresses are less restricted for the vocal or visual reader (though the silent reader will profit from "hearing" the lines with the mind's ear). A comma demands a pause, but if the comma is absent, the reader is not obliged to pause.

What punctuation there is, does not necessarily follow modern grammatical rules for written English. In the Quartos, the punctuation is "rhetorical," for spoken English. One of the most important contributions of the Quarto punctuation is that it is careful and sensitive in the major passages, and an excellent guide in interpreting these lines.

A comma generally designates a short pause, a colon or semi-colon calls for a longer pause, and a period indicates a stop. Sometimes sentences are run together with commas, indicating that there is no longer pause until a colon, semicolon, or period is reached. The quotation from *Hamlet* above demonstrates how the thought is sustained over several lines with brief pauses until the full stop, marked by the period. The comma indicates not only pauses but stresses. The typical Quarto way to punctuate a vocative is either after the name or not at all, so that the name receives the stress: "And now Laertes what's the news with you?" (*Ham.*, I, ii, 42). To insert a comma before and after the name, as do almost all modern editions, is to chop up the line into four stresses, because to keep the rhythm, "news" is stressed as well. The Quarto punctuation calls for one or two stresses, on the name and at the end.

Just as periods and commas may not appear where expected according to modern rules of grammar, so they also may be inserted contrary to these rules, in order to designate excessive pauses or stops, as when Polonius forgets his instructions to Reynaldo and the lines stumble along with the old man's mind (II, i). This type of punctuation recurs in Polonius' speeches.

Another rhetorical use of the comma is to indicate antithesis or balance in two or more lines by a pause half-way in each line:

> Though yet of Hamlet our dear brother's death
> The memory be green, and that it us befitted
> To bear our hearts in grief, and our whole kingdom . . .

(I, ii, 1-3)

The comma after "grief," omitted in texts with modern punctuation, stresses the word, emphasizes its antithesis and alliteration with "green," and gives balance and rhythm to the statement. As these are Claudius' first words in the play, the sense of a studied, artificial utterance also is conveyed.

By using the exclamation point sparingly, the original texts indicate high points of emotion. In Hamlet's first soliloquy (I, ii, 129 ff.) the Quarto indicates one exclamation point rather than the twelve used in

the 1864 Globe edition or the fourteen in a recent American edition.
Teachers will agree that the over-use of the exclamation mark in modern
texts of Shakespeare's plays hampers classroom work in oral interpretation. These also give a false sense of hysteria to what might well be a
reflective passage.

For a humorous effect, there is careful mis-punctuation in the Quarto of
A Midsummer Night's Dream. The prologue to the Pyramus interlude in Act
V, as theatrically disastrous as the rest of this playlet, is punctuated to
indicate that the thought expressed is opposite to that intended. Here is
overwhelmingly convincing testimony that the original punctuation is to
be respected rather than rejected.

This new text corrects only obvious errors in punctuation (where
possible by reference to the First Folio of 1623) or substitutes Folio
punctuation where that of the Quarto is unclear. For a fuller treatment of
the original punctuation, the reader is referred to the substance of Percy
Simpson's *Shakespearian Punctuation* and to the remarks of later British
textual editors such as John Dover Wilson, C. J. Sisson and M. J. Ridley.

The wording of the texts is also that of the Quartos, with emendation
sparingly employed only where there is obvious error. Significant depar-
tures from the Quarto text are recorded in the textual notes, as are
alternate and familiar emendations. Passages found in the First Folio but
not in the good Quartos are incorporated with the text and designated in
the notes. Also noted are the Folio's omissions or "cuts" from the longer
Quarto text, these being of particular significance in the first acting
versions of the plays, on which the Folio is based. Spelling is modernized;
the notes indicate the old spelling where it suggests pronunciation which
might be useful. By designating the standard scene and act divisions
unobtrusively, this edition attempts to give a sense of the flow of scene
into scene, as found in the Quartos and in Elizabethan staging as well as in
the best modern productions of the plays. Nor is the text interrupted with
headnotes for settings; these are indicated in the first footnote to a scene.
As an editor's stage directions are inevitably more restrictive than in-
spiring, the stage directions given here are those found only in the original
Quarto and Folio versions. Additions to these, if necessary for clarity,
are enclosed in square brackets.

The extent and wording of the footnotes are a result of the editor's
experience in working with these plays in the classroom and in the theatre.
As misreadings rarely result when the definition is readily available, it
seemed preferable to err on the side of generosity and to place all definitions within easy reach, rather than to omit explanations that could be
found elsewhere if the reader troubled to look for them. It is hoped that the
glossary provides compactly, on the same page as the text, all the explanation necessary to understand that portion of the play.

In teaching students to remember the Elizabethan meanings of words and thus to save fifty percent of their time spent consulting the glossary, I found certain mnemonic aids useful; these have been applied in working out the definitions. Sound-alikes are used liberally, both with words that have undergone phonological development—"dearest" is glossed as "direst" in "Would I had met my dearest foe. . ." (*Ham.* I, ii, 182)—and those that have undergone semantic change: "continent" is glossed as "container" in "tomb enough and continent/To hide the slain" (IV, iv, 64-5). Semantically similar modern expressions are matched to those of the text: "muddied" is glossed as "stirred up" in "the people muddied" (IV, v, 78). Expressions from specialized areas are explained as well as defined: "out of frame" is glossed as "tottering (frame=builder's framework)" in "Our state to be . . . out of frame" (I, ii, 20). Difficult constructions and figures of speech also are explicated.

The introduction to each play is designed as a point of departure for further discussion. It offers an interpretation that reviews the plot while commenting on characters, themes, and styles, and concludes with factual information on the date, text and source of the play. The general introduction extends the book's theme to other plays by Shakespeare.

Most of my enthusiasm for this project I owe to my best students, whose intelligence and perception have been my most helpful guides in working with the texts and glosses in the classroom. I also owe a debt of gratitude to my colleagues in the English Department at Lehman (formerly Hunter) College, especially to Professor David Aivaz, for their suggestions for the introductory material. Professors Erica Garcia and Michael Paull kindly advised me on the linguistics of the glossary. My thanks are due to Hunter College for its financial assistance through the George N. Shuster Faculty Fellowship and Abbie and Nora Fund, which enabled me to undertake the textual research. The project could not have been completed without the financial support of the Axe-Houghton Foundation, to which my appreciation is gratefully acknowledged with the hope that the result may justify their generosity. I should like to thank the directors and staffs of the Bodleian Library, the British Museum and the Folger Shakespeare Library for their consideration and cooperation regarding my research on the texts, and the Lehman College librarians for their general assistance. My appreciation as well as my admiration is due to my proofreaders, Henrietta Leary, Janet Perkins, Pamela Polansky, and Dorothy Streett. My greatest debt is to my husband, John Griffin, for his invaluable encouragement and inestimable patience.

A MIDSUMMER NIGHTS DREAM

A play about love in a magical and moonlit setting, *A Midsummer Night's Dream* depicts a quartet of young people falling in and out of love, choosing and changing their partners, and finally getting married. With such a subject the theme is perhaps predictable: "The course of true love never did run smooth."

The main characters are two pairs of young lovers. Before the action begins, Demetrius and Helena love each other. When the play opens, Demetrius and Lysander both love Hermia, and Helena still loves Demetrius. In the middle of the play, in the moonlit, fairyland woods, Demetrius and Lysander both love Helena, while Hermia still loves Lysander. (Only the men change their affections; each girl is faithful to the same man she loves in the beginning.) By the end of the play, the original couples get married.

What makes this play an enjoyable and valuable comment on love is the imagination, as well as the insight and understanding, with which Shakespeare presents these young people and the other characters who compare and contrast to them: the mature couples, the supernatural creatures, and the earnest workmen who stage a play about love that was originally a tragedy but that turns out, unintentionally, a comedy.

The four lovers embody the characteristic hopes and frustrations of romantic love which leads to marriage; the secondary characters provide additional viewpoints. Theseus, the Duke of Athens, and his fiancée Hippolyta, Queen of the Spartans, are both mature; they have made their reputations in the world and are now approaching marriage. Their emotions are under the control of what Theseus calls "cool reason." The already-married pair are Oberon and Titania, rulers of fairyland. The view of marriage which they demonstrate is discouraging: self-love motivates their quarrel, which is literally of world-shaking proportions. Trying to patch up his own marriage, Oberon would also like to help the young lovers, but his good intentions are misdirected by his jester, the mischievous sprite-hobgoblin Puck or Robin Goodfellow. Lastly, love as it exists in legend is represented by the tragic pair Pyramus and Thisby; as they are depicted in a "tragicall comedy" staged by inept but well-meaning amateur actors, even the tragedies of love here become part of a happier whole.

Being young, Hermia, Helena, Demetrius and Lysander are enthusiastic, exuberant, and emotional, at times excessively so. But they also are developing in maturity, even though sometimes they make the right judgment and then take the wrong action. Hermia's and Lysander's behavior is extreme, but so is the situation they face. If she does not marry Demetrius, the man her father has chosen for her, the law of Athens rules that she must either become a nun or be put to death. When she and Lysander decide to elope instead, to cut themselves off from the life they knew and to journey through an unknown woods, Lysander consoles Hermia with the observation that they are not alone in suffering hardships for love:

> The course of true love never did run smooth;
> But either it was different in blood—
>   . . .
> Or else misgraffèd in respect of years—
>   . . .
> Or else it stood upon the choice of friends—[relatives]
>   . . .
> Or if there were a sympathy in choice,
> War, death, or sickness did lay siege to it;
> Making it momentany as a sound,
> Swift as a shadow, short as any dream,
> Brief as the lightning in the collied night,
> That, in a spleen, unfolds both heaven and earth;
> And ere a man hath power to say 'Behold,'
> The jaws of darkness do devour it up:
> So quick bright things come to confusion.   (I, i, 134-149)

Helena, who has been rejected by her former lover, Demetrius, is aware that "Love looks not with the eyes, but with the mind" (I, i, 234), that is, what the lover "sees" or responds to in his beloved is a matter of how she appears not to his eyes, but to his mind. However, even though Helena realizes this, she feels that she might recapture Demetrius' love if only she could look like Hermia, could "catch," Hermia's appearance, the way one "catches" a sickness. If she cannot look like Hermia, perhaps she can act like Hermia to regain Demetrius. Hermia says that these actions of hers are to discourage Demetrius, with curses, frowns and hatred. Far from acting this same way towards him, Helena pursues Demetrius, and lamenting "I am as ugly as a bear," continues to blame her looks for his cooled passion.

When Hermia learns that both men love Helena (unaware that they are

under the influence of Puck's magic potion), she, like Hermia, decides
there must be something wrong with her looks. It occurs to her that
Helena won the former suitors because of her height. Hermia, who is
short, rages at her one-time best friend for reminding the men of this:

> Now I perceive that she hath made compare
> Between our statures, she hath urged her height,
> And with her personage, her tall personage,
> Her height (forsooth) she hath prevailed with him.
> And are you grown so high in his esteem,
> Because I am so dwarfish and so low?
> How low am I, thou painted maypole? Speak:
> How low am I? I am not yet so low,
> But that my nails can reach unto thine eyes.
>   (III, ii, 290-298)

When love makes rivals of former friends, loyalty is forgotten as both
girls and men resort to physical violence. In this scene Helena and Hermia
are forcibly parted by the men; later, an invisible Puck keeps Demetrius
and Lysander, swords drawn, from killing or at least wounding each
other.

Although love makes the two couples behave emotionally and even
violently, it also gives them a special understanding (apprehension) that
may go beyond what reason can grasp. Theseus observes that lovers,
lunatics and poets share this quality of heightened sensitivity and imagination:

> Lovers and madmen have such seething brains,
> Such shaping fantasies, that apprehend
> More than cool reason ever comprehends.
> The lunatic, the lover, and the poet,
> Are of imagination all compact.   (V, i, 4-8)

The lovers' journey through the magic woods might be considered a
symbol of their progress from youth to adulthood. When they awaken
from their sleep at the end of the journey, they decide upon their future
married lives. In some of Shakespeare's other plays, the journey also
might be related to the maturing process. In Mantua, in the apothecary's
shop, Romeo, who a few scenes earlier was weeping on the floor of Friar
Lawrence's cell, shows strength, determination, and a recognition of the
bitter realities that are part of life. Hamlet returns from his interrupted
trip to England with a strong resolution and a realization that "the readiness is all."

Because the time scheme of the play is like that of a dream, the lovers seem to grow up overnight. As in a dream, the events seem convincing and realistic as they occur, even though so much happens in the course of a single night. Puck's magic love juices, which provide instant infatuation and instant recovery, may represent short-cuts to a solution that might have evolved anyway, given time. Time is the cure for infatuation; Puck's second flower that takes "error" away and recovers Lysander and Titania from their infatuations is a quicker, more dramatic way to the same result. The flower juice, accepted as one accepts all things in a dream, has its own logic.

When the lovers awake, they look back on the events of the previous night like a dream or like occurrences of long ago, as one might reflect upon an earlier period of life: "These things seem small and undistinguishable,/Like far-off mountains turned into clouds" (IV, i, 186-7).

Their behavior on awakening is reflective and serious as well as filled with wonder. Demetrius speaks of his infatuation for Hermia as "the remembrance of an idle gaud,/Which in my childhood I did dote upon" (IV, i, 166-7), a line suggesting that the arrival of true love heralds the end of childishness. If the past seems brief, far-off and dreamlike, the future appears long but not lonely: "These couples shall eternally be knit" in marriage, a "league whose date till death shall never end" (III, ii, 373).

The final scene celebrates their weddings and that of Theseus and Hippolyta. With the fairies singing and dancing, Oberon predicts: "So shall all the couples three/Ever true in loving be." (390-1) Marriage celebrations in Shakespeare's comedies invariably include references to future children. Here Oberon, blessing the marriage beds, predicts good luck for the children of the couples: "And the issue [children] there create/ Ever shall be fortunate." (388-9) At the same time, even a fairy's blessing is aware of reality, so that along with hopes for good fortune, there is a wish for healthy, well-formed children:

> And the blots of Nature's hand
> Shall not in their issue stand.
> Never mole, harelip, nor scar,
> Nor mark prodigious, such as are
> Despisèd in nativity,
> Shall upon their children be.   (V, i, 392-7)

In this last scene, Oberon and Titania are now reconciled. For the most part of the play their domestic wrangling suggests that marriage is a beginning as well as an end, and that neither does the course of married love always "run smooth." Their quarrel concerns the upbringing of an adopted child. Oberon, jealous of Titania's affection for the little orphan boy, wants him as an attendant. Selfishness is at the root of their disagreement; each is thinking not of the boy but of self. When we first meet them in Act II, they are arguing bitterly, each blaming the other for the upset in nature that reflects the upset of their marriage:

> Therefore the winds, piping to us in vain,
> As in revenge, have sucked up from the sea
> Contagious fogs: . . .
> The ox hath therefore stretched his yoke in vain,
> The ploughman lost his sweat, and the green corn
> Hath rotted, ere his youth attained a beard:
>
> . . .
>
> The spring, the summer,
> The chiding autumn, angry winter change
> Their wonted liveries: . . .   (II, i, 88-113)

As they are fairies, their differences are resolved by magic. Oberon uses enchanted love juice to cause Titania's infatuation with a monster — Bottom the weaver who has, through magic, assumed the head of a donkey. She relinquishes the boy to her husband, renounces Bottom when (influenced by a second fairy juice) she realizes the grossness of her infatuation, and is reunited with Oberon. Although the plot against Titania is devised by Oberon through spite, all works out well in the end.

Theseus and Oberon are the two rulers, one of Athens, one of fairyland. Unlike Oberon, Theseus is also capable of ruling himself. He represents "cool reason," which prevents him from accepting as reality the lovers' account of their strange woodland adventures: "I never may believe/These antick fables, nor these fairy toys" (V, i, 2-3). At the same time he realizes that to be ruled by reason is to lack the heightened imagination which the lunatic, the lover and the poet share. His love for Hippolyta is deep, but disciplined, although he complains of time dragging until their marriage: "O, methinks how slow/This old moon wanes." Hippolyta consoles him that in four days the new moon (whose appearance heralds their marriage) will appear "like to a silver bow/New-bent in heaven . . ." (I, i, 3-10) He is a benevolent ruler who will apply the justice of the law when he feels it is necessary, as in the first scene, but who will also relax the law, as he does when he permits Hermia to marry Lysander against her father's wishes. He is tolerant of his humblest subjects' endeavors to entertain him with the play of Pyramus and Thisby, no matter how badly acted. While the other spectators heap ridicule upon the effort,

Theseus remains indulgent. Afterwards, he compliments it: ". . . it would have been a fine tragedy; and so it is truly, and very notably discharged." (V, i, 343)

Although the story of Pyramus and Thisby resembles that of Romeo and Juliet, the legendary tragic children of feuding families, here the tragedy becomes "comicall" because of the ineptness of those who perform it, the Athenian workmen headed by Bottom the weaver. A comic version of the theme "the course of true love never did run smooth," the "interlude" offered as a wedding entertainment by Bottom and his friends epitomizes many an amateur dramatic presentation, from the choice of a work inappropriate both for the occasion and for the sparse talents of the performers, right through disastrous rehearsals with lines forgotten or misread, down to a performance marred by mispunctuation (that changes the meaning), misinterpretation, unintentional bawdiness, actors stepping out of character to talk with the audience, and over-playing of the serious to the point where it becomes comic.

Incongruity, the bringing together of the incompatible or seemingly incompatible (the demands of the playlet and the talents of the amateur actors) is one of the many humorous devices that make *A Midsummer Night's Dream* a favorite with audiences. There are jokes, puns, witty observations, physical farce, parody (the dialogue of the interlude parodies the "old style" plays characterized by alliteration, declamation, and forced rhyme), and of course the character of Bottom himself.

Nick Bottom is the first of Shakespeare's great comic characters, and one of the most memorable. He is inane, but his vitality excuses much. He exudes self-confidence, but he is not conceited, only enthusiastic. He is often wrong, but he is never discouraged. Nothing fazes him. Whether enacting a classic hero or wearing an ass's head, he is a model of composure. As the paramour of the Queen of the Fairies, he is the only mortal to enter her realm and may be the only mortal in all literature to survive such an affair without after-effects. Perfectly at home sharing the rule of fairyland, he is as gracious as is Theseus to subjects of the throne:

> Mounsieur Cobweb, good mounsieur, get you your weapons in your hand, and kill me a red-hipped humblebee on the top of a thistle: and good mounsieur, bring me the honey-bag. Do not fret yourself too much in the action, mounsieur; and good mounsieur have a care the honey-bag break not, I would be loath to have you overflowen with a honey-bag, signior.
> (IV, i, 10-16)

Although he has advanced his station in life, he does not change his tastes.

He prefers customary pleasures to sophisticated offerings: the tongs and bones to fairy music, and simple food to exotic. His milieu is limitless; he is the play's only character who moves, and it is an effortless move, from subplot to main plot, from city shops to woodland to fairyland to court, and in this way contributes to the unity as well as to the comic effect of the play.

Puck's contribution to the comic effects is mainly in the realm of farce or comic physical action, like the mix-up he causes by giving the love-juice to Lysander instead of Demetrius. He sees the turn-about in love, with both men now wooing Helena instead of Hermia, as an amusement for himself and for the King of the Fairies, to whom he is jester:

> Then will two at once woo one:
> That must needs be sport alone.
> And those things do best please me
> That befall prepost'rously.   (III, ii, 118-21)

A figure out of English folklore, Puck is sometimes called Robin Goodfellow, hobgoblin or "puck," who plays mischievous tricks on the unsuspecting. He meets a fairy who describes some of these pranks:

> Are not you he
> That frights the maidens of the villagery,
> Skim milk, and sometimes labour in the quern,
> And bootless make the breathless housewife churn,
> And sometime make the drink to bear no barm [head],
> Mislead night-wanderers, laughing at their harm?
> (II, i, 34-39)

In addition to the adult, life-sized king and queen of fairyland and to the boy-actor-sized Puck and attendant fairies, are the troupes of diminutive fairies who people the dialogue. They are Shakespeare's contribution to fairy lore, as pre-Shakespearean fairies were not the exquisite, tiny spirits who attend on Titania and on Queen Mab in Mercutio's speech in *Romeo and Juliet*. These little folk are created by imaginative description: ". . .all their elves for fear/ Creep into acorn cups, and hide them there"; "Some war with reremice [bats] for their leathren wings,/ To make my small elves coats. . ." (II, i, 30-31; ii, 4-5) The sense of diminution carries over to the fairies seen on stage, so that we are quite prepared to share Bottom's concern that Cobweb might be "overflowen with a honey bag" from a bee.

The magic woods which the fairies inhabit and through which the lovers travel, are created entirely by the dialogue. Played on a stage bare of scenery, *A Midsummer Night's Dream* relies on the words to establish an atmosphere of moonlight and magic. The landscape pictured in the dialogue is moonlit, both from the moon above and from its reflection in the water below. Lysander proposes that he and Hermia elope

> Tomorrow night, when Phoebe [the moon] doth behold
> Her silver visage in the wat'ry glass,
> Decking with liquid pearl the bladed grass. . .   (I, i, 209-11)

The same image of water drops turned pearl-like by the reflection of the moon, appears when the Fairy tells Puck at the beginning of the woodland scene: "I must go seek some dewdrops here,/ And hang a pearl in every cowslip's ear" (II, i, 14-15). Personified, the moon not only is part of the beautiful setting; it responds with anger or sadness to the action. Disturbed by the quarrel between Titania and Oberon, the moon upsets nature just as the rulers of fairyland upset their marriage:

> Therefore the moon, the governess of floods,
> Pale in her anger, washes all the air,
> That rheumatic diseases do abound.   (II, i, 103-5)

The images of and allusions to the moon combine the moon's natural function in relationship to the tides with its mythological personification as a goddess (Phoebe) to create an atmosphere of beauty, "a local habitation" (which Theseus says the poet's imagination gives to "airy nothing"). Thus the moon weeps to behold Titania's infatuation with Bottom: "The moon methinks looks with a wat'ry eye:/ And when she weeps, weeps every little flower . . .   (III, i, 182-3)

Other nature pictures contribute to evoke a setting that is realistic as well as magical. Oberon's description of Titania's resting place, for example, appeals to the senses of sight, smell, and hearing (evoked by assonance, repetition of the musical vowel sounds):

> I know a bank where the wild thyme blows,
> Where oxlips and the nodding violet grows,
> Quite over-canopied with luscious woodbine,
> With sweet musk-roses, and with eglantine:. . .
>   (II, i, 249-52)

One of Shakespeare's most interesting techniques is to give a double view, one comic and one serious, of the same event or character or even passage in a play. Hal's appearance before his father in *I Henry IV*, for example, is preceded by the comic version of this meeting, with Falstaff and then Hal playing the king. So the inadvertently humorous "tragicall comedy" of Pyramus and Thisby, staged in a "great chamber" (III, i, 54) to celebrate Duke Theseus' wedding might be considered a comic parody of *A Midsummer Night's Dream* itself, so far as the circumstances of presentation are concerned. For it is believed that the *Dream* was first performed as a wedding entertainment in the great hall of a palace, to celebrate a noble wedding, possibly that of William Stanley, Earl of Derby, to Elizabeth Vere, daughter of the Earl of Oxford, on January 26, 1595. The closing dances and songs of the fairies who bless the house and the newlyweds are also in the nature of a wedding entertainment, appropriate both for the characters watching it in the play and for the real newlyweds watching them.

When the lovers awaken from their night's adventures, Hermia says, "Methinks I see these things with parted eye, /When everything seems double," to which Demetrius replies:

> Are you sure
> That we are awake? It seems to me,
> That yet we sleep, we dream.   (IV, ii, 188-93)

The epilogue spoken by Puck at the very end of the play is the final bridge between audience and actors, and suggests that, just as actors are called "shadows", so we the audience, like the four lovers and Titania and Bottom, may have been dreaming the play:

> If we shadows have offended,
> Think but this, and all is mended,
> That you have but slumbered here,
> While these visions did appear.
> And this weak and idle theme,
> No more yielding but a dream . . .   (V, i, 406-11)

Date, Text, Sources

The First Quarto published in 1600 is the most authoritative, as it is closest to the date of composition, and probably was set from Shakespeare's own draft, released to the printer once a "fair copy" had been made for his acting company. The Second Quarto, printed in 1619 but dated 1600, served (with revisions) as the text for the First Folio of 1623. Q1 is followed here, with references to Q2 and F in the textual notes for significant readings or correction of omissions and obvious misprints.

As far as is known, there is no specific source for the general plot, although the names of some of the characters can be traced to various works. Theseus appears in Chaucer's *Knight's Tale* (source of *The Two Noble Kinsmen)* and in Plutarch's *Lives* (source of the Roman plays). Oberon's name seems to be derived from the French romance *Huon of Bordeaux*, where he appears as a dwarf fairy king, and from Spenser, where he is the father of Gloriana, the Faerie Queene. Titania's name is found in Ovid's *Metamorphoses* (applied to Diana and to Circe), which also tells the Pyramus and Thisby legend in Book IV. The date of composition is generally fixed as 1594-1595, for the wedding mentioned above. Another possible clue to the date of composition is Titania's description of the upset in the seasons (II, i, 88-117), which may refer to actual occurrences of unusually bad weather in 1594, with results like those described by Shakespeare. Following the play's presentation in the great hall of the palace where the wedding celebration took place, the *Dream*, as the First Quarto testifies, subsequently was "publickely acted" by Shakespeare's company, the Lord Chamberlain's Men.

A MIDSUMMER NIGHT'S DREAM

A MIDSUMMER NIGHT'S DREAM

THESEUS, *Duke of Athens*
EGEUS, *father of* HERMIA
LYSANDER, *beloved of* HERMIA
DEMETRIUS, *in love with* HERMIA, *favoured by* EGEUS
PHILOSTRATE, *Master of the Revels to* THESEUS

PETER QUINCE, *a carpenter* (PROLOGUE)*
NICK BOTTOM, *a weaver* (PYRAMUS)*
FRANCIS FLUTE, *a bellows-mender* (THISBY)*
TOM SNOUT, *a tinker* (WALL)*
SNUG, *a joiner* (LION)*
ROBIN STARVELING, *a tailor* (MOONSHINE)*

HIPPOLYTA, *Queen of the Amazons, betrothed to* THESEUS
HERMIA, *daughter of* EGEUS, *in love with* LYSANDER
HELENA, *in love with* DEMETRIUS

OBERON, *King of the Fairies*
TITANIA, *Queen of the Fairies*
PUCK, *or* ROBIN GOODFELLOW
PEASEBLOSSOM ⎫
COBWEB ⎬ *fairies*
MOTH ⎪
MUSTARDSEED ⎭

Other fairies attending OBERON *and* TITANIA. *Attendants on* THESEUS *and* HIPPOLYTA.

SCENE: *Athens, and a wood near by*]

*characters played in the interlude

Act One

[SCENE I.]

Enter THESEUS, HIPPOLYTA, [PHILOSTRATE,] *with others.*

THESEUS. Now fair Hippolyta, our nuptial hour
Draws on apace: four happy days bring in
Another moon: but O, methinks how slow
This old moon wanes! she lingers my desires,
Like to a stepdame or a dowager,   5
Long withering out a young man's revenue.

HIPPOLYTA. Four days will quickly steep themselves in night:
Four nights will quickly dream away the time:
And then the moon, like to a silver bow
New-bent in heaven, shall behold the night   10
Of our solemnities.

THESEUS.   Go Philostrate,
Stir up the Athenian youth to merriments,
Awake the pert and nimble spirit of mirth,
Turn melancholy forth to funerals:
The pale companion is not for our pomp.   15

[Exit PHILOSTRATE.]

Hippolyta, I wooed thee with my sword,
And won thy love doing thee injuries:
But I will wed thee in another key,
With pomp, with triumph, and with revelling.

Enter EGEUS *and his daughter* HERMIA,
LYSANDER *and* DEMETRIUS.

EGEUS. Happy be Theseus, our renownèd duke.   20
THESEUS. Thanks good Egeus: what's the news with thee?

I,i Athens. The palace of Theseus   s.d. **Theseus, Hippolyta** (Theseus, legendary Greek
hero, had defeated the Amazon Queen Hippolyta in battle, captured her, brought her to
Athens, and married her)   2 **apace** quickly   4 **lingers** delays the fulfillment of   5
dowager a widow with a 'dowage' (dowery rights) in her former husband's estate   6
withering out (1) depleting (2) growing withered (both the old dowager and the young man as
he ages)   6 **revenue** income   13 **pert** lively   15 **companion** fellow (contemptuous)   19
triumph public festival, military victory procession in ancient Rome   21 **Egeus**

EGEUS.   Full of vexation come I, with complaint
          Against my child, my daughter Hermia.
          Stand forth Demetrius. My noble lord,
          This man hath my consent to marry her.   25
          Stand forth Lysander. And my gracious duke,
          This man hath bewitched the bosom of my child.
          Thou, thou Lysander, thou hast given her rhymes,
          And interchanged love tokens with my child:
          Thou hast by moonlight at her window sung,   30
          With feigning voice, verses of feigning love,
          And stol'n the impression of her fantasy
          With bracelets of thy hair, rings, gauds, conceits,
          Knacks, trifles, nosegays, sweetmeats—messengers
          Of strong prevailment in unhardened youth.   35
          With cunning hast thou filched my daughter's heart,
          Turned her obedience, which is due to me,
          To stubborn harshness. And my gracious duke,
          Be it so she will not here before your grace
          Consent to marry with Demetrius,   40
          I beg the ancient privilege of Athens:
          As she is mine, I may dispose of her:
          Which shall be, either to this gentleman,
          Or to her death, according to our law
          Immediately provided in that case.   45
THESEUS. What say you, Hermia? Be advised, fair maid.
          To you your father should be as a god:
          One that composed your beauties: yea and one
          To whom you are but as a form in wax
          By him imprinted, and within his power   50
          To leave the figure, or disfigure it:
          Demetrius is a worthy gentleman.
HERMIA.   So is Lysander.
THESEUS.   In himself he is:
          But in this kind, wanting your father's voice,
          The other must be held the worthier.   55
HERMIA.   I would my father looked but with my eyes.
THESEUS. Rather your eyes must with his judgment look.

(trisyllabic)   27 **bosom** heart   31 **feigning** . . . **feigning** (1) deceptive (2) desirous ("fain-
ing"). . . false   32 **stol'n** . . . **fantasy** stealthily imprinted your image upon her fancy (first
of three metaphors on wax impressions; cf. ll. 35, 49)   33 **gauds** trinkets   **conceits** either
(a) love poetry, or (b) love tokens   34 **Knacks** knick-knacks   35 **unhardened** easily
impressed   39 **Be it so** if it be that   45 **Immediately** precisely   46 **Be advised** consider
carefully   51 **disfigure** destroy   54 **kind** nature (as a husband)   54 **wanting**
lacking   54 **voice** approval   60 **concern** befit   68 **Know** . . . **youth** ask yourself as a

HERMIA.   I do entreat your grace to pardon me.
           I know not by what power I am made bold,
           Nor how it may concern my modesty,   60
           In such a presence, here to plead my thoughts:
           But I beseech your grace that I may know
           The worst that may befall me in this case,
           If I refuse to wed Demetrius.

THESEUS.   Either to die the death, or to abjure   65
           For ever the society of men.
           Therefore fair Hermia, question your desires,
           Know of your youth, examine well your blood,
           Whether, if you yield not to your father's choice,
           You can endure the livery of a nun,   70
           For aye to be in shady cloister mewed,
           To live a barren sister all your life,
           Chanting faint hymns to the cold fruitless moon.
           Thrice blessèd they that master so their blood,
           To undergo such maiden pilgrimage: 75
           But earthlier happy is the rose distilled,
           Than that which, withering on the virgin thorn,
           Grows, lives, and dies, in single blessedness.

HERMIA.   So will I grow, so live, so die my lord,
           Ere I will yield my virgin patent up   80
           Unto his lordship, whose unwishèd yoke
           My soul consents not to give sovereignty.

THESEUS.   Take time to pause, and by the next moon,
           The sealing day betwixt my love and me,
           For everlasting bond of fellowship,   85
           Upon that day either prepare to die
           For disobedience to your father's will,
           Or else to wed Demetrius, as he would,
           Or on Diana's altar to protest
           For aye, austerity and single life.   90

DEMETRIUS.
           Relent, sweet Hermia, and Lysander, yield
           Thy crazèd title to my certain right.

LYSANDER. You have her father's love, Demetrius:
           Let me have Hermia's: do you marry him.

---

young person   68,74 **blood** passions   70 **livery** habit   71 **aye** ever   71 **mewed** shut
up   73 **fruitless** barren   73 **moon** (the moon goddess Diana represented unmarried
chastity)   75 **pilgrimage** journey through life   76 **earthlier happy** more happy on
earth   76 **distilled** i.e. into perfume (thus its essence is passed on, as to a child)   80 **virgin
patent** privilege of being a virgin   89 **protest** vow   92 **crazed** flawed

EGEUS.   Scornful Lysander, true, he hath my love: 95
          And what is mine, my love shall render him.
          And she is mine, and all my right of her
          I do estate unto Demetrius.

LYSANDER. I am, my lord, as well derived as he,
          As well possessed: my love is more than his: 100
          My fortunes every way as fairly ranked
          (If not with vantage) as Demetrius':
          And, which is more than all these boasts can be,
          I am beloved of beauteous Hermia.
          Why should not I then prosecute my right?   105
          Demetrius, I'll avouch it to his head,
          Made love to Nedar's daughter, Helena,
          And won her soul: and she, sweet lady, dotes,
          Devoutly dotes, dotes in idolatry,
          Upon this spotted and inconstant man.   110

THESEUS. I must confess that I have heard so much,
          And with Demetrius thought to have spoke thereof:
          But being over-full of self-affairs,
          My mind did lose it. But Demetrius come,
          And come Egeus, you shall go with me: 115
          I have some private schooling for you both.
          For you fair Hermia, look you arm yourself,
          To fit your fancies to your father's will;
          Or else the law of Athens yields you up
          (Which by no means we may extenuate)   120
          To death or to a vow of single life.
          Come my Hippolyta, what cheer my love?
          Demetrius and Egeus, go along:
          I must employ you in some business
          Against our nuptial, and confer with you   125
          Of something nearly that concerns yourselves.

EGEUS.   With duty and desire we follow you.

          Exeunt. Manent LYSANDER *and* HERMIA.

LYSANDER. How now my love? Why is your cheek so pale?
          How chance the roses there do fade so fast?

HERMIA.   Belike for want of rain, which I could well   130

---

98 **estate**
transfer   99 **well derived** well born   100 **well possessed** wealthy   101 **fairly ranked**
equal in rank   102 **with vantage,** as better, than   106 **avouch . . . head** prove it to his
face   110 **spotted** stained (by betrayal of Helena)   116 **schooling** advice   117 **arm**
fortify   120 **extenuate** alleviate, lessen   125 **Against** in preparation for   126 **nearly**
closely   130 **Belike** likely   131 **Beteem** (1) pour out on (2) allow   **tempest** storm (of

Beteem them from the tempest of my eyes.

LYSANDER. Ay me, for aught that I could ever read,
Could ever hear by tale or history,
The course of true love never did run smooth;
But either it was different in blood—   135

HERMIA. O cross! too high to be enthralled to low.

LYSANDER. Or else misgraffèd in respect of years—

HERMIA. O spite! too old to be engaged to young.

LYSANDER. Or else it stood upon the choice of friends—

HERMIA. O hell! to choose love by another's eyes.   140

LYSANDER. Or if there were a sympathy in choice,
War, death, or sickness did lay siege to it;
Making it momentany as a sound,
Swift as a shadow, short as any dream,
Brief as the lightning in the collied night,   145
That, in a spleen, unfolds both heaven and earth;
And ere a man hath power to say 'Behold,'
The jaws of darkness do devour it up:
So quick bright things come to confusion.

HERMIA. If then true lovers have been ever crossed,   150
It stands as an edìct in destiny:
Then let us teach our trial patience,
Because it is a customary cross,
As due to love as thoughts and dreams and sighs,
Wishes and tears; poor Fancy's followers.   155

LYSANDER. A good persuasion: therefore hear me, Hermia:
I have a widow aunt, a dowager,
Of great revenue, and she hath no child:
From Athens is her house remote seven leagues,
And she respects me as her only son: 160
There gentle Hermia, may I marry thee,
And to that place the sharp Athenian law
Cannot pursue us. If thou lov'st me then,
Steal forth thy father's house tomorrow night:
And in the wood, a league without the town,   165
Where I did meet thee once with Helena

---

tears)   135   **blood**   birth,   social   rank   136   **cross**   frustration   **high**
highborn   **enthralled to low** made a slave to one of low birth   137 **misgraffed** badly
joined   139 **stood** depended   **friends** relatives   143 **momentany** momentary   145
collied black as coal   146 **in a spleen** impulsively, in a sudden outburst   149 **confusion**
destruction   150 **ever crossed** evermore thwarted   152 **teach. . .patience** teach ourselves fortitude to endure our trial   154 **As due to** as much a part of   **thoughts** melancholy
brooding   155 **Fancy** love (sometimes infatuation or fancied love)   160 **respects**
regards   165 **without** outside

To do observance to a morn of May,
There will I stay for thee.

HERMIA.   My good Lysander,
I swear to thee, by Cupid's strongest bow,
By his best arrow, with the golden head,   170
By the simplicity of Venus' doves,
By that which knitteth souls and prospers loves,
And by that fire which burned the Carthage queen,
When the false Troyan under sail was seen,
By all the vows that ever men have broke,   175
(In number more than ever women spoke)
In that same place thou hast appointed me,
Tomorrow truly will I meet with thee.

LYSANDER. Keep promise love: look, here comes Helena.

Enter HELENA.

HERMIA.   God speed fair Helena: whither away?   180
HELENA.   Call you me fair? That fair again unsay.
Demetrius loves your fair: O happy fair!
Your eyes are lodestars, and your tongue's sweet air
More tuneable than lark to shepherd's ear,
When wheat is green, when hawthorn buds appear.   185
Sickness is catching: O were favour so,
Yours would I catch, fair Hermia, ere I go,
My ear should catch your voice, my eye your eye,
My tongue should catch your tongue's sweet melody.
Were the world mine, Demetrius being bated,   190
The rest I'ld give to be to you translated.
O teach me how you look, and with what art
You sway the motion of Demetrius' heart.

HERMIA.   I frown upon him; yet he loves me still.
HELENA.   O that your frowns would teach my smiles such skill. 195
HERMIA.   I give him curses; yet he gives me love.

---

167 **do . . . May** celebrate May Day   168 **stay**
wait   170 **golden head** (The arrow with the gold head causes love; the lead-tipped one
causes hate)   171 **simplicity** harmlessness   **doves** (which drew Venus' chariot)   172
that . . . loves the girdle of Venus, giving the wearer the power to arouse love   173–4
Carthage Queen . . . false Troyan Dido, who burned herself to death on a funeral pyre
when Trojan Aeneas deserted her   182 **your fair** i.e. beauty (Helena being fair and Hermia
dark)   **happy** fortunate   183 **lodestars** guiding stars   184 **tuneable** tuneful   **When
. . . appear** i.e. in the spring   186 **favour** appearance   187 **Yours would**
(Hamner and others emend from "your words," poss. correct; "words" is the first of
three attributes Helena would like to catch, all dealing with speaking)   **catch** should
catch   188 **My ear . . . voice** my ear should catch the tone of your voice   **my eye your
eye** my eye should catch the way you glance   190 **bated** subtracted, excepted   191
translated transformed   193 **sway** rule   201 **your beauty** the fault of your beauty   206

HELENA.   O that my prayers could such affection move.
HERMIA.   The more I hate, the more he follows me.
HELENA.   The more I love, the more he hateth me.
HERMIA.   His folly, Helena, is no fault of mine.   200
HELENA.   None but your beauty; would that fault were mine.
HERMIA.   Take comfort: he no more shall see my face:
            Lysander and myself will fly this place.
            Before the time I did Lysander see,
            Seemed Athens as a paradise to me: 205
            O then, what graces in my love do dwell,
            That he hath turned a heaven unto a hell!
LYSANDER.   Helen, to you our minds we will unfold:
            Tomorrow night, when Phoebe doth behold
            Her silver visage in the wat'ry glass,   210
            Decking with liquid pearl the bladed grass
            (A time that lovers' flights doth still conceal)
            Through Athens gates have we devised to steal.
HERMIA.   And in the wood, where often you and I
            Upon faint primrose beds were wont to lie,   215
            Emptying our bosoms of their counsel sweet,
            There my Lysander and myself shall meet,
            And thence from Athens turn away our eyes,
            To seek new friends and stranger companies.
            Farewell, sweet playfellow: pray thou for us: 220
            And good luck grant thee thy Demetrius.
            Keep word Lysander: we must starve our sight
            From lovers' food, till morrow deep midnight.
LYSANDER.   I will my Hermia.   *Exit* HERMIA.
                      Helena adieu:
            As you on him, Demetrius dote on you.   225

                                            Exit LYSANDER.

HELENA.   How happy some, o'er other some, can be!
            Through Athens I am thought as fair as she.
            But what of that? Demetrius thinks not so:
            He will not know what all but he do know.
            And as he errs, doting on Hermia's eyes,   230
            So I, admiring of his qualities.
            Things base and vile, holding no quantity,

---

love loved one   209 **Phoebe** Diana, the moon   210 **wat'ry glass** mirror of the
water   212 **still** always   216 **counsel** secrets   219 **stranger companies** the companionship of strangers   223 **lovers' food** the sight of the loved one   232 **holding no quantity** out

Love can transpose to form and dignity.
Love looks not with the eyes, but with the mind:
And therefore is winged Cupid painted blind.   235
Nor hath Love's mind of any judgment taste:
Wings, and no eyes, figure unheedy haste.
And therefore is Love said to be a child:
Because in choice he is so oft beguiled.
As waggish boys in game themselves forswear: 240
So the boy Love is perjured everywhere.
For ere Demetrius looked on Hermia's eyne,
He hailed down oaths that he was only mine.
And when this hail some heat from Hermia felt,
So he dissolved, and show'rs of oaths did melt.   245
I will go tell him of fair Hermia's flight:
Then to the wood will he tomorrow night
Pursue her: and for this intelligence,
If I have thanks, it is a dear expense:
But herein mean I to enrich my pain,   250
To have his sight thither and back again.   *Exit.*

[SCENE II.]

Enter QUINCE *the Carpenter; and* SNUG *the Joiner;
and* BOTTOM *the Weaver; and* FLUTE *the Bellows-mender;
and* SNOUT *the Tinker; and* STARVELING *the Tailor.*

QUINCE.   Is all our company here?
BOTTOM.   You were the best to call them generally, man by man, ac-
            cording to the scrip.
QUINCE.   Here is the scroll of every man's name which is thought
            fit, through all Athens, to play in our interlude before   5
            the duke and the duchess, on his wedding-day at night.
BOTTOM.   First good Peter Quince, say what the play treats on,

---

of proportion   236 **taste** a touch   237 **figure** symbolize   240 **game** sport   242 **eyne**
eyes   248 **intelligence** information   249 **dear expense** costly outlay (on Demetrius'
part)   250-1 **But . . . sight** but I will be rewarded (if not by him) just by the sight of him.
    I,ii Quince's house s.d. (Wilson observes that their names describe their work: **Quince**
quoins, wooden wedges used in building   **Snug** fitting snugly, suiting a joiner of furniture
(carpenter)   **Bottom** bobbin or core on which yarn is wound (and the ball of yarn
itself)   **Flute** mender of fluted church organs and bellows   **Snout** spout (of the kettles he
mends)   **Starveling** (tailors being traditionally thin)   2 **generally** (Bottom, who often
mistakes the word, means the opposite: "severally, one-by-one")   5 **interlude** short play
originally performed during intervals of festivities such as state dinners   8 **grow . . . point**

then read the names of the actors: and so grow to a point.

QUINCE. Marry, our play is 'The most lamentable comedy, and
most cruel death of Pyramus and Thisby.'   10

BOTTOM. A very good piece of work I assure you, and a merry. Now
good Peter Quince, call forth your actors by the scroll.
Masters, spread yourselves.

QUINCE. Answer as I call you. Nick Bottom the weaver?

BOTTOM. Ready: name what part I am for, and proceed.   15

QUINCE. You, Nick Bottom, are set down for Pyramus.

BOTTOM. What is Pyramus? A lover, or a tyrant?

QUINCE. A lover that kills himself, most gallant, for love.

BOTTOM. That will ask some tears in the true performing of it. If I
do it, let the audience look to their eyes: I will move   20
storms: I will condole in some measure. To the rest—
yet my chief humour is for a tyrant. I could play Ercles
rarely, or a part to tear a cat in, to make all split.

> The raging rocks
> And shivering shocks,   25
> Shall break the locks
>   Of prison gates,
> And Phibbus' car
> Shall shine from far,
> And make and mar   30
>   The foolish Fates.

This was lofty. Now name the rest of the players. This is
Ercles' vein, a tyrant's vein: a lover is more condoling.

QUINCE. Francis Flute, the bellows-mender?

FLUTE. Here Peter Quince.   35

QUINCE. Flute, you must take Thisby on you.

FLUTE. What is Thisby? A wand'ring knight?

QUINCE. It is the lady that Pyramus must love.

FLUTE. Nay faith, let not me play a woman: I have a beard
coming.   40

QUINCE. That's all one: you shall play it in a mask, and you may
speak as small as you will.

BOTTOM. And I may hide my face, let me play Thisby too: I'll speak

---

either (a) come to the conclusion, or (b) get to the point   9 **Marry** indeed (mild oath,
corruption of "by the Virgin Mary")   21 **storms** i.e. of tears   **condole** lament   22
humour inclination   **Ercles** Hercules (typified by ranting as in Seneca's *Hercules
Furens*)   23 **tear . . . split** (terms for ranting and raging on the stage)   24–31 **the raging
. . . Fates** (a parody of the style of earlier English translations of Seneca)   28 **Phibbus'**
Phoebus Apollo   **car** chariot   37 **wand'ring knight** knight-errant (another favorite
character, like the tyrant)   41 **That's all one** never mind   43 **And if**

in a monstrous little voice; 'Thisne, Thisne,' 'Ah
Pyramus, my lover dear, thy Thisby dear, and lady   45
dear.'

QUINCE.   No, no, you must play Pyramus: and Flute, you Thisby.

BOTTOM.   Well, proceed.

QUINCE.   Robin Starveling, the tailor?

STARVELING.
           Here Peter Quince.   50

QUINCE.   Robin Starveling, you must play Thisby's mother. Tom
           Snout, the tinker?

SNOUT.   Here Peter Quince.

QUINCE.   You, Pyramus' father; myself, Thisby's father; Snug the
           joiner, you the lion's part: and I hope here is a play   55
           fitted.

SNUG.   Have you the lion's part written? Pray you, if it be, give
           it me: for I am slow of study.

QUINCE.   You may do it extempore: for it is nothing but roaring.

BOTTOM.   Let me play the lion' too. I will roar, that I will do any   60
           man's heart good to hear me. I will roar, that I will make
           the duke say 'Let him roar again: let him roar again.'

QUINCE.   And you should do it too terribly, you would fright the
           duchess and the ladies, that they would shriek: and
           that were enough to hang us all.   65

ALL.   That would hang us, every mother's son.

BOTTOM.   I grant you, friends, if you should fright the ladies out of
           their wits, they would have no more discretion but to
           hang us: but I will aggravate my voice so, that I will roar
           you as gently as any sucking dove: I will roar you and   70
           'twere any nightingale.

QUINCE.   You can play no part but Pyramus: for Pyramus is a
           sweet-faced man; a proper man as one shall see in a
           summer's day; a most lovely gentleman-like man: there-
           fore you must needs play Pyramus.   75

BOTTOM.   Well: I will undertake it. What beard were I best to play
           it in?

QUINCE.   Why, what you will.

BOTTOM.   I will discharge it in either your straw-colour beard, your
           orange-tawny beard, your purple-in-grain beard, or your   80
           French-crown-colour beard, your perfit yellow.

---

56 **fitted** cast
(actors fitted to the parts; also a pun on Snug's profession)   60 **that** so that   69 **aggravate**
(he means "moderate")   70 **sucking** (in the sense of "nestling")   **and 'twere** as if it
were   73 **proper** handsome   80 **purple-in-grain** dyed purple by cochineal ("grain"),

QUINCE.   Some of your French crowns have no hair at all; and
then you will play barefaced. But masters here are your
parts, and I am to entreat you, request you, and desire
you, to con them by tomorrow night: and meet me in the   85
palace wood, a mile without the town, by moonlight;
there will we rehearse: for if we meet in the city, we
shall be dogged with company, and our devices known.
In the meantime, I will draw a bill of properties, such
as our play wants. I pray you fail me not.   90

BOTTOM.   We will meet, and there we may rehearse most obscenely
and courageously. Take pain, be perfit: adieu.

QUINCE.   At the duke's oak we meet.

BOTTOM.   Enough: hold, or cut bow-strings.   *Exeunt.*

Act Two

[SCENE I.]

Enter a FAIRY *at one door, and* ROBIN GOODFELLOW [PUCK] *at
another.*

PUCK.   How now spirit, whither wander you?

FAIRY.   Over hill, over dale,
          Thorough bush, thorough brier,
          Over park, over pale,
          Thorough flood, thorough fire: 5
          I do wander everywhere,
          Swifter than the moon's sphere:
          And I serve the Fairy Queen,
          To dew her orbs upon the green.
          The cowslips tall her pensioners be,   10
          In their gold coats, spots you see:
          Those be rubies, fairy favours:

bodies of the dried *coccus* insect; ("in grain" also = permanent, fast color)   81 **French-
crown-colour** golden, like French crowns (gold coins)   82 **French crowns** bald heads
believed to be caused by syphilis, the "French" disease   85 **con** learn by heart   88
devices plans   89 **bill of properties** list of stage props   91 **obscenely** (he may mean
"fittingly," or "obscurely," or connected with "scene" in the word, "dramatically")   94
hold, or cut bow-strings (fr. archery, meaning uncertain, but equivalent to "fish, or cut bait")

II,i A wood near Athens   4 **pale** enclosure   9 **dew** bedew   9 **orbs** fairy rings (circles
of high grass)   10 **cowslips** primroses   **pensioners** royal bodyguards   12 **favours**

In those freckles live their savours.
I must go seek some dewdrops here,
And hang a pearl in every cowslip's ear.   15
Farewell thou lob of spirits: I'll be gone,
Our queen and all her elves come here anon.

PUCK.   The king doth keep his revels here tonight.
Take heed the queen come not within his sight.
For Oberon is passing fell and wrath,   20
Because that she, as her attendant, hath
A lovely boy, stol'n from an Indian king:
She never had so sweet a changeling.
And jealous Oberon would have the child
Knight of his train, to trace the forests wild.   25
But she, perforce, withholds the lovèd boy,
Crowns him with flowers, and makes him all her joy.
And now, they never meet in grove or green,
By fountain clear, or spangled starlight sheen,
But they do square, that all their elves for fear   30
Creep into acorn cups, and hide them there.

FAIRY.   Either I mistake your shape and making quite,
Or else you are that shrewd and knavish sprite
Called Robin Goodfellow. Are not you he
That frights the maidens of the villagery,   35
Skim milk, and sometimes labour in the quern,
And bootless make the breathless housewife churn,
And sometime make the drink to bear no barm,
Mislead night-wanderers, laughing at their harm?
Those that Hobgoblin call you, and sweet Puck,   40
You do their work, and they shall have good luck.
Are not you he?

PUCK.   Thou speakest aright;
I am that merry wanderer of the night.
I jest to Oberon, and make him smile,
When I a fat and bean-fed horse beguile,   45
Neighing in likeness of a filly foal;
And sometime lurk I in a gossip's bowl,

---

tokens of favor   13 **savours** perfumes   15 **pearl** dewdrop (additional jewels as "favours"
for the pensioners)   **ear** (Elizabethan men wore jewels in their ears)   16 **lob** lout,
lubber   20 **passing fell** surpassingly fierce   23 **changeling** creature exchanged by fairies
for a stolen baby (among the fairies, the stolen child)   25 **trace** traverse   26 **perforce** by
force   30 **square** quarrel   **that** so that   33 **shrewd** mischievous   36 **Skim milk** steals
the cream off the milk   **quern** handmill for grinding grain (which work Robin might help
or hinder)   37 **bootless** without result   38 **barm** foamy head (therefore the drink was
flat)   41 **You ... work** (when not being mischievous, Robin helped)   47 **gossip** old

In very likeness of a roasted crab,
And when she drinks, against her lips I bob,
And on her withered dewlap pour the ale.   50
The wisest aunt, telling the saddest tale,
Sometime for three-foot stool mistaketh me:
Then slip I from her bum, down topples she,
And 'tailor' cries, and falls into a cough;
And then the whole quire hold their hips and laugh,   55
And waxen in their mirth, and neeze, and swear
A merrier hour was never wasted there.
But room fairy: here comes Oberon.

FAIRY.   And here, my mistress. Would that he were gone.

> *Enter* [OBERON] *the* KING OF FAIRIES, *at one*
> *door with his* TRAIN; *and the* QUEEN
> [TITANIA], *at another, with hers.*

OBERON.   Ill met by moonlight, proud Titania.   60
QUEEN.   What, jealous Oberon? Fairy, skip hence.
          I have forsworn his bed and company.
OBERON.   Tarry, rash wanton. Am not I thy lord?
QUEEN.   Then I must be thy lady: but I know
          When thou has stol'n away from fairyland,   65
          And in the shape of Corin sat all day,
          Playing on pipes of corn, and versing love
          To amorous Phillida. Why are thou here
          Come from the farthest steep of India?
          But that, forsooth, the bouncing Amazon,   70
          Your buskined mistress and your warrior love,
          To Theseus must be wedded; and you come,
          To give their bed joy and prosperity.
OBERON.   How canst thou thus, for shame, Titania,
          Glance at my credit with Hippolyta,   75
          Knowing I know thy love to Theseus?
          Didst thou not lead him through the glimmering night,
          From Perigenia, whom he ravishèd?

---

dame, crony (lit. sponsor or godparent)   48 **crab** crabapple (often put into ale)   50
dewlap loose skin hanging about the throat   51 **aunt** old lady   54 **'tailor'** (variously
explained: perhaps the squatting position of the tailor, or "tailard" = one with a tail)   55
quire choir, group   55 **laugh** (Q spells "loffe," indicating its pronunciation to rhyme with
cough, sp. "coffe")   56 **waxen** increase   56 **neeze** sneeze   57 **wasted** spent   58 **room**
make room   60 **Ill met** a poor occasion for meeting   63 **Tarry, rash wanton** wait,
headstrong one   64 **lady** wife   66,68 **Corin, Phillida** (traditional names in pastoral
literature for a shepherd and his loved one, respectively)   67 **corn** wheat or oak
straws   69 **steep** mountains   70 **Amazon** Hippolyta   71 **buskined** wearing boots   75
Glance . . . credit with hint at my favors from   78–80 **Perigenia . . . Antiopa** (Plutarch's

And make him with fair Ægles break his faith,
With Ariadne, and Antiopa?   80

QUEEN.   These are the forgeries of jealousy:
And never, since the middle summer's spring,
Met we on hill, in dale, forest, or mead,
By pavèd fountain, or by rushy brook,
Or in the beachèd margent of the sea,   85
To dance our ringlets to the whistling wind,
But with thy brawls thou hast disturbed our sport.
Therefore the winds, piping to us in vain,
As in revenge, have sucked up from the sea
Contagious fogs: which falling in the land,   90
Hath every pelting river made so proud,
That they have overborne their continents.
The ox hath therefore stretched his yoke in vain,
The ploughman lost his sweat, and the green corn
Hath rotted, ere his youth attained a beard: 95
The fold stands empty in the drownèd field,
And crows are fatted with the murrion flock.
The nine men's morris is filled up with mud:
And the quaint mazes in the wanton green,
For lack of tread, are undistinguishable.   100
The human mortals want their winter here,
No night is now with hymn or carol blest;
Therefore the moon, the governess of floods,
Pale in her anger, washes all the air,
That rheumatic diseases do abound.   105
And thorough this distemperature, we see
The seasons alter: hoary-headed frosts
Fall in the fresh lap of the crimson rose,

"Life of Theseus" ascribes to him these love affairs. He seduced Perigouna (North's spelling), was beloved of Aegles, a nymph whom he left for another, and was assisted by Ariadne in threading the labyrinth and killing the Minotaur. Antiopa = Hippolyta)   82 **middle . . . spring** beginning of midsummer   84 **paved** with a pebbly bottom   85 **in** on   **margent** margin, shore   86 **ringlets** rings or round dances   88–117 **Therefore . . . original** (the disturbance in nature reflects the discord between Oberon and Titania. Some find here a reference to the abnormally bad weather in the summer of 1594)   88 **piping** blowing (music)   90 **Contagious** spreading pestilence   91 **pelting** paltry   92 **overborne their continents** overflown the banks which contain them   94 **corn** grain   95 **beard** the tassels on ripened grain   96 **fold** enclosure for livestock   97 **murrion** dead from murrain, a cattle disease   98 **nine men's morris** game played on squares cut in the grass on which stones or disks are moved   99 **quaint mazes** intricate paths   **wanton green** luxuriant grass   101 **want** lack   **here** (Q and F; though generally emended to "cheer," it makes sense as it stands: at the time most associated with carol singing and hymns, winter is lacking; cf. ll. 107-13)   103 **Therefore** (because of the discord between Oberon and Titania)   104 **washes** i.e. with moisture   105 **That** so that   **rheumatic diseases** rheumatism,

And on old Hiems' thin and icy crown,
An odorous chaplet of sweet summer buds   110
Is, as in mockery, set. The spring, the summer,
The childing autumn, angry winter change
Their wonted liveries: and the mazèd world,
By their increase, now knows not which is which:
And this same progeny of evils comes   115
From our debate, from our dissension:
We are their parents and original.

OBERON.   Do you amend it then: it lies in you.
Why should Titania cross her Oberon?
I do but beg a little changeling boy,   120
To be my henchman.

QUEEN.   Set your heart at rest.
The fairy land buys not the child of me.
His mother was a vot'ress of my order:
And in the spicèd Indian air, by night,
Full often hath she gossiped by my side,   125
And sat with me on Neptune's yellow sands,
Marking th' embarkèd traders on the flood:
When we have laughed to see the sails conceive,
And grow big-bellied with the wanton wind:
Which she, with pretty and with swimming gait,   130
Following (her womb then rich with my young squire)
Would imitate, and sail upon the land,
To fetch me trifles, and return again,
As from a voyage, rich with merchandise.
But she, being mortal, of that boy did die,   135
And for her sake, do I rear up her boy:
And for her sake, I will not part with him.

OBERON.   How long within this wood intend you stay?

QUEEN.   Perchance till after Theseus' weddding day.
If you will patiently dance in our round,   140
And see our moonlight revels, go with us:
If not, shun me, and I will spare your haunts.

OBERON.   Give me that boy, and I will go with thee.

QUEEN.   Not for thy fairy kingdom. Fairies away

---

colds   106 **distemperature** upset in nature   109 **Hiems** god of winter   109 **crown**
head   110 **odorous chaplet** sweet-smelling wreath   112 **childing** fruitful   113 **wonted**
liveries accustomed dress   **mazed** amazed   114 **increase** products   116 **debate**
quarrel   117 **original** source   119 **cross** vex   121 **henchman** attendant   123 **vot'ress**
vowed and devoted follower   127 **traders** merchant ships   129 **wanton** sportive   140
round ring. round dance   142 **spare** shun

We shall chide downright, if I longer stay.   145

Exeunt [TITANIA *and her* TRAIN].

OBERON.   Well, go thy way. Thou shalt not from this grove,
Till I torment thee for this injury.
My gentle Puck come hither: thou rememb'rest,
Since once I sat upon a promontory,
And heard a mermaid, on a dolphin's back,   150
Uttering such dulcet and harmonious breath,
That the rude sea grew civil at her song,
And certain stars shot madly from their spheres,
To hear the sea-maid's music.

PUCK.   I remember.

OBERON.   That very time, I saw (but thou couldst not)   155
Flying between the cold moon and the earth,
Cupid, all armed: a certain aim he took
At a fair Vestal, thronèd by the west,
And loosed his love-shaft smartly from his bow,
As it should pierce a hundred thousand hearts: 160
But I might see young Cupid's fiery shaft
Quenched in the chaste beams of the wat'ry moon:
And the imperial vot'ress passèd on,
In maiden meditation, fancy-free.
Yet marked I where the bolt of Cupid fell.   165
It fell upon a little western flower;
Before, milk-white; now purple with love's wound,
And maidens call it love-in-idleness.
Fetch me that flow'r: the herb I showed thee once.
The juice of it, on sleeping eyelids laid,   170
Will make or man or woman madly dote
Upon the next live creature that it sees.
Fetch me this herb, and be thou here again
Ere the leviathan can swim a league.

PUCK.   I'll put a girdle round about the earth,   175
In forty minutes.   [*Exit.*]

146 **from** go from   149 **Since**
when   150–8 **mermaid . . . west** (the details are reminiscent of the water pageantry
presented before Queen Elizabeth at Kenilworth, near Stratford in 1575, which Shakespeare
could have seen as a boy, or at Elvetham in 1591; a published account of the latter pictures the
mermaid, dolphin, fireworks, and Elizabeth's throne in the west)   152 **rude** rough   **civil**
calm   153 **stars . . . spheres** (probably referring to fireworks at a royal
entertainment)   156 **cold** chaste (moon goddess Diana represented chastity)   158**Vestal**
virgin, probable reference to Queen Elizabeth   163 **imperial vot'ress** royal devotee (Queen
Elizabeth) of Diana   164 **fancy-free** free from love   165 **bolt** arrow   168 **love-in-
idleness** heartsease or pansy   174 **leviathan** whale   175 **put . . . earth** circle the

OBERON.   Having once this juice,
          I'll watch Titania when she is asleep,
          And drop the liquor of it in her eyes:
          The next thing then she waking looks upon,
          (Be it on lion, bear, or wolf, or bull,   180
          On meddling monkey, or on busy ape)
          She shall pursue it, with the soul of love.
          And ere I take this charm from off her sight
          (As I can take it with another herb)
          I'll make her render up her page to me.   185
          But who comes here? I am invisible,
          And I will overhear their conference.

                    Enter DEMETRIUS, HELENA *following him.*

DEMETRIUS.
          I love thee not: therefore pursue me not.
          Where is Lysander and fair Hermia?
          The one I'll slay: the other slayeth me.   190
          Thou told'st me they were stol'n unto this wood:
          And here am I, and wood within this wood:
          Because I cannot meet my Hermia.
          Hence, get thee gone, and follow me no more.
HELENA.   You draw me, you hard-hearted adamant: 195
          But yet you draw not iron, for my heart
          Is true as steel. Leave you your power to draw,
          And I shall have no power to follow you.
DEMETRIUS.
          Do I entice you? Do I speak you fair?
          Or rather do I not in plainest truth   200
          Tell you I do not, nor I cannot love you?
HELENA.   And even for that, do I love you the more:
          I am your spaniel: and Demetrius,
          The more you beat me, I will fawn on you.
          Use me but as your spaniel: spurn me, strike me,   205
          Neglect me, lose me: only give me leave,
          Unworthy as I am, to follow you.
          What worser place can I beg in your love
          (And yet a place of high respect with me)

---

earth   181 **busy** mischievous   192 **and wood** and crazy   195 **adamant** (1) magnet (2)
impenetrably hard lodestone   196–7 **yet you . . . steel** although the soft heart you draw
(attract) is not made of iron, it is as true as steel   199 **you fair** to you in a kindly way   205
spurn kick   206 **Neglect** ignore

    Than to be used as you use your dog.   210
DEMETRIUS.
    Tempt not too much the hatred of my spirit,
    For I am sick, when I do look on thee.
HELENA. And I am sick, when I look not on you.
DEMETRIUS.
    You do impeach your modesty too much,
    To leave the city and commit yourself   215
    Into the hands of one that loves you not,
    To trust the opportunity of night,
    And the ill counsel of a desert place,
    With the rich worth of your virginity.
HELENA. Your virtue is my privilege: for that   220
    It is not night, when I do see your face,
    Therefore I think I am not in the night.
    Nor doth this wood lack worlds of company,
    For you, in my respect, are all the world.
    Then how can it be said I am alone,   225
    When all the world is here to look on me?
DEMETRIUS.
    I'll run from thee and hide me in the brakes,
    And leave thee to the mercy of wild beasts.
HELENA. The wildest hath not such a heart as you.
    Run when you will: the story shall be changed;   230
    Apollo flies, and Daphne holds the chase:
    The dove pursues the griffin: the mild hind
    Makes speed to catch the tiger. Bootless speed,
    When cowardice pursues, and valour flies.
DEMETRIUS.
    I will not stay thy questions. Let me go: 235
    Or if thou follow me, do not believe
    But I shall do thee mischief in the wood.

              [*Exit* DEMETRIUS.]

HELENA. Ay, in the temple, in the town, the field,
    You do me mischief. Fie Demetrius,
    Your wrongs do set a scandal on my sex: 240
    We cannot fight for love, as men may do:

---

214 **impeach** discredit 218 **desert** deserted 220
Your . . . privilege your attraction is my sanction (for coming) **for that** because 224
respect regard 227 **brakes** thickets 230 **changed** i.e. into the weak pursuing the
strong 231 **Apollo . . . Daphne** (in Ovid, Apollo pursues Daphne, who turns into a laurel
tree) 232 **griffin** legendary beast with the head of an eagle and the body of a lion **hind**

We should be wooed, and were not made to woo.
I'll follow thee and make a heaven of hell,
To die upon the hand I love so well.   *Exit.*

OBERON.   Fare thee well nymph. Ere he do leave this grove,   245
Thou shalt fly him, and he shall seek thy love.

Enter PUCK.

Hast thou the flower there? Welcome wanderer.
PUCK.   Ay, there it is.
OBERON.   I pray thee give it me.
I know a bank where the wild thyme blows,
Where oxlips and the nodding violet grows,   250
Quite over-canopied with luscious woodbine,
With sweet musk-roses, and with eglantine:
There sleeps Titania, sometime of the night,
Lulled in these flowers, with dances and delight:
And there the snake throws her enamelled skin,   255
Weed wide enough to wrap a fairy in.
And with the juice of this, I'll streak her eyes,
And make her full of hateful fantasies.
Take thou some of it, and seek through this grove:
A sweet Athenian lady is in love   260
With a disdainful youth: anoint his eyes.
But do it when the next thing he espies
May be the lady. Thou shalt know the man
By the Athenian garments he hath on.
Effect it with some care, that he may prove   265
More fond on her, than she upon her love:
And look thou meet me ere the first cock crow.
PUCK.   Fear not my lord: your servant shall do so.   *Exeunt.*

[SCENE II.]

Enter TITANIA *Queen of Fairies with her train.*

QUEEN.   Come, now a roundel and a fairy song:
Then, for the third part of a minute, hence—

---

female deer   233 **Bootless** useless   235 **stay thy questions** wait for any more talk   240
set . . . sex cast a scandalous reflection on womankind   250 **oxlips** primroses   251
woodbine honeysuckle   252 **eglantine** sweetbriar   255 **throws** casts off   256 **weed**
garment   266 **fond** doting
  II,ii Another part of the wood   1 **roundel** dance in a ring

Some to kill cankers in the musk-rose buds,
Some war with reremice for their leathren wings,
To make my small elves coats, and some keep back   5
The clamorous owl, that nightly hoots and wonders
At our quaint spirits. Sing me now asleep:
Then to your offices, and let me rest.

Fairies sing.

You spotted snakes with double tongue,
    Thorny hedgehogs be not seen,   10
Newts and blind-worms do no wrong,
    Come not near our Fairy Queen.

Philomele, with melody,
    Sing in our sweet lullaby,
Lulla, lulla, lullaby, lulla, lulla, lullaby.   15
    Never harm,
    Nor spell, nor charm,
Come our lovely lady nigh.
So good night, with lullaby.

1. FAIRY.   Weaving spiders come not here: 20
    Hence you long-legged spinners, hence:
Beetles black approach not near:
    Worm nor snail do no offence.

Philomele, with melody, &c.   *She sleeps.*
2. FAIRY. Hence away: now all is well: 25
    One aloof stand sentinel.   [*Exeunt fairies.*]

Enter OBERON [*and applies the flower
juice to* TITANIA's *eyelids*].

OBERON.   What thou seest, when thou dost wake,
    Do it for thy true love take:
    Love and languish for his sake.
    Be it ounce, or cat, or bear,   30
    Pard, or boar with bristled hair,
    In thy eye that shall appear,
    When thou wak'st, it is thy dear:

---

4 **reremice** bats   7 **quaint**
dainty   8 **offices** duties   9 **double** forked   11 **blind-worms** legless lizards   13
Philomele the nightingale (into which Philomela was transformed)   30 **ounce** lynx   **cat**
wildcat   31 **Pard** leopard   36 **troth** truth   42 **troth** true love, trothplight

Wake when some vile thing is near.   [*Exit.*]

Enter LYSANDER *and* HERMIA.

LYSANDER. Fair love, you faint with wand'ring in the wood: 35
And to speak troth I have forgot our way.
We'll rest us Hermia, if you think it good,
And tarry for the comfort of the day.

HERMIA. Be't so Lysander: find you out a bed:
For I upon this bank will rest my head.   40

LYSANDER. One turf shall serve as pillow for us both,
One heart, one bed, two bosoms, and one troth.

HERMIA. Nay good Lysander: for my sake, my dear,
Lie further off yet; do not lie so near.

LYSANDER. O take the sense, sweet, of my innocence: 45
Love takes the meaning in love's conference.
I mean that my heart unto yours is knit,
So that but one heart we can make of it:
Two bosoms interchainèd with an oath,
So then two bosoms and a single troth.   50
Then by your side no bed-room me deny:
For lying so, Hermia, I do not lie.

HERMIA. Lysander riddles very prettily.
Now much beshrew my manners and my pride,
If Hermia meant to say Lysander lied.   55
But gentle friend, for love and courtesy,
Lie further off, in human modesty:
Such separation as may well be said
Becomes a virtuous bachelor and a maid,
So far be distant, and good night sweet friend: 60
Thy love ne'er alter till thy sweet life end.

LYSANDER. Amen, amen, to that fair prayer say I,
And then end life, when I end loyalty.
Here is my bed: sleep give thee all his rest.

HERMIA. With half that wish, the wisher's eyes be pressed.   65

They sleep.

Enter PUCK.

PUCK.   Through the forest have I gone,
             But Athenian found I none,

(betrothal)   45 **take . . . innocence** understand the innocence of my remark (w. pun on
"sense" and "cence")   46 **Love . . . conference** love enables lovers to understand each
other when they converse   49 **interchained** bound   54 **beshrew** curse   65 **pressed** i.e.

On whose eyes I might approve
This flower's force in stirring love.
Night and silence. Who is here?   70
Weeds of Athens he doth wear:
This is he (my master said)
Despisèd the Athenian maid:
And here the maiden, sleeping sound,
On the dank and dirty ground.   75
Pretty soul, she durst not lie
Near this lack-love, this kill-courtesy.
Churl, upon thy eyes I throw
All the power this charm doth owe:
When thou wak'st, let love forbid   80
Sleep his seat on thy eyelid.
So awake when I am gone:
For I must now to Oberon.   *Exit.*

Enter DEMETRIUS *and* HELENA *running.*

HELENA.   Stay, thou kill me, sweet Demetrius.
DEMETRIUS.
            I charge thee hence, and do not haunt me thus.   85
HELENA.   O, wilt thou darkling leave me? Do not so.
DEMETRIUS.
            Stay on thy peril: I alone will go.   *Exit* DEMETRIUS.
HELENA.   O, I am out of breath in this fond chase:
            The more my prayer, the lesser is my grace.
            Happy is Hermia, wheresoe'er she lies: 90
            For she hath blessèd and attractive eyes.
            How came her eyes so bright? Not with salt tears:
            If so, my eyes are oft'ner washed than hers.
            No, no: I am as ugly as a bear:
            For beasts that meet me run away for fear.   95
            Therefore no marvel, though Demetrius
            Do as a monster, fly my presence thus.
            What wicked and dissembling glass of mine,
            Made me compare with Hermia's sphery eyne!
            But who is here? Lysander, on the ground?   100
            Dead, or asleep? I see no blood, no wound.

---

by sleep   68 **approve** test   71 **Weeds** garments   79 **owe** own   80–1 **forbid** . . .
eyelid make you sleepless (with love)   86 **darkling** in the dark   88 **fond** foolishly
doting   89 **my grace** favor shown to me   91 **attractive** attracting   97 **as** i.e. from   98
glass looking glass   99 **sphery** like stars (which were believed to inhabit their own
spheres)   **eyne** eyes   104 **Transparent** radiant   **nature** . . . **art** (Q; F: "nature her

> Lysander, if you live, good sir awake.

LYSANDER. [*Wakes.*] And run through fire, I will for thy sweet sake.
Transparent Helena, nature shows art,
That through thy bosom, makes me see thy heart.   105
Where is Demetrius? O how fit a word
Is that vile name to perish on my sword!

HELENA.   Do not say so, Lysander, say not so.
What though he love your Hermia? Lord, what though?
Yet Hermia still loves you: then be content.   110

LYSANDER. Content with Hermia? No: I do repent
The tedious minutes I with her have spent.
Not Hermia, but Helena I love.
Who will not change a raven for a dove?
The will of man is by his reason swayed: 115
And reason says you are the worthier maid.
Things growing are not ripe until their season:
So I, being young, till now ripe not to reason.
And touching now the point of human skill,
Reason becomes the marshal to my will,   120
And leads me to your eyes; where I o'erlook
Love's stories, written in love's richest book.

HELENA.   Wherefore was I to this keen mockery born?
When at your hands did I deserve this scorn?
Is't not enough, is't not enough, young man,   125
That I did never, no, nor never can,
Deserve a sweet look from Demetrius' eye,
But you must flout my insufficiency?
Good troth you do me wrong, good sooth you do,
In such disdainful manner me to woo.   130
But fare you well: perforce I must confess,
I thought you lord of more true gentleness.
O, that a lady, of one man refused,
Should of another, therefore be abused!   *Exit.*

LYSANDER. She sees not Hermia. Hermia, sleep thou there,   135
And never mayst thou come Lysander near.
For, as a surfeit of the sweetest things
The deepest loathing to the stomach brings:

---

shewes art")   104–5 nature . . . heart through the magic art of nature I can see through
your bosom to your heart   115 swayed ruled   118 ripe ripen, mature   119 point
peak   skill knowledge   120 marshal . . . will leader of my desires (the marshal led a royal
procession, often to stations where allegorical shows were presented, here "love's
stories")   122 Love's stories the images of true love   book (her eyes)   123 Wherefore
why   127 Deserve earn   128 flout mock   131 perforce . . . confess I am forced to
confess .   132 lord . . . gentleness more of a gentleman

	Or as the heresies that men do leave,	
	Are hated most of those they did deceive:	140
	So thou, my surfeit and my heresy,	
	Of all be hated; but the most, of me:	

And all my powers, address your love and might,
To honour Helen, and to be her knight.   *Exit.*

HERMIA.   [*Wakes.*] Help me Lysander, help me: do thy best   145
To pluck this crawling serpent from my breast.
Ay me, for pity. What a dream was here?
Lysander, look how I do quake with fear.
Methought a serpent eat my heart away,
And you sat smiling at his cruel prey.   150
Lysander: what, removed? Lysander, lord!
What, out of hearing, gone? No sound, no word?
Alack, where are you? Speak, and if you hear:
Speak, of all loves. I swoon almost with fear.
No? Then I well perceive you are not nigh: 155
Either death, or you, I'll find immediately.   *Exit.*

Act Three

[SCENE I.]

Enter the CLOWNS [QUINCE, SNUG, BOTTOM, FLUTE, SNOUT,
and STARVELING].

BOTTOM.   Are we all met?
QUINCE.   Pat, pat: and here's a marvellous convenient place for
our rehearsal. This green plot shall be our stage, this
hawthorn brake our tiring-house, and we will do it in
action, as we will do it before the duke.   5
BOTTOM.   Peter Quince?
QUINCE.   What sayest thou, bully Bottom?
BOTTOM.   There are things in this Comedy of Pyramus and Thisby
that will never please. First, Pyramus must draw a sword
to kill himself; which the ladies cannot abide. How   10
answer you that?

---

144 **knight** faithful lover   150

prey preying   154 **of** for the sake of
III, i The wood   4 **brake** thicket   **tiring-house** dressing room   7 **bully** "old

SNOUT.   By'r lakin, a parlous fear.

STARVELING.

I believe we must leave the killing out, when all is done.

BOTTOM.   Not a whit: I have a device to make all well. Write me
a prologue, and let the prologue seem to say, we will   15
do no harm with our swords, and that Pyramus is not
killed indeed: and for the more better assurance, tell
them that I Pyramus am not Pyramus, but Bottom the
weaver: this will put them out of fear.

QUINCE.   Well, we will have such a prologue, and it shall be   20
written in eight and six.

BOTTOM.   No, make it two more: let it be written in eight and
eight.

SNOUT.   Will not the ladies be afeard of the lion?

STARVELING.

I fear it, I promise you.   25

BOTTOM.   Masters, you ought to consider with yourselves, to bring
in (God shield us) a lion among ladies, is a most dreadful thing. For there is not a more fearful wild-fowl than
your lion living: and we ought to look to't.

SNOUT.   Therefore another prologue must tell he is not a lion.   30

BOTTOM.   Nay, you must name his name, and half his face must be
seen through the lion's neck, and he himself must speak
through, saying thus, or to the same defect: 'Ladies,'
or 'Fair ladies—I would wish you,' or 'I would request you,' or 'I would entreat you, not to fear,   35
not to tremble: my life for yours. If you think I come
hither as a lion, it were pity of my life. No, I am no
such thing: I am a man as other men are.' And there
indeed let him name his name, and tell them plainly he
is Snug the joiner.   40

QUINCE.   Well, it shall be so, but there is two hard things: that is,
to bring the moonlight into a chamber: for you know,
Pyramus and Thisby meet by moonlight.

SNOUT.   Doth the moon shine that night we play our play?

BOTTOM.   A calendar, a calendar: look in the almanac: find out   45
moonshine, find out moonshine.

pal"   12 **By'r lakin** mild oath, "by Our Lady"   **parlous** "awful" (lit. perilous)   21 **eight
and six** alternate lines of eight and six syllables (the ballad metre)   22 **eight and eight** ("He
cannot have too much of a good thing": Wilson)   26–8 **to bring . . . thing** (possibly an
allusion to the masque celebrating the baptism of Prince Henry of Scotland on August 30,
1594, in which a triumphal chariot was to have been drawn by a tame lion, but "because his
presence might have brought some fear," a blackamoor was substituted)   28 **wild-fowl**
(Bottom's conception of natural history, like the "sucking dove")   33 **defect** (he means

QUINCE.   Yes, it doth shine that night.

BOTTOM.   Why then may you leave a casement of the great cham-
             ber window, where we play, open; and the moon may
             shine in at the casement.   50

QUINCE.   Ay, or else one must come in with a bush of thorns and
             a lantern, and say he comes to disfigure, or to present,
             the person of Moonshine. Then, there is another thing;
             we must have a wall in the great chamber: for Pyramus
             and Thisby, says the story, did talk through the chink   55
             of a wall.

SNOUT.   You can never bring in a wall. What say you, Bottom?

BOTTOM.   Some man or other must present wall: and let him have
             some plaster, or some loam, or some rough-cast about
             him, to signify wall; and let him hold his fingers thus: 60
             and through that cranny, shall Pyramus and Thisby
             whisper.

QUINCE.   If that may be, then all is well. Come, sit down every
             mother's son, and rehearse your parts. Pyramus, you be-
             gin: when you have spoken your speech, enter into that   65
             brake, and so every one according to his cue.

                         Enter PUCK.

PUCK.   What hempen homespuns have we swagg'ring here,
             So near the cradle of the Fairy Queen?
             What, a play toward? I'll be an auditor,
             An actor too perhaps, if I see cause.   70

QUINCE.   Speak Pyramus. Thisby stand forth.

PYRAMUS.   Thisby, the flowers of odious savours sweet—

QUINCE.   'Odorous, odorous.'

PYRAMUS.   —odours savours sweet,
             So hath thy breath, my dearest Thisby dear.   75
             But hark, a voice: stay thou but here awhile,
             And by and by I will to thee appear.

                                        Exit PYRAMUS.

PUCK.   A stranger Pyramus than e'er played here.   [*Exit.*]

THISBY.   Must I speak now?

QUINCE.   Ay marry must you. For you must understand he goes   80
             but to see a noise that he heard, and is to come again.

"effect")   **48 great chamber** great hall of the palace   **51 bush of thorns** bundle of
firewood (the man in the moon was supposed to have been placed there as a punishment for
gathering wood on Sundays)   **52 disfigure** (he means "figure," symbolize)   **59 rough-
cast** coarse plaster of lime and gravel   **67 hempen homespuns** wearers of clothing spun at

THISBY.   Most radiant Pyramus, most lily-white of hue,
    Of colour like the red rose, on triumphant brier,
   Most brisky juvenal, and eke most lovely Jew,
    As true as truest horse, that yet would never tire, 85
   I'll meet thee Pyramus, at Ninny's tomb.

QUINCE.   'Ninus' tomb,' man: why, you must not speak that yet.
   That you answer to Pyramus. You speak all your part
   at once, cues and all. Pyramus, enter; your cue is past:
   it is 'never tire.' 90

THISBY.   O—As true as truest horse, that yet would never tire.

     Enter PYRAMUS *with the*
     ass-head [followed by PUCK].

PYRAMUS.   If I were fair, Thisby, I were only thine.

QUINCE.   O monstrous! O strange! We are haunted. Pray masters,
   fly masters. Help!

          the clowns all exeunt.

PUCK.   I'll follow you: I'll lead you about a round, 95
    Through bog, through bush, through brake, through
     brier.
   Sometime a horse I'll be, sometime a hound,
    A hog, a headless bear, sometime a fire,
   And neigh, and bark, and grunt, and roar, and burn,
   Like horse, hound, hog, bear, fire, at every turn. *Exit.* 100

BOTTOM.   Why do they run away? This is a knavery of them to
   make me afeared.

      Enter SNOUT.

SNOUT.   O Bottom, thou art changed. What do I see on thee?

BOTTOM.   What do you see? You see an ass-head of your own, do
   you?   [*Exit* SNOUT.] 105

      Enter QUINCE.

QUINCE.   Bless thee Bottom, bless thee. Thou art translated.

             Exit.

BOTTOM.   I see their knavery. This is to make an ass of me, to

---

home from hemp 69 **toward** in preparation 84 **brisky juvenal** lively youth **Jew** diminutive of either "juvenal" or "jewel" 87 **Ninus' tomb** (tomb of the founder of Nineveh, and meeting place of the lovers in Ovid's version of the Pyramus story) 92 **were fair,** (transposing his pause, which belongs after "were" ["were true"] Bottom unintentionally comments on his appearance) 95 **about a round** in circles, like a round dance (round about) 98, 100 **fire** will-o'-the-wisp (which misled night wanderers) 104 **You . . . own** you see something you imagine in your own stupid head 106 **translated** transformed

fright me if they could: but I will not stir from this
place, do what they can. I will walk up and down here,
and will sing that they shall hear I am not afraid.   110

[*Sings.*]

The woosel cock, so black of hue,
With orange tawny bill,
The throstle, with his note so true,
The wren, with little quill.

TITANIA.   What angel wakes me from my flow'ry bed?   115
BOTTOM.   [*Sings.*]
The finch, the sparrow, and the lark,
The plain-song cuckoo gray:
Whose note full many a man doth mark,
And dares not answer, nay.

For indeed, who would set his wit to so foolish a bird? 120
Who would give a bird the lie, though he cry 'cuckoo'
never so?
TITANIA.   I pray thee, gentle mortal, sing again.
Mine ear is much enamoured of thy note:
So is mine eye enthrallèd to thy shape,   125
And thy fair virtue's force (perforce) doth move me,
On the first view to say, to swear, I love thee.
BOTTOM.   Methinks mistress, you should have little reason for
that. And yet, to say the truth, reason and love keep
little company together now-a-days. The more the pity, 130
that some honest neighbours will not make them friends.
Nay, I can gleek upon occasion.
TITANIA.   Thou art as wise as thou art beautiful.
BOTTOM.   Not so neither: but if I had wit enough to get out of
this wood, I have enough to serve mine own turn.   135
TITANIA.   Out of this wood do not desire to go:
Thou shalt remain here, whether thou wilt or no.
I am a spirit of no common rate:
The summer still doth tend upon my state,
And I do love thee: therefore go with me.   140
I'll give thee fairies to attend on thee:

---

111   **woosel** ousel, blackbird   113 **throstle** thrush   114 **quill** piping note   117 **plain-song**
sounding a simple, unvaried note   120 **set . . . to** match his wit against   121 **Who . . . lie**
who could call a bird a liar   **'cuckoo'** (which sounded like "cuckold" = a deceived
husband)   122 **never so** i.e. often   126 **thy . . . force** the attraction of your
manliness   **perforce** by force   132 **gleek** joke satirically   138 **rate** rank, value   139
still always   **tend . . . state** serve as an attendant in my royal train   142 **deep** deepest

And they shall fetch thee jewels from the deep,
And sing, while thou on pressèd flowers dost sleep:
And I will purge thy mortal grossness so,
That thou shalt like an airy spirit go.   145
Peaseblossom, Cobweb, Moth, and Mustardseed!

Enter four FAIRIES.

PEASEBLOSSOM.
Ready.

COBWEB. And I.

MOTH.   And I.

MUSTARDSEED.   And I.

ALL.   Where shall we go?

TITANIA. Be kind and courteous to this gentleman,
Hop in his walks and gambol in his eyes,   150
Feed him with apricocks and dewberries,
With purple grapes, green figs, and mulberries.
The honey-bags steal from the humblebees,
And for night-tapers, crop their waxen thighs,
And light them at the fiery glow-worm's eyes,   155
To have my love to bed and to arise:
And pluck the wings from painted butterflies,
To fan the moonbeams from his sleeping eyes.
Nod to him elves, and do him courtesies.

PEASEBLOSSOM.
Hail, mortal.   160

COBWEB. Haii.

MOTH. Hail.

MUSTARDSEED.
Hail.

BOTTOM. I cry your worships mercy, heartily: I beseech your worship's name.   165

COBWEB. Cobweb.

BOTTOM. I shall desire you of more acquaintance, good Master
Cobweb: if I cut my finger, I shall make bold with you.
Your name, honest gentleman?

PEASEBLOSSOM.
Peaseblossom.   170

---

ocean (location of shipwrecked jewels, as in *Tempest*, I,ii,398, and *RIII*, I,iv,27.)   146 **Moth**
mote (so pronounced), tiny speck   150 **gambol in** caper before   151 **apricocks**
apricots   **dewberries** blackberries   153 **humblebees** bumblebees   154 **crop**
clip   164 **I . . . mercy** I respectfully beg your pardons   168 **cut my finger** (cobwebs were
used to stop blood)

BOTTOM.   I pray you commend me to Mistress Squash, your mother,
and to Master Peascod, your father. Good Master Peaseblossom, I shall desire you of more acquaintance, too.
Your name I beseech you sir?

MUSTARDSEED.

Mustardseed.   175

BOTTOM.   Good Master Mustardseed, I know your patience well.
That same cowardly giant-like ox beef hath devoured
many a gentleman of your house. I promise you, your
kindred hath made my eyes water ere now. I desire you
of more acquaintance, good Master Mustardseed.   180

TITANIA.   Come wait upon him: lead him to my bower.
The moon methinks looks with a wat'ry eye:
And when she weeps, weeps every little flower,
Lamenting some enforcèd chastity.
Tie up my lover's tongue, bring him silently. *Exeunt.* 185

[SCENE II.]

Enter [OBERON,] *King of Fairies, solus.*

OBERON.   I wonder if Titania be awaked;
Then what it was that next came in her eye,
Which she must dote on in extremity.

Enter PUCK.

Here comes my messenger. How now, mad spirit?
What night-rule now about this haunted grove?   5

PUCK.   My mistress with a monster is in love.
Near to her close and consecrated bower,
While she was in her dull and sleeping hour,
A crew of patches, rude mechanicals,
That work for bread upon Athenian stalls,   10
Were met together to rehearse a play,
Intended for great Theseus' nuptial day:
The shallowest thickskin of that barren sort,
Who Pyramus presented in their sport,
Forsook his scene and entered in a brake: 15

---

171 **commend me** offer my respects   **Squash** unripe peapod   172
Peascod ripe peapod   176 **patience** fortitude   179 **my eyes water** ((1) in pity (2) because
the mustard was so strong)   184 **enforced** violated

III,ii Another part of the wood   5 **night-rule** diversion ("misrule") in the night   8 **dull**
drowsy   9 **patches** fools (from the motley worn by fools)   9 **mechanicals** workers   10
stalls shops   13 **barren sort** stupid crew   14 **presented** represented   15 **brake**

When I did him at this advantage take,
An ass's nole I fixèd on his head.
Anon his Thisby must be answerèd,
And forth my mimic comes. When they him spy,
As wild geese, that the creeping fowler eye,   20
Or russet-pated choughs, many in sort,
Rising and cawing at the gun's report,
Sever themselves and madly sweep the sky,
So at his sight away his fellows fly:
And at our stamp, here o'er and o'er one falls: 25
He murder cries, and help from Athens calls.
Their sense thus weak, lost with their fears thus strong,
Made senseless things begin to do them wrong.
For briers and thorns at their apparel snatch:
Some sleeves, some hats; from yielders, all things catch. 30
I led them on in this distracted fear,
And left sweet Pyramus translated there:
When in that moment (so it came to pass)
Titania waked, and straightway loved an ass.

OBERON.   This falls out better than I could devise.   35
            But hast thou yet latched the Athenian's eyes
            With the love-juice, as I did bid thee do?

PUCK.   I took him sleeping (that is finished too)
            And the Athenian woman by his side;
            That when he waked, of force she must be eyed.   40

Enter DEMETRIUS *and* HERMIA.

OBERON.   Stand close: this is the same Athenian.

PUCK.   This is the woman: but not this the man.

DEMETRIUS.
            O why rebuke you him that loves you so?
            Lay breath so bitter on your bitter foe.

HERMIA.   Now I but chide: but I should use thee worse,   45
            For thou, I fear, hast given me cause to curse.
            If thou hast slain Lysander in his sleep,
            Being o'er shoes in blood, plunge in the deep,
            And kill me too.

---

thicket   17 **nole** head, noodle   19 **mimic** buffoon   20 **fowler** hunter of fowl   21
russet-pated choughs grey-headed jackdaws ("russet" = browns or greys)   **sort** a
flock   25 **our stamp** (the stamping of an angry goblin could be terrifying [cf.
Rumplestiltskin]. Johnson and others emend: "a stump")   28 **wrong** harm   30 **Some** i.e.
snatch   **from yielders . . . catch** (everything joins in to harm the weak)   31 **distracted**
maddened   32 **translated** transformed   36 **latched** moistened   40 **of force** by
necessity   41 **close** hidden

The sun was not so true unto the day,   50
As he to me. Would he have stolen away
From sleeping Hermia? I'll believe as soon
This whole earth may be bored, and that the moon
May through the center creep, and so displease
Her brother's noontide with th' Antipodes.   55
It cannot be but thou hast murdered him.
So should a murderer look; so dead, so grim.

DEMETRIUS.
So should the murdered look, and so should I,
Pierced through the heart with your stern cruelty.
Yet you, the murderer, look as bright, as clear,   60
As yonder Venus in her glimmering sphere.

HERMIA.   What's this to my Lysander? Where is he?
Ah good Demetrius, wilt thou give him me?

DEMETRIUS.
I had rather give his carcass to my hounds.

HERMIA.   Out dog, out cur! Thou driv'st me past the bounds   65
Of maiden's patience. Hast thou slain him then?
Henceforth be never numbered among men.
O, once tell true: tell true, even for my sake:
Durst thou have looked upon him, being awake?
And hast thou killed him sleeping? O brave touch!   70
Could not a worm, an adder, do so much?
An adder did it: for with doubler tongue
Than thine, thou serpent, never adder stung.

DEMETRIUS.
You spend your passion on a misprised mood:
I am not guilty of Lysander's blood: 75
Nor is he dead, for aught that I can tell.

HERMIA.   I pray thee, tell me then that he is well.

DEMETRIUS.
And if I could, what should I get therefore?

HERMIA.   A privilege never to see me more:
And from thy hated presence part I so: 80
See me no more, whether he be dead or no.   *Exit.*

DEMETRIUS.
There is no following her in this fierce vein.

---

53 **whole** solid   **be bored** have a hole bored through
it   55 **Her brother's . . . Antipodes** the noon of her brother sun, by appearing among the
Antipodes (the people on the other side of the earth, whose time of day and night is the
reverse of ours)   57 **dead** deadly   61 **sphere** (in the Ptolemaic system, each planet moved
in its own sphere around the earth)   69 **being** he being   70 **brave touch** splendid stroke
(ironic)   71 **worm** snake   72 **doubler tongue** (1) tongue more forked (2) more deceitful
speech   74 **on . . . mood** in mistaken anger   84 **heaviness** sadness   **heavier** (1) sadder

Here therefore for a while I will remain.
So sorrow's heaviness doth heavier grow
For debt that bankrout sleep doth sorrow owe:　　85
Which now in some slight measure it will pay,
If for his tender here I make some stay.

Lie down.

OBERON.　What hast thou done? Thou hast mistaken quite,
　　　　And laid the love-juice on some true-love's sight.
　　　　Of thy misprision must perforce ensue　　90
　　　　Some true love turned, and not a false turned true.
PUCK.　　Then fate o'errules, that one man holding troth,
　　　　A million fail, confounding oath on oath.
OBERON.　About the wood, go swifter than the wind,
　　　　And Helena of Athens look thou find.　　95
　　　　All fancy-sick she is, and pale of cheer,
　　　　With sighs of love, that costs the fresh blood dear.
　　　　By some illusion see thou bring her here:
　　　　I'll charm his eyes against she do appear.
PUCK.　　I go, I go, look how I go.　　100
　　　　Swifter than arrow from the Tartar's bow.　　*Exit.*
OBERON.　　Flower of this purple dye,
　　　　　Hit with Cupid's archery,
　　　　　Sink in apple of his eye:
　　　　　When his love he doth espy,　　105
　　　　　Let her shine as gloriously
　　　　　As the Venus of the sky.
　　　　　When thou wak'st, if she be by,
　　　　　Beg of her for remedy.

Enter PUCK.

PUCK.　　Captain of our fairy band,　　110
　　　　Helena is here at hand,
　　　　And the youth, mistook by me,
　　　　Pleading for a lover's fee.
　　　　Shall we their fond pageant see?
　　　　Lord, what fools these mortals be!　　115

---

(2) drowsier　85 **For debt. . . . owe** because sleep cannot pay the debt of repose he owes the man who is kept awake by sorrow　87 **tender** offer (fr. law)　**make some stay** wait　90 **misprision** mistake　**perforce** of necessity　92 **one . . . troth** for every one man keeping faith　93 **confounding** destroying　**oath on oath** one oath after another　96 **fancy-sick** lovesick　**cheer** face　97 **sighs . . . dear** (each sigh was believed to cost the heart a drop of blood)　98 **illusion** magic deception　99 **against . . . appear** in preparation for her appearance　101 **Tartar's bow** (the Tartars, who used powerful Oriental bows, were famed as archers)　109 **remedy** cure (for your lovesickness)　113 **fee** reward　114 **fond**

OBERON.　　Stand aside. The noise they make
　　　　　　Will cause Demetrius to awake.
PUCK.　　　Then will two at once woo one:
　　　　　　That must needs be sport alone.
　　　　　　And those things do best please me　　　120
　　　　　　That befall prepost'rously.

Enter LYSANDER *and* HELENA.

LYSANDER. Why should you think that I should woo in scorn?
　　　　　　Scorn and derision never come in tears.
　　　　　　Look when I vow, I weep: and vows so born,
　　　　　　　In their nativity all truth appears.　　　125
　　　　　　How can these things in me seem scorn to you,
　　　　　　Bearing the badge of faith to prove them true?
HELENA.　You do advance your cunning more and more.
　　　　　　When truth kills truth, O devilish-holy fray!
　　　　　　These vows are Hermia's. Will you give her o'er?　　　130
　　　　　　Weigh oath with oath, and you will nothing weigh.
　　　　　　Your vows to her and me, put in two scales,
　　　　　　Will even weigh: and both as light as tales.
LYSANDER. I had no judgment, when to her I swore.
HELENA.　Nor none, in my mind, now you give her o'er.　　　135
LYSANDER. Demetrius loves her: and he loves not you.
DEMETRIUS.
　　　　　　(*Awakes.*) O Helen, goddess, nymph, perfect, divine,
　　　　　　To what, my love, shall I compare thine eyne!
　　　　　　Crystal is muddy. O, how ripe in show,
　　　　　　Thy lips, those kissing cherries, tempting grow!　　　140
　　　　　　That pure congealèd white, high Taurus' snow,
　　　　　　Fanned with the eastern wind, turns to a crow,
　　　　　　When thou hold'st up thy hand. O let me kiss
　　　　　　This princess of pure white, this seal of bliss.
HELENA.　O spite! O hell! I see you all are bent　　　145
　　　　　　To set against me, for your merriment.
　　　　　　If you were civil, and knew courtesy,
　　　　　　You would not do me thus much injury.
　　　　　　Can you not hate me, as I know you do,

---

pageant foolish spectacle　119 **alone** singular　122 **scorn** mockery　124–5 **vows . . .
appears** vows born in weeping must be true ones　127 **badge** (1) outward signs (2) family
crest worn by servants as badges　128–9 **advance, kills, fray** (war-love metaphor common
to love poetry)　129 **truth kills truth** former true love is killed by vows of present true
love　131 **nothing weigh** (because the oaths are worthless; "weigh" also = "value")　133
tales fictitious stories　141 **Taurus** (mountain range in Asia Minor)　144 **princess . . .
white** sovereign example of whiteness (her hand)　**seal** confirmation　147 **civil** well

But you must join in souls to mock me too?   150
If you were men, as men you are in show,
You would not use a gentle lady so;
To vow, and swear, and superpraise my parts,
When I am sure you hate me with your hearts.
You both are rivals, and love Hermia: 155
And now both rivals, to mock Helena.
A trim exploit, a manly enterprise,
To conjure tears up in a poor maid's eyes
With your derision. None of noble sort
Would so offend a virgin, and extort   160
A poor soul's patience, all to make you sport.

LYSANDER. You are unkind, Demetrius: be not so.
For you love Hermia: this you know I know.
And here, with all good will, with all my heart,
In Hermia's love I yield you up my part: 165
And yours of Helena to me bequeath,
Whom I do love, and will do to my death.

HELENA.   Never did mockers waste more idle breath.

DEMETRIUS.
Lysander, keep thy Hermia: I will none.
If e'er I loved her, all that love is gone.   170
My heart to her but as guest-wise sojourned:
And now to Helen is it home returned,
There to remain.

LYSANDER.   Helen, it is not so.

DEMETRIUS.
Disparage not the faith thou dost not know,
Lest to thy peril thou aby it dear.   175
Look where thy love comes: yonder is thy dear.

Enter HERMIA.

HERMIA.   Dark night, that from the eye his function takes,
The ear more quick of apprehension makes.
Wherein it doth impair the seeing sense,
It pays the hearing double recompense.   180
Thou art not by mine eye, Lysander, found:
Mine ear, I thank it, brought me to thy sound.
But why unkindly didst thou leave me so?

---

behaved   150 **join in souls** agree in spirit   153 **parts** qualities   157 **trim** fine
(ironic)   160 **extort** wring   169 **none** have none of her   171 **to her . . . sojourned**
visited her only as a guest   175 **aby it dear** buy it at a high price

LYSANDER. Why should he stay, whom love doth press to go?
HERMIA. What love could press Lysander from my side?   185
LYSANDER. Lysander's love, that would not let him bide—
            Fair Helena: who more engilds the night
            Than all you fiery oes and eyes of light.
            Why seek'st thou me? Could not this make thee know,
            The hate I bare thee made me leave thee so?   190
HERMIA. You speak not as you think: it cannot be.
HELENA. Lo: she is one of this confederacy.
            Now I perceive they have conjoined all three,
            To fashion this false sport in spite of me.
            Injurious Hermia, most ungrateful maid,   195
            Have you conspired, have you with these contrived
            To bait me with this foul derision?
            Is all the counsel that we two have shared,
            The sisters' vows, the hours that we have spent,
            When we have chid the hasty-footed time   200
            For parting us; O, is all forgot?
            All schooldays' friendship, childhood innocence?
            We Hermia, like two artificial gods,
            Have with our needles created both one flower,
            Both on one sampler, sitting on one cushion,   205
            Both warbling of one song, both in one key;
            As if our hands, our sides, voices, and minds
            Had been incorporate. So we grew together,
            Like to a double cherry, seeming parted,
            But yet an union in partition,   210
            Two lovely berries moulded on one stem:
            So with two seeming bodies, but one heart,
            Two of the first, like coats in heraldry,
            Due but to one, and crownèd with one crest.
            And will you rent our ancient love asunder,   215
            To join with men in scorning your poor friend?
            It is not friendly, 'tis not maidenly.
            Our sex, as well as I, may chide you for it;
            Though I alone do feel the injury.
HERMIA. I am amazèd at your passionate words: 220
            I scorn you not. It seems that you scorn me.

---

188 **oes** . . . **light** stars
(punning on "o's" and "i's"; "oes" = "circles")   194 **in spite of** to spite   195 **Injurious**
insulting   197 **bait** attack (as dogs did the bear in the sport of bearbaiting)   198 **counsel**
secrets   203 **artificial** skilled in art   208 **incorporate** in one body   213–4 **Two** . . .
crest (the two bodies being) like double coats of arms joined under one crest (with one heart)
when   a   man   and   woman   marry   216 **scorning** mocking   220 **amazed**

HELENA.   Have you not set Lysander, as in scorn,
             To follow me, and praise my eyes and face?
             And made your other love, Demetrius
             (Who even but now did spurn me with his foot)   225
             To call me goddess, nymph, divine, and rare,
             Precious, celestial? Wherefore speaks he this
             To her he hates? And wherefore doth Lysander
             Deny your love, so rich within his soul,
             And tender me (forsooth) affection,   230
             But by your setting on, by your consent?
             What though I be not so in grace as you,
             So hung upon with love, so fortunate,
             But miserable most, to love unloved?
             This you should pity, rather than despise.   235

HERMIA.   I understand not what you mean by this.

HELENA.   Ay, do. Persèver, counterfeit sad looks:
             Make mouths upon me when I turn my back:
             Wink each at other, hold the sweet jest up.
             This sport well carried, shall be chronicled.   240
             If you have any pity, grace, or manners,
             You would not make me such an argument.
             But fare ye well: 'tis partly my own fault:
             Which death or absence soon shall remedy.

LYSANDER.   Stay, gentle Helena: hear my excuse,   245
             My love, my life, my soul, fair Helena.

HELENA.   O excellent!

HERMIA.   Sweet, do not scorn her so.

DEMETRIUS.
             If she cannot entreat, I can compel.

LYSANDER.   Thou canst compel no more than she entreat.
             Thy threats have no more strength than her weak
                    prayers.   250
             Helen, I love thee, by my life I do:
             I swear by that which I will lose for thee,
             To prove him false that says I love thee not.

DEMETRIUS.
             I say I love thee more than he can do.

LYSANDER.   If thou say so, withdraw, and prove it too.   255

---

dumbfounded   225 **spurn** kick   230 **tender** offer   232 **in grace** favored   237 **sad**
serious   238 **mouths upon** faces at   240 **well carried** if well carried out   **chronicled**
written down in the history books   242 **argument** subject (of your mockery)   248
entreat sway you by entreaty   252 **that** (my life)   253,5 **prove** i.e. by a duel

DEMETRIUS.
          Quick. come.

HERMIA.   Lysander, whereto tends all this?

LYSANDER. Away, you Ethiope.

DEMETRIUS.
                  No, no, sir,
Seem to break loose: take on as you would follow;
But yet come not. You are a tame man, go.

LYSANDER. Hang off, thou cat, thou burr: vile thing, let loose;   260
         Or I will shake thee from me like a serpent.

HERMIA.   Why are you grown so rude? What change is this,
         Sweet love?

LYSANDER.   Thy love? Out, tawny Tartar, out:
         Out, loathèd med'cine: O hated potion, hence!

HERMIA.   Do you not jest?

HELENA.   Yes sooth: and so do you.   265

LYSANDER. Demetrius, I will keep my word with thee.

DEMETRIUS.
         I would I had your bond. For I perceive
         A weak bond holds you. I'll not trust your word.

LYSANDER. What? Should I hurt her, strike her, kill her dead?
         Although I hate her, I'll not harm her so.   270

HERMIA.   What? Can you do me greater harm than hate?
         Hate me, wherefore? O me, what news, my love?
         Am not I Hermia? Are not you Lysander?
         I am as fair now, as I was erewhile.
         Since night, you loved me; yet since night, you left me.275
         Why then, you left me—O, the gods forbid—
         In earnest, shall I say?

LYSANDER.   Ay, by my life:
         And never did desire to see thee more.
         Therefore be out of hope, of question, of doubt:
         Be certain: nothing truer: 'tis no jest   280
         That I do hate thee, and love Helena.

HERMIA.   O me, you juggler, you canker blossom,
         You thief of love: what, have you come by night,
         And stol'n my love's heart from him?

---

257 Ethiope (because she is a brunette) 258–9 Seem. . .not you only seem to break loose
from Hermia and pretend to follow me to a duel, but you actually hold back   260 Hang off
let go   262 rude rough   263 tawny tan   266 keep my word i.e. to duel   267 bond
written agreement (punning on "your word is not as good as your bond")   268 weak bond
Hermia's weak hold   272 wherefore why   272 what news what's the matter   274
erewhile a short while ago   282 juggler deceiver   canker blossom worm that causes

HELENA.   Fine, i' faith.
    Have you no modesty, no maiden shame,   285
    No touch of bashfulness? What, will you tear
    Impatient answers from my gentle tongue?
    Fie, fie, you counterfeit, you puppet, you.
HERMIA.   Puppet? why so—ay, that way goes the game.
    Now I perceive that she hath made compare   290
    Between our statures, she hath urged her height,
    And with her personage, her tall personage,
    Her height (forsooth) she hath prevailed with him.
    And are you grown so high in his esteem,
    Because I am so dwarfish and so low?   295
    How low am I, thou painted maypole? Speak:
    How low am I? I am not yet so low,
    But that my nails can reach unto thine eyes.
HELENA.   I pray you, though you mock me, gentlemen,
    Let her not hurt me. I was never curst: 300
    I have no gift at all in shrewishness:
    I am a right maid for my cowardice:
    Let her not strike me. You perhaps may think,
    Because she is something lower than myself,
    That I can match her.
HERMIA.   Lower? Hark again.   305
HELENA.   Good Hermia, do not be so bitter with me,
    I evermore did love you Hermia,
    Did ever keep your counsels, never wronged you;
    Save that in love unto Demetrius,
    I told him of your stealth unto this wood.   310
    He followed you: for love I followed him.
    But he hath chid me hence, and threatened me
    To strike me, spurn me, nay to kill me too;
    And now, so you will let me quiet go,
    To Athens will I bear my folly back,   315
    And follow you no further. Let me go.
    You see how simple and how fond I am.
HERMIA.   Why, get you gone. Who is't that hinders you?
HELENA.   A foolish heart, that I leave here behind.
HERMIA.   What, with Lysander?

---

canker in blossoms   288 **puppet** doll-sized person (Hermia is short and Helena tall)   291
urged her height used her height as an inducement   296 **painted maypole** giant in heavy
makeup   300 **curst** bad-tempered   302 **right . . . cowardice** true woman in being
cowardly   305 **can match** am a match for (in a fight)   308 **counsels** secrets   313 **spurn**
kick   314 **so** if only   317 **fond** foolish

HELENA.   With Demetrius.   320
LYSANDER. Be not afraid: she shall not harm thee Helena.
DEMETRIUS.
          No sir: she shall not, though you take her part.
HELENA.   O when she's angry, she is keen and shrewd.
          She was a vixen when she went to school:
          And though she be but little, she is fierce.   325
HERMIA.   'Little' again? nothing but 'low' and 'little'?
          Why will you suffer her to flout me thus?
          Let me come to her.
LYSANDER.   Get you gone, you dwarf;
          You minimus, of hind'ring knot-grass made;
          You bead, you acorn.
DEMETRIUS.   You are too officious   330
          In her behalf that scorns your services.
          Let her alone: speak not of Helena,
          Take not her part. For if thou dost intend
          Never so little show of love to her,
          Thou shalt aby it.
LYSANDER.   Now she holds me not: 335
          Now follow, if thou dar'st, to try whose right,
          Of thine or mine, is most in Helena.
DEMETRIUS.
          Follow? Nay, I'll go with thee, cheek by jowl.

                    Exeunt LYSANDER *and* DEMETRIUS.

HERMIA.   You, mistress, all this coil is long of you.
          Nay, go not back.
HELENA.   I will not trust you, I,   340
          Nor longer stay in your curst company.
          Your hands than mine are quicker for a fray:
          My legs are longer though, to run away.   [*Exit.*]
HERMIA.   I am amazed, and know not what to say.   *Exit.*
OBERON.   This is thy negligence: still thou mistak'st,   345
          Or else commit'st thy knaveries wilfully.
PUCK.   Believe me, king of shadows, I mistook.
          Did not you tell me I should know the man
          By the Athenian garments he had on?

---

321 **afraid** i.e. to say you love me   322 **take her part** offer yourself as her defender   323 **keen and shrewd** sharp and malicious   327 **flout** mock   329 **minimus** smallest of creatures   **knot-grass** weed believed to stunt the growth if eaten   333 **intend** extend   335 **aby it** buy it dearly   336–7 **try . . . Helena** prove by fighting which of us has most right to Helena   339 **coil is long of** turmoil is because of   344 **amazed** dumbfounded   345 **still** always   352 **sort** turn out   356

And so far blameless proves my enterprise,   350
That I have 'nointed an Athenian's eyes:
And so far am I glad it so did sort,
As this their jangling I esteem a sport.

OBERON.   Thou seest these lovers seek a place to fight;
Hie therefore Robin, overcast the night,   355
The starry welkin cover thou anon
With drooping fog as black as Acheron,
And lead these testy rivals so astray,
As one come not within another's way.
Like to Lysander sometime frame thy tongue: 360
Then stir Demetrius up with bitter wrong:
And sometime rail thou like Demetrius:
And from each other look thou lead them thus;
Till o'er their brows death-counterfeiting sleep
With leaden legs and batty wings doth creep: 365
Then crush this herb into Lysander's eye;
Whose liquor hath this virtuous property,
To take from thence all error with his might,
And make his eyeballs roll with wonted sight.
When they next wake, all this derision   370
Shall seem a dream, and fruitless vision,
And back to Athens shall the lovers wend,
With league whose date till death shall never end.
Whiles I in this affair do thee employ,
I'll to my queen and beg her Indian boy: 375
And then I will her charmèd eye release
From monster's view, and all things shall be peace.

PUCK.   My fairy lord, this must be done with haste,
For night's swift dragons cut the clouds full fast:
And yonder shines Aurora's harbinger,   380
At whose approach, ghosts wand'ring here and there,
Troop home to churchyards: damnèd spirits all,
That in crossways and floods have burial,
Already to their wormy beds are gone:
For fear lest day should look their shames upon,   385
They wilfully themselves exile from light,
And must for aye consort with black-browed night.

---

welkin sky   357 **Acheron** Hades, specifically one of the four rivers there   358 **testy**
irritable   359 **As** so that   361 **wrong** insult   367 **virtuous** potent   369 **wonted**
(previously) accustomed   370 **derision** laughable interlude   373 **date** term   379
dragons (that pulled the chariot of night)   380 **Aurora's harbinger** the morning star
heralding Aurora, the dawn   383 **crossways** crossroads, where suicides (who were therefore damned) were buried   **floods** those who drowned without receiving final rites

OBERON.   But we are spirits of another sort.
          I with the morning's love have oft made sport,
          And like a forester, the groves may tread   390
          Even till the eastern gate all fiery red,
          Opening on Neptune, with fair blessèd beams,
          Turns into yellow gold his salt green streams.
          But notwithstanding, haste, make no delay:
          We may effect his business yet ere day.   [*Exit.*] 395
PUCK.   Up and down, up and down,
          I will lead them up and down.
          I am feared in field and town.
          Goblin, lead them up and down.
          Here comes one.   400

                    Enter LYSANDER.

LYSANDER. Where art thou, proud Demetrius? Speak thou now.
PUCK.   Here villain, drawn and ready. Where art thou?
LYSANDER. I will be with thee straight.
PUCK.   Follow me then
          To plainer ground.   [*Exit* LYSANDER.]

                    Enter DEMETRIUS.

DEMETRIUS.   Lysander, speak again.
          Thou runaway, thou coward, art thou fled?   405
          Speak: in some bush? Where dost thou hide thy head?
PUCK.   Thou coward, art thou bragging to the stars,
          Telling the bushes that thou look'st for wars,
          And wilt not come? Come recreant, come thou child,
          I'll whip thee with a rod. He is defiled   410
          That draws a sword on thee.
DEMETRIUS.   Yea, art thou there?
PUCK.   Follow my voice: we'll try no manhood here.   *Exeunt.*

                    [*Enter* LYSANDER.]

LYSANDER. He goes before me and still dares me on:
          When I come where he calls, then he is gone.
          The villain is much lighter-heeled than I;   415
          I followed fast: but faster he did fly,

---

387 **aye** ever   **consort** associate   389 **morning's . . . sport** hunted with Cephalus (beloved of Aurora and himself devoted to his wife Procris, whom he killed by accident; "sport" also = "amorous dalliance," and "love" = Aurora's love for Oberon)   393 **Turns . . . streams** (cf. Sonnet 33, *l*.4)   402 **drawn** with sword drawn   403 **straight** straightway   404 **plainer** more level   409 **recreant** oath-breaker, coward   412 **try**

That fallen am I in dark uneven way,
And here will rest me. (*Lie down.*) Come thou gentle
   day,
For if but once thou show me thy grey light,
I'll find Demetrius and revenge this spite.   [*Sleeps.*] 420

Enter PUCK *and* DEMETRIUS.

PUCK.   Ho, ho, ho! Coward, why com'st thou not?
DEMETRIUS.

Abide me, if thou dar'st, for well I wot
Thou run'st before me, shifting every place,
And dar'st not stand, nor look me in the face.
Where art thou now?
PUCK.   Come hither: I am here.   425
DEMETRIUS.

Nay then thou mock'st me. Thou shalt buy this dear,
If ever I thy face by daylight see.
Now go thy way. Faintness constraineth me
To measure out my length on this cold bed.
By day's approach look to be visited.   430

[*Lies down and sleeps.*]

Enter HELENA.

HELENA.   O weary night, O long and tedious night,
   Abate thy hours; shine comforts from the east,
That I may back to Athens by daylight,
   From these that my poor company detest:
And sleep, that sometimes shuts up sorrow's eye,   435
Steal me awhile from mine own company.   *Sleep.*
PUCK.   Yet but three? Come one more,
   Two of both kinds makes up four.
   Here she comes, curst and sad.
   Cupid is a knavish lad,   440
   Thus to make poor females mad.

Enter HERMIA.

HERMIA.   Never so weary, never so in woe,
   Bedabbled with the dew, and torn with briers:
I can no further crawl, no further go:

---

test 413 **still** constantly 422 **Abide** wait for **wot** know 423 **shifting . . . place** (F s.d.
opposite *l.* 416: "shifting places") 426 **buy this dear** pay dearly for this 432 **Abate**
shorten **shine comforts** may comforts shine 439 **curst** cross

My legs can keep no pace with my desires.   445
Here will I rest me till the break of day.
Heavens shield Lysander, if they mean a fray.
                                    [*Lies down and sleeps.*]

PUCK.   On the ground,
                              Sleep sound:
                              I'll apply   450
                              To your eye,
                    Gentle lover, remedy.
                    [*Squeezes the love-juce on* LYSANDER'S *eye-
                    lids.*]
                              When thou wak'st,
                              Thou tak'st
                              True delight   455
                              In the sight
                    Of thy former lady's eye:
                    And the country proverb known,
                    That every man should take his own,
                    In your waking shall be shown.   460
                              Jack shall have Jill:
                              Naught shall go ill:
The man shall have his mare again, and all shall be well.

                                              [*Exit.*]

                    THEY SLEEP ALL THE ACT.

Act Four

[SCENE I.]

Enter [TITANIA] QUEEN OF FAIRIES, *and* [BOTTOM THE]
CLOWN, *and* FAIRIES, *and the* KING [OBERON]
behind them [*unseen*].

TITANIA.   Come sit thee down upon this flow'ry bed,
           While I thy amiable cheeks do coy,
           And stick musk-roses in thy sleek smooth head,

---

461 **Jack . . . Jill** boy
. . . girl   463 **The man . . . again** (proverbial: "everything will turn out all right")   463
s.d. They . . . Act (from F, indicating that the lovers remained sleeping on stage until
awakened in the next act. It also suggests that there was no inner stage where the play was
performed, for if there were, the lovers could fall asleep there and the curtain be drawn.
"Act" may = "intermission")

IV,i The wood   2 **amiable** lovely   2 **coy** caress   19 **neaf** fist   20 **leave your curtsy**

And kiss thy fair large ears, my gentle joy.

BOTTOM.   Where's Peaseblossom?   5

PEASEBLOSSOM.
           Ready.

BOTTOM.   Scratch my head, Peaseblossom. Where's Mounsieur
           Cobweb?

COBWEB.   Ready.

BOTTOM.   Mounsieur Cobweb, good mounsieur, get you your weap-   10
           ons in your hand, and kill me a red-hipped humblebee on
           the top of a thistle: and good mounsieur, bring me the
           honey-bag. Do not fret yourself too much in the action,
           mounsieur: and good mounsieur have a care the honey-
           bag break not, I would be loath to have you overflowen   15
           with a honey-bag, signior. Where's Mounsieur Mustard-
           seed?

MUSTARDSEED.
           Ready.

BOTTOM.   Give me your neaf, Mounsieur Mustardseed. Pray you
           leave your curtsy, good mounsieur.   20

MUSTARDSEED.
           What's you will?

BOTTOM.   Nothing, good mounsieur, but to help Cavalery Cobweb
           to scratch. I must to the barber's mounsieur, for me-
           thinks I am marvellous hairy about the face. And I am
           such a tender ass, if my hair do but tickle me, I must   25
           scratch.

TITANIA.   What, will thou hear some music, my sweet love?

BOTTOM.   I have a reasonable good ear in music. Let's have the
           tongs and the bones.

TITANIA.   Or say, sweet love, what thou desirest to eat.   30

BOTTOM.   Truly, a peck of provender. I could munch your good
           dry oats. Methinks I have a great desire to a bottle of hay.
           Good hay, sweet hay, hath no fellow.

TITANIA.   I have a venturous fairy that shall seek
           The squirrel's hoard, and fetch thee new nuts.   35

BOTTOM.   I had rather have a handful or two of dried pease. But
           I pray you, let none of your people stir me: I have an ex-
           position of sleep come upon me.

TITANIA.   Sleep thou, and I will wind thee in my arms.

either (a) stop bowing, or (b) replace your hat   22 **Cavalery** (he means "cavalier")   29
tongs crude music made by striking tongs with a piece of metal   **bones** pieces of bone held
between the fingers and clapped together rhythmically (F s.d.: "Musicke Tongs, Rurall
Musicke")   32 **bottle** bundle   37 **exposition of** (he means "disposition to")

Fairies, be gone, and be all ways away.   40

[Exeunt FAIRIES.]

So doth the woodbine the sweet honeysuckle
Gently entwist: the female ivy so
Enrings the barky fingers of the elm.
O how I love thee! how I dote on thee!   [*They sleep.*]

Enter ROBIN GOODFELLOW [PUCK].

OBERON.   [*Advances.*] Welcome good Robin. Seest thou this sweet
                sight?   45
             Her dotage now I do begin to pity.
             For meeting her of late behind the wood,
             Seeking sweet favours for this hateful fool,
             I did upbraid her and fall out with her.
             For she his hairy temples then had rounded   50
             With coronet of fresh and fragrant flowers.
             And that same dew which sometime on the buds
             Was wont to swell like round and orient pearls,
             Stood now within the pretty flowerets' eyes,
             Like tears that did their own disgrace bewail.   55
             When I had at my pleasure taunted her,
             And she in mild terms begged my patience,
             I then did ask of her her changeling child:
             Which straight she gave me, and her fairy sent
             To bear him to my bower in fairy land.   60
             And now I have the boy, I will undo
             This hateful imperfection of her eyes.
             And gentle Puck, take this transformèd scalp
             From off the head of this Athenian swain;
             That he awaking when the other do,   65
             May all to Athens back again repair,
             And think no more of this night's accidents,
             But as the fierce vexation of a dream.
             But first I will release the Fairy Queen.
                  Be as thou wast wont to be: 70
                  See, as thou wast wont to see.
                  Dian's bud o'er Cupid's flower
                  Hath such force and blessèd power.

---

                                                        40 **all ways**
in every direction   41 **woodbine** either (a) honeysuckle (entwisting itself), or (b) morning
glory   52 **sometime** formerly   53 **Was wont to**
used to   **orient** (where the most beautiful pearls came from)   66 **repair** return   67
accidents incidents   72 **Dian's bud** bud of the *agnus castus* plant (which was thought to

	Now my Titania, wake you, my sweet queen.	
TITANIA.	My Oberon, what visions have I seen!	75
	Methought I was enamoured of an ass.	

OBERON. There lies your love.

TITANIA.   How came these things to pass?
O, how mine eyes do loathe his visage now!

OBERON. Silence awhile. Robin, take off this head:
Titania, music call, and strike more dead   80
Than common sleep of all these five the sense.

TITANIA. Music, ho music! such as charmeth sleep.

PUCK. Now, when thou wak'st, with thine own fool's eyes peep.

OBERON. Sound music: *Music still.*
                come my queen, take hands with me,
And rock the ground whereon these sleepers be.   85

                                        [*Dance.*]

Now thou and I are new in amity,
And will tomorrow midnight solemnly
Dance in Duke Theseus' house triumphantly,
And bless it to all fair prosperity.
There shall the pairs of faithful lovers be   90
Wedded, with Theseus, all in jollity.

PUCK.   Fairy King, attend and mark:
I do hear the morning lark.

OBERON.   Then my queen, in silence sad,
Trip we after the night's shade: 95
We the globe can compass soon,
Swifter than the wand'ring moon.

TITANIA.   Come my lord, and in our flight,
Tell me how it came this night,
That I sleeping here was found,   100
With these mortals on the ground.   *Exeunt.*

                                        Wind horns.

Enter THESEUS, HIPPOLYTA, EGEUS
and all his train.

---

preserve chastity, and was a symbol of Diana, goddess of chastity. Cf. II, i, 184; III, ii,
366-8) **Cupid's flower** the pansy (described in II, i, 157-68, source of the love
juice) 80–81 **strike . . . sense** make these five (the lovers and Bottom) sleep more soundly
than usual; make their sense of sleep even more deathlike than usual   84 **s.d. still**
continuously (F, at *l.* 82)   88 **triumphantly** in celebration   94 **sad** serious   101 **s.d.** (F
adds "Sleepers Lye still" as their later cue is also the sound of horns)

THESEUS. Go one of you, find out the forester:
For now our observation is performed.
And since we have the vaward of the day,
My love shall hear the music of my hounds.   105
Uncouple in the western valley, let them go:
Dispatch I say, and find the forester.

[*Exit an* ATTENDANT.]

We will, fair queen, up to the mountain's top,
And mark the musical confusion
Of hounds and echo in conjunction.   110

HIPPOLYTA.

I was with Hercules and Cadmus once,
When in a wood of Crete they bayed the bear,
With hounds of Sparta: never did I hear
Such gallant chiding. For besides the groves,
The skies, the fountains, every region near   115
Seemed all one mutual cry. I never heard
So musical a discord, such sweet thunder.

THESEUS. My hounds are bred out of the Spartan kind:
So flewed, so sanded: and their heads are hung
With ears that sweep away the morning dew,   120
Crook-kneed, and dewlapped like Thessalian bulls:
Slow in pursuit; but matched in mouth like bells,
Each under each. A cry more tuneable
Was never holloa'd to, nor cheered with horn,
In Crete, in Sparta, nor in Thessaly.   125
Judge when you hear. But soft. What nymphs are these?

EGEUS. My lord, this is my daughter here asleep,
And this Lysander, this Demetrius is,
This Helena, old Nedar's Helena.
I wonder of their being here together.   130

THESEUS. No doubt they rose up early to observe
The rite of May: and hearing our intent,
Came here in grace of our solemnity.
But speak Egeus, is not this the day

---

103 **observation**
observance of the May Day rites   104 **vaward** vanguard, earliest part   106 **Uncouple**
unleash (the dogs)   107 **Dispatch** hurry   111 **Cadmus** (mythical builder of Thebes and
slayer of the dragon whose sown teeth grew into warriors)   112 **bayed the bear** brought
the bear to bay, to its last stand   113 **hounds of Sparta** (a breed famous for their swiftness
and quick scent)   114 **chiding** clamor   119 **flewed** with hanging chaps (skin at either side
of the mouth)   **sanded** sand-colored   121 **dewlapped** with skin hanging from the
chin   122–3 **matched . . . each** with each voice matched for harmony with the next in
pitch, like bells in a chime   123 **cry** pack of dogs   126 **soft** wait   133 **grace**

That Hermia should give answer of her choice?   135
EGEUS.   It is, my lord.
THESEUS.   Go bid the huntsmen wake them with their horns.

Shout within:
wind horns. They all start up.

Good morrow, friends. Saint Valentine is past.
Begin these wood-birds but to couple now?
LYSANDER. Pardon, my lord.   [*They kneel.*]
THESEUS.   I pray you all, stand up.   140
I know you two are rival enemies.
How comes this gentle concord in the world,
That hatred is so far from jealousy,
To sleep by hate, and fear no enmity?
LYSANDER. My lord, I shall reply amazedly,   145
Half sleep, half waking. But as yet, I swear,
I cannot truly say how I came here.
But as I think—for truly would I speak,
And now I do bethink me, so it is—
I came with Hermia hither. Our intent   150
Was to be gone from Athens, where we might,
Without the peril of the Athenian law—
EGEUS.   Enough, enough, my lord: you have enough.
I beg the law, the law, upon his head:
They would have stol'n away, they would, Demetrius, 155
Thereby to have defeated you and me:
You of your wife, and me of my consent:
Of my consent that she should be your wife.
DEMETRIUS.
My lord, fair Helen told me of their stealth,
Of this their purpose hither, to this wood,   160
And I in fury hither followed them;
Fair Helena in fancy following me.
But my good lord, I wot not by what power
(But by some power it is) my love to Hermia,
Melted as the snow, seems to me now   165
As the remembrance of an idle gaud,
Which in my childhood I did dote upon:
And all the faith, the virtue of my heart,

---

honor   138–9 **Saint . . . now** (birds traditionally chose their mates on St. Valentine's
Day)   143 **jealousy** suspicion   144 **hate** one it hates   152 **Without** beyond   162 **in
fancy** out of doting love   166 **idle gaud** trifling toy

The object and the pleasure of mine eye,
Is only Helena. To her, my lord,   170
Was I betrothed ere I saw Hermia:
But like a sickness, did I loathe this food.
But as in health, come to my natural taste,
Now I do wish it, love it, long for it,
And will for evermore be true to it.   175

THESEUS.   Fair lovers, you are fortunately met.
Of this discourse we more will hear anon.
Egeus, I will overbear your will:
For in the temple, by and by, with us,
These couples shall eternally be knit.   180
And for the morning now is something worn,
Our purposed hunting shall be set aside.
Away with us to Athens. Three and three,
We'll hold a feast in great solemnity.
Come Hippolyta.   185

Exeunt DUKE [HIPPOLYTA,
EGEUS,] *and* LORDS.

DEMETRIUS.
These things seem small and undistinguishable,
Like far-off mountains turnèd into clouds.

HERMIA.   Methinks I see these things with parted eye,
When everything seems double.

HELENA.   So methinks:
And I have found Demetrius, like a jewel,   190
Mine own, and not mine own.

DEMETRIUS.   Are you sure
That we are awake? It seems to me,
That yet we sleep, we dream. Do not you think
The duke was here, and bid us follow him?

HERMIA.   Yea, and my father.

HELENA.   And Hippolyta.   195

LYSANDER. And he did bid us follow to the temple.

DEMETRIUS.
Why then, we are awake: let's follow him,
And by the way let us recount our dreams.

Exeunt Lovers.

172 **sickness** sick person   173 **come**
i.e. back   179 **by and by** immediately   181 **something worn** somewhat worn on   188
parted divided (each eye seeing a separate image)   190–1 **like . . . own** like a person who

BOTTOM.   (*Wakes*.) When my cue comes, call me, and I will answer.
My next is 'Most fair Pyramus.' Hey ho. Peter Quince? 200
Flute the bellows-mender? Snout the tinker? Starveling?
God's my life! Stol'n hence, and left me asleep? I have
had a most rare vision. I have had a dream, past the wit
of man to say what dream it was. Man is but an ass, if he
go about to expound this dream. Methought I was— 205
there is no man can tell what. Methought I was, and
methought I had—but man is but a patched fool, if he
will offer to say what methought I had. The eye of man
hath not heard, the ear of man hath not seen, man's hand is
not able to taste, his tongue to conceive, nor his 210
heart to report, what my dream was. I will get Peter
Quince to write a ballad of this dream: it shall be called
Bottom's Dream; because it hath no bottom: and I
will sing it in the latter end of our play, before the duke.
Peradventure, to make it the more gracious, I shall sing 215
it at her death.   *Exit*.

[SCENE II.]

Enter QUINCE, FLUTE, SNOUT, *and* STARVELING.

QUINCE.   Have you sent to Bottom's house? Is he come home yet?

STARVELING.
He cannot be heard of. Out of doubt he is transported.

FLUTE.   If he come not, then the play is marred. It goes not forward, doth it?

QUINCE.   It is not possible. You have not a man in all Athens able   5
to discharge Pyramus but he.

FLUTE.   No, he hath simply the best wit of any handicraft man
in Athens.

QUINCE.   Yea, and the best person too, and he is a very paramour
for a sweet voice.   10

FLUTE.   You must say 'paragon.' A paramour is (God bless us)
a thing of naught.

Enter SNUG THE JOINER.

---

finds a jewel: the finder is the owner, but insecurely so   200 **Hey, ho** (he yawns)   205 **go
about** attempt   207 **patched fool** fool dressed in motley   216 **her** Thisby's

IV, ii Athens. Quince's house   2 **transported** carried away (by spirits)   6 **discharge**
portray   7 **wit** understanding   12 **of naught** wicked, naughty

SNUG.   Masters, the duke is coming from the temple, and there
             is two or three lords and ladies more married. If our
             sport had gone forward, we had all been made men.   15
FLUTE.   O sweet bully Bottom. Thus hath he lost sixpence a day
             during his life: he could not have 'scaped sixpence a day.
             And the duke had not given him sixpence a day for play-
             ing Pyramus, I'll be hanged. He would have deserved it.
             Sixpence a day in Pyramus, or nothing.   20

                        Enter BOTTOM.

BOTTOM.   Where are these lads? Where are these hearts?
QUINCE.   Bottom! O most courageous day! O most happy hour!
BOTTOM.   Masters, I am to discourse wonders: but ask me not what.
             For if I tell you, I am not true Athenian. I will tell you
             everything, right as it fell out.   25
QUINCE.   Let us hear, sweet Bottom.
BOTTOM.   Not a word of me. All that I will tell you is, that the
             duke hath dined. Get your apparel together, good
             strings to your beards, new ribbands to your pumps, meet
             presently at the palace, every man look o'er his part: for 30
             the short and the long is, our play is preferred. In any
             case, let Thisby have clean linen: and let not him that
             plays the lion pare his nails, for they shall hang out for
             the lion's claws. And most dear actors, eat no onions nor
             garlic, for we are to utter sweet breath: and I do not 35
             doubt but to hear them say it is a sweet comedy. No more
             words: away, go away.   *Exeunt.*

Act Five

[SCENE I.]

Enter THESEUS, HIPPOLYTA, *and* PHILOSTRATE,
    and his LORDS.

HIPPOLYTA.   'Tis strange, my Theseus, that these lovers speak of.
THESEUS.   More strange than true. I never may believe

---

                                              15 **made men** men
made rich   16 **sixpence a day** i.e. as a pension   22 **courageous** (he may mean
"auspicious")   30 **presently** immediately   31 **preferred** recommended (for presentation)
    V, i The palace of Theseus s.d. (F substitutes Egeus for Philostrate throughout the

These antick fables, nor these fairy toys.
Lovers and madmen have such seething brains,
Such shaping fantasies, that apprehend   5
More than cool reason ever comprehends.
The lunatic, the lover, and the poet,
Are of imagination all compact.
One sees more devils than vast hell can hold:
That is the madman. The lover, all as frantic,   10
Sees Helen's beauty in a brow of Egypt.
The poet's eye, in a fine frenzy rolling,
Doth glance from heaven to earth, from earth to heaven.
And as imagination bodies forth
The forms of things unknown, the poet's pen   15
Turns them to shapes, and gives to airy nothing,
A local habitation and a name.
Such tricks hath strong imagination,
That if it would but apprehend some joy,
It comprehends some bringer of that joy.   20
Or in the night, imagining some fear,
How easy is a bush supposed a bear.

HIPPOLYTA. But all the story of the night told over,
And all their minds transfigured so together,
More witnesseth than fancy's images,   25
And grows to something of great constancy:
But howsoever, strange and admirable.

Enter LOVERS: LYSANDER, DEMETRIUS,
HERMIA, *and* HELENA.

THESEUS.   Here come the lovers, full of joy and mirth.
Joy, gentle friends, joy and fresh days of love
Accompany your hearts.

LYSANDER.   More than to us   30
Wait in your royal walks, your board, your bed.

THESEUS.   Come now, what masques, what dances shall we have,
To wear away this long age of three hours
Between our after-supper and bed-time?

---

scene)   1 **that** i.e. which   2 **may** can   3 **antick** fantastic   **fairy toys** trivial fairy
stories   4 **seething** boiling   5 **fantasies** imaginations   8 **of . . . compact** totally composed of imagination   11 **a brow of Egypt** the swarthy face of a gypsy (believed to come
from Egypt)   20 **comprehends** includes   25 **More . . . images** testifies that it is more
than just imagination   26 **constancy** certainty   27 **howsoever** nevertheless   **admirable**
to be wondered at   30 **More** even more (joy and love)   32,40 **masques** lavish courtly
entertainments combining song and dance   34 **after-supper** late supper

Where is our usual manager of mirth?   35
What revels are in hand? Is there no play,
To ease the anguish of a torturing hour?
Call Philostrate.

PHILOSTRATE.   Here, mighty Theseus.

THESEUS. Say, what abridgment have you for this evening?
What masque, what music? How shall we beguile   40
The lazy time, if not with some delight?

PHILOSTRATE.
There is a brief how many sports are ripe:
Make choice of which your highness will see first.

[*Gives a paper.*]

THESEUS. 'The battle with the Centaurs, to be sung
By an Athenian eunuch to the harp.'   45
We'll none of that. That have I told my love
In glory of my kinsman Hercules.
'The riot of the tipsy Bacchanals,
Tearing the Thracian singer in their rage.'
That is an old device: and it was played   50
When I from Thebes came last a conqueror.
'The thrice three Muses mourning for the death
Of Learning, late deceased in beggary.'
That is some satire keen and critical,
Not sorting with a nuptial ceremony.   55
'A tedious brief scene of young Pyramus
And his love Thisby; very tragical mirth.'
Merry and tragical? tedious and brief?
That is hot ice and wondrous strange snow.
How shall we find the concord of this discord?   60

PHILOSTRATE.
A play there is, my lord, some ten words long,
Which is as brief as I have known a play:
But by ten words, my lord, it is too long,
Which makes it tedious: for in all the play
There is not one word apt, one player fitted.   65

---

39 **abridgment**
either (a) diversion to make the hours seem shorter or (b) short entertainment   41 **lazy**
(because it moves so slowly)   42 **brief** list   **ripe** ready   44 **battle . . . Centaurs** (which
occurred at the wedding of Theseus' friend Pirithous when a drunken Centaur tried to
violate the bride. Cf. Ovid, *Metamorphoses*, Bk. XII)   48–9 **riot . . . rage** (The singer
Orpheus of Thrace was torn limb from limb by the Maenads, frenzied female priests of
Bacchus. Cf. *Metamorphoses*, Bk. XI)   52–3 **thrice . . . beggary** (perhaps a reference to the
death of Robert Greene in 1592; topicality suggested by "satire," *l.* 54)   55 **sorting with**
befitting   59 **strange** prodigious   65 **fitted** (well) cast   74 **unbreathed** unpracticed,

And tragical, my noble lord, it is:
For Pyramus therein doth kill himself.
Which when I saw rehearsed, I must confess,
Made mine eyes water; but more merry tears
The passion of loud laughter never shed.   70

THESEUS. What are they that do play it?

PHILOSTRATE.

Hard-handed men, that work in Athens here,
Which never laboured in their minds till now:
And now have toiled their unbreathed memories
With this same play, against your nuptial.   75

THESEUS. And we will hear it.

PHILOSTRATE.   No, my noble lord,
It is not for you. I have heard it over,
And it is nothing, nothing in the world;
Unless you can find sport in their intents,
Extremely stretched and conned with cruel pain,   80
To do you service.

THESEUS.   I will hear that play.
For never anything can be amiss,
When simpleness and duty tender it.
Go bring them in, and take your places, ladies.

                  [*Exit* PHILOSTRATE.]

HIPPOLYTA. I love not to see wretchedness o'ercharged,   85
And duty in his service perishing.

THESEUS. Why, gentle sweet, you shall see no such thing.

HIPPOLYTA. He says they can do nothing in this kind.

THESEUS. The kinder we, to give them thanks for nothing.
Our sport shall be to take what they mistake.   90
And what poor duty cannot do, noble respect
Takes it in might, not merit.
Where I have come, great clerks have purposèd
To greet me with premeditated welcomes;
Where I have seen them shiver and look pale,   95
Make periods in the midst of sentences,
Throttle their practised accent in their fears,
And in conclusion dumbly have broke off,

---

unexercised   75 **against** in preparation for   79 **intents** i.e. to do you service   80
stretched strained   **conned** memorized   83 **simpleness . . . tender** sincerity and devotion offer   85 **wretchedness o'ercharged** poor fellows taxing themselves too much   86
duty . . . perishing the effort destroying itself in the attempt to do service   88 **in this kind**
of this sort   90 **take** accept (graciously)   91–2 **noble . . . merit** a noble nature considers
the sincerity of effort rather than the skill of execution   93–103 **Where . . . eloquence**
(Another reference (cf. II, i, 148-54) to the entertainment of Queen Elizabeth on her royal
progresses: in almost every town a scholar welcomed her with a Latin oration)   93 **clerks**
scholars   97 **Throttle** choke on

Not paying me a welcome. Trust me, sweet,
Out of this silence yet I picked a welcome: 100
And in the modesty of fearful duty
I read as much as from the rattling tongue
Of saucy and audacious eloquence.
Love, therefore, and tongue-tied simplicity,
In least, speak most, to my capacity.   105

[Enter PHILOSTRATE.]

PHILOSTRATE.
So please your grace, the Prologue is addressed.
THESEUS.   Let him approach.

Flourish trumpets. Enter the PROLOGUE
(QUINCE).

PROLOGUE.   If we offend, it is with our good will.
That you should think, we come not to offend,
But with good will. To show our simple skill,   110
That is the true beginning of our end.
Consider then, we come but in despite.
We do not come, as minding to content you,
Our true intent is. All for your delight,
We are not here. That you should here repent you,   115
The actors are at hand: and by their show,
You shall know all, that you are like to know.
THESEUS.   This fellow doth not stand upon points.
LYSANDER.   He hath rid his prologue like a rough colt: he knows
not the stop. A good moral my lord: it is not enough 120
to speak; but to speak true.
HIPPOLYTA.   Indeed he hath played on his prologue like a child on a
recorder: a sound, but not in government.
THESEUS.   His speech was like a tangled chain: nothing impaired, but
all disordered. Who is next?   125

---

101 **fearful duty** subjects whose devotion gave them
stage fright   104 **simplicity** sincerity   105 **In** i.e. saying   **capacity** way of
thinking   106 **addressed** ready   108–17 **If . . . know** (Quince's blunders in punctuation
exactly reverse the meaning)   112 **despite** malice   113 **minding** having in mind   118
stand upon points (1) pay attention to punctuation (2) bother about the niceties (of
expression)   119 **rough** unbroken   120 **stop** (1) halt (fr. horsemanship) (2) period   123
recorder flutelike wind instrument held in a vertical position   **in government** well
managed   125 **s.d.** (F adds "Tawyer with a Trumpet before them." Tawyer served John
Heminge, who was a member of Shakespeare's acting company and coeditor of the First

Enter PYRAMUS *and* THISBY, WALL,
MOONSHINE, *and* LION.

PROLOGUE. Gentles, perchance you wonder at this show,
    But wonder on, till truth make all things plain.
This man is Pyramus, if you would know:
    This beauteous lady, Thisby is certain.
This man, with lime and rough-cast, doth present   130
    Wall, that vile wall which did these lovers sunder:
And through Wall's chink, poor souls, they are content
    To whisper. At the which, let no man wonder.
This man, with lantern, dog, and bush of thorn,
    Presenteth Moonshine. For if you will know,   135
By moonshine did these lovers think no scorn
    To meet at Ninus' tomb, there, there to woo:
This grisly beast (which Lion hight by name)
The trusty Thisby, coming first by night,
Did scare away, or rather did affright: 140
And as she fled, her mantle she did fall:
    Which Lion vile with bloody mouth did stain.
Anon comes Pyramus, sweet youth and tall,
    And finds his trusty Thisby's mantle slain:
Whereat, with blade, with bloody blameful blade,   145
    He bravely broached his boiling bloody breast.
And Thisby, tarrying in mulberry shade,
    His dagger drew, and died. For all the rest,
Let Lion, Moonshine, Wall, and lovers twain,
At large discourse, while here they do remain.   150
THESEUS. I wonder if the lion be to speak.
DEMETRIUS.
    No wonder, my lord: one lion may, when many asses do.

Exeunt [PROLOGUE, PYRAMUS,] LION,
THISBY, MOONSHINE.

WALL. In this same interlude it doth befall
That I, one Snout by name, present a wall:
And such a wall, as I would have you think,   155
That had in it a crannied hole or chink:
Through which the lovers, Pyramus and Thisby,

Folio)   130 **rough-cast** rough plaster made of lime and gravel   **present** represent   138
hight is called   141 **fall** let fall   143 **tall** brave   146 **broached** opened (Shakespeare
parodies the overuse of alliteration in the earlier bombastic Elizabethan plays)   150 **At**
large in full   151 **be to speak** is to speak   153 **interlude** short play

Did whisper often, very secretly.
This loam, this rough-cast, and this stone doth show
That I am that same wall: the truth is so.   160
And this the cranny is, right and sinister,
Through which the fearful lovers are to whisper.
THESEUS.   Would you desire lime and hair to speak better?
DEMETRIUS.It is the wittiest partition that ever I heard discourse,
my lord.   165

Enter PYRAMUS.

THESEUS.   Pyramus draws near the wall: silence.
PYRAMUS.   O grim-looked night, O night with hue so black,
O night, which ever art when day is not:
O night, O night, alack, alack, alack,
I fear my Thisby's promise is forgot.   170
And thou O wall, O sweet, O lovely wall,
That stand'st between her father's ground and mine,
Thou wall, O wall, O sweet and lovely wall,
Show me thy chink, to blink through with mine eyne.

[WALL *holds up his fingers.*]

Thanks, courteous wall. Jove shield thee well for this.   175
But what see I? No Thisby do I see.
O wicked wall, through whom I see no bliss,
Cursed be thy stones for thus deceiving me.
THESEUS.   The wall methinks being sensible, should curse again.
PYRAMUS.   No in truth sir, he should not. 'Deceiving me' is 180
Thisby's cue: she is to enter now, and I am to spy her
through the wall. You shall see it will fall pat as I told
you: yonder she comes.

Enter THISBY.

THISBY.   O Wall, full often hast thou heard my moans,
For parting my fair Pyramus and me.   185
My cherry lips have often kissed thy stones;
Thy stones with lime and hair knit up in thee.
PYRAMUS.   I see a voice: now will I to the chink,
To spy and I can hear my Thisby's face.

---

161 **right and sinister** from right to left (he probably uses the
fingers of his right and left hands to form the cranny)   164 **wittiest** most
intelligent   **partition** (1) wall (2) section of a learned book or speech   174 **eyne**
eyes   178 **stones** (1) lit. (2) testicles (one of the interlude's many bawdy undertones, of
which its actors are unaware)   179 **sensible** capable of feelings and perception   **again**
back   180 **should not** will not   182 **pat** exactly   193 **Limander** (he means

Thisby?   190

THISBY.   My love thou art, my love I think.

PYRAMUS.   Think what thou wilt, I am thy lover's grace:
             And, like Limander, am I trusty still.

THISBY.   And I like Helen, till the Fates me kill.

PYRAMUS.   Not Shafalus to Procrus, was so true.   195

THISBY.   As Shafalus to Procrus, I to you.

PYRAMUS.   O kiss me through the hole of this vile wall.

THISBY.   I kiss the wall's hole, not your lips at all.

PYRAMUS.   Wilt thou at Ninny's tomb meet me straightway?

THISBY.   Tide life, tide death, I come without delay.   200

                   [*Exeunt* PYRAMUS *and* THISBY.]

WALL.   Thus have I, Wall, my part dischargèd so;
             And being done, thus Wall away doth go.   *Exit.*

THESEUS.   Now is the mural down between the two neighbours.

DEMETRIUS.
             No remedy my lord, when walls are so wilful to hear
             without warning.   205

HIPPOLYTA.   This is the silliest stuff that ever I heard.

THESEUS.   The best in this kind are but shadows: and the worst are
             no worse, if imagination amend them.

HIPPOLYTA.   It must be your imagination then, and not theirs.

THESEUS.   If we imagine no worse of them than they of themselves, 210
             they may pass for excellent men. Here come two noble
             beasts in, a man and a lion.

                   Enter LION *and* MOONSHINE.

LION.   You ladies, you, whose gentle hearts do fear
                 The smallest monstrous mouse that creeps on floor,
             May now perchance both quake and tremble here,   215
                 When lion rough in wildest rage doth roar.
             Then know that I, as Snug the joiner am
             A lion fell, nor else no lion's dam:
             For if I should as lion come in strife
             Into this place, 'twere pity on my life.   220

THESEUS.   A very gentle beast, and of a good conscience.

DEMETRIUS.
             The very best at a beast, my lord, that e'er I saw.

"Leander")   194 **Helen** (he means "Hero")   195 **Shafalus to Procrus** (he means
"Cephalus" and "Procris" (see above, III, ii, 389 n.))   199 **Ninny** fool (he means
"Ninus")   200 **Tide** come, betide   203 **mural** wall   205 **without warning** either (a)
without warning the parents or (b) unexpectedly   207 **but shadows** only actors   218 **fell**
fierce   **nor . . . dam** and not a lioness   222 **best, beast** (pronounced similarly)

LYSANDER. This lion is a very fox for his valour.

THESEUS. True: and a goose for his discretion.

DEMETRIUS.

Not so my lord: for his valour cannot carry his discre- 225
tion, and the fox carries the goose.

THESEUS. His discretion, I am sure, cannot carry his valour: for the
goose carries not the fox. It is well: leave it to his discretion, and let us listen to the moon.

MOONSHINE.

This lanthorn doth the hornèd moon present—   230

DEMETRIUS.

He should have worn the horns on his head.

THESEUS. He is no crescent, and his horns are invisible within the
circumference.

MOONSHINE.

This lanthorn doth the hornèd moon present,
Myself, the man i' th' moon do seem to be.   235

THESEUS. This is the greatest error of all the rest; the man should
be put into the lanthorn. How is it else the man i' th'
moon?

DEMETRIUS.

He dares not come there for the candle; for you see, it
is already in snuff.   240

HIPPOLYTA. I am aweary of this moon. Would he would change.

THESEUS. It appears, by his small light of discretion, that he is in
the wane: but yet in courtesy, in all reason, we must stay
the time.

LYSANDER. Proceed, Moon.   245

MOONSHINE.

All that I have to say, is to tell you that the lanthorn is
the moon, I the man i' th' moon, this thornbush my
thornbush, and this dog my dog.

DEMETRIUS.

Why, all these should be in the lanthorn: for all these are
in the moon. But silence: here comes Thisby.   250

Enter THISBY.

THISBY. This is old Ninny's tomb. Where is my love?

223-4 **valour . . . discretion** (as Falstaff says, "the better part of valour is discretion")   **for**
regarding   230 **lanthorn** lantern (once made of horn)   230-1 **horned . . . head** (referring
to the cuckold or deceived husband, who supposedly grew horns)   232 **crescent** horned
moon (the two points being its horns)   240 **in snuff** (1) in need of snuffing (having a long,
burnt-out wick or snuff) (2) in a temper   243 **stay** await   257 **moused** shaken, as a cat

LION.   Oh!   *The* LION *roars.* THISBY *runs off.*
DEMETRIUS.
        Well roared, Lion.
THESEUS.   Well run, Thisby.
HIPPOLYTA. Well shone, Moon. Truly, the moon shines with a good 255
        grace.

                    [*The* LION *shakes* THISBY's *mantle.*]

THESEUS.   Well moused, Lion.
DEMETRIUS.
        And then came Pyramus.

                    Enter PYRAMUS. [*Exit* LION.]

LYSANDER. And so the lion vanished.
PYRAMUS.   Sweet moon, I thank thee for thy sunny beams,   260
            I thank thee, moon, for shining now so bright.
        For by thy gracious, golden, glittering gleams,
            I trust to take of truest Thisby sight.
                But stay: O spite!
                But mark, poor knight,   265
            What dreadful dole is here?
                Eyes, do you see!
                How can it be!
            O dainty duck, O dear!
                Thy mantle good,   270
                What, stained with blood?
            Approach, ye Furies fell:
                O Fates! come, come:
                Cut thread and thrum,
            Quail, crush, conclude, and quell.   275
THESEUS.   This passion, and the death of a dear friend, would go
        near to make a man look sad.
HIPPOLYTA. Beshrew my heart, but I pity the man.
PYRAMUS.   O wherefore Nature, didst thou lions frame?
            Since lion vile hath here deflowered my dear.   280
        Which is—no, no—which was the fairest dame
            That lived, that loved, that liked, that looked with
            cheer.

---

shakes a mouse   266 **dole** dolor, grief   272 **Furies** classical spirits of the underworld who
avenged murder   273 **Fates** three sisters who spun the thread of human destiny, which at
will was cut with a shears   274 **thrum** fringelike end of the warp in weaving   275 **Quail**
subdue   **quell** kill   278 **Beshrew** curse (meant lightly)   280 **deflowered**
ravished   282 **cheer** a countenance

Come tears, confound:
Out sword, and wound
The pap of Pyramus: 285
Ay, that left pap,
Where heart doth hop.   [*Stabs himself.*]
Thus die I, thus, thus, thus.
Now am I dead,
Now am I fled,   290
My soul is in the sky.
Tongue lose thy light,
Moon take thy flight,   [*Exit* MOONSHINE.]
Now die, die, die, die, die.   [*Dies.*]

DEMETRIUS.
No die, but an ace for him. For he is but one.   295
LYSANDER. Less than an ace, man. For he is dead, he is nothing.
THESEUS. With the help of a surgeon, he might yet recover, and
prove an ass.
HIPPOLYTA. How chance Moonshine is gone before Thisby comes
back and finds her lover?   300

Enter THISBY.

THESEUS. She will find him by starlight. Here she comes, and her
passion ends the play.
HIPPOLYTA. Methinks she should not use a long one for such a
Pyramus: I hope she will be brief.

DEMETRIUS.
A mote will turn the balance, which Pyramus, which 305
Thisby, is the better: he for a man, God warr'nt us;
she for a woman,' God bless us.
LYSANDER. She hath spied him already with those sweet eyes.

DEMETRIUS.
And thus she means, videlicet—

THISBY.   Asleep my love?   310
What, dead, my dove?
O Pyramus, arise,
Speak, speak. Quite dumb?
Dead, dead? A tomb
Must cover thy sweet eyes.   315
These lily lips,

---

283 **confound** destroy   285 **pap** breast   292-3
Tongue . . . Moon (he reverses the two subjects)   295 **die** (singular of "dice")   **ace** a
throw of one at dice   **but one** (1) unique (2) one person   298 **ass** (w. pun on "ace")   305
mote speck of dust   **which . . . which** whether . . . or   306 **warr'nt** warrant,
protect   309 **means** (1) laments (2) lodges a formal complaint (fr. law)   **videlicet**

This cherry nose,
These yellow cowslip cheeks,
Are gone, are gone:
Lovers, make moan: 320
His eyes were green as leeks.
O Sisters Three,
Come, come to me,
With hands as pale as milk,
Lay them in gore,   325
Since you have shore
With shears his thread of silk.
Tongue, not a word:
Come trusty sword,
Come blade, my breast imbrue: 330

                                        [*Stabs herself.*]

And farewell friends:
Thus Thisby ends:
Adieu, adieu, adieu.   [*Dies.*]

THESEUS. Moonshine and Lion are left to bury the dead.

DEMETRIUS.
           Ay, and Wall too.   335

BOTTOM. [*Starts up.*] No, I assure you, the wall is down that parted
their fathers. Will it please you to see the Epilogue, or
to hear a Bergomask dance between two of our company?

THESEUS. No epilogue, I pray you; for your play needs no excuse.
Never excuse: for when the players are all dead, there 340
need none to be blamed. Marry, if he that writ it had
played Pyramus and hanged himself in Thisby's garter,
it would have been a fine tragedy: and so it is truly, and
very notably discharged. But come, your Bergomask:
let your Epilogue alone.   [*A dance.*] 345
The iron tongue of midnight hath told twelve.
Lovers, to bed, 'tis almost fairy time.
I fear we shall outsleep the coming morn,
As much as we this night have overwatched.
This palpable gross play hath well beguiled   350
The heavy gait of night. Sweet friends, to bed.

---

namely   318 **cowslip** yellow primrose   322 **Sisters Three** the Fates (above, l. 273
n.)   330 **imbrue** stain with gore   338 **Bergomask** exaggerated country dance (named
after the people of Bergamo, Italy, noted for rustic behavior)   346 **iron tongue** i.e. of the
bell   **told** counted (w. pun on "tolled")   347 **fairy time** (from midnight to
daybreak)   349 **overwatched** stayed up too late   350 **palpable gross** obvious and
crude   351 **heavy** (1) slow (2) drowsy

A fortnight hold we this solemnity,
In nightly revels, and new jollity.   *Exeunt.*

Enter PUCK [*with a broom*].

PUCK.   Now the hungry lion roars,
    And the wolf behowls the moon;   355
Whilst the heavy ploughman snores,
    All with weary task fordone.
Now the wasted brands do glow,
    Whilst the screech-owl, screeching loud,
Puts the wretch that lies in woe   360
    In remembrance of a shroud.
Now it is the time of night,
    That the graves, all gaping wide,
Every one lets forth his sprite,
    In the church-way paths to glide.   365
And we fairies, that do run
    By the triple Hecate's team,
From the presence of the sun,
    Following darkness like a dream,
Now are frolic: not a mouse   370
Shall disturb this hallowed house.
I am sent with broom before,
To sweep the dust behind the door.

Enter KING *and* QUEEN OF FAIRIES, *with all
their train.*

OBERON.   Through the house give glimmering light,
    By the dead and drowsy fire,   375
Every elf and fairy sprite,
    Hop as light as bird from brier,
And this ditty after me,
Sing, and dance it trippingly.

TITANIA.   First rehearse your song by rote,   380
To each word a warbling note.
Hand in hand, with fairy grace,
Will we sing and bless this place.   [*Song and dance.*]

---

356 **heavy** sleepy   357 **fordone** worn out, "done in"   358 **wasted brands** burnt logs   359 **screech-owl** (bird of ill omen)   360 **wretch . . . woe** sick person   364 **sprite** spirit, ghost   367 **triple Hecate** the moon goddess, identified as Cynthia in heaven, Diana on earth, and Hecate in hell   **team** dragons that pull the chariot of the night moon   370 **frolic** frolicsome   373 **To sweep the dust** (Puck often

OBERON.   Now, until the break of day,
           Through this house each fairy stray.   385
           To the best bride-bed will we,
           Which by us shall blessèd be:
           And the issue there create,
           Ever shall be fortunate:
           So shall all the couples three   390
           Ever true in loving be:
           And the blots of Nature's hand
           Shall not in their issue stand.
           Never mole, harelip, nor scar,
           Nor mark prodigious, such as are   395
           Despisèd in nativity,
           Shall upon their children be.
           With this field-dew consecrate,
           Every fairy take his gait,
           And each several chamber bless,   400
           Through this palace, with sweet peace;
           And the owner of it blest,
           Ever shall in safety rest.
           Trip away: make no stay:
           Meet me all by break of day.   405

                    Exeunt [all but PUCK].

PUCK.   If we shadows have offended,
           Think but this, and all is mended,
           That you have but slumbered here,
           While these visions did appear.
           And this weak and idle theme,   410
           No more yielding but a dream,
           Gentles, do not reprehend.
           If you pardon, we will mend.
           And as I am an honest Puck,
           If we have unearnèd luck,   415
           Now to scape the serpent's tongue,
           We will make amends, ere long:

---

helped with household chores)   **behind** from behind   388,393 **issue** children   388
create created   392 **blots . . . hand** birth defects   395 **mark prodigious** unnatural
birthmark   398 **consecrate** consecrated   400 **several** separate   402–3 **And the . . . rest**
(Singer em.; lines transposed in Q and F)   406 **shadows** actors   410 **idle** foolish   411
No . . . but yielding nothing more than   413 **mend** improve   415 **unearned luck** better
luck than we deserve   416 **serpent's tongue** hissing of the audience

Else the Puck a liar call.
So, good night unto you all.
Give me your hands, if we be friends: 420
And Robin shall restore amends.   [*Exit.*]

FINIS.

Textual Notes

I,i   10 **New** Rowe em.; Q: "Now"   24,26 **Stand forth** Rowe em.; s.d. in Q & F   216
sweet Theobald em.; Q, F: "sweld"   219 **stranger companies** Theobald em.; Q, F:
"strange companions," obvious error because of the lack of rhyme
    II,i   109 **thin** Tyrwhitt em.; Q, F: "chinne"   190 **slay . . . slayeth** Theobald em.; Q,
F: "stay . . . stayeth"
    II,ii   49 **interchained** Q; F: "interchanged"
    III,i   73 **Odorous, odorous** Collier em.; F: "Odours, odours"; Q: "Odours,
odorous"   163 **Mustard seed. Hail.** Capell em.; Q, F omit   180 **of more** Collier em.; Q,
F: "you more"
    III,ii   80 **so** Pope em.; F, Q omit   85 **sleep** Rowe em.; Q: "slippe"; F: "slip"   213 **like**
Theobald em.; Q, F: "life"   220 **passionate** F; not in Q   250 **prayers** Theobald em.; Q,
F: "praise"   257 **No, no, sir** F; Q: "heele" for "sir"   264 **potion** Q; F: "poison"   451 **To**
Rowe em.; Q and F omit
    IV,i   81 **five** Theobald em.; Q, F: "fine"   89 **prosperity** Q; F: "posterity"   214 **our**
Walker em.; Q, F: "a"
    V,i   187 **up in thee** F; Q: "now againe"   203 **mural down** Pope em.; Q: "Moon used";
F: "morall downe"   262 **gleams** Knight em.; Q, F: "beams", probably from l. 260   263
take . . . sight Q; F: "taste of truest Thisbies sight" is possibly correct, as Bottom confuses
the senses   355 **behowls** Warburton em.; Q, F: "beholds"   402-3 **And the . . . rest**
Singer em.; lines transposed in Q and F

                                                                420 **hands**
applause   421 **restore amends** do better in the future (a conventional promise in epilogues)

ROMEO AND JULIET

Romeo and Juliet depicts young love against a background of old hatreds, which destroy the lovers but which in turn are wiped out by their sacrifice. The tone of the play is lyric, moving from rapture to despair as symbolized by a dominant poetic image of incandescence surrounded by darkness. The story develops by contrasts in language, characterization, and action. Impetuous, selfless, dedicated to perfect love, Romeo and Juliet are contrasted with the rational Friar Lawrence, with their possessive parents, and with their bawdy confidants, the Nurse and Mercutio. Ominous, brooding over all in the darkness surrounding the light, are the contrary stars.

Romeo and Juliet has always been one of Shakespeare's most popular plays; audiences in every age group seem to find the hero and heroine irresistibly sympathetic as they struggle to attain love in a hostile world. The opening scene introduces us to that world, a brawling society in which hatred between two families—Capulet and Montague—erupts in the street: servant cudgels servant, gentleman duels with gentleman, Montague abuses Capulet. It is a materialistic society, where money and position are a major concern in marriage arrangements; the Capulets are pleased with Paris's "noble parentage" and "fair demesnes" (domains) and the Nurse brags of Juliet's dowery: ". . . he that can lay hold of her/ Shall have the chinks" (coin). It bustles with the petty activities of daily life. The fighting crowd in the street and the dancing couples at Capulet's party represent the world from which Romeo and Juliet withdraw to seek a happiness bound solely by each other's presence; as soon as they meet, they are oblivious to everyone else. Their love develops in isolation from the society whose blood feud finally destroys that love.

Although their world of love is confined within intimate bounds, they express that love with extravagant abandon; cosmic imagery describes the wonder and splendor of a love that is both physical and spiritual. At their first meeting, Romeo can hardly contain his eagerness to touch Juliet and then to kiss her. Along with the rapture of their love declarations in the balcony scene (II, ii) is the agony at being physically separated (Juliet is on the upper stage, as the text indicates). After they are married, the tone of Juliet's epithalamium (hymn in celebration of a marriage; III, ii, 1-31) is one of eager longing for consummation. Ennobled by love, they grow under its influence to rich if brief maturity.

As love sets them apart from the rest of the world, so the lovers measure time emotionally, not realistically: ". . . in a minute there are many days" (III, v, 45); a lifetime of sorrow cannot counter-balance "the exchange of joy/ That one short minute gives me in her sight" (II, vi, 4-5). On the other hand, constantly aware of impending expiration of time, as in a contract, they express their premonitions in time-business metaphors: the "fearful date" the party presages; the "contract" which is "too rash, too unadvised, too sudden" (II, ii, 117-18), and, in the tomb, Romeo's "dateless bargain to engrossing death" (V, iii, 115).

Their loss is all the more pitiable because Shakespeare has transformed them from dupes of Fortune (as they are depicted in Brooke's poem, the source of the play) to independent young people responsible for their actions. Brooke editorially, and through the Friar's remarks, stresses that Romeo and Juliet are punished because they have allowed emotion to overcome reason and because they have disobeyed their parents. The retribution at work in Shakespeare's play is a punishment directed not at the children, but at the parents.

The Romeo of the earlier scenes is, to use a convenient expression, more in love with love than with Rosaline. He displays such traditional traits of the literary type of courtly lover as desire for solitude, sleeplessness, and extravagant declarations of commitment to the lady. The artificiality of his expressions of love for Rosaline contrasts with the simplicity of his first impression of Juliet: "O she doth teach the torches to burn bright" (I, v, 42). Although love drives him to emotional extremes, Romeo is reputed to be well-balanced and well-behaved, as Capulet himself reports: "Verona brags of him/ To be a virtuous and well-governed youth" (65-66). The post-banishment hysteria, weeping and throwing himself on the floor of the friar's cell, tends to overshadow Romeo's solid effort to appease Tybalt by accepting his insults meekly and—with dire results—by playing the peacemaker even while Tybalt and Mercutio fight.

It is perhaps typical of one on the threshold of maturity to draw allusions from childhood, which is still close to youth in time, but far removed in outlook. Romeo relates his present experience in love to his schoolboy past: "Love goes toward love as schoolboys from their books,/ But love from love, toward school with heavy looks" (II, ii 157-58).

Romeo's change of locale may be indicative of a change in character, for in Mantua he demonstrates a new maturity. Whereas he succumbed to emotion when told of his banishment, he receives the report of Juliet's death with resolve and a challenge to the stars that have crossed him. His cheeks may be pale, as his servant notes, but Romeo has the strength of will to force the apothecary to sell him poison, and the bitter insight to comment that the gold offered is "worse poison to men's souls" (V, i, 80).

When Paris appears at the tomb, Romeo, as he did with Tybalt, again attempts in vain to pacify a challenger whom he is forced to kill. Nothing can deter him from his resolve to die with Juliet. World-weary, but possessed by the same sense of wonder that filled him at their first meeting, he again describes her beauty in terms of dazzling brightness set off by darkness, a beauty that makes "This vault a feasting presence full of light" (V, iii, 86). He drinks the poison as if it were a toast: "Here's to my love."

Under the influence of love, Juliet matures more swiftly than does Romeo. In her first scene, when Lady Capulet suggests marriage, Juliet replies, "It is an honour that I dream not of" (I, iii, 66), but in the balcony scene, it is she, not Romeo, who first proposes marriage. In the earlier scene, Juliet remarks that she will show favor to Paris only insofar as her mother consents, but once she has met Romeo, at the end of the party she employs guile in questioning the Nurse to discover his identity by first pretending to be interested in two other partygoers. Although fourteen was a marriageable age in days when the period of life expectancy was considerably shorter, Juliet is still very young, and therefore her plight is all the more poignant. The incident in Juliet's babyhood recalled by the Nurse is not only her bawdy contribution to the subject of Juliet's prospective marriage, but also a reminder that it is only eleven years since Juliet was weaned. As Romeo does, Juliet will sometimes allude to childhood, indicating both a proximity to that period and an awareness that she is past it. Longing for Romeo to join her on their wedding night, she compares the tediousness of the day to that of "the night before some festival,/ To an impatient child that hath new robes/ And may not wear them" (III, ii, 29-31).

Although impetuousity is characteristic of both the lovers, it is Juliet who in the balcony scene fears they may be acting too suddenly and too rashly, and who interjects into the lyrical declarations of love the everyday details of a time and a place for the marriage.

Once she meets Romeo, love for him is the single motivation of all her actions. Her inheritance (so important to her father in I, ii, 15) she will lay at Romeo's feet, and "follow . . . [him] my lord throughout the world" (II, ii, 148). Love gives her the inner strength she maintains under the emotional stress of the confrontation with her father and the taking of the potion. Even when she succumbs to emotion in her outburst on hearing that Romeo has killed Tybalt, she regains control of herself by rationalizing that "My husband lives that Tybalt would have slain" (III, ii, 105). With her mother in III, v, and in the next scene with Paris in the Friar's cell, Juliet displays the ability to conceal her true feelings and at the same time express them ironically, in words that have one meaning for the listener and another for herself. Isolation has been a condition of her love, and, therefore, when she realizes that father, mother, and even the Nurse have deserted her, there is no self-pity. She says, "My dismal scene I needs must act alone" (IV, iii, 19), and prepares to take the vial which the Friar has given her. Despite her fearful imaginings of waking in the tomb (drawn mostly from the source), she nevertheless carries out her resolve and drinks the potion. The Friar arrives at the tomb in time to save her, but refusal is inevitable from the woman into whom Juliet has grown. There is a world of sad maturity in her reply, "Go get thee hence, for I will not away" (V, iii, 160).

Action, characterization, and language are structured on an almost formal series of contrasts. The opening scene is a patterned one, as servants, young men, and elders from the feuding households encounter their opposite numbers. Soon the hating Capulet and Montague are contrasted to their loving children in age and outlook. In the style, the use of antithesis reinforces the contrast in characterization and action. In addition to the more formal oxymoron (seeming contradiction) of "O brawling love, O loving hate" are such lines as Juliet's response when she learns Romeo's indentity: "My only love sprung from my only hate,/ Too early seen unknown, and known too late" (I, v, 136-37). The families' "ancient grudge" stretching back over the years, there follow with breath-taking swiftness, the love, marriage, and death of Romeo and Juliet in less than a week.

Scene is juxtaposed with scene to underscore the dramatic irony. Mercutio's coarse jests in his mock conjuration of Romeo precede the lyrical utterances of the balcony scene, and Juliet's epithalamium celebrating marriage directly follows the sentencing of Romeo to banishment. On the lower stage, Capulet sets the date for Juliet's wedding to Paris, while on the upper stage, which represents Juliet's bedroom, the curtains are drawn across the lovers' consummation of their marriage. Juliet lies in that same room drugged by the potion, while the servants and Capulet bustle about below, preparing for festivities which never take place. Most deeply poignant is the contrast between the lovers' hopes and their fate.

In contrast to Romeo's intensity is the aimlessness of his young friends, who idle in the summer's heat, crash parties, exchange ribaldries, and fight in the streets. They also contribute to the sense of realism in the action surrounding the love story. Although the old people may be weary of the feud and, as Capulet indicates to Paris, are inclined to let it subside, there are younger, hotter bloods, like Tybalt, anxious to maintain the dispute. As humorless as he is irascible, Tybalt is a ready target for Mercutio, who ridicules Tybalt's punctilious adherence to the minutiae of the dueling code. Whether or not, as Dryden charged, Shakespeare killed off Mercutio to save the unity of the play, the vividness and appeal of this character is indisputable. Mercutio's cynical comments on the romantic action place it in a realistic perspective. His "Queen Mab" speech (I, iv, 53 ff.), an aria during which the action stands still, has been suspiciously regarded as a leftover from *A Midsummer Night's Dream*, and staunchly defended on the grounds that dreams and imaginings are very much a part of *Romeo and Juliet*. Though it is difficult (but not impossible) to consider the passage a revelation of character, it is easy to appreciate its verbal virtuosity, a talent with which Mercutio is plentifully endowed. Its content, like Mercutio himself, defies classification. The passage begins with exquisite description of tiny fairy folk (the diminution of fairies being Shakespeare's own invention), proceeds to commentary on dreams as expressions of unfulfilled desires, and concludes with the bawdy mockery that is Mercutio's trademark. He applies his keen wit to the most serious subjects, even to death itself, and he dies as gaily as he lived, with a pun on his lips (". . . ask for me tomorrow, and you shall find me a grave man"), but also with a curse on the houses of Capulet and Montague (III, i, 93-94, 102).

From the nurse in the source, who is a talkative, practical, and bawdy go-between, Shakespeare develops his intensely human Nurse, who combines sense and sentimentality, garrulity and good intentions. Her humor stems as much from her circumlocution as from her bawdiness. She has a zest for living, reminiscent of Chaucer's Wife of Bath (whom the nurse in the source resembles even more closely). Like Mercutio, the Nurse equates love with its physical expression and is so insensitive to Juliet's feelings as to advise her to marry Paris, with the suggestion that Romeo still may visit her by stealth. Old, earthy, prosaic, slow, and realistic, she is an obvious contrast to her young charge.

Materialistic, stubbornly insistent that he knows what is best for his child, old Capulet is representative of all four parents in the play and of a young person's view of parents in general. He also is individualized. A good host who provides plentifully, reminisces with the older relatives, and encourages the younger ones to dance, he can begin with plans for a small wedding reception and end up hiring twenty cooks. His is the restraining influence on Tybalt, who would like to turn the party into a continuation of the fight that was interrupted in the opening scene. A doting parent at first, Capulet becomes harsh and unrelenting. Not only does Juliet's refusal thwart his will, but it threatens his standing with Paris, to whom Capulet has made a "desperate tender" (offer) of Juliet's love. At the end it is Capulet who makes the first gesture of reconciliation.

Contrast is implicit in the theme of the play: the triumph of love over hate, the spiritual victory of the lovers despite earthly defeat. Prevalent throughout is the motif of *Liebestod,* death in love that carries with it the seeds of its own destruction. Before they meet, during their exchanges of love, and at their parting, the lovers have premonitions of death that prove true. Before going to Capulet's party, Romeo fears an "untimely [early] death" (I, iv, 111), and Juliet in the balcony scene, likens their love to "the lightning which doth cease to be,/ Ere one can say, 'It lightens' " (II, ii, 119-20). The motif intensifies as the play progresses. Romeo begs the Friar to marry them so that "love-devouring Death" may then do his worst: "It is enough I may but call her mine" (II, vi, 7-8). Seeing Romeo below, in their final farewell, Juliet says he looks "as one dead in the bottom of a tomb" (III, v, 56). In the first scene of Act V, Romeo's dream of his death and revival by kisses from Juliet foreshadows the actual merging of love and death in the final scene in the tomb. Here, as in the previous love scenes, declarations of love light up the surrounding darkness. But in contrast to those scenes, the lovers are first separated and then joined. Their union in love is realized only through union in death.

That reason should control the emotions is constantly emphasized in the source poem. In the play this thought is voiced by the Friar, but it is demonstrated by the lovers in achieving a maturity no longer at the mercy of emotion. The fickleness of Fortune and the inevitability of Fate as stressed in the source are strains appearing also in the play.

In its style, *Romeo and Juliet* is both patterned and poetic, marked by the lyric virtuosity characteristic of plays written about the same time, such as *Richard II.* Act. II, Scene ii, is almost entirely lyrical, and the choruses to Acts I and II are in sonnet form, as is the dialogue of the lovers when they meet in I, v. Rhyme occurs throughout, even in the final speeches. Among the many rhetorical devices are oxymoron and antithesis as mentioned above.

While their expression is unique, the metaphors, with some exceptions, are those common to Renaissance poetry, such as the lover as a worshipper at the shrine of the lady or as a boat tossed on the perilous sea of love. In the sonnet which they speak upon meeting, the pilgrim metaphor expresses not only Romeo's desire to touch Juliet (the shrine) but also his worship of her, thus combining the physical and spiritual aspects of love. The ship image, a favorite of Petrarchan sonneteers, is used by Romeo first in the balcony scene:

> I am no pilot, yet wert thou as far
> As that vast shore washed with the farthest sea,
> I should adventure for such merchandise.   (II, ii, 82-84)

It is echoed at his death:

Come bitter conduct, come unsavoury guide,
Thou desperate pilot, now at once run on
The dashing rocks, thy seasick weary bark . . .(V, iii, 116-18)

Another convention is the comparison of a person to a book, with which
Lady Capulet praises Paris to Juliet (I, iii, 81-92), but book metaphors
used by Romeo and Juliet carry the additional implication that the figure
comes naturally to them because they have completed their education but
recently.

Caroline Spurgeon points out that the play's dominant image is that of
light, as the ardor of the lovers is "the irradiating glory of sunlight and
starlight in a dark world." Imagery from the balcony scene is echoed in the
tomb scene; in the former, Juliet is the "bright angel" who is "glorious to
this night" (II, ii, 26-27), and in the latter, she makes the vault "a feasting
presence full of light" (V, iii, 86).

Mark Van Doren observes that night is friendly to the lovers and day is
hostile to them, that night joins them and day parts them. In her
epithalamium in III, ii, Juliet invokes the night, which will bring Romeo
to her. The following dawn, their reluctance to admit that night is over
begins on a plaintive note and ends in desperation: "More light and light,
more dark and dark our woes" (III, v, 36).

At the other end of the scale in this play, one of Shakespear's most
lyrical and at the same time one of his most bawdy, are Mercutio's
comments on love. He personifies Love not as Cupid but as an idiot, and,
in innumerable puns on sexual organs, equates love with sex.

Romeo and Juliet express in figurative language the whole gamut of
their emotional experience: impatience—"Love's heralds should be
thoughts" (II, v, 4); physical longing—"O that I were a glove upon that
hand" (II, ii 24); intoxication—"My ears have not yet drunk a hundred
words" (58); ecstasy—"It is my soul that calls upon my name./ How
silver-sweet sound lovers' tongues by night" (165-66); and grief—"Dry
sorrow drinks our blood" (III, v, 59).

Ironically, the stars not only symbolize Fate, which is adverse to the
"star-crossed" lovers, but also represent the brightness of love. If Juliet's
eyes and the stars were to change places, says Romeo, "The brightness of
her cheek would shame those stars/ As daylight doth a lamp" (II, ii, 19-20).
If Romeo at death is "cut . . . out in little stars," says Juliet, "all the world
will be in love with night" (III, ii, 22-24).

As accompaniment to the *Liebestod* motif, there are recurrent images of
death. Death is personified as a devourer, a conqueror, and a lover or
bridegroom. The last metaphor is most often associated with Juliet:
"Death, not Romeo, take my maidenhead" (III, ii, 137); "I would the fool

were married to her grave" (III, v, 141); ". . . make the bridal bed/ In that dim monument where Tybalt lies" (202-3); "Flower as she was, deflowered by him:/ Death is my son-in-law" (IV, v, 37-38); "Sweet flower, with flowers thy bridal bed I strew/ O woe, thy canopy is dust and stones" (V, iii, 12-13); "Shall I believe/ That unsubstantial Death is amorous,/ And that the lean abhorred monster keeps/ Thee here in dark to be his paramour?" (102-5).

Date, Text, Source

A likely date of composition is 1595, during the period in which Shakespeare wrote such other highly lyrical plays, marked by an almost self-conscious display of poetic technique, as *Richard II* and *A Midsummer Night's Dream*. The most reliable text, on which the present one is based (with significant alternate readings noted), is that of the Second Quarto (Q2), published in 1599. That it was set from Shakespeare's own manuscript is a probability suggested by the presence of false starts and of original passages included along with their rewritten versions. Q1, published in 1597, is considered a "bad" Quarto (perhaps a reconstruction by unscrupulous actors), faulty in most areas, although occasionally helpful for correction of obvious errors and for its fairly full stage directions, such as "Tibalt under Romeos arme thrusts Mercutio in and flyes" (III, i, 86). The First Folio of 1623, the first collection of the plays, is based upon Q3 (1609), which was printed from Q2. Q3 and Q4 are occasionally helpful.

Published in 1562, Arthur Brooke's *The Tragical History of Romeus and Juliet* (based on the story told by Bandello and translated into French by Boaistuau) is a poem of some six thousand lines, rhyming *abcb*, the *c* line in tetrameter and the others in trimeter. It is preceded by a sonnet, which gives "The Argument," or synopsis, of the story. In the inclusion and sequence of incidents, Shakespeare follows this source more closely than he does any other on which he bases a play, although in transforming the poem to a drama, he telescopes the time, develops suspense, deepens characterization, and lifts the expression to poetic heights never achieved by Brooke. Mercutio, although he appears briefly at Capulet's party in the original, is a Shakespearean creation; the Nurse is further developed from a lively portrayal in the original. Here and there the dialogue is suggested or even identical. In the original, which is consciously medieval in tone, the tragedy is clearly due to a reversal of fortune, an idea repeated many times:

> For Fortune changeth more
> Than fickle fantasy;
> In nothing Fortune constant is,
> Save in unconstancy.

As the workmanlike narrative is converted to dramatic poetry, Shake-speare transforms the central pair from conventional medieval lovers to vivid and appealing individuals, whose names ever since have symbolized the joys and sorrows of young love.

ROMEO AND JULIET

ROMEO AND JULIET

ESCALUS, *Prince of Verona*

PARIS, *a young count, kinsman to the* PRINCE

MONTAGUE
CAPULET
} *heads of two houses at enmity with each other*

An old Man of the Capulet family

ROMEO, *son to* MONTAGUE

MERCUTIO, *kinsman to the* PRINCE *and friend to* ROMEO

BENVOLIO, *nephew to* MONTAGUE *and friend to* ROMEO

TYBALT, *nephew to* LADY CAPULET

FRIAR LAWRENCE
FRIAR JOHN
} *Franciscans*

BALTHASAR, *servant to* ROMEO

ABRAHAM, *servant to* MONTAGUE

SAMPSON
GREGORY
} *servants to* CAPULET

PETER, *servant to* JULIET'S *nurse*

Page to PARIS

An Apothecary

Three Musicians

An Officer

CHORUS

LADY MONTAGUE, *wife to* MONTAGUE

LADY CAPULET, *wife to* CAPULET

JULIET, *daughter to* CAPULET

Nurse to JULIET

Citizens of Verona, men and women of both houses, Maskers, Guards, Watchmen, Servants, and Attendants

SCENE: *Verona and Mantua*]

The Prologue

CHORUS. Two households both alike in dignity,
    (In fair Verona where we lay our scene)
From ancient grudge, break to new mutiny,
    Where civil blood makes civil hands unclean:
From forth the fatal loins of these two foes,   5
    A pair of star-crossed lovers take their life:
Whose misadventured piteous overthrows,
    Doth with their death bury their parents' strife.
The fearful passage of their death-marked love,
    And the continuance of their parents' rage,   10
Which but their children's end naught could remove,
    Is now the two hours' traffic of our stage.
The which if you with patient ears attend,
What here shall miss, our toil shall strive to mend.

Prologue, s.d. **Chorus** (a character who introduced the action to follow. This and the speech preceding Act II are in sonnet form)   1 **dignity** rank   3 **mutiny** discord   4 **civil** citizens'   5 **fatal** (1) ill-fated (2) death-producing   6 **star-crossed** destined from birth to be thwarted by unfavorable stars   7 **misadventured** unfortunate   9 **fearful** fear-inspiring **passage** course   11 **but** except for   12 **two hours' traffic** (the usual length of Elizabethan plays, because there was no scenery to change)   14 **here** i.e. in the play   **miss** be lacking   **our toil** i.e. in acting

Act One

Enter SAMPSON *and* GREGORY, *with swords and bucklers, of the house of* CAPULET.

SAMPSON. Gregory, on my word we'll not carry coals.

GREGORY. No, for then we should be colliers.

SAMPSON. I mean, and we be in choler, we'll draw.

GREGORY. Ay while you live, draw your neck out of collar.

SAMPSON. I strike quickly, being moved. 5

GREGORY. But thou art not quickly moved to strike.

SAMPSON. A dog of the house of Montague moves me.

GREGORY. To move is to stir, and to be valiant, is to stand: therefore if thou art moved, thou runn'st away.

SAMPSON. A dog of that house shall move me to stand: I will take 10 the wall of any man or maid of Montague's.

GREGORY. That shows thee a weak slave, for the weakest goes to the wall.

SAMPSON. 'Tis true, and therefore women being the weaker vessels are ever thrust to the wall: therefore I will push Mon- 15 tague's men from the wall, and thrust his maids to the wall.

GREGORY. The quarrel is between our masters, and us their men.

SAMPSON. 'Tis all one, I will show myself a tyrant: when I have fought with the men, I will be cruel with the maids, I 20 will cut off their heads.

GREGORY. The heads of the maids?

SAMPSON. Ay, the heads of the maids, or their maidenheads, take it in what sense thou wilt.

GREGORY. They must take it in sense that feel it. 25

SAMPSON. Me they shall feel while I am able to stand, and 'tis known I am a pretty piece of flesh.

GREGORY. 'Tis well thou art not fish: if thou hadst, thou hadst been

---

I, i s.d. Verona. A public place   **bucklers** small shields   1 **carry coals** do dirty work, be put upon or insulted   2 **colliers** (1) coal carriers (2) cheaters (associated with coal dealing) 3 **and** if   **choler** anger   **draw** i.e. our swords   4 **collar** the hangman's noose ("collier," "choler," and "collar" were pronounced similarly)   5 **moved** angered   6 **quickly moved** easily motivated   8 **stand** i.e. my ground   10-11 **take the wall** get the better of (by walking near the walls of houses, as a gutter ran down the street. To "give the wall" was a courtesy, "take the wall" and force another into the gutter, an insult.)   12-13 **goes . . . wall** is pushed out (proverbial)   14 **weaker vessels** (1 Pet. III.7)   25 **sense** (1) lit. (2) sensuality   28 **fish** slang for "whore"

93

poor-John: draw thy tool, here comes two of the house of
Montagues.   30

Enter two other Servingmen [ABRAHAM *and*
BALTHASAR].

SAMPSON. My naked weapon is out: quarrel, I will back thee.

GREGORY. How, turn thy back and run?

SAMPSON. Fear me not.

GREGORY. No marry, I fear thee.

SAMPSON. Let us take the law of our sides, let them begin.   35

GREGORY. I will frown as I pass by, and let them take it as they list.

SAMPSON. Nay, as they dare: I will bite my thumb at them, which
is disgrace to them if they bear it.

ABRAHAM. Do you bite your thumb at us sir?

SAMPSON. I do bite my thumb sir.   40

ABRAHAM. Do you bite your thumb at us sir?

SAMPSON. [*Aside to* GREGORY.] Is the law of our side if I say ay?

GREGORY. [*Aside to* SAMPSON.] No.

SAMPSON. No sir, I do not bite my thumb at you sir, but I bite my
thumb sir.   45

GREGORY. Do you quarrel sir?

ABRAHAM. Quarrel sir? No sir.

SAMPSON. But if you do sir, I am for you, I serve as good a man as
you.

ABRAHAM. No better.   50

SAMPSON. Well sir.

Enter BENVOLIO.

GREGORY. [*Aside to* SAMPSON.] Say "better," here comes one of my
master's kinsmen.

SAMPSON. Yes, better sir.

ABRAHAM. You lie.   55

SAMPSON. Draw if you be men. Gregory, remember thy washing
blow.   *They fight.*

BENVOLIO. Part fools,   [*Beats down their swords.*]
Put up your swords, you know not what you do.

Enter TYBALT.

TYBALT. What, art thou drawn among these heartless hinds?   60

---

29 **poor-John** cheap dried cod   29 **tool**
(1) weapon (2) sex organ   31 **back thee** i.e. up   33 **Fear me not** have no fears about me
35 **take . . . sides** be on the right side of the law   36 **list** please   37 **bite my thumb**
(insulting gesture made by jerking the thumbnail from behind the upper teeth)   56
washing (1) swashing or slashing forcefully (2) beating clothes in the wash   60 **drawn** (1)

Turn thee Benvolio, look upon thy death.
BENVOLIO. I do but keep the peace, put up thy sword,
Or manage it to part these men with me.
TYBALT. What, drawn and talk of peace? I hate the word,
As I hate hell, all Montagues and thee: 65
Have at thee, coward.   [*They*] *fight.*

Enter three or four CITIZENS *with clubs or
partisans* [*and an officer.*]

OFFICER. Clubs, bills and partisans, strike, beat them down.
CITIZENS. Down with the Capulets, down with the Montagues!

Enter old CAPULET *in his gown, and his*
WIFE.

CAPULET. What noise is this? Give me my long sword, ho!
WIFE. A crutch, a crutch, why call you for a sword?   70
CAPULET. My sword I say, old Montague is come,
And flourishes his blade in spite of me.

Enter old MONTAGUE *and his* WIFE.

MONTAGUE.
Thou villain Capulet!—Hold me not, let me go.
MONTAGUE'S WIFE.
Thou shalt not stir one foot to seek a foe.

Enter PRINCE ESCALUS, *with his train.*

PRINCE. Rebellious subjects, enemies to peace,   75
Profaners of this neighbour-stainèd steel—
Will they not hear? What ho, you men, you beasts,
That quench the fire of your pernicious rage,
With purple fountains issuing from your veins:
On pain of torture, from those bloody hands,   80
Throw your mistempered weapons to the ground,
And hear the sentence of your movèd prince.
Three civil brawls bred of an airy word,
By thee old Capulet and Montague,
Have thrice disturbed the quiet of our streets,   85
And made Verona's ancient citizens

---

with sword drawn (2) chased from cover (fr. hunting)   **heartless** (1) cowardly (2) hartless
(without a stag for protection)   **hinds** (1) menials (2) female deer   62 **put up**
sheathe   63 **manage** handle   66 s.d. **partisans** broad-bladed pikes   67 **bills**
axe-headed spears   68 s.d. **gown** dressing gown   69 **long sword** old-fashioned medieval
weapon   72 **spite** defiance   76 **neighbour-stained steel** steel stained with the blood
of neighbors   81 **mistempered** (1) tempered for evil (2) bad-tempered   82 **moved**
angered

Cast by their grave beseeming ornaments,
To wield old partisans, in hands as old,
Cankered with peace, to part your cankered hate:
If ever you disturb our streets again,   90
Your lives shall pay the forfeit of the peace.
For this time all the rest depart away:
You Capulet, shall go along with me,
And Montague, come you this afternoon,
To know our farther pleasure in this case,   95
To old Freetown, our common judgment place:
Once more on pain of death, all men depart.

Exeunt [*all but* MONTAGUE, *his* WIFE,
and BENVOLIO].

MONTAGUE. Who set this ancient quarrel new abroach?
Speak nephew, were you by when it began?
BENVOLIO. Here were the servants of your adversary   100
And yours, close fighting ere I did approach:
I drew to part them: in the instant came
The fiery Tybalt, with his sword prepared,
Which as he breathed defiance to my ears,
He swung about his head and cut the winds,   105
Who nothing hurt withal, hissed him in scorn:
While we were interchanging thrusts and blows,
Came more and more, and fought on part and part,
Till the prince came, who parted either part.
MONTAGUE'S WIFE.
O where is Romeo? Saw you him today?   110
Right glad I am, he was not at this fray.
BENVOLIO. Madam, an hour before the worshipped sun
Peered forth the golden window of the east,
A troubled mind drave me to walk abroad,
Where underneath the grove of sycamore,   115
That westward rooteth from this city side,
So early walking did I see your son:
Towards him I made, but he was ware of me,
And stole into the covert of the wood:
I, measuring his affections by my own,   120

87 **grave beseeming** befitting the sober-minded   89 **Cankered . . . peace** corroded by disuse   **cankered** consuming   96 **Freetown** (Brooke's translation of *Villa Franca* in Bandello's Italian version)   98 **new abroach** running again ("broach" = to tap a cask and let the wine run out)   102 **drew** i.e. my sword   104 **breathed** uttered   106 **withal** thereby   108 **part and part** one side and the other   109 **either part** both sides   114 **abroad** away from home   118 **ware** aware, wary   120 **affections** feelings

Which then most sought, where most might not be found,
Being one too many by my weary self,
Pursued my humour, not pursuing his,
And gladly shunned who gladly fled from me.
MONTAGUE. Many a morning hath he there been seen,   125
With tears augmenting the fresh morning's dew,
Adding to clouds, more clouds with his deep sighs,
But all so soon as the all-cheering sun
Should in the farthest east begin to draw
The shady curtains from Aurora's bed,   130
Away from light steals home my heavy son,
And private in his chamber pens himself,
Shuts up his windows, locks fair daylight out,
And makes himself an artificial night:
Black and portentous must this humour prove,   135
Unless good counsel may the cause remove.
BENVOLIO. My noble uncle, do you know the cause?
MONTAGUE. I neither know it, nor can learn of him.
BENVOLIO. Have you importuned him by any means?
MONTAGUE. Both by myself and many other friends,   140
But he, his own affections' counsellor,
Is to himself (I will not say how true)
But to himself so secret and so close,
So far from sounding and discovery,
As is the bud bit with an envious worm,   145
Ere he can spread his sweet leaves to the air,
Or dedicate his beauty to the sun.
Could we but learn from whence his sorrows grow,
We would as willingly give cure as know.

Enter ROMEO.

BENVOLIO. See where he comes, so please you step aside,   150
I'll know his grievance or be much denied.
MONTAGUE. I would thou wert so happy by thy stay,
To hear true shrift: come madam, let's away.

Exeunt [MONTAGUE *and* WIFE].

BENVOLIO. Good morrow cousin.

---

121 **where most** a place where most people   123 **humour** inclination, mood   **not by**
not   130 **Aurora** goddess of the dawn   131 **heavy** sad (w. pun on "light")   133
windows shutters   135 **humour** mood   141 **his . . . counsellor** the confidant of his
own feelings   143 **close** reserved   144 **sounding** fathoming   145 **envious**
malicious   151 **denied** refused   152 **happy** fortunate   153 **To . . . shrift** as to hear a

ROMEO.   Is the day so young?

BENVOLIO. But new struck nine.

ROMEO.   Ay me, sad hours seem long: 155
Was that my father that went hence so fast?

BENVOLIO. It was: what sadness lengthens Romeo's hours?

ROMEO.   Not having that, which having, makes them short.

BENVOLIO. In love?

ROMEO.   Out.   160

BELVOLIO. Of love?

ROMEO.   Out of her favour where I am in love.

BENVOLIO. Alas that Love, so gentle in his view,
Should be so tyrannous and rough in proof.

ROMEO.   Alas that Love, whose view is muffled still,   165
Should without eyes, see pathways to his will.
Where shall we dine? O me! What fray was here?
Yet tell me not, for I have heard it all:
Here's much to do with hate, but more with love:
Why then O brawling love, O loving hate,   170
O anything of nothing first create:
O heavy lightness, serious vanity,
Misshapen chaos of well-seeming forms,
Feather of lead, bright smoke, cold fire, sick health,
Still-waking sleep, that is not what it is.   175
This love feel I, that feel no love in this.
Dost thou not laugh?

BELVOLIO.   No coz, I rather weep.

ROMEO.   Good heart, at what?

BELVOLIO.   At thy good heart's oppression.

ROMEO.   Why such is love's transgression:
Griefs of mine own lie heavy in my breast,   180
Which thou wilt propagate to have it prest
With more of thine: this love that thou hast shown,
Doth add more grief, to too much of mine own.
Love is a smoke made with the fume of sighs:
Being purged, a fire sparkling in lovers' eyes: 185
Being vexed, a sea nourished with lovers' tears:
What is it else? a madness most discreet,

true confession   163,5 **Love** Cupid, the god of love   163 **view** appearance   164 **in
proof** when experienced   165 **view . . . still** eyes are always blindfolded ("love is
blind")   169 **more with love** more applicable to my state of chaos caused by love (in the
following lines he continues the paradox of love's warring emotions, a favorite device of the
Petrarchan sonneteers)   172 **heavy lightness** sad frivolity   175 **Still-waking**
ever-wakeful   176 **in this** (1) in return (2) in this feud   177 **coz** cousin (applied to any
relative)   181 **to have it** by having it   185 **purged** cleared away   188 **gall**

A choking gall, and a preserving sweet:
Farewell, my coz.
BENVOLIO.   Soft, I will go along:
And if you leave me so, you do me wrong.   190
ROMEO.   Tut, I have lost myself, I am not here,
This is not Romeo, he's some other where.
BENVOLIO. Tell me in sadness, who is that you love?
ROMEO.   What, shall I groan and tell thee?
BENVOLIO.   Groan? Why no:
But sadly tell me who.   195
ROMEO.   A sick man. in sadness makes his will:
A word ill urged to one that is so ill:
In sadness cousin, I do love a woman.
BENVOLIO. I aimed so near, when I supposed you loved.
ROMEO.   A right good markman, and she's fair I love.   200
BENVOLIO. A right fair mark, fair coz, is soonest hit.
ROMEO.   Well, in that hit you miss, she'll not be hit
With Cupid's arrow, she hath Dian's wit:
And in strong proof of chastity well armed,
From Love's weak childish bow she lives unharmed.   205
She will not stay the siege of loving terms,
Nor bide th' encounter of assailing eyes,
Nor ope her lap to saint-seducing gold.
O she is rich in beauty, only poor
That when she dies, with beauty dies her store.   210
BENVOLIO. Then she hath sworn that she will still live chaste?
ROMEO.   She hath, and in that sparing makes huge waste:
For beauty, starved with her severity,
Cuts beauty off from all posterity.
She is too fair, too wise, wisely too fair,   215
To merit bliss by making me despair:
She hath forsworn to love, and in that vow,
Do I live dead, that live to tell it now.
BENVOLIO. Be ruled by me, forget to think of her.

---

bitterness   189 **Soft** wait a minute   193 **sadness** seriousness (Romeo interprets as
"sorrow")   197 **ill urged** inopportunely mentioned (because the sick man should not be
reminded that death is near)   201 **mark . . . hit** (bawdy double meaning for copulation)   202 **miss** i.e. the target   203 **Dian's wit** the wisdom of Diana, goddess of
chastity   204 **proof** armor   206 **stay** abide   **siege** (the lady as a castle besieged by the
lover is a common metaphor)   207 **assailing eyes** loving looks shot at her   208 **ope . . .**
gold (like Danaë seduced by Zeus disguised as a shower of gold)   209-10 **poor . . . store**
when she dies unmarried, her capital ("store") of beauty will not be bequeathed to children
(cf. Sonnets 1-14)   211 **still** always   212 **sparing** (1) preserving (2) thrift   213 **starved**
killed   214 **beauty** the inheritance of beauty   215 **wisely too fair** too wisely virtuous
216 **merit bliss** earn salvation

ROMEO.   O teach me how I should forget to think.   220
BENVOLIO. By giving liberty unto thine eyes,
           Examine other beauties.
ROMEO.   'Tis the way
           To call hers (exquisite) in question more:
           These happy masks that kiss fair ladies' brows,
           Being black, puts us in mind they hide the fair: 225
           He that is strucken blind, cannot forget
           The precious treasure of his eyesight lost:
           Show me a mistress that is passing fair,
           What doth her beauty serve but as a note,
           Where I may read who passed that passing fair: 230
           Farewell, thou canst not teach me to forget.
BENVOLIO. I'll pay that doctrine, or else die in debt.   *Exeunt.*

[SCENE II.]

Enter CAPULET, COUNTY PARIS, *and the* CLOWN [SERVANT].

CAPULET.   But Montague is bound as well as I,
           In penalty alike, and 'tis not hard I think,
           For men so old as we to keep the peace.
PARIS.   Of honourable reckoning are you both,
           And pity 'tis, you lived at odds so long: 5
           But now my lord, what say you to my suit?
CAPULET.   But saying o'er what I have said before,
           My child is yet a stranger in the world,
           She hath not seen the change of fourteen years,
           Let two more summers wither in their pride,   10
           Ere we may think her ripe to be a bride.
PARIS.   Younger than she are happy mothers made.
CAPULET.   And too soon marred are those so early made:
           Earth hath swallowed all my hopes but she,
           She's the hopeful lady of my earth: 15

---

223 **call . . . in question** bring . . . to thought   224
masks black half-masks worn by ladies in public   228,230 **passing** surpassingly   229
note reminder   230 **passed** surpassed   **that** i.e. one who is   232 **pay that doctrine**
furnish that instruction and pay you what you deserve   **die in debt** ("debt" and "death"
were pronounced alike and often metaphorically related)

     I, ii s.d. a street. **Clown** oafish rustic (Capulets' servant, probably Peter, played by Will
Kempe, the company comedian) 1 **bound** obliged (to keep the peace)   4 **reckoning**
reputation   11 **ripe** ready   13 **marred** (1) lit. (2) married ("make" and "mar" are favorites
in Elizabethan word play)   14 **Earth . . . she** all my other children are buried   15
hopeful . . . earth (1) lady who will inherit my land ("earth") (2) one on whom my body's

But woo her gentle Paris, get her heart,
My will to her consent is but a part.
And she agreed, within her scope of choice
Lies my consent and fair according voice:
This night I hold an old accustomed feast,   20
Whereto I have invited many a guest,
Such as I love, and you among the store,
One more, most welcome, makes my number more:
At my poor house, look to behold this night,
Earth-treading stars, that make dark heaven light: 25
Such comfort as do lusty young men feel,
When well-apparelled April on the heel
Of limping Winter treads, even such delight
Among fresh female buds shall you this night
Inherit at my house: hear all, all see,   30
And like her most, whose merit most shall be:
Which on more view, of many, mine being one,
May stand in number, though in reck'ning none.
Come, go with me: [*To* SERVANT, *giving him a paper.*]
    go sirrah, trudge about
Through fair Verona, find those persons out   35
Whose names are written there, and to them say,
My house and welcome on their pleasure stay.

                          Exeunt [CAPULET *and* PARIS.]

SERVANT. Find them out whose names are written here. It is written that the shoemaker should meddle with his yard and
the tailor with his last, the fisher with his pencil, and the   40
painter with his nets. But I am sent to find those persons
whose names are here writ, and can never find what
names the writing person hath here writ: I must to the
learned. In good time.

                  Enter BENVOLIO *and* ROMEO.

BENVOLIO. Tut man, one fire burns out another's burning,   45
    One pain is lessened by another's anguish:

("earth") hopes for posterity are placed   19 **fair according** favorably consenting   20
feast (pronounced "fest")   25 **stars** (ladies)   26 **lusty** vigorous   30 **Inherit**
possess   31 **whose . . . be** who most merits your liking   32-3 **mine . . . none** my
daughter will hold her own, though (proverbially) one among many counts as none   34
sirrah (term used with inferiors)   37 **stay** wait   39-41 **shoemaker . . . nets** (he means
that each should deal with what he knows best — as a servant should not be expected to read
— but he assigns the tools to the wrong trades)   39 **meddle** busy himself (plus bawdy
double meaning)   **yard** yardstick   45-6 **one fire . . . anguish** (proverbial
expressions)   46 **another's** another pain's

Turn giddy, and be holp by backward turning:
   One desperate grief cures with another's languish:
Take thou some new infection to thy eye,
And the rank poison of the old will die.   50

ROMEO. Your plantain leaf is excellent for that.

BENVOLIO. For what, I pray thee?

ROMEO.   For your broken shin.

BENVOLIO. Why Romeo, art thou mad?

ROMEO. Not mad, but bound more than a madman is:
Shut up in prison, kept without my food,   55
Whipped and tormented, and—God-den, good fellow.

SERVANT. God gi'god-den, I pray sir, can you read?

ROMEO. Ay, mine own fortune in my misery.

SERVANT. Perhaps you have learned it without book: but I pray,
can you read any thing you see?   60

ROMEO. Ay, if I know the letters and the language.

SERVANT. Ye say honestly, rest you merry.

ROMEO. Stay fellow, I can read.   *He reads the letter.*

   'Signior Martino and his wife and daughters:
   County Anselmo and his beauteous sisters: 65
   The lady widow of Vitruvio:
   Signior Placentio and his lovely nieces:
   Mercutio and his brother Valentine:
   Mine uncle Capulet, his wife and daughters:
   My fair niece Rosaline, Livia: 70
   Signior Valentio and his cousin Tybalt:
   Lucio and the lively Helena.'
A fair assembly, whither should they come?

SERVANT. Up.

ROMEO. Whither? To supper?   75

SERVANT. To our house.

ROMEO. Whose house?

SERVANT. My master's.

ROMEO. Indeed I should have asked you that before.

SERVANT. Now I'll tell you without asking. My master is the great 80
rich Capulet, and if you be not of the house of Mon-

---

                                      47 **holp** helped   48 **languish**
anguish   49 **eye** (in the belief that one fell in love through sight)   51 **plantain leaf**
broad-leafed marsh plant (used to staunch the blood of minor wounds)   52 **bro ken** where
the skin is broken   54-6 **bound . . . tormented** (the conventional treatment of the madman describes Romeo's love-suffering)   56 **God-den** good evening, good afternoon   57
God gi' god-den God give you good evening (used after noon)   59 **without book** by
heart   62 **rest you merry** keep happy (expression at parting)   82 **crush** drink

tagues, I pray come and crush a cup of wine. Rest you
merry.   [*Exit.*]

BENVOLIO. At this same ancient feast of Capulet's,
Sups the fair Rosaline whom thou so loves,   85
With all th' admirèd beauties of Verona:
Go thither, and with unattained eye,
Compare her face with some that I shall show,
And I will make thee think thy swan a crow.

ROMEO. When the devout religion of mine eye   90
Maintains such falsehood, then turn tears to fires:
And these who often drowned, could never die,
Transparent heretics be burnt for liars.
One fairer than my love: the all-seeing sun
Ne'er saw her match, since first the world begun.   95

BENVOLIO. Tut, you saw her fair, none else being by,
Herself poised with herself in either eye:
But in that crystal scales let there be weighed
Your lady's love against some other maid,
That I will show you shining at this feast,   100
And she shall scant show well that now seems best.

ROMEO. I'll go along, no such sight to be shown,
But to rejoice in splendour of mine own.   [*Exeunt.*]

[SCENE III.]

Enter CAPULET'S WIFE *and* NURSE.

WIFE.   Nurse, where's my daughter? Call her forth to me.
NURSE. Now by my maidenhead at twelve year old,
I bade her come. What, lamb: what, ladybird:
(God forbid.) Where's this girl? What, Juliet!

Enter JULIET.

JULIET. How now, who calls?
NURSE.   Your mother.
JULIET.   Madam I am here,   5
What is your will?

---

down   84 **ancient** traditional   87 **unattainted** unimpaired (by love)   92 **these** i.e.
eyes   93 **Transparent** (1) bright (2) easily seen through   **heretics** (because of worshipping false deities; burning was the customary punishment)   97-8 **poised . . . weighed** (In
this conceit or elaborate metaphor, Romeo's eyes are the two pans of the scale with the image
of Rosaline weighed — "poised" — in both, i.e. against herself)   99 **lady's love** ladylove
101 **scant** scarcely   103 **by** i.e. lady
I,iii Capulet's house   2 **by . . . old** by my virginity until the age of twelve   3 **ladybird**
(1) sweetheart (2) loose woman (a meaning she apologizes for in the next line)

WIFE.   This the matter. Nurse, give leave awhile,
          We must talk in secret. Nurse, come back again,
          I have remembered me, thou's hear our counsel.
          Thou knowest my daughter's of a pretty age.   10
NURSE.   Faith, I can tell her age unto an hour.
WIFE.   She's not fourteen.
NURSE.   I'll lay fourteen of my teeth—
          And yet to my teen be it spoken, I have but four—
          She's not fourteen. How long is it now
          To Lammas-tide?
WIFE.   A fortnight and odd days.   15
NURSE.   Even or odd, of all days in the year,
          Come Lammas Eve at night shall she be fourteen.
          Susan and she (God rest all Christian souls)
          Were of an age. Well, Susan is with God,
          She was too good for me. But as I said,   20
          On Lammas Eve at night shall she be fourteen,
          That shall she, marry, I remember it well.
          'Tis since the earthquake now eleven years,
          And she was weaned (I never shall forget it)
          Of all the days of the year upon that day: 25
          For I had then laid wormwood to my dug,
          Sitting in the sun under the dovehouse wall.
          My lord and you were then at Mantua,
          Nay, I do bear a brain. But as I said,
          When it did taste the wormwood on the nipple   30
          Of my dug, and felt it bitter, pretty fool,
          To see it tetchy and fall out with the dug.
          'Shake,' quoth the dovehouse: 'twas no need I trow
          To bid me trudge:
          And since that time it is eleven years,   35
          For then she could stand high-lone, nay, by th' rood,
          She could have run and waddled all about:
          For even the day before, she broke her brow,
          And then my husband (God be with his soul,
          'A was a merry man) took up the child: 40

9 thou's
thou shalt   counsel private talk   10 pretty apt   12 lay bet   13 teen sorrow   15
Lammas-tide August 1, a holiday celebrating the wheat harvest   18 Susan her own
daughter (as she would actually nurse the new baby [ll. 24 ff.], she would have a child about
the same age)   22 marry (mild oath, corruption of "by the Virgin Mary")   23 earthquake . . . years (some scholars believe the London earthquake of 1580 is referred to, and so
date the play 1591)   26 wormwood a bitter herb   29 bear a brain have quite a
mind   32 tetchy touchy, fretful   fall out quarrel   33 'Shake' (the shaking
dovehouse was a warning to "get moving" or "shake a leg")   36 high-lone alone   rood
Holy Cross   38 broke broke the skin on or bruised

'Yea,' quoth he, 'dost thou fall upon thy face?
Thou wilt fall backward when thou hast more wit,
Wilt thou not, Jule?' And by my holidam,
The pretty wretch left crying, and said 'Ay.'
To see now how a jest shall come about: 45
I warrant, and I should live a thousand years,
I never should forget it: 'Wilt thou not, Jule?' quoth he,
And pretty fool it stinted, and said 'Ay.'

WIFE.   Enough of this, I pray thee hold thy peace.

NURSE.   Yes madam, yet I cannot choose but laugh,   50
To think it should leave crying and say 'Ay:'
And yet I warrant it had upon it brow
A bump as big as a young cock'rel's stone:
A perilous knock, and it cried bitterly.
'Yea,' quoth my husband, 'fall'st upon thy face?   55
Thou wilt fall backward when thou comest to age:
Wilt thou not, Jule?' It stinted, and said 'Ay'.

JULIET.   And stint thou too, I pray thee nurse, say I.

NURSE.   Peace, I have done: God mark thee to his grace,
Thou wast the prettiest babe that e'er I nursed,   60
And I might live to see thee married once,
I have my wish.

WIFE.   Marry, that 'marry' is the very theme
I came to talk of: tell me daughter Juliet,
How stands your disposition to be married?   65

JULIET.   It is an honour that I dream not of.

NURSE.   An honour: were not I thine only nurse,
I would say thou hadst sucked wisdom from thy teat.

WIFE.   Well, think of marriage now, younger than you
Here in Verona, ladies of esteem,   70
Are made already mothers. By my count
I was your mother, much upon these years
That you are now a maid. Thus then in brief:
The valiant Paris seeks you for his love.

NURSE.   A man, young lady, lady, such a man   75
As all the world. Why, he's a man of wax.

WIFE.   Verona's summer hath not such a flower.

NURSE.   Nay, he's a flower, in faith a very flower.

---

42 **fall backward** i.e. under the
embrace of a man   43 **by my holidam** (originally an oath by a sacred relic; popularly
considered a reference to the Virgin Mary)   48,57,58 **stint(ed)** stop(ped)   53 **cock'rel**
rooster   **stone** testicle   59 **mark** choose   65 **disposition** inclination   68 **thy** the
Nurse's   72 **much . . . years** at the same age   76 **of wax** as perfect and handsome as a

WIFE.   What say you, can you love the gentleman?
           This night you shall behold him at our feast,   80
           Read o'er the volume of young Paris' face,
           And find delight writ there with beauty's pen:
           Examine every married lineament,
           And see how one another lends content:
           And what obscured in this fair volume lies,   85
           Find written in the margent of his eyes.
           This precious book of love, this unbound lover,
           To beautify him, only lacks a cover.
           The fish lives in the sea, and 'tis much pride
           For fair without, the fair within to hide.   90
           That book in many's eyes doth share the glory,
           That in gold clasps locks in the golden story:
           So shall you share all that he doth possess,
           By having him, making yourself no less.

NURSE.   No less? Nay, bigger: women grow by men.   95
WIFE.   Speak briefly, can you like of Paris' love?
JULIET.   I'll look to like, if looking liking move.
           But no more deep will I endart mine eye,
           Than your consent gives strength to make it fly.

                    Enter SERVINGMAN.

SERVINGMAN.
           Madam, the guests are come, supper served up, you   100
           called, my young lady asked for, the nurse cursed in
           the pantry, and everything in extremity: I must hence
           to wait, I beseech you follow straight.

                              Exit [SERVINGMAN].

WIFE.   We follow thee. Juliet, the county stays.
NURSE.   Go girl, seek happy nights to happy days.   *Exeunt.* 105

---

waxen model   81 **volume** (the metaphor develops a comparison of Paris to a book)   83
married harmonious   84 **one . . . content** the perfection of one adds to that of the
others   86 **written . . . eyes** as explanations of obscure passages are written in the margin,
so his eyes express his hidden love   87 **unbound** (1) as a book (2) outside the bonds of
marriage   88 **Cover** (in the sense of "being bound to a wife")   89-90 **The fish . . . hide** it
is natural for the fish to live in the sea, but it is unnatural pride for a fair lady to keep to herself
without a handsome husband   91-92 **That book . . . story** both the book's cover and its
pages (or the man and wife) benefit from each other and share the glory of public
esteem   95 **grow** become pregnant   97 **look** be prepared   **move** prompt   98 **en-
dart** shoot like a dart   103 **straight** straightway   104 **county** count (fr. Italian:"*conte*")

[SCENE IV.]

Enter ROMEO, MERCUTIO, BENVOLIO, *with five or six other*
MASKERS, TORCHBEARERS.

ROMEO.   What, shall this speech be spoke for our excuse?
            Or shall we on without apology?
BENVOLIO.   The date is out of such prolixity,
            We'll have no Cupid, hoodwinked with a scarf,
            Bearing a Tartar's painted bow of lath,   5
            Scaring the ladies like a crow-keeper,
            Nor no without-book prologue, faintly spoke
            After the prompter, for our entrance:
            But let them measure us by what they will,
            We'll measure them a measure and be gone.   10
ROMEO.   Give me a torch, I am not for this ambling,
            Being but heavy I will bear the light.
MERCUTIO.   Nay gentle Romeo, we must have you dance.
ROMEO.   Not I, believe me, you have dancing shoes
            With nimble soles, I have a soul of lead   15
            So stakes me to the ground I cannot move.
MERCUTIO.   You are a lover, borrow Cupid's wings,
            And soar with them above a common bound.
ROMEO.   I am too sore enpiercèd with his shaft,
            To soar with his light feathers, and so bound: 20
            I cannot bound a pitch above dull woe,
            Under love's heavy burden do I sink.
MERCUTIO.   And to sink in it should you burden love,
            Too great oppression for a tender thing.
ROMEO.   Is love a tender thing? It is too rough,   25
            Too rude, too boist'rous and it pricks like thorn.
MERCUTIO.   If love be rough with you, be rough with love,
            Prick love for pricking, and you beat love down.

I, iv s.d. A street   **Maskers** (it was a social custom for a group of young men to dress up
in costume, "crash" a party after sending a "presenter" to announce them, and dance with the
ladies)   1 **speech** i.e. by the presenter   3 **The date . . . of** it is out of date to have   4
Cupid (a favorite costume for the boy presenter)   **hoodwinked** blindfolded   5 **Tartar's**
(Cupid's lip-shaped bow is likened to the Tartar's, to differentiate it from the Elizabethan
circular one)   **lath** wood   6 **crow-keeper** boy hired to keep the crows off a field   7
without-book memorized   8 **After the prompter** being continually prompted   9
measure estimate   10 **measure . . . measure** dance a measure (stately figure) with
them   11 **torch** (torchbearers accompanied the maskers, as in *MV*, but did not join the
dance)   12 **heavy** sad (w. pun on "light")   18 **bound** (1) referring to "stakes," l. 16 (2)
boundary   20 **bound** restricted   21 **bound** leap, as in dancing   **pitch** greatest height
to which a falcon soars to swoop at its prey   23 **in** into   **should you** you
would   **burden** i.e. with your weight upon it   28 **for** (1) in return for (2) for the purpose

Give me a case to put my visage in,
A visor for a visor: what care I   30
What curious eye doth quote deformities?
Here are the beetle brows shall blush for me.

BENVOLIO. Come knock and enter, and no sooner in,
But every man betake him to his legs.

ROMEO. A torch for me, let wantons light of heart   35
Tickle the senseless rushes with their heels,
For I am proverbed with a grandsire phrase:
I'll be a candle-holder and look on,
The game was ne'er so fair, and I am done.

MERCUTIO. Tut, dun's the mouse, the constable's own word: 40
If thou art Dun, we'll draw thee from the mire
Or (save your reverence) love, wherein thou stick'st
Up to the ears. Come, we burn daylight, ho!

ROMEO. Nay, that's not so.

MERCUTIO.   I mean sir, in delay
We waste our lights in vain, like lights by day: 45
Take our good meaning, for our judgment sits
Five times in that, ere once in our five wits.

ROMEO. And we mean well in going to this masque,
But 'tis no wit to go.

MERCUTIO.   Why, may one ask?

ROMEO. I dreamt a dream tonight.

MERCUTIO.   And so did I.   50

ROMEO. Well, what was yours?

MERCUTIO.   That dreamers often lie.

ROMEO. In bed asleep while they do dream things true.

MERCUTIO. O then I see Queen Mab hath been with you:
She is the fairies' midwife, and she comes
In shape no bigger than an agate stone,   55
On the forefinger of an alderman,

---

of   **pricking** (1) sticking you with thorns (2) copulation   29 **case** mask   30 **visor for a
visor** mask for a face as ugly as the mask   31 **quote** note   32 **beetle** overhanging   34
betake . . . legs dance   36 **senseless** lacking the sense of feeling   **rushes** (used as
floor-covering)   37 **proverbed . . . phrase** ("A good candle-holder [onlooker] proves a
good gamester" is the proverb)   39 **done** (1) (w. pun on "dun" or dark, cf. to "fair") (2) done
with it   40 **dun's . . . word** be like the dun-colored mouse, quiet, unseen, and an
appropriate watchword for a constable   41 **Dun** (name for a horse)   **draw . . . mire** (as
often had to be done with horses)   42 **Or . . . love** or with all due apologies, your love
(which is sticky as mud)   43 **burn daylight** waste time   46-7 **Take . . . wits** understand
the meaning with your mind, for that is worth more than the sound of the words taken in by
the senses   49 **wit** intelligence   50 **dream** (one of the many forebodings in the
play)   50 **tonight** last night   53 **Mab** (1) a variant of Maeve, Celtic legendary queen (2)
slang for "slut", as is "quean"   54 **midwife** (because she assists in the birth of dreams)   55
agate stone the tiny figure carved in the agate of a seal ring (first of the passage's

Drawn with a team of little atomi,
Over men's noses as they lie asleep:
Her wagon spokes made of long spinners' legs:
The cover, of the wings of grasshoppers,   60
Her traces of the smallest spider web,
Her collars of the moonshine's wat'ry beams,
Her whip of cricket's bone, the lash of film,
Her wagoner a small grey-coated gnat,
Not half so big as a round little worm,   65
Pricked from the lazy finger of a man.
Her chariot is an empty hazelnut,
Made by the joiner squirrel or old grub,
Time out o' mind, the fairies' coachmakers:
And in this state she gallops night by night,   70
Through lovers' brains, and then they dream of love.
On courtiers' knees, that dream on curtsies straight,
O'er lawyers' fingers who straight dream on fees,
O'er ladies' lips who straight on kisses dream,
Which oft the angry Mab with blisters plagues,   75
Because their breaths with sweetmeats tainted are.
Sometime she gallops o'er a courtier's nose,
And then dreams he of smelling out a suit:
And sometime comes she with a tithe-pig's tail,
Tickling a parson's nose as 'a lies asleep,   80
Then dreams he of another benefice.
Sometime she driveth o'er a soldier's neck,
And then dreams he of cutting foreign throats,
Of breaches, ambuscadoes, Spanish blades,
Of healths five fathom deep: and then anon   85
Drums in his ear, at which he starts and wakes,
And being thus frighted, swears a prayer or two,
And sleeps again: this is that very Mab
That plats the manes of horses in the night:
And bakes the elf-locks in foul sluttish hairs,   90
Which once untangled, much misfortune bodes.

---

diminutives)   57 **atomi** atoms, tiny creatures (Latin plural)   59 **spinners** spiders   61
traces harness   62 **wat'ry** (because it engendered dew)   63 **film** gossamer   65-6
worm . . . finger (it was believed that worms bred in one's idle fingers)   68 **joiner**
cabinetmaker   70 **state** stately magnificence   72,73,74 **straight** straightway   76
sweetmeats "kissing -comfits" (*MWW*), which sweeten the breath   78 **smelling . . . suit**
searching for someone who would pay to have his suit presented at court   79 **tithe-pig**
(every tenth pig went to the parson for his tithe)   81 **benefice** income   84 **ambuscadoes**
ambushes   **blades** swords (for which Toledo was famous)   89 **plats** plaits   90 **bakes**
. . . **hairs** causes the knotted hair of the unclean   91 **once . . . bodes** (it was thought to be

This is the hag, when maids lie on their backs,
That presses them and learns them first to bear,
Making them women of good carriage:
This is she—

ROMEO.   Peace, peace, Mercutio peace,   95
Thou talk'st of nothing.

MERCUTIO.   True, I talk of dreams:
Which are the children of an idle brain,
Begot of nothing but vain fantasy:
Which is as thin of substance as the air,
And more inconstant than the wind who woos   100
Even now the frozen bosom of the north:
And being angered, puffs away from thence,
Turning his side to the dew-dropping south.

BENVOLIO. This wind you talk of, blows us from ourselves:
Supper is done, and we shall come too late.   105

ROMEO.   I fear too early, for my mind misgives,
Some consequence yet hanging in the stars,
Shall bitterly begin his fearful date
With this night's revels, and expire the term
Of a despisèd life closed in my breast,   110
By some vile forfeit of untimely death.
But he that hath the steerage of my course,
Direct my sail: on, lusty gentlemen.

BENVOLIO. Strike, drum.

They march about the stage,

[SCENE V.]

and servingmen come forth with napkins.

1. SERVINGMAN.

Where's Potpan, that he helps not to take away? He
shift a trencher, he scrape a trencher?

2. SERVINGMAN.

When good manners shall lie all in one or two men's

---

bad luck to untangle elf-locks)   93 **bear** (1) a man's weight (2) children   97 **idle** foolish
98 **vain fantasy** empty imagination   102 **angered** i.e. at her coldness   103 **dew-
dropping south** rainy south wind   104 **ourselves** our intentions   107 **consequence**
event to follow   108 **date** duration   109-10 **expire . . . life** cause the expiration of the
bond of my hated life (fr. business)   111 **By . . . forfeit** by having to forfeit that vile life
itself

I, v s.d.   (the action is continuous with that of scene iv)   2 **trencher** wooden dish
(cleaned by scraping)   5 **join-stools** stools carefully made of joined parts (they are clearing

hands and they unwashed too, 'tis a foul thing.

I. SERVINGMAN.

>Away with the join-stools, remove the court-cubbert,   5
>look to the plate. Good thou, save me a piece of march-
>pane, and as thou loves me, let the porter let in Susan
>Grindstone and Nell. Anthony and Potpan!

[Enter 3. SERVINGMAN.]

3. SERVINGMAN.

>Ay boy, ready.

I. SERVINGMAN.

>You are looked for, and called for, asked for, and sought   10
>for, in the great chamber.

3. SERVINGMAN.

>We cannot be here and there too. Cheerly boys, be
>brisk awhile, and the longer liver take all.   *Exeunt.*

Enter CAPULET, *his* WIFE, JULIET, TYBALT,
and all the GUESTS *and* GENTLEWOMEN
to the MASKERS.

CAPULET. Welcome gentlemen, ladies that have their toes
Unplagued with corns will walk a bout with you: 15
Ah my mistresses, which of you all
Will now deny to dance? She that makes dainty,
She I'll swear hath corns: am I come near ye now?
Welcome gentlemen, I have seen the day
That I have worn a visor and could tell   20
A whispering tale in a fair lady's ear,
Such as would please: 'tis gone, 'tis gone, 'tis gone.
You are welcome gentlemen, come, musicians play.
A hall, a hall, give room, and foot it girls.

Music plays and they dance.

More light you knaves, and turn the tables up: 25
And quench the fire, the room is grown too hot.
Ah sirrah, this unlooked-for sport comes well:
Nay sit, nay sit, good cousin Capulet,
For you and I are past our dancing days:

---

the floor for dancing)   **court-cubbert** court cupboard, sideboard   **6 marchpane**
marzipan (confection of sugar and almonds)   13 **longer . . . all** (proverbial encouragement
to be cheerful)   15 **walk a bout** have a dance   17 **makes dainty** coyly hesitates   18
am . . . ye have I hit the mark   20 **worn a visor** been a masker   24 **A hall** clear the
floor   25 **knaves** fellows   **turn . . . up** dismantle the tables (made of boards on trestles)
and take them away   27 **sirrah** (term of familiar address)

How long is't now since last yourself and I   30
Were in a mask?

2. CAPULET.   By'r Lady, thirty years.

CAPULET. What man, 'tis not so much, 'tis not so much:
'Tis since the nuptial of Lucentio,
Come Pentecost as quickly as it will,
Some five-and-twenty years, and then we masked.   35

2. CAPULET.
'Tis more, 'tis more, his son is elder, sir:
His son is thirty.

CAPULET.   Will you tell me that?
His son was but a ward two years ago.

ROMEO. [To a SERVINGMAN.] What lady's that which doth enrich
the hand
Of yonder knight?   40

SERVINGMAN.
I know not sir.

ROMEO. O she doth teach the torches to burn bright:
It seems she hangs upon the cheek of night
As a rich jewel in an Ethiop's ear,
Beauty too rich for use, for earth too dear: 45
So shows a snowy dove trooping with crows,
As yonder lady o'er her fellows shows:
The measure done, I'll watch her place of stand,
And touching hers, make blessèd my rude hand.
Did my heart love till now? Forswear it sight,   50
For I ne'er saw true beauty till this night.

TYBALT. This by his voice, should be a Montague.
Fetch me my rapier, boy. What dares the slave
Come hither covered with an antic face,
To fleer and scorn at our solemnity?   55
Now by the stock and honour of my kin,
To strike him dead, I hold it not a sin.

CAPULET. Why how now kinsman, wherefore storm you so?

TYBALT. Uncle, this is a Montague, our foe:
A villain that is hither come in spite,   60
To scorn at our solemnity this night.

CAPULET. Young Romeo is it?

TYBALT.   'Tis he, that villain Romeo.

CAPULET. Content thee gentle coz, let him alone,

34 **Pentecost** Whitsunday
(seventh Sunday after Easter)   38 **ward** minor   49 **rude** rough   54 **antic face**
grotesque mask   55 **fleer** sneer   56 **stock and honour** honorable stock   60 **spite**
insulting defiance   61 **solemnity** celebration   64 **portly** of good deportment   69

'A bears him like a portly gentleman:
And to say truth, Verona brags of him   65
To be a virtuous and well-governed youth:
I would not for the wealth of all this town,
Here in my house do him disparagement:
Therefore be patient, take no note of him,
It is my will, the which if thou respect,   70
Show a fair presence, and put off these frowns,
An ill-beseeming semblance for a feast.

TYBALT.   It fits when such a villain is a guest,
I'll not endure him.

CAPULET.   He shall be endured.
What, goodman boy, I say he shall, go to,   75
Am I the master here or you? Go to,
You'll not endure him, God shall mend my soul,
You'll make a mutiny among my guests:
You will set cock-a-hoop, you'll be the man.

TYBALT.   Why uncle, 'tis a shame.

CAPULET.   Go to, go to,   80
You are a saucy boy, is't so indeed?
This trick may chance to scathe you, I know what,
You must contrary me, marry, 'tis time—
Well said, my hearts—you are a princox, go,
Be quiet, or—more light, more light—for shame,   85
I'll make you quiet—what, cheerly my hearts.

TYBALT.   Patience perforce, with wilful choler meeting,
Makes my flesh tremble in their different greeting:
I will withdraw, but this intrusion shall
Now seeming sweet, convert to bitt'rest gall.   *Exit.* 90

ROMEO.   If I profane with my unworthiest hand,
     This holy shrine, the gentle sin is this,
My lips, two blushing pilgrims ready stand,
     To smooth that rough touch with a tender kiss.

JULIET.   Good pilgrim, you do wrong your hand too much,   95
     Which mannerly devotion shows in this,

---

patient forbearing   71 **presence** demeanor   75 **goodman boy** (insult implying immaturity; "goodman"=title applied to those of rank lower than gentleman)   78 **mutiny** disturbance   79 **set cock-a-hoop** lose all restraint (of uncertain origin, perhaps a ref. to cockfighting)   **be the man** take charge of things   81 **saucy** insolent   82 **scathe** harm   83 **contrary** act contrary to   84 **my hearts** (he addresses the guests here and in l. 86)   **princox** coxcomb, impertinent boy   87 **Patience perforce** forced endurance   88 **different** hostile   91–104 **If I . . . take** (the lovers' first encounter is expressed in the form of an Elizabethan sonnet)   92 **shrine** (her hand, which, in Brooke, Romeo holds, and here, in l. 49, has planned to touch. The metaphor or conceit of the sonnet is that of a pilgrim worshipping at a shrine)   **gentle sin** (of kissing her hand)   96

For saints have hands, that pilgrims' hands do touch,
   And palm to palm is holy palmers' kiss.

ROMEO.   Have not saints lips and holy palmers too?

JULIET.   Ay pilgrim, lips that they must use in prayer.   100

ROMEO.   O then dear saint, let lips do what hands do,
   They pray, grant thou, lest faith turn to despair.

JULIET.   Saints do not move, though grant for prayers' sake.

ROMEO.   Then move not while my prayer's effect I take.
   Thus from my lips, by thine my sin is purged.   105

                         [*Kisses her.*]

JULIET.   Then have my lips the sin that they have took.

ROMEO.   Sin from my lips? O trespass sweetly urged:
   Give me my sin again.   [*Kisses her.*]

JULIET.   You kiss by th' book.

NURSE.   Madam, your mother craves a word with you.

ROMEO.   What is her mother?

NURSE.   Marry, bachelor,   110
   Her mother is the lady of the house,
   And a good lady, and a wise and virtuous,
   I nursed her daughter that you talked withal:
   I tell you, he that can lay hold of her
   Shall have the chinks.

ROMEO.   Is she a Capulet?   115
   O dear account! my life is my foe's debt.

BENVOLIO. Away be gone, the sport is at the best.

ROMEO.   Ay so I fear, the more is my unrest.

CAPULET.   Nay gentlemen, prepare not to be gone,
   We have a trifling foolish banquet towards: 120
   Is it e'en so? Why then I thank you all.
   I thank you honest gentlemen, good night:

                       [*Exeunt* MASKERS.]

More torches here, come on, then let's to bed.
Ah sirrah, by my fay it waxes late,
I'll to my rest.   [*Exeunt all but* JULIET *and* NURSE.] 125

---

mannerly well-mannered   97 **saints** images of saints   98 **palmers** pilgrims to the Holy Land (who carried a palm branch)   103 **move . . . sake** take the initiative, though they may answer prayers   104 **effect** fulfillment   105 **s.d.** (it was not unusual to kiss in greeting; cf. *Oth*, II, i, 96)   107 **urged** mentioned   108 **by th' book** as if this were a ritual   113 **withal** with   115 **the chinks** plenty of coin   116 **dear account** costly bill   **is . . . debt** is at the mercy of my foe (because his life depends on Juliet)   120 **foolish** insignificant   **banquet** light refreshments   **towards** upcoming   122 **honest**

JULIET.   Come hither nurse, what is yond gentleman?
NURSE.   The son and heir of old Tiberio.
JULIET.   What's he that now is going out of door?
NURSE.   Marry, that I think be young Petruchio.
JULIET.   What's he that follows here that would not dance?   130
NURSE.   I know not.
JULIET.   Go ask his name: if he be marrièd,
             My grave is like to be my wedding bed.
NURSE.   His name is Romeo, and a Montague,
             The only son of your great enemy.   135
JULIET.   My only love sprung from my only hate,
             Too early seen unknown, and known too late,
             Prodigious birth of love it is to me,
             That I must love a loathèd enemy.
NURSE.   What's this? What's this?
JULIET.   A rhyme I learnt even now   140
             Of one I danced withal.   *One calls within, 'Juliet.'*
NURSE.   Anon, anon:
             Come let's away, the strangers all are gone.   *Exeunt.*

[Act Two]

[*Enter* CHORUS.]

CHORUS.   Now old desire doth in his deathbed lie,
                 And young affection gapes to be his heir:
             That fair for which love groaned for and would die,
                 With tender Juliet matched, is now not fair.
             Now Romeo is beloved, and loves again,   5
                 Alike bewitchèd by the charm of looks:
             But to his foe supposed he must complain,
                 And she steal love's sweet bait from fearful hooks:
             Being held a foe, he may not have access
                 To breathe such vows as lovers use to swear,   10
             And she as much in love, her means much less,
                 To meet her new belovèd anywhere:

honorable   124 **fay** faith   **waxes** grows   138 **Prodigious birth** like the birth of a
deformed child   141 **Anon** right away
    II Prologue   1 **old desire** Romeo's old love for Rosaline   2 **gapes** is openmouthed and
eager   3 **fair** Rosaline   6 **Alike** mutually   8 **fearful** fear-inspiring   10 **use** are

But passion lends them power, time means to meet,
Temp'ring extremities with extreme sweet.   [*Exit.*]

[SCENE I.]

Enter ROMEO *alone.*

ROMEO.   Can I go forward when my heart is here?
Turn back dull earth, and find thy center out.
                                            [*Withdraws.*]

Enter BENVOLIO *with* MERCUTIO.

BENVOLIO. Romeo! my cousin Romeo! Romeo!
MERCUTIO.   He is wise,
And on my life hath stol'n him home to bed.
BENVOLIO. He ran this way and leapt this orchard wall.   5
Call, good Mercutio.
MERCUTIO.   Nay, I'll conjure too.
Romeo, humours, madman, passion, lover!
Appear thou in the likeness of a sigh,
Speak but one rhyme and I am satisfied:
Cry but 'Ay me,' pronounce but 'love' and 'dove',   10
Speak to my gossip Venus one fair word,
One nickname for her purblind son and heir,
Young Abraham Cupid, he that shot so true,
When King Cophetua loved the beggar maid.
He heareth not, he stirreth not, he moveth not,   15
The ape is dead, and I must conjure him.
I conjure thee by Rosaline's bright eyes,
By her high forehead, and her scarlet lip,
By her fine foot, straight leg, and quivering thigh,
And the demesnes that there adjacent lie,   20
That in thy likeness thou appear to us.
BENVOLIO. And if he hear thee, thou wilt anger him.
MERCUTIO. This cannot anger him, 'twould anger him

---

used   14 **Temp'ring . . . sweet** making the meeting even sweeter because of the dangerous situation
    II, i Capulet's orchard   2 **dull earth** heavy body   **center** heart, Juliet   2 **s.d.** (he
probably hides behind one of the pillars supporting the roof of the outer stage)   5 **orchard**
garden   6 **conjure** invoke, as with a spirit   7 **Romeo . . . lover** (various names were
incanted; the spirit replied to the right one)   **humours** moods   9 **Speak** (he parodies the
traditional behavior of the courtly lover)   11 **gossip** friendly old dame   12 **purblind**
totally blind   13 **Abraham** (beggars who pretended to be lunatics were called "Abraham
men," so the term was applied to cheats and dissemblers)   14 **King Cophetua** the ballad
king who is struck by Cupid's arrow and falls in love with a beggar   16 **ape** creature (term
of affection)   20 **demesnes** regions, domains   24–26 **circle, stand, laid** magic circle,

                To raise a spirit in his mistress' circle,
                Of some strange nature, letting it there stand   25
                Till she had laid it, and conjùred it down,
                That were some spite. My invocation
                Is fair and honest: in his mistress' name,
                I conjure only but to raise up him.
BENVOLIO.   Come, he hath hid himself among these trees   30
                To be consorted with the humorous night:
                Blind is his love, and best befits the dark.
MERCUTIO.   If love be blind, love cannot hit the mark.
                Now will he sit under a medlar tree,
                And wish his mistress were that kind of fruit   35
                As maids call medlars, when they laugh alone.
                O Romeo, that she were, O that she were
                An open et cetera, thou a pop'rin pear.
                Romeo good night, I'll to my truckle-bed,
                This field-bed is too cold for me to sleep.   40
                Come, shall we go?
BENVOLIO.   Go then, for 'tis in vain
                To seek him here that means not to be found.   *Exeunt.*

                [SCENE II.]

                [ROMEO *comes forward.*]

ROMEO.   He jests at scars that never felt a wound,
                But soft, what light through yonder window breaks?
                It is the east, and Juliet is the sun.
                Arise fair sun and kill the envious moon,
                Who is already sick and pale with grief,   5
                That thou her maid art far more fair than she:
                Be not her maid since she is envious,
                Her vestal livery is but sick and green,
                And none but fools do wear it: cast it off.

                        [*Enter* JULIET *above.*]

                It is my lady, O it is my love,   10

<hr>

stay, exorcised (with bawdy double meanings)   25 **strange** stranger's   27 **spite**
vexation   31 **consorted** associated   **humorous** (1) damp (2) moody   33 **hit the mark**
(1) hit the bull's eye with his arrow (2) copulate   34 **medlar** (1) pearlike fruit (2) slang for
"pudendum"   38 **pop'rin pear** (1) variety of pear from Poperinghe, Flanders (2)
phallus   39 **truckle** trundle (small bed stored under the main bed)
    II, ii s.d. (Romeo's completion of the rhymed couplet indicates that he has not left the
stage)   4 **moon** Diana, goddess of chastity   5 **sick** sickly in color   6 **her maid** (all
virgins were votaries of Diana)   8 **vestal** virginal   **livery** follower's uniform   8 **sick**

O that she knew she were:
She speaks, yet she says nothing, what of that?
Her eye discourses, I will answer it:
I am too bold, 'tis not to me she speaks:
Two of the fairest stars in all the heaven,   15
Having some business, do entreat her eyes
To twinkle in their spheres till they return.
What if her eyes were there, they in her head,
The brightness of her cheek would shame those stars,
As daylight doth a lamp: her eyes in heaven,   20
Would through the airy region stream so bright,
That birds would sing, and think it were not night:
See how she leans her cheek upon her hand.
O that I were a glove upon that hand,
That I might touch that cheek.

JULIET.   Ay me.

ROMEO.   She speaks.   25
O speak again bright angel, for thou art
As glorious to this night being o'er my head,
As is a wingèd messenger of heaven
Unto the white-upturnèd wond'ring eyes
Of mortals that fall back to gaze on him,   30
When he bestrides the lazy-pacing clouds,
And sails upon the bosom of the air.

JULIET.   O Romeo, Romeo, wherefore art thou Romeo?
Deny thy father and refuse thy name:
Or if thou wilt not, be but sworn my love,   35
And I'll no longer be a Capulet.

ROMEO.   [Aside.] Shall I hear more, or shall I speak at this?

JULIET.   'Tis but thy name that is my enemy:
Thou art thyself, though not a Montague,
What's Montague? It is nor hand nor foot,   40
Nor arm nor face, nor any other part
Belonging to a man. O be some other name.
What's in a name? That which we call a rose,
By any other word would smell as sweet:
So Romeo would, were he not Romeo called,   45
Retain that dear perfection which he owes

---

and green sickly and greenish, like the complexion of adolescent girls suffering from
greensickness, a type of anemia   17 **spheres** (according to Ptolemaic astronomy, each
planet was contained in a hollow sphere rotating around the earth)   21 **stream** beam   29
white-upturned turned up, so that the whites show   33 **wherefore** why   39 **Thou . . .
Montague** even without the name of Montague you would still be yourself   46 **owes**

Without that title. Romeo, doff thy name,
And for thy name which is no part of thee,
Take all myself.

ROMEO.   I take thee at thy word:
Call me but love, and I'll be new baptized,   50
Henceforth I never will be Romeo.

JULIET.   What man art thou, that thus bescreened in night
So stumblest on my counsel?

ROMEO.   By a name,
I know not how to tell thee who I am:
My name dear saint, is hateful to myself,   55
Because it is an enemy to thee:
Had I it written, I would tear the word.

JULIET.   My ears have yet not drunk a hundred words
Of thy tongue's uttering, yet I know the sound.
Art thou not Romeo, and a Montague?   60

ROMEO.   Neither fair maid, if either thee dislike.

JULIET.   How cam'st thou hither, tell me, and wherefore?
The orchard walls are high and hard to climb,
And the place death, considering who thou art,
If any of my kinsmen find thee here.   65

ROMEO.   With love's light wings did I o'erperch these walls,
For stony limits cannot hold love out,
And what love can do, that dares love attempt:
Therefore thy kinsmen are no stop to me.

JULIET.   If they do see thee, they will murder thee.   70

ROMEO.   Alack, there lies more peril in thine eye,
Than twenty of their swords: look thou but sweet,
And I am proof against their enmity.

JULIET.   I would not for the world they saw thee here.

ROMEO.   I have night's cloak to hide me from their eyes,   75
And but thou love me, let them find me here:
My life were better ended by their hate,
Than death proroguèd, wanting of thy love.

JULIET.   By whose direction found'st thou out this place?

ROMEO.   By love that first did prompt me to enquire,   80
He lent me counsel, and I lent him eyes:
I am no pilot, yet wert thou as far
As that vast shore washed with the farthest sea,

---

owns   48 **for** in exchange for   53 **counsel** secret thoughts   55 **dear saint** (a reminder
of their earlier meeting)   61 **dislike** displease   66 **o'erperch** fly over   73 **proof** pro-
tected (by love's armor)   76 **but** unless   78 **prorogued** postponed   **wanting of**
lacking

I should adventure for such merchandise.
JULIET.   Thou knowest the mask of night is on my face,   85
Else would a maiden blush bepaint my cheek,
For that which thou hast heard me speak tonight:
Fain would I dwell on form, fain, fain, deny
What I have spoke, but farewell compliment.
Dost thou love me? I know thou wilt say 'Ay:'   90
And I will take thy word, yet if thou swearst,
Thou mayst prove false: at lovers' perjuries,
They say Jove laughs. O gentle Romeo,
If thou dost love, pronounce it faithfully:
Or if thou thinkest I am too quickly won,   95
I'll frown and be perverse, and say thee nay,
So thou wilt woo, but else not for the world.
In truth fair Montague, I am too fond,
And therefore thou mayst think my haviour light:
But trust me gentleman, I'll prove more true,   100
Than those that have more cunning to be strange:
I should have been more strange, I must confess,
But that thou overheardst, ere I was ware,
My true-love passion, therefore pardon me,
And not impute this yielding to light love,   105
Which the dark night hath so discoverèd.
ROMEO.   Lady, by yonder blessèd moon I vow,
That tips with silver all these fruit-tree tops—
JULIET.   O swear not by the moon, th' inconstant moon,
That monthly changes in her circled orb,   110
Lest that thy love prove likewise variable.
ROMEO.   What shall I swear by?
JULIET.   Do not swear at all:
Or if thou wilt, swear by thy gracious self,
Which is the god of my idolatry,
And I'll believe thee.
ROMEO.   If my heart's dear love—   115
JULIET.   Well, do not swear: although I joy in thee,
I have no joy of this contract tonight,
It is too rash, too unadvised, too sudden,
Too like the lightning which doth cease to be,

---

84 **adventure** (the "merchant adventurers" took great risks in seeking out exotic merchandise)   88 **Fain** gladly   **form** formal convention   89 **compliment** convention, ceremony   97 **So** i.e. that   98 **fond** foolishly affectionate   99 **light** loose   101 **cunning** skill   **strange** reserved   105 **light** (1) loose (2) worthless (3) contrast to "dark"   106 **Which** (refers to "yielding")   **discovered** revealed   110 **orb** sphere (cf. l. 17n.)   117 **contract** betrothal, based on an exchange of vows, and considered a contract (accent on second syllable)   118 **unadvised** unconsidered   131 **frank** generous   141

Ere one can say, 'It lightens.' Sweet, good night: 120
This bud of love, by summer's ripening breath,
May prove a beauteous flower when next we meet:
Good night, good night, as sweet repose and rest
Come to thy heart, as that within my breast.

ROMEO.   O wilt thou leave me so unsatisfied?   125
JULIET.   What satisfaction canst thou have tonight?
ROMEO.   Th' exchange of thy love's faithful vow for mine.
JULIET.   I gave thee mine before thou didst request it:
                 And yet I would it were to give again.
ROMEO.   Wouldst thou withdraw it? for what purpose, love?   130
JULIET.   But to be frank and give it thee again,
                 And yet I wish but for the thing I have:
                 My bounty is as boundless as the sea,
                 My love as deep, the more I give to thee
                 The more I have, for both are infinite: 135
                 I hear some noise within, dear love adieu—

                      [NURSE] *calls within*.

Anon, good nurse—sweet Montague, be true:
Stay but a little, I will come again.   [*Exit*.]
ROMEO.   O blessed, blessèd night! I am afeard
                 Being in night, all this is but a dream,   140
                 Too flattering sweet to be substantial.

                      [*Enter* JULIET *above*.]

JULIET.   Three words dear Romeo, and good night indeed:
                 If that thy bent of love be honourable,
                 Thy purpose marriage, send me word tomorrow,
                 By one that I'll procure to come to thee,   145
                 Where and what time thou wilt perform the rite,
                 And all my fortunes at thy foot I'll lay,
                 And follow thee my lord throughout the world.
NURSE.   (*Within*.) Madam!
JULIET.   I come, anon.—But if thou meanest not well,   150
                 I do beseech thee—
NURSE.   (*Within*.) Madam!
JULIET.   By and by I come.—
                 To cease thy strife, and leave me to my grief.
                 Tomorrow will I send.

---

substantial of real substance (as opposed to the dream, or "shadow" of reality, a favorite
contrast in Shakespeare)   143 **bent** intentions   145 **procure** arrange   152 **By and by**
at once   153 **strife** striving

ROMEO.   So thrive my soul—
JULIET.   A thousand times good night.   *Exit.* 155
ROMEO.   A thousand times the worse, to want thy light:
Love goes toward love as schoolboys from their books,
But love from love, toward school with heavy looks.

Enter JULIET *again [above].*

JULIET.   Hist Romeo, hist: O for a falconer's voice,
To lure this tassel-gentle back again: 160
Bondage is hoarse, and may not speak aloud,
Else would I tear the cave where Echo lies,
And make her airy tongue more hoarse than mine,
With repetition of my 'Romeo.'
ROMEO.   It is my soul that calls upon my name.   165
How silver-sweet sound lovers' tongues by night,
Like softest music to attending ears.
JULIET.   Romeo.
ROMEO.   My dear.
JULIET.   What o'clock tomorrow
Shall I send to thee?
ROMEO.   By the hour of nine.
JULIET.   I will not fail, 'tis twenty year till then: 170
I have forgot why I did call thee back.
ROMEO.   Let me stand here till thou remember it.
JULIET.   I shall forget, to have thee still stand there,
Rememb'ring how I love thy company.
ROMEO.   And I'll still stay, to have thee still forget, 175
Forgetting any other home but this.
JULIET.   'Tis almost morning, I would have thee gone,
And yet no farther than a wanton's bird,
That lets it hop a little from his hand,
Like a poor prisoner in his twisted gyves,   180
And with a silken thread, plucks it back again,
So loving-jealous of his liberty.
ROMEO.   I would I were thy bird.
JULIET.   Sweet, so would I,
Yet I should kill thee with much cherishing:
Good night, good night. Parting is such sweet sorrow, 185
That I shall say good night, till it be morrow.   *[Exit.]*

---

154 **So . . . soul** as I hope to be saved   156 **want**
lack   158 **heavy** sad   160 **tassel-gentle** tercel-gentle, male falcon   161 **Bondage. . .**
aloud duty to my father prevents me from speaking too loudly   162 **Echo** nymph who
after her fruitless pursuit of Narcissus pined away in caves until only her voice was
left   167 **attending** listening   173 **still** always   178 **wanton** spoiled, capricious

ROMEO.　　Sleep dwell upon thine eyes, peace in thy breast.
　　　　　　Would I were sleep and peace, so sweet to rest.
　　　　　　Hence will I to my ghostly friar's close cell,
　　　　　　His help to crave, and my dear hap to tell.　　*Exit.* 190

[SCENE III.]

Enter FRIAR [LAWRENCE] *alone with a basket.*

FRIAR.　　The grey-eyed morn smiles on the frowning night,
　　　　　　Check'ring the eastern clouds with streaks of light,
　　　　　　And fleckèd darkness like a drunkard reels,
　　　　　　From forth day's path, and Titan's fiery wheels:
　　　　　　Now ere the sun advance his burning eye,　　　　　5
　　　　　　The day to cheer, and night's dank dew to dry,
　　　　　　I must up-fill this osier cage of ours,
　　　　　　With baleful weeds, and precious-juicèd flowers.
　　　　　　The earth that's nature's mother is her tomb,
　　　　　　What is her burying grave, that is her womb:　　　10
　　　　　　And from her womb children of divers kind
　　　　　　We sucking on her natural bosom find:
　　　　　　Many for many virtues excellent:
　　　　　　None but for some, and yet all different.
　　　　　　O mickle is the powerful grace that lies　　　　　15
　　　　　　In plants, herbs, stones, and their true qualities:
　　　　　　For naught so vile that on the earth doth live,
　　　　　　But to the earth some special good doth give:
　　　　　　Nor aught so good but strained from that fair use,
　　　　　　Revolts from true birth, stumbling on abuse.　　　20
　　　　　　Virtue itself turns vice, being misapplied,
　　　　　　And vice sometime by action dignified.

Enter ROMEO.

　　　　　　Within the infant rind of this weak flower
　　　　　　Poison hath residence, and medicine power:

---

child　180 **gyves** fetters (formed by thread tied to the bird's leg)　189 **ghostly** spiritual　**close** secret　190 **dear hap** good fortune
　　II, iii　Friar Lawrence's Cell　3 **flecked** blotchy or dappled with light spots　4 **Titan** the sun god　**wheels** i.e. of Titan's chariot (cutting a path as it is driven across the sky)　7 **osier cage** wicker basket　**ours** his order's　9–10 **The earth . . . womb** from the earth, which receives the dead, grows new life　11 **children** plants　14 **some** i.e. purpose　15 **mickle** great　**grace** beneficial quality　18 **earth** inhabitants of the earth　19 **strained** constrained, forced (away)　20 **birth** nature　**stumbling on** being made to fall by　22 **by action dignified** may be dignified by a good act　24 **medicine**

For this being smelt with that part, cheers each part: 25
Being tasted, stays all senses with the heart.
Two such opposèd kings encamp them still,
In man as well as herbs—grace and rude will:
And where the worser is predominant,
Full soon the canker death eats up that plant.   30

[ROMEO *comes forward.*]

ROMEO.   Good morrow father.
FRIAR.   Benedicite.
What early tongue so sweet saluteth me?
Young son, it argues a distempered head,
So soon to bid good morrow to thy bed:
Care keeps his watch in every old man's eye,   35
And where care lodges, sleep will never lie:
But where unbruisèd youth with unstuffed brain
Doth couch his limbs, there golden sleep doth reign.
Therefore thy earliness doth me assure
Thou art uproused with some distemp'rature,   40
Or if not so, then here I hit it right:
Our Romeo hath not been in bed tonight.
ROMEO.   That last is true, the sweeter rest was mine.
FRIAR.   God pardon sin: wast thou with Rosaline?
ROMEO.   With Rosaline, my ghostly father? No,   45
I have forgot that name, and that name's woe.
FRIAR.   That's my good son, but where hast thou been then?
ROMEO.   I'll tell thee ere thou ask it me again:
I have been feasting with mine enemy,
Where on a sudden one hath wounded me,   50
That's by me wounded: both our remedies
Within thy help and holy physic lies:
I bear no hatred, blessed man: for lo,
My intercession likewise steads my foe.
FRIAR.   Be plain good son, and homely in thy drift,   55
Riddling confession finds but riddling shrift.
ROMEO.   Then plainly known my heart's dear love is set

---

power healing has power   25 **that part** the odorous part   **cheers each part** strengthens each part of the body   26 **stays** suspends   27 **still** always   28 **grace** virtue, by which man may receive divine grace   **rude will** ungoverned lust   30 **canker** cankerworm   31 **Benedicite** God bless you   32 **early** awake early   33, 40 **distempered,-ature** sick, -ness (caused by an improper tempering or mixture of the four bodily fluids or humors)   37 **unbruised** untouched by the hard knocks of life   45 **ghostly** spiritual   50 **wounded** (common love-battle metaphor)   52 **physic** healing power (by performing the marriage)   54 **steads** benefits   55 **homely** plain   56 **shrift**

On the fair daughter of rich Capulet:
As mine on hers, so hers is set on mine,
And all combined, save what thou must combine 60
By holy marriage: when and where, and how,
We met, we wooed, and made exchange of vow,
I'll tell thee as we pass, but this I pray,
That thou consent to marry us today.

FRIAR. Holy Saint Francis what a change is here. 65
Is Rosaline that thou didst love so dear,
So soon forsaken? Young men's love then lies
Not truly in their hearts, but in their eyes.
Jesu Maria, what a deal of brine
Hath washed thy sallow cheeks for Rosaline. 70
How much salt water thrown away in waste,
To season love, that of it doth not taste.
The sun not yet thy sighs from heaven clears,
Thy old groans yet ring in mine ancient ears:
Lo here upon thy cheek the stain doth sit, 75
Of an old tear that is not washed off yet.
If e'er thou wast thyself, and these woes thine,
Thou and these woes were all for Rosaline.
And art thou changed? Pronounce this sentence then:
Women may fall, when there's no strength in men. 80

ROMEO. Thou chid'st me oft for loving Rosaline.

FRIAR. For doting, not for loving, pupil mine.

ROMEO. And bad'st me bury love.

FRIAR.   Not in a grave,
To lay one in, another out to have.

ROMEO. I pray thee chide me not, her I love now 85
Doth grace for grace, and love for love allow:
The other did not so.

FRIAR.   O she knew well
Thy love did read by rote, that could not spell:
But come young waverer, come go with me,
In one respect I'll thy assistant be: 90
For this alliance may so happy prove,
To turn your households' rancour to pure love.

absolution 60 **combined** agreed 72 **season** (1) preserve (2) flavor **of it . . . taste** no longer tastes like love 73 **The sun . . . clears** the sun has not yet cleared away the clouds formed by your deep sighs 79 **sentence** maxim 80 **may** i.e. be allowed to 86 **grace** favor 88 **did read . . . spell** was only pretense, like a child pretending to read but actually reciting from memory 90 **In one respect** for one consideration 91 **happy** fortunate 93 **stand** insist

ROMEO.   O let us hence, I stand on sudden haste.

FRIAR.   Wisely and slow, they stumble that run fast.   *Exeunt.*

[SCENE IV.]

Enter BENVOLIO *and* MERCUTIO.

MERCUTIO. Where the devil should this Romeo be?
Came he not home tonight?

BENVOLIO. Not to his father's, I spoke with his man.

MERCUTIO. Why that same pale hard-hearted wench, that Rosaline,
Torments him so, that he will sure run mad.   5

BENVOLIO. Tybalt, the kinsman to old Capulet,
Hath sent a letter to his father's house.

MERCUTIO. A challenge, on my life.

BENVOLIO. Romeo will answer it.

MERCUTIO. Any man that can write may answer a letter.   10

BENVOLIO. Nay, he will answer the letter's master how he dares,
being dared.

MERCUTIO. Alas poor Romeo, he is already dead, stabbed with a
white wench's black eye, run through the ear with a love
song, the very pin of his heart cleft with the blind bow-   15
boy's butt-shaft, and is he a man to encounter Tybalt?

BENVOLIO. Why what is Tybalt?

MERCUTIO. More than Prince of Cats. O he's the courageous
captain of compliments: he fights as you sing pricksong, keeps time, distance, and proportion: he rests   20
his minim rests, one, two, and the third in your
bosom: the very butcher of a silk button, a duellist, a
duellist, a gentleman of the very first house, of the first
and second cause: ah the immortal passado, the punto
reverso, the hay.   25

BENVOLIO. The what?

MERCUTIO. The pox of such antic, lisping, affecting fantasticoes,

---

II, iv A street   3 **man** servant   9, 11 **answer** (1) accept the challenge (2) reply to the
letter   11, 12 **dare(s, d)** (1) show courage (2) challenge   15 **pin** center of the target   16
butt-shaft unbarbed arrow used for target practice   18 **Prince of Cats** (in the beast fables
the cat's name was Tybert or Thibaut)   19 **captain of compliments** master of
etiquette   19–20 **as you sing pricksong** with close attention to detail, like singing not
from memory but from music written down in "pricks" or "dots"   20 **time** movement of
the feet   **distance** i.e. from the opponent   **proportion** rhythm   20–2 **rests his
minim . . . bosom** after two feints with short pauses ("minim-rests") between, he strikes for
the bosom   22 **silk button** (an expert fencer could aim for a certain button on his
opponent)   23–4 **very first . . . cause** best school of fencing which gives instruction in the
acceptable reasons for a duel, according to the code (cf. *AYLI*, V, iv, 65 ff.)   24 **passado**
forward thrust   **punto reverso** backhanded stroke   25 **hay** home thrust   27 **antic**
absurd, grotesque   **lisping** speaking affectedly   **affecting fantasticoes** affected

these new tuners of accent: 'By Jesu, a very good blade,
a very tall man, a very good whore.' Why, is not this a
lamentable thing, grandsir, that we should be thus af-   30
flicted with these strange flies: these fashion-mongers,
these pardon-me's, who stand so much on the new form,
that they cannot sit at ease on the old bench. O their
bones, their bones.

Enter ROMEO.

BENVOLIO. Here comes Romeo, here comes Romeo.   35
MERCUTIO. Without his roe, like a dried herring. O flesh, flesh, how
art thou fishified. Now is he for the numbers that
Petrarch flowed in: Laura, to his lady, was a kitchen
wench, marry, she had a better love to berhyme her:
Dido a dowdy, Cleopatra a gypsy, Helen and Hero   40
hildings and harlots: Thisby a gray eye or so, but not
to the purpose. Signior Romeo, *bon jour*, there's a
French salutation to your French slop: you gave us the
counterfeit fairly last night.
ROMEO. Good morrow to you both. What counterfeit did I give   45
you?
MERCUTIO. The slip sir, the slip, can you not conceive?
ROMEO. Pardon good Mercutio, my business was great, and
in such a case as mine, a man may strain courtesy.
MERCUTIO. That's as much as to say, such a case as yours con-   50
strains a man to bow in the hams.
ROMEO. Meaning to curtsy.
MERCUTIO. Thou hast most kindly hit it.
ROMEO. A most courteous exposition.
MERCUTIO. Nay, I am the very pink of courtesy.   55

---

fops   28 **new . . . accent** users of fashionable new terms and inflections   29 **tall**
brave   30 **grandsir** old man, grandsire   32 **stand** (1) insist (2) lit. meaning, to contrast
with "sit"   **form** (1) style (2) bench   34 **bones** (possibly a pun on the French "*bon*" and
the aching bones resulting from the "old bench")   36 **roe . . . herring** "dried herring" =
(1) one that had cast its roe (2) a thin, spiritless person, and "Romeo" without "Ro" leaves
only a sigh of woe   37 **numbers** meters   38 **Petrarch** the fourteenth-century Italian
poet (and father of the English sonnet), who addressed his love poems to Laura   **to**
compared to   40 **Dido** queen of Carthage (who loved and was forsaken by
Aeneas)   **gypsy** dusky Egyptian   **Helen** (whose elopement with Paris caused the Trojan
War)   **Hero** beloved of Leander (who drowned while swimming the Hellespont to see
her)   41 **hildings** good-for-nothings   **Thisby** (loved by Pyramus, son of an enemy
family; their deaths through misunderstanding have been compared to the ending of *Romeo
and Juliet*)   41–2 **not to the purpose** of no importance   43 **slop** loose-fitting
breeches   47 **slip** (1) lit. (2) counterfeit coin   **conceive** (1) understand (2) breed (leads to
the bawdy double meaning of "case" as the upper front section of the trousers)   52 **curtsy**
pronounced the same as "courtesy" (ll. 49, 55)   53 **kindly** (1) graciously (2) according to
nature   53 **hit it** (1) arrived (at my meaning) (2) copulated   55 **pink** (1) height (2) rapier

ROMEO.   Pink for flower.

MERCUTIO. Right.

ROMEO.   Why, then is my pump well flowered.

MERCUTIO. Sure wit: follow me this jest now till thou hast worn
            out thy pump, that when the single sole of it is worn,   60
            the jest may remain after the wearing, solely singular.

ROMEO.   O single-soled jest, solely singular for the singleness.

MERCUTIO. Come between us good Benvolio, my wits faint.

ROMEO.   Swits and spurs, swits and spurs, or I'll cry a match.

MERCUTIO. Nay, if our wits run the wild-goose chase, I am done: 65
            for thou hast more of the wild goose in one of thy wits,
            than I am sure I have in my whole five. Was I with
            you there for the goose?

ROMEO.   Thou wast never with me for any thing, when thou wast
            not there for the goose.   70

MERCUTIO. I will bite thee by the ear for that jest.

ROMEO.   Nay good goose, bite not.

MERCUTIO. Thy wit is a very bitter sweeting, it is a most sharp sauce.

ROMEO.   And is it not then well served in to a sweet goose?

MERCUTIO. O here's a wit of cheveril, that stretches from an inch   75
            narrow to an ell broad.

ROMEO.   I stretch it out for that word 'broad,' which added to
            the goose, proves thee far and wide a broad goose.

MERCUTIO. Why, is not this better now than groaning for love?
            Now art thou sociable, now art thou Romeo: now art   80
            thou what thou art, by art as well as by nature, for this
            drivelling love is like a great natural that runs lolling up
            and down to hide his bauble in a hole.

BENVOLIO. Stop there, stop there.

MERCUTIO. Thou desirest me to stop in my tale against the hair.   85

BENVOLIO. Thou wouldst else have made thy tale large.

---

thrust (continuing the bawdy double meaning)   58 **pump well flowered** dancing shoe
"pinked" or punched with holes in a decorative pattern and therefore "flowered"   59 **Sure
wit** very witty   60 **single sole** i.e. of the pump   61 **solely** absolutely   62 **single-soled**
weak-souled   **singleness** (1) singularity (2) feebleness   63 **Come between us** (as a
second in this duel of wits)   64 **Swits and spurs** (use) switches and spurs to drive your
horse (wit) faster   64 **cry a match** claim to have won the contest   65 **wild-goose chase** a
follow-the-leader (like geese) race or sport   66 **goose** (equated with silliness)   67 **with
you** even with you   70 **goose** slang for "prostitute"   72 **good . . . not** (proverbial call for
mercy when the opponent is weak)   73 **sweeting** kind of apple, here a tart one   **sauce**
applesauce   74 **sweet goose** (a sour sauce was traditional with a sweet meat)   75
cheveril kid leather (easily stretched, as Romeo is stretching out jests on the word
"goose")   76 **ell** forty-five inches   **broad** (1) wide (2) obvious   77 **for** to make it
fit   78 **broad** indecent   81 **by art** by conscious effort   82 **natural** i.e. born
idiot   **lolling** sticking out his tongue and his bauble   83 **bauble** (1) court fool's stick (2)
phallus   85 **tale** (w. pun on "tail")   **hair** (1) grain (2) pubic hair   86 **large** (1) indecent

MERCUTIO. O thou art deceived, I would have made it short, for I
was come to the whole-depth of my tale, and meant
indeed to occupy the argument no longer.

Enter NURSE *and her* MAN [PETER].

ROMEO. Here's goodly gear—a sail, a sail.   90

MERCUTIO. Two, two: a shirt and a smock.

NURSE. Peter:

PETER. Anon.

NURSE. My fan, Peter.

MERCUTIO. Good Peter, to hide her face, for her fan's the fairer
face.   95

NURSE. God ye good morrow, gentlemen.

MERCUTIO. God ye good-den, fair gentlewoman.

NURSE. Is it good-den?

MERCUTIO. 'Tis no less I tell ye, for the bawdy hand of the dial is   100
now upon the prick of noon.

NURSE. Out upon you, what a man are you?

ROMEO. One, gentlewoman, that God hath made, himself to
mar.

NURSE. By my troth it is well said, 'For himself to mar,' quoth   105
'a? Gentlemen, can any of you tell me where I may find
the young Romeo?

ROMEO. I can tell you, but young Romeo will be older when you
have found him, than he was when you sought him: I am
the youngest of that name, for fault of a worse.   110

NURSE. You say well.

MERCUTIO. Yea, is the worst well? Very well took, i' faith, wisely,
wisely.

NURSE. If you be he sir, I desire some confidence with you.

BENVOLIO. She will indite him to some supper.   115

MERCUTIO. A bawd, a bawd, a bawd. So ho!

ROMEO. What hast thou found?

MERCUTIO. No hare sir, unless a hare sir in a lenten pie, that is
something stale and hoar ere it be spent.

He walks by them and sings.

---

(2) i.e. in size (bawdy innuendo)   89 **occupy** (1) treat (2) slang for "copulate"   90 **goodly
gear** good fun at hand   91 **shirt ... smock** man and a woman ("smock" = loose
petticoat)   93 **Anon** right away   96 **God ye** God give you   97 **good-den** good evening
(used anytime after noon)   100 **dial** clock   101 **prick** (1) point (2) phallus   102 **what**
i.e. kind of   103 **himself** leaving it to himself   110 **fault** the lack   112 **took**
understood   114 **confidence** (she means "conference")   115 **indite** (he matches her
mistaken word)   116 **bawd** go-between, procuress   **So ho** (hunter's cry on sighting the
quarry)   118 **hare** (1) the animal (2) slang for "prostitute"   **lenten pie** either (a) pie
without meat, or (b) rabbit pie left over into Lent and therefore growing mouldy   119, 125

An old hare hoar,   120
And an old hare hoar,
Is very good meat in Lent.
But a hare that is hoar
Is too much for a score,
When it hoars ere it be spent.   125

Romeo, will you come to your father's? We'll to dinner
thither.

ROMEO.   I will follow you.

MERCUTIO.   Farewell ancient lady, farewell [*Sings.*] 'Lady, lady, lady.'

> *Exeunt* MERCUTIO, BENVOLIO.

NURSE.   I pray you sir, what saucy merchant was this that was so 130
             full of his ropery?

ROMEO.   A gentleman, nurse, that loves to hear himself talk, and
             will speak more in a minute than he will stand to in a
             month.

NURSE.   And 'a speak anything against me, I'll take him down, 135
             and 'a were lustier than he is, and twenty such Jacks: and
             if I cannot, I'll find those that shall: scurvy knave, I am
             none of his flirt-gills, I am none of his skains-mates,
             and thou must stand by too and suffer every knave to
             use me at his pleasure.   140

PETER.   I saw no man use you at his pleasure: if I had, my
             weapon should quickly have been out: I warrant you,
             I dare draw as soon as another man, if I see occasion in
             a good quarrel, and the law on my side.

NURSE.   Now afore God, I am so vexed that every part about me 145
             quivers, scurvy knave: pray you sir, a word: and as I
             told you, my young lady bid me enquire you out: what
             she bid me say, I will keep to myself: but first let me tell
             ye, if ye should lead her in a fool's paradise, as they
             say, it were a very gross kind of behaviour as they say: 150
             for the gentlewoman is young: and therefore, if you

---

spent consumed   120 **hoar** (1) mouldy (2) grey-haired (referring to the Nurse) (3) w. pun
on "whore"   124 **too . . . score** not good enough to have to pay for   129 **"lady, lady,
lady"** (line from a ballad praising the virtues of the heroine in the story of Susanna and the
Elders)   131 **ropery** knavish talk Q2; Q1: "roperipe" = ready for the hangman's
noose)   133 **stand to** make good   136 **Jacks** jackanapes   138 **flirt-gills** come-hither
prostitutes   **skains-mates** cutthroat companions   139 **suffer** allow   141–2 **use,
weapon** (both with bawdy double meaning: "copulate," "sex organ")   149 **lead . . .
paradise** seduce her by falsely promising to marry her (proverbial)   **in** into   152 **double**

	should deal double with her, truly it were an ill thing	
	to be offered to any gentlewoman, and very weak dealing.	
ROMEO.	Nurse, commend me to thy lady and mistress. I protest	
	unto thee—	155
NURSE.	Good heart, and i' faith I will tell her as much: Lord,	
	Lord, she will be a joyful woman.	
ROMEO.	What wilt thou tell her, nurse? Thou dost not mark me.	
NURSE.	I will tell her sir, that you do protest, which as I take	
	it, is a gentlemanlike offer.	160
ROMEO.	Bid her devise	
	Some means to come to shrift this afternoon,	
	And there she shall at Friar Lawrence' cell	
	Be shrived and married: here is for thy pains.	
NURSE.	No truly sir, not a penny.	165
ROMEO.	Go to, I say you shall.	
NURSE.	This afternoon sir, well, she shall be there.	
ROMEO.	And stay good nurse behind the abbey wall,	
	Within this hour my man shall be with thee,	
	And bring thee cords made like a tackled stair,	170
	Which to the high topgallant of my joy	
	Must be my convoy in the secret night.	
	Farewell, be trusty, and I'll quit thy pains:	
	Farewell, commend me to thy mistress.	
NURSE.	Now God in heaven bless thee, hark you sir.	175
ROMEO.	What say'st thou, my dear nurse?	
NURSE.	Is your man secret? Did you ne'er hear say,	
	Two may keep counsel, putting one away?	
ROMEO.	Warrant thee my man's as true as steel.	
NURSE.	Well sir, my mistress is the sweetest lady. Lord, Lord, 180	
	when 'twas a little prating thing — O there is a noble-	
	man in town, one Paris, that would fain lay knife	
	aboard: but she good soul had as lief see a toad, a very	
	toad, as see him: I anger her sometimes, and tell her that	
	Paris is the properer man, but I'll warrant you, when I 185	
	say so, she looks as pale as any clout in the versal world.	

---

with duplicity   153 **weak** (she may mean "wicked")   154 **commend me** give my
regards   154 **protest** declare, vow   158 **mark** heed   162 **shrift** confession   164
shrived absolved   **here . . . pains** (offering her money)   170 **tackled stair** rope
ladder   171 **topgallant** platform on the top mast of a ship   173 **quit** requite,
reward   178 **counsel** a secret   **one** i.e. of them   182–3 **lay knife aboard** (1) stake a
claim (a diner reserved his place at a tavern table by laying down his own knife) (2) **get** on
board (in the physical sense; cf. *Oth*, I, ii, 50)   185 **properer** handsomer   186 **clout**
cloth   **versal** universal

Doth not rosemary and Romeo begin both with a letter?

ROMEO.   Ay nurse, what of that? Both with an R.

NURSE.   Ah mocker, that's the dog-name. R is for the—no,
I know it begins with some other letter: and she hath 190
the prettiest sententious of it, of you and rosemary, that
it would do you good to hear it.

ROMEO.   Commend me to thy lady.

NURSE.   Ay, a thousand times. [*Exit* ROMEO.] Peter.

PETER.   Anon.   195

NURSE.   Before and apace.   *Exeunt.*

[SCENE V.]

Enter JULIET.

JULIET.   The clock struck nine when I did send the nurse,
In half an hour she promised to return,
Perchance she cannot meet him: that's not so:
O she is lame, Love's heralds should be thoughts,
Which ten times faster glides than the sun's beams,   5
Driving back shadows over low'ring hills.
Therefore do nimble-pinioned doves draw Love,
And therefore hath the wind-swift Cupid wings:
Now is the sun upon the highmost hill
Of this day's journey, and from nine till twelve,   10
Is three long hours, yet she is not come.
Had she affections and warm youthful blood,
She would be as swift in motion as a ball,
My words would bandy her to my sweet love,
And his to me,   15
But old folks, many feign as they were dead:
Unwieldy, slow, heavy, and pale as lead.

Enter NURSE [*and* PETER].

O God, she comes: O honey nurse, what news?
Hast thou met with him? Send thy man away.

NURSE.   Peter, stay at the gate.   [*Exit* PETER.] 20

---

187 **rosemary** herb symbolizing remembrance   **a** the
same   189 **dog-name** (because "R" sounds like a dog growling)   191 **sententious** (she
means "sentence" [maxim])   196 **apace** hurry up
II, v Capulet's orchard   6 **low'ring** dark, threatening   7 **nimble-pinioned**
swift-winged   **draw Love** draw the chariot of Venus   12 **affections** passions   14
bandy strike back and forth (as in tennis)   15 **his** i.e. words (would bandy her back)   25

JULIET.	Now good sweet nurse: O Lord, why look'st thou sad?
	Though news be sad, yet tell them merrily.
	If good, thou shamest the music of sweet news
	By playing it to me with so sour a face.
NURSE.	I am aweary, give me leave awhile, 25
	Fie, how my bones ache, what a jaunce have I.
JULIET.	I would thou hadst my bones, and I thy news:
	Nay come, I pray thee speak, good good nurse, speak.
NURSE.	Jesu what haste, can you not stay awhile?
	Do you not see that I am out of breath? 30
JULIET.	How art thou out of breath, when thou hast breath
	To say to me that thou art out of breath?
	The excuse that thou dost make in this delay
	Is longer than the tale thou dost excuse.
	Is thy news good or bad? Answer to that, 35
	Say either, and I'll stay the circumstance:
	Let me be satisfied, is't good or bad?
NURSE.	Well, you have made a simple choice, you know not
	how to choose a man: Romeo, no, not he. Though his
	face be better than any man's, yet his leg excels all men's, 40
	and for a hand and a foot and a body, though they be
	not to be talked on, yet they are past compare: he is not
	the flower of courtesy, but I'll warrant him, as gentle as
	a lamb: go thy ways wench, serve God. What, have you
	dined at home? 45
JULIET.	No, no. But all this did I know before.
	What says he of our marriage, what of that?
NURSE.	Lord, how my head aches, what a head have I.
	It beats as it would fall in twenty pieces.
	My back o' t' other side, ah my back, my back: 50
	Beshrew your heart for sending me about
	To catch my death with jauncing up and down.
JULIET.	I' faith I am sorry that thou art not well.
	Sweet, sweet, sweet nurse, tell me what says my love?
NURSE.	Your love says like an honest gentleman, and a 55
	courteous, and a kind, and a handsome, and I warrant
	a virtuous— where is your mother?
JULIET.	Where is my mother? Why she is within,
	Where should she be? How oddly thou repliest:

---

give me leave let me alone   26 **jaunce** jaunt   29, 69 **stay(s)** wait(s)   36 **stay the circumstance** wait for the details   38 **simple** silly   41–42 **be not . . . on** are not worth talking about   51 **Beshrew** curse   55 **honest** honorable

'Your love says like an honest gentleman,   60
"Where is your mother?"'

NURSE.   O God's Lady dear,
Are you so hot? Marry come up I trow,
Is this the poultice for my aching bones?
Henceforward do your messages yourself.

JULIET.   Here's such a coil, come, what says Romeo?   65

NURSE.   Have you got leave to go to shrift today?

JULIET.   I have.

NURSE.   Then hie you hence to Friar Lawrence' cell,
There stays a husband to make you a wife:
Now comes the wanton blood up in your cheeks,   70
They'll be in scarlet straight at any news:
Hie you to church, I must another way,
To fetch a ladder by the which your love
Must climb a bird's nest soon when it is dark:
I am the drudge, and toil in your delight,   75
But you shall bear the burden soon at night.
Go, I'll to dinner, hie you to the cell.

JULIET.   Hie to high fortune, honest nurse, farewell.   *Exeunt.*

[SCENE VI.]

Enter FRIAR [LAWRENCE] *and* ROMEO.

FRIAR.   So smile the heavens upon this holy act,
That after hours with sorrow chide us not.

ROMEO.   Amen, amen, but come what sorrow can,
It cannot countervail the exchange of joy
That one short minute gives me in her sight: 5
Do thou but close our hands with holy words,
Then love-devouring Death do what he dare,
It is enough I may but call her mine.

FRIAR.   These violent delights have violent ends,
And in their triumph die: like fire and powder,   10
Which as they kiss consume. The sweetest honey
Is loathsome in his own deliciousness,
And in the taste confounds the appetite.

---

62 **Marry come up**
(expression of angry impatience)   65 **coil** fuss   68 **hie** hurry   70 **wanton**
uncontrolled   71 **be in . . . straight** blush immediately ' 74 **climb** i.e. to   **a bird's**
nest (Juliet's room)   75 **in** for
II, vi Friar Lawrence's cell   1 **smile** let smile   3 **come . . . can** whatever sorrow may
bring   4 **countervail** counterbalance   10 **triumph, fire, powder** (the association of
these three words suggests the fireworks displays featured at royal triumphs or
celebrations)   13 **confounds** destroys   14 **long** long-lasting   17 **flint** i.e. of the

Therefore love moderately, long love doth so,
Too swift arrives as tardy as too slow.   15

Enter JULIET.

Here comes the lady. O so light a foot
Will ne'er wear out the everlasting flint:
A lover may bestride the gossamers
That idles in the wanton summer air,
And yet not fall, so light is vanity.   20

JULIET. Good even to my ghostly confessor.

FRIAR. Romeo shall thank thee daughter, for us both,

JULIET. As much to him, else is his thanks too much.

ROMEO. Ah Juliet, if the measure of thy joy
Be heaped like mine, and that thy skill be more   25
To blazon it, then sweeten with thy breath
This neighbour air, and let rich music's tongue
Unfold the imagined happiness that both
Receive in either, by this dear encounter.

JULIET. Conceit more rich in matter than in words,   30
Brags of his substance, not of ornament:
They are but beggars that can count their worth,
But my true love is grown to such excess,
I cannot sum up sum of half my wealth.

FRIAR. Come, come with me, and we will make short work,   35
For by your leaves, you shall not stay alone,
Till Holy Church incorporate two in one.   [*Exeunt.*]

[Act Three]

[SCENE I.]

Enter MERCUTIO, BENVOLIO, *and* MEN.

BENVOLIO. I pray thee good Mercutio, let's retire,
The day is hot, the Capulets abroad:
And if we meet, we shall not scape a brawl,

---

path   18 **gossamers** spiders' threads   19 **wanton** sportive   20 **vanity** trivial earthly
joy   21 **ghostly** spiritual   23 **As much** the same   25 **that** if   26 **blazon** describe (as
in heraldry)   26–28 **sweeten . . . Unfold** speak   29 **in either** from the other   30
Conceit conception   31 **ornament** ornamental words   32 **worth** wealth   34 **sum up**
sum add up the total
  III, i A public place   2 **abroad** around the town

For now these hot days, is the mad blood stirring.

MERCUTIO. Thou art like one of these fellows, that when he enters   5
the confines of a tavern, claps me his sword upon the
table, and says 'God send me no need of thee:' and by
the operation of the second cup, draws him on the
drawer, when indeed there is no need.

BENVOLIO. Am I like such a fellow?   10

MERCUTIO. Come, come, thou art as hot a Jack in thy mood as any
in Italy: and as soon moved to be moody, and as soon
moody to be moved.

BENVOLIO. And what to?

MERCUTIO. Nay, and there were two such, we should have none   15
shortly, for one would kill the other: thou, why thou
wilt quarrel with a man that hath a hair more or a hair
less in his beard than thou hast: thou wilt quarrel with
a man for cracking nuts, having no other reason but
because thou hast hazel eyes: what eye but such an eye   20
would spy out such a quarrel? Thy head is as full of
quarrels as an egg is full of meat, and yet thy head hath
been beaten as addle as an egg for quarrelling: thou
hast quarrelled with a man for coughing in the street,
because he hath wakened thy dog that hath lain asleep   25
in the sun. Didst thou not fall out with a tailor for
wearing his new doublet before Easter, with another for
tying his new shoes with old ribband, and yet thou wilt
tutor me from quarrelling?

BENVOLIO. And I were so apt to quarrel as thou art, any man should   30
buy the fee-simple of my life for an hour and a quarter.

MERCUTIO. The fee-simple? O simple.

Enter TYBALT, PETRUCHIO, *and* OTHERS.

BENVOLIO. By my head, here come the Capulets.

MERCUTIO. By my heel, I care not.

TYBALT. Follow me close, for I will speak to them.   35
Gentlemen, good-den, a word with one of you.

MERCUTIO. And but one word with one of us? Couple it with something, make it a word and a blow.

TYBALT. You shall find me apt enough to that sir, and you will
give me occasion.   40

7–8 **by. . . cup** as soon as his second
drink takes effect   8 **draws him** draws his sword   9 **drawer** tapster   11 **hot**
hot-tempered   **Jack** fellow, jackanapes   12 **moved to be moody** provoked to be
angry   13 **moody** irascible   15 **and** if   23 **addle as an egg** muddled as a rotten
egg   26 **fall out** quarrel   28 **ribband** shoelaces   31 **fee-simple** absolute possession (fr.

MERCUTIO. Could you not take some occasion without giving?

TYBALT.   Mercutio, thou consortest with Romeo.

MERCUTIO. Consort? What, dost thou make us minstrels? And thou
           make minstrels of us, look to hear nothing but discords:
           here's my fiddlestick, here's that shall make you dance: 45
           zounds, consort.

BENVOLIO. We talk here in the public haunt of men:
           Either withdraw unto some private place,
           Or reason coldly of your grievances,
           Or else depart: here all eyes gaze on us.   50

MERCUTIO. Men's eyes were made to look, and let them gaze.
           I will not budge for no man's pleasure, I.

                        Enter ROMEO.

TYBALT.   Well, peace be with you sir, here comes my man.

MERCUTIO. But I'll be hanged sir, if he wear your livery:
           Marry, go before to field, he'll be your follower,   55
           Your worship in that sense may call him man.

TYBALT.   Romeo, the love I bear thee can afford
           No better term than this: thou art a villain.

ROMEO.   Tybalt, the reason that I have to love thee,
           Doth much excuse the appertaining rage   60
           To such a greeting: villain am I none.
           Therefore farewell, I see thou knowest me not.

TYBALT.   Boy, this shall not excuse the injuries
           That thou hast done me, therefore turn and draw.

ROMEO.   I do protest I never injured thee,   65
           But love thee better than thou canst devise,
           Till thou shalt know the reason of my love:
           And so good Capulet, which name I tender
           As dearly as mine own, be satisfied.

MERCUTIO. O calm, dishonourable, vile submission: 70
           Alla stoccata carries it away.   [*Draws.*]
           Tybalt, you rat-catcher, will you walk?

TYBALT.   What wouldst thou have with me?

MERCUTIO. Good King of Cats, nothing but one of your nine lives:

real estate)   32 **simple** foolish   36 **good-den** good evening   39 **apt** ready   40 **occasion** opportunity   42 **consortest** (1) associate with (2) combine in harmony, like minstrels (so Mercutio interprets)   45 **fiddlestick** (his sword)   46 **zounds** (oath: "by God's wounds")   49 **coldly** calmly, dispassionately   54 **livery** servant's outfit (interpreting "man" as "servant")   55 **field** (in the sense of "dueling spot")   58 **villain** base fellow, servant (an insult intended as a challenge)   60 **appertaining rage** absence of rage which should appertain   63 **Boy** (implying immaturity, used disparagingly)   68 **tender** cherish   71 **Alla stoccata** at the thrust (fr. fencing)   **carries it away** wins the game   72 **rat-catcher** referring to Tybert the cat in beast fables

that I mean to make bold withal, and as you shall use 75
me hereafter, dry-beat the rest of the eight. Will you
pluck your sword out of his pilcher by the ears? Make
haste, lest mine be about your ears ere it be out.

TYBALT.   I am for you.   [*Draws.*]

ROMEO.   Gentle Mercutio, put thy rapier up.   80

MERCUTIO. Come sir, your *passado*.   [*They fight.*]

ROMEO.   Draw Benvolio, beat down their weapons,
Gentlemen, for shame, forbear this outrage:
Tybalt, Mercutio, the prince expressly hath
Forbid this bandying in Verona streets.   85
Hold, Tybalt: good Mercutio—

> TYBALT *under* ROMEO's *arm thrusts*
> MERCUTIO *in and flies.*

MERCUTIO.   I am hurt.
A plague o' both your houses, I am sped:
Is he gone and hath nothing?

BENVOLIO.   What, are thou hurt?

MERCUTIO. Ay, ay, a scratch, a scratch, marry 'tis enough,
Where is my page? Go villain, fetch a surgeon.   90

> [*Exit* PAGE.]

ROMEO.   Courage man, the hurt cannot be much.

MERCUTIO. No, 'tis not so deep as a well, nor so wide as a church
door, but 'tis enough, 'twill serve: ask for me tomorrow,
and you shall find me a grave man. I am peppered, I
warrant, for this world: a plague o' both your houses. 95
Zounds, a dog, a rat, a mouse, a cat, to scratch a man
to death: a braggart, a rogue, a villain, that fights by the
book of arithmetic. Why the devil came you between us?
I was hurt under your arm.

ROMEO.   I thought all for the best.   100

MERCUTIO. Help me into some house Benvolio,
Or I shall faint: a plague o' both your houses.
They have made worms' meat of me,
I have it, and soundly too—your houses.

> *Exit* [*helped by* BENVOLIO].

ROMEO.   This gentleman, the prince's near ally,   105
My very friend, hath got this mortal hurt

---

76 **dry-beat** thrash, as
with the flat of a sword, without drawing blood   77 **pilcher** leather garment (contemptuous for "scabbard")   **ears** hilt   81 **passado** thrust, with one foot extended (fr.
fencing)   85 **bandying** exchanging blows   87 **sped** done for   90 **villain** term of address for a servant   94 **peppered** finished   95 **for** as concerns   98 **book of arithmetic**
rules and theories of fencing   105 **ally** relative   106 **very** true (fr. French:

In my behalf: my reputation stained
With Tybalt's slander, Tybalt that an hour
Hath been my cousin: O sweet Juliet,
Thy beauty hath made me effeminate,   110
And in my temper softened valour's steel.

Enter BENVOLIO.

BENVOLIO. O Romeo, Romeo, brave Mercutio's dead,
That gallant spirit hath aspired the clouds,
Which too untimely here did scorn the earth.
ROMEO. This day's black fate, on moe days doth depend,   115
This but begins the woe others must end.

Enter TYBALT.

BENVOLIO. Here comes the furious Tybalt back again.
ROMEO. Alive in triumph, and Mercutio slain?
Away to heaven, respective lenity,
And fire-eyed Fury be my conduct now.   120
Now Tybalt, take the 'villain' back again
That late thou gavest me, for Mercutio's soul
Is but a little way above our heads,
Staying for thine to keep him company:
Either thou or I, or both, must go with him.   125
TYBALT. Thou, wretched boy that didst consort him here,
Shalt with him hence.
ROMEO.   This shall determine that.

They fight. TYBALT *falls.*

BENVOLIO. Romeo, away be gone:
The citizens are up, and Tybalt slain,
Stand not amazed, the prince will doom thee death   130
If thou art taken: hence, be gone away.
ROMEO. O! I am Fortune's fool.
BENVOLIO.   Why dost thou stay?

Exit ROMEO.

Enter CITIZENS.

CITIZEN. Which way ran he that killed Mercutio?

"*vrai*")   **mortal** deadly   110 **effeminate** weak   111 **temper** (1) disposition, which is
weak (2) the tempering of a sword blade to harden it   111 **softened** (rather than
hardened)   112 **brave** fine   113 **aspired** mounted to   114 **scorn** scoff at   115 **moe**
more (in the future)   **depend** hang over, threaten   119 **respective lenity** considerate
leniency   120 **Fury** goddess of revenge   **conduct** guide   126 **consort** associate
with   129 **up** i.e. in arms   130 **amazed** dumbfounded   **doom thee** sentence you
to   132 **fool** dupe

Tybalt, that murderer, which way ran he?
BENVOLIO. There lies that Tybalt.
CITIZEN.   Up sir, go with me: 135
I charge thee in the prince's name obey.

Enter PRINCE, OLD MONTAGUE,
CAPULET, *their* WIVES, *and* ALL.

PRINCE.   Where are the vile beginners of this fray?
BENVOLIO. O noble prince, I can discover all
The unlucky manage of this fatal brawl:
There lies the man slain by young Romeo,   140
That slew thy kinsman, brave Mercutio.
CAPULET'S WIFE.
Tybalt, my cousin, O my brother's child,
O prince, O cousin, husband, O the blood is spilled
Of my dear kinsman! Prince, as thou art true,
For blood of ours shed blood of Montague.   145
O cousin, cousin!
PRINCE.   Benvolio, who began this bloody fray?
BENVOLIO. Tybalt here slain, whom Romeo's hand did slay,
Romeo that spoke him fair, bid him bethink
How nice the quarrel was, and urged withal   150
Your high displeasure: all this utterèd
With gentle breath, calm look, knees humbly bowed,
Could not take truce with the unruly spleen
Of Tybalt deaf to peace, but that he tilts
With piercing steel at bold Mercutio's breast,   155
Who all as hot, turns deadly point to point,
And with a martial scorn, with one hand beats
Cold death aside, and with the other sends
It back to Tybalt, whose dexterity
Retorts it. Romeo he cries aloud,   160
'Hold friends, friends part,' and swifter than his
          tongue,
His agile arm beats down their fatal points,
And 'twixt them rushes, underneath whose arm,
An envious thrust from Tybalt hit the life
Of stout Mercutio, and then Tybalt fled,   165

---

135 **Up** get up   138 **discover** reveal   139 **manage**
conduct   144 **true** just   149 **spoke him fair** spoke civilly to him   150 **nice**
trivial   **urged withal** mentioned in addition   153 **take truce** make peace   **spleen**
irascibility   154 **tilts** thrusts   160 **Retorts it** throws it back in reply   164 **envious**
malicious   165, 169 **stout** stout-hearted   166 **by and by** shortly   167 **newly** . . .

But by and by comes back to Romeo,
Who had but newly entertained revenge,
And to't they go like lightning, for ere I
Could draw to part them, was stout Tybalt slain:
And as he fell, did Romeo turn and fly: 170
This is the truth, or let Benvolio die.

CAPULET'S WIFE.
He is a kinsman to the Montague,
Affection makes him false, he speaks not true:
Some twenty of them fought in this black strife,
And all those twenty could but kill one life.   175
I beg for justice, which thou prince, must give:
Romeo slew Tybalt, Romeo must not live.

PRINCE.   Romeo slew him, he slew Mercutio:
Who now the price of his dear blood doth owe?

MONTAGUE.
Not Romeo, prince, he was Mercutio's friend,   180
His fault concludes but what the law should end,
The life of Tybalt.

PRINCE.   And for that offence
Immediately we do exile him hence:
I have an interest in your hate's proceeding:
My blood for your rude brawls doth lie a-bleeding.   185
But I'll amerce you with so strong a fine,
That you shall all repent the loss of mine.
I will be deaf to pleading and excuses,
Nor tears nor prayers shall purchase out abuses.
Therefore use none, let Romeo hence in haste,   190
Else when he is found, that hour is his last.
Bear hence this body, and attend our will:
Mercy but murders, pardoning those that kill.   *Exeunt.*

[SCENE II.]

Enter JULIET *alone.*

JULIET.   Gallop apace, you fiery-footed steeds,
Towards Phoebus' lodging: such a wagoner

---

revenge recently entertained thoughts of revenge   179 **Who . . . owe?** Who now has to
pay the price with his dear blood?   181 **but** only   185 **blood** i.e. relation   186 **amerce**
penalize   187 **mine** my blood   189 **Nor . . . nor** neither . . . nor   **purchase out** buy
pardon for   193 **murders** encourages other murders (by)
    III, ii Capulet's house   1 **apace** quickly   **fiery-footed steeds** horses of the sun god,
Phoebus Apollo   2 **lodging** resting-place for the night in the west, below the

As Phaëton would whip you to the west,
And bring in cloudy night immediately.
Spread thy close curtain, love-performing night, 5
That runaways' eyes may wink, and Romeo
Leap to these arms, untalked of and unseen.
Lovers can see to do their amorous rites
By their own beauties, or if love be blind,
It best agrees with night: come civil night, 10
Thou sober-suited matron all in black,
And learn me how to lose a winning match,
Played for a pair of stainless maidenhoods.
Hood my unmanned blood bating in my cheeks,
With thy black mantle, till strange love grow bold, 15
Think true love acted simple modesty:
Come night, come Romeo, come thou day in night,
For thou wilt lie upon the wings of night,
Whiter than new snow upon a raven's back:
Come gentle night, come loving, black-browed night, 20
Give me my Romeo, and when he shall die,
Take him and cut him out in little stars,
And he will make the face of heaven so fine,
That all the world will be in love with night,
And pay no worship to the garish sun. 25
O I have bought the mansion of a love,
But not possessed it, and though I am sold,
Not yet enjoyed: so tedious is this day,
As is the night before some festival,
To an impatient child that hath new robes 30
And may not wear them. O here comes my nurse:

Enter NURSE *with cords.*

And she brings news, and every tongue that speaks
But Romeo's name, speaks heavenly eloquence:
Now nurse, what news? What hast thou there, the cords
That Romeo bid thee fetch?

---

horizon **wagoner** charioteer 3 **Phaëton** Apollo's son (who tried to drive the sun-chariot but could not restrain the horses from galloping wildly away) 5 **close curtain** curtain of darkness that gives privacy **love-performing** for performing the acts of love 6 **runaways' eyes** eyes of the curious who might try to look in if night's curtains were not closed (a famous crux. Other interpretations of "runaway" include the sun, Phaëton, the stars) **wink** be unable to see (lit. close the eyes and keep them so) 10 **civil** sober 14 **Hood** cover (fr. falconry: method of calming an excited hawk) **unmanned** (1) untrained (fr. falconry) (2) without a man **bating** beating (fr. falconry: flapping the wings) 15 **strange** unfamiliar 34 **cords** rope ladder 38 **undone** ruined 40 **envi-**

NURSE.	Ay, ay, the cords. 35

[Throws them down.]

JULIET.	Ay me, what news? Why dost thou wring thy hands?
NURSE.	Ah weraday, he's dead, he's dead, he's dead,
	We are undone lady, we are undone.
	Alack the day, he's gone, he's killed, he's dead!
JULIET.	Can heaven be so envious?
NURSE.	Romeo can, 40
	Though heaven cannot. O Romeo, Romeo,
	Who ever would have thought it Romeo?
JULIET.	What devil art thou that dost torment me thus?
	This torture should be roared in dismal hell:
	Hath Romeo slain himself? Say thou but 'ay,' 45
	And that bare vowel 'I' shall poison more
	Than the death-darting eye of cockatrice.
	I am not I, if there be such an 'ay,'
	Or those eyes shut that makes thee answer 'ay.'
	If he be slain, say 'ay,' or if not, 'no.' 50
	Brief sounds determine of my weal or woe.
NURSE.	I saw the wound, I saw it with mine eyes,
	God save the mark, here on his manly breast:
	A piteous corse, a bloody piteous corse,
	Pale, pale as ashes, all bedaubed in blood, 55
	All in gore blood, I swounded at the sight.
JULIET.	O break my heart, poor bankrout break at once!
	To prison, eyes, ne'er look on liberty.
	Vile earth, to earth resign, end motion here,
	And thou and Romeo press one heavy bier. 60.
NURSE.	O Tybalt, Tybalt, the best friend I had,
	O courteous Tybalt, honest gentleman,
	That ever I should live to see thee dead.
JULIET.	What storm is this that blows so contrary?
	Is Romeo slaughtered? and is Tybalt dead? 65
	My dearest cousin, and my dearer lord?
	Then dreadful trumpet sound the general doom,

ous malicious   45–6 'ay' . . . 'I' (common wordplay, as "ay" was written "I"; "eye," l. 47, is a third variation)   46 poison more have more power to kill (myself)   47 cockatrice basilisk (fabulous serpent that killed with a glance)   49 those eyes (Romeo's)   shut i.e. in death   51 determine decide   weal happiness, welfare   53 God . . . mark apology preceding a remark that might offend   54 corse corpse   56 gore clotted   swounded swooned   57 bankrout bankrupt, having lost everything   break (wordplay: being "broke" when bankrupt)   59 Vile earth body   to earth to a grave   62 honest honorable   67 general doom end of the world, Day of Judgment

	For who is living, if those two are gone?	
NURSE.	Tybalt is gone and Romeo banishèd,	
	Romeo that killed him, he is banishèd.	70
JULIET.	O God! Did Romeo's hand shed Tybalt's blood?	
NURSE.	It did, it did, alas the day, it did.	
JULIET.	O serpent heart, hid with a flow'ring face.	
	Did ever dragon keep so fair a cave?	
	Beautiful tyrant, fiend angelical:	75
	Dove-feathered raven, wolvish-ravening lamb,	
	Despisèd substance of divinest show:	
	Just opposite to what thou justly seem'st,	
	A damnèd saint, an honourable villain:	
	O nature, what hadst thou to do in hell	80
	When thou didst bower the spirit of a fiend	
	In mortal paradise of such sweet flesh?	
	Was ever book containing such vile matter	
	So fairly bound? O that deceit should dwell	
	In such a gorgeous palace.	
NURSE.	There's no trust,	85
	No faith, no honesty in men, all perjured,	
	All forsworn, all naught, all dissemblers.	
	Ah where's my man? Give me some aqua vitæ:	
	These griefs, these woes, these sorrows make me old.	
	Shame come to Romeo.	
JULIET.	Blistered be thy tongue	90
	For such a wish, he was not born to shame:	
	Upon his brow shame is ashamed to sit:	
	For 'tis a throne where honour may be crowned	
	Sole monarch of the universal earth.	
	O what a beast was I to chide at him.	95
NURSE.	Will you speak well of him that killed your cousin?	
JULIET.	Shall I speak ill of him that is my husband?	
	Ah poor my lord, what tongue shall smooth thy name,	
	When I thy three-hours wife have mangled it?	
	But wherefore villain didst thou kill my cousin?	100
	That villain cousin would have killed my husband:	
	Back foolish tears, back to your native spring,	
	Your tributary drops belong to woe,	

74 **keep** inhabit   **so
fair a cave** a cave that seemed so full of treasure   77 **substance** reality   **show**
appearance   78 **justly** truly   81 **bower** lodge   87 **naught** wicked   88 **man**
servant   **aqua vitae** spirits   90 **Blistered . . . tongue** (proverbially, slanderers were so
punished)   98 **smooth** (1) speak well of (2) smooth out (in contrast to "mangled")   104

Which you mistaking offer up to joy:
My husband lives that Tybalt would have slain,   105
And Tybalt's dead that would have slain my husband:
All this is comfort, wherefore weep I then?
Some word there was, worser than Tybalt's death
That murdered me, I would forget it fain,
But O it presses to my memory   110
Like damnèd guilty deeds to sinners' minds,
'Tybalt is dead and Romeo banishèd.'
That 'banishèd,' that one word 'banishèd,'
Hath slain ten thousand Tybalts: Tybalt's death
Was woe enough if it had ended there: 115
Or if sour woe delights in fellowship,
And needly will be ranked with other griefs,
Why followed not when she said 'Tybalt's dead,'
'Thy father' or 'thy mother,' nay or both,
Which modern lamentation might have moved?   120
But with a rearward following Tybalt's death,
'Romeo is banishèd:' to speak that word,
Is father, mother, Tybalt, Romeo, Juliet,
All slain, all dead: 'Romeo is banishèd,'
There is no end, no limit, measure, bound,   125
In that word's death, no words can that woe sound.
Where is my father and my mother, nurse?

NURSE.   Weeping and wailing over Tybalt's corse,
Will you go to them? I will bring you thither.

JULIET.   Wash they his wounds with tears? Mine shall be spent, 130
When theirs are dry, for Romeo's banishment.
Take up those cords, poor ropes, you are beguiled,
Both you and I, for Romeo is exiled:
He made you for a highway to my bed,
But I a maid, die maiden-widowèd.   135
Come cords, come nurse, I'll to my wedding bed,
And Death, not Romeo, take my maidenhead.

NURSE.   Hie to your chamber, I'll find Romeo
To comfort you, I wot well where he is:
Hark ye, your Romeo will be here at night,   140
I'll to him, he is hid at Lawrence' cell.

---

joy i.e. that Romeo is alive   109 fain gladly   116 sour bitter   woe . . . fellowship
misery loves companionship   117 needly of necessity   120 modern ordinary   121
rearward (1) rear guard (continuing the military metaphor of "ranked") (2) (wordplay:
"rear-word")   126 that word's death the death involved in that word   139 wot know

JULIET.   O find him, give this ring to my true knight,
           And bid him come, to take his last farewell.   *Exeunt.*

           [SCENE III.]

           Enter FRIAR [LAWRENCE].

FRIAR.   Romeo come forth, come forth thou fearful man:
           Affliction is enamoured of thy parts,
           And thou art wedded to calamity.

                        Enter ROMEO.

ROMEO.   Father, what news? What is the prince's doom?
           What sorrow craves acquaintance at my hand,   5
           That I yet know not?
FRIAR.   Too familiar
           Is my dear son with such sour company:
           I bring thee tidings of the prince's doom.
ROMEO.   What less than doomsday is the prince's doom?
FRIAR.   A gentler judgment vanished from his lips,   10
           Not body's death, but body's banishment.
ROMEO.   Ha, banishment? Be merciful, say 'death:'
           For exile hath more terror in his look,
           Much more than death: do not say 'banishment.'
FRIAR.   Hence from Verona art thou banishèd: 15
           Be patient, for the world is broad and wide.
ROMEO.   There is no world without Verona walls,
           But purgatory, torture, hell itself:
           Hence 'banishèd' is banished from the world,
           And world's exile is death. Then 'banishèd'   20
           Is death, mistermed: calling death 'banishèd,'
           Thou cut'st my head off with a golden axe,
           And smilest upon the stroke that murders me.
FRIAR.   O deadly sin, O rude unthankfulness!
           Thy fault our law calls death, but the kind prince 25
           Taking thy part, hath rushed aside the law,
           And turned that black word 'death' to 'banishment.'
           This is dear mercy, and thou seest it not.
ROMEO.   'Tis torture and not mercy: heaven is here
           Where Juliet lives, and every cat and dog,   30

III, iii Friar Lawrence's cell   **2 parts** personal qualities   **4 doom** judgment   **7 sour**
bitter   **9 doomsday** (in the sense of "death")   **10 vanished** issued   **17 without**
outside   **20 world's exile** exile from the world   **26 part** side   **28 dear** great

And little mouse, every unworthy thing
Live here in heaven, and may look on her,
But Romeo may not. More validity,
More honourable state, more courtship lives
In carrion flies than Romeo: they may seize   35
On the white wonder of dear Juliet's hand,
And steal immortal blessing from her lips,
Who even in pure and vestal modesty
Still blush, as thinking their own kisses sin.
But Romeo may not, he is banishèd.   40
This may flies do, when I from this must fly:
They are free men, but I am banishèd.
And sayest thou yet, that exile is not death?
Hadst thou no poison mixed, no sharp-ground knife,
No sudden mean of death, though ne'er so mean,   45
But 'banishèd' to kill me: 'banishèd'?
O friar, the damnèd use that word in hell,
Howling attends it: how hast thou the heart,
Being a divine, a ghostly confessor,
A sin-absolver, and my friend professed,   50
To mangle me with that word 'banishèd'?

FRIAR.   Thou fond mad man, hear me a little speak.
ROMEO.   O thou wilt speak again of banishment.
FRIAR.   I'll give thee armour to keep off that word,
Adversity's sweet milk, philosophy,   55
To comfort thee though thou art banishèd.
ROMEO.   Yet 'banishèd'? Hang up philosophy,
Unless philosophy can make a Juliet,
Displant a town, reverse a prince's doom,
It helps not, it prevails not, talk no more.   60
FRIAR.   O then I see that madmen have no ears.
ROMEO.   How should they when that wise men have no eyes?
FRIAR.   Let me dispute with thee of thy estate.
ROMEO.   Thou canst not speak of that thou dost not feel:
Wert thou as young as I, Juliet thy love,   65
An hour but married, Tybalt murderèd,
Doting like me, and like me banishèd,
Then mightst thou speak, then mightst thou tear thy
            hair,

---

33 **validity** value 34 **state** position **courtship** courtliness (w. pun on "wooing") 38
vestal virgin 39 **Still blush** always are red **their own kisses** the "kisses" one lip gives
another 45 **mean ... mean** means ... base 49 **ghostly** spiritual 52 **fond**
foolish 57 **Yet** still 59 **Displant a town** replant Verona (in my place of
banishment) 63 **dispute ... estate** reason with you about your situation 64 **that** i.e.

And fall upon the ground as I do now,
Taking the measure of an unmade grave.   70

Knock [*within*].

FRIAR.   Arise, one knocks, good Romeo, hide thyself.
ROMEO.   Not I, unless the breath of heartsick groans
Mist-like infold me from the search of eyes.   *Knock.*
FRIAR.   Hark how they knock—Who's there?—Romeo arise,
Thou wilt be taken.—Stay awhile.—Stand up. *Knock.* 75
Run to my study:—By and by.—God's will,
What simpleness is this:—I come, I come.   *Knock.*
Who knocks so hard? Whence come you? What's your
will?
NURSE.   [*Within.*] Let me come in, and you shall know my errand:
I come from Lady Juliet.
FRIAR.   Welcome then.   80

Enter NURSE.

NURSE.   O holy friar, O tell me holy friar,
Where's my lady's lord? Where's Romeo?
FRIAR.   There on the ground, with his own tears made drunk.
NURSE.   O he is even in my mistress' case,
Just in her case. O woeful sympathy: 85
Piteous predicament, even so lies she,
Blubb'ring and weeping, weeping and blubb'ring.
Stand up, stand up, stand and you be a man,
For Juliet's sake, for her sake rise and stand:
Why should you fall into so deep an O?   90
ROMEO.   [*Rises.*] Nurse—
NURSE.   Ah sir, ah sir, death's the end of all.
ROMEO.   Spakest thou of Juliet? how is it with her?
Doth not she think me an old murderer,
Now I have stained the childhood of our joy   95
With blood removed but little from her own?
Where is she? and how doth she? and what says
My còncealed lady to our cancelled love?
NURSE.   O she says nothing sir, but weeps and weeps,
And now falls on her bed, and then starts up,   100
And Tybalt calls, and then on Romeo cries,
And then down falls again.

which   70 **Taking the measure** indicating the measurements for   75 **Stay** wait   77
simpleness foolishness   85 **woeful sympathy** agreement in woe   90 **O** (1) a moan (2)
bawdy pun on pudendum, as is "case," l.84   94 **old** (1) hardened (2) aged   98 **concealed**

ROMEO.   As if that name
Shot from the deadly level of a gun,
Did murder her, as that name's cursèd hand
Murdered her kinsman. O tell me friar, tell me,   105
In what vile part of this anatomy
Doth my name lodge? Tell me, that I may sack
The hateful mansion.

                    He offers to stab himself.

FRIAR.   Hold thy desperate hand:
Art thou a man? Thy form cries out thou art:
Thy tears are womanish, thy wild acts denote   110
The unreasonable fury of a beast.
Unseemly woman in a seeming man,
And ill-beseeming beast in seeming both,
Thou hast amazed me. By my holy order,
I thought thy disposition better tempered.   115
Hast thou slain Tybalt? Wilt thou slay thyself?
And slay thy lady that in thy life lives,
By doing damnèd hate upon thyself?
Why railest thou on thy birth, the heaven and earth?
Since birth and heaven and earth all three do meet   120
In thee at once, which thou at once wouldst lose.
Fie, fie, thou shamest thy shape, thy love, thy wit,
Which like a usurer abound'st in all:
And usest none in that true use indeed,
Which should bedeck thy shape, thy love, thy wit: 125
Thy noble shape is but a form of wax,
Digressing from the valour of a man:
Thy dear love sworn but hollow perjury,
Killing that love which thou hast vowed to cherish:
Thy wit, that ornament to shape and love,   130
Misshapen in the conduct of them both,
Like powder in a skilless soldier's flask,
Is set afire by thine own ignorance,

---

lady secret wife   98 **cancelled** annulled (fr. law)   101 **cries** i.e. out against   103 **level**
line of aim   113 **ill-beseeming . . . both** unnatural monster, by seeming to be both man
and woman   114 **amazed** dumbfounded   115 **better tempered** made up of better
qualities   118 **damned** (through suicide)   120 **birth . . . meet** at one's birth, the body
(earth) and soul (heaven) are united   121 **lose** i.e. through suicide   122, 125 **wit** intelligence, judgment   123–5 **like a usurer . . . wit** a usurer increases his bounty unnaturally
by taking interest, but you are as bad by withholding from their rightful use your endowments of good looks, love, and judgment   126 **a form of wax** like a waxen figure (as it
shows no manly valor)   129 **Killing** because you will kill (by your suicide)   130 **that
ornament to** that which ornaments   131 **Misshapen . . . both** forced from its true

And thou dismembered with thine own defence.
What, rouse thee man, thy Juliet is alive,   135
For whose dear sake thou wast but lately dead.
There art thou happy. Tybalt would kill thee,
But thou slewest Tybalt, there art thou happy.
The law that threatened death becomes thy friend,
And turns it to exile, there art thou happy.   140
A pack of blessings light upon thy back,
Happiness courts thee in her best array,
But like a misbehaved and sullen wench,
Thou pouts upon thy fortune and thy love:
Take heed, take heed, for such die miserable.   145
Go get thee to thy love as was decreed,
Ascend her chamber, hence and comfort her:
But look thou stay not till the watch be set,
For then thou canst not pass to Mantua,
Where thou shalt live till we can find a time   150
To blaze your marriage, reconcile your friends,
Beg pardon of the prince and call thee back,
With twenty hundred thousand times more joy
Than thou went'st forth in lamentation.
Go before, nurse, commend me to thy lady,   155
And bid her hasten all the house to bed,
Which heavy sorrow makes them apt unto.
Romeo is coming.

NURSE.   O Lord, I could have stayed here all the night,
To hear good counsel: O what learning is!   160
My lord, I'll tell my lady you will come.

ROMEO.   Do so, and bid my sweet prepare to chide.

NURSE.   Here sir, a ring she bid me give you sir:
Hie you, make haste, for it grows very late.

                                        [*Exit* NURSE.]

ROMEO.   How well my comfort is revived by this.   165

FRIAR.   Go hence, good night, and here stands all your state:
Either be gone before the watch be set,
Or by the break of day disguised from hence:
Sojourn in Mantua, I'll find out your man,

nature, and unable to guide your physical and emotional endowments 134 **dismembered
. . . defence** blown to pieces by the wrong use of judgment (the "powder") which is meant
for your defense   137 **happy** fortunate   146 **decreed** arranged   148 **watch be set**
guard be stationed at the city gates   151 **blaze** make public   **friends** kinsmen   157 **apt**
inclined   164 **Hie** hurry   166 **here . . . state** your fortune depends on acting as

And he shall signify from time to time,   170
Every good hap to you that chances here:
Give me thy hand, 'tis late, farewell, good night.

ROMEO.   But that a joy past joy calls out on me,
It were a grief, so brief to part with thee:
Farewell.   *Exeunt.* 175

[SCENE IV.]

Enter OLD CAPULET, his WIFE *and* PARIS.

CAPULET.   Things have fall'n out sir so unluckily,
That we have had no time to move our daughter:
Look you, she loved her kinsman Tybalt dearly,
And so did I. Well, we were born to die.
'Tis very late, she'll not come down tonight: 5
I promise you, but for your company,
I would have been abed an hour ago.

PARIS.   These times of woe afford no time to woo:
Madam good night, commend me to your daughter.

LADY.   I will, and know her mind early tomorrow,   10
Tonight she's mewed up to her heaviness.

CAPULET.   Sir Paris, I will make a desperate tender
Of my child's love: I think she will be ruled
In all respects by me: nay more, I doubt it not.
Wife, go you to her ere you go to bed,   15
Acquaint her here of my son Paris' love,
And bid her (mark you me?) on Wednesday next—
But soft, what day is this?

PARIS.   Monday, my lord.

CAPULET.   Monday, ha ha: well Wednesday is too soon,
O' Thursday let it be: o' Thursday tell her   20
She shall be married to this noble earl:
Will you be ready? do you like this haste?
We'll keep no great ado, a friend or two:
For hark you, Tybalt being slain so late,
It may be thought we held him carelessly,   25
Being our kinsman, if we revel much:
Therefore we'll have some half a dozen friends,

---

follows   171 **good hap** favorable happening   174 **brief** hastily
   III, iv Capulet's house   2 **move** make the proposal to   11 **mewed . . . heaviness** shut
up with her grief ("mew"=cage)   12 **make . . . tender** risk making an offer   16 **son**
son-in-law   19 **ha ha** uh-huh   23 **keep . . . ado** make no great fuss   24 **late**
lately   25 **held him carelessly** cared little about him

And there an end. But what say you to Thursday?
PARIS.   My lord, I would that Thursday were tomorrow.
CAPULET.   Well, get you gone: o' Thursday be it then: 30
Go you to Juliet ere you go to bed,
Prepare her, wife, against this wedding day.
Farewell my lord. Light to my chamber ho:
Afore me, it is so very late that we
May call it early by and by. Good night.   35

Exeunt.

[SCENE V.]

Enter ROMEO *and* JULIET *aloft at the window.*

JULIET.   Wilt thou be gone? It is not yet near day:
It was the nightingale, and not the lark,
That pierced the fearful hollow of thine ear,
Nightly she sings on yond pomegranate tree,
Believe me love, it was the nightingale.   5
ROMEO.   It was the lark, the herald of the morn,
No nightingale: look love, what envious streaks
Do lace the severing clouds in yonder east:
Night's candles are burnt out, and jocund day
Stands tiptoe on the misty mountain tops: 10
I must be gone and live, or stay and die.
JULIET.   Yond light is not daylight, I know it, I:
It is some meteor that the sun exhales
To be to thee this night a torchbearer,
And light thee on thy way to Mantua.   15
Therefore stay yet, thou need'st not to be gone.
ROMEO.   Let me be ta'en, let me be put to death,
I am content, so thou wilt have it so.
I'll say yon grey is not the morning's eye,
'Tis but the pale reflex of Cynthia's brow.   20
Nor that is not the lark whose notes do beat
The vaulty heaven so high above our heads,
I have more care to stay than will to go:

---

32 **against** in anticipation of   35 **by and by** very soon
III, v Juliet's chamber   3 **fearful** fear-filled   7 **envious** malicious   7–8 **streaks . . .
clouds** (1) the clouds are being severed by the streaks of light (2) the lovers are being parted
by the streaked sky of dawn   9 **Night's candles** the stars   13 **meteor . . . exhales**
(meteors were believed to be formed by vapors drawn up and ignited by the sun)   20 **reflex**

Come death and welcome, Juliet wills it so.
How is't, my soul? Let's talk, it is not day.   25

JULIET.   It is, it is, hie hence, be gone away:
It is the lark that sings so out of tune,
Straining harsh discords and unpleasing sharps.
Some say the lark makes sweet division:
This doth not so: for she divideth us.   30
Some say the lark and loathèd toad change eyes,
O now I would they had changed voices too:
Since arm from arm that voice doth us affray,
Hunting thee hence, with hunt's-up to the day.
O now be gone, more light and light it grows.   35

ROMEO.   More light and light, more dark and dark our woes.

Enter NURSE *hastily.*

NURSE.   Madam!
JULIET.   Nurse?
NURSE.   Your lady mother is coming to your chamber,
The day is broke, be wary, look about.   [*Exit.*] 40
JULIET.   Then window let day in, and let life out.
ROMEO.   Farewell, farewell, one kiss and I'll descend.

He goeth down.

JULIET.   Art thou gone so? Love, lord, ay husband, friend,
I must hear from thee every day in the hour,
For in a minute there are many days: 45
O by this count I shall be much in years,
Ere I again behold my Romeo.

ROMEO.   Farewell:
I will omit no opportunity
That may convey my greetings love, to thee.   50

JULIET.   O think'st thou we shall ever meet again?
ROMEO.   I doubt it not, and all these woes shall serve
For sweet discourses in our times to come.
JULIET.   O God! I have an ill-divining soul,
Methinks I see thee, now thou art so low,   55
As one dead in the bottom of a tomb:
Either my eyesight fails, or thou look'st pale.

reflection   **Cynthia** the moon   22 **vaulty** arched   28 **sharps** shrill sounds   29
division execution of a rapid melodic passage (fr. music)   31 **change eyes** (because the
toad's eyes were thought to be more beautiful)   33 **affray** startle, make afraid   34
hunt's-up early morning song to summon hunters (as the lark does the day) and also to
awaken newlyweds   43 **friend** lover   46 **count** method of counting   54 **ill-divining**

ROMEO. And trust me love, in my eye so do you:
        Dry sorrow drinks our blood. Adieu, adieu.   *Exit.*

JULIET. O Fortune, Fortune, all men call thee fickle: 60
        If thou art fickle, what dost thou with him
        That is renowned for faith? Be fickle, Fortune:
        For then I hope thou wilt not keep him long,
        But send him back.

LADY.   [*Within.*] Ho daughter, are you up?   65

JULIET. Who is't that calls? It is my lady mother.
        Is she not down so late, or up so early?
        What unaccustomed cause procures her hither?

                    Enter MOTHER.

LADY.   Why how now Juliet?

JULIET.   Madam, I am not well.

LADY.   Evermore weeping for your cousin's death?   70
        What, wilt thou wash him from his grave with tears?
        And if thou couldst, thou couldst not make him live:
        Therefore have done—some grief shows much of love,
        But much of grief shows still some want of wit.

JULIET. Yet let me weep for such a feeling loss.   75

LADY.   So shall you feel the loss, but not the friend
        Which you weep for.

JULIET.   Feeling so the loss,
        I cannot choose but ever weep the friend.

LADY.   Well girl, thou weep'st not so much for his death,
        As that the villain lives which slaughtered him.   80

JULIET. What villain, madam?

LADY.   That same villain Romeo.

JULIET. [*Aside.*] Villain and he be many miles asunder.—
        God pardon him, I do with all my heart:
        And yet no man like he, doth grieve my heart.

LADY.   That is because the traitor murderer lives.   85

JULIET. Ay madam, from the reach of these my hands:
        Would none but I might venge my cousin's death.

LADY.   We will have vengeance for it, fear thou not.
        Then weep no more, I'll send to one in Mantua,
        Where that same banished runagate doth live,   90

forseeing misfortune   59 **Dry** thirsty   **sorrow . . . blood** (it was believed that grief
drained the blood away)   61 **dost thou** is your concern   **him** Romeo   67 **down** lying
down in bed   73 **shows . . . love** is a sign of great love   74 **still** always   **want of wit**
lack of wisdom   75 **feeling** heartfelt   78 **friend** (Juliet interprets as "lover." Through
1.103, Juliet combines two meanings, one for her mother and the other covertly expressing
her love for Romeo)   84 **like** so much as   86 **from** away from   90 **runagate**

Shall give him such an unaccustomed dram,
That he shall soon keep Tybalt company:
And then I hope thou wilt be satisfied.

JULIET.   Indeed I never shall be satisfied
With Romeo, till I behold him—dead—   95
Is my poor heart so for a kinsman vexed:
Madam, if you could find out but a man
To bear a poison, I would temper it:
That Romeo should upon receipt thereof,
Soon sleep in quiet. O how my heart abhors   100
To hear him named and cannot come to him,
To wreak the love I bore my cousin,
Upon his body that hath slaughtered him.

LADY.   Find thou the means, and I'll find such a man.
But now I'll tell thee joyful tidings, girl.   105

JULIET.   And joy comes well in such a needy time:
What are they, beseech your ladyship?

LADY.   Well, well, thou hast a careful father, child,
One who to put thee from thy heaviness,
Hath sorted out a sudden day of joy   110
That thou expects not, nor I looked not for.

JULIET.   Madam, in happy time, what day is that?

LADY.   Marry my child, early next Thursday morn,
The gallant, young, and noble gentleman,
The County Paris at Saint Peter's Church,   115
Shall happily make thee there a joyful bride.

JULIET.   Now by Saint Peter's Church, and Peter too,
He shall not make me there a joyful bride.
I wonder at this haste, that I must wed
Ere he that should be husband comes to woo: 120
I pray you tell my lord and father, madam,
I will not marry yet, and when I do, I swear
It shall be Romeo, whom you know I hate,
Rather than Paris. These are news indeed.

LADY.   Here comes your father, tell him so yourself: 125
And see how he will take it at your hands.

Enter CAPULET *and* NURSE.

CAPULET.   When the sun sets, the earth doth drizzle dew,

---

renegade   91 **unaccustomed** strange   95 **dead** (applied, for the mother, to "Romeo";
for herself, to "heart")   98 **temper** (1) mix (2) modify   106 **needy** needful (of
happiness)   108 **careful** caring   109 **heaviness** sadness   110 **sorted out**
chosen   112 **in . . . time** (customary greeting to good fortune)

But for the sunset of my brother's son,
It rains downright.
How now, a conduit, girl? What, still in tears?   130
Evermore show'ring? In one little body
Thou counterfeits a bark, a sea, a wind:
For still thy eyes, which I may call the sea,
Do ebb and flow with tears: the bark thy body is,
Sailing in this salt flood, the winds thy sighs,   135
Who raging with thy tears and they with them,
Without a sudden calm will overset
Thy tempest-tossèd body. How now wife?
Have you delivered to her our decree?

LADY.   Ay sir, but she will none, she gives you thanks,   140
           I would the fool were married to her grave.

CAPULET.   Soft, take me with you, take me with you wife,
           How, will she none? Doth she not give us thanks?
           Is she not proud? Doth she not count her blest,
           Unworthy as she is, that we have wrought   145
           So worthy a gentleman to be her bride?

JULIET.   Not proud you have, but thankful that you have:
           Proud can I never be of what I hate,
           But thankful even for hate that is meant love.

CAPULET.   How, how, how, how, chopt-logic? what is this?   150
           'Proud' and 'I thank you,' and 'I thank you not,'
           And yet 'not proud'? Mistress minion you,
           Thank me no thankings, nor proud me no prouds,
           But fettle your fine joints 'gainst Thursday next,
           To go with Paris to Saint Peter's Church: 155
           Or I will drag thee on a hurdle thither.
           Out you green-sickness carrion, out you baggage,
           You tallow-face!

LADY.   Fie, fie, what, are you mad?

JULIET.   Good father, I beseech you on my knees,
           Hear me with patience, but to speak a word.   160

CAPULET.   Hang thee young baggage, disobedient wretch,

130 **conduit** fountain
(often emitting from a statue)   130, 133 **still** continually   132 **counterfeits**
imitates   137 **Without** unless there is   **overset** overturn, overwhelm   139 **decree**
decision   140 **will none** will have none of it   142 **Soft . . . you** just a minute; let me
understand you   145 **wrought** worked to find   150 **chopt-logic** hair-splitting
argument   152 **minion** spoiled darling   154 **fettle** get ready   **'gainst** in preparation
for   156 **hurdle** vehicle that brought traitors to execution   157 **green-sickness** form of
anemia afflicting adolescent girls (he alludes to her paleness)   **carrion** dead flesh   157,
161 **baggage** hussy   158 **tallow** yellowish-white   165 **My fingers itch** i.e. to hit

I tell thee what, get thee to church o' Thursday,
Or never after look me in the face.
Speak not, reply not, do not answer me.
My fingers itch: wife, we scarce thought us blest   165
That God had lent us but this only child,
But now I see this one is one too much,
And that we have a curse in having her:
Out on her, hilding!

NURSE.   God in heaven bless her:
You are to blame, my lord, to rate her so.   170

CAPULET.   And why, my Lady Wisdom? Hold your tongue,
Good Prudence, smatter with your gossips, go.

NURSE.   I speak no treason.

CAPULET.   O Godigoden.

NURSE.   May not one speak?

CAPULET.   Peace, you mumbling fool,
Utter your gravity o'er a gossip's bowl,   175
For here we need it not.

LADY.   You are too hot.

CAPULET.   God's bread, it makes me mad:
Day, night, hour, tide, time, work, play,
Alone, in company, still my care hath been
To have her matched, and having now provided   180
A gentleman of noble parentage,
Of fair demesnes, youthful and nobly trained,
Stuffed as they say, with honourable parts,
Proportioned as one's thought would wish a man,
And then to have a wretched puling fool,   185
A whining mammet, in her fortune's tender,
To answer 'I'll not wed, I cannot love:
I am too young, I pray you pardon me.'
But and you will not wed, I'll pardon you.
Graze where you will, you shall not house with me: 190
Look to't, think on't, I do not use to jest.
Thursday is near, lay hand on heart, advise:
And you be mine, I'll give you to my friend,
And you be not, hang, beg, starve, die in the streets,

you   169 **hilding** good-for-nothing   170 **rate** berate   172 **smatter** chatter   172, 175
gossips cronies   173 **Godigoden** God give you good evening   175 **gravity** wisdom
(ironic)   177 **God's bread** by the holy sacrament   179 **still** always   182 **demesnes**
domains   183 **parts** personal qualities   185 **puling** whimpering   186 **mammet** doll,
baby   **in . . . tender** upon the offer of good fortune   189 **pardon you** give you leave to
depart   191 **do not use** am not used   192 **lay . . . heart** take it to heart   **advise** think it

| | For by my soul I'll ne'er acknowledge thee, | 195 |

For by my soul I'll ne'er acknowledge thee,   195
Nor what is mine shall never do thee good:
Trust to't, bethink you, I'll not be forsworn.   *Exit.*

JULIET.   Is there no pity sitting in the clouds
That sees into the bottom of my grief?
O sweet my mother, cast me not away,   200
Delay this marriage for a month, a week,
Or if you do not, make the bridal bed
In that dim monument where Tybalt lies.

LADY.   Talk not to me, for I'll not speak a word,
Do as thou wilt, for I have done with thee.   *Exit.*   205

JULIET.   O God! O nurse, how shall this be prevented?
My husband is on earth, my faith in heaven:
How shall that faith return again to earth,
Unless that husband send it me from heaven,
By leaving earth? Comfort me, counsel me: 210
Alack, alack, that heaven should practise stratagems
Upon so soft a subject as myself.
What say'st thou, hast thou not a word of joy?
Some comfort, nurse.

NURSE.   Faith here it is,
Romeo is banished, and all the world to nothing,   215
That he dares ne'er come back to challenge you:
Or if he do, it needs must be by stealth.
Then since the case so stands as now it doth,
I think it best you married with the county.
O he's a lovely gentleman: 220
Romeo's a dishclout to him: an eagle, madam,
Hath not so green, so quick, so fair an eye
As Paris hath. Beshrew my very heart,
I think you are happy in this second match,
For it excels your first, or if it did not,   225
Your first is dead, or 'twere as good he were,
As living here, and you no use of him.

JULIET.   Speak'st thou from thy heart?

NURSE.   And from my soul too,
Else beshrew them both.

JULIET.   Amen.

---

over carefully   196 **what** i.e. property   197 **forsworn** false to my oath   203 **monument** burial vault   207 **faith** marriage vow (recorded)   208 **to earth** i.e. to be made in another marriage   210 **leaving earth** dying   211 **stratagems** violent deeds   216 **challenge** claim   221 **dishclout** dishrag   222 **green** (such eyes were regarded as beautiful)   **quick** lively   223 **Beshrew** curse   224 **happy** fortunate   227

NURSE.   What?

JULIET.   Well, thou hast comforted me marvellous much.   230
              Go in, and tell my lady I am gone,
              Having displeased my father, to Lawrence' cell,
              To make confession and to be absolved.

NURSE.   Marry I will, and this is wisely done.   [*Exit.*]

JULIET.   Ancient damnation, O most wicked fiend!   235
              Is it more sin to wish me thus forsworn,
              Or to dispraise my lord with that same tongue
              Which she hath praised him with above compare,
              So many thousand times? Go counsellor,
              Thou and my bosom henceforth shall be twain: 240
              I'll to the friar to know his remedy,
              If all else fail, myself have power to die.   *Exit.*

[Act Four]

[SCENE I.]

Enter FRIAR [LAWRENCE] *and* COUNTY PARIS.

FRIAR.   On Thursday sir: the time is very short.
PARIS.   My father Capulet will have it so,
              And I am nothing slow to slack his haste.
FRIAR.   You say you do not know the lady's mind?
              Uneven is the course, I like it not.   5
PARIS.   Immoderately she weeps for Tybalt's death,
              And therefore have I little talked of love,
              For Venus smiles not in a house of tears.
              Now sir, her father counts it dangerous
              That she do give her sorrow so much sway: 10
              And in his wisdom hastes our marriage,
              To stop the inundation of her tears,
              Which too much minded by herself alone,
              May be put from her by society.

---

here in this world   235 **Ancient damnation** damned old woman   236 **forsworn** false
to my marriage vows   240 **bosom** secrets   **twain** divided
    IV, i Friar Lawrence's cell   2 **father** father-in-law   3 **nothing slow to** not so reluc-
tant as to   5 **Uneven** irregular   8 **Venus . . . tears** (1) grief is not an encouraging
atmosphere for love (2) the planet Venus is not favorable when in one of the watery divisions
(houses) of the Zodiac   10 **sway** rule   13 **minded . . . alone** on her mind when she is
alone   14 **society** companionship

	Now do you know the reason of this haste.	15
FRIAR.	[*Aside.*] I would I knew not why it should be slowed.—	
	Look sir, here comes the lady toward my cell.	

Enter JULIET.

PARIS.	Happily met, my lady and my wife.	
JULIET.	That may be sir, when I may be a wife.	
PARIS.	That 'may be' must be, love, on Thursday next.	20
JULIET.	What must be shall be.	
FRIAR.	That's a certain text.	
PARIS.	Come you to make confession to this father?	
JULIET.	To answer that, I should confess to you.	
PARIS.	Do not deny to him that you love me.	
JULIET.	I will confess to you that I love him.	25
PARIS.	So will ye, I am sure, that you love me.	
JULIET.	If I do so, it will be of more price,	
	Being spoke behind your back, than to your face.	
PARIS.	Poor soul, thy face is much abused with tears.	
JULIET.	The tears have got small victory by that,	30
	For it was bad enough before their spite.	
PARIS.	Thou wrong'st it more than tears with that report.	
JULIET.	That is no slander sir, which is a truth,	
	And what I spake, I spake it to my face.	
PARIS.	Thy face is mine, and thou hast slandered it.	35
JULIET.	It may be so, for it is not mine own.	
	Are you at leisure, holy father now,	
	Or shall I come to you at evening mass?	
FRIAR.	My leisure serves me, pensive daughter, now.	
	My lord, we must entreat the time alone.	40
PARIS.	God shield I should disturb devotion:	
	Juliet, on Thursday early will I rouse ye,	
	Till then adieu, and keep this holy kiss. *Exit.*	
JULIET.	O shut the door, and when thou hast done so,	
	Come weep with me, past hope, past cure, past help.	45
FRIAR.	O Juliet, I already know thy grief,	
	It strains me past the compass of my wits:	
	I hear thou must, and nothing may prorogue it,	
	On Thursday next be married to this county.	
JULIET.	Tell me not friar, that thou hear'st of this,	50
	Unless thou tell me how I may prevent it:	

27 **price** value   29 **abused** marred   31 **spite**
injury   34 **to my face** (1) not behind my back (2) about my face   36 **it . . . own** (because
it is Romeo's)   40 **entreat . . . alone** beg you to let us have this time alone   41 **shield**
prevent   47 **strains . . . wits** drives me beyond my wits' end   48 **prorogue**

	If in thy wisdom thou canst give no help,	
	Do thou but call my resolution wise,	
	And with this knife I'll help it presently.	
	God joined my heart and Romeo's, thou our hands:	55
	And ere this hand by thee to Romeo's sealed,	
	Shall be the label to another deed,	
	Or my true heart with treacherous revolt	
	Turn to another, this shall slay them both:	
	Therefore out of thy long-experienced time,	60
	Give me some present counsel, or behold	
	'Twixt my extremes and me, this bloody knife	
	Shall play the umpire, arbitrating that,	
	Which the commission of thy years and art,	
	Could to no issue of true honour bring:	65
	Be not so long to speak, I long to die,	
	If what thou speak'st, speak not of remedy.	
FRIAR.	Hold daughter, I do spy a kind of hope,	
	Which craves as desperate an execution	
	As that is desperate which we would prevent.	70
	If rather than to marry County Paris,	
	Thou hast the strength of will to slay thyself,	
	Then is it likely thou wilt undertake	
	A thing like death to chide away this shame,	
	That cop'st with death himself to scape from it:	75
	And if thou dar'st, I'll give thee remedy.	
JULIET.	O bid me leap, rather than marry Paris,	
	From off the battlements of any tower,	
	Or walk in thievish ways, or bid me lurk	
	Where serpents are: chain me with roaring bears,	80
	Or shut me nightly in a charnel house,	
	O'ercovered quite with dead men's rattling bones,	
	With reeky shanks and yellow chapless skulls:	
	Or bid me go into a new-made grave,	
	And hide me with a dead man in his shroud,	85
	Things that to hear them told, have made me tremble,	
	And I will do it without fear or doubt,	
	To live an unstained wife to my sweet love.	
FRIAR.	Hold then, go home, be merry, give consent	

postpone   54 **presently** immediately   57 **label** strip fixed to a deed to hold the legalizing seal   59 **this** i.e. knife   59 **both** (hand and heart)   62 **extremes** extremities of suffering   **bloody** blood-bringing   63 **umpire** third party called in to decide a matter under arbitration   64 **commission** authority   65 **issue** resolution   74 **chide away** rebuke and drive away   75 **cop'st** deals   79 **thievish ways** roads where thieves lurk   81 **charnel house** vault housing stray bones unearthed in digging new graves   83 **reeky** reeking   **chapless** jawless   89 **be merry** cheer up

To marry Paris: Wednesday is tomorrow,   90
Tomorrow night look that thou lie alone,
Let not the nurse lie with thee in thy chamber:
Take thou this vial being then in bed,
And this distilling liquor drink thou off,
When presently through all thy veins shall run   95
A cold and drowsy humour: for no pulse
Shall keep his native progress, but surcease,
No warmth, no breath, shall testify thou livest,
The roses in thy lips and cheeks shall fade
To wanny ashes, thy eyes' windows fall,   100
Like death when he shuts up the day of life.
Each part deprived of supple government,
Shall stiff and stark and cold appear like death,
And in this borrowed likeness of shrunk death
Thou shalt continue two and forty hours,   105
And then awake as from a pleasant sleep.
Now when the bridegroom in the morning comes,
To rouse thee from thy bed, there art thou dead:
Then as the manner of our country is,
In thy best robes uncovered on the bier,   110
Thou shalt be borne to that same ancient vault,
Where all the kindred of the Capulets lie:
In the meantime, against thou shalt awake,
Shall Romeo by my letters know our drift,
And hither shall he come, and he and I   115
Will watch thy waking, and that very night
Shall Romeo bear thee hence to Mantua.
And this shall free thee from this present shame,
If no inconstant toy nor womanish fear
Abate thy valour in the acting it.   120

JULIET.   Give me, give me, O tell not me of fear.

FRIAR.   Hold, get you gone, be strong and prosperous
          In this resolve: I'll send a friar with speed
          To Mantua, with my letters to thy lord.

JULIET.   Love give me strength, and strength shall help afford: 125
          Farewell dear father.   *Exeunt.*

---

94 **distilling** permeating
(the body)   96 **drowsy humour** sleep-inducing fluid   97 **native progress** natural
motion   100 **wanny** pale   **windows** shutters (eyelids)   101 **shuts up the day** ends the
daylight (the metaphor is of closing up the shutters at night)   102 **supple government**
control that makes it supple   110 **uncovered** with face uncovered   113 **against** in
anticipation of the time that   114 **drift** intent   119 **inconstant toy** whim that makes you
waver   120 **Abate** diminish

[SCENE II.]

Enter FATHER CAPULET, MOTHER, NURSE, *and*
SERVINGMEN, *two or three.*

CAPULET.   So many guests invite as here are writ.

[*Exit a* SERVINGMAN.]

Sirrah, go hire me twenty cunning cooks.

SERVINGMAN.
You shall have none ill sir, for I'll try if they can lick
their fingers.

CAPULET.   How canst thou try them so?   5

SERVINGMAN.
Marry sir, 'tis an ill cook that cannot lick his own fingers: therefore he that cannot lick his fingers goes not
with me.

CAPULET.   Go be gone,   *Exit* SERVINGMAN.
We shall be much unfurnished for this time: 10
What, is my daughter gone to Friar Lawrence?

NURSE.   Ay forsooth.

CAPULET.   Well, he may chance to do some good on her:
A peevish self-willed harlotry it is.

Enter JULIET.

NURSE.   See where she comes from shrift with merry look.   15

CAPULET.   How now my headstrong, where have you been
gadding?

JULIET.   Where I have learnt me to repent the sin
Of disobedient opposition
To you and your behests, and am enjoined
By holy Lawrence, to fall prostrate here,   20
To beg your pardon, pardon I beseech you,
Henceforward, I am ever ruled by you.

CAPULET.   Send for the county, go tell him of this,
I'll have this knot knit up tomorrow morning.

JULIET.   I met the youthful lord at Lawrence' cell,   25
And gave him what becomèd love I might,
Not stepping o'er the bounds of modesty.

IV, ii Capulet's house   2 **cunning** skillful   3 **ill** bad   6 **cannot . . . fingers**
(because he will lick his fingers if the food is good)   10 **unfurnished** short of
provisions   14 **peevish** childish, silly   **harlotry** wench (affectionate)   15 **shrift**
confession   **merry** cheerful   26 **becomed** fitting, becoming

CAPULET.   Why, I am glad on't, this is well, stand up,
            This is as't should be, let me see the county:
            Ay marry, go I say, and fetch him hither.   30
            Now afore God, this reverend holy friar,
            All our whole city is much bound to him.
JULIET.   Nurse, will you go with me into my closet,
            To help me sort such needful ornaments,
            As you think fit to furnish me tomorrow?   35
MOTHER.   No, not till Thursday, there is time enough.
CAPULET.   Go nurse, go with her, we'll to church tomorrow.

                            Exeunt JULIET *and* NURSE.

MOTHER.   We shall be short in our provision,
            'Tis now near night.
CAPULET.   Tush, I will stir about,
            And all things shall be well, I warrant thee wife: 40
            Go thou to Juliet, help to deck up her,
            I'll not to bed tonight, let me alone:
            I'll play the housewife for this once, what ho?
            They are all forth: well, I will walk myself
            To County Paris, to prepare up him   45
            Against tomorrow. My heart is wondrous light,
            Since this same wayward girl is so reclaimed.   *Exeunt.*

[SCENE III.]

Enter JULIET *and* NURSE.

JULIET.   Ay, those attires are best, but gentle nurse
            I pray thee leave me to myself tonight:
            For I have need of many orisons,
            To move the heavens to smile upon my state,
            Which well thou knowest, is cross and full of sin.   5

                            Enter MOTHER.

MOTHER.   What, are you busy, ho? need you my help?
JULIET.   No madam, we have culled such necessaries
            As are behoveful for our state tomorrow:
            So please you, let me now be left alone,
            And let the nurse this night sit up with you,   10

---

                                                        32 **bound**
indebted   33 **closet** private room   34 **sort** select   46 **Against** in anticipation of
    IV, iii Juliet's chamber   3 **orisons** prayers   5 **cross** contrary (refers to "the heavens";
"full of sin" refers to "my state")   8 **behoveful** useful   **state** pomp, ceremony   15

> For I am sure you have your hands full all,
> In this so sudden business.

MOTHER.   Good night.
> Get thee to bed and rest, for thou hast need.   *Exeunt.*

JULIET.   Farewell, God knows when we shall meet again.
> I have a faint cold fear thrills through my veins,   15
> That almost freezes up the heat of life:
> I'll call them back again to comfort me.
> Nurse!—What should she do here?
> My dismal scene I needs must act alone.
> Come vial.   20
> What if this mixture do not work at all?
> Shall I be married then tomorrow morning?
> No, no, this shall forbid it. Lie thou there:

> *[Lays down her knife.]*

> What if it be a poison which the friar
> Subtilly hath ministered to have me dead,   25
> Lest in this marriage he should be dishonoured,
> Because he married me before to Romeo?
> I fear it is, and yet methinks it should not,
> For he hath still been tried a holy man.
> How if when I am laid into the tomb,   30
> I wake before the time that Romeo
> Come to redeem me? There's a fearful point:
> Shall I not then be stifled in the vault,
> To whose foul mouth no healthsome air breathes in,
> And there die strangled ere my Romeo comes?   35
> Or if I live, is it not very like,
> The horrible conceit of death and night,
> Together with the terror of the place,
> As in a vault, an ancient receptàcle,
> Where for this many hundred years the bones   40
> Of all my buried ancestors are packed,
> Where bloody Tybalt yet but green in earth,
> Lies festering in his shroud, where as they say,
> At some hours in the night, spirits resort:
> Alack, alack, is it not like that I   45
> So early waking—what with loathsome smells,

---

faint causing faintness   thrills pierces   29 still been tried always proved to be   36
like likely that   37 conceit conception   39 As in being in   receptacle sepulchre
(accent on first and third syllables)   42 green in earth recently put in his grave   43
festering decaying

And shrieks like mandrakes torn out of the earth,
That living mortals hearing them, run mad—
O if I wake, shall I not be distraught,
Environèd with all these hideous fears,   50
And madly play with my forefathers' joints,
And pluck the mangled Tybalt from his shroud,
And in this rage, with some great kinsman's bone,
As with a club dash out my desp'rate brains.
O look, methinks I see my cousin's ghost,   55
Seeking out Romeo that did spit his body
Upon a rapier's point: stay Tybalt, stay!
Romeo I come: this do I drink to thee.

> *She falls upon her bed within the curtains.*

[SCENE IV.]

Enter LADY OF THE HOUSE *and* NURSE.

LADY.   Hold, take these keys and fetch more spices, nurse.
NURSE.   They call for dates and quinces in the pastry.

> *Enter* OLD CAPULET.

CAPULET. Come, stir, stir, stir, the second cock hath crowed.
          The curfew bell hath rung, 'tis three o'clock:
          Look to the baked meats, good Angelica,   5
          Spare not for cost.
NURSE.   Go you cot-quean, go,
          Get you to bed, faith you'll be sick tomorrow
          For this night's watching.
CAPULET. No, not a whit: what, I have watched ere now,
          All night for lesser cause, and ne'er been sick.   10
LADY.   Ay, you have been a mouse-hunt in your time,
          But I will watch you from such watching now.

> *Exeunt* LADY *and* NURSE.

CAPULET. A jealous-hood, a jealous-hood.

> *Enter three or four* [FELLOWS] *with
> spits and logs and baskets.*

---

47 **mandrakes . . . earth** (the forked root of the plant mandragora
was supposed to resemble the human form and when uprooted to emit shrieks that drove the
hearer mad)   49 **distraught** driven mad   53 **rage** madness
   IV, iv Capulet's house   2 **pastry** pastry room   3 **second cock** (at 3 a.m.)   4 **curfew**
(signalling morning)   5 **baked meats** meat pies   6 **cot-quean** man who acts like a

Now fellow, what is there?

FELLOW.		Things for the cook sir, but I know not what.		15

CAPULET.		Make haste, make haste. [*Exit* FELLOW.] Sirrah, fetch
				drier logs.
			Call Peter, he will show thee where they are.

FELLOW.		I have a head sir, that will find out logs,
			And never trouble Peter for the matter.

CAPULET.		Mass and well said, a merry whoreson, ha,		20
			Thou shalt be loggerhead; [*Exit* FELLOW.] good
				father, 'tis day.
			The county will be here with music straight,
			For so he said he would.				*Play music.*
						I hear him near.
			Nurse! Wife! What ho? what, nurse I say!

				Enter NURSE.

			Go waken Juliet, go and trim her up,			25
			I'll go and chat with Paris: hie, make haste,
			Make haste, the bridegroom he is come already:
			Make haste I say.					[*Exeunt.*]

[SCENE V.]

[*Enter* NURSE.]

NURSE.		Mistress, what, mistress? Juliet? Fast, I warrant her, she.
			Why lamb, why lady, fie, you slug-a-bed,
			Why love I say, madam, sweetheart, why bride:
			What, not a word? You take your pennyworths now,
			Sleep for a week, for the next night I warrant		5
			The County Paris hath set up his rest,
			That you shall rest but little: God forgive me.
			Marry and amen: how sound is she asleep:
			I needs must wake her: Madam, madam, madam,
			Ay, let the county take you in your bed,			10

---

housewife (lit. wife in a cottage)   8 **watching** staying awake   11 **mouse-hunt**
woman-chaser   12 **watch** prevent   13 **jealous-hood** jealousy, jealous person   20
whoreson bastard   21 **loggerhead** the blockhead   22 **straight** straightway
	IV, v Juliet's chamber 1 **Fast** i.e. asleep 2 **slug-a-bed** sleepy head 4 **You take**
see that you take   6 **set . . . rest** (1) resovled, staked everything (fr. cards) (2) bawdy pun

He'll fright you up i' faith. Will it not be?

        [Draws the curtains.]

What, dressed, and in your clothes, and down again?
I must needs wake you: Lady, lady, lady!
Alas, alas, help, help, my lady's dead!
O weraday that ever I was born,   15
Some aqua vitæ ho! My lord, my lady!

       Enter MOTHER.

MOTHER. What noise is here?
NURSE.   O lamentable day!
MOTHER. What is the matter?
NURSE.   Look, look, O heavy day!
MOTHER. O me, O me, my child, my only life!
Revive, look up, or I will die with thee: 20
Help, help, call help.

       Enter FATHER.

CAPULET. For shame, bring Juliet forth, her lord is come.
NURSE. She's dead: deceased, she's dead: alack the day!
MOTHER. Alack the day, she's dead, she's dead, she's dead!
CAPULET. Ha? Let me see her: out alas, she's cold,   25
Her blood is settled, and her joints are stiff:
Life and these lips have long been separated:
Death lies on her like an untimely frost,
Upon the sweetest flower of all the field.
NURSE. O lamentable day!
MOTHER.   O woeful time!   30
CAPULET. Death that hath ta'en her hence to make me wail,
Ties up my tongue and will not let me speak.

       Enter FRIAR [LAWRENCE] *and the* COUNTY
       [PARIS] *with musicians.*

FRIAR. Come, is the bride ready to go to church?
CAPULET. Ready to go, but never to return.
O son, the night before thy wedding day   35
Hath Death lain with thy wife: there she lies,
Flower as she was, deflowerèd by him:
Death is my son-in-law, Death is my heir,
My daughter he hath wedded. I will die,

---

on "wrest" = tuning instrument   15 **weraday** alas   16 **aqua vitae** spirits   18 **heavy**
sorrowful   26 **settled** no longer flowing   37 **deflowered** ravished (the medieval theme

	And leave him all: life, living, all is Death's.	40
PARIS.	Have I thought long to see this morning's face,	
	And doth it give me such a sight at this?	
MOTHER.	Accursed, unhappy, wretched, hateful day,	
	Most miserable hour that e'er time saw	
	In lasting labour of his pilgrimage,	45
	But one poor one, one poor and loving child,	
	But one thing to rejoice and solace in,	
	And cruel Death hath catched it from my sight.	
NURSE.	O woe, O woeful, woeful, woeful day,	
	Most lamentable day, most woeful day	50
	That ever, ever, I did yet behold!	
	O day, O day, O day, O hateful day,	
	Never was seen so black a day as this,	
	O woeful day, O woeful day!	
PARIS.	Beguiled, divorcèd, wrongèd, spited, slain,	55
	Most detestable Death, by thee beguiled,	
	By cruel, cruel thee, quite overthrown:	
	O love, O life; not life, but love in death!	
CAPULET.	Despised, distressèd, hated, martyred, killed!	
	Uncomfortable time, why cam'st thou now,	60
	To murder, murder our solemnity?	
	O child, O child, my soul and not my child,	
	Dead art thou, alack, my child is dead,	
	And with my child my joys are burièd.	
FRIAR.	Peace ho for shame, confusion's cure lives not	65
	In these confusions: heaven and yourself	
	Had part in this fair maid, now heaven hath all,	
	And all the better is it for the maid:	
	Your part in her you could not keep from death,	
	But heaven keeps his part in eternal life:	70
	The most you sought was her promotion,	
	For 'twas your heaven she should be advanced,	
	And weep ye now, seeing she is advanced	
	Above the clouds, as high as heaven itself?	
	O in this love, you love your child so ill,	75
	That you run mad, seeing that she is well:	
	She's not well married, that lives married long,	

---

of death ravishing the bride continues through l. 40)   40 **living** possessions   41 **thought long** longed   45 **In . . . pilgrimage** in his unceasing, toilsome journey   48 **catched** snatched   58 **not life . . . death** no longer my life, but still my love, even in death   60 **Uncomfortable** discomforting   61 **solemnity** festivity   65 **confusion** calamity   69 **Your part** (the body)   71 **promotion** social advancement   72 **advanced** raised up   76

But she's best married, that dies married young.
Dry up your tears, and stick your rosemary
On this fair corse, and as the custom is,   80
All in her best array bear her to church:
For though fond nature bids us all lament,
Yet nature's tears are reason's merriment.

CAPULET.   All things that we ordainèd festival,
Turn from their office to black funeral: 85
Our instruments to melancholy bells,
Our wedding cheer to a sad burial feast:
Our solemn hymns to sullen dirges change:
Our bridal flowers serve for a buried corse:
And all things change them to the contrary.   90

FRIAR.   Sir go you in, and madam go with him,
And go Sir Paris, every one prepare
To follow this fair corse unto her grave.
The heavens do low'r upon you for some ill:
Move them no more, by crossing their high will.   95

Exeunt. Manent [musicians and
NURSE].

1. MUSICIAN.
Faith, we may put up our pipes and be gone.

NURSE.   Honest good fellows, ah put up, put up,
For well you know this is a pitiful case.   [*Exit.*]

FIDDLER.   Ay by my troth, the case may be amended.

Enter PETER.

PETER.   Musicians, O musicians, 'Heart's ease,' 'Heart's ease,'   100
O, and you will have me live, play 'Heart's ease.'

FIDDLER.   Why 'Heart's ease'?

PETER.   O musicians, because my heart itself plays 'My heart is
full of woe.' O play me some merry dump to comfort
me.   105

---

well (well-off) in heaven   79 rosemary evergreen, symbolizing remembrance (used at
both weddings and funerals)   80 corse corpse   82 fond foolishly doting   nature
natural affection   83 nature's . . . merriment what we weep for because of natural
affection, reason makes us rejoice at   84 festival festal   85 office function   87 cheer
meal   88 solemn ceremonial   sullen mournful   94 low'r frown, look dark and
threatening   ill wrongdoing   95 s.d (Q1: "they all but the Nurse go forth, casting
rosemary upon her and shutting the curtains.")   96 put . . . pipes shut up, put away our
instruments   98 case event   99 case . . . amended (1) event may be improved (2)
instrument case may be repaired (3) bawdy pun on "case" = pudendum   100 Heart's ease
(a current song)   103–4 My heart . . . woe (a refrain from another song, "Ballad of Two
Lovers")   104 dump mournful air   109 give . . . soundly let you have it good and

MINSTRELS.
> Not a dump we, 'tis no time to play now.

PETER.   You will not then?

1. MINSTREL.
> No.

PETER.   I will then give it you soundly.

1. MINSTREL.
> What will you give us?   110

PETER.   No money on my faith, but the gleek. I will give you the
minstrel.

1. MINSTREL.
> Then will I give you the serving-creature.

PETER.   Then will I lay the serving-creature's dagger on your
pate. I will carry no crotchets, I'll re you, I'll fa you, do 115
you note me?

1. MINSTREL.
> And you re us and fa us, you note us.

2. MINSTREL.
> Pray you put up your dagger, and put out your wit.

PETER.
> Then have at you with my wit. I will dry-beat you with
> an iron wit, and put up my iron dagger. Answer me like 120
> men.
>   'When griping grief the heart doth wound,
>   And doleful dumps the mind oppress,
>   Then music with her silver sound'—
> Why 'silver sound'? Why 'music with her silver sound'? 125
> What say you, Simon Catling?

1. MINSTREL.
> Marry sir, because silver hath a sweet sound.

PETER.   Pretty. What say you, Hugh Rebeck?

2. MINSTREL.
> I say 'silver sound' because musicians sound for silver.

PETER.   Pretty too. What say you, James Soundpost?   130

3. MINSTREL.
> Faith, I know not what to say.

---

proper (w. pun on "sound")   111 **gleek** gibe, insult   111–12 **give . . . minstrel** call you
a ne'er-do-well (minstrels being considered vagabonds)   113 **serving-creature** servant
(insulting)   115 **pate** head   **carry no crotchets** (1) endure none of your whims (2) not
carry a tune in quarter notes   **re . . . fa . . . note** (more puns on musical terms)   117
note us set us to music   118 **up** away   **put out** display   119 **dry-beat** beat without
drawing blood, as with the flat of a sword   122–24 **When . . . sound** (from "In Commendation of Music," a poem by Richard Edwards)   123 **dumps** sorrows   126 **Catling**
catgut (lutestring)   128 **Pretty** apt   **Rebeck** three-stringed fiddle   130 **Soundpost**

PETER.   O I cry you mercy, you are the singer. I will say for you;
it is 'music with her silver sound' because musicians
have no gold for sounding:
    'Then music with her silver sound   135
        With speedy help doth lend redress.'   *Exit.*

1. MINSTREL.
    What a pestilent knave is this same.

2. MINSTREL.
    Hang him Jack, come, we'll in here, tarry for the
mourners, and stay dinner.   *Exeunt.*

[Act Five]

[SCENE I.]

Enter ROMEO.

ROMEO.   If I may trust the flattering truth of sleep,
My dreams presage some joyful news at hand:
My bosom's lord sits lightly in his throne,
And all this day an unaccustomed spirit
Lifts me above the ground with cheerful thoughts.   5
I dreamt my lady came and found me dead
(Strange dream that gives a dead man leave to think)
And breathed such life with kisses in my lips,
That I revived and was an emperor.
Ah me, how sweet is love itself possessed,   10
When but love's shadows are so rich in joy.

            Enter Romeo's MAN BALTHASAR, *booted.*

News from Verona, how now Balthasar,
Dost thou not bring me letters from the friar?
How doth my lady? Is my father well?
How fares my Juliet? That I ask again,   15
For nothing can be ill if she be well.

MAN.   Then she is well and nothing can be ill,

---

peg of wood beneath the bridge of a violin   **132 cry you mercy** beg your pardon   **say**
speak (because you only sing)   **134 have . . . sounding** are not paid in gold for playing
138 Jack the jackanapes   **138–9 tarry, stay** wait for

V, i Mantua. A street   **1 If . . . sleep** if I can trust in good dreams to come true   **3**
bosom's lord heart   **11 love's shadows** dreams of love   **17 well** well-off in

Her body sleeps in Capel's monument,
And her immortal part with angels lives.
I saw her laid low in her kindred's vault,   20
And presently took post to tell it you:
O pardon me for bringing these ill news,
Since you did leave it for my office, sir.

ROMEO.   Is it e'en so? Then I deny you, stars.
Thou knowest my lodging, get me ink and paper,   25
And hire posthorses, I will hence tonight.

MAN.   I do beseech you sir, have patience:
Your looks are pale and wild, and do import
Some misadventure.

ROMEO.   Tush, thou art deceived,
Leave me, and do the thing I bid thee do.   30
Hast thou no letters to me from the friar?

MAN.   No my good lord.

ROMEO.   No matter: get thee gone,
And hire those horses, I'll be with thee straight.

                                          Exit [MAN].

Well Juliet, I will lie with thee tonight:
Let's see for means, O mischief thou art swift   35
To enter in the thoughts of desperate men.
I do remember an apothecary,
And hereabouts 'a dwells which late I noted,
In tattered weeds with overwhelming brows,
Culling of simples; meager were his looks,   40
Sharp misery had worn him to the bones:
And in his needy shop a tortoise hung,
An alligator stuffed, and other skins
Of ill-shaped fishes, and about his shelves,
A beggarly account of empty boxes,   45
Green earthen pots, bladders and musty seeds,
Remnants of packthread, and old cakes of roses
Were thinly scattered, to make up a show.
Noting this penury, to myself I said,
'An if a man did need a poison now,   50
Whose sale is present death in Mantua,
Here lives a caitiff wretch would sell it him.'

---

heaven   21 **presently** immediately   **post** posthorses   23 **office** duty   29 **misadventure** misfortune   39 **weeds** clothes   **overwhelming** overhanging   40 **Culling of
simples** sorting medicinal herbs   47 **packthread** twine   **cakes of roses** dried rose
petals pressed into sachet cakes (used for perfuming)   51 **present death** immediate death
(the apothecary's fate in Brooke's poem)   52 **caitiff** miserable

O this same thought did but forerun my need,
And this same needy man must sell it me.
As I remember, this should be the house: 55
Being holiday, the beggar's shop is shut.
What ho, apothecary!

Enter APOTHECARY.

APOTHECARY.   Who calls so loud?
ROMEO.   Come hither man, I see that thou art poor.
Hold, there is forty ducats, let me have
A dram of poison, such soon-speeding gear,   60
As will disperse itself through all the veins,
That the life-weary taker may fall dead,
And that the trunk may be discharged of breath,
As violently as hasty powder fired
Doth hurry from the fatal cannon's womb.   65
APOTHECARY.
Such mortal drugs I have, but Mantua's law
Is death to any he that utters them.
ROMEO.   Art thou so bare and full of wretchedness,
And fearest to die? Famine is in thy cheeks,
Need and oppression starveth in thy eyes,   70
Contempt and beggary hangs upon thy back:
The world is not thy friend, nor the world's law,
The world affords no law to make thee rich:
Then be not poor, but break it and take this.
APOTHECARY.
My poverty, but not my will consents.   75
ROMEO.   I pay thy poverty and not thy will.
APOTHECARY.
Put this in any liquid thing you will
And drink it off, and if you had the strength
Of twenty men, it would dispatch you straight.
ROMEO.   There is thy gold, worse poison to men's souls,   80
Doing more murder in this loathsome world,
Than these poor compounds that thou mayst not sell:
I sell thee poison, thou hast sold me none,
Farewell, buy food, and get thyself in flesh.
Come cordial, and not poison, go with me   85
To Juliet's grave, for there must I use thee.   *Exeunt.*

59 **ducats** gold
coins   60 **gear** stuff   63 **trunk** body   66 **mortal** death-bringing   67 **utters**
issues   70 **starveth in** look out hungrily from   71 **Contempt and beggary**

[SCENE II.]

Enter FRIAR JOHN *to* FRIAR LAWRENCE.

JOHN.　　Holy Franciscan friar, brother, ho!

Enter FRIAR LAWRENCE.

LAWRENCE. This same should be the voice of Friar John.
　　　　Welcome from Mantua, what says Romeo?
　　　　Or if his mind be writ, give me his letter.

JOHN.　　Going to find a barefoot brother out,　　　　　　5
　　　　One of our order to associate me,
　　　　Here in this city visiting the sick,
　　　　And finding him, the searchers of the town,
　　　　Suspecting that we both were in a house
　　　　Where the infectious pestilence did reign,　　　　10
　　　　Sealed up the doors, and would not let us forth,
　　　　So that my speed to Mantua there was stayed.

LAWRENCE.
　　　　Who bare my letter then to Romeo?

JOHN.　　I could not send it—here it is again—
　　　　Nor get a messenger to bring it thee,　　　　　　15
　　　　So fearful were they of infection.

LAWRENCE.
　　　　Unhappy fortune: by my brotherhood,
　　　　The letter was not nice, but full of charge,
　　　　Of dear import, and the neglecting it
　　　　May do much danger: Friar John go hence,　　　　20
　　　　Get me an iron crow and bring it straight
　　　　Unto my cell.

JOHN.　　　　　　Brother, I'll go and bring it thee.　　*Exit.*

LAWRENCE. Now must I to the monument alone,
　　　　Within this three hours will fair Juliet wake,
　　　　She will beshrew me much that Romeo　　　　　25
　　　　Hath had no notice of these accidents:
　　　　But I will write again to Mantua,
　　　　And keep her at my cell till Romeo come,
　　　　Poor living corse, closed in a dead man's tomb.　*Exit.*

---

contemptible beggary　79 **dispatch** kill　84 **get thyself in flesh** put on some
weight　85 **cordial** restorative
　V,ii Friar Lawrence's cell　6 **associate** travel with (a rule of the Franciscan order)　8
searchers health investigators of causes of death　11 **Sealed . . . doors** quarantined the
premises (a practice in London during plagues)　18 **nice** trivial　**charge** weight　19
dear great　21 **crow** crowbar　**straight** straightway　25 **beshrew** curse, rebuke　26
accidents events

[SCENE III.]

Enter PARIS *and his* PAGE *with flowers* [*and a torch*].

PARIS.   Give me thy torch boy, hence and stand aloof,
            Yet put it out, for I would not be seen:
            Under yond yew trees lay thee all along,
            Holding thine ear close to the hollow ground,
            So shall no foot upon the churchyard tread,   5
            Being loose, unfirm with digging up of graves,
            But thou shalt hear it: whistle then to me
            As signal that thou hear'st something approach.
            Give me those flowers, do as I bid thee, go.

PAGE.   [*Aside.*] I am almost afraid to stand alone,   10
            Here in the churchyard, yet I will adventure.
                                                   [*Withdraws.*]

PARIS.   Sweet flower, with flowers thy bridal bed I strew—
            O woe, thy canopy is dust and stones—
            Which with sweet water nightly I will dew,
            Or wanting that, with tears distilled by moans: 15
            The obsequies that I for thee will keep,
            Nightly shall be to strew thy grave and weep.

                                           Whistle BOY.

            The boy gives warning, something doth approach:
            What cursed foot wanders this way tonight,
            To cross my obsequies and true love's rite?   20
            What, with a torch? Muffle me night awhile.

                                               [*Withdraws.*]

                Enter ROMEO *and* BALTHASAR *with a*
                torch, a mattock, and a crow of iron.

ROMEO.   Give me that mattock and the wrenching iron:
            Hold, take this letter, early in the morning
            See thou deliver it to my lord and father.
            Give me the light; upon thy life I charge thee,   25
            Whate'er thou hearest or seest, stand all aloof,
            And do not interrupt me in my course.

V, iii A churchyard   1, 26 **stand aloof** keep away   3 **yew** (symbolizing
mourning)   11 **adventure** risk it   13 **canopy** i.e. (1) of the bridal bed (2) of Juliet   14
Which the flowers   **sweet** perfumed   15 **wanting** lacking   16, 20 **obsequies** rites for
the dead   16 **keep** hold   20 **cross** thwart   21 **Muffle** hide (by wrapping me in your

Why I descend into this bed of death,
Is partly to behold my lady's face:
But chiefly to take thence from her dead finger,   30
A precious ring: a ring that I must use
In dear employment, therefore hence be gone:
But if thou jealous dost return to pry
In what I farther shall intend to do,
By heaven I will tear thee joint by joint,   35
And strew this hungry churchyard with thy limbs:
The time and my intents are savage-wild,
More fierce and more inexorable far,
Than empty tigers, or the roaring sea.

BALTHASAR.
I will be gone sir, and not trouble ye.   40

ROMEO.   So shalt thou show me friendship: take thou that,
Live and be prosperous, and farewell good fellow.

BALTHASAR.
[*Aside.*] For all this same, I'll hide me hereabout,
His looks I fear, and his intents I doubt.   [*Withdraws.*]

ROMEO.   Thou detestable maw, thou womb of death,   45
Gorged with the dearest morsel of the earth:
Thus I enforce thy rotten jaws to open,
And in despite I'll cram thee with more food.

                                                Opens the tomb.

PARIS.   This is that banished haughty Montague
That murdered my love's cousin, with which grief   50
It is supposèd the fair creature died,
And here is come to do some villainous shame
To the dead bodies: I will apprehend him.
Stop thy unhallowed toil, vile Montague:
Can vengeance be pursued further than death?   55
Condemnèd villain, I do apprehend thee.
Obey and go with me, for thou must die.

ROMEO.   I must indeed, and therefore came I hither:
Good gentle youth, tempt not a desp'rate man,
Fly hence and leave me, think upon these gone,   60
Let them affright thee. I beseech thee youth,

---

darkness)   21 s.d. **mattock** pickaxe   32 **dear** important   33 **jealous** being
suspicious   36 **hungry** devouring   39 **empty** hungry   41 **that** (money)   44 **doubt**
suspect   45 **maw** gullet, stomach   **womb** belly   47 **rotten jaws** (the door of the
tomb)   48 **in despite** out of spite (as you are already full)   48 s.d. **tomb** (possibly an
inner stage)   53 **apprehend** arrest   55 **vengeance** i.e. on Tybalt   60 **gone** dead

Put not another sin upon my head,
By urging me to fury, O be gone:
By heaven I love thee better than myself,
For I come hither armed against myself: 65
Stay not, be gone, live, and hereafter say,
A madman's mercy bid thee run away.

PARIS.   I do defy thy conjuration,
And apprehend thee for a felon here.

ROMEO.   Wilt thou provoke me? Then have at thee boy.   70

They fight.

PAGE.   O Lord, they fight, I will go call the watch.

[*Exit.* PARIS *falls.*]

PARIS.   O I am slain! If thou be merciful,
Open the tomb, lay me with Juliet.   [*Dies.*]

ROMEO.   In faith I will, let me peruse this face:
Mercutio's kinsman, noble County Paris.   75
What said my man, when my betossèd soul
Did not attend him as we rode? I think
He told me Paris should have married Juliet,
Said he not so? Or did I dream it so?
Or am I mad, hearing him talk of Juliet,   80
To think it was so? O give me thy hand,
One writ with me in sour misfortune's book,
I'll bury thee in a triumphant grave.
A grave; O no. A lanthorn, slaughtered youth:
For here lies Juliet, and her beauty makes   85
This vault a feasting presence full of light.
Death, lie thou there, by a dead man interred.

[*Lays* PARIS *in the tomb.*]

How oft when men are at the point of death,
Have they been merry, which their keepers call
A lightning before death. O how may I   90
Call this a lightning? O my love, my wife,
Death that hath sucked the honey of thy breath,
Hath had no power yet upon thy beauty:

---

68 **conjuration** entreaty   70 **provoke** challenge   **boy** (insult implying immaturity)   76
betossed tossing   77 **attend** listen to   78 **should** was to   84 **lanthorn** lighthouse or
windowed turret on the roof of a hall (in each the translucent part was made of horn)   86
feasting presence palace hall set out for a feast   87 **Death** (Paris)   89 **keepers** (1) nurses
of the sick (2) jailers of the condemned   90 **lightning** i.e. of the spirit   91 **lightning** (the

Thou art not conquered, beauty's ensign yet
Is crimson in thy lips and in thy cheeks,   95
And death's pale flag is not advancèd there.
Tybalt, liest thou there in thy bloody sheet?
O what more favour can I do to thee,
Than with that hand that cut thy youth in twain,
To sunder his that was thine enemy?   100
Forgive me cousin. Ah dear Juliet,
Why art thou yet so fair? Shall I believe
That unsubstantial Death is amorous,
And that the lean abhorrèd monster keeps
Thee here in dark to be his paramour?   105
For fear of that I still will stay with thee,
And never from this palace of dim night
Depart again; here, here will I remain,
With worms that are thy chambermaids: O here
Will I set up my everlasting rest: 110
And shake the yoke of inauspicious stars,
From this world-wearied flesh: eyes look your last:
Arms take your last embrace: and lips, O you
The doors of breath, seal with a righteous kiss
A dateless bargain to engrossing death: 115
Come bitter conduct, come unsavoury guide,
Thou desperate pilot, now at once run on
The dashing rocks, thy seasick weary bark:
Here's to my love. [*Drinks.*] O true apothecary!
Thy drugs are quick. Thus with a kiss I die.   *Falls.* 120

>   *Enter* FRIAR [LAWRENCE] *with lanthorn,*
>   *crow, and spade.*

FRIAR.   Saint Francis be my speed, how oft tonight
           Have my old feet stumbled at graves. Who's there?
BALTHASAR.
           Here's one, a friend, and one that knows you well.
FRIAR.   Bliss be upon you. Tell me good my friend
           What torch is yond that vainly lends his light   125
           To grubs and eyeless skulls? As I discern,

---

light of her beauty)   94 **ensign** banner (red was the signal for battle; the metaphor, through
l. 96, was usually associated with love)   96 **advanced** raised   97 **sheet** winding
sheet   103 **unsubstantial** shadowy   104 **lean** skeletal   106 **still** always   110 **set
. . . rest** (1) take my final rest (2) stake everything (fr. cards)   111 **shake** i.e. off   115
dateless endless   **engrossing** monopolizing (by buying in gross; fr. business)   116
conduct (the poison)   118 **dashing rocks** rocks against which boats are dashed   **bark**
(his body)   121 **speed** protector   122 **stumbled** (a bad omen)   125 **vainly** for no

It burneth in the Capels' monument.

BALTHASAR.

It doth so, holy sir, and there's my master,
One that you love.

FRIAR.   Who is it?

BALTHASAR.   Romeo.

FRIAR.   How long hath he been there?

BALTHASAR.   Full half an hour.   130

FRIAR.   Go with me to the vault.

BALTHASAR.   I dare not sir.

My master knows not but I am gone hence,
And fearfully did menance me with death
If I did stay to look on his intents.

FRIAR.   Stay then, I'll go alone, fear comes upon me.   135
O much I fear some ill unthrifty thing.

BALTHASAR.

As I did sleep under this yew tree here,
I dreamt my master and another fought,
And that my master slew him.

FRIAR.   Romeo!
Alack, alack, what blood is this which stains   140
The stony entrance of this sepulchre?
What mean these masterless and gory swords
To lie discoloured by this place of peace?

                                        [*Enters the tomb.*]

Romeo, O pale! Who else? What, Paris too?
And steeped in blood? Ah what an unkind hour   145
Is guilty of this lamentable chance!
The lady stirs.   JULIET *rises.*

JULIET.   O comfortable friar, where is my lord?
I do remember well where I should be:
And there I am: where is my Romeo?   '   150

FRIAR.   I hear some noise lady, come from that nest
Of death, contagion, and unnatural sleep:
A greater power than we can contradict
Hath thwarted our intents, come, come away,
Thy husband in thy bosom there lies dead: 155
And Paris too, come, I'll dispose of thee,
Among a sisterhood of holy nuns:

---

reason   132 **but** i.e. that   136 **unthrifty** unfortunate   148 **comfortable**
comforting   149 **should** was to   162 **timeless** untimely   163 **churl** miser   164

     Stay not to question, for the watch is coming,
     Come go good Juliet, I dare no longer stay.
JULIET. Go get thee hence, for I will not away. *Exit* [FRIAR]. 160
     What's here? A cup closed in my true love's hand?
     Poison I see hath been his timeless end:
     O churl, drunk all, and left no friendly drop
     To help me after? I will kiss thy lips,
     Haply some poison yet doth hang on them,   165
     To make me die with a restorative. [*Kisses him.*]
     Thy lips are warm.
CHIEF WATCHMAN.
     [*Within.*] Lead boy, which way?
JULIET. Yea, noise? Then I'll be brief. O happy dagger,

       [*Snatches* ROMEO's *dagger.*]

     This is thy sheath, there rust and let me die. 170

       She stabs herself and falls.
     Enter [PARIS'S] BOY *and* WATCH.
BOY. This is the place, there where the torch doth burn.
CHIEF WATCHMAN.
     The ground is bloody, search about the churchyard.
     Go some of you, whoe'er you find attach.

      [*Exeunt some of the* WATCH.]

     Pitiful sight, here lies the county slain,
     And Juliet bleeding, warm, and newly dead, 175
     Who here hath lain this two days burièd.
     Go tell the prince, run to the Capulets,
     Raise up the Montagues, some others search.

      [*Exeunt others of the* WATCH.]

     We see the ground whereon these woes do lie,
     But the true ground of all these piteous woes 180
     We cannot without circumstance descry.
       Enter [A WATCHMAN *with*]
       Romeo's MAN [BALTHASAR].
2. WATCHMAN.
     Here's Romeo's man, we found him in the churchyard.
CHIEF WATCHMAN.
     Hold him in safety till the prince come hither.

---

after follow after 165 **Haply** perhaps 169 **happy** opportune 170 **This** (her
bosom) 173 **attach** arrest 179 **woes** woeful bodies 180 **ground** cause (with wordplay on l. 179) 181 **circumstance** details **descry** discover

Enter FRIAR [LAWRENCE] *and another*
WATCHMAN.

3. WATCHMAN.
　　　　Here is a friar that trembles, sighs, and weeps:
　　　　We took this mattock and this spade from him,   185
　　　　As he was coming from this churchyard's side.
CHIEF WATCHMAN.
　　　　A great suspicion, stay the friar too.

　　　　　　Enter the PRINCE [*with others*].

PRINCE.   What misadventure is so early up,
　　　　That calls our person from our morning rest?

　　　　　　Enter CAPULET *and his* WIFE.

CAPULET.   What should it be that is so shrieked abroad?   190
WIFE.   O the people in the street cry 'Romeo,'
　　　　Some 'Juliet,' and some 'Paris,' and all run
　　　　With open outcry toward our monument.
PRINCE.   What fear is this which startles in your ears?
CHIEF WATCHMAN.
　　　　Sovereign, here lies the County Paris slain,   195
　　　　And Romeo dead, and Juliet dead before,
　　　　Warm and new killed.
PRINCE.   Search, seek, and know how this foul murder comes.
CHIEF WATCHMAN.
　　　　Here is a friar, and slaughtered Romeo's man,
　　　　With instruments upon them fit to open   200
　　　　These dead men's tombs.
CAPULET.   O heavens! O wife, look how our daughter bleeds!
　　　　This dagger hath mista'en, for lo his house
　　　　Is empty on the back of Montague,
　　　　And it mis-sheathèd in my daughter's bosom.   205
WIFE.   O me, this sight of death is as a bell
　　　　That warns my old age to a sepulchre.

　　　　　　Enter MONTAGUE.

PRINCE.   Come Montague, for thou art early up
　　　　To see thy son and heir more early down.
MONTAGUE.
　　　　Alas my liege, my wife is dead tonight,   210

---

187 **stay** detain   188
misadventure misfortune   190 **should** could   194 **startles** sounds startling   203
mista'en made a mistake   **house** sheath   204 **back** (where daggers were worn)   207

Grief of my son's exile hath stopped her breath.
What further woe conspires against mine age?

PRINCE.   Look and thou shalt see.

MONTAGUE.

O thou untaught, what manners is in this,
To press before thy father to a grave?   215

PRINCE.   Seal up the mouth of outrage for a while,
Till we can clear these ambiguities,
And know their spring, their head, their true descent,
And then will I be general of your woes,
And lead you even to death: meantime forbear,   220
And let mischance be slave to patience.
Bring forth the parties of suspicion.

FRIAR.   I am the greatest, able to do least,
Yet most suspected, as the time and place
Doth make against me, of this direful murder: 225
And here I stand both to impeach and purge
Myself condemnèd and myself excused.

PRINCE.   Then say at once what thou dost know in this.

FRIAR.   I will be brief, for my short date of breath
Is not so long as is a tedious tale.   230
Romeo there dead, was husband to that Juliet,
And she there dead, that Romeo's faithful wife:
I married them, and their stol'n marriage day
Was Tybalt's doomsday, whose untimely death
Banished the new-made bridegroom from this city,   235
For whom, and not for Tybalt, Juliet pined.
You to remove that siege of grief from her
Betrothed and would have married her perforce
To County Paris. Then comes she to me,
And with wild looks bid me devise some mean   240
To rid her from this second marriage:
Or in my cell there would she kill herself.
Then gave I her (so tutored by my art)
A sleeping potion, which so took effect
As I intended, for it wrought on her   245

warns (1) calls (2) sounds a warning that death is near   214 untaught
bad-mannered   216 Seal . . . outrage (1) possibly an indication to close the curtains of an
inner stage or "mouth" of the tomb (2) cease the lamentations   218 spring, head, descent
origin (all three mean the same thing)   219–20 general . . . death the leader in discover-
ing the cause and punishing the wrongdoers (fr. battle)   221 mischance . . . patience
your misfortunes be ruled by patient endurance   222 of under   223 greatest most
suspect   225 make against implicate   226–7 impeach . . . excused accuse myself (of
some matters) and exonerate myself (from others)   229 date of breath term of life (before
expiration)   238 perforce by force   243 art knowledge of medicine

The form of death. Meantime I writ to Romeo
That he should hither come as this dire night
To help to take her from her borrowed grave,
Being the time the potion's force should cease.
But he which bore my letter, Friar John,   250
Was stayed by accident, and yesternight
Returned my letter back: then all alone
At the prefixèd hour of her waking
Came I to take her from her kindred's vault,
Meaning to keep her closely at my cell,   255
Till I conveniently could send to Romeo.
But when I came, some minute ere the time
Of her awaking, here untimely lay
The noble Paris, and true Romeo dead.
She wakes, and I entreated her come forth   260
And bear this work of heaven with patience:
But then a noise did scare me from the tomb,
And she, too desperate, would not go with me:
But as it seems, did violence on herself.
All this I know, and to the marriage   265
Her nurse is privy: and if aught in this
Miscarried by my fault, let my old life
Be sacrificed some hour before his time,
Unto the rigour of severest law.

PRINCE. We still have known thee for a holy man.   270
Where's Romeo's man? What can he say to this?

BALTHASAR.

I brought my master news of Juliet's death,
And then in post he came from Mantua,
To this same place, to this same monument.
This letter he early bid me give his father,   275
And threatened me with death, going in the vault,
If I departed not, and left him there.

PRINCE. Give me the letter, I will look on it.
Where is the county's page that raised the watch?
Sirrah, what made your master in this place?   280

BOY. He came with flowers to strew his lady's grave,
And bid me stand aloof, and so I did:
Anon comes one with light to ope the tomb,
And by and by my master drew on him,

---

247 as this this
very   251 stayed detained   255 closely secretly   261 patience fortitude   266 is
privy i.e. to, has secret knowledge of   267 Miscarried went astray   270 still
always   273 in post by posthorse   280 made did   282 stand aloof keep away   284

And then I ran away to call the watch.   285
PRINCE.   This letter doth make good the friar's words,
Their course of love, the tidings of her death,
And here he writes, that he did buy a poison
Of a poor pothecary, and therewithal,
Came to this vault to die, and lie with Juliet.   290
Where be these enemies? Capulet, Montague,
See what a scourge is laid upon your hate,
That heaven finds means to kill your joys with love;
And I for winking at your discords too,
Have lost a brace of kinsmen, all are punished.   295
CAPULET.   O brother Montague, give me thy hand,
This is my daughter's jointure, for no more
Can I demand.
MONTAGUE.   But I can give thee more,
For I will raise her statue in pure gold,
That whiles Verona by that name is known,   300
There shall no figure at such rate be set,
As that of true and faithful Juliet.
CAPULET.   As rich shall Romeo's by his lady's lie,
Poor sacrifices of our enmity.
PRINCE.   A glooming peace this morning with it brings,   305
The sun for sorrow will not show his head:
Go hence to have more talk of these sad things,
Some shall be pardoned, and some punishèd.
For never was a story of more woe,
Than this of Juliet and her Romeo.   *Exeunt omnes.* 310

FINIS.

---

by and by immediately   **drew** i.e. his sword   293 **joys** (children)   294 **winking at**
closing my eyes to   295 **kinsmen** Mercutio and Paris   297 **This** i.e. hand
clasp   **jointure** marriage portion (given by the bridegroom)   299 **raise** have made (as the
statues are recumbent, l. 303)   301 **rate** value   303 **Romeo's** (effigy)   305 **glooming**
gloomy

Textual Notes

I, i 20 **cruel** Q4; Q2: "civil" 147 **sun** Theobald em.; Q2: "same", prob. misreading of "sunne" 173 **well-seeming** Q4; Q2: "welseeing" 184 **made** Q2; Q1: "raisde" 185 **lovers'** Q1; Q2: "loving" 191 **lost** Q2; Q1: "left" 205 **unharmed** Q1; Q2: "uncharm'd"

I, ii 29 **female** Q1; Q2: "fennell".

I, iii 66, 67 **honour** Q1; Q2: "houre"

I, iv 7–8 Q1; not in Q2 39 **done** Q1, F; Q2: "dum" 45 **like lights** Johnson em.; Q2: "lights lights"; Q1: "like lamps" 47 **five** Malone em.; Q2: "fine" 57 **atomi** Q1; Q2: "ottamie" 66 **man** Q2, F; Q1: "maid" 90 **elf-locks** Q1; Q2: "elklocks" 113 **sail** Q1; Q2: "sute"

II, i 10 **dove** Q1; Q2, F: "day" 38 **open et cetera** Q1; Q2: "open, or" for which some eds. read "open-arse," a synonym for "medlar"; "open O" is another possibility, the letter being slang for "pudendum"

II, ii 16 **do** Q1; Q2: "to" 31 **lazy-pacing** Q1; Q2: "lazie puffing"; some eds. suggest "lazy passing" 40–3 **What's . . . name** Malone's conflation of Q1 and Q2, in which "nor any other part" is omitted, and "O be some other name" is on the half-line following "face" 44 **word** Q2; Q1: "name" 69 **stop** Q2; Q1: "let" = obstacle 75 **eyes** Q2; Q1: "sight" 101 **cunning** Q1; Q2: "coying" 110 **circled** Q1; Q2: "circle" 163 **mine** Q1; not in Q2 168 **dear** Q4; F: "sweete"; Q2: "Neece", prob. misreading of "deere", with "c", as often, confused with "r" and "N" with "d"

II, iii 1–4 **The grey . . . wheels** Q2 gives these lines, in slightly different forms, to Romeo at the end of the preceding scene, as well as to Friar Lawrence here. They may represent a rewritten and an original version that was not deleted, or simply a printer's oversight in setting lines indicated for deletion. There has been much controversy over which is the better version 3 **flecked** Q1; Q2: "fleckted" and "fleckeld" 4 **fiery** Q1; Q2: "burning" 23 **weak** Q2; Q1: "small" 26 **stays** Q2; Q1: "slaies" 74 **ring** Q1; Q2: "ringing" 85 **chide . . . her** Q2; Q1: "chide not, she whom"

III, i 86 s.d. Q1; Q2: "Away Tybalt." 87 **o' both your** Dyce em.; Q2: "a both"; Q1: "on your"; cf. ll. 95, 102 118 **Alive** Q1; Q2: "He gan" 120 **fire-eyed** Q1; Q2: "fier end" 162 **agile** Q1; Q2: "aged" 184 **hate's** Q1; Q2: "hearts"

III, ii 6 **runaways'** Q2: "runnawayes;" F: "run-awayes" 9 **By** Q4; Q2: "And by" 21 **he** Q4; Q2: "I" 49 **shut** Capell em.; Q2: "shot" 76 **Dove-feathered** Theobald em.; Q2: "Ravenous dovefeatherd" 79 **damned** Q4; Q2: "dimme"

III, iii 41–43 **This may . . . death** l. 41 appears twice in Q2 in slightly different forms, leading to various editorial arrangements 52 **Thou** Q1; Q2: "Then" 110 **denote** Q1; Q2: "deuote" 117 **lives** F4, suggested in Q1; Q2: "lies" 143 **misbehaved** Q1; Q2: "mishaued"; F: "mishaped" 144 **pouts upon** Q4; Q2: "puts up"

III, v 83 **him** Q4; not in Q2 146 **bride** Q2; F: "bridegroom" 182 **trained** Q1; Q2: "liand", for which "limb'd" has been proposed. F: "Allied"

IV, i 45 **cure** Q1; Q2: "care" 72 **slay** Q1; Q2: "stay" 85 **shroud** Q4; not in Q2 100 **wanny** Q2; F: "many" 110 Q2 follows this line with "Be borne to buriall in thy kindreds graue:"—evidently an earlier version of l. 111 116 **waking** Q3; Q2: "walking"

IV iii 58 **Romeo . . . do I** Q1; Q2: "Romeo, Romeo, Romeo, heeres drinke, I"

IV, v 41 **thought long** Q3 and Brooke; Q2: "thought loue" 65 **cure** Theobald em.; Q2: "care" The same Q2 error occurs in IV, i, 45 81 **All** Q1; Q2: "And" 82 **fond** F2; Q2: "some" 99 s.d. **Peter** Q4; Q2: "Will Kemp," the company's leading comedian 104 **of woe** Q4; Q2 omits 128 **Pretty** Q1; Q2: "Prates"

V, i 15 **fares my Juliet** Q1; Q2: "doth my lady Juliet," caught from l. 14 24 **deny** Q2; Q1 and Brooke: "defie" 76 **pay** Q1; Q2: "pray"

V, iii 3 **yew** Q1; Q2: "young" (also in l. 137) 21 s.d. **Balthasar** Q1; Q2: "Peter" 68 **conjuration** Q1 (plural); Q2: "commiration" 102 **"Shall I believe"** Q2 precedes with "I will believe," evidently a false start 107 **palace** Q3; Q2: "pallat" 108 **Depart again** this begins four lines in Q2 in which Romeo drinks the potion, evidently a first version, later expanded through l. 120, but undeleted from the MS. given the printer 170 **rust** Q2; Q1: "Rest" 190 **shrieked** Daniel em.; Q2: "shrike"; F: "they so shrike" 209 **more early** Q1; Q2: "now earling" 299 **raise** Q4; Q2: "raie"

KING HENRY THE FOURTH PART I

The central theme of *Henry IV Part 1* is Prince Hal's progress from irresponsibility to maturity; its appeal is the universal one of a Cinderella or ugly duckling transformed to a glittering heroic figure. Hal's activities link the two plots of the play and give unity to the structure. The action centers on one of the uprisings which plagued the reign of Hal's father, Henry IV. The Percy family — Northumberland and his son Hotspur — who had been instrumental in crowning Henry king, now feel that Henry is their enemy. The main plot, set in the political arena where England's fate is decided, treats the Percys' 1402-1403 rebellion, its plotting, inception and defeat, culminating in the Battle of Shrewsbury. The comic underplot, set in the everyday world of ordinary life, depicts the eating, drinking, cheating, robbing and jesting that go on there as usual, until interrupted by the call to arms. Then, as the subplot grows less comic, new abuses are revealed, such as Falstaff's misusing the draft law, clothing his conscripts by theft, and leading his troops where they are "peppered." Hal moves effortlessly from court to tavern to battlefield, changing along the way from princely guise to buckram disguise to bright armor, and shifting with ease from prose to blank verse as the occasion demands.

Although the presentation of Hal may reflect, as has been suggested, the education of the Renaissance prince or the redemption of the prodigal son, the heart of his situation is human and familiar — the misunderstanding between parent and youthful offspring on the threshold of maturity. It is as typical for youth to rebel against parental authority as it is for the father to worry about his son. Nor is it unusual for the parent to draw unfavorable comparisons between his son and himself at the same age, and between his son and a rival youth of higher reputation and greater achievement. Although Hal realizes the sacrifice is inevitable, he is understandably reluctant to exchange a carefree life for a burdensome one. In Hal's case the responsibilities — those of a kingdom — are intensified, and so is the wildness.

In the sources Shakespeare consulted, which include historical accounts and a play, Hal undergoes an overnight conversion from blaspheming swaggerer to model king. But Shakespeare makes the change credible because it is gradual, beginning as early as the soliloquy at the end of the play's second scene. Here, Hal informs the audience that he knows his companions for the idlers and drinkers they are, and that he intends to reform and win men's admiration by throwing off his loose behavior and redeeming his heretofore wasted time. Time is the subject with which the scene opens and closes, contrasting Falstaff's disregard of present time with Hal's promise to use future time more wisely. The soliloquy, and even the joking which precedes it, indicates a certain detachment on Hal's part; he is with them but not of them, although tavern life, especially if presided over by a lord of misrule like Falstaff, can be very attractive to one who is destined to spend the rest of his days on serious matters of court and state. Falstaff and the prince both have a sense of humor, an attribute lacking in King Henry IV. And the wit, gaiety and irresponsibility that Falstaff embodies are all the more attractive to Hal because he soon must bid them farewell.

Hal's tavern life might be considered unusual though effective curriculum in the education of a Renaissance prince. In the confrontation scene with his son (III, ii), King Henry confesses that when he was still Henry Bolingbroke, he "stole all courtesy from heaven" and "dressed" himself in humility in his courtship of the common people to gain their love; Hal joins them. Because he is not egocentric, Hal is sensitive to the humanity of others: "I am sworn brother to a leash of drawers, and can call them all by their christen names. . . . They take it already upon their salvation, that though I be but Prince of Wales, yet I am the king of courtesy . . . and when I am King of England I shall command all the good lads in Eastcheap" (II, iv, 8-13).

As sometimes happens when the father is self-made, the inheritor is an improvement on his elder. Whereas Bolingbroke in *Richard II* was forced to be suspicious, his son Hal possesses the easy nonchalance of security. Whereas Bolingbroke's virtues were action, drive, and dedication to a particular aim, Hal's good qualities are in repose, enhancing his behavior and deepening his character. Hal can be honest, self-aware, modest and magnanimous, as Bolingbroke, fighting and wary on his way up, could not afford to be.

When it comes to honor, Hal represents the mean or middle way between Hotspur's fanaticism and Falstaff's cynicism. Although the king has characterized his son as weak, Hal's statement of his intention to defeat Hotspur reflects the toughness of a soldier: "I will tear the reckoning from his heart" (III, ii, 152). By that victory Hal gains all Hotspur's honors. Yet Hal seeks not the fame honor confers, but the inner satisfaction it brings. He is content to allow the fame (to Hotspur the paramount aspect of honor) to go to Falstaff, who has behaved the least honorably. Hal has something more precious—the sophistication to appreciate the irony of a situation in which the reluctant soldier Falstaff can bluff his way to heroism. It is ironic too that Hotspur's hard-won honors go to his supposed vanquisher.

Shakespeare deliberately makes Hotspur younger than he was historically, to contrast with Hal. Both are rebels, but Hotspur is more dangerous. Hal's rebellion against authority damages his own reputation; Hotspur's would divide and destroy England. When King Henry is upbraiding his son, he uses Hotspur as an example to shame Hal, but as matters turn out, Henry is also rightly suspicious of the hot-tempered youth. Hotspur's impatience, plain speaking and total commitment to honor make him a lively and engaging character, but his irrational extremes indicate that his fortunes may be as unstable as his emotions. His dedication to honor is impressive, but egotistical; he will share honor with no one, but will wear "without corrival all her dignities" (I, iii, 207). When he dies, he grieves the loss not of his life but of his "proud titles" to Hal. In reprimanding Hotspur's rash and stubborn behavior with the Welsh leader Glendower, Worcester objectively explains why the character of Hotspur is an appealing one, but also why it neither earns nor deserves total approval:

> You must needs learn lord to amend this fault:
> Though sometimes it show greatness, courage, blood,
> And that's the dearest grace it renders you,
> Yet oftentimes it doth present harsh rage,
> Defect of manners, want of government,
> Pride, haughtiness, opinion, and disdain. . . (III, i, 179-84)

The parting of Hotspur and his wife in II, iii, adds dimension to his character and to the play, which has no other such domestic scene. Despite Hotspur's teasing of Kate in III, i, which goes from praise for certain of her abilities ("thou art perfect in lying down") to criticism of others ("Heart, you swear like a comfit-maker's wife"), mutual love and respect in marriage is apparent in this relationship as nowhere else in the play.

Hotspur and Falstaff are extremists; yet Hal — and we — are more indulgent of Falstaff. If Hal cannot resist the fat knight, how can the audience be expected to do so, to judge the extraordinary by ordinary standards? By the end of Part 2, Hal (then Henry V) will have to reach a moral decision and reject Falstaff, but as Part 1 ends, Falstaff carries off, with the prince's complicity, the honors of the day.

Critics have seen Falstaff as the descendant of the Vice or comic tempter of the medieval morality plays, as the lord of misrule of folk festivals who turned sobriety topsy-turvy, as the *miles gloriosus* or braggart soldier of Roman comedy. The effect of his first appearance is magnetic, and he never lets go his hold on the audience.

For all his respectable literary derivations, Falstaff's humanity is what we respond to, and just as his body is larger than life, so are his vices and his better qualities. The vices are not crimes, but magnified human failings, which in less exaggerated form are found in more respectable citizens: over-indulgence in food and drink, laziness, ribaldry, cheating the government, and reluctance to expose one's person to danger in an impersonal cause. His more deserving qualities — also magnified out of all proportion, like his body — are not necessarily those we possess, but those which we would like to own: zest for life, wit, honest self-appraisal, a superb sense of humor, youthful enthusiasm and gaiety despite advanced age, dexterity in getting out of tight situations, and objectivity about everything, including oneself. As Hal remarks in their first scene, Falstaff has no reason to ask what time it is, for he lives in the present, and being totally irresponsible, he spends all his time enjoying himself.

Like Hotspur, whom we can admire and blame at the same time, Falstaff lacks moderation. An observation that honor is worth little to those who die in its cause (V, i) may be taken as objective, but to refuse to take war seriously and to carry a bottle of sack instead of a pistol into battle seems childish. On one level, Falstaff plays at war like a child, falling down and pretending to be dead or stabbing a body that cannot feel it. On another level, he is cynical about the destruction of his troops and quick to save his own skin. In between the practical cynicism and the childish horseplay is an understandably human reluctance to face the dangers of battle. As the clash approaches, Falstaff responds with neither the eagerness of Hotspur nor the resolution of Hal, but with a wish that "'twere bedtime Hal, and all well" (V, i, 125). His "catechism" on honor that follows and his tavern play (II, iv) rehearsing Hal's interview with the king, both exemplify Falstaff's irreverence towards respected conventions and ceremonies. In the former Falstaff concludes that honor is only a symbol ("scutcheon") displayed at one's funeral, and in the latter, he parodies court ceremony by using the fashionable style of studied prose known as "euphuism." Both scenes comment comically on subjects treated seriously elsewhere in the play. The speech on honor is in counterpoint to Hotspur's (I, iii, 195 ff.), and the tavern play not only parallels the actual interview between Hal and the king, but enacts in jest the reality of the sentence of banishment with which Part 2 ends.

Of Falstaff's lies, as colossal as he is himself, it should be noted that he does not expect anyone to really believe that he fought a small army at Gadshill; the fun is in the enormity of the lie, which Falstaff enjoys as much as the others. He and Hal both know who killed Hotspur, but that Hal will "gild" Falstaff's lie is a stroke of luck for the fat knight, who gains repute as a warrior to whom others surrender (in Part 2) without a blow.

His alleged cowardice, which is related to his lying, is a topic much discussed by critics of the nineteenth century, who defend him from the charge of being a coward, and by critics of the twentieth century, who contend that he earns the title, although perhaps the point hardly seems worth so much serious debate. Falstaff, just as he will lie in the tavern to save his face, will lie down on the field of battle to save his skin. By doing so, he might be considered neither unique among men nor a setter of example for the prince of the realm. Falstaff's singularity lies in the wit and ingenuity of his explanations for his actions.

Besides being both witty and the cause of wit in others, Falstaff is involved in comic situations because of his size; he is forced to laboriously wheeze along when Hal and Poins hide his horse, and when Hal tells him to lie on the ground to listen for the tread of travelers, Falstaff replies, "Have you any levers to lift me up again, being down?" (II, ii, 31)

His individualistic prose, filled with allusions to everyday objects and topics, can be turned with equal skill to parody courtly euphuism or moralistic Puritanisms. He is fond of the mock-heroic style, of rhetorical questions, and the techniques of formal argument. He and Hal bring the conventional Elizabethan comedy of insult to its pinnacle. When Hal calls him "This sanguine coward, this bed-presser, this horse-back-breaker, this huge hill of flesh," Falstaff retaliates with: ". . . you starveling, you elf-skin, you dried neat's tongue, you bull's pizzle, you stockfish" (II, iv, 221-5). His expressions are as exaggerated as his failings and his size; hyperbole is a favorite rhetorical device, as is the use of incongruity. Although he is banished by the end of Part 2, Part 1 ends with Falstaff a national hero. Perhaps this is why Part 1 is preferred by audiences.

Some observers see Falstaff as the substitute father whom Hal prefers, at least in the beginning of the play. In jest Falstaff assumes the role of the king in the tavern rehearsal of the serious confrontation scene which follows.

Hal's wild behavior is only one of King Henry's problems. The king's opening words apply both to the country and to himself: "So shaken as we are, so wan with care." After Henry ascended the throne of Richard, reports the historian Holinshed, there were wars with the Welsh and the Scots, atmospheric disturbances regarded as portents, an attempt on Henry's life, and a threat of war with France. As the opening speech proceeds to describe the horrors of civil war, it becomes apparent that Bolingbroke, the somewhat ambiguous and calculating man of action in *Richard II*, is now a king deeply concerned with the welfare of the country. Because the political strife seems to stem from Henry's own act in assuming the kingship when Richard II was deposed, Henry suffers from the double burden of worry and guilt. Henry feels he is being punished personally as well as politically. While the nobles are rising against him, his son is rioting with low companions. Tired, worried, and ill, the king envies Northumberland his model son Hotspur. Hal, misunderstood by his father, is accused of being another Richard II (III, ii, 94) who was deposed for his irresponsibility.

Civil war, of which Henry paints an abhorrent picture at the play's opening, erupts; Richard's prophecy of Northumberland's revolt comes true. As Henry owes his throne to political maneuvering, he both fears and distrusts the kingmakers, as they do him. Henry knows that, having learned how to depose a king, they might try it again; they know he knows and that he will take measures to forestall such an occurrence.

Convinced by Hal of his seriousness and impressed with the bravery shown by his sons Hal and John on the field of battle, the king is depicted in V, iv, in a closer relationship with the two boys than has been seen heretofore. He brags of them to Douglas, and when that warrior threatens the king's life, Hal saves his father and immediately starts off to do further battle. The king detains him briefly, and, in a few words of gratitude, voices his pride and faith in Hal. He predicts at the end of the play that with Hal's help, "Rebellion in this land shall lose his sway" (V, v, 41). But it will not be that easy.

Beginning with *Richard II*, each of the eight plays in the chronicle cycle (of which *Henry IV* is the second) depicts an assembly of nobles who rebel against the king. Some rebels are retained from former plays, others are added or shift sides; but a group is always there, as rebellious action succeeds former revolt and is, in turn, followed by new rebellions, until York joins with Lancaster in the marriage of Richmond and Elizabeth York after the defeat of Richard III, at the chronological conclusion of Shakespeare's series of plays on this period of English history. According to the "Tudor myth," the union of the two families ends the divine retribution for the deposition of Richard II, and prosperity returns to the land.

Northumberland and Hotspur are continued from *Richard II*, the father older and more cautious, the son grown to a prominence that rivals that of the Prince of Wales. Shrewd in the advice he gives Hotspur to curb his temper, and so suspicious of the king as to reject his lenity in favor of war, Worcester contrasts with poetic, superstitious, temperamental Glendower, the Welsh leader. Aspiring to rule with Glendower and Hotspur an England divided into three parts, Mortimer has some individuality as an ardent bridegroom but is politically relatively colorless, despite being Richard's declared heir to the throne.

Douglas, the famous Scottish hero, is more lightly sketched than Hotspur, though a parallel to him in honor and rashness. Douglas is shown performing bravely in the battle, killing Blunt, attacking King Henry, and temporarily vanquishing Falstaff. When taken prisoner, Douglas is magnanimously freed by the prince: "His valours . . . Have taught us how to cherish such high deeds" (V, v, 29-30). The loyal Blunt, who sacrifices his life to save the king's and earns the epitaph of "gallant" from Hotspur, stands in contrast to the expedient Worcester, who, to save his own skin, falsifies Henry's message to the rebels and precipitates the Battle of Shrewsbury. While the main characters feel the urgency of time, the people of the underplot—the gentlemanly loiterer Poins, drunken, red-nosed Bardolph, garrulous Mistress Quickly—are unconcerned about the time they waste. They survive to entertain again in Part 2 of *Henry IV*.

Shakespeare's prose in *1 Henry IV* is reporting at its best. We get a varied and vivid picture of Elizabethan life and speech on its everyday level, from the ramblings of Mistress Quickly to the intricate stylishness of Falstaff, to the realistic idiom of the complaining carriers who have to get up at dawn to deliver the goods they carry (II, i). In addition, Falstaff, as noted, adapts his prose to the situation, which may call forth the cadence of a sermon or a catalog of insults that leaves him breathless. Many of the references used by or associated with the corpulent Sir John are drawn from food: ribs, tallow, butter, chops, roasted Manningtree ox. He loves to apply to himself allusions to thin or small things: "I was not an eagle's talon in the waist, I could have crept into any alderman's thumb-ring"; "I am a shotten herring"; "I am a peppercorn." His dialogue is livened with juxtaposition ("I am accursed to rob in that thief's company"), and, as mentioned, with hyperbole and incongruity (". . . thy father's beard is turned white with the news, you may buy land now as cheap as stinking mackerel").

Prince Hal can match blank verse with anyone at court, and prose with anyone in the tavern. His account of his camaraderie with the drawers (II, iv) is easy-going and colloquial; his banter with Falstaff pointed and satiric. The blank verse in the play is vigorous, fluid, and rich, yet never departing from the natural cadence of speech, and Shakespeare adapts the verse, as he does the prose, to fit the characters.

The recurrent images which appear in *Henry IV* include some of those to be found in all Shakespeare's history plays; the horrors of civil war and the comparison of the king to the sun are two of these. Henry's opening speech about civil war combines the image of the earth drinking "her own children's blood" with allusions to "intestine," "civil butchery," and a sword that cuts its wearer to suggest the physical mutilation of land and people in time of such war. The medieval sun-king metaphor is associated primarily with Hal. In his soliloquy at the end of I, ii, he thinks of himself in terms of the sun that is deliberately allowing the clouds to mar his visage, so that when he breaks through them and appears in all his magnificence, he will be more "wondered at." The second half of the soliloquy employs a new but related simile: his reformation will be "like bright metal on a sullen ground . . . glitt'ring o'er my fault" to "attract more eyes" (192-4). To describe Hal's appearance on the field of battle, Vernon alludes to both the sun and the glitter: "Glittering in golden coats . . . gorgeous as the sun at midsummer" (IV, i, 100-2). Unaware of Hal's intention to reform, Henry IV, in chastising him, applies almost the same image as the prince used in his soliloquy: "Such as is bent on sun-like majesty,/ When it shines seldom in admiring eyes" (III, ii, 79-80).

Date, Text, Sources

A likely date for the composition of *1 Henry IV* is 1596. A Quarto first appeared in 1598, in two editions. There is only a fragment of one of these (QO). The other (Q1), which is followed here as the most authoritative text, was possibly based on a "fair copy" of Shakespeare's own manuscript. Significant alternate readings are recorded in the textual notes. Subsequent Quarto editions, each based on the preceding one, were Q2, 1599; Q3, 1604; Q4, 1608; Q5, 1615; Q6, 1622. The First Folio text (1623) was printed from Q5 with some revisions.

There are three main sources: Holinshed's *Chronicles* in the second edition of 1587, Samuel Daniel's *The Civil Wars* (1595), and an anonymous chronicle play published in 1598, at which time it was about ten years old, *The Famous Victories of Henry V.* Details of the Percys' rebellion, the Battle of Shrewsbury, and the interview and reconciliation between Henry and Hal are found in Holinshed, as are all the historical characters. Daniel first makes Hal and Hotspur the same age (Hotspur and Henry IV were contemporaries) and brings them together at the Battle of Shrewsbury. The prince's wild escapades are dramatized in *The Famous Victories*, where he is engaged in a robbery and tavern brawl with disreputable companions, among them Sir John Oldcastle. The interview and reconciliation between king and prince also appear in the older play. Alternating comic and serious scenes of the prince in the tavern and then at court, and transporting the comic characters to the battle scenes, are devices common to both the old play and Shakespeare's. In scene iv of *Famous Victories*, the chief comic character Dereck stages a play-within-the-play parody of the serious action, perhaps a forerunner of Hal's and Falstaff's tavern play. The character of Oldcastle, which bears little resemblance to Falstaff, was based on the historical Sir John, who was a Lollard, a follower of Wycliffe, and a Protestant martyr. In Shakespeare's day the descendants of Oldcastle were the wealthy and powerful Cobham family, who evidently objected to Shakespeare's portrayal, and required the author to change the name of his character. In Holinshed he found the name of Sir John Fastolfe as a lieutenant of Henry V and later, under Henry VI, a deserter in battle. One of the puns on the original name remains in the text: ". . . my old lad of the castle" Hal calls Falstaff in I, ii 39. In Part 2, one of Falstaff's speeches was prefixed "*Old.*" and the Epilogue assures the audience that "Oldcastle died a martyr, and this is not the man."

HENRY THE IV PART I

THE HISTORY OF HENRY THE FOURTH

[THE NAMES OF THE ACTORS

KING HENRY THE FOURTH
HENRY, PRINCE OF WALES ⎱
PRINCE JOHN OF LANCASTER ⎰ *sons to the king*
EDMUND MORTIMER, *Earl of March*
RALPH NEVILLE, *Earl of Westmoreland*
HENRY PERCY, *Earl of Northumberland*
THOMAS PERCY, *Earl of Worcester, his brother*
HENRY PERCY, *surnamed* HOTSPUR, NORTHUMBERLAND'S *son*
ARCHIBALD, *Earl of Douglas*
RICHARD SCROOP, *Archbishop of York*
OWEN GLENDOWER
SIR WALTER BLUNT
SIR RICHARD VERNON
SIR JOHN FALSTAFF
SIR MICHAEL, *a friend to the Archbishop of York*
EDWARD POINS ⎞
PETO   ⎟
          ⎬ *companions of the Prince of Wales and of* FALSTAFF
GADSHILL   ⎟
BARDOLPH ⎠
FRANCIS, *a tavern drawer*

LADY PERCY, *wife to* HOTSPUR *and sister to* MORTIMER
LADY MORTIMER, *wife to* MORTIMER *and daughter to*
    GLENDOWER
MISTRESS QUICKLY, *hostess of the Boar's Head Tavern*

Lords, Officers, Sheriff, Vintner, Chamberlain,
    Drawers, Carriers, Ostler, Travellers, and Attendants

SCENE: *England and Wales.*]

Act One

Enter the KING, *Lord* JOHN OF LANCASTER, *Earl of*
WESTMORELAND, *with others.*

KING.

So shaken as we are, so wan with care,
Find we a time for frighted peace to pant,
And breathe short-winded accents of new broils
To be commenced in stronds afar remote:
No more the thirsty entrance of this soil   5
Shall daub her lips with her own children's blood,
No more shall trenching war channel her fields,
Nor bruise her flow'rets with the armèd hoofs
Of hostile paces: those opposèd eyes,
Which like the meteors of a troubled heaven,   10
All of one nature, of one substance bred,
Did lately meet in the intestine shock
And furious close of civil butchery,
Shall now in mutual well-beseeming ranks,
March all one way, and be no more opposed   15
Against acquaintance, kindred and allies.
The edge of war, like an ill-sheathèd knife,
No more shall cut his master: therefore friends,
As far as to the sepulchre of Christ—
Whose soldier now, under whose blessèd cross   20
We are impressèd and engaged to fight—

I, i Westminster. The King's palace   1 **we** (the royal plural, meaning the king and the
country)   4 **stronds** strands, shores   5-6 **entrance . . . blood** (the earth is personified as a
mother drinking the blood of her own children)   7 **trenching** trench-cutting **channel** make
channels in   8-9 **armed . . . paces** tread of war horses in battle trappings   9 **opposed
eyes** eyes of opposed warriors   10 **meteors . . . heaven** shooting stars, lightning, and other
phenomena of the atmosphere (that presaged or reflected disturbances on earth)   12
intestine internal (enforces "butchery," l. 13)   13 **close** grapple   14 **mutual well-
beseeming** united and well-ordered   21 **impressed** conscripted   **engaged** pledged

Forthwith a power of English shall we levy,
Whose arms were moulded in their mothers' womb,
To chase these pagans in those holy fields,
Over whose acres walked those blessèd feet,   25
Which fourteen hundred years ago were nailed,
For our advantage on the bitter cross.
But this our purpose now is twelve month old,
And bootless 'tis to tell you we will go:
Therefore we meet not now. Then let me hear   30
Of you my gentle cousin Westmoreland,
What yesternight our council did decree
In forwarding this dear expedience.

WESTMORELAND.
My liege, this haste was hot in question,
And many limits of the charge set down   35
But yesternight, when all athwart there came
A post from Wales, loaden with heavy news,
Whose worst was that the noble Mortimer,
Leading the men of Herefordshire to fight
Against the irregular and wild Glendower,   40
Was by the rude hands of that Welshman taken,
A thousand of his people butcherèd,
Upon whose dead corpse there was such misuse,
Such beastly shameless transformation
By those Welshwomen done, as may not be   45
Without much shame, retold, or spoken of.
KING.   It seems then that the tidings of this broil
Brake off our business for the Holy Land.

WESTMORELAND.
This matched with other did, my gracious lord,
For more uneven and unwelcome news   50
Came from the north, and thus it did import:
On Holy-rood day, the gallant Hotspur there,
Young Harry Percy, and brave Archibald,

---

22 **power** army   28 **purpose . . . old** (at the end of *R II*, when the king learns of Richard's murder, he vows to make this journey "to wash the blood off from my guilty hand")   29 **bootless** needless   31 **cousin** kinsman   33 **dear expedience** important expedition   34 **hot in question** hotly debated   35 **limits of the charge** assignments of duties and expenditures   36 **athwart** thwarting   37 **post** messenger   38 **Mortimer** Edmund Mortimer, Earl of March, declared heir to the throne by Richard II (Shakespeare, following Holinshed, confuses Edmund with his uncle of the same name, who married Glendower's daughter; he also is confused with his father Roger, who was Hotspur's brother-in-law)   40 **irregular** lawless   44 **transformation** mutilation   50 **uneven** disagreeable   52 **Holy-rood day** Holy Cross Day, September 14   54 **approved** of proved

That ever valiant and approvèd Scot,
At Holmedon met,   55
Where they did spend a sad and bloody hour:
As by discharge of their artillery,
And shape of likelihood the news was told:
For he that brought them, in the very heat
And pride of their contention, did take horse,   60
Uncertain of the issue any way.

KING.   Here is a dear, a true industrious friend,
Sir Walter Blunt, new lighted from his horse,
Stained with the variation of each soil
Betwixt that Holmedon and this seat of ours,   65
And he hath brought us smooth and welcome news:
The Earl of Douglas is discomfited,
Ten thousand bold Scots, two and twenty knights,
Balked in their own blood did Sir Walter see
On Holmedon's plains. Of prisoners Hotspur took   70
Mordake Earl of Fife, and eldest son
To beaten Douglas, and the Earl of Athol,
Of Murray, Angus, and Menteith:
And is not this an honorable spoil?
A gallant prize? Ha cousin, is it not?   75

WESTMORELAND.
In faith
It is, a conquest for a prince to boast of.

KING.   Yea, there thou mak'st me sad, and mak'st me sin
In envy, that my Lord Northumberland
Should be the father to so blest a son: 80
A son who is the theme of honour's tongue,
Amongst a grove, the very straightest plant,
Who is sweet Fortune's minion and her pride,
Whilst I by looking on the praise of him,
See riot and dishonour stain the brow   85
Of my young Harry. O that it could be proved
That some night-tripping fairy had exchanged
In cradle-clothes our children where they lay,
And called mine Percy, his Plantagenet,
Then would I have his Harry, and he mine: 90

worth   55 **Holmedon** Humbleton, Northumberland   57 **by** judging by   58 **shape of
likelihood** evidence of probability   60 **pride** highest pitch (fr. falconry)   62 **true industrious** loyal and zealous   66 **smooth** pleasant   69 **Balked** (1) piled up in ridges (2)
thwarted   71 **Mordake** (Murdoch was actually the son of the Duke of Albany, Regent of
Scotland; faulty punctuation in Holinshed caused the misreading)   83 **minion**

But let him from my thoughts. What think you coz
Of this young Percy's pride? The prisoners
Which he in this adventure hath surprised,
To his own use he keeps and sends me word
I shall have none but Mordake Earl of Fife.   95

WESTMORELAND.
This is his uncle's teaching. This is Worcester,
Malevolent to you in all aspècts,
Which makes him prune himself, and bristle up
The crest of youth against your dignity.

KING.   But I have sent for him to answer this: 100
And for this cause awhile we must neglect
Our holy purpose to Jerusalem.
Cousin, on Wednesday next our council we
Will hold at Windsor, so inform the lords:
But come yourself with speed to us again,   105
For more is to be said and to be done,
Than out of anger can be utterèd.

WESTMORELAND.
I will my liege.   *Exeunt.*

[SCENE II.]

Enter PRINCE OF WALES *and* SIR JOHN FALSTAFF.

FALSTAFF. Now Hal, what time of day is it lad?

PRINCE.   Thou art so fat-witted with drinking of old sack, and
unbuttoning thee after supper, and sleeping upon benches
after noon, that thou hast forgotten to demand that truly
which thou wouldst truly know. What a devil hast thou to   5
do with the time of the day? Unless hours were cups of
sack, and minutes capons, and clocks the tongues of
bawds, and dials the signs of leaping-houses, and the
blessed sun himself a fair hot wench in flame-coloured
taffeta, I see no reason why thou shouldst be so super-   10
fluous to demand the time of the day.

FALSTAFF. Indeed you come near me now Hal, for we that take

darling   91 **coz** cousin   97 **Malevolent . . . aspects** malicious against you whenever he
has influence (fr. astrology)   98 **Which** who   **prune** preen (fr. falconry)
   I, ii Westminster. A public wating room at court   7 **sack** Spanish white wine   8 **bawds**
pimps   **dials** clock faces   8 **leaping-houses** brothels   9-10 **flame-coloured taffeta**
(worn by prostitutes)   10 **superfluous** (1) overly curious (2) self-indulgent   12 **come near
me** come near the mark (fr. fencing)

purses go by the moon and the seven stars, and not by
Phoebus, he, that wandering knight so fair: and I prithee
sweet wag when thou art king, as God save thy   15
grace—majesty I should say, for grace thou wilt have
none.

PRINCE.   What, none?

FALSTAFF. No by my troth, not so much as will serve to be prologue
to an egg and butter.   20

PRINCE.   Well, how then? Come roundly, roundly.

FALSTAFF. Marry then sweet wag, when thou art king, let not us that
are squires of the night's body, be called thieves of the
day's beauty: let us be Diana's foresters, gentlemen of the
shade, minions of the moon, and let men say we be men of 25
good government, being governed as the sea is, by our
noble and chaste mistress the moon, under whose countenance we steal.

PRINCE.   Thou sayest well, and it holds well too, for the fortune of
us that are the moon's men, doth ebb and flow like the sea, 30
being governed as the sea is, by the moon. As for proof
now, a purse of gold most resolutely snatched on Monday
night and most dissolutely spent on Tuesday morning,
got with swearing 'Lay by' and spent with crying 'Bring
in', now in as low an ebb as the foot of the ladder, and by 35
and by in as high a flow as the ridge of the gallows.

FALSTAFF. By the Lord thou sayest true lad, and is not my hostess of
the tavern a most sweet wench?

PRINCE.   As the honey of Hybla my old lad of the castle, and is not a
buff jerkin a most sweet robe of durance?   40

FALSTAFF. How now, how now mad wag? what, in thy quips and thy
quiddities? What a plague have I to do with a buff jerkin?

PRINCE.   Why, what a pox have I to do with my hostess of the
tavern?

---

13 **go by** (1) tell the time by (2) go by the light
of   **seven stars** the Pleiades   14 **Phoebus** the sun   **wandering knight** (probably a
reference to the Knight of the Sun, hero of a popular romance)   16-20 **grace** (1) your
highness (2) spiritual grace (3) prayer before a meal   21 **roundly** plainly   23 **squires . . .
body** attendants of the night (w. pun on "knight")   25 **minions** darlings   26 **of good
government** (1) well-behaved (2) serving a good governor   27 **countenance** (1) patronage
(2) face   34 **'Lay by'** (cry of highwaymen to their victims)   **'Bring in'** i.e. the
wine   35,36 **ladder, ridge** i.e. of the gallows (the condemned climbed a ladder to the
"ridge," crossbeam from which he dropped)   39 **Hybla** Sicilian town famous for
honey   37 **By the Lord** (Q; F omits profanity throughout, as its usage on stage was
censored in 1606   39 **old . . . castle** (1) w. pun on "Oldcastle," Falstaff's original, historical
name, as used in the source play *The Famous Victories of Henry V* (2) the "Castle," a famous
brothel in Southwark   40 **buff jerkin** leather jacket worn by constables   **of durance** (1) of
durability (2) to lead to a prison term   42 **quiddities** word plays, puns

FALSTAFF.   Well, thou hast called her to a reckoning many a time and   45
            oft.
PRINCE.   Did I ever call for thee to pay thy part?
FALSTAFF.   No, I'll give thee thy due, thou hast paid all there.
PRINCE.   Yea and elsewhere, so far as my coin would stretch, and
            where it would not, I have used my credit.   50
FALSTAFF.   Yea, and so used it that were it not here apparent that thou
            art heir-apparent—But I prithee sweet wag, shall there be
            gallows standing in England when thou art king? and
            resolution thus fubbed as it is with the rusty curb of old
            Father Antic the law? Do not thou when thou art king,   55
            hang a thief.
PRINCE.   No, thou shalt.
FALSTAFF.   Shall I? O rare! By the Lord I'll be a brave judge.
PRINCE.   Thou judgest false already, I mean thou shalt have the
            hanging of the thieves, and so become a rare hangman.   60
FALSTAFF.   Well Hal, well, and in some sort it jumps with my humour
            as well as waiting in the court I can tell you.
PRINCE.   For obtaining of suits?
FALSTAFF.   Yea, for obtaining of suits, whereof the hangman hath no
            lean wardrobe. 'Sblood I am as melancholy as a gib-cat, or   65
            a lugged bear.
PRINCE.   Or an old lion, or a lover's lute.
FALSTAFF.   Yea, or the drone of a Lincolnshire bagpipe.
PRINCE.   What sayest thou to a hare, or the melancholy of Moor
            ditch?   70
FALSTAFF.   Thou hast the most unsavoury similes, and art indeed the
            most comparative rascalliest sweet young prince. But
            Hal, I prithee trouble me no more with vanity: I would to
            God thou and I knew where a commodity of good names
            were to be bought: an old lord of the council rated me the   75
            other day in the street about you sir, but I marked him
            not, and yet he talked very wisely, but I regarded him not,
            and yet he talked wisely, and in the street too.

---

45 **called** . . .
reckoning (1) called her to account (2) asked for the bill (3) bawdy double meaning   51-2
here, heir (similarly pronounced)   54 **resolution thus fubbed** enterprise thus
thwarted   55 **Antic** buffoon, joker   58 **brave** fine   61 **jumps** agrees   **humour**
temperament   63-4 **suits** (1) petitions to the king (2) suits of clothing worn by the hanged
man, which went to the executioner   65 **gib-cat** tomcat (whose wail was melancholy)   66
lugged baited   69 **hare** (associated with melancholy)   **Moor ditch** a foul-smelling ditch
which drained Moorfields in the suburbs of London   72 **comparative** inventive in witty
comparisons   74 **commodity** supply   76-8 **I marked** . . . **too** (at times he uses the

PRINCE.   Thou didst well, for wisdom cries out in the streets and no
            man regards it.   80

FALSTAFF.   O thou hast damnable iteration, and art indeed able to
            corrupt a saint: thou hast done much harm upon me Hal,
            God forgive thee for it. Before I knew thee Hal, I knew
            nothing, and now am I, if a man should speak truly, little
            better than one of the wicked: I must give over this life,   85
            and I will give it over: by the Lord and I do not, I am a
            villain. I'll be damned for never a king's son in Christen-
            dom.

PRINCE.   Where shall we take a purse tomorrow Jack?

FALSTAFF.   'Zounds, where thou wilt lad, I'll make one, and I do not,   90
            call me villain and baffle me.

PRINCE.   I see a good amendment of life in thee, from praying to
            purse-taking.

FALSTAFF.   Why Hal, 'tis my vocation Hal, 'tis no sin for a man to
            labour in his vocation.   95

                          Enter POINS.

            Poins: now shall we know if Gadshill have set a match. O
            if men were to be saved by merit, what hole in hell were
            hot enough for him? This is the most omnipotent villain
            that ever cried 'Stand' to a true man.

PRINCE.   Good morrow Ned.   100

POINS.   Good morrow sweet Hal. What says Monsieur Remorse?
            What says Sir John Sack-and-Sugar, Jack? How agrees
            the devil and thee about thy soul that thou soldest him on
            Good Friday last, for a cup of Madeira and a cold capon's
            leg?   105

PRINCE.   Sir John stands to his word, the devil shall have his
            bargain, for he was never yet a breaker of proverbs: he will
            give the devil his due.

POINS.   Then art thou damned for keeping thy word with the
            devil.   110

PRINCE.   Else he had been damned for cozening the devil.

scriptural style of an overzealous Puritan)   79-80 **wisdom . . . it** (Prov. I. 20, 24: "Wisdom
crieth without; she uttereth her voice in the streets." "Because I have called, and ye refused; I
have stretched out my hand, and no man regarded")   81 **damnable iteration** trick of
repeating the Scriptures for a wicked purpose   85-6 **I must . . . over** (he parodies the
Puritan idiom)   **over** up   **and** if   91 **baffle** publicly disgrace (as traitorous knights, by
being hung up by the heels)   96 **Gadshill** (the character, based on one in *Famous Victories*, is
named for a place famous for robberies)   **set a match** planned a robbery   99 **'Stand'**
(thief's cry to his victim)   **true** honest   102 **Sack-and-Sugar** (the mixture characterized
old age)   107 **breaker** disprover   111 **cozening** cheating

POINS.   But my lads, my lads, tomorrow morning, by four o'clock
            early at Gadshill, there are pilgrims going to Canterbury
            with rich offerings, and traders riding to London with fat
            purses. I have vizards for you all, you have horses for   115
            yourselves, Gadshill lies tonight in Rochester, I have
            bespoke supper tomorrow night in Eastcheap, we may do
            it as secure as sleep: if you will go I will stuff your purses
            full of crowns: if you will not, tarry at home and be
            hanged.   120

FALSTAFF.   Hear ye Yedward, if I tarry at home and go not, I'll hang
            you for going.

POINS.   You will, chops.

FALSTAFF.   Hal, wilt thou make one?

PRINCE.   Who, I rob? I a thief? Not I by my faith.   125

FALSTAFF.   There's neither honesty, manhood, nor good fellowship
            in thee, nor thou cam'st not of the blood royal, if thou
            darest not stand for ten shillings.

PRINCE.   Well then, once in my days I'll be a madcap.

FALSTAFF.   Why, that's well said.   130

PRINCE.   Well, come what will, I'll tarry at home.

FALSTAFF.   By the Lord, I'll be a traitor then, when thou art king.

PRINCE.   I care not.

POINS.   Sir John, I prithee leave the prince and me alone: I will lay
            him down such reasons for this adventure that he shall go. 135

FALSTAFF.   Well, God give thee the spirit of persuasion and him the
            ears of profiting, that what thou speakest, may move; and
            what he hears, may be believed, that the true prince may
            (for recreation sake) prove a false thief, for the poor abuses
            of the time want countenance: farewell, you shall find me   140
            in Eastcheap.

PRINCE.   Farewell the latter spring, farewell Allhallown summer.

                                          [*Exit* FALSTAFF.]

POINS.   Now my good sweet honey lord, ride with us tomorrow. I
            have a jest to execute, that I cannot manage alone. Falstaff,
            Bardolph, Peto, and Gadshill shall rob those men that we   145
            have already waylaid, yourself and I will not be there: and
            when they have the booty, if you and I do not rob them,

115 **vizards** masks   117
bespoke ordered   121 **Yedward** Edward   123 **chops** fat jaws   127 **royal** (1) lit. (2) coin
worth 10s.   128 **stand for** (1) be worth (2) give the robber's cry "stand" for   136-40 **God
. . . countenance** (another mimicry of Puritan idiom)   139 **abuses** deceptions   140 **want
countenance** need encouragement   142 **latter spring . . . summer** (1) end of the season (2)

cut this head off from my shoulders.

PRINCE. How shall we part with them in setting forth?

POINS. Why, we will set forth before or after them, and appoint 150
them a place of meeting, wherein it is at our pleasure to
fail; and then will they adventure upon the exploit themselves, which they shall have no sooner achieved but we'll
set upon them.

PRINCE. Yea but 'tis like that they will know us by our horses, by 155
our habits, and by every other appointment to be ourselves.

POINS. Tut, our horses they shall not see, I'll tie them in the
wood: our vizards we will change after we leave them: and
sirrah, I have cases of buckram for the nonce, to immask 160
our noted outward garments.

PRINCE. Yea, but I doubt they will be too hard for us.

POINS. Well, for two of them, I know them to be as true-bred
cowards as ever turned back: and for the third, if he fight
longer than he sees reason, I'll forswear arms. The virtue 165
of this jest will be the incomprehensible lies that this same
fat rogue will tell us when we meet at supper, how thirty
at least he fought with, what wards, what blows, what
extremities he endured, and in the reproof of this lives the
jest.   170

PRINCE. Well, I'll go with thee, provide us all things necessary, and
meet me tomorrow night in Eastcheap, there I'll sup:
farewell.

POINS. Farewell my lord.   *Exit* POINS.

PRINCE. I know you all, and will awhile uphold   175
The unyoked humour of your idleness,
Yet herein will I imitate the sun,
Who doth permit the base contagious clouds
To smother up his beauty from the world,
That when he please again to be himself,   180
Being wanted, he may be more wondered at
By breaking through the foul and ugly mists
Of vapours that did seem to strangle him.
If all the year were playing holidays,

Indian summer or youthfulness in old age   156 **habits** clothes   **appointment** piece of
equipment   160 **cases of buckram** suits of stiffened coarse cloth   **nonce** occasion   161
noted well-known   162 **doubt** fear   168 **wards** defenses (fr. fencing)   169 **extremities**
perils   **reproof** refutation   176 **unyoked humour** unbridled caprices   **idleness**
folly   177 **sun** king of the heavens (favorite metaphor for royalty, along with the eagle and
the lion)   178 **contagious** breeding contagion   181 **wanted** needed, lacked

To sport would be as tedious as to work;   185
But when they seldom come, they wished for come,
And nothing pleaseth but rare accidents:
So when this loose behaviour I throw off,
And pay the debt I never promisèd,
By how much better than my word I am,   190
By so much shall I falsify men's hopes,
And like bright metal on a sullen ground,
My reformation glitt'ring o'er my fault,
Shall show more goodly, and attract more eyes
Than that which hath no foil to set it off.   195
I'll so offend, to make offence a skill,
Redeeming time when men think least I will.   *Exit.*

[SCENE III.]

Enter the KING, NORTHUMBERLAND, WORCESTER, HOTSPUR,
          SIR WALTER BLUNT, *with others.*

KING.   My blood hath been too cold and temperate,
          Unapt to stir at these indignities,
          And you have found me, for accordingly
          You tread upon my patience: but be sure
          I will from henceforth rather be myself,   5
          Mighty, and to be feared, than my condition,
          Which hath been smooth as oil, soft as young down,
          And therefore lost that title of respect,
          Which the proud soul ne'er pays but to the proud.

WORCESTER.
          Our house, my sovereign liege, little deserves   10
          The scourge of greatness to be used on it,
          And that same greatness too, which our own hands
          Have holp to make so portly.

NORTHUMBERLAND.
          My lord—

---

187 **acci-
dents** events   191 **hopes** expectations   192 **sullen ground** dark background   195 **foil**
thin leaf of metal placed under a jewel to make it shine more brightly   197 **Redeeming time**
making up for lost time

I, iii Windsor Castle   3 **found me** i.e. out   6 **condition** natural disposition   8 **title of**
claim to   13 **portly** stately   17 **peremptory** imperative   19 **moody . . . brow** sullen
defiance of a frowning subject   **frontier** (1) forehead (2) border fortress   26 **delivered**

KING.   Worcester get thee gone, for I do see   15
                 Danger and disobedience in thine eye:
                 O sir, your presence is too bold and peremptory,
                 And majesty might never yet endure
                 The moody frontier of a servant brow,
                 You have good leave to leave us. When we need   20
                 Your use and counsel we shall send for you.

                                          Exit WORCESTER.

                 [*To Northumberland.*] You were about to speak.
NORTHUMBERLAND.   Yea my good lord.
                 Those prisoners in your highness' name demanded,
                 Which Harry Percy here at Holmedon took,
                 Were as he says, not with such strength denied   25
                 As is delivered to your majesty.
                 Either envy therefore, or misprision,
                 Is guilty of this fault, and not my son.
HOTSPUR.   My liege, I did deny no prisoners,
                 But I remember when the fight was done,   30
                 When I was dry with rage, and extreme toil,
                 Breathless and faint, leaning upon my sword,
                 Came there a certain lord, neat and trimly dressed,
                 Fresh as a bridegroom, and his chin new reaped,
                 Showed like a stubble-land at harvest home.   35
                 He was perfumèd like a milliner,
                 And 'twixt his finger and his thumb he held
                 A pouncet-box, which ever and anon
                 He gave his nose, and took't away again,
                 Who therewith angry, when it next came there   40
                 Took it in snuff: and still he smiled and talked,
                 And as the soldiers bore dead bodies by,
                 He called them untaught knaves, unmannerly,
                 To bring a slovenly unhandsome corse
                 Betwixt the wind and his nobility: 45
                 With many holiday and lady terms
                 He questioned me, amongst the rest demanded
                 My prisoners in your majesty's behalf.

---

reported   27 **envy** malice   **misprision** misunderstanding   34 **new reaped** with a
newly clipped beard   36 **milliner** haberdasher (who perfumed his wares)   38 **pouncet-
box** perforated box containing sweet-smelling powder   40 **Who** the nose   41 **in snuff** (1)
as an offense (2) as snuff   44 **corse** corpse   46 **holiday** choice

I then, all smarting with my wounds being cold,
To be so pestered with a popinjay,   50
Out of my grief and my impatience
Answered neglectingly, I know not what,
He should, or he should not, for he made me mad
To see him shine so brisk, and smell so sweet,
And talk so like a waiting-gentlewoman,   55
Of guns, and drums, and wounds, God save the mark;
And telling me the sovereign'st thing on earth
Was parmacity, for an inward bruise,
And that it was great pity, so it was,
This villainous saltpetre should be digged   60
Out of the bowels of the harmless earth,
Which many a good tall fellow had destroyed
So cowardly, and but for these vile guns
He would himself have been a soldier.
This bald unjointed chat of his, my lord,   65
I answered indirectly, as I said,
And I beseech you, let not his report
Come current for an accusation
Betwixt my love and your high majesty.

BLUNT.   The circumstance considered, good my lord,   70
What e'er Lord Harry Percy then had said
To such a person, and in such a place,
At such a time, with all the rest retold,
May reasonably die, and never rise
To do him wrong, or any way impeach   75
What then he said, so he unsay it now.

KING.   Why yet he doth deny his prisoners,
But with proviso and exception,
That we at our own charge shall ransom straight
His brother-in-law, the foolish Mortimer,   80
Who on my soul, hath wilfully betrayed
The lives of those that he did lead to fight
Against that great magician, damned Glendower,
Whose daughter as we hear, that Earl of March

---

50 **popinjay** parrot, idle
chatterer   51 **grief** pain   56 **God . . . mark** (expression of apology, here impatience,
made originally to avert evil)   58 **parmacity** spermaceti or whale sperm (credited with
curing coagulated blood)   62 **tall** brave   63 **guns** cannons   65 **bald . . . chat** petty
disjointed chatter   66 **indirectly** heedlessly   68 **Come current** be accepted (as valid
currency)   75 **impeach** discredit   78 **But with proviso** except on condition   79 **charge**
expense   **ransom** (the custom with noble prisoners)   80,84 **brother-in-law, Earl of**

Hath lately married: shall our coffers then   85
Be emptied, to redeem a traitor home?
Shall we buy treason? and indent with fears,
When they have lost and forfeited themselves?
No, on the barren mountains let him starve:
For I shall never hold that man my friend,   90
Whose tongue shall ask me for one penny cost
To ransom home revolted Mortimer.

HOTSPUR. Revolted Mortimer?
He never did fall off, my sovereign liege,
But by the chance of war: to prove that true   95
Needs no more but one tongue for all those wounds,
Those mouthèd wounds which valiantly he took,
When on the gentle Severn's sedgy bank,
In single opposition hand to hand,
He did confound the best part of an hour,   100
In changing hardiment with great Glendower:
Three times they breathed, and three times did they drink
Upon agreement, of swift Severn's flood,
Who then affrighted with their bloody looks,
Ran fearfully among the trembling reeds,   105
And hid his crisp head in the hollow bank,
Bloodstainèd with these valiant combatants.
Never did bare and rotten policy
Colour her working with such deadly wounds,
Nor never could the noble Mortimer   110
Receive so many, and all willingly:
Then let not him be slandered with revolt.

KING. Thou dost belie him Percy, thou dost belie him,
He never did encounter with Glendower:
I tell thee,   115
He durst as well have met the devil alone,
As Owen Glendower for an enemy.
Art thou not ashamed? But sirrah, henceforth
Let me not hear you speak of Mortimer:
Send me your prisoners with the speediest means,   120
Or you shall hear in such a kind from me

March (cf. I, i, 38 n.)   86 **redeem** ransom   87 **indent** make an agreement
(indenture)   94 **fall off** rebel   97 **mouthed wounds** wounds that speak in his
behalf   100 **confound** consume   101 **changing hardiment** exchanging valor   102
breathed paused for breath   103 **flood** river   106 **crisp** curled, rippled   108 **bare**
obvious   **policy** cunning   109 **Colour** disguise   121 **kind** way

As will displease you. My Lord Northumberland,
We license your departure with your son:
Send us your prisoners, or you will hear of it.

Exit KING [*with* BLUNT *and train*].

HOTSPUR.   And if the devil come and roar for them   125
I will not send them: I will after straight
And tell him so, for I will ease my heart,
Albeit I make a hazard of my head.

NORTHUMBERLAND.
What? drunk with choler? Stay, and pause
awhile,
Here comes your uncle.

Enter WORCESTER.

HOTSPUR.   Speak of Mortimer?   130
'Zounds I will speak of him, and let my soul
Want mercy if I do not join with him:
Yea on his part I'll empty all these veins,
And shed my dear blood, drop by drop in the dust,
But I will lift the down-trod Mortimer   135
As high in the air as this unthankful king,
As this ingrate and cankered Bolingbroke.

NORTHUMBERLAND.
Brother, the king hath made your nephew mad.

WORCESTER.
Who struck this heat up after I was gone?

HOTSPUR.   He will forsooth have all my prisoners,   140
And when I urged the ransom once again
Of my wife's brother, then his cheek looked pale,
And on my face he turned an eye of death,
Trembling even at the name of Mortimer.

WORCESTER.
I cannot blame him, was not he proclaimed   145
By Richard that dead is, the next of blood?

NORTHUMBERLAND.
He was, I heard the proclamation:
And then it was, when the unhappy king,

---

128 **Albeit** . . .
hazard of although I risk   129 **choler** anger   132 **Want** lack   137 **cankered** rotten at
the core   **Bolingbroke** (King Henry's name before he was crowned)   143 **of death** of
deadly fear   146 **of blood** of royal blood, in succession to the throne

(Whose wrongs in us God pardon) did set forth
Upon his Irish expedition;   150
From whence he intercepted did return
To be deposed, and shortly murderèd.

WORCESTER.
And for whose death, we in the world's wide mouth
Live scandalized and foully spoken of.

HOTSPUR. But soft I pray you, did King Richard then   155
Proclaim my brother Edmund Mortimer
Heir to the crown?

NORTHUMBERLAND.   He did, myself did hear it.

HOTSPUR. Nay then I cannot blame his cousin king,
That wished him on the barren mountains starve:
But shall it be that you that set the crown   160
Upon the head of this forgetful man,
And for his sake wear the detested blot
Of murderous subornation—shall it be
That you a world of curses undergo,
Being the agents, or base second means,   165
The cords, the ladder, or the hangman rather?
O pardon me, that I descend so low,
To show the line and the predicament
Wherein you range under this subtle king!
Shall it for shame be spoken in these days,   170
Or fill up chronicles in time to come,
That men of your nobility and power
Did gage them both in an unjust behalf.
(As both of you, God pardon it, have done)
To put down Richard, that sweet lovely rose,   175
And plant this thorn, this canker Bolingbroke?
And shall it in more shame be further spoken,
That you are fooled, discarded, and shook off
By him, for whom these shames ye underwent?
No, yet time serves, wherein you may redeem   180
Your banished honours, and restore yourselves
Into the good thoughts of the world again:

---

149 **Whose wrongs
in us** for the wrongs we did to whom   156 **brother** brother-in-law (actually the nephew of
Hotspur's brother-in-law; cf. I, i, 38 n.)   163 **murderous subornation** suborning others to
commit murder   168 **line** degree   **predicament** (1) category (2) dangerous
position   169 **range** rank   173 **gage them** pledge your nobility and power   176 **canker**
either (1) inferior wild rose or (2) cankerworm causing plant disease

Revenge the jeering and disdained contempt
Of this proud king, who studies day and night
To answer all the debt he owes to you,   185
Even with the bloody payment of your deaths:
Therefore I say—
WORCESTER.   Peace cousin, say no more.
And now I will unclasp a secret book,
And to your quick-conceiving discontents
I'll read you matter deep and dangerous,   190
As full of peril and adventurous spirit,
As to o'er-walk a current roaring loud,
On the unsteadfast footing of a spear.
HOTSPUR.   If he fall in, good night, or sink or swim.
Send danger from the east unto the west,   195
So honour cross it, from the north to south,
And let them grapple: O the blood more stirs
To rouse a lion than to start a hare.

NORTHUMBERLAND.
Imagination of some great exploit
Drives him beyond the bounds of patience.   200
HOTSPUR.   By heaven methinks it were an easy leap,
To pluck bright honour from the pale-faced moon,
Or dive into the bottom of the deep,
Where fathom-line could never touch the ground,
And pluck up drownèd honour by the locks,   205
So he that doth redeem her thence might wear
Without corrival all her dignities:
But out upon this half-faced fellowship.

WORCESTER.
He apprehends a world of figures here,
But not the form of what he should attend: 210
Good cousin give me audience for a while.
HOTSPUR.   I cry you mercy.
WORCESTER.   Those same noble Scots
That are your prisoners—
HOTSPUR.   I'll keep them all;

---

183 **disdained**
disdainful   186 **deaths** (1) pronounced similar to "debts" (2) proverbial: "death pays all
debts"   192-3 **o'er-walk . . . spear** walk over a raging torrent on a bridge made from a spear
(a feat found in medieval romance)   194 **good night** so be it   **or . . . swim** either sink or
swim   196 **So** i.e. that   198 **rouse, start** (fr. hunting: driving an animal from its lair,
"start" for the smaller game and "rouse" for the larger)   204 **fathom-line** sounding
rope   207 **corrival** equal partner   208 **half-faced fellowship** half-and-half, incomplete
sharing (fr. coining)   209 **apprehends** imagines   **figures** images   210 **form** essential
principle

By God he shall not have a Scot of them,
No, if a Scot would save his soul he shall not.   215
I'll keep them, by this hand.
WORCESTER.   You start away,
And lend no ear unto my purposes:
Those prisoners you shall keep.
HOTSPUR.   Nay I will: that's flat:
He said he would not ransom Mortimer,
Forbade my tongue to speak of Mortimer,   220
But I will find him when he lies asleep,
And in his ear I'll holla 'Mortimer:'
Nay,
I'll have a starling shall be taught to speak
Nothing but 'Mortimer,' and give it him   225
To keep his anger still in motion.
WORCESTER.
Hear you cousin a word.
HOTSPUR.   All studies here I solemnly defy,
Save how to gall and pinch this Bolingbroke,
And that same sword-and-buckler Prince of Wales,   230
But that I think his father loves him not,
And would be glad he met with some mischance,
I would have him poisoned with a pot of ale.
WORCESTER.
Farewell kinsman, I'll talk to you
When you are better tempered to attend.   235
NORTHUMBERLAND.
Why what a wasp-stung and impatient fool
Art thou, to break into this woman's mood,
Tying thine ear to no tongue but thine own.
HOTSPUR.   Why look you, I am whipped and scourged with rods,
Nettled, and stung with pismires, when I hear   240
Of this vile politician Bolingbroke.
In Richard's time—what do you call the place?
A plague upon't, it is in Gloucestershire;
'Twas where the madcap duke his uncle kept,
His uncle York, where I first bowed my knee   245
Unto this king of smiles, this Bolingbroke—
'Sblood,

214-5 **Scot** (1) lit. (2) small payment   226 **still** always   230 **sword-and-buckler** swashbuckler, commoner (gentlemen wore rapiers)   236 **wasp-stung** irascible   240 **Nettled** irritated (as if stung by nettles)   **pismires** ants

When you and he came back from Ravenspurgh.
NORTHUMBERLAND.
    At Berkeley Castle.
HOTSPUR. You say true.   250
    Why what a candy deal of courtesy
    This fawning greyhound then did proffer me.
    'Look when his infant fortune came to age,'
    And 'gentle Harry Percy,' and 'kind cousin:'
    O the devil take such cozeners. God forgive me,   255
    Good uncle tell your tale, I have done.
WORCESTER.
    Nay, if you have not, to it again,
    We'll stay your leisure.
HOTSPUR.   I have done i' faith.
WORCESTER.
    Then once more to your Scottish prisoners,
    Deliver them up without their ransom straight,   260
    And make the Douglas' son your only mean
    For powers in Scotland, which for divers reasons
    Which I shall send you written, be assured
    Will easily be granted. [*To Northumberland.*] You my
        lord,
    Your son in Scotland being thus employed,   265
    Shall secretly into the bosom creep
    Of that same noble prelate well beloved,
    The archbishop.
HOTSPUR. Of York, is it not?
WORCESTER.
    True, who bears hard   270
    His brother's death at Bristol, the Lord Scroop.
    I speak not this in estimation,
    As what I think might be, but what I know
    Is ruminated, plotted, and set down,
    And only stays but to behold the face   275
    Of that occasion that shall bring it on.
HOTSPUR. I smell it. Upon my life it will do well.
NORTHUMBERLAND.
    Before the game's afoot thou still let'st slip.

---

251 **candy** sugary-sweet (often associated with fawning dogs, as in l. 252)   253 **Look when** whenever   255 **cozeners** (1) cheats (2) w. pun on "cousin"   260 **Deliver . . . up** free   262 **powers** troops   266 **into . . . creep** gain the trust   271 **Lord Scroop** (executed for treason in 1399, he was actually the archbishop's cousin. Shakespeare follows Holinshed's mistake)   276 **occasion** opportunity   278 **thou . . . slip** you always let the

HOTSPUR.   Why, it cannot choose but be a noble plot,
          And then the power of Scotland, and of York,   280
          To join with Mortimer, ha.
WORCESTER.   And so they shall.
HOTSPUR.   In faith it is exceedingly well aimed.
WORCESTER.
          And 'tis no little reason bids us speed,
          To save our heads by raising of a head,
          For bear ourselves as even as we can,   285
          The king will always think him in our debt,
          And think we think ourselves unsatisfied,
          Till he hath found a time to pay us home.
          And see already how he doth begin
          To make us strangers to his looks of love.   290
HOTSPUR.   He does, he does, we'll be revenged on him.
WORCESTER.
          Cousin farewell. No further go in this,
          Than I by letters shall direct your course.
          When time is ripe, which will be suddenly,
          I'll steal to Glendower and Lord Mortimer,   295
          Where you and Douglas, and our powers at once,
          As I will fashion it, shall happily meet,
          To bear our fortunes in our own strong arms,
          Which now we hold at much uncertainty.
NORTHUMBERLAND.
          Farewell good brother, we shall thrive I trust.   300
HOTSPUR.   Uncle adieu: O let the hours be short,
          Till fields, and blows, and groans, applaud our sport.

                                           Exeunt.

Act Two

[SCENE I.]

Enter a CARRIER *with a lantern in his hand.*

I. CARRIER.

          Heigh-ho. An it be not four by the day, I'll be hanged.
          Charles' wain is over the new chimney, and yet our horse

---

hounds loose (fr. hunting)   282 **aimed** planned   284 **a head** an army   285 **even**
prudently   288 **home** in full   294 **suddenly** at once   296 **at once** all together
    II, i An inn-yard at Rochester s.d. **Carrier** transporter of merchandise and produce   1
Heigh-ho (a yawn)   2 **Charles' wain** big dipper, Great Bear

not packed. What, ostler!

OSTLER.   [*Within.*] Anon, anon.

1. CARRIER.

I prithee Tom, beat Cut's saddle, put a few flocks in the   5
point: poor jade is wrung in the withers, out of all cess.

Enter another CARRIER.

2. CARRIER.

Peas and beans are as dank here as a dog, and that is the
next way to give poor jades the bots: this house is turned
upside down since Robin Ostler died.

1. CARRIER.

Poor fellow never joyed since the price of oats rose, it was   10
the death of him.

2. CARRIER.

I think this be the most villainous house in all London road
for fleas: I am stung like a tench.

1. CARRIER.

Like a tench? By the mass, there is ne'er a king christen
could be better bit than I have been since the first cock.   15

2. CARRIER.

Why, they will allow us ne'er a jordan, and then we leak in
your chimney, and your chamber-lye breeds fleas like a
loach.

1. CARRIER.

What, ostler! Come away and be hanged, come away.

2. CARRIER.

I have a gammon of bacon, and two razes of ginger, to be   20
delivered as far as Charing Cross.

1. CARRIER.

God's body, the turkeys in my pannier are quite starved.
What, ostler? A plague on thee, hast thou never an eye in
thy head? Canst not hear? And 'twere not as good deed as
drink to break the pate on thee, I am a very villain. Come   25
and be hanged, hast no faith in thee?

Enter GADSHILL.

---

3 **ostler** stableboy   5 **Cut**
name for workhorse with a cropped tail   5-6 **put . . . point** put some wool into the head of
the saddle   6 **jade** nag   **wrung** chafed   **withers** shoulders   **out of all cess** to
excess   7 **dank** damp   8 **next** surest   **bots** worms   13 **tench** fish with spots that
looked like vermin bites   14 **king christen** Christian king   16 **jordan** chamber pot   17
chimney fireplace   **chamber-lye** urine   18 **loach** fish supposed to breed fleas   19 **away**
i.e. from where you are   20 **razes** roots   21 **Charing Cross** then a village outside
London   22 **pannier** larger wicker basket   25 **pate** head   26 **faith**

GADSHILL. Good morrow carriers, what's o'clock?

1. CARRIER.

    I think it be two o'clock.

GADSHILL. I prithee lend me thy lantern, to see my gelding in the
    stable.   30

1. CARRIER.

    Nay by God, soft, I know a trick worth two of that, i'
    faith.

GADSHILL. I pray thee lend me thine.

2. CARRIER.

    Ay, when, canst tell? Lend me thy lantern, quoth he.
    Marry I'll see thee hanged first.   35

GADSHILL. Sirrah carrier, what time do you mean to come to Lon-
    don?

2. CARRIER.

    Time enough to go to bed with a candle, I warrant thee.
    Come neighbour Mugs, we'll call up the gentlemen, they
    will along with company, for they have great charge.   40

Exeunt [CARRIERS].

Enter CHAMBERLAIN.

GADSHILL. What ho, chamberlain?

CHAMBERLAIN.

    At hand, quoth pickpurse.

GADSHILL. That's even as fair as 'at hand, quoth the chamberlain:' for
    thou variest no more from picking of purses, than giving
    direction doth from labouring: thou layest the plot how.   45

CHAMBERLAIN.

    Good morrow Master Gadshill, it holds current that I told
    you yesternight. There's a franklin in the wild of Kent
    hath brought three hundred marks with him in gold: I
    heard him tell it to one of his company last night at supper;
    a kind of auditor, one that hath abundance of charge too,   50
    God knows what. They are up already, and call for eggs
    and butter, they will away presently.

GADSHILL. Sirrah, if they meet not with Saint Nicholas' clerks, I'll

---

trustworthiness   40,50 **charge** money, luggage   40 **s.d. Chamberlain** inn-servant, in
charge of bedrooms   43 **fair** apt   43-5 **for thou . . . labouring** (chamberlains had the
reputation of being in league, as this one is, with highwaymen)   46 **holds current** is still
valid   47 **franklin** wealthy landowner   **wild** weald, forest   48 **three hundred marks**
£200 (a mark=13s. 4d).   53 **St. Nicholas' clerks** highwaymen, whose patron saint pro-
tected children, travelers, wandering scholars (clerks), and thence perhaps vagabonds and
highwaymen

give thee this neck.

CHAMBERLAIN.

No, I'll none of it, I pray thee keep that for the hangman,   55
for I know thou worshippest Saint Nicholas as truly as a
man of falsehood may.

GADSHILL. What talkest thou to me of the hangman? If I hang, I'll
make a fat pair of gallows: for if I hang, old Sir John hangs
with me, and thou knowest he is no starveling. Tut, there   60
are other Trojans that thou dream'st not of, the which for
sport sake are content to do the profession some grace, that
would (if matters should be looked into) for their own
credit sake make all whole. I am joined with no foot
land-rakers, no long-staff sixpenny strikers, none of these   65
mad mustachio purple-hued malt-worms; but with nobility and tranquillity, burgomasters and great oneyers, such
as can hold in, such as will strike sooner than speak, and
speak sooner than drink, and drink sooner than pray: and
yet, zounds, I lie, for they pray continually to their saint   70
the commonwealth, or rather not pray to her, but prey on
her, for they ride up and down on her, and make her their
boots.

CHAMBERLAIN.

What, the commonwealth their boots? Will she hold out
water in foul way?   75

GADSHILL. She will, she will, justice hath liquored her: we steal as in a
castle, cock-sure: we have the receipt of fern-seed, we
walk invisible.

CHAMBERLAIN.

Nay by my faith, I think you are more beholding to the
night than to fern-seed, for your walking invisible.   80

GADSHILL. Give me thy hand, thou shalt have a share in our purchase
as I am a true man.

CHAMBERLAIN.

Nay rather let me have it, as you are a false thief.

GADSHILL. Go to, *homo* is a common name to all men: bid the ostler
bring my gelding out of the stable. Farewell, you muddy   85
knave.

Exeunt.

---

61 **Trojans** sporting fellows   62 **profession** i.e. of highwayman   64
whole right   65 **land-rakers** vagabonds   **long-. . . strikers** low-class thieves armed with
poles   66 **malt-worms** drunkards   67 **oneyers** ones   68 **hold in** (1) keep a secret (2) stick
together (3) stick to the quarry (fr. hunting)   **speak** hold up, rob   73 **boots** booty (the
reply interprets as "shoes")   75 **in foul way** on a muddy road   76 **liquored** (1) greased to
keep out water (2) made intoxicated (3) bribed   76 **as in a castle** (without danger)   77

[SCENE II.]

Enter PRINCE, POINS, *and* PETO.

POINS.   Come shelter, shelter, I have removed Falstaff's horse,
            and he frets like a gummed velvet.
PRINCE.   Stand close.

Enter FALSTAFF.

FALSTAFF.   Poins! Poins, and be hanged. Poins!
PRINCE.   Peace, ye fat-kidneyed rascal, what a brawling dost thou   5
            keep.
FALSTAFF.   Where's Poins, Hal?
PRINCE.   He is walked up to the top of the hill, I'll go seek him.

                                                    [*Withdraws.*]

FALSTAFF.   I am accursed to rob in that thief's company: the rascal
            hath removed my horse, and tied him I know not where: if   10
            I travel but four foot by the squire further afoot, I shall
            break my wind. Well, I doubt not but to die a fair death for
            all this, if I 'scape hanging for killing that rogue. I have
            forsworn his company hourly any time this two and
            twenty years, and yet I am bewitched with the rogue's   15
            company. If the rascal have not given me medicines to
            make me love him, I'll be hanged. It could not be else, I
            have drunk medicines. Poins! Hal! a plague upon you
            both. Bardolph! Peto! I'll starve ere I'll rob a foot further.
            And 'twere not as good a deed as drink to turn true man,   20
            and to leave these rogues, I am the veriest varlet that ever
            chewed with a tooth. Eight yards of uneven ground is
            threescore and ten miles afoot with me, and the stony-
            hearted villains know it well enough. A plague upon it
            when thieves can not be true one to another. *They whistle.* 25
            Whew: a plague upon you all, give me my horse you
            rogues, give me my horse and be hanged.
PRINCE.   [*Coming forward.*] Peace ye fat guts, lie down, lay thine ear
            close to the ground, and list if thou canst hear the tread of
            travellers.   30

---

receipt of fern-seed formula for finding fern-seed (believed to make the wearer
invisible)   81 **purchase** stolen goods (thieves' jargon)   84 **homo** Latin for "man" (which
he is entitled to call himself)   85 **muddy** dull-witted
    II, ii Gadshill   2 **frets . . . velvet** chafes, as cheap gummed velvet frays (frets)   3 **close**
hidden   11 **squire** square, measure   16 **medicines** love potions   20 **true** honest   26
Whew (Falstaff's unsuccessful attempt to whistle back)

FALSTAFF. Have you any levers to lift me up again, being down?
'Sblood, I'll not bear mine own flesh so far afoot again for
all the coin in thy father's exchequer. What a plague mean
ye to colt me thus?

PRINCE. Thou liest, thou art not colted, thou art uncolted.   35

FALSTAFF. I prithee good prince, Hal, help me to my horse, good
king's son.

PRINCE. Out ye rogue, shall I be your ostler?

FALSTAFF. Hang thyself in thine own heir-apparent garters. If I be
ta'en, I'll peach for this: and I have not ballads made on   40
you all, and sung to filthy tunes, let a cup of sack be my
poison: when a jest is so forward, and afoot too, I hate it.

Enter GADSHILL [*and* BARDOLPH].

GADSHILL. Stand!

FALSTAFF. So I do, against my will.

POINS. O 'tis our setter, I know his voice: Bardolph, what news?   45

BARDOLPH. Case ye, case ye, on with your vizards, there's money of
the king's coming down the hill, 'tis going to the king's
exchequer.

FALSTAFF. You lie ye rogue, 'tis going to the king's tavern.

GADSHILL. There's enough to make us all.   50

FALSTAFF. To be hanged.

PRINCE. Sirs you four shall front them in the narrow lane: Ned
Poins and I will walk lower; if they 'scape from your
encounter, then they light on us.

PETO. How many be there of them?   55

GADSHILL. Some eight or ten.

FALSTAFF. 'Zounds, will they not rob us?

PRINCE. What, a coward, Sir John Paunch?

FALSTAFF. Indeed I am not John of Gaunt your grandfather, but yet
no coward, Hal.   60

PRINCE. Well, we leave that to the proof.

POINS. Sirrah Jack, thy horse stands behind the hedge: when thou
needst him, there thou shalt find him: farewell, and stand
fast.

FALSTAFF. Now can not I strike him if I should be hanged.   65

PRINCE. [*Aside to Poins.*] Ned, where are our disguises?

POINS. [*Aside to Prince.*] Here, hard by, stand close.

---

34 **colt** trick   35 **uncolted**
unhorsed   40 **peach** turn informer   **ballads** (which treated memorable or notorious
events)   42 **so forward** goes so far   45 **setter** informant (thieves' jargon)   46 **Case ye**
mask yourselves   48 **exchequer** (as in *Famous Victories*)   50 **make** i.e. rich   61 **proof**
test   67 **close** hidden

[Prince and Poins withdraw.]

FALSTAFF. Now my masters, happy man be his dole, say I: every
man to his business.

Enter the TRAVELLERS.

1. TRAVELLER.
Come neighbour, the boy shall lead our horses down the   70
hill: we'll walk afoot awhile and ease our legs.

THIEVES. Stand!

TRAVELLERS.
Jesus bless us.

FALSTAFF. Strike, down with them, cut the villains' throats; ah
whoreson caterpillars, bacon-fed knaves, they hate us   75
youth, down with them, fleece them.

TRAVELLERS.
O we are undone, both we and ours for ever.

FALSTAFF.
Hang ye gorbellied knaves, are ye undone? No, ye fat
chuffs, I would your store were here: on bacons, on, what,
ye knaves, young men must live: you are grand-jurors, are   80
ye? We'll jure ye, faith.

Here they rob them and bind them. Exeunt.

Enter the PRINCE *and* POINS.

PRINCE. The thieves have bound the true men: now could thou and
I rob the thieves, and go merrily to London, it would be
argument for a week, laughter for a month, and a good jest
for ever.   85

POINS. Stand close, I hear them coming.

Enter the thieves again.

FALSTAFF. Come my masters, let us share and then to horse before
day: and the Prince and Poins be not two arrant cowards
there's no equity stirring. There's no more valour in that
Poins, than in a wild duck.   90

PRINCE. Your money!

POINS. Villains!

As they are sharing, the Prince and Poins set upon them.

---

68 **happy . . . dole** may happiness be each one's portion   77
undone ruined   78 **gorbellied** fat-bellied   79 **chuffs** misers   **your store** all your
property   **bacons** fatties   80 **grand-jurors** men of wealth (a requirement for becoming a
grand juror)   82 **true** honest   84 **argument** subject matter   89 **equity stirring**

They all run away, and Falstaff after a blow or two runs
away too, leaving the booty behind them.

PRINCE.   Got with much ease. Now merrily to horse:
The thieves are all scattered and possessed with fear
So strongly, that they dare not meet each other: 95
Each takes his fellow for an officer.
Away good Ned, Falstaff sweats to death,
And lards the lean earth as he walks along:
Were't not for laughing I should pity him.

POINS.   How the fat rogue roared.   *Exeunt.*

[SCENE III.]

Enter HOTSPUR *solus, reading a letter.*

HOTSPUR. 'But for mine own part, my lord, I could be well contented to be there, in respect of the love I bear your house.'

He could be contented: why is he not then? In the respect
of the love he bears our house: he shows in this, he loves
his own barn better than he loves our house. Let me see   5
some more.

[*Reads.*]
'The purpose you undertake is dangerous—'

Why that's certain, 'tis dangerous to take a cold, to sleep,
to drink, but I tell you, my lord fool, out of this nettle
danger, we pluck this flower safety.   10

[*Reads.*]
'The purpose you undertake is dangerous, the friends you
have named uncertain, the time itself unsorted, and your
whole plot too light, for the counterpoise of so great an
opposition.'

Say you so, say you so: I say unto you again, you are a   15
shallow cowardly hind and you lie: what a lack-brain is

judgment extant   98 **lards** (sweat was thought to be melted body fat)
    II, iii Warkworth Castle, Northumberland   2 **house** family   12 **unsorted**
ill-chosen   16 **hind** slave   19 **expectation** promise

this. By the Lord our plot is a good plot as ever was laid,
our friends true and constant: a good plot, good friends,
and full of expectation: an excellent plot, very good
friends; what a frosty-spirited rogue is this. Why, my lord   20
of York commends the plot, and the general course of the
action. 'Zounds, and I were now by this rascal I could
brain him with his lady's fan. Is there not my father, my
uncle, and myself; Lord Edmund Mortimer, my lord of
York, and Owen Glendower? Is there not besides the   25
Douglas? Have I not all their letters to meet me in arms by
the ninth of the next month, and are they not some of them
set forward already? What a pagan rascal is this, an in-
fidel. Ha, you shall see now in very sincerity of fear and
cold heart, will he to the king, and lay open all our   30
proceedings. O, I could divide myself, and go to buffets,
for moving such a dish of skim milk with so honourable an
action. Hang him, let him tell the king, we are prepared: I
will set forward tonight.

Enter his LADY.

How now Kate, I must leave you within these two hours.   35

LADY PERCY.

O my good lord, why are you thus alone?
For what offence have I this fortnight been
A banished woman from my Harry's bed?
Tell me sweet lord, what is't that takes from thee
Thy stomach, pleasure, and thy golden sleep?   40
Why dost thou bend thine eyes upon the earth,
And start so often when thou sit'st alone?
Why hast thou lost the fresh blood in thy cheeks,
And given my treasures and my rights of thee
To thick-eyed musing, and curst melancholy?   45
In thy faint slumbers I by thee have watched,
And heard thee murmur tales of iron wars,
Speak terms of manage to thy bounding steed,
Cry courage to the field. And thou hast talked
Of sallies and retires, of trenches, tents,   50
Of palisadoes, frontiers, parapets,

28 **pagan** unbelieving   31 **divide
... buffets** divide myself in two and let the halves fight eachother   40 **stomach**
appetite   44 **rights** (perhaps "rites," in the sense of "amorous rites" as in *R&J*, III, ii, 8;
spellings were interchangeable)   45 **thick-eyed** dull-eyed   **curst** bad-tempered   46
watched stayed awake   48 **manage** horsemanship   51 **palisadoes** stakes hammered into
the ground as defenses   **frontiers** outlying parts of a fort

Of basilisks, of cannon, culverin,
Of prisoners' ransom, and of soldiers slain,
And all the currents of a heady fight.
Thy spirit within thee hath been so at war,   55
And thus hath so bestirred thee in thy sleep,
That beads of sweat have stood upon thy brow
Like bubbles in a late-disturbèd stream;
And in thy face strange motions have appeared,
Such as we see when men restrain their breath,   60
On some great sudden hest. O what portènts are these?
Some heavy business hath my lord in hand,
And I must know it, else he loves me not.

HOTSPUR.   What ho! [*Enter* SERVANT.] Is Gilliams with the
                packet gone?
SERVANT.   He is my lord, an hour ago.   65
HOTSPUR.   Hath Butler brought those horses from the sheriff?
SERVANT.   One horse my lord he brought even now.
HOTSPUR.   What horse? A roan, a crop-ear is it not?
SERVANT.   It is my lord.
HOTSPUR.   That roan shall be my throne.
            Well, I will back him straight. O Esperance!   70
            Bid Butler lead him forth into the park.

                                            [*Exit* SERVANT.]

LADY PERCY.
            But hear you my lord.
HOTSPUR.   What sayst thou my lady?
LADY PERCY.
            What is it carries you away?
HOTSPUR.   Why, my horse, my love, my horse.   75
LADY PERCY.
            Out, you mad-headed ape,
            A weasel hath not such a deal of spleen
            As you are tossed with. In faith
            I'll know your business Harry, that I will.
            I fear my brother Mortimer doth stir   80
            About his title, and hath sent for you
            To line his enterprise, but if you go—

---

52 **basilisks . . . culverin** the
heaviest,   medium,   and   smallest   cannons   54 **currents** occurrences   **heady**
headlong   61 **hest** behest, command   70 **Esperance** (motto of the Percy family: "Esperance ma comforte")   77 **spleen** irritability (associated with weasels)   82 **line** support,
strengthen

HOTSPUR.   So far afoot, I shall be weary, love.

LADY PERCY.

         Come, come you paraquito, answer me

         Directly unto this question that I ask.   85

         In faith I'll break thy little finger Harry,

         And if thou wilt not tell me all things true.

HOTSPUR.   Away,

         Away you trifler: love, I love thee not,

         I care not for thee Kate, this is no world   90

         To play with mammets, and to tilt with lips,

         We must have bloody noses, and cracked crowns,

         And pass them current too: God's me, my horse.

         What sayst thou Kate? What wouldst thou have with me?

LADY PERCY.

         Do you not love me? do you not indeed?   95

         Well, do not then, for since you love me not,

         I will not love myself. Do you not love me?

         Nay tell me if you speak in jest 'or no.

HOTSPUR.   Come, wilt thou see me ride?

         And when I am a-horseback I will swear   100

         I love thee infinitely. But hark you Kate,

         I must not have you henceforth question me

         Whither I go, nor reason whereabout.

         Whither I must, I must: and to conclude,

         This evening must I leave you gentle Kate.   105

         I know you wise, but yet no farther wise

         Than Harry Percy's wife: constant you are,

         But yet a woman, and for secrecy

         No lady closer, for I well believe

         Thou wilt not utter what thou dost not know,   110

         And so far will I trust thee gentle Kate.

LADY PERCY.

         How, so far?

HOTSPUR.   Not an inch further. But hark you Kate,

         Whither I go, thither shall you go too:

         Today will I set forth, tomorrow you,   115

         Will this content you Kate?

LADY PERCY.

                     It must of force.   *Exeunt.*

---

     91 **play with mammets** dally amorously   **tilt with lips** kiss   92 **crowns** (1)
heads (2) currency which could not "pass current" (as legal tender) if cracked   93 **God's me**
God save me   110 **wilt . . . know** (proverbial)   116 **force** necessity

SCENE IV.

Enter PRINCE *and* POINS.

PRINCE.   Ned, prithee come out of that fat room, and lend me thy
           hand to laugh a little.

POINS.   Where hast been Hal?

PRINCE.   With three or four loggerheads, amongst three or four
           score hogsheads. I have sounded the very base-string of   5
           humility. Sirrah, I am sworn brother to a leash of draw-
           ers, and can call them all by their christen names, as Tom,
           Dick, and Francis. They take it already upon their salva-
           tion, that though I be but Prince of Wales, yet I am the
           king of courtesy, and tell me flatly I am no proud Jack like 10
           Falstaff, but a Corinthian, a lad of mettle, a good boy (by
           the Lord so they call me) and when I am King of England I
           shall command all the good lads in Eastcheap. They call
           drinking deep 'dyeing scarlet,' and when you breathe in
           your watering they cry 'hem!' and bid you play it off. To   15
           conclude, I am so good a proficient in one quarter of an
           hour that I can drink with any tinker in his own language,
           during my life. I tell thee Ned thou hast lost much hon-
           our, that thou wert not with me in this action; but sweet
           Ned, to sweeten which name of Ned, I give thee this   20
           pennyworth of sugar, clapped even now into my hand by
           an underskinker, one that never spake other English in his
           life than 'Eight shillings and six-pence,' and 'You are
           welcome,' with this shrill addition, 'Anon, anon sir; score
           a pint of bastard in the Half-moon,' or so. But Ned, to   25
           drive away the time till Falstaff come, I prithee do thou
           stand in some by-room, while I question my puny drawer
           to what end he gave me the sugar, and do thou never leave
           calling 'Francis!' that his tale to me may be nothing but
           'Anon.' Step aside and I'll show thee a precedent.   30

POINS.   Francis!

PRINCE.   Thou art perfect.

POINS.   Francis!   [*Exit* POINS.]

II, iv The Boar's Head Tavern, Eastcheap, London,   1 **fat** (1) vat (2) stuffy   4
loggerheads blockheads   6 **drawers** tapsters   10 **Jack** fellow (with reference to Falstaff's
Christian name)   11 **Corinthian** good sport   **mettle** spirit   14-15 **breathe . . . water-
ing** pause for breath when drinking   15 **play it off** drink it down   22 **underskinker**
assistant tapster   24 **Anon** right away   **score** chalk up   25 **Half-moon** name of a room
in the tavern   27 **puny** inexperienced   30 **precedent** example   34 **Pomgarnet**

Enter DRAWER [FRANCIS].

FRANCIS.   Anon, anon sir. Look down into the Pomgarnet, Ralph.

PRINCE.   Come hither Francis.   35

FRANCIS.   My lord.

PRINCE.   How long hast thou to serve, Francis?

FRANCIS.   Forsooth, five years, and as much as to—

POINS.   [*Within.*] Francis!

FRANCIS.   Anon, anon sir.   40

PRINCE.   Five years, by'r lady a long lease for the clinking of pew-
           ter; but Francis, darest thou be so valiant, as to play the
           coward with thy indenture, and show it a fair pair of heels,
           and run from it?

FRANCIS.   O Lord sir, I'll be sworn upon all the books in England, I 45
           could find in my heart—

POINS.   [*Within.*] Francis!

FRANCIS.   Anon sir.

PRINCE.   How old art thou Francis?

FRANCIS.   Let me see, about Michaelmas next I shall be—   50

POINS.   [*Within.*] Francis!

FRANCIS.   Anon sir, pray stay a little my lord.

PRINCE.   Nay but hark you Francis, for the sugar thou gavest me,
           'twas a pennyworth, was't not?

FRANCIS.   O Lord, I would it had been two.   55

PRINCE.   I will give thee for it a thousand pound: ask me when thou
           wilt, and thou shalt have it.

POINS.   [*Within.*] Francis!

FRANCIS.   Anon, anon.

PRINCE.   Anon Francis? No Francis, but tomorrow Francis; or   60
           Francis o' Thursday; or indeed Francis when thou wilt.
           But Francis.

FRANCIS.   My lord?

PRINCE.   Wilt thou rob this leathern-jerkin, crystal-button, not-
           pated, agate-ring, puke-stocking, caddis-garter, smooth- 65
           tongue, Spanish pouch?

FRANCIS.   O Lord sir, who do you mean?

PRINCE.   Why then your brown bastard is your only drink, for look

---

Pomegranate (another tavern room)   37 **to serve** i.e. as an apprentice (the full term was
seven years)   43 **indenture** contract of apprenticeship   45 **books** Bibles or prayer
books   64–6 **Wilt . . . pouch** (he describes the characteristic appearance of an
innkeeper)   64–5 **not-pated** short-haired   65 **agate-ring** wearing a seal ring with a carved
agate   **puke-stocking** wearing dark heavy woolen stockings   **caddis-garter**
worsted-gartered   66 **Spanish pouch** with a pouch of Spanish leather, as worn by
innkeepers   68–70 **brown bastard . . . much** (nonsense patter by the prince to confuse
Francis)

you Francis, your white canvas doublet will sully. In
Barbary sir, it cannot come to so much.   70

FRANCIS.   What sir?

POINS.   [*Within.*] Francis!

PRINCE.   Away you rogue, dost thou not hear them call?

> *Here they both call him; the Drawer stands
> amazed, not knowing which way to go.*

Enter VINTNER.

VINTNER.   What, stand'st thou still and hear'st such a calling? Look to
the guests within.   75

> [*Exit* FRANCIS.]

My lord, old Sir John with half a dozen more are at the
door: shall I let them in?

PRINCE.   Let them alone awhile, and then open the door. [*Exit*
VINTNER.] Poins!

POINS.   [*Within.*] Anon, anon sir.   80

Enter POINS.

PRINCE.   Sirrah, Falstaff and the rest of the thieves are at the door,
shall we be merry?

POINS.   As merry as crickets my lad, but hark ye, what cunning
match have you made with this jest of the drawer? Come,
what's the issue?   85

PRINCE.   I am now of all humours that have showed themselves
humours since the old days of goodman Adam, to the
pupil age of this present twelve o'clock at midnight.
> [*Enter* FRANCIS.]

What's o'clock, Francis?

FRANCIS.   Anon, anon sir.   [*Exit.*]   90

PRINCE.   That ever this fellow should have fewer words than a
parrot, and yet the son of a woman. His industry is
upstairs and downstairs, his eloquence the parcel of a
reckoning. I am not yet of Percy's mind, the Hotspur of
the North, he that kills me some six or seven dozen of   95

---

84 **match** game   86–7 **of all humours . . . Adam** I am now in the mood to
indulge in all the whims that man has had since Adam   88 **pupil age** youth   93-4 **parcel
. . . reckoning** items on a bill   97 **work** a really good fight   99 **a drench** bran and
water   102 **Rivo** expression used in drinking bouts (possibly fr. Spanish *arriba*, "up"
[drink up])   107 **nether-stocks** stockings   110-12 **Titan . . . sun's** the sun (Titan) kissing
the butter and melting it is like Falstaff's full red face looking over the melted butter of his

Scots at a breakfast, washes his hands, and says to his
wife, 'Fie upon this quiet life, I want work.' 'O my sweet
Harry,' says she, 'how many hast thou killed today?' 'Give
my roan horse a drench,' says he, and answers, 'Some
fourteen,' an hour after: 'a trifle, a trifle.' I prithee call in 100
Falstaff: I'll play Percy, and that damned brawn shall play
Dame Mortimer his wife. 'Rivo!' says the drunkard. Call
in Ribs, call in Tallow.

Enter FALSTAFF, [BARDOLPH, PETO, *and*
GADSHILL. FRANCIS *follows with drink*].

POINS.   Welcome Jack, where hast thou been?
FALSTAFF.   A plague of all cowards I say, and a vengeance too, marry 105
and amen: give me a cup of sack, boy. Ere I lead this life
long, I'll sew nether-stocks and mend them, and foot them
too. A plague of all cowards. Give me a cup of sack, rogue:
is there no virtue extant?

He drinketh.

PRINCE.   Didst thou never see Titan kiss a dish of 110
butter—pitiful-hearted Titan—that melted at the sweet
tale of the sun's? If thou didst, then behold that com-
pound.
FALSTAFF.   You rogue, here's lime in this sack too: there is nothing but
roguery to be found in villainous man, yet a coward is 115
worse than a cup of sack with lime in it. A villainous
coward. Go thy ways old Jack, die when thou wilt: if
manhood, good manhood, be not forgot upon the face of
the earth, then am I a shotten herring: there lives not three
good men unhanged in England, and one of them is fat, 120
and grows old. God help the while, a bad world I say. I
would I were a weaver, I could sing psalms, or anything.
A plague of all cowards I say still.
PRINCE.   How now wool-sack, what mutter you?
FALSTAFF.   A king's son? If I do not beat thee out of thy kingdom with 125
a dagger of lath, and drive all thy subjects afore thee like a
flock of wild geese, I'll never wear hair on my face more.
You Prince of Wales?
PRINCE.   Why you whoreson round man, what's the matter?

perspiring body   114 **lime** (used to make wine dry and sparkling)   119 **shotten** thin,
because it has just spawned   122 **weaver** (weavers traditionally sang at their work; many
were Puritans who sang psalms)   126 **dagger of lath** wooden sword (weapon used by the
Vice, character in morality plays, to strike others)

FALSTAFF. Are not you a coward? Answer me to that, and Poins 130
there.

POINS. 'Zounds ye fat paunch, and ye call me coward, by the
Lord I'll stab thee.

FALSTAFF. I call thee coward? I'll see thee damned ere I call thee
coward, but I would give a thousand pound I could run as 135
fast as thou canst. You are straight enough in the shoulders, you care not who sees your back: call you that
backing of your friends? A plague upon such backing, give
me them that will face me. Give me a cup of sack. I am a
rogue if I drunk today.   140

PRINCE. O villain, thy lips are scarce wiped since thou drunk'st
last.

FALSTAFF. All is one for that. (He drinketh.) A plague of all cowards
still say I.

PRINCE. What's the matter?   145

FALSTAFF. What's the matter? there be four of us here have ta'en a
thousand pound this day morning.

PRINCE. Where is it Jack? where is it?

FALSTAFF. Where is it? Taken from us it is: a hundred upon poor four
of us.   150

PRINCE. What, a hundred, man?

FALSTAFF. I am a rogue if I were not at half-sword with a dozen of
them two hours together. I have 'scaped by miracle. I am
eight times thrust through the doublet, four through the
hose, my buckler cut through and through, my sword 155
hacked like a handsaw, *ecce signum*. I never dealt better
since I was a man: all would not do. A plague of all
cowards: let them speak; if they speak more or less than
truth, they are villains, and the sons of darkness.

PRINCE. Speak sirs, how was it?   160

GADSHILL. We four set upon some dozen—

FALSTAFF. Sixteen at least my lord.

GADSHILL. And bound them.

PETO. No, no, they were not bound.

FALSTAFF. You rogue, they were bound, every man of them, or I am a 165
Jew else: an Ebrew Jew.

GADSHILL. As we were sharing, some six or seven fresh men set upon
us—

---

152 **half-sword** (in the sense of "close
quarters")   154 **doublet** jacket   155 **hose** breeches   **buckler** small shield   156 **ecce
signum** behold the sign   157 **do** i.e. so

FALSTAFF.	And unbound the rest, and then come in the other.	
PRINCE.	What, fought you with them all?	170
FALSTAFF.	All? I know not what you call all, but if I fought not with fifty of them, I am a bunch of radish: if there were not two or three and fifty upon poor old Jack, then am I no two-legged creature.	
PRINCE.	Pray God you have not murdered some of them.	175
FALSTAFF.	Nay, that's past praying for, I have peppered two of them. Two I am sure I have paid, two rogues in buckram suits: I tell thee what Hal, if I tell thee a lie, spit in my face, call me horse: thou knowest my old ward: here I lay, and thus I bore my point; four rogues in buckram let drive at me—	180
PRINCE.	What, four? Thou saidst but two even now.	
FALSTAFF.	Four Hal, I told thee four.	
POINS.	Ay, ay, he said four.	
FALSTAFF.	These four came all a-front, and mainly thrust at me; I made me no more ado, but took all their seven points in my target, thus.	185
PRINCE.	Seven? Why, there were but four even now.	
FALSTAFF.	In buckram?	
POINS.	Ay, four in buckram suits.	
FALSTAFF.	Seven, by these hilts, or I am a villain else.	190
PRINCE.	Prithee let him alone, we shall have more anon.	
FALSTAFF.	Dost thou hear me Hal?	
PRINCE.	Ay, and mark thee too, Jack.	
FALSTAFF.	Do so, for it is worth the listening to: these nine in buckram that I told thee of—	195
PRINCE.	So, two more already.	
FALSTAFF.	Their points being broken—	
POINS.	Down fell their hose.	
FALSTAFF.	Began to give me ground: but I followed me close, came in, foot and hand, and with a thought, seven of the eleven I paid.	200
PRINCE.	O monstrous! Eleven buckram men grown out of two.	
FALSTAFF.	But as the devil would have it, three misbegotten knaves in Kendal green came at my back, and let drive at me, for it was so dark Hal, that thou couldst not see thy hand.	205
PRINCE.	These lies are like their father that begets them, gross as a	

---

177 **paid** killed (paid in full)   179 **ward** posture of defense (fr. fencing)   180 **bore my point** pointed my sword   185 **points** (1) i.e. of swords (2) laces that fastened the hose to the doublet, as interpreted in l. 197   206 **gross** obvious

mountain, open, palpable. Why thou clay-brained guts, thou knotty-pated fool, thou whoreson obscene greasy tallow-catch—

FALSTAFF.   What, art thou mad? art thou mad? Is not the truth the 210 truth?

PRINCE.   Why, how couldst thou know these men in Kendal green when it was so dark thou couldst not see thy hand? Come tell us your reason. What sayest thou to this?

POINS.   Come, your reason Jack, your reason.   215

FALSTAFF.   What, upon compulsion? 'Zounds, and I were at the strappado, or all the racks in the world, I would not tell you on compulsion. Give you a reason on compulsion? If reasons were as plentiful as blackberries, I would give no man a reason upon compulsion, I.   220

PRINCE.   I'll be no longer guilty of this sin. This sanguine coward, this bed-presser, this horse-back-breaker, this huge hill of flesh—

FALSTAFF.   'Sblood, you starveling, you elf-skin, you dried neat's-tongue, you bull's pizzle, you stockfish: O for 225 breath to utter what is like thee: you tailor's yard, you sheath, you bow-case, you vile standing tuck—

PRINCE.   Well, breathe awhile, and then to it again, and when thou hast tired thyself in base comparisons, hear me speak but this.   230

POINS.   Mark, Jack.

PRINCE.   We two saw you four set on four, and bound them and were masters of their wealth: mark now how a plain tale shall put you down. Then did we two set on you four, and with a word, outfaced you from your prize, and have it, 235 yea and can show it you here in the house: and Falstaff, you carried your guts away as nimbly, with as quick dexterity, and roared for mercy and still run and roared, as ever I heard bull-calf. What a slave art thou to hack thy sword as thou hast done, and then say it was in fight. 240 What trick? what device? what starting-hole canst thou now find out, to hide thee from this open and apparent shame?

---

208 **knotty-pated** wooden-headed   209 **tallow-catch** tub or lump of fat supplied by the butcher to the candlemaker   217 **strappado** (a torture device)   219 **reasons . . . blackberries** (w. pun on similar pronunciation of "reason" and "raisin")   221 **sanguine** ruddy-faced (the exchange of insults was a favorite comic device)   224 **elf-skin** so thin your skin would fit an elf   225 **neat** ox   **stockfish** dried cod   226 **yard** yardstick   227 **bow-case** long holder for musical bows   **standing tuck** small rapier so stiff it stands on end   235 **outfaced** bluffed   241 **starting-hole** hole which shelters a hunted animal   249

POINS.   Come, let's hear, Jack: what trick hast thou now?

FALSTAFF.   By the Lord, I knew ye as well as he that made ye. Why, 245
              hear you my masters, was it for me to kill the heir-
              apparent? Should I turn upon the true prince? Why, thou
              knowest I am as valiant as Hercules: but beware instinct,
              the lion will not touch the true prince: instinct is a great
              matter. I was now a coward on instinct: I shall think the 250
              better of myself, and thee, during my life: I for a valiant
              lion, and thou for a true prince. But by the Lord, lads, I
              am glad you have the money. Hostess, clap to the doors:
              watch tonight, pray tomorrow. Gallants, lads, boys,
              hearts of gold, all the titles of good fellowship come to 255
              you. What, shall we be merry? shall we have a play
              extempore?

PRINCE.   Content, and the argument shall be thy running away.

FALSTAFF.   Ah, no more of that Hal, and thou lovest me.

                         Enter HOSTESS.

HOSTESS.   O Jesu, my lord the prince!   260

PRINCE.   How now my lady the hostess, what say'st thou to me?

HOSTESS.   Marry my lord, there is a nobleman of the court at door
              would speak with you: he says he comes from your father.

PRINCE.   Give him as much as will make him a royal man, and send
              him back again to my mother.   265

FALSTAFF.   What manner of man is he?

HOSTESS.   An old man.

FALSTAFF.   What doth gravity out of his bed at midnight? Shall I give
              him his answer?

PRINCE.   Prithee do Jack.   270

FALSTAFF.   Faith, and I'll send him packing.   *Exit*.

PRINCE.   Now sirs, by'r lady you fought fair, so did you Peto, so
              did you Bardolph: you are lions too, you ran away upon
              instinct, you will not touch the true prince; no, fie.

BARDOLPH.   Faith, I ran when I saw others run.   275

PRINCE.   Tell me now in earnest, how came Falstaff's sword so
              hacked?

PETO.   Why, he hacked it with his dagger, and said he would
              swear truth out of England, but he would make you

---

lion . . . prince (idea traceable to Pliny: the king of the beasts recognized the king of
men)   254 watch . . . tomorrow Matt. XXVI.41; "watch" = (1) stay awake (2)
carouse   256-7 play extempore (a common tavern pastime; cf. 343-442)   264 royal (w.
pun on "noble," I. 62, coin worth 6s. 3 d., and "royal," worth 10s.)

believe it was done in fight, and persuaded us to do the 280
like.

BARDOLPH. Yea, and to tickle our noses with speargrass, to make them
bleed, and then to beslubber our garments with it, and
swear it was the blood of true men. I did that I did not this
seven year before, I blushed to hear his monstrous de- 285
vices.

PRINCE. O villain, thou stolest a cup of sack eighteen years ago and
wert taken with the manner, and ever since thou hast
blushed extempore: thou hadst fire and sword on thy side,
and yet thou ranst away; what instinct hadst thou for it? 290

BARDOLPH. [*Points to his own face.*] My lord, do you see these
meteors? do you behold these exhalations?

PRINCE. I do.

BARDOLPH. What think you they portend?

PRINCE. Hot livers, and cold purses.   295

BARDOLPH. Choler, my lord, if rightly taken.

PRINCE. No, if rightly taken, halter.

Enter FALSTAFF.

Here comes lean Jack, here comes bare-bone. How now
my sweet creature of bombast, how long is't ago Jack since
thou sawest thine own knee?   300

FALSTAFF. My own knee? When I was about thy years, Hal, I was not
an eagle's talon in the waist, I could have crept into any
alderman's thumb-ring: a plague of sighing and grief, it
blows a man up like a bladder. There's villainous news
abroad: here was Sir John Bracy from your father; you 305
must to the court in the morning. That same mad fellow of
the North, Percy, and he of Wales that gave Amamon the
bastinado and made Lucifer cuckold, and swore the devil
his true liegeman upon the cross of a Welsh hook: what a
plague call you him?   310

POINS. O, Glendower.

FALSTAFF. Owen, Owen, the same, and his son-in-law Mortimer,
and old Northumberland, and that sprightly Scot of
Scots, Douglas, that runs a-horseback up a hill perpen-
dicular.   315

282–3 tickle . . .
bleed (from *Famous Victories*, scene 19)   288 the manner (1) stealing (2) drinking   289
blushed extempore had the drunkard's red nose and ruddy face   fire (his red face)   295
Hot . . . purses (two results of habitual drinking; "cold" = empty)   296 Choler excess of
choler, indicating irascibility   rightly taken properly diagnosed   297 rightly taken
justly arrested   halter (w. pun on "choler"—"collar" = halter, hanging)   299 bombast
cotton stuffing   303 thumb-ring (worn by well-to-do citizens)   307 Amamon a
devil   308 bastinado cudgelling   309 liegeman subject   309 Welsh hook pike with a

PRINCE.   He that rides at high speed, and with his pistol kills a
             sparrow flying.
FALSTAFF.   You have hit it.
PRINCE.   So did he never the sparrow.
FALSTAFF.   Well, that rascal hath good mettle in him, he will not run.   320
PRINCE.   Why, what a rascal art thou then, to praise him so for
             running.
FALSTAFF.   A-horseback, ye cuckoo, but afoot he will not budge a
             foot.
PRINCE.   Yes Jack, upon instinct.   325
FALSTAFF.   I grant ye upon instinct: well, he is there too, and one
             Mordake, and a thousand blue-caps more. Worcester is
             stolen away tonight, thy father's beard is turned white
             with the news, you may buy land now as cheap as stinking
             mackerel.   330
PRINCE.   Why then, it is like if there come a hot June, and this civil
             buffeting hold, we shall buy maidenheads as they buy
             hobnails, by the hundreds.
FALSTAFF.   By the mass lad thou sayest true, it is like we shall have
             good trading that way: but tell me Hal, art not thou 335
             horrible afeard? Thou being heir-apparent, could the
             world pick thee out three such enemies again as that fiend
             Douglas, that spirit Percy, and that devil Glendower? Art
             thou not horribly afraid? doth not thy blood thrill at it?
PRINCE.   Not a whit i' faith, I lack some of thy instinct.   340
FALSTAFF.   Well, thou wilt be horribly chid tomorrow when thou
             comest to thy father: if thou love me, practise an answer.
PRINCE.   Do thou stand for my father and examine me upon the
             particulars of my life.
FALSTAFF.   Shall I? content. This chair shall be my state, this dagger 345
             my sceptre, and this cushion my crown.
PRINCE.   Thy state is taken for a joined-stool, thy golden sceptre for
             a leaden dagger, and thy precious rich crown for a pitiful
             bald crown.
FALSTAFF.   Well, and the fire of grace be not quite out of thee, now 350
             shalt thou be moved. Give me a cup of sack to make my
             eyes look red, that it may be thought I have wept, for I
             must speak in passion, and I will do it in King Cambyses
             vein.

hook at the point (hiltless and therefore without a cross)   327 **blue-caps** Scots, who wore
blue bonnets   331–3 **hot June . . . hundreds** between the hot weather and the excitement
of civil war, we can get girls by the hundreds   339 **thrill** shiver   345 **state** throne   347
joined put together carefully by a joiner   353 **King Cambyses' vein** the bombastic, ranting
style of Thomas Preston's *Cambyses* of 1569 (often parodied)

PRINCE.   Well, here is my leg.   355
FALSTAFF. And here is my speech; stand aside nobility.
HOSTESS.   O Jesu, this is excellent sport i' faith.
FALSTAFF. Weep not sweet queen, for trickling tears are vain.
HOSTESS.   O the father, how he holds his countenance.
FALSTAFF. For God's sake lords, convey my tristful queen,   360
           For tears do stop the floodgates of her eyes.
HOSTESS.   O Jesu, he doth it as like one of these harlotry players as
           ever I see.
FALSTAFF. Peace good pintpot, peace good tickle-brain. Harry, I do
           not only marvel where thou spendest thy time, but also   365
           how thou art accompanied. For though the camomile, the
           more it is trodden on, the faster it grows: yet youth, the
           more it is wasted, the sooner it wears. That thou art my
           son, I have partly thy mother's word, partly my own
           opinion, but chiefly a villainous trick of thine eye, and a   370
           foolish hanging of thy nether lip, that doth warrant me. If
           then thou be son to me, here lies the point: why, being son
           to me, art thou so pointed at? Shall the blessed sun of
           heaven prove a micher, and eat blackberries? a question
           not to be asked. Shall the son of England prove a thief, and 375
           take purses? a question to be asked. There is a thing
           Harry, which thou hast often heard of, and it is known to
           many in our land by the name of pitch. This pitch (as
           ancient writers do report) doth defile, so doth the com-
           pany thou keepest: for Harry, now I do not speak to thee   380
           in drink, but in tears; not in pleasure, but in passion: not in
           words only, but in woes also: and yet there is a virtuous
           man, whom I have often noted in thy company, but I
           know not his name.
PRINCE.   What manner of man, and it like your majesty?   385
FALSTAFF. A goodly portly man i' faith, and a corpulent, of a cheerful
           look, a pleasing eye, and a most noble carriage, and as I
           think his age some fifty, or by'r lady inclining to three-
           score, and now I remember me, his name is Falstaff: if that
           man should be lewdly given, he deceiveth me. For Harry   390

---

355 **leg** bow   359 **holds his
countenance** keeps a straight face   364 **tickle-brain** strong liquor   364–82 **Harry . . .
also** (Falstaff adopts the elaborate prose style of Lyly's *Euphues* of 1578, with its balance,
alliteration, unnatural natural history, antithesis, etc., a style Shakespeare uses elsewhere in
prose comedy scenes, as in *MV* and *AYLI*)   366 **camomile** a strong-scented creeping
plant   370 **trick** trait   372 **son** (w. pun on "sun," metaphor for royalty)   373 **pointed at**
i.e. in scorn   374 **micher** truant (often associated with blackberrying)   381 **passion**
sorrow   390 **lewdly given** wickedly inclined

I see virtue in his looks: if then the tree may be known by
the fruit, as the fruit by the tree, then peremptorily I speak
it, there is virtue in that Falstaff: him keep with, the rest
banish. And tell me now thou naughty varlet, tell me
where hast thou been this month?   395

PRINCE.   Dost thou speak like a king? Do thou stand for me, and I'll
play my father.

FALSTAFF.   Depose me? if thou dost it half so gravely, so majestically,
both in word and matter, hang me up by the heels for a
rabbit-sucker, or a poulter's hare.   400

PRINCE.   Well, here I am set.

FALSTAFF.   And here I stand: judge, my masters.

PRINCE.   Now Harry, whence come you?

FALSTAFF.   My noble lord, from Eastcheap.

PRINCE.   The complaints I hear of thee are grievous.   405

FALSTAFF.   'Sblood, my lord, they are false. Nay, I'll tickle ye for a
young prince i' faith.

PRINCE.   Swearest thou, ungracious boy? henceforth ne'er look on
me: thou art violently carried away from grace: there is a
devil haunts thee in the likeness of an old fat man, a tun of 410
man is thy companion: why dost thou converse with that
trunk of humours, that bolting-hutch of beastliness, that
swoln parcel of dropsies, that huge bombard of sack, that
stuffed cloak-bag of guts, that roasted Manningtree ox
with the pudding in his belly, that reverend vice, that grey 415
iniquity, that father ruffian, that vanity in years? Wherein
is he good, but to taste sack and drink it? wherein neat and
cleanly, but to carve a capon and eat it? wherein cunning,
but in craft? wherein crafty, but in villainy? wherein
villainous, but in all things? wherein worthy, but in 420
nothing?

FALSTAFF.   I would your grace would take me with you, whom means
your grace?

PRINCE.   That villainous abominable misleader of youth, Falstaff,

---

392 **peremptorily** conclusively 400
rabbit-sucker suckling rabbit   **poulter's hare** hare hanging in a poultry shop (he enjoys
comparing himself to small, thin things)   406-7 **I'll tickle . . . prince** my impersonation of
a young prince will tickle you   408 **ungracious** graceless   409 **grace** the grace of
God   410 **tun** (1) large barrel (2) ton   412 **trunk of humours** excess of bodily fluids,
causing diseases   **bolting-hutch** bin for bolted (sifted) flour   413 **bombard** big leather
wine container   414 **cloak-bag** large traveling bag   **Manningtree ox** (Manningtree,
Essex, was famous for its oxen roasted whole at celebrations)   415 **pudding**
stuffing   415-6 **vice, iniquity, vanity** personified as characters in morality plays   416
ruffian ruffin, the devil   **in years** in old age (also implied by "reverend," "grey," and
"father")   418 **cunning** skillful   422 **take . . . you** let me follow your meaning

that old white-bearded Satan.   425

FALSTAFF. My lord, the man I know.

PRINCE.   I know thou dost.

FALSTAFF. But to say I know more harm in him than in myself, were
to say more than I know. That he is old, the more the pity,
his white hairs do witness it: but that he is (saving your 430
reverence) a whoremaster, that I utterly deny. If sack and
sugar be a fault, God help the wicked; if to be old and
merry be a sin, then many an old host that I know is
damned: if to be fat be to be hated, then Pharaoh's lean
kine are to be loved. No my good lord, banish Peto, banish 435
Bardolph, banish Poins, but for sweet Jack Falstaff, kind
Jack Falstaff, true Jack Falstaff, valiant Jack Falstaff, and
therefore more valiant being as he is old Jack Falstaff,
banish not him thy Harry's company, banish not him thy
Harry's company; banish plump Jack, and banish all the 440
world.

PRINCE.   I do, I will.

Enter BARDOLPH *running.*

BARDOLPH. O my lord, my lord, the sheriff with a most monstrous
watch is at the door.

FALSTAFF. Out ye rogue: play out the play, I have much to say in the 445
behalf of that Falstaff.

Enter the HOSTESS.

HOSTESS.   O Jesu, my lord, my lord!

PRINCE.   Heigh, heigh, the devil rides upon a fiddlestick: what's the
matter?

HOSTESS.   The sheriff and all the watch are at the door: they are come 450
to search the house, shall I let them in?

FALSTAFF. Dost thou hear, Hal? Never call a true piece of gold a
counterfeit: thou art essentially made, without seeming
so.

PRINCE.   And thou a natural coward, without instinct.   455

FALSTAFF. I deny your major: if you will deny the sheriff, so: if not,
let him enter. If I become not a cart as well as another man,

---

                                                                430-1
saving your reverence asking your pardon (for an offensive statement to follow)   434-5
Pharaoh's lean kine (Gen. XLI.19-21)   443 monstrous watch large guard   448 devil . . .
fiddlestick (proverbial: "the devil's leading the dance")   452-4 Never . . . seeming so
don't denounce me (a true piece of gold) to the sheriff as a counterfeit thief. You also are the
genuine article, though you do not seem so.   456 major major premise (that natural
cowards are so without instinct)   457 become not a cart am not a credit to the hangman's

a plague on my bringing up: I hope I shall as soon be
strangled with a halter as another.

PRINCE.   Go hide thee behind the arras, the rest walk up above. 460
Now my masters, for a true face and good conscience.

FALSTAFF.   Both which I have had, but their date is out, and therefore
I'll hide me.   *Exit.*

PRINCE.   Call in the sheriff.

Enter SHERIFF *and the* CARRIER.

Now master sheriff, what is your will with me?   465

SHERIFF.   First pardon me my lord. A hue and cry
Hath followed certain men unto this house.

PRINCE.   What men?

SHERIFF.   One of them is well known my gracious lord,
A gross fat man.   470

CARRIER.   As fat as butter.

PRINCE.   The man I do assure you is not here,
For I myself at this time have employed him:
And sheriff, I will engage my word to thee,
That I will by tomorrow dinnertime   470
Send him to answer thee or any man,
For any thing he shall be charged withal,
And so let me entreat you leave the house.

SHERIFF.   I will my lord: there are two gentlemen
Have in this robbery lost three hundred marks.   480

PRINCE.   It may be so: if he have robbed these men,
He shall be answerable, and so farewell.

SHERIFF.   Good night my noble lord.

PRINCE.   I think it is good morrow is it not?

SHERIFF.   Indeed my lord I think it be two o'clock.   485

Exit [with CARRIER].

PRINCE.   This oily rascal is known as well as Paul's: go call him
forth.

PETO.   Falstaff! Fast asleep behind the arras, and snorting like a
horse.

PRINCE.   Hark how hard he fetches breath: search his pockets.   490
*He searcheth his pocket, and findeth certain
papers.*

cart   458 **bringing up** (1) breeding (2) being called up before the court   460 **arras** hanging
tapestry (at the rear of the stage)   461 **true** honest   462 **out** expired   472 **here** at this
spot (as he is behind the arras)   474 **engage** pledge   486 **Paul's** St. Paul's
Cathedral

What hast thou found?

PETO. Nothing but papers my lord.

PRINCE. Let's see what they be: read them.

PETO.

> Item a capon ....2s. 2d.
> Item sauce 4d. 495
> Item sack two gallons ....5s. 8d.
> Item anchovies and sack after supper .....2s. 6d.
> Item bread ....ob.

PRINCE. O monstrous! but one halfpenny-worth of bread to this intolerable deal of sack? What there is else, keep close, 500 we'll read it at more advantage; there let him sleep till day. I'll to the court in the morning. We must all to the wars, and thy place shall be honourable. I'll procure this fat rogue a charge of foot, and I know his death will be a march of twelve score. The money shall be paid back 505 again with advantage; be with me betimes in the morning, and so good morrow Peto.

PETO. Good morrow, good my lord.   *Exeunt.*

Act Three

[SCENE I.]

Enter HOTSPUR, WORCESTER, LORD MORTIMER,
OWEN GLENDOWER.

MORTIMER. These promises are fair, the parties sure,
And our induction full of prosperous hope.

HOTSPUR. Lord Mortimer, and Cousin Glendower,
Will you sit down? And Uncle Worcester;
A plague upon it, I have forgot the map.   5

GLENDOWER.

No, here it is; sit cousin Percy,
Sit good Cousin Hotspur, for by that name
As oft as Lancaster doth speak of you,
His cheek looks pale, and with a rising sigh,
He wisheth you in heaven.   10

---

498 **ob.** half-penny (obolus)   500 **intolerable** excessively great   500 **close**
secret   502 **advantage** opportunity   504 **charge of foot** infantry command   505 **twelve**
score 240 yards (fr. archery)   506 **advantage** interest   **betimes** early
III, i North Wales. Glendower's castle   2 **induction** beginning   8 **Lancaster** King

HOTSPUR.   And you in hell, as oft as he hears
              Owen Glendower spoke of.
GLENDOWER.
              I cannot blame him; at my nativity
              The front of heaven was full of fiery shapes
              Of buring cressets, and at my birth   15
              The frame and huge foundation of the earth
              Shaked like a coward.
HOTSPUR.   Why so it would have done at the same season if your
              mother's cat had but kittened, though yourself had never
              been born.   20
GLENDOWER.
              I say the earth did shake when I was born.
HOTSPUR.   And I say the earth was not of my mind,
              If you suppose as fearing you it shook.
GLENDOWER.
              The heavens were all on fire, the earth did tremble.
HOTSPUR.   O then the earth shook to see the heavens on fire,   25
              And not in fear of your nativity.
              Diseasèd nature oftentimes breaks forth
              In strange eruptions; oft the teeming earth
              Is with a kind of colic pinched and vexed,
              By the imprisoning of unruly wind   30
              Within her womb, which for enlargement striving,
              Shakes the old beldam earth, and topples down
              Steeples and moss-grown towers. At your birth
              Our grandam earth, having this distemp'rature,
              In passion shook.
GLENDOWER.   Cousin, of many men   35
              I do not bear these crossings: give me leave
              To tell you once again that at my birth
              The front of heaven was full of fiery shapes,
              The goats ran from the mountains, and the herds
              Were strangely clamorous to the frighted fields.   40
              These signs have marked me extraordinary,
              And all the courses of my life do show
              I am not in the roll of common men:
              Where is he living, clipped in with the sea

Henry   14 **front** forehead, face   14–15 **fiery . . . cressets** shooting stars resembling the
fire in swinging iron baskets burning oil   18 **season** time   28–33 **oft . . . towers** (this
explanation of earthquakes caused by wind imprisoned in the earth goes back to classical
times)   28 **teeming** pregnant   31 **enlargement** release   32 **beldam** grandmother   34
distemp'rature upset   35 **passion** suffering   36 **crossings** vexations   **44 clipped in with**

That chides the banks of England, Scotland, Wales,   45
Which calls me pupil or hath read to me?
And bring him out that is but woman's son,
Can trace me in the tedious ways of art,
And hold me pace in deep experiments.

HOTSPUR. I think there's no man speaks better Welsh: 50
I'll to dinner.

MORTIMER. Peace Cousin Percy, you will make him mad.

GLENDOWER.
          I can call spirits from the vasty deep.

HOTSPUR. Why so can I, or so can any man,
But will they come when you do call for them?   55

GLENDOWER.
          Why I can teach you, cousin, to command
The devil.

HOTSPUR. And I can teach thee, coz, to shame the devil,
By telling truth. 'Tell truth and shame the devil:'
If thou have power to raise him, bring him hither,   60
And I'll be sworn I have power to shame him hence:
O while you live, tell truth and shame the devil.

MORTIMER. Come, come, no more of this unprofitable chat.

GLENDOWER.
          Three times hath Henry Bolingbroke made head
Against my power: thrice from the banks of Wye   65
And sandy-bottomed Severn have I sent him
Bootless home, and weather-beaten back.

HOTSPUR. Home without boots, and in foul weather too,
How 'scapes he agues, in the devil's name?

GLENDOWER.
          Come, here is the map, shall we divide our right,   70
According to our threefold order ta'en?

MORTIMER. The archdeacon hath divided it
Into three limits very equally:
England, from Trent and Severn hitherto,
By south and east is to my part assigned: 75
All westward, Wales beyond the Severn shore,
And all the fertile land within that bound,
To Owen Glendower: and dear coz to you

surrounded by   45 **chides** rushes against   46 **read to** taught   48 **trace** follow   49
hold me pace keep pace with me   50 **better Welsh** (1) the language better (2) bigger
brags   59 **Tell . . . devil** (proverbial)   64 **made head** sent an army   67 **Bootless**
profitless   **weather-beaten** in storms (raised by Glendower's magic)   70 **right** rightful
lands   71 **threefold order ta'en** agreement made for a three-part division

The remnant northward lying off from Trent.
And our indentures tripartite are drawn,   80
Which being sealèd interchangeably,
(A business that this night may execute)
Tomorrow, Cousin Percy, you and I
And my good Lord of Worcester will set forth
To meet your father and the Scottish power,   85
As is appointed us, at Shrewsbury.
My father Glendower is not ready yet,
Nor shall we need his help these fourteen days.
[*To Glendower*.] Within that space you may have drawn
    together
Your tenants, friends, and neighbouring gentlemen.   90

GLENDOWER.

A shorter time shall send me to you lords,
And in my conduct shall your ladies come,
From whom you now must steal and take no leave,
For there will be a world of water shed,
Upon the parting of your wives and you.   95

HOTSPUR.   Methinks my moiety north from Burton here,
In quantity equals not one of yours:
See how this river comes me cranking in,
And cuts me from the best of all my land,
A huge half-moon, a monstrous cantle out.   100
I'll have the current in this place dammed up,
And here the smug and silver Trent shall run
In a new channel fair and evenly:
It shall not wind with such a deep indent,
To rob me of so rich a bottom here.   105

GLENDOWER.

Not wind? it shall, it must, you see it doth.

MORTIMER. Yea, but
Mark how he bears his course, and runs me up
With like advantage on the other side,
Gelding the opposèd continent as much   110
As on the other side it takes from you.

WORCESTER.

Yea, but a little charge will trench him here,

---

80 **indentures
tripartite** reciprocal agreements in triplicate   81 **sealed interchangeably** i.e. by each party
signing   each   copy   87 **father** father-in-law   92 **conduct** escort   96 **moiety**
portion   98 **cranking** winding   100 **cantle** segment   102 **smug** neat, smooth   105
bottom valley   110 **Gelding . . . continent** cutting from the opposite land   112 **charge**
expenditure

And on this north side win this cape of land,
And then he runs straight and even.

HOTSPUR.   I'll have it so, a little charge will do it.   115
GLENDOWER.
        I'll not have it altered.
HOTSPUR.   Will not you?
GLENDOWER.
        No, nor you shall not.
HOTSPUR.   Who shall say me nay?
GLENDOWER.
        Why that will I.
HOTSPUR.   Let me not understand you then, speak it in Welsh.
GLENDOWER.
        I can speak English, lord, as well as you,   120
        For I was trained up in the English court,
        Where being but young I framèd to the harp
        Many an English ditty lovely well,
        And gave the tongue a helpful ornament,
        A virtue that was never seen in you.   125
HOTSPUR.   Marry,
        And I am glad of it with all my heart.
        I had rather be a kitten and cry mew,
        Than one of these same metre ballad-mongers:
        I had rather hear a brazen canstick turned,   130
        Or a dry wheel grate on the axletree,
        And that would set my teeth nothing on edge,
        Nothing so much as mincing poetry;
        'Tis like the forced gait of a shuffling nag.
GLENDOWER.
        Come, you shall have Trent turned.   135
HOTSPUR.   I do not care, I'll give thrice so much land
        To any well-deserving friend:
        But in the way of bargain, mark ye me,
        I'll cavil on the ninth part of a hair.
        Are the indentures drawn? Shall we be gone?   140
GLENDOWER.
        The moon shines fair, you may away by night:
        I'll haste the writer, and withal
        Break with your wives of your departure hence:

---

124 **gave ... ornament** ornamented and contributed to the English
language   129 **metre ballad-mongers** writers of ballads in forced rhyme   130 **brazen
canstick turned** the noise of a brass candlestick being scraped to polish it   133 **mincing**
tripping along with an affectation of elegance   142 **writer** i.e. of the indentures   143
Break with inform

I am afraid my daughter will run mad,
So much she doteth on her Mortimer.   *Exit.* 145
MORTIMER. Fie Cousin Percy, how you cross my father.
HOTSPUR. I cannot choose: sometime he angers me
With telling me of the moldwarp and the ant,
Of the dreamer Merlin and his prophecies,
And of a dragon and a finless fish,   150
A clip-winged griffin and a moulten raven,
A couching lion and a ramping cat,
And such a deal of skimble-skamble stuff,
As puts me from my faith. I tell you what,
He held me last night at least nine hours   155
In reckoning up the several devils' names
That were his lackeys: I cried 'hum,' and 'Well, go to,'
But marked him not a word. O he is as tedious
As a tired horse, a railing wife,
Worse than a smoky house. I had rather live   160
With cheese and garlic in a windmill far,
Than feed on cates and have him talk to me,
In any summer-house in Christendom.
MORTIMER. In faith he is a worthy gentleman,
Exceedingly well read and profited   165
In strange concealments, valiant as a lion,
And wondrous affable; and as bountiful
As mines of India. Shall I tell you cousin,
He holds your temper in a high respect
And curbs himself even of his natural scope,   170
When you come cross his humour, faith he does.
I warrant you that man is not alive
Might so have tempted him as you have done,
Without the taste of danger and reproof:
But do not use it oft, let me entreat you.   175
WORCESTER.
In faith my lord you are too wilful-blame,
And since your coming hither have done enough
To put him quite beside his patience.

---

148 **moldwarp**
mole   149 **Merlin** Welsh prophet and magician of the King Arthur legends   151 **griffin**
legendary animal with the head and wings of an eagle and the body of a lion **moulten**
moulting   152 **couching** reclining ("couchant" in heraldry)   **ramping** upright ("rampant"
in heraldry)   153 **deal of skimble-skamble** lot of nonsense   154 **puts me from** makes me
skeptical of   **faith** belief (1) in what he says (2) in God   156 **several** different   162 **cates**
delicacies   163 **summer-house** (regarded as a luxury)   165 **profited** proficient   166
strange concealments wondrous mysteries   171 **humour** disposition, inclination   176
wilful-blame wilful and therefore blamable

You must needs learn lord to amend this fault:
Though sometimes it show greatness, courage, blood,   180
And that's the dearest grace it renders you,
Yet oftentimes it doth present harsh rage,
Defect of manners, want of government,
Pride, haughtiness, opinion, and disdain,
The least of which haunting a nobleman,   185
Loseth men's hearts and leaves behind a stain
Upon the beauty of all parts besides,
Beguiling them of commendation.

HOTSPUR.   Well, I am schooled: good manners be your speed;
Here come our wives, and let us take our leave.   190

Enter GLENDOWER *with the* LADIES.

MORTIMER.   This is the deadly spite that angers me,
My wife can speak no English, I no Welsh.

GLENDOWER.
My daughter weeps, she'll not part with you,
She'll be a soldier too, she'll to the wars.

MORTIMER.   Good father, tell her that she and my Aunt Percy   195
Shall follow in your conduct speedily.

Glendower speaks to her in Welsh, and she
answers him in the same.

GLENDOWER.
She is desperate here, a peevish self-willed harlotry, one
that no persuasion can do good upon.

The lady speaks in Welsh.

MORTIMER.   I understand thy looks: that pretty Welsh
Which thou pourest down from these swelling heavens, 200
I am too perfect in, and but for shame
In such a parley should I answer thee.

The lady again in Welsh.

I understand thy kisses, and thou mine,
And that's a feeling disputation,
But I will never be a truant, love,   205

---

180 **blood** spirit   181 **dearest** most
valuable   182 **present** represent   183 **government** self-control   184 **opinion**
stubbornness   185 **haunting** frequenting   188 **Beguiling** cheating   189 **be your speed**
bring you success   191 **spite** vexation   197 **harlotry** foolish girl   199 **Welsh** i.e.
tears   200 **swelling heavens** eyes   202 **such a parley** a like manner of speaking   204
feeling disputation exchange of emotions (in place of words)

Till I have learnt thy language, for thy tongue
Makes Welsh as sweet as ditties highly penned,
Sung by a fair queen in a summer's bower,
With ravishing division to her lute.

GLENDOWER.

    Nay, if you melt, then will she run mad.   210

The lady speaks again in Welsh.

MORTIMER. O I am ignorance itself in this.

GLENDOWER.

    She bids you on the wanton rushes lay you down,
    And rest your gentle head upon her lap,
    And she will sing the song that pleaseth you,
    And on your eyelids crown the god of sleep,   215
    Charming your blood with pleasing heaviness,
    Making such difference 'twixt wake and sleep,
    As is the difference betwixt day and night,
    The hour before the heavenly-harnessed team
    Begins his golden progress in the east.   220

MORTIMER. With all my heart I'll sit and hear her sing:
    By that time will our book I think be drawn.

GLENDOWER.

    Do so,
    And those musicians that shall play to you
    Hang in the air a thousand leagues from hence,   225
    And straight they shall be here: sit and attend.

HOTSPUR. Come Kate, thou art perfect in lying down:
    Come quick, quick, that I may lay my head in thy lap.

LADY PERCY.

    Go, ye giddy goose.

The music plays.

HOTSPUR. Now I perceive the devil understands Welsh,   230
    And 'tis no marvel he is so humorous,
    By'r lady he is a good musician.

LADY PERCY.

    Then should you be nothing but musical, for you are
    altogether governed by humours. Lie still ye thief, and

---

207 **highly**
ingeniously   209 **division** passage of rapid short notes founded on a simpler passage of
longer notes (fr. music)   212 **wanton** luxurious   216 **heaviness** drowsiness   219
heavenly-harnessed team horses that draw the chariot of the sun across the sky   220
progress (1) lit. (2) royal journey (the sun-king metaphor)   222 **book** indenture   225
Hang . . . hence (are sprites at my command)   231 **humorous** capricious

hear the lady sing in Welsh.   235
HOTSPUR. I had rather hear Lady my branch howl in Irish.
LADY PERCY.
         Wouldst thou have thy head broken?
HOTSPUR. No.
LADY PERCY.
         Then be still.
HOTSPUR. Neither, 'tis a woman's fault.   240
LADY PERCY.
         Now God help thee.
HOTSPUR. To the Welsh lady's bed.
LADY PERCY.
         What's that?
HOTSPUR. Peace, she sings.

                            Here the lady sings a Welsh song.

HOTSPUR. Come Kate, I'll have your song too.   245
LADY PERCY.
         Not mine in good sooth.
HOTSPUR. Not yours 'in good sooth?' Heart, you swear like a
         comfit-maker's wife. Not you, 'in good sooth,' and 'as true
         as I live,' and 'as God shall mend me,' and 'as sure as day:'
         And givest such sarcenet surety for thy oaths,   250
         As if thou never walk'st further than Finsbury.
         Swear me Kate like a lady as thou art,
         A good mouth-filling oath, and leave 'in sooth'
         And such protest of pepper gingerbread
         To velvet guards, and Sunday citizens.   255
         Come sing.
LADY PERCY.
         I will not sing.
HOTSPUR. 'Tis the next way to turn tailor, or be redbreast-teacher:
         and the indentures be drawn, I'll away within these two
         hours, and so come in when ye will.   260

                                                    Exit.
GLENDOWER.
         Come, come, Lord Mortimer, you are as slow,
         As hot Lord Percy is on fire to go:

---

                                                     236 **brach**
bitch (dog)   246 **in good sooth** (like the others Hotspur mentions, a genteel expression used
by the middle classes in place of an oath)   248 **comfit-maker** confectioner   250 **sarcenet**
insubstantial (as thin silk)   251 **Finsbury** Finsbury Fields (a favorite recreation area for
Londoners on Sundays)   254 **pepper** coarse (hence crumbling)   255 **guards**
trimmings   258 **turn . . . teacher** turn into a tailor (noted for their singing) or a teacher of

By this our book is drawn, we'll but seal,
And then to horse immediately.

MORTIMER.   With all my heart. *Exeunt.*

[SCENE II.]

Enter the KING, PRINCE OF WALES, *and others.*

KING.   Lords give us leave, the Prince of Wales and I
Must have some private conference, but be near at hand,
For we shall presently have need of you.

Exeunt lords.

I know not whether God will have it so
For some displeasing service I have done,   5
That in his secret doom, out of my blood
He'll breed revengement and a scourge for me:
But thou dost in thy passages of life,
Make me believe that thou art only marked
For the hot vengeance and the rod of heaven,   10
To punish my mistreadings. Tell me else
Could such inordinate and low desires,
Such poor, such bare, such lewd, such mean attempts,
Such barren pleasures, rude society
As thou art matched withal, and grafted to,   15
Accompany the greatness of thy blood,
And hold their level with thy princely heart?
PRINCE.   So please your majesty, I would I could
Quit all offences with as clear excuse,
As well as I am doubtless I can purge   20
Myself of many I am charged withal:
Yet such extenuation let me beg,
As in reproof of many tales devised,
Which oft the ear of greatness needs must hear,
By smiling pickthanks and base newsmongers,   25
I may for some things true, wherein my youth

---

songbirds   263 **book is drawn** agreement is drawn up
    III, ii Westminster. The palace   6 **doom** judgment   8 **passages of** courses of action
in   11 **mistreadings** transgressions   12 **inordinate** unworthy of your station   13 **bare**
. . . **lewd** wretched . . . wicked   **attempts** activities   15 **grafted** attached   17 **hold**
their level put themselves on a level   19 **Quit** acquit myself of   20 **doubtless** without
doubt   22–8 **such extenuation. . . submission** "let me beg so much extenuation that upon
confutation of many false charges I may be pardoned some that are true": Johnson   25
pickthanks . . . **newsmongers** flatterers . . . rumor spreaders

Hath faulty wandered, and irregular,
Find pardon on my true submission.

KING.   God pardon thee, yet let me wonder, Harry,
At thy affections, which do hold a wing   30
Quite from the flight of all thy ancestors.
Thy place in council thou hast rudely lost,
Which by thy younger brother is supplied,
And art almost an alien to the hearts
Of all the court and princes of my blood.   35
The hope and expectation of thy time
Is ruined, and the soul of every man
Prophetically do forethink thy fall:
Had I so lavish of my presence been,
So common-hackneyed in the eyes of men,   40
So stale and cheap to vulgar company,
Opinion, that did help me to the crown,
Had still kept loyal to possession,
And left me in reputeless banishment,
A fellow of no mark nor likelihood.   45
By being seldom seen, I could not stir
But like a comet I was wondered at,
That men would tell their children 'This is he:'
Others would say, 'Where, which is Bolingbroke?'
And then I stole all courtesy from heaven,   50
And dressed myself in such humility
That I did pluck allegiance from men's hearts,
Loud shouts and salutations from their mouths,
Even in the presence of the crownèd king.
Thus did I keep my person fresh and new,   55
My presence like a robe pontifical,
Ne'er seen but wondered at: and so my state,
Seldom, but sumptuous, showed like a feast,
And won by rareness such solemnity.
The skipping king, he ambled up and down,   60
With shallow jesters, and rash bavin wits,
Soon kindled, and soon burnt, carded his state,
Mingled his royalty with cap'ring fools,

---

30 **affections**
inclinations   32 **rudely** because of rudeness   36 **time** life, reign   42 **Opinion** public
opinion   43 **possession** i.e. of Richard II   45 **likelihood** promise   50 **stole . . . heaven**
acted as courteous as heaven itself (Richard comments on this "courtship to the common
people," *RII*, I, iv, 24-36)   56 **robe pontifical** bishop's or archbishop's robe worn on special
occasions   57 **state** magnificence   58 **showed like a feast** was a cause for
celebration   59 **solemnity** sense of occasion   61 **rash bavin** quick-burning kindling   62

Had his great name profanèd with their scorns,
And gave his countenance against his name   65
To laugh at gibing boys, and stand the push
Of every beardless vain comparative;
Grew a companion to the common streets,
Enfeoffed himself to popularity,
That being daily swallowed by men's eyes,   70
They surfeited with honey, and began
To loathe the taste of sweetness, whereof a little
More than a little, is by much too much.
So when he had occasion to be seen,
He was but as the cuckoo is in June,   75
Heard, not regarded: seen, but with such eyes
As sick and blunted with community,
Afford no extraordinary gaze,
Such as is bent on sun-like majesty,
When it shines seldom in admiring eyes,   80
But rather drowsed, and hung their eyelids down,
Slept in his face, and rendered such aspèct
As cloudy men use to their adversaries,
Being with his presence glutted, gorged, and full.
And in that very line Harry standest thou,   85
For thou hast lost thy princely privilege
With vile participation. Not an eye
But is aweary of thy common sight,
Save mine, which hath desired to see thee more,
Which now doth that I would not have it do,   90
Make blind itself with foolish tenderness.

PRINCE.   I shall hereafter my thrice gracious lord,
            Be more myself.

KING.   For all the world,
As thou art to this hour was Richard then,
When I from France set foot at Ravenspurgh,   95
And even as I was then, is Percy now:
Now by my sceptre, and my soul to boot,
He hath more worthy interest to the state
Than thou, the shadow of succession.

---

carded adulterated, debased by indiscriminate mingling   62 **state** majesty   65 **against
his name** (1) contrary to his dignity (2) to the injury of his title   66–7 **stand . . . comparative** compete on equal terms in joking with foolish youths   69 **Enfeoffed . . . popularity**
bound himself to low company   77 **community** familiarity   79 **sun-like** (king-sun
metaphor)   82 **face** presence   83 **cloudy** sullen, frowning   87 **vile participation**
association with low company   90 **that** i.e. which   91 **Make blind** weep   94 **to** up
to   97 **to boot** in addition   98 **more . . . state** more of a claim, based on worth, to succeed
to the throne   99 **the shadow of succession** who are but a shadow of what a successor to the

For of no right, nor colour like to right,   100
He doth fill fields with harness in the realm,
Turns head against the lion's armèd jaws,
And being no more in debt to years than thou,
Leads ancient lords and reverend bishops on
To bloody battles, and to bruising arms.   105
What never-dying honour hath he got
Against renownèd Douglas, whose high deeds,
Whose hot incursions, and great name in arms,
Holds from all soldiers chief majority
And military title capital   110
Through all the kingdoms that acknowledge Christ.
Thrice hath this Hotspur, Mars in swathling clothes,
This infant warrior, in his enterprises
Discomfited great Douglas, ta'en him once,
Enlargèd him, and made a friend of him,   115
To fill the mouth of deep defiance up,
And shake the peace and safety of our throne.
And what say you to this? Percy, Northumberland,
The Archbishop's grace of York, Douglas, Mortimer,
Capitulate against us, and are up.   120
But wherefore do I tell these news to thee?
Why Harry do I tell thee of my foes,
Which art my nearest and dearest enemy?
Thou that art like enough through vassal fear,
Base inclination, and the start of spleen,   125
To fight against me under Percy's pay,
To dog his heels, and curtsy at his frowns,
To show how much thou art degenerate.

PRINCE.   Do not think so, you shall not find it so,
And God forgive them that so much have swayed   130
Your majesty's good thoughts away from me.
I will redeem all this on Percy's head,
And in the closing of some glorious day
Be bold to tell you that I am your son,
When I will wear a garment all of blood,   135
And stain my favours in a bloody mask,

---

throne should be   100 **colour** pretext   101 **harness** men in armor   102 **Turns head**
leads an army   102 **lion** king (a common metaphor)   103 **no more . . . thou** (the historical
Hotspur was twenty-three years older than Hal)   108 **incursions** raids   109 **majority**
preeminence   110 **capital** paramount   112 **swathling** swaddling   115 **Enlarged him**
set him free   116 **To fill the mouth . . . up** to satisfy the appetite of   120 **Capitulate**
agree   120 **up** i.e. in arms   123 **dearest** (1) most loved (2) direst   124 **vassal**
slavish   125 **start of spleen** fit of temper   128 **degenerate** a traitor to your royal blood

Which washed away, shall scour my shame with it:
And that shall be the day, whene'er it lights,
That this same child of honour and renown,
This gallant Hotspur, this all-praisèd knight,   140
And your unthought-of Harry chance to meet:
For every honour sitting on his helm,
Would they were multitudes, and on my head
My shames redoubled. For the time will come
That I shall make this northern youth exchange   145
His glorious deeds for my indignities.
Percy is but my factor, good my lord,
To engross up glorious deeds on my behalf.
And I will call him to so strict account,
That he shall render every glory up,   150
Yea, even the slightest worship of his time,
Or I will tear the reckoning from his heart.
This in the name of God I promise here,
The which if he be pleased I shall perform,
I do beseech your majesty may salve   155
The long-grown wounds of my intemperance:
If not, the end of life cancels all bands,
And I will die a hundred thousand deaths
Ere break the smallest parcel of this vow.
KING. A hundred thousand rebels die in this: 160
Thou shalt have charge and sovereign trust herein.

Enter BLUNT.

How now good Blunt? Thy looks are full of speed.
BLUNT. So hath the business that I come to speak of.
Lord Mortimer of Scotland hath sent word
That Douglas and the English rebels met   165
The eleventh of this month at Shrewsbury:
A mighty and a fearful head they are,
If promises be kept on every hand,
As ever offered foul play in a state.
KING. The Earl of Westmoreland set forth today,   170
With him my son Lord John of Lancaster,
For this advertisement is five days old.

---

136 **favours** features   142–3
honour . . . **multitudes** (because the victor gained the honors previously held by the
vanquished)   147–8 **factor** . . . **behalf** agent . . . collecting honors for my account (fr.
commerce, as are ll. 149-52)   152 **reckoning** total sum   157 **bands** bonds (proverbial:
"death pays all debts")   159 **parcel** portion   161 **charge** command   167 **head**
army   172 **advertisement** news

On Wednesday next, Harry you shall set forward,
On Thursday we ourselves will march. Our meeting
Is Bridgnorth, and Harry, you shall march   175
Through Gloucestershire, by which account,
Our business valuèd, some twelve days hence
Our general forces at Bridgnorth shall meet:
Our hands are full of business, let's away,
Advantage feeds him fat while men delay.   180

Exeunt.

[SCENE III.]

Enter FALSTAFF *and* BARDOLPH.

FALSTAFF. Bardolph, am I not fallen away vilely since this last action?
Do I not bate? Do I not dwindle? Why, my skin hangs
about me like an old lady's loose gown. I am withered like
an old apple-john. Well, I'll repent and that suddenly,
while I am in some liking: I shall be out of heart shortly,   5
and then I shall have no strength to repent. And I have not
forgotten what the inside of a church is made of, I am a
peppercorn, a brewer's horse: the inside of a church.
Company, villainous company, hath been the spoil of me.

BARDOLPH. Sir John, you are so fretful you cannot live long.   10

FALSTAFF. Why, there is it; come sing me a bawdy song, make me
merry. I was as virtuously given as a gentleman need to be;
virtuous enough, swore little, diced not above seven times
a week, went to a bawdy-house not above once in a
quarter—of an hour, paid money that I borrowed—three   15
or four times, lived well, and in good compass, and now I
live out of all order, out of all compass.

BARDOLPH. Why, you are so fat Sir John, that you must needs be out
of all compass: out of all reasonable compass, Sir John.

FALSTAFF. Do thou amend thy face, and I'll amend my life: thou art   20
our admiral, thou bearest the lantern in the poop, but 'tis

177 **Our business valued** weighing the necessary preparation
      III, iii Eastcheap. The Boar's Head Tavern   1 **action** (the robbery at Gadshill)   2 **bate**
lose weight   4 **apple-john** apple that shriveled as it ripened   **suddenly** at once   5 **liking**
(1) health (2) mood for it   **out of heart** (1) in poor health (2) out of the mood   6 **strength** (1)
of body (2) of purpose   8 **brewer's horse** old, tired workhorse   10 **fretful** (1) worried (2)
eroded   16 **in good compass** within proper bounds   20 **face** (the red of a habitual
drunkard)   21 **admiral** flagship (suggested by "compass")   22 **Knight . . . Lamp**

in the nose of thee: thou art the Knight of the Burning
Lamp.

BARDOLPH. Why, Sir John, my face does you no harm.

FALSTAFF. No I'll be sworn, I make as good use of it as many a man 25
doth of a death's head, or a *memento mori*. I never see thy
face, but I think upon hell-fire, and Dives that lived in
purple: for there he is in his robes burning, burning. If
thou wert any way given to virtue, I would swear by thy
face: my oath should be 'By this fire that's God's angel.' 30
But thou art altogether given over: and wert indeed but for
the light in thy face, the son of utter darkness. When thou
ran'st up Gadshill in the night to catch my horse, if I did
not think thou hadst been an *ignis fatuus,* or a ball of
wildfire, there's no purchase in money. O thou art a 35
perpetual triumph, an everlasting bonfire-light: thou hast
saved me a thousand marks in links and torches, walking
with thee in the night betwixt tavern and tavern: but the
sack that thou has drunk me would have bought me lights
as good cheap at the dearest chandler's in Europe. I have 40
maintained that salamander of yours with fire any time
this two and thirty years, God reward me for it.

BARDOLPH. 'Sblood, I would my face were in your belly.

FALSTAFF. God-a-mercy, so should I be sure to be heartburned.

Enter HOSTESS.

How now Dame Parlet the hen, have you inquired yet 45
who picked my pocket?

HOSTESS. Why Sir John, what do you think Sir John? Do you think I
keep thieves in my house? I have searched, I have inquired, so has my husband, man by man, boy by boy,
servant by servant: the tithe of a hair was never lost in my 50
house before.

FALSTAFF. Ye lie hostess, Bardolph was shaved, and lost many a hair,
and I'll be sworn my pocket was picked: go to, you are a
woman, go.

(paraphrase of the Knight of the Burning Sword, hero of a chivalric romance)   26
memento mori reminder of death (as was the skull)   27 **Dives** rich man in the parable of
Dives and Lazarus in Luke XVI. 19-31   30 **God's angel** the angel of death   31 **given over**
i.e. to the devil   32 **utter** outer   34 **ignis fatuus** will o' the wisp   35 **wildfire** (1)
fireworks used in entertainments (2) burning ball of gunpowder used in naval wars   36
triumph pageant (because he is always lit, like the fireworks and bonfires that accompanied
these celebrations)   37 **links** small torches   40 **dearest chandler's** most expensive
candlemakers   41 **salamander** (his nose) lizard (which, being cold-blooded, supposedly
lived in fire)   45 **Dame Partlet** hen in the beast fable (term applied to fussy, "clucking"
women)   50 **tithe** tenth   52 **shaved** infected with syphilis (baldness being a result)

HOSTESS. Who I? No, I defy thee: God's light, I was never called so   55
in mine own house before.

FALSTAFF. Go to. I know you well enough.

HOSTESS. No, Sir John, you do not know me, Sir John, I know you
Sir John: you owe me money Sir John, and now you pick a
quarrel to beguile me of it: I bought you a dozen of shirts   60
to your back.

FALSTAFF. Dowlas, filthy dowlas. I have given them away to bakers'
wives, they have made bolters of them.

HOSTESS. Now as I am a true woman, holland of eight shillings an
ell. You owe money here besides, Sir John, for your diet,   65
and by-drinkings, and money lent you, four and twenty
pound.

FALSTAFF. He had his part of it, let him pay.

HOSTESS. He? alas, he is poor, he hath nothing.

FALSTAFF. How? poor? look upon his face. What call you rich? Let   70
them coin his nose, let them coin his cheeks, I'll not pay a
denier. What, will you make a younker of me? Shall I not
take mine ease in mine inn, but I shall have my pocket
picked? I have lost a seal-ring of my grandfather's worth
forty mark.   75

HOSTESS. O Jesu, I have heard the prince tell him I know not how
oft, that that ring was copper.

FALSTAFF. How? the prince is a Jack, a sneak-up, 'Sblood, and he
were here, I would cudgel him like a dog if he would say
so.   80

> *Enter the* PRINCE *marching* [*with* PETO],
> *and* FALSTAFF *meets him, playing upon his
> truncheon like a fife.*

FALSTAFF. How now lad? Is the wind in that door i' faith, must we all
march?

BARDOLPH. Yea, two and two, Newgate fashion.

HOSTESS. My lord, I pray you hear me.

PRINCE. What sayest thou Mistress Quickly? How doth thy hus-   85

62

Dowlas coarse linen   63 **bolters** sifting cloths   64 **holland** fine lawn   66 **by-drinkings**
drinks between meals   70 **rich** i.e. color   72 **denier** one-tenth of a penny   **younker**
gullible youth, dupe   78 **Jack** jackanapes   **sneak-up** cowardly rascal (Q; F: "sneak-cup",
one who shirks his share of drinking)   80 s.d. **truncheon** short stick   83 **Newgate** a
London prison

band? I love him well, he is an honest man.

HOSTESS.   Good my lord, hear me.

FALSTAFF.   Prithee let her alone, and list to me.

PRINCE.   What say'st thou Jack?

FALSTAFF.   The other night I fell asleep here, behind the arras, and   90
            had my pocket picked: this house is turned bawdy-house,
            they pick pockets.

PRINCE.   What didst thou lose Jack?

FALSTAFF.   Wilt thou believe me Hal, three or four bonds of forty
            pound apiece, and a seal-ring of my grandfather's.   95

PRINCE.   A trifle, some eightpenny matter.

HOSTESS.   So I told him my lord, and I said I heard your grace say so:
            and my lord, he speaks most vilely of you, like a foul-
            mouthed man as he is, and said he would cudgel you.

PRINCE.   What? he did not.   100

HOSTESS.   There's neither faith, truth, nor womanhood in me else.

FALSTAFF.   There's no more faith in thee than in a stewed prune, nor
            no more truth in thee than in a drawn fox, and for woman-
            hood, Maid Marian may be the deputy's wife of the ward
            to thee. Go you thing, go.   105

HOSTESS.   Say what thing, what thing?

FALSTAFF.   What thing? Why, a thing to thank God on.

HOSTESS.   I am no thing to thank God on, I would thou shouldst
            know it: I am an honest man's wife, and setting thy
            knighthood aside, thou art a knave to call me so.   110

FALSTAFF.   Setting thy womanhood aside, thou art a beast to say
            otherwise.

HOSTESS.   Say, what beast, thou knave thou?

FALSTAFF.   What beast? Why, an otter.

PRINCE.   An otter, Sir John? why an otter?   115

FALSTAFF.   Why? She's neither fish nor flesh, a man knows not
            where to have her.

HOSTESS.   Thou art an unjust man in saying so, thou or any man
            knows where to have me, thou knave thou.

PRINCE.   Thou say'st true hostess, and he slanders thee most 120
            grossly.

HOSTESS.   So he doth you my lord, and said this other day you ought
            him a thousand pound.

---

102 **stewed prune** (associated with brothels)   103 **drawn** i.e. from his
hole, when cunningly trying to escape   104–105 **Maid Marian . . .thee** you make the
ungainly character in the morris dances seem as decorous as a deputy alderman's
wife   116-7 **where . . . her** how to understand her (with a bawdy double meaning)   119
where . . . me how to get the better of me   122 **ought** owed

PRINCE.   Sirrah, do I owe you a thousand pound?

FALSTAFF.   A thousand pound Hal? A million. Thy love is worth a 125
            million, thou owest me thy love.

HOSTESS.   Nay my lord, he called you Jack, and said he would cudgel
            you.

FALSTAFF.   Did I, Bardolph?

BARDOLPH.   Indeed Sir John you said so.   130

FALSTAFF.   Yea, if he said my ring was copper.

PRINCE.   I say 'tis copper, darest thou be as good as thy word now?

FALSTAFF.   Why Hal, thou knowest as thou art but man I dare, but as
            thou art prince, I fear thee as I fear the roaring of the lion's
            whelp.   135

PRINCE.   And why not as the lion?

FALSTAFF.   The king himself is to be feared as the lion: dost thou think
            I'll fear thee as I fear thy father? Nay and I do, I pray God
            my girdle break.

PRINCE.   O, if it should, how would thy guts fall about thy knees. 140
            But sirrah, there's no room for faith, truth, nor honesty, in
            this bosom of thine. It is all filled up with guts and midriff.
            Charge an honest woman with picking thy pocket? Why,
            thou whoreson, impudent, embossed rascal, if there were
            anything in thy pocket but tavern reckonings, memoran- 145
            dums of bawdy-houses, and one poor pennyworth of
            sugar-candy to make thee long-winded—if thy pocket
            were enriched with any other injuries but these, I am a
            villain; and yet you will stand to it, you will not pocket up
            wrong. Art thou not ashamed?   150

FALSTAFF.   Dost thou hear, Hal? Thou knowest in the state of inno-
            cency Adam fell, and what should poor Jack Falstaff do in
            the days of villainy? Thou seest I have more flesh than
            another man, and therefore more frailty. You confess then
            you picked my pocket?   155

PRINCE.   It appears so by the story.

FALSTAFF.   Hostess, I forgive thee, go make ready breakfast, love thy
            husband, look to thy servants, cherish thy guests: thou
            shalt find me tractable to any honest reason: thou seest I
            am pacified still. Nay prithee be gone.   160

                                                   Exit HOSTESS.

---

127 **Jack**
jackanapes   134-5 **lion's whelp** (king-lion metaphor)   139 **girdle** belt   144 **embossed**
swollen   145 **reckonings** bills   147 **sugar . . . winded** (fighting cocks were fed sugar to
extend their breaths)   148 **injuries** items whose loss would be an injury   153 **days of
villainy** present evil times   160 **pacified still** always easy to pacify

Now Hal, to the news at court: for the robbery lad, how is
that answered?

PRINCE.   O my sweet beef, I must still be good angel to thee. The
money is paid back again.

FALSTAFF.   O I do not like that paying back, 'tis a double labour.   165

PRINCE.   I am good friends with my father and may do anything.

FALSTAFF.   Rob me the exchequer the first thing thou dost, and do it
with unwashed hands too.

BARDOLPH.   Do my lord.

PRINCE.   I have procured thee Jack, a charge of foot.   170

FALSTAFF.   I would it had been of horse. Where shall I find one that
can steal well? O for a fine thief of the age of two and
twenty or thereabouts: I am heinously unprovided. Well,
God be thanked for these rebels, they offend none but the
virtuous; I laud them, I praise them.   175

PRINCE.   Bardolph.

BARDOLPH.   My lord.

PRINCE.   Go bear this letter to Lord John of Lancaster, to my
brother John, this to my Lord of Westmoreland. Go Peto,
to horse, to horse, for thou and I have thirty miles to ride 180
yet ere dinner time. Jack, meet me tomorrow in the Temple Hall at two o'clock in the afternoon.
There shalt thou know thy charge, and there receive
Money and order for their furniture.
The land is burning, Percy stands on high,   185
And either we or they must lower lie.

FALSTAFF.   Rare words, brave world. Hostess, my breakfast, come:
O I could wish this tavern were my drum!

Exeunt omnes.

Act Four

[SCENE I.]

Enter HARRY HOTSPUR, WORCESTER, *and* DOUGLAS.

HOTSPUR.   Well said my noble Scot: if speaking truth
In this fine age were not thought flattery,

---

168 **with . . . hands**
at once, without pausing to wash your hands   170 **charge of foot** command of
infantry   173 **unprovided** poorly equipped   181-2 **Temple Hall** hall of the Inner Temple, a law school in London   184 **furniture** furnishings   187 **brave** fine   188 **drum**
drummer (to accompany me to battle)
    IV, i,   2 **fine** refined

Such attribution should the Douglas have,
As not a soldier of this season's stamp
Should go so general current through the world.   5
By God, I cannot flatter, I do defy
The tongues of soothers, but a braver place
In my heart's love hath no man than yourself.
Nay, task me to my word, approve me, lord.

DOUGLAS.   Thou art the king of honour: 10
No man so potent breathes upon the ground,
But I will beard him.

HOTSPUR.   Do so, and 'tis well.

Enter one with letters.

What letters hast thou there? [*To Douglas.*] I can but
    thank you.

MESSENGER.
These letters come from your father.

HOTSPUR.   Letters from him, why comes he not himself?   15

MESSENGER.
He cannot come, my lord, he is grievous sick.

HOTSPUR.   'Zounds, how has he the leisure to be sick
In such a justling time? Who leads his power?
Under whose government come they along?

MESSENGER.
His letters bears his mind, not I my lord.   20

WORCESTER.
I prithee tell me, doth he keep his bed?

MESSENGER.
He did my lord, four days ere I set forth,
And at the time of my departure thence,
He was much feared by his physicians.

WORCESTER.
I would the state of time had first been whole,   25
Ere he by sickness had been visited:
His health was never better worth than now.

HOTSPUR.   Sick now? droop now? this sickness doth infect
The very life-blood of our enterprise,
'Tis catching hither even to our camp.   30

---

3 **attribution** citation of worth   4 **stamp** coinage   5 **so
general current** as sterling currency   6 **defy** distrust   7 **soothers** flatterers **braver**
finer   9 **task . . . word** put my word to the test   9 **approve** test   12 **beard** oppose
18   **justling** jostling, busy   24 **feared** feared for   25 **whole** healthy, wholesome

He writes me here that inward sickness—
And that his friends by deputation could not
So soon be drawn, nor did he think it meet
To lay so dangerous and dear a trust
On any soul removed, but on his own.   35
Yet doth he give us bold advertisement,
That with our small conjunction we should on,
To see how fortune is disposed to us,
For as he writes there is no quailing now,
Because the king is certainly possessed   40
Of all our purposes. What say you to it?

WORCESTER.

Your father's sickness is a maim to us.

HOTSPUR.   A perilous gash, a very limb lopped off,
And yet in faith it is not: his present want
Seems more than we shall find it. Were it good   45
To set the exact wealth of all our states
All at one cast? to set so rich a main
On the nice hazard of one doubtful hour?
It were not good, for therein should we read
The very bottom and the soul of hope,   50
The very list, the very utmost bound
Of all our fortunes.

DOUGLAS.   Faith, and so we should.
Where now remains a sweet reversion,
We may boldly spend upon the hope of what
Is to come in: 55
A comfort of retirement lives in this.

HOTSPUR.   A rendezvous, a home to fly unto,
If that the devil and mischance look big
Upon the maidenhead of our affairs.

WORCESTER.

But yet I would your father had been here: 60
The quality and hair of our attempt
Brooks no division: it will be thought
By some that know not why he is away,

---

32 **deputation** a deputy   33 **drawn** i.e. together   35 **removed** less inti-
mately concerned   36 **advertisement** advice   37 **conjunction** joint armies   44 **want**
lack   46 **set** risk (fr. dicing)   47 **cast** throw of the dice **main** (1) stake in gambling (2)
army   48 **nice** precise   **hazard** (1) chance (2) dice game   49–52 **therein . . . fortunes** if
we did, we would learn the limits of our hopes and the boundaries of our fortunes   53
Where whereas   **reversion** promise of inheritance   56 **comfort of retirement** support
which we may fall back on   58 **big** threateningly   61 **hair** nature   62 **Brooks**
permits

That wisdom, loyalty, and mere dislike
Of our proceedings kept the earl from hence: 65
And think how such an apprehension
May turn the tide of fearful faction,
And breed a kind of question in our cause:
For well you know we of the off'ring side
Must keep aloof from strict arbitrement,   70
And stop all sight-holes, every loop from whence
The eye of reason may pry in upon us:
This absence of your father's draws a curtain
That shows the ignorant a kind of fear
Before not dreamt of.

HOTSPUR.   You strain too far.   75
I rather of his absence make this use,
It lends a lustre and more great opinion,
A larger dare to our great enterprise
Than if the earl were here, for men must think,
If we without his help can make a head   80
To push against a kingdom, with his help
We shall o'erturn it topsy-turvy down:
Yet all goes well, yet all our joints are whole.

DOUGLAS.   As heart can think: there is not such a word
Spoke of in Scotland as this term of fear.   85

Enter SIR RICHARD VERNON.

HOTSPUR.   My cousin Vernon, welcome by my soul.
VERNON.   Pray God my news be worth a welcome lord,
The Earl of Westmoreland seven thousand strong
Is marching hitherwards, with him Prince John.
HOTSPUR.   No harm, what more?
VERNON.   And further I have learned,   90
The king himself in person is set forth,
Or hitherwards intended speedily
With strong and mighty preparation.
HOTSPUR.   He shall be welcome too: where is his son,
The nimble-footed madcap Prince of Wales,   95
And his comrades that daffed the world aside
And bid it pass?

---

64 **mere** pure   67 **fearful faction** timorous division   68 **breed . . . cause**
generate investigation of our cause   69 **off'ring side** side taking the offensive   70 **strict**
arbitrement judicial inquiry   71 **loop** loophole   73 **draws** i.e. aside   74–5 **a kind . . .**
dreamt of that we fear, which never occurred to them before   77 **opinion** reputation   80
make a head (1) raise an army (2) advance against the enemy
95 **nimble-footed** (Holinshed points out Hal's skill as a runner; Hotspur implies the prince
will run from battle)

VERNON.   All furnished, all in arms:
                 All plumed like estridges that with the wind
                 Bated like eagles having lately bathed,
                 Glittering in golden coats like images,   100
                 As full of spirit as the month of May,
                 And gorgeous as the sun at midsummer,
                 Wanton as youthful goats, wild as young bulls:
                 I saw young Harry with his beaver on,
                 His cushes on his thighs, gallantly armed,   105
                 Rise from the ground like feathered Mercury,
                 And vaulted with such ease into his seat,
                 As if an angel dropped down from the clouds,
                 To turn and wind a fiery Pegasus,
                 And witch the world with noble horsemanship.   110
HOTSPUR.   No more, no more, worse than the sun in March,
                 This praise doth nourish agues: let them come,
                 They come like sacrifices in their trim,
                 And to the fire-eyed maid of smoky war,
                 All hot and bleeding will we offer them: 115
                 The mailèd Mars shall on his altar sit
                 Up to the ears in blood. I am on fire
                 To hear this rich reprisal is so nigh,
                 And yet not ours. Come let me taste my horse,
                 Who is to bear me like a thunderbolt   120
                 Against the bosom of the Prince of Wales.
                 Harry to Harry shall, hot horse to horse,
                 Meet and ne'er part till one drop down a corse.
                 O that Glendower were come.
VERNON.   There is more news:
                 I learned in Worcester as I rode along,   125
                 He cannot draw his power this fourteen days.
DOUGLAS.   That's the worst tidings that I hear of yet.
WORCESTER.
                 Ay by my faith, that bears a frosty sound.
HOTSPUR.   What may the king's whole battle reach unto?

---

96 **daffed** threw   97–110 **furnished . . . horsemanship** (the passage is rich in imagery that suggests the future hero in the young prince: gold, royalty, and classical myth)   97 **furnished** equipped   98–9 **estridges . . . bathed** ostriches that beat ("bated") their wings in the wind like eagles that had just bathed   100 **images** gilded statues of warriors   103 **Wanton** spirited   104 **beaver** helmet   105 **cushes** thigh armor   107 **vaulted . . . seat** (a test of horsemanship; cf. Macbeth's "vaulting ambition")   109 **wind** wheel   110 **witch** bewitch   112 **nourish agues** breed chills and fever (as it was believed the spring sun did)   113 **sacrifices . . . trim** decked out like animals to be sacrificed   114 **fire-eyed . . . war** Bellona, goddess of war   116 **mailed** wearing mail armor   118 **reprisal** prize   119 **taste** test   123 **corse** corpse   129 **battle** army

VERNON.   To thirty thousand.

HOTSPUR.   Forty let it be,   130
            My father and Glendower being both away,
            The powers of us may serve so great a day.
            Come let us take a muster speedily:
            Doomsday is near; die all, die merrily.

DOUGLAS.   Talk not of dying, I am out of fear   135
            Of death or death's hand for this one half year.

                                                        Exeunt.

            [SCENE II.]

            Enter FALSTAFF *and* BARDOLPH.

FALSTAFF.   Bardolph, get thee before to Coventry, fill me a bottle of
            sack, our soldiers shall march through. We'll to Sutton
            Co'fil' tonight.

BARDOLPH.   Will you give me money captain?

FALSTAFF.   Lay out, lay out.   5

BARDOLPH.   This bottle makes an angel.

FALSTAFF.   And if it do, take it for thy labour; and if it make twenty,
            take them all, I'll answer the coinage. Bid my lieutenant
            Peto meet me at town's end.

BARDOLPH.   I will captain, farewell.   *Exit.*   10

FALSTAFF.   If I be not ashamed of my soldiers, I am a soused gurnet: I
            have misused the king's press damnably. I have got in
            exchange of a hundred and fifty soldiers three hundred
            and odd pounds. I press me none but good householders,
            yeomen's sons, inquire me out contracted bachelors, such   15
            as had been asked twice on the banns: such a commodity
            of warm slaves, as had as lief hear the devil as a drum, such
            as fear the report of a caliver worse than a struck fowl or a
            hurt wild duck: I pressed me none but such toasts-and-
            butter with hearts in their bellies no bigger than pins'   20
            heads, and they have bought out their services, and now
            my whole charge consists of ancients, corporals, lieuten-
            ants, gentlemen of companies: slaves as ragged as Lazarus

---

IV, ii Warwickshire. The Coventry Road   2–3 **Sutton Co'fil'** Sutton Coldfield, (near
Birmingham and twenty miles past Coventry [Camb.; Q, F: "Sutton Cop-hill"])   5 **Lay
out** lay it out yourself   6 **makes an angel** brings the total outlay to 10s. (Falstaff interprets
as "will make an angel for me")   8 **I'll . . . coinage** if the bottle can make angels (coins), go
ahead, and I'll take the responsibility   11 **soused gurnet** small pickled fish   12 **king's
press** royal warrant for conscripting soldiers   15 **contracted** engaged   16 **banns**
marriage banns   **commodity** supply   17 **warm** well-off   18 **caliver** musket   19
toasts-and-butter timid souls   20 **hearts** (in the sense of "courage")   21 **bought . . .
services** paid to be released from serving (a practice not unusual)   22 **charge**

in the painted cloth, where the glutton's dogs licked his
sores, and such as indeed were never soldiers, but dis-   25
carded, unjust serving-men, younger sons to younger
brothers, revolted tapsters, and ostlers trade-fallen, the
cankers of a calm world and a long peace, ten times more
dishonourable ragged than an old fazed ancient; and such
have I to fill up the rooms of them as have bought out their 30
services, that you would think that I had a hundred and
fifty tattered prodigals, lately come from swine-keeping,
from eating draff and husks. A mad fellow met me on the
way, and told me I had unloaded all the gibbets, and
pressed the dead bodies. No eye hath seen such scare-   35
crows. I'll not march through Coventry with them, that's
flat: nay, and the villains march wide betwixt the legs as if
they had gyves on, for indeed I had the most of them out of
prison: there's not a shirt and a half in all my company,
and the half shirt is two napkins tacked together, and   40
thrown over the shoulders like a herald's coat without
sleeves, and the shirt to say the truth, stolen from my host
at Saint Alban's, or the red-nose inn-keeper of Daventry.
But that's all one, they'll find linen enough on every
hedge.   45

Enter the PRINCE *and the*
LORD OF WESTMORELAND.

PRINCE.   How now blown Jack? how now quilt?

FALSTAFF.   What Hal, how now mad wag? What a devil dost thou in
            Warwickshire? My good Lord of Westmoreland, I cry
            you mercy, I thought your honour had already been at
            Shrewsbury.   50

WESTMORELAND.
            Faith Sir John, 'tis more than time that I were there, and
            you too, but my powers are there already. The king, I can
            tell you, looks for us all, we must away all night.

FALSTAFF.   Tut, never fear me, I am as vigilant as a cat to steal cream.

PRINCE.   I think to steal cream indeed, for thy theft hath already 55

---

command   **ancients** ensigns, flag bearers   23 **gentlemen of companies** men of indeter-
minate rank above a private, similar to a noncommissioned officer   24 **painted cloth**
imitation tapestry, cheap wall hanging   26 **unjust** dishonest   27 **revolted**
runaway   **trade-fallen** unemployed   28 **cankers** parasites, cankerworms (which preyed
on healthy plants)   29 **fazed ancient** frayed flag   32 **prodigals** (referring to the parable of
the prodigal son, in Luke XV. 16)   33 **draff** pig swill   34 **gibbets** gallows, where the dead
were left hanging   35 **pressed** conscripted   38 **gyves** iron rings that fettered the
legs   43 **Saint Alban's, Daventry** towns on the road from London to Coventry   44–5
find . . . hedge steal the linen drying on hedges   46 **blown** i.e. up   **quilt** (w. pun on
"jack," the soldier's quilted jacket)   49 **cry you mercy** beg your pardon

made thee butter: but tell me Jack, whose fellows are these
that come after?

FALSTAFF.   Mine, Hal, mine.

PRINCE.   I did never see such pitiful rascals.

FALSTAFF.   Tut, tut, good enough to toss, food for powder, food for   60
powder: they'll fill a pit as well as better; tush man, mortal
men, mortal men.

WESTMORELAND.
Ay but Sir John, methinks they are exceeding poor and
bare, too beggarly.

FALSTAFF.   Faith, for their poverty I know not where they had that,   65
and for their bareness I am sure they never learned that of
me.

PRINCE.   No I'll be sworn, unless you call three fingers in the ribs
bare. But sirrah make haste, Percy is already in the field.

FALSTAFF.   What, is the king encamped?   70

WESTMORELAND.
He is Sir John, I fear we shall stay too long.   [*Exit.*]

FALSTAFF.   Well,
To the latter end of a fray, and the beginning of a feast,
Fits a dull fighter and a keen guest.   *Exeunt.*

[SCENE III.]

Enter HOTSPUR, WORCESTER, DOUGLAS, *and* VERNON.

HOTSPUR.   We'll fight with him tonight.

WORCESTER.   It may not be.

DOUGLAS.   You give him then advantage.

VERNON.   Not a whit.

HOTSPUR.   Why say you so, looks he not for supply?

VERNON.   So do we.

HOTSPUR.   His is certain, ours is doubtful.

WORCESTER.
Good cousin be advised, stir not tonight.   5

VERNON.   Do not, my lord.

DOUGLAS.   You do not counsel well:
You speak it out of fear, and cold heart.

VERNON.   Do me no slander, Douglas: by my life,
And I dare well maintain it with my life,

---

56 **butter**
fat   60 **toss** blow into the air   **powder** gunpowder   64 **bare** threadbare   68 **three**
. . . **ribs** being covered with fat the width of three fingers on the ribs   73–4 **To . . . guest**
(proverbial)
     IV, iii Near Shrewsbury. The rebel camp   3 **supply** reinforcements   10

| | If well-respected honour bid me on, | 10 |

                If well-respected honour bid me on,   10
                I hold as little counsel with weak fear,
                As you my lord, or any Scot that this day lives.
                Let it be seen tomorrow in the battle
                Which of us fears.
DOUGLAS.   Yea, or tonight.
VERNON.   Content.
HOTSPUR.   Tonight say I.   15
VERNON.   Come, come, it may not be. I wonder much,
                Being men of such great leading as you are,
                That you foresee not what impediments
                Drag back our expedition: certain horse
                Of my cousin Vernon's are not yet come up,   20
                Your uncle Worcester's horses came but today,
                And now their pride and mettle is asleep,
                Their courage with hard labour tame and dull,
                That not a horse is half the half of himself.
HOTSPUR.   So are the horses of the enemy   25
                In general journey-bated and brought low,
                The better part of ours are full of rest.
WORCESTER.
                The number of the king exceedeth ours:
                For God's sake cousin, stay till all come in.

                            The trumpet sounds a parley.

                        Enter SIR WALTER BLUNT.

BLUNT.   I come with gracious offers from the king,   30
                If you vouchsafe me hearing and respect.
HOTSPUR.   Welcome Sir Walter Blunt: and would to God
                You were of our determination.
                Some of us love you well, and even those some
                Envy your great deservings and good name,   35
                Because you are not of our quality,
                But stand against us like an enemy.
BLUNT.   And God defend but still I should stand so,
                So long as out of limit and true rule
                You stand against anointed majesty.   40
                But to my charge. The king hath sent to know
                The nature of your griefs, and whereupon
                You conjure from the breast of civil peace

---

well-respected well-considered   17 **great leading** experienced leadership   22 **mettle**
spirit   26 **journey-bated** worn out from travel   29 **stay** wait   33 **determination** mind
(faction)   35 **Envy** begrudge   36 **quality** company   38 **defend** forbid   **still**
always   39 **out of limit** beyond the bounds (of allegiance)   42 **whereupon** why

Such bold hostility, teaching his duteous land
Audacious cruelty. If that the king   45
Have any way your good deserts forgot,
Which he confesseth to be manifold,
He bids you name your griefs, and with all speed
You shall have your desires with interest,
And pardon absolute for yourself, and these   50
Herein misled by your suggestion.

HOTSPUR.   The king is kind, and well we know the king
Knows at what time to promise, when to pay:
My father and my uncle and myself,
Did give him that same royalty he wears,   55
And when he was not six and twenty strong,
Sick in the world's regard, wretched and low,
A poor unminded outlaw sneaking home,
My father gave him welcome to the shore:
And when he heard him swear and vow to God,   60
He came but to be Duke of Lancaster,
To sue his livery, and beg his peace
With tears of innocency, and terms of zeal,
My father in kind heart and pity moved,
Swore him assistance, and performed it too.   65
Now when the lords and barons of the realm
Perceived Northumberland did lean to him,
The more and less came in with cap and knee,
Met him in boroughs, cities, villages,
Attended him on bridges, stood in lanes,   70
Laid gifts before him, proffered him their oaths,
Gave him their heirs as pages, followed him,
Even at the heels, in golden multitudes.
He presently, as greatness knows itself,
Steps me a little higher than his vow   75
Made to my father while his blood was poor
Upon the naked shore at Ravenspurgh,
And now forsooth takes on him to reform
Some certain edicts, and some strait decrees,
That lie too heavy on the commonwealth,   80
Cries out upon abuses, seems to weep

---

51 **suggestion** incitement 62 **sue his livery** sue for the delivery of his rightful inheritance
(which Richard II had seized)   63 **terms of zeal** pronouncements of his loyalty   68 **The
more and less** those of high and low estate   68 **with . . . knee** respectfully removing their
hats and bowing their knees   70 **lanes** rows crowding both sides of a passage   73 **golden**
richly decked   74 **knows itself** comes to know itself as great   76 **his . . . poor** he was
humble in spirit   79 **strait** strict   81 **Cries out upon** denounces

Over his country's wrongs, and by this face,
This seeming brow of justice, did he win
The hearts of all that he did angle for:
Proceeded further, cut me off the heads   85
Of all the favourites that the absent king
In deputation left behind him here,
When he was personal in the Irish war.

BLUNT.   Tut, I came not to hear this.

HOTSPUR.   Then to the point.
In short time after, he deposed the king,   90
Soon after that, deprived him of his life,
And in the neck of that, tasked the whole state:
To make that worse, suffered his kinsman March
(Who is, if every owner were well placed,
Indeed his king) to be engaged in Wales,   95
There without ransom to lie forfeited:
Disgraced me in my happy victories,
Sought to entrap me by intelligence,
Rated mine uncle from the council-board,
In rage dismissed my father from the court,   100
Broke oath on oath, committed wrong on wrong,
And in conclusion drove us to seek out
This head of safety, and withal to pry
Into his title, the which we find
Too indirect for long continuance.   105

BLUNT.   Shall I return this answer to the king?

HOTSPUR. Not so, Sir Walter. We'll withdraw awhile.
Go to the king, and let there be impawned
Some surety for a safe return again,
And in the morning early shall mine uncle   110
Bring him our purposes, and so farewell.

BLUNT.   I would you would accept of grace and love.

HOTSPUR. And may be so we shall.

BLUNT.   Pray God you do.

Exeunt.

---

87 **In deputation** as
deputies   88 **personal** personally   92 **in the neck of** immediately following   **tasked**
taxed   93 **March** Mortimer, the Earl of March   94 **well** rightfully   95 **engaged** held as
hostage   98 **intelligence** reports from spies   99 **Rated** berated   103 **head of safety**
army for our safety   103 **withal** at the same time   105 **Too indirect** in too indirect a line of
succession   108 **impawned** left as security   111 **purposes** proposals

[SCENE IV].

Enter the ARCHBISHOP OF YORK *and* SIR MICHAEL.

ARCHBISHOP.

    Hie good Sir Michael, bear this sealèd brief
    With wingèd haste to the lord marshal,
    This to my cousin Scroop, and all the rest
    To whom they are directed. If you knew
    How much they do import, you would make haste.   5

SIR MICHAEL.

    My good lord,
    I guess their tenour.

ARCHBISHOP.   Like enough you do.

    Tomorrow good Sir Michael is a day,
    Wherein the fortune of ten thousand men
    Must bide the touch. For sir at Shrewsbury,   10
    As I am truly given to understand,
    The king with mighty and quick-raisèd power
    Meets with Lord Harry: and I fear Sir Michael
    What with the sickness of Northumberland,
    Whose power was in the first proportion,   15
    And what with Owen Glendower's absence thence,
    Who with them was a rated sinew too,
    And comes not in, o'er-ruled by prophecies,
    I fear the power of Percy is too weak
    To wage an instant trial with the king.   20

SIR MICHAEL.

    Why my good lord, you need not fear,
    There is Douglas, and Lord Mortimer.

ARCHBISHOP.

    No, Mortimer is not there.

SIR MICHAEL.

    But there is Mordake, Vernon, Lord Harry Percy,
    And there is my Lord of Worcester, and a head   25
    Of gallant warriors, noble gentlemen.

ARCHBISHOP.

    And so there is: but yet the king hath drawn
    The special head of all the land together,

    IV, iv, York. The Archbishop's palace   1 **brief** letter   2 **lord marshal** Thomas
Mowbray (son of the Mowbray banished in *RII* and one of the rebels in *2 HIV*)   7 **tenour**
intent   10 **bide the touch** be put to the test ("touch"=touchstone, which tested gold)   15
first highest   17 **a rated sinew** a strength on which we counted   18 **prophecies** (in
keeping with his belief in portents; this may identify him as the Welsh captain who fails
Richard II for the same reason)   25 **head** army   28 **head** (1) army (2) nobility,

The Prince of Wales, Lord John of Lancaster,
The noble Westmoreland, and warlike Blunt,   30
And many moe corrivals and dear men
Of estimation and command in arms.

SIR MICHAEL.

Doubt not my lord: they shall be well opposed.

ARCHBISHOP.

I hope no less, yet needful 'tis to fear,
And to prevent the worst, Sir Michael speed: 35
For if Lord Percy thrive not, ere the king
Dismiss his power, he means to visit us,
For he hath heard of our confederacy,
And 'tis but wisdom to make strong against him:
Therefore make haste, I must go write again   40
To other friends, and so farewell Sir Michael.   *Exeunt.*

Act Five

[SCENE I.]

Enter the KING, PRINCE OF WALES, LORD JOHN OF LANCASTER,
    EARL OF WESTMORELAND, SIR WALTER BLUNT, *and*
    FALSTAFF.

KING.

How bloodily the sun begins to peer
Above yon busky hill, the day looks pale
    At his distemp'rature.

PRINCE.   The southern wind
Doth play the trumpet to his purposes,
And by his hollow whistling in the leaves   5
Foretells a tempest and a blust'ring day.

KING.

Then with the losers let it sympathize,
For nothing can seem foul to those that win.

                                    The trumpet sounds.

                    Enter WORCESTER [*and* VERNON].

How now my Lord of Worcester, 'tis not well,
That you and I should meet upon such terms   10
As now we meet. You have deceived our trust,
And made us doff our easy robes of peace,
To crush our old limbs in ungentle steel,

---

leaders   31 **moe** more   **corrivals** partners   **dear** valued   32 **estimation** reputation
37 **means . . . us** (foreshadowing the events of *2 HIV*)
V, i Shrewsbury. The King's camp   2 **busky** wooded   3 **his distemp'rature** the sun's
disorder (unusually flushed appearance)   4 **his purposes** the sun's portents (of coming
tempest)

This is not well my lord, this is not well.
What say you to it? Will you again unknit   15
This churlish knot of all-abhorrèd war,
And move in that obedient orb again,
Where you did give a fair and natural light,
And be no more an èxhaled meteor,
A prodigy of fear, and a portent   20
Of broachèd mischief to the unborn times?

WORCESTER.

Hear me my liege:
For mine own part I could be well content
To entertain the lag-end of my life
With quiet hours. For I do protest   25
I have not sought the day of this dislike.

KING.   You have not sought it, how comes it then?

FALSTAFF. Rebellion lay in his way, and he found it.

PRINCE.   Peace chewet, peace.

WORCESTER.

It pleased your majesty to turn your looks   30
Of favour from myself, and all our house,
And yet I must remember you my lord,
We were the first and dearest of your friends:
For you my staff of office did I break
In Richard's time, and posted day and night   35
To meet you on the way, and kiss your hand,
When yet you were in place and in account
Nothing so strong and fortunate as I.
It was myself, my brother and his son,
That brought you home, and boldly did outdare   40
The dangers of the time. You swore to us,
And you did swear that oath at Doncaster,
That you did nothing purpose 'gainst the state,
Nor claim no further than your new-fall'n right,
The seat of Gaunt, dukedom of Lancaster: 45
To this we swore our aid: but in short space
It rained down fortune show'ring on your head,
And such a flood of greatness fell on you—

---

17 **obedient orb** sphere of obedience (the Ptolemaic conception of the planets fixed in orbs revolving around the earth)   19 **exhaled** drawn forth (1) by the sun from vapors (2) from the "obedient orb" (l. 17)   21 **broached mischief** unleashed evil   24 **entertain** employ   29 **chewet** (1) jackdaw (chatterer) (2) minced meat   32 **remember** remind   34 **staff . . . break** (sign of resignation of office)   43 **purpose** intend   44 **new-fall'n** newly fallen due to you   45 **seat** estate

What with our help, what with the absent king,
What with the injuries of a wanton time,   50
The seeming sufferances that you had borne,
And the contrarious winds that held the king
So long in his unlucky Irish wars,
That all in England did repute him dead—
And from this swarm of fair advantages,   55
You took occasion to be quickly wooed
To gripe the general sway into your hand,
Forgot your oath to us at Doncaster,
And being fed by us, you used us so
As that ungentle gull the cuckoo's bird   60
Useth the sparrow: did oppress our nest,
Grew by our feeding to so great a bulk,
That even our love durst not come near your sight,
For fear of swallowing: but with nimble wing
We were enforced for safety sake to fly   65
Out of your sight, and raise this present head,
Whereby we stand opposèd by such means
As you yourself have forged against yourself
By unkind usage, dangerous countenance,
And violation of all faith and troth   70
Sworn to us in your younger enterprise.

KING.   These things indeed you have articulate,
Proclaimed at market-crosses, read in churches,
To face the garment of rebellion
With some fine colour that may please the eye   75
Of fickle changelings and poor discontents,
Which gape and rub the elbow at the news
Of hurlyburly innovation:
And never yet did insurrection want
Such water-colours to impaint his cause,   80
Nor moody beggars starving for a time
Of pell-mell havoc and confusion.

PRINCE.   In both your armies there is many a soul
Shall pay full dearly for this encounter

---

50 **injuries** wrongs   **wanton** turbulent   51 **sufferances** sufferings   57 **gripe . . . sway** grasp the rule of the whole country   60 **bird** nestling   61 **sparrow** (in whose nest the cuckoo lays its eggs, and then its fledglings crowd out the baby sparrows)   64 **swallowing** being swallowed   66 **head** army   69 **dangerous** threatening   71 **younger** beginning   72 **articulate** itemized in articles   74 **face** trim   75 **colour** (1) lit. (2) pretext   77 **rub the elbow** hug themselves (with joy)   78 **innovation** revolution   79 **want** lack   80 **water-colours** weak (1) colors (2) excuses   82 **pell-mell havoc** indiscriminate pillage   **confusion** destruction

If once they join in trial. Tell your nephew   85
The Prince of Wales doth join with all the world
In praise of Henry Percy: by my hopes,
This present enterprise set off his head,
I do not think a braver gentleman,
More active-valiant, or more valiant-young,   90
More daring, or more bold, is now alive
To grace this latter age with noble deeds.
For my part I may speak it to my shame,
I have a truant been to chivalry,
And so I hear he doth account me too;   95
Yet this before my father's majesty—
I am content that he shall take the odds
Of his great name and estimation,
And will, to save the blood on either side,
Try fortune with him in a single fight.   100

KING.   And Prince of Wales, so dare we venture thee,
Albeit considerations infinite
Do make against it: no, good Worcester, no,
We love our people well, even those we love
That are misled upon your cousin's part,   105
And will they take the offer of our grace,
Both he, and they, and you, yea every man
Shall be my friend again, and I'll be his,
So tell your cousin, and bring me word
What he will do. But if he will not yield,   110
Rebuke and dread correction wait on us,
And they shall do their office. So be gone:
We will not now be troubled with reply,
We offer fair, take it advisedly.

                Exit WORCESTER [with VERNON].

PRINCE.   It will not be accepted, on my life,   115
The Douglas and the Hotspur both together
Are confident against the world in arms.

KING.   Hence therefore, every leader to his charge,
For on their answer will we set on them,
And God befriend us as our cause is just.   120

                Exeunt. Manent Prince and Falstaff.

FALSTAFF.   Hal, if thou see me down in the battle and bestride me, so,

87 hopes i.e. of salvation 88 set . . . head excepted 98 estimation reputation   102
Albeit yet   105 cousin kinsman   part side   111 wait on serve   121 bestride
(common battle practice to protect a fallen comrade)

'tis a point of friendship.

PRINCE.   Nothing but a colossus can do thee that friendship, say
thy prayers, and farewell.

FALSTAFF. I would 'twere bedtime Hal, and all well.   125

PRINCE.   Why, thou owest God a death.   [*Exit.*]

FALSTAFF. 'Tis not due yet, I would be loath to pay him before his
day: what need I be so forward with him that calls not on
me? Well, 'tis no matter, honour pricks me on; yea, but
how if honour prick me off when I come on? how then? 130
Can honour set to a leg? No: or an arm? No: or take away
the grief of a wound? No: honour hath no skill in surgery
then? No. What is honour? A word. What is in that word
honour? What is that honour? Air: a trim reckoning. Who
hath it? He that died o' Wednesday. Doth he feel it? No. 135
Doth he hear it? No. 'Tis insensible then? Yea, to the
dead. But will it not live with the living? No. Why?
Detraction will not suffer it, therefore I'll none of it.
Honour is a mere scutcheon, and so ends my catechism.

Exit.

[SCENE II.]

Enter WORCESTER *and* SIR RICHARD VERNON.

WORCESTER.
O no, my nephew must not know Sir Richard,
The liberal and kind offer of the king.

VERNON.   'Twere best he did.

WORCESTER.   Then are we all undone.
It is not possible, it cannot be
The king should keep his word in loving us: 5
He will suspect us still, and find a time
To punish this offence in other faults:
Supposition all our lives shall be stuck full of eyes,
For treason is but trusted like the fox,
Who never so tame, so cherished and locked up,   10
Will have a wild trick of his ancestors:
Look how we can, or sad or merrily,

---

123 **colossus** giant statue whose legs
spanned the harbor of ancient Rhodes   126–7 **death . . . due** (punning on similar sound of
"death" and "debt")   129 **pricks** spurs   130 **prick me off** check (or prick with a pin) my
name among those who are to die   131 **set to a leg** set a broken leg   132 **grief** pain   134
trim reckoning fine score (ironic)   136 **insensible** imperceptible to the senses   138 **suffer**
allow   139 **scutcheon** tablet displaying the coat of arms of a deceased person
V, ii The rebel camp   6 **still** always   8 **Supposition** Rumor (personified in *2
HIV*)   **stuck . . . eyes** painted with watchful eyes   11 **trick** trait   12 **or . . . or** either

Interpretation will misquote our looks,
And we shall feed like oxen at a stall,
The better cherished still the nearer death.   15
My nephew's trespass may be well forgot,
It hath the excuse of youth and heat of blood,
And an adopted name of privilege,
A hare-brained Hotspur, governed by a spleen:
All his offences live upon my head   20
And on his father's. We did train him on,
And his corruption being ta'en from us,
We as the spring of all shall pay for all:
Therefore good cousin, let not Harry know
In any case the offer of the king.   25

VERNON.   Deliver what you will, I'll say 'tis so.
Here comes your cousin.

Enter HOTSPUR [*and* DOUGLAS].

HOTSPUR.   My uncle is returned,
Deliver up my Lord of Westmoreland.
Uncle, what news?   30

WORCESTER.
The King will bid you battle presently.

DOUGLAS.   Defy him by the Lord of Westmoreland.
HOTSPUR.   Lord Douglas, go you and tell him so.
DOUGLAS.   Marry and shall, and very willingly.

Exit DOUGLAS.

WORCESTER.
There is no seeming mercy in the king.   35
HOTSPUR.   Did you beg any? God forbid.
WORCESTER.
I told him gently of our grievances,
Of his oath-breaking, which he mended thus,
By now forswearing that he is forsworn:
He calls us rebels, traitors, and will scourge   40
With haughty arms this hateful name in us.

Enter DOUGLAS.

DOUGLAS.   Arm gentlemen, to arms, for I have thrown
A brave defiance in King Henry's teeth,

. . . or   18 **adopted** . . . **privilege** nickname that gives him the privilege of living up to
it   19 **spleen** hot temper   31 **presently** immediately   35 **seeming** pretense of   38
mended amended   39 **forswearing** swearing falsely   44 **engaged** held as a hostage   51

And Westmoreland that was engaged did bear it,
Which cannot choose but bring him quickly on.   45
WORCESTER.
        The Prince of Wales stepped forth before the king,
        And nephew, challenged you to single fight.
HOTSPUR.   O would the quarrel lay upon our heads,
        And that no man might draw short breath today
        But I and Harry Monmouth; tell me, tell me,   50
        How showed his tasking? Seemed it in contempt?
VERNON.   No, by my soul I never in my life
        Did hear a challenge urged more modestly,
        Unless a brother should a brother dare
        To gentle exercise and proof of arms.   55
        He gave you all the duties of a man,
        Trimmed up your praises with a princely tongue,
        Spoke your deservings like a chronicle,
        Making you ever better than his praise,
        By still dispraising praise valued with you: 60
        And which became him like a prince indeed,
        He made a blushing cital of himself,
        And chid his truant youth with such a grace
        As if he mastered there a double spirit
        Of teaching and of learning instantly: 65
        There did he pause, but let me tell the world,
        If he outlive the envy of this day,
        England did never owe so sweet a hope,
        So much misconstrued in his wantonness.
HOTSPUR.   Cousin I think thou art enamourèd   70
        On his follies: never did I hear
        Of any prince so wild a liberty.
        But be he as he will, yet once ere night
        I will embrace him with a soldier's arm,
        That he shall shrink under my courtesy.   75
        Arm, arm with speed, and fellows, soldiers, friends,
        Better consider what you have to do
        Than I that have not well the gift of tongue
        Can lift your blood up with persuasion.

tasking challenging   56 **duties of** due respect   57 **Trimmed up** embellished   58
chronicle history book (which appraised character as well as reported events)   60 **disprais-
ing . . . you** censuring praise as inadequate to describe your worth   62 **blushing cital**
modest recital   65 **instantly** at the same instant   67 **envy** ill will   68 **owe** own   72 **so
wild a liberty** such reckless license   77–9 **Better . . . persuasion** consider what actions you
have to perform, and that will rouse your blood better than I can, lacking the talents of an
orator

Enter a MESSENGER.

MESSENGER.
    My lord, here are letters for you.   80
HOTSPUR. I cannot read them now.
    O gentlemen the time of life is short;
    To spend that shortness basely were too long
    If life did ride upon a dial's point,
    Still ending at the arrival of an hour: 85
    And if we live, we live to tread on kings,
    If die, brave death when princes die with us.
    Now for our consciences, the arms are fair
    When the intent of bearing them is just.

Enter another MESSENGER.

MESSENGER.
    My lord prepare, the king comes on apace.   90
HOTSPUR. I thank him that he cuts me from my tale,
    For I profess not talking: only this,
    Let each man do his best. And here draw I
    A sword whose temper I intend to stain
    With the best blood that I can meet withal,   95
    In the adventure of this perilous day.
    Now Esperance Percy! and set on,
    Sound all the lofty instruments of war,
    And by that music let us all embrace,
    For heaven to earth, some of us never shall   100
    A second time do such a courtesy.
            Here they embrace. The trumpets sound. [*Exeunt.*]

[SCENE III.]

The KING *enters with his power* [*over the stage, and exeunt*].
Alarum to the battle. Then enter DOUGLAS *and* SIR WALTER BLUNT.

BLUNT.   What is thy name, that in battle thus
    Thou crossest me? What honour dost thou seek
    Upon my head?
DOUGLAS.   Know then my name is Douglas,
    And I do haunt thee in the battle thus
    Because some tell me that thou art a king.   5

83–5 **were too long . . . hour** would make
life too long, even if it lasted only an hour   84 **dial's point** hand of a clock   87 **brave**
splendid   88 **for** as for   89 **intent of** cause for   90 **apace** swiftly   97 **Esperance** (first
word of the Percy motto, and their battle cry; the final "e" is pronounced)   100 **heaven to**
earth the odds being as heaven is to earth

BLUNT.   They tell thee true.

DOUGLAS.   The Lord of Stafford dear today hath bought
Thy likeness, for instead of thee King Harry,
This sword hath ended him, so shall it thee
Unless thou yield thee as my prisoner.   10

BLUNT.   I was not born a yielder thou proud Scot,
And thou shalt find a king that will revenge
Lord Stafford's death.

They fight. Douglas kills Blunt.

Then enter HOTSPUR.

HOTSPUR.   O Douglas, hadst thou fought at Holmedon thus,
I never had triumphed upon a Scot.   15

DOUGLAS.   All's done, all's won, here breathless lies the king.

HOTSPUR.   Where?

DOUGLAS.   Here.

HOTSPUR.   This Douglas? No, I know this face full well,
A gallant knight he was, his name was Blunt,   20
Semblably furnished like the king himself.

DOUGLAS.   Ah 'fool' go with thy soul whither it goes,
A borrowed title hast thou bought too dear.
Why didst thou tell me that thou wert a king?

HOTSPUR.   The king hath many marching in his coats.   25

DOUGLAS.   Now by my sword I will kill all his coats.
I'll murder all his wardrobe, piece by piece,
Until I meet the king.

HOTSPUR.   Up and away,
Our soldiers stand full fairly for the day.   *Exeunt.*

Alarum. Enter FALSTAFF *solus.*

FALSTAFF.   Though I could 'scape shot-free at London, I fear the shot   30
here, here's no scoring but upon the pate. Soft, who are
you? Sir Walter Blunt—there's honour for you: here's no
vanity. I am as hot as molten lead, and as heavy too: God
keep lead out of me, I need no more weight than mine own
bowels. I have led my ragamuffins where they are pep-   35
pered, there's not three of my hundred and fifty left alive,
and they are for the town's end, to beg during life: but who
comes here?

V, iii The battlefield   6 **true** (in customary battle practice, some nobles dressed like the
king or leader to act as decoys. Cf. *JC*, V, iv; *RIII*, V, iv, 11-12)   21 **Semblably furnished
like** equipped to resemble   22 **'fool'** . . . **goes** the title of "fool" accompany your soul to the
next world   25,26 **coats** (1) the sleeveless surcoat (2) the coat of arms on that tunic   29
stand . . . **day** look as if they are in a fair way to win today   30 **shot-free** (1) free from being
shot (2) without paying the bill   31 **scoring** (1) charging the bill (2) cutting   31 **pate**
head   37 **town's** . . . **life** (some returned soldiers became beggars at the town gates)

Enter the PRINCE.

PRINCE.   What, stand'st thou idle here? Lend me thy sword.
            Many a nobleman lies stark and stiff,   40
            Under the hoofs of vaunting enemies,
            Whose deaths are yet unrevenged. I prithee lend me thy
                sword.

FALSTAFF.   O Hal, I prithee give me leave to breathe awhile: Turk
            Gregory never did such deeds in arms as I have done this
            day. I have paid Percy, I have made him sure.   45

PRINCE.   He is indeed, and living to kill thee: I prithee lend me thy
            sword.

FALSTAFF.   Nay, before God Hal, if Percy be alive thou get'st not my
            sword, but take my pistol if thou wilt.

PRINCE.   Give it me: what, is it in the case?   50

FALSTAFF.   Ay Hal, 'tis hot, 'tis hot, there's that will sack a city.

                                    *The Prince draws it out, and
                                    finds it to be a bottle of sack.*

PRINCE.   What, is it a time to jest and dally now?

                                    He throws the bottle at him. Exit.

FALSTAFF.   Well, if Percy be alive, I'll pierce him: if he do come in my
            way, so: if he do not, if I come in his willingly, let him
            make a carbonado of me. I like not such grinning honour   55
            as Sir Walter hath. Give me life, which if I can save, so: if
            not, honour comes unlooked for, and there's an end.

                                                        Exit.

            [SCENE IV.]

            Alarum, excursions. Enter the KING, *the* PRINCE,
            LORD JOHN OF LANCASTER, EARL OF WESTMORELAND.

KING.   I prithee
            Harry withdraw thyself, thou bleedest too much:
            Lord John of Lancaster go you with him.

JOHN.   Not I my lord, unless I did bleed too.

PRINCE.   I do beseech your majesty make up,   5
            Lest your retirement do amaze your friends.

---

43 **Turk Gregory** either Pope Gregory VII or Gregory XIII (whose names were synonyms
for violence. "Turk" implies cruelty)   45 **paid** killed   51 **hot** i.e. from having fired so
often   53 **pierce** (pronounced "perse," a pun on "Percy")   55 **carbonado** meat slashed all
over for broiling
V, iv Another part of the battlefield   5 **make up** advance

KING.   I will do so.
             My lord of Westmoreland, lead him to his tent.
WESTMORELAND.
             Come my lord, I'll lead you to your tent.
PRINCE.   Lead me my lord? I do not need your help,   10
             And God forbid a shallow scratch should drive
             The Prince of Wales from such a field as this,
             Where stained nobility lies trodden on,
             And rebels' arms triumph in massacres.
JOHN.   We breathe too long: come Cousin Westmoreland,   15
             Our duty this way lies: for God's sake come.

                    [*Exeunt* LORD JOHN *and* WESTMORELAND.]

PRINCE.   By God, thou hast deceived me Lancaster,
             I did not think thee lord of such a spirit:
             Before, I loved thee as a brother, John,
             But now I do respect thee as my soul.   20
KING.   I saw him hold Lord Percy at the point,
             With lustier maintenance than I did look for
             Of such an ungrown warrior.
PRINCE.   O this boy
             Lends mettle to us all.   *Exit.*

                    Enter DOUGLAS.

DOUGLAS.   Another king? They grow like Hydra's heads: 25
             I am the Douglas, fatal to all those
             That wear those colours on them. What art thou
             That counterfeit'st the person of a king?
KING.   The king himself, who Douglas, grieves at heart,
             So many of his shadows thou hast met   30
             And not the very king. I have two boys
             Seek Percy and thyself about the field,
             But seeing thou fall'st on me so luckily,
             I will assay thee: so defend thyself.
DOUGLAS.   I fear thou art another counterfeit,   35
             And yet in faith thou bear'st thee like a king:
             But mine I am sure thou art, whoe'er thou be,
             And thus I win thee.

             They fight, the king being in danger, enter PRINCE OF WALES.

---

6 amaze dismay   13
stained (1) bloodstained (2) dishonored   15 **breathe** pause for breath   24 **mettle**
spirit   25 **Hydra's heads** (in the myth, whenever a head was cut off, the Hydra grew two in
its place)   27 **those colours** that coat of arms   34 **assay thee** put you to the trial

PRINCE.   Hold up thy head vile Scot, or thou art like
          Never to hold it up again: the spirits   40
          Of valiant Shirley, Stafford, Blunt are in my arms,
          It is the Prince of Wales that threatens thee,
          Who never promiseth but he means to pay.

                              They fight. Douglas flieth.

          Cheerly my lord, how fares your grace?
          Sir Nicholas Gawsey hath for succour sent,   45
          And so hath Clifton: I'll to Clifton straight.
KING.   Stay and breathe awhile.
          Thou hast redeemed thy lost opinion,
          And showed thou mak'st some tender of my life,
          In this fair rescue thou hast brought to me.   50
PRINCE.   O God they did me too much injury,
          That ever said I hearkened for your death.
          If it were so, I might have let alone
          The insulting hand of Douglas over you,
          Which would have been as speedy in your end   55
          As all the poisonous potions in the world,
          And saved the treacherous labour of your son.
KING.   Make up to Clifton, I'll to Sir Nicholas Gawsey.

                              Exit KING.

                         Enter HOTSPUR.

HOTSPUR. If I mistake not, thou art Harry Monmouth.
PRINCE.   Thou speak'st as if I would deny my name.   60
HOTSPUR. My name is Harry Percy.
PRINCE.   Why then I see
          A very valiant rebel of the name;
          I am the Prince of Wales, and think not Percy
          To share with me in glory any more:
          Two stars keep not their motion in one sphere,   65
          Nor can one England brook a double reign
          Of Harry Percy and the Prince of Wales.
HOTSPUR. Nor shall it Harry, for the hour is come
          To end the one of us, and would to God
          Thy name in arms were now as great as mine.   70

---

43 **pay** (1) lit. (with "promiseth") (2) kill   47 **breathe** catch your breath   48 **opinion** reputation   49 **mak'st some tender of** cherish   52 **hearkened for** hoped to hear of   54 **insulting** exulting   58 **Make up** advance   65 **keep ... sphere** (according to the Ptolemaic system, each star remained fixed in its sphere as it revolved around the earth)   66, 74, 78 **brook** endure   70 **were now as great** (because the victor gained the

PRINCE.   I'll make it greater ere I part from thee,
            And all the budding honours on thy crest
            I'll crop to make a garland for my head.
HOTSPUR.   I can no longer brook thy vanities.   *They fight.*

                        Enter FALSTAFF.

FALSTAFF.   Well said Hal, to it Hal. Nay you shall find no boy's play   75
            here, I can tell you.

                        Enter DOUGLAS.
                        He fighteth with Falstaff, who
                falls down as if he were dead. [*Exit* DOUGLAS.]

                                The Prince killeth Percy.

HOTSPUR.   O Harry, thou hast robbed me of my youth:
            I better brook the loss of brittle life
            Than those proud titles thou hast won of me,
            They wound my thoughts worse than thy sword my
                flesh: 80
            But thought's the slave of life, and life, time's fool;
            And time that takes survey of all the world
            Must have a stop. O I could prophesy,
            But that the earthy and cold hand of death
            Lies on my tongue: no Percy, thou art dust   85
            And food for—   [*Dies.*]
PRINCE.   For worms, brave Percy. Fare thee well great heart:
            Ill-weaved ambition, how much art thou shrunk:
            When that this body did contain a spirit,
            A kingdom for it was too small a bound,   90
            But now two paces of the vilest earth
            Is room enough: this earth that bears thee dead,
            Bears not alive so stout a gentleman.
            If thou wert sensible of courtesy,
            I should not make so dear a show of zeal,   95
            But let my favours hide thy mangled face,
            And even in thy behalf I'll thank myself,
            For doing these fair rites of tenderness.

---

honors previously earned by the vanquished)   75 **said** done   81–3 **But thought's** . . .
stop as life is master of thought and is in turn servant to time, so time, even though it rules all
the world, must come to an end (F punctuation)   83 **prophesy** (it was believed that dying
men foresaw the future)   88 **Ill-weaved** . . . **shrunk** ambition, faulty in your conception,
how, like poorly woven cloth, you have shrunk   90 **bound** boundary   92 **room enough**
i.e. for a grave   93 **stout** brave   94 **sensible of** capable of feeling   95 **dear** deep   **zeal**
admiration   96 **favours** a scarf, or possibly the feathered plumes of his helmet

Adieu, and take thy praise with thee to heaven,
Thy ignominy sleep with thee in the grave,   100
But not remembered in thy epitaph.

He spieth Falstaff on the ground.

What, old acquaintance, could not all this flesh
Keep in a little life? Poor Jack farewell,
I could have better spared a better man:
O I should have a heavy miss of thee,   105
If I were much in love with vanity:
Death hath not struck so fat a deer today,
Though many dearer in this bloody fray:
Embowelled will I see thee by and by,
Till then in blood by noble Percy lie.   *Exit.* 110

Falstaff riseth up.

FALSTAFF. Embowelled? if thou embowel me today, I'll give you
leave to powder me and eat me too tomorrow. 'Sblood,
'twas time to counterfeit, or that hot termagant Scot had
paid me scot and lot too. Counterfeit? I lie, I am no
counterfeit; to die is to be a counterfeit, for he is but the 115
counterfeit of a man, who hath not the life of a man: but to
counterfeit dying when a man thereby liveth, is to be no
counterfeit, but the true and perfect image of life indeed.
The better part of valour is discretion, in the which better
part I have saved my life. 'Zounds, I am afraid of this 120
gunpowder Percy, though he be dead. How if he should
counterfeit too and rise? By my faith, I am afraid he would
prove the better counterfeit, therefore I'll make him sure,
yea, and I'll swear I killed him. Why may not he rise as
well as I? Nothing confutes me but eyes, and nobody sees 125
me: therefore sirrah [*Stabs him.*], with a new wound in
your thigh, come you along with me.

He takes up Hotspur on his back.

Enter PRINCE *and* JOHN OF LANCASTER.

PRINCE.   Come brother John, full bravely hast thou fleshed

---

105 **heavy** (1) sad (2) referring to Falstaff's weight   109 **Embowelled** (1) disembowelled for
embalming (2) cut up, as with a slain deer (l. 107)   110 **in blood** in vigor (also fr.
hunting)   112 **powder** salt for pickling   113 **termagant** mythical Saracen god, depicted
in medieval drama as ranting and violent   114 **paid . . . lot** paid (killed) me in full (referring
to parish taxes)   125 **Nothing . . . eyes** only an eye-witness could contradict me   128

Thy maiden sword.

JOHN.   But soft, whom have we here?
Did you not tell me this fat man was dead?   130
PRINCE.   I did, I saw him dead,
Breathless and bleeding on the ground. Art thou alive?
Or is it fantasy that plays upon our eyesight?
I prithee speak, we will not trust our eyes
Without our ears: thou art not what thou seem'st.   135
FALSTAFF.   No, that's certain, I am not a double man: but if I be not
Jack Falstaff, then am I a Jack: there is Percy [*Throws down
the body.*], if your father will do me any honour, so: if not,
let him kill the next Percy himself: I look to be either earl
or duke, I can assure you.   140
PRINCE.   Why, Percy I killed myself, and saw thee dead.
FALSTAFF.   Didst thou? Lord, Lord, how this world is given to lying.
I grant you I was down, and out of breath, and so was he,
but we rose both at an instant, and fought a long hour by
Shrewsbury clock. If I may be believed, so: if not, let   145
them that should reward valour, bear the sin upon their
own heads. I'll take it upon my death, I gave him this
wound in the thigh: if the man were alive, and would deny
it, 'zounds, I would make him eat a piece of my sword.
JOHN.   This is the strangest tale that ever I heard.   150
PRINCE.   This is the strangest fellow, brother John.
Come bring your luggage nobly on your back.
For my part, if a lie may do thee grace,
I'll gild it with the happiest terms I have.

A retreat is sounded.

The trumpet sounds retreat, the day is ours: 155
Come brother, let us to the highest of the field,
To see what friends are living, who are dead.   *Exeunt.*
FALSTAFF.   I'll follow as they say, for reward. He that rewards me,
God reward him. If I do grow great, I'll grow less, for I'll
purge and leave sack, and live cleanly as a nobleman   160
should do.

*Exit [bearing
off the body].*

---

fleshed initiated (by smearing with blood; fr. hunting)   133 **fantasy** imagination   136
double man (1) apparition of a living person (2) twice the size of one man (3) two men, with
Hotspur on my back   137 **a Jack** a jackanapes   144 **at an instant** at the same
instant   153 **a lie** i.e. of yours   **do thee grace** gain you rewards   159 **grow great** (1) get
fat (2) receive advancement   **less** thin   160 **purge** (1) repent (2) take purgatives to grow
thin

[SCENE V.]

The trumpets sound. Enter the KING, PRINCE OF WALES,
    LORD JOHN OF LANCASTER, EARL OF WESTMORELAND, *with*
    WORCESTER *and* VERNON *prisoners.*

KING.   Thus ever did rebellion find rebuke.
             Ill-spirited Worcester, did not we send grace,
             Pardon, and terms of love to all of you?
             And wouldst thou turn our offers contrary?
             Misuse the tenour of thy kinsman's trust?   5
             Three knights upon our party slain today,
             A noble earl and many a creature else,
             Had been alive this hour,
             If like a Christian thou hadst truly borne
             Betwixt our armies true intelligence.   10

WORCESTER.
             What I have done my safety urged me to:
             And I embrace this fortune patiently,
             Since not to be avoided it falls on me.

KING.   Bear Worcester to the death and Vernon too:
             Other offenders we will pause upon.   15

                        Exeunt WORCESTER *and* VERNON [*guarded*].

             How goes the field?

PRINCE.   The noble Scot Lord Douglas, when he saw
             The fortune of the day quite turned from him,
             The noble Percy slain and all his men
             Upon the foot of fear, fled with the rest,   20
             And falling from a hill, he was so bruised,
             That the pursuers took him. At my tent
             The Douglas is: and I beseech your grace
             I may dispose of him.

KING.   With all my heart.

PRINCE.   Then brother John of Lancaster, to you   25
             This honourable bounty shall belong,
             Go to the Douglas and deliver him
             Up to his pleasure, ransomless and free:
             His valours shown upon our crests today

V, v Another part of the battlefield   1 **rebuke** check   2 **Ill-spirited** malicious   5
Misuse the tenour misinterpret the intent   20 **Upon . . . fear** fleeing in fear   29 **valours**

	Have taught us how to cherish such high deeds,	30
	Even in the bosom of our adversaries.	
JOHN.	I thank your grace for this high courtesy,	
	Which I shall give away immediately.	
KING.	Then this remains, that we divide our power.	
	You son John, and my cousin Westmoreland	35
	Towards York shall bend you, with your dearest speed	
	To meet Northumberland and the prelate Scroop,	
	Who as we hear are busily in arms:	
	Myself and you son Harry will towards Wales,	
	To fight with Glendower and the Earl of March.	40
	Rebellion in this land shall lose his sway,	
	Meeting the check of such another day,	
	And since this business so fair is done,	
	Let us not leave till all our own be won. *Exeunt.*	

FINIS.

Textual Notes

I, i   50 **For** Q; F: "Far"   51 **import** Q; F: "report"   80 **to** Q; F: "of"
I, ii   145 **Bardolph, Peto** Theobald em.; Q, F: "Harvey, Rossill," prob. vestiges of the characters' original names
I, iii   108 **bare** Q; F: "base"   128 **Albeit . . . hazard of** Q; F: "Although it be with hazard of"   236 **wasp-stung** Q; F: "Waspe-tongu'd"
II, ii   100 **fat** QO; not in Q or F
II, iv   8 **salvation** Q; F: "confidence"   122 **psalms, or anything** Q; F; "all manner of songs"   328 **tonight** Q; F: "by night"   453 **made** Q, F; F3: "mad"
III, i   32 **topples** Q; F: "tombles"
III, ii   112 **swathling** Q; F: "swathing"   156 **intemperance** Q; F: "intemperature"
III, iii   50 **tithe** Theobald em.; Q, F: "tight"
IV, i   20 **my lord** Capell em.; Q: "my mind"; F: "his mind"   119 **taste** Q; F: "take"   122 **hot** Q; F: "not"   134 **merrily** Q; F: "merely"
V, i   2 **busky** F; Q: "bulky"
V, ii   94 **whose** Q; F: "Whose worthy"
V, iv   62 **the** Q; F: "that"   159 **great** Q; F: "great again"
V, v   41 **sway** Q; F: "way"

---

valorous deeds   33 **give away** announce   36 **dearest** utmost   44 **leave** i.e. off

HAMLET

It is *we* who are Hamlet, observes William Hazlitt, in explaining why this particular play strikes a responsive note in all who read or see it. No other fictional character seems to touch us so deeply as it reflects both the individually pertinent and the universally true.

In many ways Hamlet is all of us on the threshold of maturity. And Hamlet is a *young* man. Asserting this fact and refuting those critics who claim Hamlet is older, Dr. Jacob Bronowski says that Hamlet is at that age where maturity begins, with the realization that the individual must make his own decisions, decisions which in the past were made for him. The fascination of the play lies in seeing a gifted character at this stage in his life called upon to make momentous decisions that will affect life, death and kingdom.

Hamlet is intelligent, courageous, kind, witty and clever. He is also tense, rebellious, sarcastic, self-doubting, moody and at times of great emotional stress, nearly hysterical. None of these characteristics is unusual in a member of his age group, which the Elizabethans would think of as about sixteen, based on the fact that he is a student at the university, which one usually entered between the ages of fourteen and sixteen.* But while we can identify with Hamlet as a person, his situation is unique. It is a dramatic example of the reversal of fortune which is basic to Greek, medieval and Renaissance tragedies. From a secure and enviable position where he is loved by parents, sweetheart and subjects, Hamlet is catapulted by events beyond his control to a situation where he finds himself rejected and unloved, his future as king usurped by the same man who has usurped his mother's love. Returning home from the university because of the death of his father, Hamlet finds awaiting him a different world from the one he left. His father gone, his uncle Claudius, whom Hamlet hates and distrusts, on the throne, Hamlet cannot turn to his mother for comfort, for Gertrude married Claudius within a month of her first husband's death, and sides with him against Hamlet in denying his wish to return to school. In his first soliloquy, Hamlet reveals his grief and resentment over his mother's remarriage. The world is to him "weary, stale, flat and unprofitable" because of his mother's behavior, seemingly to love Hamlet's father, and then within a month, to "post" (rush) to a marriage bed with his uncle, an incestuous relationship according to Church law which forbade marriage between a widow and her husband's

---

* The records of Oxford University give the ages at which three of Shakespeare's contemporary playwrights entered: John Marston at 16, Fulke Greville at 14, and Francis Beaumont at 12.

brother. To Hamlet, revolted by the physical aspects of this marriage, his uncle is a "satyr," the half-man half-goat creature who symbolized lust.

Swiftly, the world which centered upon Hamlet has disappeared, and he is an outsider. But two greater shocks are to come. Hamlet is told by a ghost claiming to be the spirit of Hamlet's father that he did not die from a bite by a serpent, as had been reported, but that "the serpent that did sting thy father's life/ Now wears his crown:" Claudius murdered his brother to gain the throne. The ghost also reveals that Gertrude and Claudius had an "adulterate" relationship before the murder (I, v, 39-42). Third, and most shattering of all, the ghost calls upon Hamlet to revenge the murder by killing Claudius according to the primitive blood code which demanded a life for a life taken, an eye for an eye and a tooth for a tooth.

All of the four characters who see this ghost, including Hamlet, realize that, according to beliefs of Shakespeare's day, it might be either an "honest" ghost, that is, really the spirit of the dead king, or an evil spirit, a "goblin damned," in disguise, calling upon Hamlet to commit murder and thus damn his soul. Therefore, Hamlet must test the ghost's word by proving Claudius' guilt by means of the play, "The Murder of Gonzago," in which Hamlet will insert "some dozen or sixteen lines."

Testing the ghost's word is only one instance where Hamlet must discover for himself the reality or truth behind an appearance which may be deceiving. In a world which young people suddenly learn is full of deception, truth may be difficult to recognize. Part of Hamlet's training at the university will have dealt in general with this search for truth, so it is natural for him to debate "shadow" and substance" with Rosencrantz and Guildenstern, his former schoolmates:

> Then are our beggars bodies [substance], and our
> monarchs and outstretched heroes the beggars' shadows.
> (II, ii, 258-9)

But the differentiation between shadow and substance, appearance and reality, truth and deception, is no longer a topic for hypothetical discussion. Hamlet has returned to face the problem in the real world of Denmark. No teacher stands by with the answer; the student himself must find it, not for a grade, but to preserve his own life, and the penalty for failure could be death.

In Hamlet's soliloquies, the conflict between appearance and reality is a recurrent theme. Hamlet's first soliloquy, beginning "O that this too too sullied flesh . . ." voices his disgust at his mother's remarriage, and at her deception in seeming to love his father, seeming to mourn his death, and then hastily remarrying:

> she would hang on him
> As if increase of appetite had grown
> By what it fed on, and yet within a month—
> ....
> Ere yet the salt of most unrighteous tears
> Had left the flushing in her galled eyes,
> She married.   (I, ii, 143-56)

Hamlet resolves to hide his real feelings, as his mother apparently did hers: "break my heart, for I must hold my tongue" (159). Following the shock of his mother's hasty marriage comes the ghost's revelation of Claudius' act of murder, deceptively reported as accident:

> the whole ear of Denmark
> Is by a forged process of my death
> Rankly abused [deceived]:   (I, v, 36-8)

The ghost's departure is followed by a second soliloquy and an excited parody of an act performed many times in calmer moments in which the student writes down some thought, some conclusion he has arrived at in his search for truth. Here it is a realization of the ugliness that may hide behind a smiling mask: "That one may smile, and smile, and be a villain" (I, v, 108).

If one's elders, who should represent the model of behavior, have used deception, so Hamlet will "put an antic disposition on," play mad as counter-deception. To Hamlet, in the "rotten" state of Denmark none of the Establishment—"seeming-virtuous" Gertrude, murdering Claudius or scheming Polonius—is to be trusted. Among those of Hamlet's generation, he dare confide only in Horatio. Ophelia is a tool of Polonius; Laertes, Rosencrantz and Guildenstern are tools of Claudius.

As Hamlet is learning that nothing is what it seems to be, both the ghost's honesty and Claudius' dishonesty must be proven, for the appearances of both are deceptive. And Hamlet will enlist seeming or illusion in trying to arrive at the truth.

Perhaps Hamlet is so fascinated by the theatre because there at least everyone recognizes illusion as illusion. Or is theatre more than illusion when it presents a scene that is "something like" a real murder? Hamlet will use illusion to re-enact reality; the play "The Murder of Gonzago" is to be the means Hamlet will use to unmask the ugly truth Claudius hides beneath smiles.

When the players arrive and deliver a sample speech, the passage about the fall of Troy moves the actor to tears, even though, as Hamlet's third soliloquy states, the emotion is brought about by "a fiction . . . a dream of passion" (II, ii, 526). What a challenge, thinks Hamlet, his own real-life role would be to the actor, with an actual rather than fictional "cue for passion."

Before the murder play is staged, Hamlet reflects on death: "To be, or not to be," (III, i, 56) that is, to live or not to live. This fourth soliloquy is the most general in its application to "us all" and the most universal in its subject, one often present in Hamlet's mind—death. Death has the appearance of sleep, but who can know its reality? Is it merely "to sleep"? Or "perchance to dream" in that "undiscovered country"? The theme of death, on a more specific and macabre note, will be taken up again in the graveyard scene and will reach its conclusion with Hamlet's being arrested by "sergeant Death."

The play, Hamlet's illusion-trick, succeeds, and the king's "occulted guilt" is "unkenneled." But perhaps the greatest trick illusion plays on Hamlet is that he, being too young to distrust the semblance of piety, mistakes for reality the appearance of Claudius at prayer. Had he but known Claudius was merely saying words that "without thoughts never to heaven go," (III, iii, 98) Hamlet might have achieved his revenge then and there, and at the cost of one life, saved seven others.

In the following scene in his mother's "closet" (chamber), Hamlet is again deceived by appearance: the arras-concealed voice and movement he takes to be Claudius'. Hamlet springs into action, kills immediately, and discovers it is Polonius, who has made a second and fatal attempt to turn what appears to be a private conference into evidence against one of the conferees.

Hamlet's compulsory trip to England is ostensibly on official business, but in reality Claudius intends it to transport Hamlet to the "undiscovered country from whose bourn/No traveller returns." As he prepares to embark, in his final soliloquy he is conscious of the comparison between himself and his peer, Fortinbras of Norway. Although he contrasts his own inaction to the action of Fortinbras' soldiers, who, "for a fantasy and trick [illusion] of fame/Go to their graves like beds . . ." (IV, iv, 61-2), he is also aware that their actions may bring them death as well as fame.

Two final deceptions remain. One, the commission, written in flowery terms of amity, is actually a death warrant, a deception Hamlet turns back on Rosencrantz and Guildenstern. And the last, fatal deception is the conspiracy of Claudius and Laertes. What is supposed to be a fencing-match is actually a death-trap: the sword's tip, apparently "bated," is actually untipped, and "the point envenomed too," so that what will seem "a pass of practice" will really be a death wound. Should the first subterfuge fail, there is a standby also involving poison, a favorite tool of murder by deception. The drink, intended to revive, will actually contain deadly poison along with, ironically, a pearl ("union") symbolizing kingship.

The fencing match, in which Laertes holds the untipped, poisoned sword is, in a sense, a visualization of the battle Hamlet has been waging against odds throughout the play. Through skill, intelligence and moral courage, he finally wins the battle, although he sacrifices his own life to achieve his father's wishes and in so doing, releases Denmark from the grip of a dissimulating murderer. The play's arch-pretender, Claudius, is hoist with his own petar as Hamlet stabs him with the unbated, envenomed sword, forces him to drink the poisoned wine, and turns Claudius' deceitful union with the kingship into the reality of a union with death.

Hamlet's much-debated "delay" in carrying out the ghost's command, then, is partly due to his search for reality behind the appearance, starting with that of the ghost. But the question "why does Hamlet delay?" is one that has fascinated critics through the ages.

In the words of Goethe in the 18th century, Hamlet's "lovely, pure, noble and most moral nature . . . sinks beneath a burden which it cannot bear and must not cast away." The English Romantic writers see Hamlet in this light too, as a typical Byronic hero. Coleridge, who himself had some difficulty in completing tasks and finished only one of his major poems, says that Hamlet delays because he prefers the world of the mind to that of action. Some modern critics feel that Hamlet is too conscientious and civilized to carry out a murder which is part of an ancient barbaric code. Ernest Jones, a disciple of Freud, claims that Hamlet's delay is due to excessive subconscious erotic attachment to his mother, which prevents Hamlet from killing Claudius because Claudius has done what Hamlet and others afflicted with an Oedipus Complex subconsciously desire to do: get rid of the father and marry the mother. For Hamlet to kill Claudius would be to kill himself, says Jones.

Yet Hamlet tells us in his own words that before acting he must prove the ghost's words.

> The spirit that I have seen
> May be a devil, and the devil hath power
> T' assume a pleasing shape, yea, and perhaps
> Out of my weakness, and my melancholy,
> As he is very potent with such spirits,
> Abuses me to damn me;   (II, ii, 573-81)

But why does Hamlet delay *after* the play scene, in which Claudius' reaction proves his guilt? The best opportunity for killing Claudius is in III, iii, as Hamlet comes unseen upon the king who kneels in prayer. But Hamlet reflects that it would be "hire and salary, not revenge," (79) to send to heaven a man making his peace by prayer when Hamlet's own father had no such opportunity and is therefore suffering in purgatory. Hamlet defers the killing to a time "That has no relish of salvation in't"; (92) then he will kill Claudius and send him to hell. His reason has been criticized as savage, explained as necessary under the code of revenge, and declared a cover-up for a true reason. Some say that the melancholy mentioned by Hamlet in the lines quoted above is a real affliction, which the Elizabethans called "melancholy adust" which paralyzes his action. Others contend that as a civilized man of the Renaissance, he cannot bring himself to murder a man at prayer.

It might be pointed out that Hamlet could be taken at his word that he will kill Claudius at a time when he is not making his peace with heaven. The deferment is brief. A few moments later, in the Queen's chamber, Hamlet thrusts his sword through the arras in the belief that he is killing Claudius ("Is it the king?" III, iv, 26), and fatally wounds Polonius. A pattern of behavior in which inaction is followed by action occurs else-where in the play, and one explanation is that when Hamlet is deliberating ("thinking too precisely on th' event": IV, iv, 41), he cannot act, and that when he does act, it is on impulse and not as a result of thought. This is indicated in a number of situations: killing Polonius; appropriating the commission to England; boarding the pirate ship; leaping into Ophelia's grave; and finally, killing Claudius.

An explanation for Hamlet's hesitation also may be found in Dr. Bronowski's theory that being called upon to make major decisions causes conflict in a youth on his way to maturity. The less mature, like Laertes, rush into action without consideration. But as the young person ap-proaches adulthood, his decision-making involves also an appreciation of what Hamlet calls "the event", the result of the action that the decision leads to. He becomes aware that the process is complex: considering beforehand the evidence and the probable outcome; the decision itself and the action that results; and after the action, acceptance of the result. Realizing all the implications involved might well lead to hesitation and delay, which "lose the name of action."

As Hamlet's characteristic behavior is that of a youth, why do some critics say he is thirty? In the graveyard scene, the gravedigger says he became a grave-maker the day "young Hamlet was born," and later in that passage says he has been there "thirty years." (V, i, 134, 148)

There are many explanations for this one part of the text which seems at odds with the character's youthfulness in the rest of the play. It may have been carelessness on Shakespeare's part (In *As You Like It*, Rosalind is at one point described as being taller than her cousin; in another part, she is shorter); it may be a mistake in typesetting: perhaps "xx" was written for twenty, and the setter added another "x"; perhaps Shakespeare did not mean the figure literally, any more than he meant it literally when he says Hamlet walks "four hours" in the lobby. Or it may be a conscious insertion in the text at this point to make the role conform to the age of the actor who played it, Richard Burbage, who was the chief tragedian of

Shakespeare's company. Burbage created the role of Hamlet along with those of the more mature tragic heroes, Lear, Othello and Macbeth. The actor was in his thirties when he first played Hamlet, and if the age is an insertion, it is a practice which still exists in the theatre today when an age or even a nationality of a character may be changed to fit the actor performing it. (John Gielgud, playing Oscar Wilde's Ernest, changed the character's stated age from 29 to 35). A reference to "three and twenty" (Q1 prints "this dozen") a few lines later would also be such a change.

It seems that the typesetter of the Folio text of the play (1623) was somewhat confused in his figures, because he prints the word "sexton" as "sixteene": "I have bin sixteene heere, man and Boy thirty yeares." A fascinating conjecture is that "sixteene" is a vestige of the original wording, for in other texts, like *Romeo and Juliet*, the typesetter set both an original word and the revision.

But the most convincing evidence that Hamlet is indeed young lies in the text itself. The other characters think of Hamlet as young; it is the first adjective describing him: "Let us impart what we have seen tonight/Unto young Hamlet" (I, i, 169-70). As mentioned, he is home from the university. Polonius stresses Hamlet's youth in his warning to Ophelia: "Believe so much in him that he is young" (I, iii, 124). The ghost says that to tell his story would freeze Hamlet's "young blood," and youth is probably one of the reasons Hamlet does not receive the election to the throne (election was the Danish practice, although the Elizabethans would probably look on duly-elected Claudius as a usurper). Accepting all of these references to Hamlet's youth and thinking of him as sixteen or seventeen also solves many problems which have puzzled critics who take him to be thirty. When a mother re-marries, a teen-aged son might react as Hamlet does, rejecting the step-father and resenting the marriage, especially its sexual aspects. Add to this Hamlet's discovery of the mother's adulterous behavior while married to his own idolized father, and his revulsion as expressed in the scene alone with his mother need not be attributed to an Oedipus Complex. What would and still does upset someone in his teens, a middle-aged person with more experience of the ways of the world, including remarriage, would accept with more equanimity. Behavior which seems normal and acceptable for a teen-ager becomes abnormal only if Hamlet is thought of as being thirty, which would be well into middle age in Elizabethan days. Shakespeare himself married at eighteen, had three children by the time he was twenty-one, and died a sick old man, as evidenced from the shaky signature on his will, when he was fifty-two. When Shakespeare wrote *Hamlet* in 1600 or 1601, his own son Hamnet, who died when he was eleven, would have been fifteen or sixteen, the age of his surviving twin sister Judith.

In contrast to Hamlet's uniqueness, the other characters are based upon established dramatic types. Horatio is the confidant, but he is also a man whose balance and composure (upset only by the appearance of the ghost) Hamlet appreciates, admires, and lacks. Cynical, wry, detached where Hamlet is involved, and rational where Hamlet is passionate, Horatio is governed by the very qualities in which Hamlet, in his present state, is deficient.

On the other hand, Laertes, a dramatic parallel to Hamlet in years and in duty to revenge, displays some of the prince's failings which, carried to the extreme, become vices. Hamlet is emotional, but has the strength of will to gain control over his passion (as in the third soliloquy, II, ii, 557-63). Laertes is so headstrong that he almost kills Claudius; shortly thereafter he allows himself to be dominated by Claudius in plotting Hamlet's death. Hamlet disguises his feelings to protect himself, whereas Laertes uses deception to hide intended murder. In the final scenes, Laertes' self-interest is a foil to Hamlet's magnanimity, which almost arouses Laertes' conscience to reveal the deception.

Ophelia rises above her purely dramatic function as the hero's beloved to become one of the most pathetic of Shakespeare's hapless victims of circumstance. Her youth and her dependence upon and complete obedience to her father, even when ordered to give up the man she loves, contribute to the madness that seems inevitable after Polonius is killed by Hamlet. Her reaction to the same situation in which Hamlet finds himself—the murder of a father—is actual, not assumed, madness. Why does Hamlet treat Ophelia as he does? Hamlet's bitterness to her, in their first confrontation (III, i), may reflect his disgust with Gertrude transferred to womankind in general. He sees their make-up as a symbol of their deceptiveness: "God hath given you one face, and you make yourselves another . . . (143)". Some critics believe that during this scene with Ophelia, Hamlet becomes aware that Claudius and Polonius are hiding behind the arras, and unleashes his contempt for her deceit in playing decoy to trap him. In the play scene, Hamlet, pretending to be mad, is both critical of women in general and bawdy to Ophelia in particular—conduct that might persuade the court that the prince, whose manners were once models to be "observed of all observers," must be out of his senses to so address a lady in public. Here as in the earlier scene with Ophelia, Hamlet castigates women for their loose moral behavior. His treatment of Ophelia may be his way of protecting her, of breaking off the relationship. For to continue it while pursuing the revenge, would be to expose her to the danger he faces. That he truly loves Ophelia he testifies himself, in the letter which Polonius reads and by Hamlet's cry as he leaps into her grave, "I loved Ophelia" (V, i, 252).

Rosencrantz and Guildenstern, in contrast to Horatio, are the false friends, willing to betray Hamlet to curry favor with the king. That they are always out-smarted by Hamlet, right up to their last and fatal maneuver, demonstrates Hamlet's adroitness and quick wit in evading intended harm.

In their elementary dramatic functions, Claudius is the villain and Polonius the pantaloon or foolish old man, but each becomes an unforgettable individual. Second in the play only to Hamlet in complexity, Claudius is a mixture of wickedness and weakness, one who gives the impression of having more administrative ability than he probably possesses, a man whose heart yearns for salvation, but whose mind realizes that salvation can come only from true penitence and sacrifice of the prizes gained by the crime: "May one be pardoned and retain th' offence?" (III, iii, 56) That the kingdom suffers under the ruler who attains the throne by murder, that "something is rotten in the state of Denmark," is echoed in Claudius' own remarks about the people as "distracted" and "Thick and unwholesome in their thoughts" (IV, v, 79).

Polonius is recognizably human in combining wisdom and foolishness. It is through the exaggeration of both these traits that the character becomes dramatically impressive. At one moment he is the fatuous dotard, but in the next, Claudius is reminding us how important Polonius has been to the state; after giving his son sage advice that has never been bettered, Polonius embarks on a garrulous disquisition, lacking brevity and wit, on Hamlet's madness.

Gertrude is perhaps the most original of the secondary characters, in that the erring wife, often a subject for comedy, is here developed not only seriously but with great clarity and consistency. The key to her character is suggested in Hamlet's "Frailty, thy name is woman" (I, ii, 146). While she may not be the hypocrite Hamlet accuses her of being, she lacks a strong will. She is inclined to be ruled by emotion, whether it is her love for Hamlet, or for Claudius, or, from Hamlet's testimony, for the former king.

Text, Date, Source

The first factual evidence of this play is an announcement of intention to print it, listed in the Stationer's Register by James Roberts in July 1602, which suggests a date of composition in 1600 or 1601. However, before Roberts printed the play in Quarto in 1604 (Q2) there appeared in 1603 a "bad" or garbled Quarto (Q1) evidently based on a reconstruction of the script made by an actor, or actors, from memory. This pirated version must have hastened the 1604 edition, advertised on the title page as being "enlarged . . . according to the true and perfect copy." It was probably printed from Shakespeare's own manuscript, from which a "fair copy" previously would have been made to serve as the playhouse prompt copy, after which the manuscript itself could be turned over to a printer.

Demonstrating the play's popularity, a third and fourth Quarto, each a reprint of the earlier, appeared before the version in the Folio collection of all the plays, published in 1623. The Folio, evidently based on the acting script, supplies a stage version of the play as cut for production, and therefore omits some passages found in Q2; it also affords some alternate readings to those in Q2. Being the earliest authentic text, Q2 is considered to be the most reliable, and is generally followed here, with the inclusion, from the Folio, of readings and passages not found in Q2, or found there in garbled form. Important alternate readings and emendations are given in the textual notes.

In an early version of the Hamlet story, Saxo Grammaticus in his Latin *Historia Danica*, compiled in the late twelfth century, tells of Amleth, son of Horwendil, Governor of Jutland. Horwendil is murdered openly by his brother Feng, who seizes the office and (incestuously) marries the wife, Gerutha. Amleth, a child at the time, grows up dedicated to revenge. For protection, he assumes madness, but the suspicious uncle tests it in various ways—plotting with a woman friend to seduce Amleth, hiding a friend in the mother's room, whom Amleth discovers and kills, and sending Amleth, accompanied by two seeming-friends, to a planned death in England. Amleth, who outsmarts the uncle each time, returns from England to literally trap him and all his drinking companions in the banquet hall, and then to set it on fire. Although the uncle escapes from the fire, Amleth first exchanges swords (his own having been tampered with) and then kills him. The story is retold in French by François de Belleforest in *Histoires Tragiques*, published in 1576 and 1582. This work may or may not have been known to Shakespeare.

Shakespeare's more direct source was evidently an earlier Hamlet play (no longer in existence but referred to by scholars as the Ur-Hamlet), just as older plays were the sources of *King Lear* and *Measure for Measure*. The Ur-Hamlet, possibly written by Thomas Kyd, was obviously quite popular, as three extant contemporary references testify. Thomas Nashe in 1589 remarks that *"English Seneca* . . . will afford you whole *Hamlets* . . ."
Philip Henslowe, a producer, records in his diary that the play was performed on June 11, 1594; and in 1596, Thomas Lodge states that a devil looked "as pale as the Visard of the ghost which cried so miserably at the Theatre, like an oyster wife, 'Hamlet, revenge.' " The Ur-Hamlet, therefore, was evidently a revenge tragedy with a ghost, based on the Hamlet legend. A German play, possibly a version of the Ur-Hamlet, was printed in 1781 from a 1710 manuscript now lost. It is a crude work, called *Der bestrafte Brudermord* (Fratricide Punished), and might have been translated from the Ur-Hamlet, which could have been taken to Germany by an English touring troupe in the fifteen-eighties or fifteen-nineties.

THE TRAGEDY OF HAMLET
Prince of Denmark

THE
TRAGEDY OF HAMLET
PRINCE OF DENMARK

[THE NAMES OF THE ACTORS

CLAUDIUS, *King of Denmark*
HAMLET, *son to the former, and nephew to the present King*
POLONIUS, *Lord Chamberlain*
HORATIO, *friend to* HAMLET
LAERTES, *son to* POLONIUS
VALTEMAND
CORNELIUS
ROSENCRANTZ } *courtiers*
GUILDENSTERN
OSRIC
A Gentleman
A Priest
MARCELLUS } *officers*
BERNARDO
FRANCISCO, *a soldier*
REYNALDO, *servant to* POLONIUS
Players
Two Clowns, gravediggers

FORTINBRAS, *Prince of Norway*
A Norwegian Captain
English Ambassadors

GERTRUDE, *Queen of Denmark, mother to* HAMLET
OPHELIA, *daughter to* POLONIUS

Ghost of HAMLET'S *Father*

Lords, Ladies, Officers, Soldiers, Sailors, Messengers, Attendants

SCENE: *Elsinore*]

Act One

SCENE I.

Enter BARNARDO *and* FRANCISCO, *two Sentinels.*

BARNARDO. Who's there?

FRANCISCO. Nay, answer me. Stand and unfold yourself.

BARNARDO. Long live the king.

FRANCISCO. Barnado?

BARNARDO. He.   5

FRANCISCO. You come most carefully upon your hour.

BARNARDO. 'Tis now struck twelve, get thee to bed Francisco.

FRANCISCO. For this relief much thanks, 'tis bitter cold,
        And I am sick at heart.

BARNARDO. Have you had quiet guard?

FRANCISCO.   Not a mouse stirring.   10

BARNARDO. Well, good night:
        If you do meet Horatio and Marcellus,
        The rivals of my watch, bid them make haste.

Enter HORATIO *and* MARCELLUS.

FRANCISCO. I think I hear them. Stand ho, who is there?

HORATIO.   Friends to this ground.

MARCELLUS.   And liegemen to the Dane.   15

FRANCISCO. Give you good night.

MARCELLUS.   O, farewell honest soldier,
        Who hath relieved you?

FRANCISCO.   Barnardo hath my place;
        Give you good night.   *Exit* FRANCISCO.

MARCELLUS.   Holla, Barnardo!

BARNARDO.   Say,
        What, is Horatio there?

HORATIO.   A piece of him.

BARNARDO. Welcome Horatio, welcome good Marcellus.   20

HORATIO.   What, has this thing appeared again tonight?

I, i a platform before the castle   2 **unfold** reveal   13 **rivals** partners   15 **liegeman**
subjects   15 **Dane** King of Denmark

BARNARDO. I have seen nothing.
MARCELLUS.
        Horatio says 'tis but our fantasy,
        And will not let belief take hold of him,
        Touching this dreaded sight twice seen of us,   25
        Therefore I have entreated him along
        With us to watch the minutes of this night,
        That if again this apparition come,
        He may approve our eyes and speak to it.
HORATIO. Tush, tush, 'twill not appear.
BARNARDO.   Sit down awhile,   30
        And let us once again assail your ears,
        That are so fortified against our story,
        What we have two nights seen.
HORATIO.   Well, sit we down,
        And let us hear Barnardo speak of this.
BARNARDO. Last night of all,   35
        When yon same star that's westward from the pole
        Had made his course t'illume that part of heaven
        Where now it burns, Marcellus and myself,
        The bell then beating one —

                    Enter GHOST.

MARCELLUS.
        Peace, break thee off, look where it comes again.   40
BARNARDO. In the same figure like the king that's dead.
MARCELLUS.
        Thou art a scholar, speak to it Horatio.
BARNARDO. Looks a' not like the king? mark it Horatio.
HORATIO. Most like, it harrows me with fear and wonder.
BARNARDO. It would be spoke to.
MARCELLUS.   Question it Horatio.   45
HORATIO. What art thou that usurp'st this time of night,
        Together with that fair and warlike form,
        In which the majesty of buried Denmark
        Did sometimes march? by heaven I charge thee speak.
MARCELLUS.
        It is offended.
BARNARDO.   See, it stalks away.   50

                                    23 **fantasy** imagination   29 **approve** prove
reliable   31, 32 **assail, fortified** (metaphor based on the siege of a fortress)   36 **pole** North
Star   42 **scholar** (with the knowledge to deal with spirits)   46 **usurp'st** wrongfully
occupy (both the time and the shape of the dead king)   48 **buried Denmark** the buried
King of Denmark   49 **sometimes** formerly   57 **sensible . . . avouch** assurance of the

HORATIO. Stay, speak, speak, I charge thee speak.

Exit GHOST.

MARCELLUS.
    'Tis gone and will not answer.

BARNARDO. How now Horatio, you tremble and look pale,
    Is not this something more than fantasy?
    What think you on't?   55

HORATIO. Before my God I might not this believe,
    Without the sensible and true avouch
    Of mine own eyes.

MARCELLUS.   Is it not like the king?

HORATIO. As thou art to thyself.
    Such was the very armour he had on,   60
    When he the ambitious Norway combated:
    So frowned he once, when in an angry parle
    He smote the sledded Polacks on the ice.
    'Tis strange.

MARCELLUS.
    Thus twice before, and jump at this dead hour,   65
    With martial stalk hath he gone by our watch.

HORATIO. In what particular thought to work, I know not,
    But in the gross and scope of mine opinion,
    This bodes some strange eruption to our state.

MARCELLUS.
    Good now sit down, and tell me he that knows,   70
    Why this same strict and most observant watch
    So nightly toils the subject of the land,
    And why such daily cast of brazen cannon
    And foreign mart, for implements of war,
    Why such impress of shipwrights, whose sore task   75
    Does not divide the Sunday from the week,
    What might be toward that this sweaty haste
    Doth make the night joint-labourer with the day,
    Who is't that can inform me?

HORATIO.   That can I.
    At least the whisper goes so; our last king,   80
    Whose image even but now appeared to us,

---

truth of the senses   61 **Norway** King of Norway   62 **parle** parley, verbal battle   63
sledded Polacks Poles on sleds   65 **jump** just   67 **particular** specific   68 **gross and
scope** general view   71 **watch** sleeplessness   72 **toils the subject** makes the subjects
toil   74 **mart** trade   75 **impress** conscription   **sore** difficult   77 **toward**

Was as you know by Fortinbras of Norway,
Thereto pricked on by a most emulate pride,
Dared to the combat; in which our valiant Hamlet
(For so this side of our known world esteemed him)   85
Did slay this Fortinbras, who by a sealed compact,
Well ratified by law and heraldy,
Did forfeit (with his life) all those his lands
Which he stood seized of, to the conqueror:
Against the which a moiety competent   90
Was gagèd by our king, which had returned
To the inheritance of Fortinbras,
Had he been vanquisher; as by the same co-mart,
And carriage of the article designed,
His fell to Hamlet; now sir, young Fortinbras,   95
Of unimprovèd mettle hot and full,
Hath in the skirts of Norway here and there
Sharked up a list of lawless resolutes
For food and diet to some enterprise
That hath a stomach in't, which is no other,   100
As it doth well appear unto our state,
But to recover of us by strong hand
And terms compulsatory, those foresaid lands
So by his father lost; and this I take it,
Is the main motive of our preparations,   105
The source of this our watch, and the chief head
Of this post-haste and romage in the land.

BARNARDO. I think it be no other, but e'en so;
Well may it sort that this portentous figure
Comes armèd through our watch so like the king   110
That was and is the question of these wars.

HORATIO.   A mote it is to trouble the mind's eye:
In the most high and palmy state of Rome,
A little ere the mightiest Julius fell,
The graves stood tenantless, and the sheeted dead   115
Did squeak and gibber in the Roman streets,
As stars with trains of fire, and dews of blood,

forthcoming   83 emulate rivalling   85 this side . . . world all of Europe   86 compact
treaty   87 law and heraldy heraldic law regulating combats   89 seized possessed   90
moiety competent equal amount   91 gaged pledged   93 co-mart joint bargain   94
carriage . . . designed intent of the treaty drawn up   96 unimproved mettle untested (1)
metal (2) spirit   97 skirts outskirts   98 Sharked up gathered up indiscriminately (as a
shark preys)   lawless resolutes determined outlaws   100 stomach show of
courage   106 head fountainhead   107 romage bustle (rummage)   109 sort turn
out   111 question subject   112 mote speck of dust   113 palmy triumphant   114
Julius Caesar   117 stars . . . fire meteors   118 Disasters unfavorable portents   moist

Disasters in the sun; and the moist star,
Upon whose influence Neptune's empire stands,
Was sick almost to doomsday with eclipse.   120
And even the like precurse of feared events,
As harbingers preceding still the fates
And prologue to the omen coming on,
Have heaven and earth together demonstrated
Unto our climatures and countrymen.   125

                    Enter GHOST.

But soft, behold, lo where it comes again.
I'll cross it though it blast me: *Spreads his arms.*
                    stay illusion,
If thou hast any sound or use of voice,
Speak to me.
If there be any good thing to be done   130
That may to thee do ease, and grace to me,
Speak to me.
If thou art privy to thy country's fate
Which happily foreknowing may avoid,
O speak: 135
Or if thou hast uphoarded in thy life
Extorted treasure in the womb of earth,
For which they say you spirits oft walk in death,
                              The cock crows.
Speak of it, stay and speak. Stop it Marcellus.

MARCELLUS.
          Shall I strike at it with my partisan?   140
HORATIO.   Do, if it will not stand.
BARNARDO.   'Tis here.
HORATIO.   'Tis here.
MARCELLUS.
          'Tis gone.   *Exit* GHOST.
We do it wrong being so majestical,
To offer it the show of violence,
For it is as the air, invulnerable,   145
And our vain blows malicious mockery.

---

star moon   120 **sick . . . doomsday** almost completely dark (as on doomsday)   121
precurse portent   121 **feared** dreaded   122 **harbingers** forerunners   **still**
always   123 **omen** disaster   125 **climatures** regions   127 **cross** (1) cross its path (2)
spread my arms to make a cross of my body (to ward against evil)   **blast** destroy   131
grace (1) honor (2) blessedness   133 **art privy** know secretly of   134 **happily**
perhaps   140 **partisan** spear   146 **vain** fruitless   **malicious mockery** mockery because
they only imitate harm

BARNARDO. It was about to speak when the cock crew.

HORATIO.   And then it started like a guilty thing,
              Upon a fearful summons; I have heard,
              The cock that is the trumpet to the morn,   150
              Doth with his lofty and shrill-sounding throat
              Awake the god of day, and at his warning
              Whether in sea or fire, in earth or air,
              Th'extravagant and erring spirit hies
              To his confine, and of the truth herein   155
              This present object made probation.

MARCELLUS.
              It faded on the crowing of the cock.
              Some say that ever 'gainst that season comes
              Wherein our Saviour's birth is celebrated
              This bird of dawning singeth all night long,   160
              And then they say no spirit dare stir abroad,
              The nights are wholesome, then no planets strike,
              No fairy takes, nor witch hath power to charm,
              So hallowed, and so gracious is that time.

HORATIO.   So have I heard and do in part believe it.   165
              But look, the morn in russet mantle clad
              Walks o'er the dew of yon high eastward hill:
              Break we our watch up and by my advice
              Let us impart what we have seen tonight
              Unto young Hamlet, for upon my life   170
              This spirit dumb to us, will speak to him:
              Do you consent we shall acquaint him with it,
              As needful in our loves, fitting our duty?

MARCELLUS.
              Let's do't I pray, and I this morning know
              Where we shall find him most convenient.   *Exeunt.*

              SCENE II.

              Flourish. Enter CLAUDIUS *King of Denmark*, GERTRUDE *the*
              Queen [members of the] Council: as POLONIUS; *and his son*
              LAERTES, HAMLET, [VALTEMAND *and* CORNELIUS,] *cum*
              aliis.

KING.   Though yet of Hamlet our dear brother's death

---

147 **cock crew** (traditional signal for ghosts to return to their
confines)   149 **fearful** fearsome   150 **trumpet** trumpeter   153 **sea . . .
air** the four
elements (inhabited by spirits, each indigenous to a particular element)   154 **extravagant**
and erring going beyond its bounds (vagrant) and wandering   **hies** hastens   156 **made**
probation gave proof   158 **'gainst** just before   160 **bird of dawning** cock   162
wholesome healthy (night air was considered unhealthy)   **strike** exert evil influence   163
takes bewitches   164 **gracious** blessed   166 **russet** reddish coarse cloth   173 **needful**
. . . loves urged by our friendship
     I, ii a room of state in the castle   s.d. *cum aliis* with others   2 **that** though   5 **nature**

The memory be green, and that it us befitted
To bear our hearts in grief, and our whole kingdom
To be contracted in one brow of woe,
Yet so far hath discretion fought with nature,   5
That we with wisest sorrow think on him
Together with remembrance of ourselves:
Therefore our sometime sister, now our queen,
Th'imperial jointress to this warlike state,
Have we as 'twere with a defeated joy,   10
With an auspicious, and a dropping eye,
With mirth in funeral, and with dirge in marriage,
In equal scale weighing delight and dole,
Taken to wife: nor have we herein barred
Your better wisdoms, which have freely gone   15
With this affair along—for all, our thanks.
Now follows that you know, young Fortinbras,
Holding a weak supposal of our worth,
Or thinking by our late dear brother's death
Our state to be disjoint and out of frame,   20
Colleaguèd with this dream of his advantage,
He hath not failed to pester us with message
Importing the surrender of those lands
Lost by his father, with all bands of law,
To our most valiant brother—so much for him: 25
Now for ourself, and for this time of meeting,
Thus much the business is. We have here writ
To Norway, uncle of young Fortinbras—
Who impotent and bed-rid scarcely hears
Of this his nephew's purpose—to suppress   30
His further gait herein, in that the levies,
The lists, and full proportions are all made
Out of his subject: and we here dispatch
You good Cornelius, and you Valtemand,
For bearers of this greeting to old Norway,   35
Giving to you no further personal power
To business with the king, more than the scope

---

natural impluse (of grief)   6 **we** (royal plural)   7 **remembrance of ourselves** reminder of
our duties   8 **sometime** former   **sister** sister-in-law   9 **jointress** widow who inherits
the estate (jointure)   10 **defeated** marred   11 **auspicious . . . eye** one eye happy, the
other tearful   13 **dole** sorrow   14–15 **barred . . . wisdoms** failed to seek and abide by
your good advice   17 **that** i.e. which   18 **weak . . . worth** low opinion of my ability in
office   20 **state** administration   **out of frame** tottering ("frame"=builder's
framework)   21 **Colleagued** supported   **advantage** superiority   24 **bands**
bonds   28 **Norway** the King of Norway   31 **gait** progress   31–3 **levies . . . subject**
taxes, conscriptions, and supplies are all obtained from his subjects   37 **To** i.e. do

Of these delated articles allow:
Farewell, and let your haste commend your duty.

CORNELIUS, VALTEMAND.

In that, and all things, will we show our duty.   40

KING.   We doubt it nothing, heartily farewell.

Exeunt VALTEMAND *and* CORNELIUS.

And now Laertes what's the news with you?
You told us of some suit, what is't Laertes?
You cannot speak of reason to the Dane
And lose your voice; what wouldst thou beg Laertes,   45
That shall not be my offer, not thy asking?
The head is not more native to the heart,
The hand more instrumental to the mouth,
Than is the throne of Denmark to thy father.
What wouldst thou have Laertes?

LAERTES.   My dread lord,   50
Your leave and favour to return to France,
From whence, though willingly I came to Denmark,
To show my duty in your coronation,
Yet now I must confess, that duty done,
My thoughts and wishes bend again toward France,   55
And bow them to your gracious leave and pardon.

KING.   Have you your father's leave? What says Polonius?

POLONIUS.   He hath my lord wrung from me my slow leave
By laboursome petition, and at last
Upon his will I sealed my hard consent.   60
I do beseech you give him leave to go.

KING.   Take thy fair hour Laertes, time be thine,
And thy best graces spend it at thy will.
But now my cousin Hamlet, and my son—

HAMLET.   [*Aside.*] A little more than kin, and less than kind.   65

KING.   How is it that the clouds still hang on you?

HAMLET.   Not so my lord, I am too much in the sun.

---

38 **delated** accusing 39 **haste . . . duty** prompt departure signify your respect   44 **Dane**
King of Denmark   45 **lose your voice** speak in vain   46 **offer . . . asking** grant even
before requested   47 **native** related by nature   48 **instrumental** serviceable   51 **leave
and favour** kind permission   56 **pardon** allowance   58 **slow leave** reluctant
permission   60 **Upon . . . consent** (1) at his request, I gave my grudging consent (2) on the
soft sealing wax of his (legal) will, I stamped my approval   63 **graces** qualities   64 **cousin**
kinsman (used for relatives outside the immediate family)   65 **more than kin** too much of a
kinsman, being both uncle and stepfather   **less than kind** (1) unkind because of: being a kin
(proverbial) and taking the throne from the former king's son (2) unnatural (as it was
considered incest to marry the wife of one's dead brother)   67 **in the sun** (1) in the presence

QUEEN.	Good Hamlet cast thy nighted colour off
	And let thine eye look like a friend on Denmark,
	Do not for ever with thy vailèd lids 70
	Seek for thy noble father in the dust,
	Thou know'st 'tis common, all that lives must die,
	Passing through nature to eternity.
HAMLET.	Ay madam, it is common.
QUEEN.	If it be,
	Why seems it so particular with thee? 75
HAMLET.	Seems, madam? nay it is, I know not 'seems.'
	'Tis not alone my inky cloak good mother,
	Nor customary suits of solemn black,
	Nor windy suspiration of forced breath,
	No, nor the fruitful river in the eye, 80
	Nor the dejected haviour of the visage,
	Together with all forms, moods, shapes of grief,
	That can denote me truly: these indeed seem,
	For they are actions that a man might play,
	But I have that within which passes show, 85
	These but the trappings and the suits of woe.
KING.	'Tis sweet and commendable in your nature Hamlet,
	To give these mourning duties to your father:
	But you must know your father lost a father,
	That father lost, lost his, and the survivor bound 90
	In filial obligation for some term
	To do obsequious sorrow: but to persever
	In obstinate condolement, is a course
	Of impious stubbornness, 'tis unmanly grief,
	It shows a will most incorrect to heaven, 95
	A heart unfortified, a mind impatient,
	An understanding simple and unschooled:
	For what we know must be, and is as common
	As any the most vulgar thing to sense,
	Why should we in our peevish opposition 100

of the king (often associated metaphorically with the sun) (2) proverbial: "out of heaven's blessing into the warm sun" (3) of a "son"   68 **nighted colour** black (mourning)   69 **Denmark** the King of Denmark   70 **vailed** downcast   72 **common** i.e. to all   73 **nature** natural life   74 **common** (1) general (2) referring to her behavior in remarrying: "commoner"=prostitute (cf. V,2,64: "whored my mother")   75 **particular** personal   79–80 **windy . . . eye** (hyperbole used to describe exaggerated sighs and tears)   80 **fruitful** abundant   81 **haviour** behavior   84 **play** act   85 **passes** surpasses   86 **trappings . . . woe** costumes of mourning (rather than the inward emotion)   92 **do obsequious sorrow** express sorrow befitting obsequies or funerals   93 **condolement** grief   95 **incorrect** uncorrected   96 **impatient** lacking fortitude   99 **As any . . . sense** as the most ordinary thing the senses can perceive   100 **peevish** foolish, childish

Take it to heart? Fie, 'tis a fault to heaven,
A fault against the dead, a fault to nature,
To reason most absurd, whose common theme
Is death of fathers, and who still hath cried
From the first corse, till he that died today,   105
'This must be so.' We pray you throw to earth
This unprevailing woe, and think of us
As of a father, for let the world take note
You are the most immediate to our throne,
And with no less nobility of love   110
Than that which dearest father bears his son,
Do I impart toward you. For your intent
In going back to school in Wittenberg,
It is most retrograde to our desire,
And we beseech you, bend you to remain   115
Here in the cheer and comfort of our eye,
Our chiefest courtier, cousin, and our son.

QUEEN.   Let not thy mother lose her prayers Hamlet,
I pray thee stay with us, go not to Wittenberg.

HAMLET.   I shall in all my best obey you madam.   120

KING.   Why 'tis a loving and a fair reply,
Be as ourself in Denmark. Madam come,
This gentle and unforced accord of Hamlet
Sits smiling to my heart, in grace whereof,
No jocund health that Denmark drinks today,   125
But the great cannon to the clouds shall tell,
And the king's rouse the heaven shall bruit again,
Re-speaking earthly thunder; come away.

Flourish. Exeunt all but HAMLET.

HAMLET.   O that this too too sullied flesh would melt,
Thaw and resolve itself into a dew,   130
Or that the Everlasting had not fixed

101–3 **fault to . . . absurd** sin against: the will of God, the dead (by not accepting
their death), universal natural order which includes both life and death, and against reason,
by foolishly refusing to accept the inevitable   104 **still** always   105 **corse** corpse (of Abel,
also, ironically, the first fratricide)   107 **unprevailing** useless   109 **most immediate** next
in succession (though Danish kings were elected by the council, an Elizabethan audience
might feel that Hamlet, not Claudius, should be king)   112 **impart** express (myself)   113
Wittenberg (the University of Wittenberg, associated with Luther)   114 **retrograde**
movement (of planets) in a reverse direction (fr. astrology)   115 **beseech . . . you** hope you
will be inclined   118 **lose her prayers** ask in vain (she intervenes when Hamlet does not
reply to Claudius)   124 **grace** honor   125 **Denmark** the King of Denmark   127 **rouse**
toast that empties the wine cup   **bruit** sound   129 **sullied** tainted (Q spells

His canon 'gainst self-slaughter. O God, God,
How weary, stale, flat, and unprofitable
Seem to me all the uses of this world!
Fie on't, ah fie, 'tis an unweeded garden   135
That grows to seed, things rank and gross in nature
Possess it merely. That it should come to this,
But two months dead, nay not so much, not two,
So excellent a king, that was to this
Hyperion to a satyr, so loving to my mother,   140
That he might not beteem the winds of heaven
Visit her face too roughly—heaven and earth,
Must I remember? why, she would hang on him
As if increase of appetite had grown
By what it fed on, and yet within a month—   145
Let me not think on't: Frailty, thy name is woman—
A little month or ere those shoes were old
With which she followed my poor father's body
Like Niobe all tears, why she, even she—
O God, a beast that wants discourse of reason   150
Would have mourned longer—married with my uncle,
My father's brother, but no more like my father
Than I to Hercules: within a month,
Ere yet the salt of most unrighteous tears
Had left the flushing in her gallèd eyes,   155
She married. O most wicked speed, to post
With such dexterity to incestuous sheets:
It is not, nor it cannot come to good,
But break my heart, for I must hold my tongue.

> *Enter* HORATIO, MARCELLUS *and*
> BARNARDO.

HORATIO.   Hail to your lordship.
HAMLET.   I am glad to see you well;   160
            Horatio, or I do forget my self.
HORATIO.   The same my lord, and your poor servant ever.

"sallied")   130 **resolve** dissolve   132 **canon** divine edict   136 **rank** (1) luxuriant, excessive (2) bad-smelling   137 **merely** entirely   139 **this** Claudius   140 **Hyperion** god of
the sun (metaphor of the sun-king)   **satyr** part-goat, part-man woodland deity (noted for
lust)   141 **beteem** allow   144–5 **As if . . . on** as if the more she fed, the more her appetite
increased (the closer physically, the greater her sexual appetite)   149 **Niobe** (who boasted
of her children before Leto and was punished by their destruction; Zeus changed the
weeping mother to a stone dropping continual tears)   150 **wants** lacks   154 **unrighteous**
(because untrue)   155 **flushing** redness   **galled** rubbed sore   156 **post** rush   157
incestuous (the church forbade marriage to one's brother's widow)   161 **I . . . myself** I
would forget myself rather than you

HAMLET.   Sir my good friend, I'll change that name with you:
And what make you from Wittenberg, Horatio?
Marcellus.   165

MARCELLUS.
My good lord.

HAMLET.   I am very glad to see you: good even, sir.
But what in faith make you from Wittenberg?

HORATIO.   A truant disposition, good my lord.

HAMLET.   I would not hear your enemy say so,   170
Nor shall you do mine ear that violence
To make it truster of your own report
Against yourself. I know you are no truant,
But what is your affair in Elsinore?
We'll teach you to drink deep ere you depart.   175

HORATIO.   My lord, I came to see your father's funeral.

HAMLET.   I prithee do not mock me, fellow student,
I think it was to see my mother's wedding.

HORATIO.   Indeed my lord it followed hard upon.

HAMLET.   Thrift, thrift, Horatio, the funeral baked meats   180
Did coldly furnish forth the marriage tables.
Would I had met my dearest foe in heaven
Or ever I had seen that day Horatio.
My father, methinks I see my father.

HORATIO.   Where my lord?

HAMLET.   In my mind's eye Horatio.   185

HORATIO.   I saw him once, a' was a goodly king.

HAMLET.   A' was a man, take him for all in all,
I shall not look upon his like again.

HORATIO.   My lord, I think I saw him yesternight.

HAMLET.   Saw? Who?   190

HORATIO.   My lord, the king your father.

HAMLET.   The king my father?

HORATIO.   Season your admiration for a while
With an attent ear till I may deliver
Upon the witness of these gentlemen
This marvel to you.

HAMLET.   For God's love let me hear!   195

HORATIO.   Two nights together had these gentlemen,

---

163 **change** exchange (and be called your
friend)   164 **make you from** are you doing away from   169 **truant disposition** inclination
to truancy   175 **to drink deep** (a custom Elizabethans associated with Denmark)   180
baked meats meat pies   181 **coldly** when cold   182 **dearest** direst   186 **goodly**
handsome   192 **Season your admiration** control your wonder   198 **waste** void   200 **at**

Marcellus and Barnardo, on their watch
In the dead waste and middle of the night,
Been thus encountered. A figure like your father
Armed at point exactly, cap-a-pe,   200
Appears before them, and with solemn march,
Goes slow and stately by them; thrice he walked
By their oppressed and fear-surprisèd eyes
Within his truncheon's length, whilst they distilled
Almost to jelly with the act of fear,   205
Stand dumb and speak not to him; this to me
In dreadful secrecy impart they did,
And I with them the third night kept the watch,
Where as they had delivered, both in time,
Form of the thing, each word made true and good,   210
The apparition comes: I knew your father,
These hands are not more like.

HAMLET.   But where was this?
MARCELLUS.
My lord upon the platform where we watch.
HAMLET.   Did you not speak to it?
HORATIO.   My lord I did,
But answer made it none, yet once methought   215
It lifted up it head, and did address
Itself to motion like as it would speak:
But even then the morning cock crew loud,
And at the sound it shrunk in haste away
And vanished from our sight.
HAMLET.   'Tis very strange.   220
HORATIO.   As I do live my honoured lord 'tis true,
And we did think it writ down in our duty
To let you know of it.
HAMLET.   Indeed indeed sirs, but this troubles me.
Hold you the watch tonight?
ALL.   We do my lord.   225
HAMLET.   Armed say you?
ALL.   Armed my lord.
HAMLET.   From top to toe?

---

point . . . cap-a-pe in every detail, head to foot   **203 oppressed** overcome by horror   **204
truncheon** staff (of office)   **distilled** dissolved   **207 in dreadful secrecy** as a dread
secret   **213 platform** open walk on the battlements for guards or cannons   **216 it**
its   **216–17 address . . . motion** start to move   **222 writ down in** prescribed as

ALL.   My lord from head to foot.
HAMLET.   Then saw you not his face.
HORATIO. O yes my lord, he wore his beaver up.   230
HAMLET.   What, looked he frowningly?
HORATIO. A countenance more in sorrow than in anger.
HAMLET.   Pale, or red?
HORATIO. Nay, very pale.
HAMLET.   And fixed his eyes upon you?
HORATIO. Most constantly.
HAMLET.   I would I had been there.   235
HORATIO. It would have much amazed you.
HAMLET.   Very like, very like, stayed it long?
HORATIO. While one with moderate haste might tell a hundred.
MARCELLUS, BARNARDO.
          Longer, longer.
HORATIO. Not when I saw't.
HAMLET.   His beard was grizzled, no?   240
HORATIO. It was as I have seen it in his life,
          A sable silvered.
HAMLET.   I will watch tonight;
          Perchance 'twill walk again.
HORATIO.   I warr'nt it will.
HAMLET.   If it assume my noble father's person,
          I'll speak to it though hell itself should gape   245
          And bid me hold my peace; I pray you all
          If you have hitherto concealed this sight
          Let it be tenable in your silence still,
          And whatsomever else shall hap tonight,
          Give it an understanding but no tongue.   250
          I will requite your loves, so fare you well:
          Upon the platform 'twixt eleven and twelve
          I'll visit you.
ALL.   Our duty to your honour.
HAMLET.   Your loves, as mine to you: farewell.   *Exeunt.*
          My father's spirit (in arms) all is not well,   255
          I doubt some foul play, would the night were come;
          Till then sit still my soul, foul deeds will rise,
          Though all the earth o'erwhelm them, to men's eyes.

                                                       Exit.

---

230 **beaver** visor 238 **tell** count 240 **grizzled** grey 242 **A sable silvered** black flecked
with grey   245–6 **though hell . . . peace** despite the risk of hell (for speaking to a demon)
warning me to be silent   245 **gape** (suggesting the huge "mouth of hell" of morality
plays)   248 **tenable** held onto   251 **requite your loves** reward your friendship   254

SCENE III.

Enter LAERTES *and* OPHELIA *his sister.*

LAERTES.   My necessaries are embarked, farewell,
            And sister, as the winds give benefit
            And convoy is assistant, do not sleep
            But let me hear from you.
OPHELIA.   Do you doubt that?
LAERTES.   For Hamlet, and the trifling of his favour,   5
            Hold it a fashion, and a toy in blood,
            A violet in the youth of primy nature,
            Forward, not permanent, sweet, not lasting,
            The perfume and suppliance of a minute,
            No more.
OPHELIA.   No more but so?
LAERTES.   Think it no more.   10
            For nature crescent does not grow alone
            In thews and bulk, but as this temple waxes
            The inward service of the mind and soul
            Grows wide withal. Perhaps he loves you now,
            And now no soil nor cautel doth besmirch   15
            The virtue of his will: but you must fear,
            His greatness weighed, his will is not his own,
            For he himself is subject to his birth:
            He may not as unvalued persons do,
            Carve for himself, for on his choice depends   20
            The sanctity and health of this whole state,
            And therefore must his choice be circumscribed
            Unto the voice and yielding of that body
            Whereof he is the head. Then if he says he loves you,
            It fits your wisdom so far to believe it   25
            As he in his particular act and place
            May give his saying deed, which is no further

Your loves . . . you offer your friendship (rather than duty) in exchange for mine   256
doubt fear
    I, iii a room in Polonius's house   3 **convoy** conveyance   6 **fashion** passing fancy   6
toy in blood whim of the passions   7 **youth of primy nature** early spring   8 **Forward**
premature   9 **suppliance of** supplying diversion for   11 **nature crescent** man as he
grows   12 **thews and bulk** sinews and body   **temple waxes** body grows (1 Cor.
VI.19)   13 **inward service** mind and soul within the body, like a religious service in the
temple   14 **withal** at the same time   15 **cautel** deceit   16 **will** desire   17 **weighed**
considered   19 **unvalued persons** common people   20 **Carve** choose (as does the one
who carves the food)   23 **voice and yielding** approving vote   26–7 **in his . . . deed**
limited by personal responsibilities and rank, may perform what he promises

Than the main voice of Denmark goes withal.
Then weigh what loss your honour may sustain
If with too credent ear you list his songs,   30
Or lose your heart, or your chaste treasure open
To his unmast'red importunity.
Fear it Ophelia, fear it my dear sister,
And keep you in the rear of your affection,
Out of the shot and danger of desire.   35
The chariest maid is prodigal enough
If she unmask her beauty to the moon.
Virtue itself 'scapes not calumnious strokes.
The canker galls the infants of the spring
Too oft before their buttons be disclosed,   40
And in the morn and liquid dew of youth
Contagious blastments are most imminent.
Be wary then, best safety lies in fear,
Youth to itself rebels, though none else near.

OPHELIA.   I shall the effect of this good lesson keep   45
As watchman to my heart: but good my brother,
Do not as some ungracious pastors do,
Show me the steep and thorny way to heaven,
Whiles like a puffed and reckless libertine
Himself the primrose path of dalliance treads,   50
And recks not his own rede.
                    Enter POLONIUS.

LAERTES.   O fear me not,
I stay too long, but here my father comes:
A double blessing is a double grace,
Occasion smiles upon a second leave.

POLONIUS.   Yet here Laertes? aboard, aboard for shame,   55
The wind sits in the shoulder of your sail,
And you are stayed for: there, my blessing with thee,
And these few precepts in thy memory
Look thou character. Give thy thoughts no tongue,

---

30 **credent**
credulous   **list** listen to   31–2 **your chaste . . . importunity** lose your virginity to his
uncontrolled persistence   34–5 **keep . . . desire** (1) restrain your natural emotions, which
could lead to desire (2) keep your emotions in the rear lines where they won't be shot at and
conquered by desire   36 **chariest** most cautious   39 **canker . . . infants** cankerworm or
caterpillar harms the young plants   40 **buttons** buds   42 **blastments** blights   44 **to
itself rebels** lusts by nature   45 **effect** moral   47 **ungracious** lacking God's grace   49
puffed surfeit-swollen   50 **dalliance** pleasure   51 **recks . . . rede** does not follow his
own advice   **fear me not** don't worry about me   53 **grace** (1) blessing (2) favor   54
Occasion . . . leave opportunity favors a second leave-taking   58 **few precepts** (such
parental advice-giving was common in literature)   59 **character** write   60

Nor any unproportioned thought his act: 60
Be thou familiar, but by no means vulgar:
Those friends thou hast, and their adoption tried,
Grapple them unto thy soul with hoops of steel,
But do not dull thy palm with entertainment
Of each new-hatched unfledged comrade. Beware   65
Of entrance to a quarrel, but being in,
Bear't that th'opposèd may beware of thee.
Give every man thy ear, but few thy voice:
Take each man's censure, but reserve thy judgment.
Costly thy habit as thy purse can buy,   70
But not expressed in fancy; rich, not gaudy,
For the apparel oft proclaims the man,
And they in France of the best rank and station,
Are of a most select and generous chief in that:
Neither a borrower nor a lender be,   75
For loan oft loses both itself and friend,
And borrowing dulls the edge of husbandry;
This above all, to thine own self be true
And it must follow as the night the day,
Thou canst not then be false to any man.   80
Farewell, my blessing season this in thee.

LAERTES. Most humbly do I take my leave my lord.
POLONIUS. The time invites you, go, your servants tend.
LAERTES. Farewell Ophelia, and remember well
What I have said to you.
OPHELIA.   'Tis in my memory locked,   85
And you yourself shall keep the key of it.
LAERTES. Farewell.   *Exit* LAERTES.
POLONIUS. What is't Ophelia he hath said to you?
OPHELIA. So please you, something touching the Lord Hamlet.
POLONIUS. Marry, well bethought: 90
'Tis told me he hath very oft of late
Given private time to you, and you yourself
Have of your audience been most free and bounteous.
If it be so, as so 'tis put on me,
And that in way of caution, I must tell you,   95

---

unproportioned out of proportion with reason   61 familiar friendly   vulgar indiscriminately friendly   62 adoption tried loyalty proved   63 hoops of steel bands that bind the
staves of a barrel   64 dull get calluses on   65 new-hatched, unfledged new and untested
(metaphor from nesting)   67 Bear't assure by your conduct   69 censure opinion   70
habit clothing   71 expressed in fancy so fantastic as to be ridiculous   74 select . . . chief
judicious and noble eminence   77 husbandry thrift   81 season bring to maturity   83
tend attend, wait   94 on to

You do not understand yourself so clearly
As it behoves my daughter, and your honour.
What is between you? give me up the truth.

OPHELIA. He hath my lord of late made many tenders
Of his affection to me.   100

POLONIUS. Affection, puh, you speak like a green girl
Unsifted in such perilous circumstance.
Do you believe his tenders as you call them?

OPHELIA. I do not know my lord what I should think.

POLONIUS. Marry, I will teach you; think yourself a baby   105
That you have ta'en these tenders for true pay
Which are not sterling. Tender yourself more dearly,
Or (not to crack the wind of the poor phrase,
Running it thus) you'll tender me a fool.

OPHELIA. My lord he hath importuned me with love   110
In honourable fashion.

POLONIUS. Ay, fashion you may call it, go to, go to.

OPHELIA. And hath given countenance to his speech, my lord,
With almost all the holy vows of heaven.

POLONIUS. Ay, springes to catch woodcocks. I do know   115
When the blood burns, how prodigal the soul
Lends the tongue vows: these blazes daughter,
Giving more light than heat, extinct in both,
Even in their promise, as it is a-making,
You must not take for fire. From this time   120
Be something scanter of your maiden presence,
Set your entreatments at a higher rate
Than a command to parle; for Lord Hamlet,
Believe so much in him that he is young,
And with a larger tether may he walk   125
Than may be given you: in few Ophelia,
Do not believe his vows, for they are brokers
Not of that dye which their investments show,

---

99 **tenders** offers (cf. 11. 106-9)   102 **Unsifted** untested   106 **tenders** offers (of money)   107 **sterling** genuine (currency)   **Tender... dearly** hold yourself at a higher value   108–9 **crack ... thus** make the phrase lose its breath (like a horse driven too hard)   109 **tender ... fool** (1) make me look foolish (2) present me with a baby ("fool"=affectionate term for baby or child)   111 **fashion** form (Polonius interprets as "whim")   113 **countenance** confirmation   115 **springes** snares   **woodcocks** snipelike birds (believed to be stupid and therefore easily trapped)   116 **prodigal** liberally   117 **blazes** flashes of passion   118–19 **extinct ... a-making** losing both appearance, because of brevity, and substance, because of broken promises   122–3 **Set ... parle** don't rush to negotiate a surrender as soon as the besieger asks for a parley, or discussion of terms (common metaphor based on besieged castle)   126 **few** i.e. words   127 **brokers** (1) agents (fr. business) (2) procurers   128 **investments** (1)

But mere implorators of unholy suits,
Breathing like sanctified and pious bonds,   130
The better to beguile. This is for all,
I would not in plain terms from this time forth
Have you so slander any moment leisure
As to give words or talk with the Lord Hamlet.
Look to't I charge you, come your ways.   135
OPHELIA. I shall obey, my lord.   *Exeunt.*

[SCENE IV.]

Enter HAMLET, HORATIO *and* MARCELLUS.

HAMLET.   The air bites shrewdly, it is very cold.
HORATIO. It is a nipping and an eager air.
HAMLET.   What hour now?
HORATIO.   I think it lacks of twelve.
MARCELLUS.
          No, it is struck.
HORATIO. Indeed? I heard it not: it then draws near the season,   5
          Wherein the spirit held his wont to walk.

              A flourish of trumpets, and two pieces
              [*of ordnance*] *go off.*

          What does this mean my lord?
HAMLET.   The king doth wake tonight and takes his rouse,
          Keeps wassail and the swagg'ring up-spring reels:
          And as he drains his draughts of Rhenish down,   10
          The kettle-drum and trumpet thus bray out
          The triumph of his pledge.
HORATIO.   Is it a custom?
HAMLET.   Ay marry is't,
          But to my mind, though I am native here
          And to the manner born, it is a custom   15
          More honoured in the breach than the observance.

---

lit. (2) vestments, clothes   129 **mere** absolute   **implorators of** solicitors or implorers
for   130 **Breathing** speaking softly   **bonds** pledges   133 **slander** disgrace   **moment**
momentary   135 **come your ways** come along
    I, iv the platform   1 **shrewdly** piercingly   2 **eager** sharp   8 **wake** stay
awake   **rouse** drinks that empty the cup   9 **Keeps wassail** holds drinking
bouts   **up-spring** a vigorous German dance   10 **Rhenish** Rhine wine   12 **triumph . . .
pledge** victory of emptying the cup with one draught   15 **to . . . born** accustomed to the
practice since birth   16 **More . . . observance** better to break than to observe

This heavy-headed revel east and west
Makes us traduced and taxed of other nations:
They clepe us drunkards, and with swinish phrase
Soil our addition, and indeed it takes   20
From our achievements, though performed at height,
The pith and marrow of our attribute.
So oft it chances in particular men,
That for some vicious mole of nature in them,
As in their birth, wherein they are not guilty   25
(Since nature cannot choose his origin),
By the o'ergrowth of some complexion,
Oft breaking down the pales and forts of reason,
Or by some habit, that too much o'er-leavens
The form of plausive manners—that these men,   30
Carrying I say the stamp of one defect,
Being nature's livery, or fortune's star,
His virtues else be they as pure as grace,
As infinite as man may undergo,
Shall in the general censure take corruption   35
From that particular fault: the dram of evil
Doth all the noble substance of a doubt,
To his own scandal.

                    Enter GHOST.

HORATIO.   Look my lord, it comes.
HAMLET.   Angels and ministers of grace defend us:
            Be thou a spirit of health, or goblin damned,   40
            Bring with thee airs from heaven, or blasts from hell,
            Be thy intents wicked, or charitable,
            Thou com'st in such a questionable shape,
            That I will speak to thee. I'll call thee Hamlet,
            King, father, royal Dane. O answer me,   45

                                                                  17–38
(omitted in F, possibly because James I was married to a Dane)   18 **traduced and taxed of**
defamed and taken to task by   19 **clepe** call   19–20 **with swinish . . . addition** blemish
our reputation by comparing us to swine (traditional comparison for drunkards)   21 **at**
height to the maximum   22 **attribute** reputation   23 **particular** individual   24 **mole of**
nature natural blemish   25 **in their birth** being born with it (first of three ways in which
these blemishes originate)   27 **o'er growth . . . complexion** overbalance of one of the
body's four humors or fluids believed to determine temperament   28 **pales** defensive
enclosures   29 **too much o'erleavens** excessively modifies (like too much leaven in
bread)   30 **plausive** pleasing   32 **nature's livery** marked by nature   **fortune's star**
destined by chance   33 **grace** blessedness   35 **general censure** public opinion   36–8
the dram . . . scandal the minute quantity of evil (Q spells "eale") casts doubt upon his noble
nature, to his shame   39 **ministers of grace** agents of God's grace   40 **spirit . . . damned**
true ghost or demon from hell   43 **questionable** question-raising   47 **canonized** buried

Let me not burst in ignorance, but tell
Why thy canonized bones hearsèd in death
Have burst their cerements? why the sepulchre,
Wherein we saw thee quietly interred
Hath oped his ponderous and marble jaws,   50
To cast thee up again? What may this mean
That thou, dead corse, again in complete steel
Revisits thus the glimpses of the moon,
Making night hideous, and we fools of nature
So horridly to shake our disposition   55
With thoughts beyond the reaches of our souls,
Say why is this? wherefore? what should we do?

Ghost beckons Hamlet.

HORATIO.   It beckons you to go away with it,
As if it some impartment did desire
To you alone.
MARCELLUS.   Look with what courteous action   60
It waves you to a more removèd ground,
But do not go with it.
HORATIO.   No, by no means.
HAMLET.   It will not speak, then I will follow it.
HORATIO.   Do not my lord.
HAMLET.   Why what should be the fear?
I do not set my life at a pin's fee,   65
And for my soul, what can it do to that
Being a thing immortal as itself;
It waves me forth again, I'll follow it.
HORATIO.   What if it tempt you toward the flood my lord,
Or to the dreadful summit of the cliff   70
That beetles o'er his base into the sea,
And there assume some other horrible form
Which might deprive your sovereignty of reason,
And draw you into madness? think of it,
The very place puts toys of desperation,   75
Without more motive, into every brain
That looks so many fathoms to the sea

in accordance with church edict   **hearsed** entombed   48 **cerements** waxed cloth
wrappings   51 **cast** vomit   54 **fools of nature** mocked by our natural limitations when
faced with the supernatural   59 **some . . . desire** desired to impart something   61
removed distant   65 **fee** value   68, 78 **waves** beckons   69 **flood** sea   71 **beetles o'er**
overhangs   72 **assume . . . form** change its shape to one more horrible   73 **deprive . . .**
reason dethrone your reason from its sovereignty   75 **toys of desperation** desperate
impulses (to throw oneself over)

And hears it roar beneath.

HAMLET.   It waves me still:
Go on, I'll follow thee.

MARCELLUS.
You shall not go my lord.

HAMLET.   Hold off your hands.   80

HORATIO. Be ruled, you shall not go.

HAMLET.   My fate cries out,
And makes each petty artire in this body
As hardy as the Nemean lion's nerve;
Still am I called, unhand me gentlemen,
By heaven I'll make a ghost of him that lets me: 85
I say away; go on, I'll follow thee.

Exeunt GHOST *and* HAMLET.

HORATIO. He waxes desperate with imagination.

MARCELLUS.
Let's follow, 'tis not fit thus to obey him.

HORATIO. Have after—to what issue will this come?

MARCELLUS.
Something is rotten in the state of Denmark.   90

HORATIO. Heaven will direct it.

MARCELLUS.   Nay, let's follow him.

Exeunt.

[SCENE V.]

Enter GHOST *and* HAMLET.

HAMLET. Whither wilt thou lead me? Speak, I'll go no further.

GHOST. Mark me.

HAMLET.   I will.

GHOST.   My hour is almost come
When I to sulphurous and tormenting flames
Must render up myself.

HAMLET.   Alas poor ghost.

GHOST. Pity me not, but lend thy serious hearing   5
To what I shall unfold.

---

81 **My fate cries out** I am fated to go   82 **artire**
ligament   83 **Nemean lion** (killed by Hercules as one of his twelve labors)   **nerve**
sinew   85 **lets** prevents   87 **waxes desperate** grows frantic
I, v another part of the platform   2 **hour** time   6 **bound** obliged by duty   11 **fast** do

HAMLET.   Speak, I am bound to hear.
GHOST.   So art thou to revenge, when thou shalt hear.
HAMLET.   What?
GHOST.   I am thy father's spirit,
           Doomed for a certain term to walk the night,   10
           And for the day confined to fast in fires,
           Till the foul crimes done in my days of nature
           Are burnt and purged away: but that I am forbid
           To tell the secrets of my prison-house,
           I could a tale unfold whose lightest word   15
           Would harrow up thy soul, freeze thy young blood,
           Make thy two eyes like stars start from their spheres,
           Thy knotted and combinèd locks to part,
           And each particular hair to stand an end,
           Like quills upon the fretful porpentine: 20
           But this eternal blazon must not be
           To ears of flesh and blood; list, list, O list:
           If thou didst ever thy dear father love—
HAMLET.   O God!
GHOST.   Revenge his foul and most unnatural murder.   25
HAMLET.   Murder?
GHOST.   Murder most foul, as in the best it is,
           But this most foul, strange and unnatural.
HAMLET.   Haste me to know't, that I with wings as swift
           As meditation or the thoughts of love,   30
           May sweep to my revenge.
GHOST.   I find thee apt,
           And duller shouldst thou be than the fat weed
           That rots itself in ease on Lethe wharf,
           Wouldst thou not stir in this; now Hamlet hear,
           'Tis given out, that sleeping in my orchard,   35
           A serpent stung me, so the whole ear of Denmark
           Is by a forgèd process of my death
           Rankly abused: but know thou noble youth,
           The serpent that did sting thy father's life
           Now wears his crown.

---

penance   12 **crimes . . . nature** sins committed during my life on earth   13 **purged** (he is
in purgatory)   15 **lightest** least important   16 **young** (this, and I, iii, 7 and 124, testify to
Hamlet's youth)   17 **spheres** (1) orbits (according to Ptolemy, each planet was confined to
a sphere revolving around the earth) (2) sockets   19 **an** on   20 **fretful porpentine** angry
porcupine (with quills erect)   21 **eternal blazon** revelation about eternity   27 **in** at   28
unnatural (against natural fraternal affection)   31 **apt** ready   32 **fat** slimy   33 **Lethe
wharf** the banks of Lethe (river in Hades from which spirits drank to forget their past
lives)   35 **orchard** garden   37 **process** account   38 **abused** deceived

HAMLET.   O my prophetic soul!   40
              My uncle?
GHOST.   Ay, that incestuous, that adulterate beast,
              With witchcraft of his wit, with traitorous gifts,
              O wicked wit and gifts, that have the power
              So to seduce; won to his shameful lust   45
              The will of my most seeming-virtuous queen;
              O Hamlet, what a falling-off was there,
              From me whose love was of that dignity
              That it went hand in hand, even with the vow
              I made to her in marriage, and to decline   50
              Upon a wretch whose natural gifts were poor
              To those of mine;
              But virtue, as it never will be moved,
              Though lewdness court it in a shape of heaven,
              So lust, though to a radiant angel linked,   55
              Will sate itself in a celestial bed
              And prey on garbage.
              But soft, methinks I scent the morning air,
              Brief let me be; sleeping within my orchard,
              My custom always of the afternoon,   60
              Upon my secure hour thy uncle stole
              With juice of cursèd hebona in a vial,
              And in the porches of my ears did pour
              The leperous distilment, whose effect
              Holds such an enmity with blood of man,   65
              That swift as quicksilver it courses through
              The natural gates and alleys of the body,
              And with a sudden vigour it doth posset
              And curd, like eager droppings into milk,
              The thin and wholesome blood; so did it mine,   70
              And a most instant tetter barked about
              Most lazar-like with vile and loathsome crust
              All my smooth body.
              Thus was I sleeping by a brother's hand,

---

40 **prophetic**
soul (because he has instinctively hated Claudius)   42 **adulterate** adulterous (the relationship between Claudius and Gertrude while King Hamlet was still alive)   50-1 **decline**
Upon descend to   51 **natural gifts** endowments of nature (as looks and bearing)   52 **To**
compared to   54 **shape of heaven** angelic appearance   61 **secure** unsuspecting   62
hebona poisonous sap of the ebony or henbane   64 **leperous** leprosy-causing   66 **courses**
runs (like a horse running through a town)   67 **gates and alleys** entrances and
passages   68 **posset** curdle   69 **eager** sour   70 **wholesome** healthy   71 **tetter** skin
eruption   **barked about** covered (like bark on a tree)   72 **lazar** leper   75 **dispatched** (1)
deprived (2) killed   77 **Unhouseled . . . unaneled** without final sacrament, unprepared

Of life, of crown, of queen at once dispatched,   75
Cut off even in the blossoms of my sin,
Unhouseled, disappointed, unaneled,
No reck'ning made, but sent to my account
With all my imperfections on my head;
O horrible, O horrible, most horrible!   80
If thou hast nature in thee bear it not,
Let not the royal bed of Denmark be
A couch for luxury and damnèd incest.
But howsomever thou pursues this act,
Taint not thy mind, nor let thy soul contrive   85
Against thy mother aught; leave her to heaven,
And to those thorns that in her bosom lodge
To prick and sting her. Fare thee well at once,
The glow-worm shows the matin to be near
And 'gins to pale his uneffectual fire: 90
Adieu, adieu, adieu, remember me.   *Exit.*

HAMLET.   O all you host of heaven! O earth! what else?
And shall I couple hell? O fie! Hold, hold my heart,
And you my sinews, grow not instant old,
But bear me stiffly up; remember thee?   95
Ay thou poor ghost, whiles memory holds a seat
In this distracted globe. Remember thee?
Yea, from the table of my memory
I'll wipe away all trivial fond recòrds,
All saws of books, all forms, all pressures past   100
That youth and observation copied there,
And thy commandment all alone shall live
Within the book and volume of my brain,
Unmixed with baser matter, yes by heaven:
O most pernicious woman!   105
O villain, villain, smiling damnèd villain!
My tables, meet it is I set it down
That one may smile, and smile, and be a villain,
At least I am sure it may be so in Denmark.

(without confession) and lacking extreme unction (anointing) (cf. III, iii, 81)   78 **reck'ning** (1) accounting (2) payment of my bill (3) confession and absolution   78 **account** (1) accounting at the Last Judgment (2) accounting for debts   80 (though Q and F assign this line to the ghost, it is often given to Hamlet in production)   81 **nature** natural filial affection   83 **luxury** lust   86 **aught** anything   87 **those thorns** (in the sense of "her own conscience")   89 **matin** dawn   90 **'gins . . . fire** his light becomes ineffective, made pale by day   93 **couple** engage in a contest against   97 **distracted globe** (his head)   98, 107 **table** tablet, "table-book" (II, ii, 136) (from university life, cf 1. 103)   99 **fond** foolish   100 **saws of books** maxims copied from books   **forms, pressures** ideas, impressions   107 **meet** fitting

So uncle, there you are: now to my word,   110
It is 'Adieu, adieu, remember me.'
I have sworn't.

Enter HORATIO *and* MARCELLUS.

HORATIO.   My lord, my lord!
MARCELLUS.   Lord Hamlet!
HORATIO.   Heaven secure him.
HAMLET.   So be it.
MARCELLUS.
            Illo, ho, ho, my lord!   115
HAMLET.   Hillo, ho, ho, boy, come bird, come.
MARCELLUS.
            How is't my noble lord?
HORATIO.   What news my lord?
HAMLET.   O, wonderful!
HORATIO.   Good my lord, tell it.
HAMLET.   No, you will reveal it.
HORATIO.   Not I my lord, by heaven.
MARCELLUS.   Nor I my lord.   120
HAMLET.   How say you then, would heart of man once think it?
            But you'll be secret?
BOTH.   Ay, by heaven, my lord.
HAMLET.   There's ne'er a villain dwelling in all Denmark
            But he's an arrant knave.
HORATIO.   There needs no ghost my lord, come from the grave   125
            To tell us this.
HAMLET.   Why right, you are in the right,
            And so without more circumstance at all
            I hold it fit that we shake hands and part,
            You, as your business and desire shall point you,
            For every man hath business and desire   130
            Such as it is, and for my own poor part,
            Look you, I will go pray.
HORATIO.   These are but wild and whirling words my lord.
HAMLET.   I am sorry they offend you, heartily,
            Yes faith, heartily.
HORATIO.   There's no offence my lord.   135
HAMLET.   Yes by Saint Patrick, but there is Horatio,
            And much offence too: touching this vision here,

---

110 **word** motto (to guide my actions)   113 **secure**
protect   116 **Hillo . . . come** (falconer's cry with which Hamlet replies to their
calls)   124 **arrant** thoroughgoing   127 **circumstance** ceremony   138 **honest** true (not a

It is an honest ghost that let me tell you:
For your desire to know what is between us,
O'ermaster't as you may. And now good friends,　　140
As you are friends, scholars, and soldiers,
Give me one poor request.

HORATIO.　What is't, my lord? we will.

HAMLET.　Never make known what you have seen tonight.

BOTH.　My lord we will not.

HAMLET.　　　　　　　　　Nay, but swear't.

HORATIO.　　　　　　　　　　　In faith　　145
My lord, not I.

MARCELLUS.　　　　　　Nor I my lord, in faith.

HAMLET.　Upon my sword.

MARCELLUS.　　　　　We have sworn my lord already.

HAMLET.　Indeed, upon my sword, indeed.

GHOST.　Swear.　　　　　　　*Ghost cries under the stage.*

HAMLET.　Ha, ha, boy, say'st thou so, art thou there,
　　　　truepenny?　　　　　　　　　　　　　150
Come on, you hear this fellow in the cellarage,
Consent to swear.

HORATIO.　　　　　　　　Propose the oath my lord.

HAMLET.　Never to speak of this that you have seen.
Swear by my sword.

GHOST.　[*Beneath.*] Swear.　　　　　　　　155

HAMLET.　Hic et ubique? then we'll shift our ground:
Come hither gentlemen,
And lay your hands again upon my sword,
Swear by my sword
Never to speak of this that you have heard.　　160

GHOST.　[*Beneath.*] Swear by his sword.

HAMLET.　Well said old mole, canst work i'th' earth so fast?
A worthy pioner—once more remove, good friends.

HORATIO.　O day and night, but this is wondrous strange.

HAMLET.　And therefore as a stranger give it welcome.　　165
There are more things in heaven and earth Horatio,
Than are dreamt of in your philosophy.
But come,
Here as before, never so help you mercy,

devil in disguise)　　147 **We have . . . already** ("in faith" was tantamount to an oath)　　148
sword (the cross-shaped hilt)　　150 **truepenny** old pal　　156 **Hic et ubique** here and
everywhere　　163 **pioner** digger (army trencher)　　**remove** move elsewhere　　165 **as a
. . . welcome** welcome it as you would a stranger, without questioning　　167 **your
philosophy** this science (which discredits ghosts)

How strange or odd some'er I bear myself,   170
(As I perchance hereafter shall think meet
To put an antic disposition on)
That you at such times seeing me, never shall
With arms encumbered thus, or this head-shake,
Or by pronouncing of some doubtful phrase,   175
As 'Well, well, we know,' or 'We could and if
    we would,'
Or 'If we list to speak,' or 'There be and if they might,'
Or such ambiguous giving out, to note
That you know aught of me; this do swear,
So grace and mercy at your most need help you.   180

GHOST.   [*Beneath.*] Swear.
HAMLET.   Rest, rest, perturbed spirit: so gentlemen,
            With all my love I do commend me to you,
            And what so poor a man as Hamlet is,
            May do t'express his love and friending to you   185
            God willing shall not lack: let us go in together,
            And still your fingers on your lips I pray.
            The time is out of joint: O cursèd spite,
            That ever I was born to set it right.
            Nay come, let's go together.   *Exeunt.* 190

Act Two

SCENE I.

Enter old POLONIUS *with his man* REYNALDO.

POLONIUS.   Give him this money, and these notes Reynaldo.
REYNALDO.   I will my lord.
POLONIUS.   You shall do marvellous wisely, good Reynaldo,
            Before you visit him, to make inquire
            Of his behaviour.
REYNALDO.   My lord, I did intend it.   5
POLONIUS.   Marry, well said, very well said; look you sir,
            Inquire me first what Danskers are in Paris,

---

171 **meet** fitting   172 **put . . . on**
assume a mad or grotesque behavior   174 **encumbered** folded   177 **list** please   183
commend . . . you put myself in your hands   187 **still** always   190 **go together** walk as
equals (instead of Hamlet first)
II, i a room in Polonius's house   1 **notes** instructions   3 **marvellous** wonderfully   7

And how, and who, what means, and where they keep,
What company, at what expense, and finding
By this encompassment and drift of question   10
That they do know my son, come you more nearer
Than your particular demands will touch it,
Take you as 'twere some distant knowledge of him,
As thus, 'I know his father, and his friends,
And in part him'—do you mark this, Reynaldo?   15

REYNALDO. Ay, very well my lord.

POLONIUS. 'And in part him, but,' you may say, 'not well,
But if't be he I mean, he's very wild,
Addicted so and so;' and there put on him
What forgeries you please, marry none so rank   20
As may dishonour him, take heed of that,
But sir, such wanton, wild, and usual slips,
As are companions noted and most known
To youth and liberty.

REYNALDO.   As gaming my lord.

POLONIUS. Ay, or drinking, fencing, swearing,   25
Quarrelling, drabbing—you may go so far.

REYNALDO. My lord, that would dishonour him.

POLONIUS. Faith no, as you may season it in the charge.
You must not put another scandal on him,
That he is open to incontinency,   30
That's not my meaning, but breathe his faults so quaintly
That they may seem the taints of liberty,
The flash and outbreak of a fiery mind,
A savageness in unreclaimèd blood,
Of general assault.

REYNALDO.   But my good lord—   35

POLONIUS. Wherefore should you do this?

REYNALDO.   Ay my lord,
I would know that.

POLONIUS.   Marry sir, here's my drift,
And I believe it is a fetch of warrant:
You laying these slight sullies on my son,
As 'twere a thing a little soiled i'th' working,   40

Danskers Danes   8 **means** income   **keep** lodge   10 **encompassment** roundabout
way   **question** conversation   12 **particular demands** specific questions   20 **forgeries**
inventions   **rank** excessive   23 **noted** observed   26 **drabbing** whoring   28 **season**
. . . **charge** temper the charge as you make it   30 **incontinency** uncontrolled lechery   31
quaintly delicately   32 **taints of** blemishes due to   34 **unreclaimed blood** unbridled
passion   35 **general assault** attacking all (young men)   36 **Wherefore** why   37 **drift**
aim   38 **fetch of warrant** trick guaranteed to succeed   39 **sullies** taints   40 **working**
handling

Mark you, your party in converse, him you would sound,
Having ever seen in the prenominate crimes
The youth you breathe of guilty, be assured
He closes with you in this consequence,
'Good sir,' or so, or 'friend,' or 'gentleman,' 45
According to the phrase, or the addition
Of man and country.

REYNALDO. Very good my lord.

POLONIUS. And then sir, does a' this, a' does, what was
I about to say?
By the mass I was about to say something,
Where did I leave?

REYNALDO. At 'closes in the consequence,' 50
At 'friend, or so, and gentleman.'

POLONIUS. At 'closes in the consequence,' ay marry,
He closes thus, 'I know the gentleman,
I saw him yesterday, or th'other day,
Or then, or then, with such or such, and as you say, 55
There was a' gaming, there o'ertook in's rouse,
There falling out at tennis,' or perchance
'I saw him enter such a house of sale,'
Videlicet, a brothel, or so forth. See you now,
Your bait of falsehood takes this carp of truth, 60
And thus do we of wisdom, and of reach,
With windlasses, and with assays of bias,
By indirections find directions out:
So by my former lecture and advice
Shall you my son; you have me, have you not? 65

REYNALDO. My lord I have.

POLONIUS. God bye ye, fare ye well.

REYNALDO. Good my lord.

POLONIUS. Observe his inclination in yourself.

REYNALDO. I shall my lord.

POLONIUS. And let him ply his music.

REYNALDO. Well my lord. 70

POLONIUS. Farewell. *Exit* REYNALDO.

---

41 **sound** i.e. out   42 **Having ever seen** if he has ever seen   **prenominate crimes** aforenamed sins   44 **closes . . . consequence** comes to terms with you as follows   46 **addition** title, form of address   48 '**a** he   56 **o'ertook in's rouse** overcome by drunkenness   57 **falling out** quarreling   59 **Videlicet** namely   61 **reach** far-reaching knowledge   62 **windlasses** roundabout approaches, circling to intercept game (fr. hunting)   **assays of bias** indirect attempts (fr. bowling: "bias" = a curve on the ball)   63 **find . . . out** find out directions to take   68 **in yourself** personally   70 **ply** practice   74

Enter OPHELIA.

        How now Ophelia, what's the matter?

OPHELIA.   O my lord, my lord, I have been so affrighted.

POLONIUS. With what, i'th'name of God?

OPHELIA.   My lord, as I was sewing in my closet,

        Lord Hamlet with his doublet all unbraced,   75

        No hat upon his head, his stockings fouled,

        Ungart'red, and down-gyvèd to his ankle,

        Pale as his shirt, his knees knocking each other,

        And with a look so piteous in purport

        As if he had been loosèd out of hell   80

        To speak of horrors, he comes before me.

POLONIUS. Mad for thy love?

OPHELIA.   My lord I do not know,

        But truly I do fear it.

POLONIUS.   What said he?

OPHELIA.   He took me by the wrist, and held me hard,

        Then goes he to the length of all his arm,   85

        And with his other hand thus o'er his brow,

        He falls to such perusal of my face

        As a' would draw it; long stayed he so,

        At last, a little shaking of mine arm,

        And thrice his head thus waving up and down,   90

        He raised a sigh so piteous and profound

        As it did seem to shatter all his bulk,

        And end his being; that done, he lets me go,

        And with his head over his shoulder turned

        He seemed to find his way without his eyes,   95

        For out adoors he went without their helps,

        And to the last bended their light on me.

POLONIUS. Come, go with me, I will go seek the king,

        This is the very ecstasy of love,

        Whose violent property fordoes itself,   100

        And leads the will to desperate undertakings

        As oft as any passion under heaven

        That does afflict our natures: I am sorry.

        What, have you given him any hard words of late?

OPHELIA.   No my good lord, but as you did command   105

---

closet private room   75 **doublet all unbraced** jacket all unfastened   76 **fouled** dirty   77 **down-gyved** down around his ankles (like prisoners' fetters or gyves)   82 **for thy love** because of love for you   85 **goes . . . arm** holds me at arm's length   88 **As** as if   92 **bulk** body   99 **ecstasy** madness   100 **Whose . . . itself** that, by its violent nature, destroys the one afflicted

I did repel his letters, and denied
His access to me.
POLONIUS.   That hath made him mad.
I am sorry that with better heed and judgment
I had not quoted him. I feared he did but trifle
And meant to wrack thee, but beshrew my jealousy: 110
By heaven it is as proper to our age
To cast beyond ourselves in our opinions,
As it is common for the younger sort
To lack discretion; come, go we to the king,
This must be known, which being kept close, might   115
    move
More grief to hide, than hate to utter love.   *Exeunt.*

SCENE II.

Flourish. Enter KING *and* QUEEN, ROSENCRANTZ
and GUILDENSTERN, *cum aliis.*

KING.   Welcome dear Rosencrantz and Guildenstern.
Moreover that we much did long to see you,
The need we have to use you did provoke
Our hasty sending. Something have you heard
Of Hamlet's transformation—so call it,   5
Sith nor th'exterior nor the inward man
Resembles that it was. What it should be,
More than his father's death, that thus hath put him
So much from th'understanding of himself,
I cannot dream of: I entreat you both,   10
That being of so young days brought up with him,
And sith so neighboured to his youth and haviour,
That you vouchsafe your rest here in our court
Some little time, so by your companies
To draw him on to pleasures, and to gather   15
So much as from occasion you may glean,

---

109 **quoted** noted, observed   110 **wrack** ruin   **beshrew my jealousy**
curse my suspicion   111–12 **proper . . . opinions** natural for old people to read more into
something than is actually there   115-16 **being kept . . . love** if kept secret, might cause
more grief than if we risked the king's displeasure (by telling him that the prince loves a
commoner)
    II, ii a room in the castle   2 **Moreover** in addition to the fact   7 **that** that which   11
of . . . days from your early days   12 **neighboured** near   **haviour** behavior   13 **vouch-**
safe your rest agree to stay   16 **occasion** opportunity   18 **opened** discovered   21

Whether aught to us unknown afflicts him thus,
That opened lies within our remedy.

QUEEN.   Good gentlemen, he hath much talked of you,
And sure I am, two men there are not living   20
To whom he more adheres. If it will please you
To show us so much gentry and good will,
As to expend your time with us awhile,
For the supply and profit of our hope,
Your visitation shall receive such thanks   25
As fits a king's remembrance.

ROSENCRANTZ.   Both your majesties
Might by the sovereign power you have of us,
Put your dread pleasures more into command
Than to entreaty.

GUILDENSTERN.   But we both obey,
And here give up ourselves in the full bent,   30
To lay our service freely at your feet
To be commanded.

KING.   Thanks Rosencrantz, and gentle Guildenstern.

QUEEN.   Thanks Guildenstern, and gentle Rosencrantz.
And I beseech you instantly to visit   35
My too much changèd son. Go some of you
And bring these gentlemen where Hamlet is.

GUILDENSTERN.
Heavens make our presence and our practices
Pleasant and helpful to him.

QUEEN.   Ay, amen.

Exeunt ROSENCRANTZ *and* GUILDENSTERN.

Enter POLONIUS.

POLONIUS. Th' ambassadors from Norway my good lord,   40
Are joyfully returned.

KING.   Thou still hast been the father of good news.

POLONIUS. Have I, my lord? Assure you, my good liege,
I hold my duty as I hold my soul,
Both to my God and to my gracious king;   45
And I do think, or else this brain of mine
Hunts not the trail of policy so sure

---

adheres is attached   22 **gentry** courtesy   30 **in the full bent** to the utmost (fr. archery:
bending the bow)   38 **practices** (1) actions (2) plots   42 **still** always   44-5 **hold my duty**
. . . **king** consider my duty to both God and the king as important as my soul   47 **policy** (1)
statecraft (2) strategy   52 **fruit** dessert

As it hath used to do, that I have found
The very cause of Hamlet's lunacy.
KING.   O speak of that, that do I long to hear.   50
POLONIUS. Give first admittance to th' ambassadors,
My news shall be the fruit to that great feast.
KING.   Thyself do grace to them, and bring them in.

[*Exit* POLONIUS.]

He tells me my dear Gertrude, he hath found
The head and source of all your son's distemper.   55
QUEEN.   I doubt it is no other but the main,
His father's death and our o'erhasty marriage.
KING.   Well, we shall sift him.

Enter POLONIUS, VALTEMAND, *and* CORNELIUS.

Welcome, my good friends.
Say Valtemand, what from our brother Norway?
VALTEMAND.
Most fair return of greetings and desires;   60
Upon our first, he sent out to suppress
His nephew's levies, which to him appeared
To be a preparation 'gainst the Polack,
But better looked into, he truly found
It was against your highness, whereat grieved   65
That so his sickness, age, and impotence
Was falsely borne in hand, sends out arrests
On Fortinbras, which he in brief obeys,
Receives rebuke from Norway, and in fine,
Makes vow before his uncle never more   70
To give th'assay of arms against your majesty:
Whereon old Norway, overcome with joy,
Gives him threescore thousand crowns in annual fee,
And his commission to employ those soldiers
So levied (as before) against the Polack,   75
With an entreaty herein further shown,
That it might please you to give quiet pass
Through your dominions for this enterprise,
On such regards of safety and allowance
As therein are set down.   [*Giving a paper.*]
KING.   It likes us well,   80

---

53 **grace** honor   55 **head**
fountainhead   **distemper** sickness   56 **doubt** suspect   61 **first** first presentation   67
borne in hand deceived   69 **fine** finishing   71 **assay** assault   77 **pass** passage   80

And at our more considered time, we'll read,
Answer, and think upon this business:
Meantime, we thank you for your well-took labour,
Go to your rest, at night we'll feast together.
Most welcome home.   *Exeunt* AMBASSADORS.

POLONIUS.   This business is well ended.   85
My liege and madam, to expostulate
What majesty should be, what duty is,
Why day is day, night night, and time is time,
Were nothing but to waste night, day, and time.
Therefore since brevity is the soul of wit,   90
And tediousness the limbs and outward flourishes,
I will be brief. Your noble son is mad:
Mad call I it, for to define true madness,
What is't but to be nothing else but mad?
But let that go.

QUEEN.   More matter, with less art.   95
POLONIUS. Madam, I swear I use no art at all:
That he is mad 'tis true: 'tis true, 'tis pity,
And pity 'tis 'tis true: a foolish figure,
But farewell it, for I will use no art.
Mad let us grant him then, and now remains   100
That we find out the cause of this effect,
Or rather say, the cause of this defect,
For this effect defective comes by cause:
Thus it remains, and the remainder thus.
Perpend.   105
I have a daughter, have while she is mine,
Who in her duty and obedience, mark,
Hath given me this, now gather and surmise.
[*Reads.*] 'To the celestial, and my soul's idol, the most
beautified Ophelia,'—   110
That's an ill phrase, a vile phrase, 'beautified' is a vile
phrase, but you shall hear. Thus: [*Reads.*]
        'In her excellent white bosom, these, &c.'—

QUEEN.   Came this from Hamlet to her?
POLONIUS. Good madam stay awhile, I will be faithful.   [*Reads.*] 115
        'Doubt thou the stars are fire,

---

likes pleases   81 **at . . . time** when time is available for consideration   86 **expostulate**
discuss   90 **wit** understanding   91 **tediousness . . . flourishes** embellishments and
flourishes cause tedium   95 **More . . . art** more content and fewer "flourishes"   98
figure rhetorical figure   105 **Perpend** consider   110 **beautified** endowed with
beauty   113 **bosom** (ref. to a blouse pocket where women kept letters)   **these** these
lines

> Doubt that the sun doth move,
> Doubt truth to be a liar,
> But never doubt I love.
> O dear Ophelia, I am ill at these numbers, I have not 120
> art to reckon my groans, but that I love thee best, O
> most best, believe it. Adieu.
> > Thine evermore, most dear lady, whilst
> > this machine is to him, Hamlet.'
> This in obedience hath my daughter shown me, 125
> And more above hath his solicitings,
> As they fell out by time, by means, and place,
> All given to mine ear.

KING.　　　　　　　　　　But how hath she
Received his love?

POLONIUS.　　　　　　　　What do you think of me?

KING.　As of a man faithful and honourable. 130

POLONIUS.　I would fain prove so. But what might you think
When I had seen this hot love on the wing,
As I perceived it (I must tell you that)
Before my daughter told me, what might you,
Or my dear majesty your queen here think, 135
If I had played the desk or table-book,
Or given my heart a winking mute and dumb,
Or looked upon this love with idle sight,
What might you think? No, I went round to work,
And my young mistress thus I did bespeak, 140
'Lord Hamlet is a prince out of thy star,
This must not be:' and then I prescripts gave her
That she should lock herself from his resort,
Admit no messengers, receive no tokens:
Which done, she took the fruits of my advice, 145
And he repellèd, a short tale to make,
Fell into a sadness, then into a fast,
Thence to a watch, thence into a weakness,
Thence to a lightness, and by this declension,
Into the madness wherein now he raves, 150
And all we mourn for.

---

117 **move** (as it was believed to do, around the earth)　118 **Doubt** suspect　121
reckon express in meter (lit. count)　124 **machine** body　**to** attached to　126 **above**
besides　136 **played . . . book** kept it concealed as in a desk or personal notebook　137
given . . . winking had my heart shut its eyes to the matter　138 **idle** unseeing　139
round frankly　141 **out . . . star** out of your sphere (above you in station)　142 **prescripts**
orders　143 **resort** company　148 **watch** sleeplessness　149 **lightness**
lightheadedness　**declension** decline　159 **center** center of the earth　**try** test　160

KING.   Do you think 'tis this?

QUEEN.   It may be very like.

POLONIUS.   Hath there been such a time, I would fain know that,
            That I have positively said ''Tis so,'
            When it proved otherwise?

KING.   Not that I know.   155

POLONIUS.   Take this, from this, if this be otherwise;
                  [*Points to his head and shoulder.*]
            If circumstances lead me, I will find
            Where truth is hid, though it were hid indeed
            Within the center.

KING.   How may we try it further?

POLONIUS.   You know sometimes he walks four hours together   160
            Here in the lobby.

QUEEN.   So he does indeed.

POLONIUS.   At such a time, I'll loose my daughter to him,
            Be you and I behind an arras then,
            Mark the encounter: if he love her not,
            And be not from his reason fall'n thereon,   165
            Let me be no assistant for a state,
            But keep a farm and carters.

KING.   We will try it.

            Enter HAMLET *reading on a book.*

QUEEN.   But look where sadly the poor wretch comes reading.

POLONIUS.   Away, I do beseech you both away,
            I'll board him presently, O give me leave.   170

            Exeunt KING *and* QUEEN.

            How does my good Lord Hamlet?

HAMLET.   Well, God-a-mercy.

POLONIUS.   Do you know me, my lord?

HAMLET.   Excellent well, you are a fishmonger.

POLONIUS.   Not I my lord.   175

HAMLET.   Then I would you were so honest a man.

POLONIUS.   Honest, my lord?

HAMLET.   Ay sir, to be honest as this world goes, is to be one
            man picked out of ten thousand.

POLONIUS.   That's very true, my lord.   180

---

four some (indefinite number)   162 **loose** (1) release (2) turn loose (fr. cattle
breeding)   163 **arras** hanging tapestry   166 **assistant . . . state** state official   170
board him presently approach him immediately   174 **fishmonger** (1) fish dealer (2)
pimp   176 **honest** (1) respectable (2) moral

HAMLET.   For if the sun breed maggots in a dead dog, being a good
           kissing carrion—have you a daughter?
POLONIUS. I have my lord.
HAMLET.   Let her not walk i'th'sun: conception is a blessing, but as
           your daughter may conceive, friend look to't.   185
POLONIUS. [*Aside.*] How say you by that? Still harping on my daugh-
           ter, yet he knew me not at first, a' said I was a fishmonger.
           A' is far gone, far gone, and truly in my youth, I suffered
           much extremity for love, very near this. I'll speak to him
           again. What do you read my lord?   190
HAMLET.   Words, words, words.
POLONIUS. What is the matter my lord?
HAMLET.   Between who?
POLONIUS. I mean the matter that you read, my lord.
HAMLET.   Slanders, sir; for the satirical rogue says here, that old men 195
           have grey beards, that their faces are wrinkled, their eyes
           purging thick amber and plum-tree gum, and that they
           have a plentiful lack of wit, together with most weak
           hams. All which sir, though I most powerfully and po-
           tently believe, yet I hold it not honesty to have it thus set 200
           down, for yourself sir shall grow old as I am: if like a crab
           you could go backward.
POLONIUS. [*Aside.*] Though this be madness, yet there is method
           in't.
           Will you walk out of the air my lord?   205
HAMLET.   Into my grave.
POLONIUS. [*Aside.*] Indeed that's out of the air; how pregnant
           sometimes his replies are, a happiness that often
           madness hits on, which reason and sanity could not so
           prosperously be delivered of. I will leave him, and   210
           suddenly contrive the means of meeting between him
           and my daughter. My honourable lord, I will most
           humbly take leave of you.
HAMLET.   You cannot sir take from me anything that I will more
           willingly part withal: except my life, except my life, ex- 215
           cept my life.

---

181 **breed maggots** (in the belief that the rays
of the sun caused maggots to breed in dead flesh)   182 **kissing carrion** piece of flesh for
kissing   184 **Let . . . sun** (1) (proverbial: "out of God's blessing, into the warm sun") (2)
because the sun is a breeder (3) don't let her go near me (w. pun on "sun" and
"son")   **conception** (1) understanding (2) pregnancy   194 **matter** (1) content (Polonius's
meaning) (2) cause of a quarrel (Hamlet's interpretation)   197–8 **purging . . . gum** exuding
a viscous yellowish discharge   199 **hams** haunches   200 **honesty** decency   205 **out
. . . air** (in the belief that fresh air was bad for the sick)   207 **pregnant** full of
meaning   208 **happiness** aptness   210 **prosperously** successfully   211 **suddenly**

POLONIUS. Fare you well my lord.

HAMLET.   These tedious old fools.

Enter ROSENCRANTZ *and* GUILDENSTERN.

POLONIUS. You go to seek the Lord Hamlet, there he is.

ROSENCRANTZ.

    [*To Polonius.*] God save you sir.   220

[*Exit* POLONIUS.]

GUILDENSTERN.

    My honoured lord.

ROSENCRANTZ.

    My most dear lord.

HAMLET.   My excellent good friends, how dost thou Guildenstern?
    Ah Rosencrantz, good lads, how do you both?

ROSENCRANTZ.

    As the indifferent children of the earth.   225

GUILDENSTERN.

    Happy, in that we are not over-happy:
    On Fortune's cap we are not the very button.

HAMLET.   Nor the soles of her shoe?

ROSENCRANTZ.

    Neither my lord.

HAMLET.   Then you live about her waist, or in the middle of her 230
    favours?

GUILDENSTERN.

    Faith, her privates we.

HAMLET.   In the secret parts of Fortune? O most true, she is a
    strumpet. What news?

ROSENCRANTZ.

    None my lord, but that the world's grown honest.   235

HAMLET.   Then is doomsday near: but your news is not true. Let me
    question more in particular: what have you my good
    friends, deserved at the hands of Fortune, that she sends
    you to prison hither?

GUILDENSTERN.

    Prison, my lord?   240

HAMLET.   Denmark's a prison.

ROSENCRANTZ.

    Then is the world one.

---

immediately   225 **indifferent** ordinary   227 **on Fortune's . . . button** we are not at the
height of our fortunes   232 **privates** (1) intimate friends (2) private parts   234 **strumpet**
(so Fortune was depicted, giving favor to many and constancy to none)

HAMLET.   A goodly one, in which there are many confines, wards,
and dungeons; Denmark being one o'th'worst.

ROSENCRANTZ.
We think not so my lord.   245

HAMLET.   Why then 'tis none to you; for there is nothing either good
or bad, but thinking makes it so: to me it is a prison.

ROSENCRANTZ.
Why then your ambition makes it one: 'tis too narrow for
your mind.

HAMLET.   O God, I could be bounded in a nutshell, and count 250
myself a king of infinite space; were it not that I have bad
dreams.

GUILDENSTERN.
Which dreams indeed are ambition: for the very substance
of the ambitious, is merely the shadow of a dream.

HAMLET.   A dream itself is but a shadow.   255

ROSENCRANTZ.
Truly, and I hold ambition of so airy and light a quality,
that it is but a shadow's shadow.

HAMLET.   Then are our beggars bodies, and our monarchs and out-
stretched heroes the beggars' shadows: shall we to th'
court? for by my fay, I cannot reason.   260

BOTH.   We'll wait upon you.

HAMLET.   No such matter. I will not sort you with the rest of my
servants: for to speak to you like an honest man, I am most
dreadfully attended. But in the beaten way of friendship,
what make you at Elsinore?   265

ROSENCRANTZ.
To visit you my lord, no other occasion.

HAMLET.   Beggar that I am, I am even poor in thanks, but I thank
you, and sure dear friends, my thanks are too dear a
halfpenny: were you not sent for? is it your own inclining?
is it a free visitation? come, come, deal justly with me, 270
come, come, nay speak.

GUILDENSTERN.
What should we say my lord?

HAMLET.   Anything but to th'purpose: you were sent for, and there

---

places of confinement   243 **wards** cells   248 **ambition** thwarted ambition (not being
king)   258-9 **Then are . . . shadows** then beggars are the true substance and ambitious
kings and heroes the elongated shadows of beggars' bodies (for only a real substance can cast a
shadow)   260 **fay** faith   261 **wait upon** attend   262 **sort** class   264 **dreadfully
attended** poorly supplied with attendants   **beaten** well-worn   265 **make you** are you
doing   268-9 **too dear a halfpenny** worth not even a halfpenny (as I have no
influence)   270 **free** voluntary   **justly** truly   274 **modesties** senses of decency   278

is a kind of confession in your looks, which your modesties
have not craft enough to colour: I know the good king and 275
queen have sent for you.

ROSENCRANTZ.

To what end my lord?

HAMLET.   That you must teach me: but let me conjure you, by the
rights of our fellowship, by the consonancy of our youth,
by the obligation of our ever-preserved love, and by what 280
more dear a better proposer can charge you withal, be
even and direct with me whether you were sent for or no.

ROSENCRANTZ.

[*Aside to Guildenstern.*] What say you?

HAMLET.   Nay then, I have an eye of you: If you love me, hold not
off.   285

GUILDENSTERN.

My lord, we were sent for.

HAMLET.   I will tell you why, so shall my anticipation prevent your
discovery, and your secrecy to the king and queen moult
no feather. I have of late, but wherefore I know not, lost all
my mirth, forgone all custom of exercises: and indeed it 290
goes so heavily with my disposition, that this goodly
frame the earth, seems to me a sterile promontory, this
most excellent canopy the air, look you, this brave
o'erhanging firmament, this majestical roof fretted with
golden fire, why it appeareth nothing to me but a foul and 295
pestilent congregation of vapours. What a piece of work is
a man! How noble in reason, how infinite in faculties, in
form and moving, how express and admirable in action,
how like an angel in apprehension, how like a god: the
beauty of the world; the paragon of animals; and yet to 300
me, what is this quintessence of dust? Man delights not
me, no, nor woman neither, though by your smiling, you
seem to say so.

ROSENCRANTZ.

My lord, there was no such stuff in my thoughts.

HAMLET.   Why did ye laugh then, when I said 'man delights not me'? 305

conjure appeal to   279 consonancy . . . youth agreement in our ages   281 proposer
speaker   withal with   282 even straightforward   284 of on   287 prevent forestall
288 discovery disclosure   288–9 moult no feather change in no way (as losing feathers
alters a bird's looks)   290 forgone given up   exercises sports   292 frame
structure   sterile promontory barren rock projecting into the sea   293 brave
splendid   294 fretted ornamented with fretwork   295 golden fire stars   296 pestilent
. . . vapours (clouds were believed to carry contagion)   296–301 What a . . . dust (punctuation follows Q2)   296 piece masterpiece   297 faculties physical powers   298 express
well framed   301 quintessence fifth and finest essence (fr. alchemy)

ROSENCRANTZ.

> To think, my lord, if you delight not in man, what lenten
> entertainment the players shall receive from you: we coted
> them on the way, and hither are they coming to offer you
> service.

HAMLET. He that plays the king shall be welcome, his majesty shall 310
have tribute of me, the adventurous knight shall use his
foil and target, the lover shall not sigh gratis, the humorous man shall end his part in peace, the clown shall make
those laugh whose lungs are tickle o'th'sere, and the lady
shall say her mind freely: or the blank verse shall halt for't. 315
What players are they?

ROSENCRANTZ.

> Even those you were wont to take such delight in, the
> tragedians of the city.

HAMLET. How chances it they travel? Their residence both in reputation and profit was better both ways. 320

ROSENCRANTZ.

> I think their inhibition comes by the means of the late
> innovation.

HAMLET. Do they hold the same estimation they did when I was in
the city; are they so followed?

ROSENCRANTZ.

> No indeed are they not. 325

HAMLET. How comes it? Do they grow rusty?

ROSENCRANTZ.

> Nay, their endeavour keeps in the wonted pace; but there
> is sir an aery of children, little eyases, that cry out on the
> top of question, and are most tyrannically clapped for't:
> these are now the fashion, and so berattle the common 330
> stages (so they call them) that many wearing rapiers are

306–7 **lenten
entertainment** meager treatment   307 **coted** passed   311 **adventurous knight** knight
errant (a popular stage character; ridiculed in *The Knight of the Burning Pestle*)   312 **foil and
target** sword blunted for stage fighting, and small shield   312 **gratis** (without
applause)   **humorous man** eccentric character with a dominant trait, caused by an excess
of one of the four humours, or bodily fluids, liked melancholy)   313 **in peace** without
interruption   **clown** comedian   314 **tickle o' th' sere** attuned to respond to laughter, as
the finely adjusted gunlock responds to the touch of the trigger (fr. hunting)   **lady**
(women's roles were played by boy actors)   315 **halt** limp (if she adds her own opinions and
spoils the meter)   319 **residence** i.e. in a city theatre   321–2 **inhibition . . . innovation**
hinderance is due to the recent novelty (of the children's companies)   328 **aery** nest (of
birds of prey)   **eyases** young hawks   328–9 **that cry . . . question** whose shrill voices can
be heard above all others (in the "War of the Theatres" between the child and adult
companies, 1601-1602)   329 **tyrannically** strongly   330 **berattle** berate   **common
stages** public playhouses (the children's companies performed in private theatres)   331

afraid of goose-quills, and dare scarce come thither.

HAMLET.   What, are they children? Who maintains 'em? How are
they escoted? Will they pursue the quality no longer than
they can sing? Will they not say afterwards if they should 335
grow themselves to common players (as it is most like, if
their means are not better) their writers do them wrong, to
make them exclaim against their own succession?

ROSENCRANTZ.
Faith, there has been much to-do on both sides: and the
nation holds it no sin to tarre them to controversy. There 340
was for a while, no money bid for argument, unless the
poet and the player went to cuffs in the question.

HAMLET.   Is't possible?

GUILDENSTERN.
O there has been much throwing about of brains.

HAMLET.   Do the boys carry it away?   345

ROSENCRANTZ.
Ay, that they do my lord, Hercules and his load too.

HAMLET.   It is not very strange, for my uncle is king of Denmark,
and those that would make mows at him while my father
lived, give twenty, forty, fifty, a hundred ducats apiece
for his picture in little. 'Sblood, there is something in this 350
more than natural, if philosophy could find it out.

A flourish for the Players.

GUILDENSTERN.
There are the players.

HAMLET.   Gentlemen, you are welcome to Elsinore: your hands,
come then, th'appurtenance of welcome is fashion and
ceremony; let me comply with you in this garb, lest my 355
extent to the players, which I tell you must show fairly
outwards, should more appear like entertainment than
yours. You are welcome: but my uncle-father, and aunt-
mother, are deceived.

---

wearing rapiers (worn by gentlemen)   332 **goose-quills** pens (of satirical dramatists who
wrote for the children)   334 **escoted** supported   334-5 **pursue . . . sing** stay in the
profession only until their voices change   336 **common** public   338 **succession**
inheritance   340 **tarre** provoke   341 **bid for argument** paid for the plot of a proposed
play   342 **went . . . question** came to blows on the subject   345 **carry it away** carry off
the prize   346 **Hercules . . . too** (Shakespeare's own company at the Globe Theatre,
whose sign was Hercules carrying the globe of the world)   348 **mows** mouths,
grimaces   350 **little** a miniature   350 **'Sblood** by God's blood   351 **philosophy**
science   354 **appurtenance** accessory   355 **comply . . . garb** observe the formalities
with you in this style   356 **extent** i.e. of welcome   357-8 **should . . . yours** should
appear more hospitable than yours

GUILDENSTERN.
     In what my dear lord? 360
HAMLET.   I am but mad north-north-west; when the wind is south-
     erly, I know a hawk from a handsaw.

Enter POLONIUS.

POLONIUS. Well be with you, gentlemen.
HAMLET.   Hark you Guildenstern, and you too, at each ear a hearer:
     that great baby you see there is not yet out of his swad- 365
     dling clouts.
ROSENCRANTZ.
     Happily he is the second time come to them, for they say
     an old man is twice a child.
HAMLET.   I will prophesy, he comes to tell me of the players, mark
     it.—You say right sir, a Monday morning, 'twas then 370
     indeed.
POLONIUS. My lord, I have news to tell you.
HAMLET.   My lord, I have news to tell you. When Roscius was an
     actor in Rome—
POLONIUS. The actors are come hither, my lord. 375
HAMLET.   Buz, buz.
POLONIUS. Upon my honour.
HAMLET.   Then came each actor on his ass—
POLONIUS. The best actors in the world, either for tragedy, comedy,
     history, pastoral, pastoral-comical, historical-pastoral, 380
     tragical-historical, tragical-comical-historical-pastoral,
     scene individable, or poem unlimited. Seneca cannot be
     too heavy, nor Plautus too light for the law of writ, and the
     liberty: these are the only men.
HAMLET.   O Jephthah, judge of Israel, what a treasure hadst thou. 385
POLONIUS. What a treasure had he, my lord?
HAMLET.   Why
     'One fair daughter and no more,
       The which he lovèd passing well.'
POLONIUS. [*Aside.*] Still on my daughter. 390

---

362 **I know . . . handsaw** I can tell the difference
between two things that are unlike ("hawk" = (1) bird of prey (2) mattock, pickaxe;
"handsaw" = (1) hernshaw or heron bird (2) small saw) 365–6 **swaddling clouts** strips of
cloth binding a newborn baby 367 **Happily** perhaps 373 **Roscius** famous Roman
actor 376 **Buz, buz** (contemptuous) 382 **scene individable** play observing the unities
(time, place, action) 382 **poem unlimited** play ignoring the unities 382–3 **Seneca,
Plautus** Roman writers of tragedy and comedy respectively (revered by
Elizabethans) 383–4 **law . . . liberty** "rules" regarding the unities and those exercising
freedom from the unities 385 **Jephthah** (who was forced to sacrifice his only daughter
because of a rash promise: Judg. XI. 29-39) 388-9 **One . . . well** (from a popular ballad on

HAMLET.   Am I not i'th' right, old Jephthah?

POLONIUS. If you call me Jephthah my lord, I have a daughter that I
           love passing well.

HAMLET.   Nay, that follows not.

POLONIUS. What follows then, my lord?   395

HAMLET.   Why
                'As by lot, God wot,'
           and then you know
                'It came to pass, as most like it was:'
           the first row of the pious chanson will show you more, for 400
           look where my abridgement comes.

                   Enter four or five PLAYERS.

           You are welcome masters, welcome all. I am glad to see
           thee well: welcome, good friends. O my old friend, why
           thy face is valanced since I saw thee last, com'st thou to
           beard me in Denmark? What, my young lady and mis- 405
           tress? by'r lady, your ladyship is nearer to heaven than
           when I saw you last, by the altitude of a chopine. Pray
           God your voice, like a piece of uncurrent gold, be not
           cracked within the ring. Masters, you are all welcome:
           we'll e'en to't like French falconers, fly at any thing we see: 410
           we'll have a speech straight. Come give us a taste of your
           quality: come, a passionate speech.

1. PLAYER. What speech, my good lord?

HAMLET.   I heard thee speak me a speech once, but it was never
           acted, or if it was, not above once, for the play I remember 415
           pleased not the million, 'twas caviary to the general, but it
           was (as I received it, and others, whose judgments in such
           matters cried in the top of mine) an excellent play, well
           digested in the scenes, set down with as much modesty as
           cunning. I remember one said there were no sallets in the 420
           lines, to make the matter savoury, nor no matter in the
           phrase that might indict the author of affection, but called
           it an honest method, as wholesome as sweet, and by very

Jephthah)   389 **passing** surpassingly   390 **Still** constantly   399 **like** likely   400 **row**
stanza   401 **abridgment** (the players who will cut short my song)   404 **valanced** fringed
with a beard   405 **lady** boy playing women's roles   407 **chopine** thick-soled
shoe   408 **uncurrent** not legal tender   409 **ring** (1) ring enclosing the design on a gold coin (to
crack it within the ring [to steal the gold] made it "uncurrent") (2) sound   410 **French** (the
reputed experts in falconry)   410 **fly . . . see** undertake any difficulty   412 **quality**
professional skill   416 **caviary . . . general** like caviar, too rich for the general
public   418 **cried . . . mine** spoke with more authority than mine   419–20 **modesty as
cunning** moderation as skill   420 **sallets** spicy bits   422 **indict . . . of** charge . . .
with

much more handsome than fine: one speech in't I chiefly
loved, 'twas Æneas' tale to Dido, and thereabout of it   425
especially where he speaks of Priam's slaughter. If it live in
your memory begin at this line, let me see, let me see:
    'The rugged Pyrrhus, like th'Hyrcanian beast'—
'tis not so: it begins with Pyrrhus—
    'The rugged Pyrrhus, he whose sable arms,   430
Black as his purpose, did the night resemble
When he lay couchèd in th'ominous horse,
Hath now this dread and black complexion smeared
With heraldy more dismal: head to foot
Now is he total gules, horridly tricked   435
With blood of fathers, mothers, daughters, sons,
Baked and impasted with the parching streets,
That lend a tyrannous and damnèd light
To their lord's murder. Roasted in wrath and fire,
And thus o'er-sizèd with coagulate gore,   440
With eyes like carbuncles, the hellish Pyrrhus
Old grandsire Priam seeks;'
So proceed you.

POLONIUS. 'Fore God, my lord, well spoken, with good accent and
good discretion.   445

1. PLAYER. 'Anon he finds him,
Striking too short at Greeks, his antique sword,
Rebellious to his arm, lies where it falls,
Repugnant to command; unequal matched,
Pyrrhus at Priam drives, in rage strikes wide,   450
But with the whiff and wind of his fell sword,
Th'unnerved father falls: then senseless Ilium,
Seeming to feel this blow, with flaming top
Stoops to his base; and with a hideous crash
Takes prisoner Pyrrhus' ear. For lo, his sword   455
Which was declining on the milky head

---

424 **handsome than fine** dignified than finely wrought   426 **Priam's slaughter** the
murder of the King of Troy (as told in the *Aeneid*, Bk. II)   428 **Pyrrhus** son of Achilles (the
highly rhetorical style differentiates the verse of the quotation from that of the action and
somewhat resembles the style of Marlowe, co-author of the play *Dido*)   **Hyrcanian beast**
tiger noted for fierceness (from Hyrcania, north of the Caspian Sea)   430 **sable**
black   432 **horse** the hollow wooden horse used by the Greeks to enter Troy   435 **gules**
red (fr. heraldry)   **horridly tricked** horribly decorated (fr. heraldry)   437 **impasted**
coagulated   **parching** (because the city was on fire)   440 **o'er-sized** covered over, as by
glue   441 **carbuncles** red gems, as garnets or rubies   445 **discretion**
interpretation   447 **antique** ancient   449 **Repugnant to command** refusing to obey its
commander   451 **fell** savage   452 **senseless** incapable of feeling   **Ilium** Troy   458

Of reverend Priam, seemed i'th'air to stick;
So as a painted tyrant Pyrrhus stood,
And like a neutral to his will and matter,
Did nothing: 460
But as we often see, against some storm,
A silence in the heavens, the rack stand still,
The bold winds speechless, and the orb below
As hush as death, anon the dreadful thunder
Doth rend the region, so after Pyrrhus' pause,   465
A rousèd vengeance sets him new awork,
And never did the Cyclops' hammers fall
On Mars's armour, forged for proof eterne,
With less remorse than Pyrrhus' bleeding sword
Now falls on Priam.   470
Out, out, thou strumpet Fortune: all you gods,
In general synod take away her power,
Break all the spokes and fellies from her wheel,
And bowl the round nave down the hill of heaven
As low as to the fiends.'   475

POLONIUS. This is too long.

HAMLET. It shall to the barber's with your beard; prithee say on: he's
for a jig, or a tale of bawdry, or he sleeps. Say on, come to
Hecuba.

1. PLAYER. 'But who, ah woe, had seen the mobled queen—'   480

HAMLET. 'The mobled queen'?

POLONIUS. That's good, 'mobled queen' is good.

1. PLAYER. 'Run barefoot up and down, threat'ning the flames
With bisson rheum, a clout upon that head
Where late the diadem stood, and for a robe,   485
About her lank and all o'er-teemèd loins,
A blanket in the alarm of fear caught up—
Who this had seen, with tongue in venom steeped,
'Gainst Fortune's state would treason have pronounced;
But if the gods themselves did see her then,   490
When she saw Pyrrhus make malicious sport

---

painted pictured   459 **like . . . matter** unmoved by either his purpose or its
achievement   461 **against** before   462 **rack** clouds   463 **orb** earth   465 **region** sky,
air   467 **Cyclops** workmen of Vulcan, armorer of the gods   468 **for proof eterne** to be
eternally invincible   471 **strumpet** (who first favored and then deserted)   472 **synod**
assembly   473 **fellies . . . wheel** curved pieces of the rim of the wheel that Fortune turns,
representing a man's fortunes   474 **nave** hub   475 **fiends** i.e. of hell   478 **jig** comic
song-and-dance afterpiece to a play   480 **mobled** muffled in a scarf   484 **bisson rheum**
blinding tears   **clout** cloth   486 **o'erteemed** worn out by excessive childbearing   489
state reign

In mincing with his sword her husband's limbs,
The instant burst of clamour that she made,
Unless things mortal move them not at all,
Would have made milch the burning eyes of heaven,   495
And passion in the gods.'

POLONIUS. Look whe'r he has not turned his colour, and has tears in's
eyes, prithee no more.

HAMLET. 'Tis well, I'll have thee speak out the rest of this soon.
Good my lord, will you see the players well bestowed; do   500
you hear, let them be well used, for they are the abstract
and brief chronicles of the time; after your death you were
better have a bad epitaph than their ill report while you
live.

POLONIUS. My lord, I will use them according to their desert.   505

HAMLET. God's bodkin man, much better. Use every man after his
desert, and who shall 'scape whipping? Use them after
you own honour and dignity: the less they deserve, the
more merit is in your bounty. Take them in.

POLONIUS. Come sirs.   *Exeunt* POLONIUS *and* PLAYERS.   510

HAMLET. Follow him friends, we'll hear a play tomorrow; [*Stops the
First Player.*] dost thou hear me, old friend, can you play
The Murder of Gonzago?

I. PLAYER. Ay my lord.

HAMLET. We'll ha't tomorrow night. You could for a need study a   515
speech of some dozen or sixteen lines, which I would set
down and insert in't, could you not?

I. PLAYER. Ay my lord.

HAMLET. Very well, follow that lord, and look you mock him not.
                                        [*Exit First* PLAYER.]
[*To Rosencrantz and Guildenstern.*] My good friends, I'll   520
leave you till night, you are welcome to Elsinore.

ROSENCRANTZ.
Good my lord.   [*Exeunt.*]

HAMLET. Ay so, God bye to you, now I am alone.
O what a rogue and peasant slave am I.
Is it not monstrous that this player here,   525
But in a fiction, in a dream of passion,
Could force his soul so to his own conceit

---

495 **milch** milky, moist   **eyes** stars   497 **turned** changed   500 **bestowed**
lodged   501 **abstract** summary (noun)   502 **brief chronicles** history in brief   503 **ill**
bad   505 **desert** merit   506 **God's bodkin** God's little body, the communion wafer (an
oath)   **after** according to   515 **for a need** if necessary   524 **rogue** wretched
creature   **peasant** base   526 **dream of passion** portrayal of emotion   527 **conceit**

That from her working all his visage wanned,
Tears in his eyes, distraction in his aspect,
A broken voice, and his whole function suiting   530
With forms to his conceit; and all for nothing,
For Hecuba.
What's Hecuba to him, or he to Hecuba,
That he should weep for her? what would he do,
Had he the motive and the cue for passion   535
That I have? he would drown the stage with tears,
And cleave the general ear with horrid speech,
Make mad the guilty and appal the free,
Confound the ignorant, and amaze indeed
The very faculties of eyes and ears; yet I,   540
A dull and muddy-mettled rascal, peak
Like John-a-dreams, unpregnant of my cause,
And can say nothing; no, not for a king,
Upon whose property and most dear life,
A damned defeat was made: am I a coward?   545
Who calls me villain, breaks my pate across,
Plucks off my beard and blows it in my face,
Tweaks me by the nose, gives me the lie i'th'throat
As deep as to the lungs, who does me this?
Ha, 'swounds, I should take it: for it cannot be   550
But I am pigeon-livered, and lack gall
To make oppression bitter, or ere this
I should ha' fatted all the region kites
With this slave's offal: bloody, bawdy villain,
Remorseless, treacherous, lecherous, kindless villain! 555
O vengeance!
Why what an ass am I, this is most brave,
That I, the son of a dear father murdered,
Prompted to my revenge by heaven and hell,

---

imagination   528 **wanned** grew pale   530 **function** bearing   531 **With forms** in appearance   **conceit** imagination   535 **motive, cue** motivation of a character; word or gesture leading to another actor's speech or action (fr. theatre)   537 **general ear** ears of all in the audience   **horrid** horrible   538 **guilty** i.e. of the crime described   **free** innocent   539 **confound the ignorant** confuse those incapable of understanding   **amaze** stun   540 **faculties . . . ears** powers of sight and hearing   541 **muddy-mettled** dull-spirited   **peak** pine, mope   542 **John-a-dreams** a daydreaming fellow   **unpregnant of** unstirred, not generated (into action) by   544 **property** possessions   546 **pate** head   547 **Plucks . . . beard** (a way of giving insult)   548-9 **gives . . . lungs** insults me by calling me a liar of the worst kind (the lungs being deeper than the throat)   550 **'swounds** God's wounds   551 **pigeon-livered** meek and uncourageous (the liver was believed to be the seat of the passions, including courage; pigeons were believed to lack gall, the cause of bitterness)   553 **region kites** vultures of the upper air   555 **kindless** unnatural   557 **brave** fine

Must like a whore unpack my heart with words,   560
And fall a-cursing like a very drab,
A scullion, fie upon't, foh.
About, my brains; hum, I have heard,
That guilty creatures sitting at a play,
Have by the very cunning of the scene   565
Been struck so to the soul, that presently
They have proclaimed their malefactions:
For murder, though it have no tongue, will speak
With most miraculous organ: I'll have these players
Play something like the murder of my father   570
Before mine uncle, I'll observe his looks,
I'll tent him to the quick, if a' do blench
I know my course. The spirit that I have seen
May be a devil, and the devil hath power
T'assume a pleasing shape, yea, and perhaps   575
Out of my weakness, and my melancholy,
As he is very potent with such spirits,
Abuses me to damn me; I'll have grounds
More relative than this: the play's the thing
Wherein I'll catch the conscience of the king.   *Exit.*

[Act Three]

[SCENE I.]

Enter KING, QUEEN, POLONIUS, OPHELIA,
        ROSENCRANTZ, GUILDENSTERN, *and Lords.*

KING.   And can you by no drift of conference
           Get from him why he puts on this confusion,
           Grating so harshly all his days of quiet
           With turbulent and dangerous lunacy?

ROSENCRANTZ.
           He does confess he feels himself distracted,   5

---

561 **drab** whore   562 **scullion** kitchen
wench   565 **cunning** skill   566 **presently** immediately   572 **tent** probe   **blench**
flinch   577 **spirits** temperaments   578 **Abuses** deceives   **damn me** condemn my soul
to hell   579 **relative** i.e. to the fact
III, i a room in the castle   1 **drift of conference** turn of conversation   2 **puts . . .
confusion** seems so distracted ("puts on" indicates the king's private suspicion that Hamlet is
playing mad and echoes Hamlet's own words: "put an antic disposition on")   7 **forward**

But from what cause, a' will by no means speak.

GUILDENSTERN.
　　　Nor do we find him forward to be sounded,
　　　But with a crafty madness keeps aloof
　　　When we would bring him on to some confession
　　　Of his true state.

QUEEN.　　　　　　　　Did he receive you well?　　　　10

ROSENCRANTZ.
　　　Most like a gentleman.

GUILDENSTERN.
　　　But with much forcing of his disposition.

ROSENCRANTZ.
　　　Niggard of question, but of our demands
　　　Most free in his reply.

QUEEN.　　　　　　　　Did you assay him
　　　To any pastime?　　　　　　　　　　　　　15

ROSENCRANTZ.
　　　Madam, it so fell out that certain players
　　　We o'er-raught on the way: of these we told him,
　　　And there did seem in him a kind of joy
　　　To hear of it: they are here about the court,
　　　And as I think, they have already order　　　20
　　　This night to play before him.

POLONIUS.　　　　　　　　　　'Tis most true,
　　　And he beseeched me to entreat your majesties
　　　To hear and see the matter.

KING.　　　With all my heart, and it doth much content me
　　　To hear him so inclined.　　　　　　　　25
　　　Good gentlemen, give him a further edge,
　　　And drive his purpose into these delights.

ROSENCRANTZ.
　　　We shall my lord.

Exeunt ROSENCRANTZ *and* GUILDENSTERN.

KING.　　　　　　　Sweet Gertrude, leave us too,
　　　For we have closely sent for Hamlet hither,
　　　That he, as 'twere by accident, may here　　　30
　　　Affront Ophelia;

. . . **sounded** disposed to be sounded out　　10 **state** (1) i.e. of mind (2) ambition to be king　　12 **forcing . . . disposition** forcing himself to be so　　13 **question** talk　　13 **demands** questions　　14–15 **assay him To** try to interest him in　　17 **o'er-raught** overtook　　23 **matter** i.e. of the play　　26 **give . . . edge** encourage his keen interest　　29 **closely** secretly　　31 **Affront** meet face to face with

Her father and myself, lawful espials,
Will so bestow ourselves, that seeing unseen,
We may of their encounter frankly judge,
And gather by him as he is behaved,   35
If't be th'affliction of his love or no
That thus he suffers for.

QUEEN.   I shall obey you.
And for your part Ophelia, I do wish
That your good beauties be the happy cause
Of Hamlet's wildness, so shall I hope your virtues   40
Will bring him to his wonted way again,
To both your honours.

OPHELIA.   Madam, I wish it may.

                                                  [*Exit* QUEEN.]

POLONIUS.   Ophelia, walk you here—Gracious, so please you,
We will bestow ourselves—read on this book,
That show of such an exercise may colour   45
Your loneliness; we are oft to blame in this,
'Tis too much proved, that with devotion's visage
And pious action, we do sugar o'er
The devil himself.

KING.   [*Aside.*] O 'tis too true,
How smart a lash that speech doth give my conscience.   50
The harlot's cheek, beautied with plast'ring art,
Is not more ugly to the thing that helps it,
Than is my deed to my most painted word:
O heavy burden!

POLONIUS.   I hear him coming, let's withdraw my lord.   55

                                                  Exeunt.

                      Enter HAMLET.

HAMLET.   To be, or not to be, that is the question,
Whether 'tis nobler in the mind to suffer
The slings and arrows of outrageous fortune,

---

32 **espials** spies   33, 44 **bestow**
place, stow   34 **frankly** freely   35 **is behaved** behaves   40 **wildness** agitation   41
wonted customary   43 **Gracious** i.e. sir   44 **book** (of prayer)   45 **exercise** religious
exercise   45 **colour** make appear plausible   47 **'Tis . . . proved** it is all too apparent   49
'tis too true (the king's first indication that he is guilty)   50 **lash** whipping (the punishment
for prostitutes)   51–3 **harlot's cheek . . . word** just as the harlot's cheek is even uglier by
contrast to the makeup that tries to beautify it, so my deed is uglier by contrast to the
hypocritical words under which I hide it   52 **to** compared to   56 **To be, or not to be** to
live, or not to live (critics are divided as to whether Hamlet is actually contemplating suicide
or expressing his melancholy over the general condition of man)   57 **nobler in the mind**

Or to take arms against a sea of troubles,
And by opposing, end them: to die, to sleep,   60
No more; and by a sleep, to say we end
The heart-ache, and the thousand natural shocks
That flesh is heir to; 'tis a consummation
Devoutly to be wished. To die, to sleep,
To sleep, perchance to dream; ay there's the rub,   65
For in that sleep of death what dreams may come
When we have shuffled off this mortal coil
Must give us pause—there's the respect
That makes calamity of so long life:
For who would bear the whips and scorns of time,   70
Th'oppressor's wrong, the proud man's contumely,
The pangs of disprized love, the law's delay,
The insolence of office, and the spurns
That patient merit of th'unworthy takes,
When he himself might his quietus make   75
With a bare bodkin; who would fardels bear,
To grunt and sweat under a weary life,
But that the dread of something after death,
The undiscovered country, from whose bourn
No traveller returns, puzzles the will,   80
And makes us rather bear those ills we have,
Than fly to others that we know not of.
Thus conscience does make cowards of us all,
And thus the native hue of resolution
Is sicklied o'er with the pale cast of thought,   85
And enterprises of great pitch and moment,
With this regard their currents turn awry,
And lose the name of action. Soft you now,
The fair Ophelia—Nymph, in thy orisons
Be all my sins remembered.

best, according to "sovereign" reason (followed by two choices: "to suffer", to live and accept the blows of fortune; or "to take arms", to fight and end them by ending oneself)   60 **to die** to die is   65 **rub** obstacle (fr. bowling: any impediment on the bowling grass or green)   67 **shuffled** cast   **mortal coil** (1) turmoil of mortal life (2) coil of flesh encircling the body (as the skin shed by a snake)   68 **respect** consideration   69 **of so long life** so long-lived   70 **time** the times   72 **law's delay** longevity of law suits   73 **office** officials, bureaucrats   75 **quietus** settlement of his debt (fr. law; "death" and "debt", pronounced similarly, were often associated by Elizabethans)   76 **bare bodkin** mere dagger   76 **fardels** burdens   79 **undiscovered** unexplored   **bourn** boundary   80 **puzzles** confuses   83 **conscience** reflection, consideration   **us all** (an indication that Hamlet is thinking not only of himself)   84 **native hue** natural ruddy complexion   85 **thought** melancholy, brooding   86 **pitch** height, excellence (fr. falconry: the highest point to which a falcon soars before swooping on its prey)   **moment** importance   87 **regard** consideration   **their currents turn awry** change their course   89 **orisons** prayers (referring to her prayer book)

OPHELIA.   Good my lord,   90
How does your honour for this many a day?

HAMLET. I humbly thank you: well, well, well.

OPHELIA. My lord, I have remembrances of yours
That I have longèd long to re-deliver,
I pray you now receive them.

HAMLET.   No, not I,   95
I never gave you aught.

OPHELIA. My honoured lord, you know right well you did,
And with them words of so sweet breath composed
As made the things more rich: their perfume lost,
Take these again, for to the noble mind   100
Rich gifts wax poor when givers prove unkind.
There my lord.

HAMLET. Ha, ha, are you honest?

OPHELIA. My lord.

HAMLET. Are you fair?   105

OPHELIA. What means your lordship?

HAMLET. That if you be honest and fair, your honesty should admit
no discourse to your beauty.

OPHELIA. Could beauty my lord, have better commerce than with
honesty?   110

HAMLET. Ay truly, for the power of beauty will sooner transform
honesty from what it is to a bawd, than the force of
honesty can translate beauty into his likeness. This was
sometime a paradox, but now the time gives it proof. I did
love you once.   115

OPHELIA. Indeed my lord, you made me believe so.

HAMLET. You should not have believed me, for virtue cannot so
inoculate our old stock, but we shall relish of it. I loved
you not.

OPHELIA. I was the more deceived.   120

HAMLET. Get thee to a nunnery, why wouldst thou be a breeder of
sinners? I am myself indifferent honest, but yet I could
accuse me of such things, that it were better my mother
had not borne me: I am very proud, revengeful, ambi-

91 this . . . day all these days   98 breath speech   101 wax
grow   103 honest (1) chaste (2) truthful   105 fair (1) beautiful (2) honorable   107–8 admit
. . . beauty (1) not allow communication with your beauty (2) not allow your beauty to be
used as a trap (Hamlet may have overheard the Polonius-Claudius plot or spotted their
movement behind the arras)   109 commerce conversation   112 honesty
chastity   bawd procurer, pimp   113 translate transform   his chastity's   114
sometime once   time times   118 inoculate . . . it change our sinful nature (as a tree is
grafted to improve it) but we will keep our old taste (as will the fruit of the grafted tree)   121
nunnery (1) lit. (2) slang for "brothel" (cf. "bawd" above)   122 indifferent honest reasona-

tious, with more offences at my beck, than I have thoughts 125
to put them in, imagination to give them shape, or time to
act them in: what should such fellows as I do, crawling
between earth and heaven? We are arrant knaves all,
believe none of us, go thy ways to a nunnery. Where's
your father?   130

OPHELIA.   At home my lord.

HAMLET.   Let the doors be shut upon him, that he may play the fool
no where but in's own house. Farewell.

OPHELIA.   O help him, you sweet heavens.

HAMLET.   If thou dost marry, I'll give thee this plague for thy dowry: 135
be thou as chaste as ice, as pure as snow, thou shalt not
escape calumny; get thee to a nunnery, go, farewell. Or if
thou wilt needs marry, marry a fool, for wise men know
well enough what monsters you make of them: to a nunnery go, and quickly too, farewell.   140

OPHELIA.   O heavenly powers, restore him.

HAMLET.   I have heard of your paintings too, well enough. God hath
given you one face, and you make yourselves another: you
jig, you amble, and you lisp, you nick-name God's creatures, and make your wantonness your ignorance; go to, 145
I'll no more on't, it hath made me mad. I say we will have
no moe marriage. Those that are married already, all but
one shall live, the rest shall keep as they are: to a nunnery,
go.

Exit HAMLET.

OPHELIA.   O what a noble mind is here o'erthrown!   150
The courtier's, soldier's, scholar's, eye, tongue, sword,
Th'expectancy and rose of the fair state,
The glass of fashion, and the mould of form,
Th'observed of all observers, quite quite down,
And I of ladies most deject and wretched,   155
That sucked the honey of his music vows,
Now see that noble and most sovereign reason
Like sweet bells jangled, out of tune and harsh,

bly virtuous   124 **ambitious** (he adopts Rosencrantz's and Guildenstern's suggested cause
of his madness)   125 **beck** beckoning   128 **arrant** absolute   135 **plague** curse   139
monsters horned cuckolds (men whose wives were unfaithful)   144 **jig** walk in a mincing
way   145 **lisp** put on affected speech   **nickname** substitute whimsical names for ordinary ones   145 **make your . . . ignorance** excuse your caprices as being due to
ignorance   147 **moe** more   148 **one** Claudius (an indication that Hamlet knows he is
overheard)   151 **eye, tongue, sword** (of the courtier, scholar, and soldier,
respectively)   152 **expectancy and rose** fair hope   153 **glass** mirror   **mould**
model   **form** manners   157 **sovereign** (because it should rule)   159 **form and feature**

That unmatched form and feature of blown youth
Blasted with ecstasy. O woe is me,   160
T'have seen what I have seen, see what I see.

Enter KING *and* POLONIUS.

KING.   Love? his affections do not that way tend,
               Nor what he spake, though it lacked form a little,
               Was not like madness. There's something in his soul
               O'er which his melancholy sits on brood,   165
               And I do doubt, the hatch and the disclose
               Will be some danger; which for to prevent,
               I have in quick determination
               Thus set it down: he shall with speed to England,
               For the demand of our neglected tribute: 170
               Haply the seas, and countries different,
               With variable objects, shall expel
               This something-settled matter in his heart,
               Whereon his brains still beating puts him thus
               From fashion of himself. What think you on't?   175
POLONIUS.   It shall do well. But yet do I believe
               The origin and commencement of his grief
               Sprung from neglected love. How now Ophelia?
               You need not tell us what Lord Hamlet said,
               We heard it all. My lord, do as you please,   180
               But if you hold it fit, after the play,
               Let his queen-mother all alone entreat him
               To show his grief, let her be round with him,
               And I'll be placed (so please you) in the ear
               Of all their conference. If she find him not,   185
               To England send him: or confine him where
               Your wisdom best shall think.
KING.   It shall be so,
               Madness in great ones must not unwatched go.

                                                        Exeunt.

behavior and bodily proportion   **blown** flowering   160 **Blasted with ecstasy** blighted by
madness   162 **affections** emotions, afflictions   165–6 **on brood . . . hatch . . . disclose**
(metaphor of a hen sitting on eggs; "disclose"=disclosure when the shell breaks)   166
doubt fear   167 **prevent** forestall   170 **neglected** (being unpaid)   171 **Haply**
perhaps   172 **variable** varied   173 **something-** somewhat-   174 **still** always   175
fashion of himself his usual self   178 **neglected** unrequited   183 **show** reveal the cause
of   **round** direct   184–5 **in the ear Of** so as to overhear   185 **find** find out
  III, ii a hall in the castle   1 **the speech** i.e. that Hamlet has inserted   2 **mouth it** hold it
in the mouth a long time and deliver it slowly and over-emphatically   7 **acquire and beget**

[SCENE II.]

Enter HAMLET *and three of the* PLAYERS.

HAMLET.   Speak the speech I pray you as I pronounced it to you,
           trippingly on the tongue, but if you mouth it as many of
           your players do, I had as lief the town-crier spoke my
           lines. Nor do not saw the air too much with your hand
           thus, but use all gently, for in the very torrent, tempest, 5
           and as I may say, whirlwind of your passion, you must
           acquire and beget a temperance that may give it smooth-
           ness. O it offends me to the soul, to hear a robustious
           periwig-pated fellow tear a passion to tatters, to very rags,
           to split the ears of the groundlings, who for the most part 10
           are capable of nothing but inexplicable dumb shows and
           noise: I would have such a fellow whipped for o'erdoing
           Termagant: it out-herods Herod, pray you avoid it.

1. PLAYER. I warrant you honour.

HAMLET.   Be not too tame neither, but let your own discretion be 15
           your tutor, suit the action to the word, the word to the
           action, with this special observance, that you o'erstep not
           the modesty of nature: for any thing so o'erdone, is from
           the purpose of playing, whose end both at the first, and
           now, was and is, to hold as 'twere the mirror up to nature, 20
           to show virtue her own feature, scorn her own image, and
           the very age and body of the time his form and pressure.
           Now this overdone, or come tardy off, though it make the
           unskilful laugh, cannot but make the judicious grieve, the
           censure of the which one, must in your allowance 25
           o'erweigh a whole theatre of others. O there be players
           that I have seen play, and heard others praise, and that
           highly (not to speak it profanely) that neither having

---

achieve for yourself and instill in other actors   **temperance** moderation   8 **robustious**
boisterous   9 **periwig-pated** wig-wearing   10 **groundlings** audience who paid least and
stood on the ground floor   11 **capable of** able to understand   11 **dumb shows** pantomimed
synopses of the action to follow (as below)   13 **Termagant** violent, ranting character in the
guild or mystery plays (believed to be a Saracen god)   **out-herods Herod** outdoes even
Herod, King of Judea (who commanded the slaughter of the innocents and who was a ranting
tyrant in the mystery plays)   18 **modesty** moderation   **from** away from   19 **at the first**
in earlier days   21 **feature** form   **scorn** that which should be scorned   22 **age . . .
pressure** shape of the times in its accurate depiction   **pressure** impression   23 **come
tardy off** understated, underdone   24 **unskilful** unsophisticated   25 **one** the
judicious   **allowance** estimation

th'accent of Christians, nor the gait of Christian, pagan,
nor man, have so strutted and bellowed, that I have   30
thought some of nature's journeymen had made men, and
not made them well, they imitated humanity so abominably.

1. PLAYER.   I hope we have reformed that indifferently with us, sir.

HAMLET.   O reform it altogether, and let those that play your clowns   35
speak no more than is set down for them, for there be of
them that will themselves laugh, to set on some quantity
of barren spectators to laugh too, though in the mean time,
some necessary question of the play be then to be considered: that's villainous, and shows a most pitiful ambition   40
in the fool that uses it. Go make you ready.

Exeunt PLAYERS.

Enter POLONIUS, ROSENCRANTZ,
and GUILDENSTERN.

How now my lord, will the king hear this piece of work?

POLONIUS.   And the queen too, and that presently.

HAMLET.   Bid the players make haste.

Exit POLONIUS.

Will you two help to hasten them?   45

ROSENCRANTZ.

Ay my lord.   *Exeunt they two.*

HAMLET.   What ho, Horatio!

Enter HORATIO.

HORATIO.   Here sweet lord, at your service.

HAMLET.   Horatio, thou art e'en as just a man
As e'er my conversation coped withal.   50

HORATIO.   O my dear lord.

HAMLET.   Nay, do not think I flatter,
For what advancement may I hope from thee,
That no revenue hast but thy good spirits
To feed and clothe thee? Why should the poor be flattered?
No, let the candied tongue lick absurd pomp,   55

31 **journeymen** artisans working for others and not yet
masters of their trades   32 **abominably** (F and Q spell "abhominably," with the Latin sense
of *ab homine*—contrary to the nature of man)   34 **indifferently** reasonably well   36 **speak
no more . . . them** stick to their lines (and not extemporize for laughs)   38 **barren**
witless   39 **question** dialogue   42 **piece** masterpiece   43 **presently** immediately   49
just well-balanced   50 **coped withal** had to do with   55–7 **candied . . . fawning**
(metaphor of a dog licking and fawning for candy)   55 **candied** sugary, flattering   **lick**

And crook the pregnant hinges of the knee
Where thrift may follow fawning. Dost thou hear,
Since my dear soul was mistress of her choice,
And could of men distinguish her election,
Sh'hath sealed thee for herself, for thou hast been   60
As one in suff'ring all that suffers nothing,
A man that Fortune's buffets and rewards
Hast ta'en with equal thanks; and blest are those
Whose blood and judgment are so well co-mingled,
That they are not a pipe for Fortune's finger   65
To sound what stop she please: give me that man
That is not passion's slave, and I will wear him
In my heart's core, ay in my heart of heart,
As I do thee. Something too much of this.
There is a play tonight before the king,   70
One scene of it comes near the circumstance
Which I have told thee of my father's death.
I prithee when thou seest that act afoot,
Even with the very comment of thy soul
Observe my uncle: if his occulted guilt   75
Do not itself unkennel in one speech,
It is a damnèd ghost that we have seen,
And my imaginations are as foul
As Vulcan's stithy; give him heedful note,
For I mine eyes will rivet to his face,   80
And after we will both our judgments join
In censure of his seeming.

HORATIO.   Well my lord,
If a' steal aught the whilst this play is playing,
And 'scape detecting, I will pay the theft.

                                Sound a flourish.

HAMLET.   They are coming to the play. I must be idle,   85
Get you a place.

                Enter Trumpets and Kettledrums, KING,
                QUEEN, POLONIUS, OPHELIA, ROSENCRANTZ,

---

pay court to   56–7 **crook . . . fawning** obsequiously kneel when personal profit may
ensue   56 **pregnant** quick in motion   59 **election** choice   60 **sealed** confirmed   62
buffets blows   64 **blood** passions   **judgment** reason   66 **sound . . . please** play whatever tune she likes   **stop** finger hole in wind instrument for varying the sound   69
Something somewhat   74 **very comment** acutest observation   75 **occulted** hidden   76
unkennel force from hiding (fr. hunting: a fox driven from its hole)   **one speech** (Hamlet's
addition)   77 **damned ghost** devil (not the ghost of my father)   78 **imaginations** i.e. about
my uncle   79 **Vulcan's stithy** the forge of the blacksmith of the gods   82 **censure . . .
seeming** (1) judgment of his appearance (2) disapproval of his pretending   84 **pay** i.e.
for   85 **be idle** act mad

GUILDENSTERN, *and other* LORDS *attendant,*
with his GUARD *carrying torches. Danish March.*

KING.   How fares our cousin Hamlet?

HAMLET.   Excellent i'faith, of the chameleon's dish: I eat the air,
            promise-crammed, you cannot feed capons so.

KING.   I have nothing with this answer Hamlet, these words are   90
            not mine.

HAMLET.   No, nor mine now. [*To Polonius.*] My lord, you played
            once i'th'university you say?

POLONIUS.   That did I my lord, and was accounted a good actor.

HAMLET.   What did you enact?   95

POLONIUS.   I did enact Julius Caesar, I was killed i'th' Capitol, Brutus
            killed me.

HAMLET.   It was a brute part of him to kill so capital a calf there. Be
            the players ready?

ROSENCRANTZ.
            Ay my lord, they stay upon your patience.   100

QUEEN.   Come hither my dear Hamlet, sit by me.

HAMLET.   No, good mother, here's metal more attractive.

POLONIUS.   [*To the King.*] O ho, do you mark that?

HAMLET.   Lady, shall I lie in your lap?

OPHELIA.   No my lord.   105

HAMLET.   I mean, my head upon your lap?

OPHELIA.   Ay my lord.

HAMLET.   Do you think I meant country matters?

OPHELIA.   I think nothing my lord.

HAMLET.   That's a fair thought to lie between maids' legs.   110

OPHELIA.   What is, my lord?

HAMLET.   Nothing.

OPHELIA.   You are merry my lord.

HAMLET.   Who, I?

OPHELIA.   Ay my lord.   115

HAMLET.   O God, your only jig-maker: what should a man do but be
            merry, for look you how cheerfully my mother looks, and
            my father died within's two hours.

---

88 **eat the air** (interpreting "fares" as "eats") (1) so believed of the
chameleon (2) pun on "heir"   89 **promise-crammed** (filled with the king's promise that
Hamlet will succeed to the throne)   **you cannot . . . so** (1) even a capon cannot feed on air
(and your promises) (2) like a capon stuffed with food before being killed, I am stuffed (fed
up) with promises   90 **nothing with** nothing to do with   91 **not mine** not in answer to my
question   98 **part** (1) deed (2) role   100 **stay . . . patience** await your permission   102
metal (w. pun on "mettle"=stuff)   108 **country** sexual (such obscenity would be construed
as madness)   110 **thought** (1) trifle (2) idea   112 **Nothing** (1) nought, zero (2) bawdy
meaning associated with O   116 **jig-maker** writer of comic song and dance routines   121

OPHELIA.   Nay, 'tis twice two months my lord.

HAMLET.   So long? Nay then let the devil wear black, for I'll have a 120
           suit of sables; O heavens, die two months ago, and not
           forgotten yet? Then there's hope a great man's memory
           may outlive his life half a year, but by'r lady a' must build
           churches then, or else shall a' suffer not thinking on, with
           the hobby-horse, whose epitaph is 'For O, for O, the 125
           hobby-horse is forgot.'

The trumpets sound. The Dumb Show follows.

*Enter a King and a Queen, very lovingly, the Queen embracing him,
and he her. She kneels and makes show of protestation unto him. He
takes her up, and declines his head upon her neck. He lies him down
upon a bank of flowers; she seeing him asleep leaves him: anon comes
in another man, takes off his crown, kisses it, pours poison in the
sleeper's ears, and leaves him: the Queen returns, finds the King
dead, and makes passionate action. The poisoner with some three or
four mutes comes in again, seeming to condole with her. The dead
body is carried away. The poisoner wooes the Queen with gifts: she
seems harsh and unwilling awhile, but in the end accepts his love.*

Exeunt.

OPHELIA.   What means this, my lord?

HAMLET.   Marry, this is miching mallecho, it means mischief.

OPHELIA.   Belike this show imports the argument of the play.

Enter PROLOGUE.

HAMLET.   We shall know by this fellow: the players cannot keep 130
           counsel, they'll tell all.

OPHELIA.   Will a' tell us what this show meant?

HAMLET.   Ay, or any show that you will show him. Be not you
           ashamed to show, he'll not shame to tell you what it
           means.   135

OPHELIA.   You are naught, you are naught, I'll mark the play.

PROLOGUE. For us and for our tragedy,
           Here stooping to your clemency,
           We beg your hearing patiently.   [*Exit.*]

---

sables (1) rich fur (2) synonym for black mourning garb   123 **by'r lady** by Our Lady (the
Virgin Mary)   124 **not thinking on** being forgotten   125 **hobby-horse** (1) character in the
May games (which the Puritans were trying to suppress) (2) slang for "prostitute"   125–6 **For
. . . forgot** (line from a popular ballad)   126 **s.d. Dumb Show** pantomimed synopsis of
the action to follow   126 **s.d. mutes** actors without speaking parts   128 **miching
mallecho** skulking iniquity ("*mallecho*" [Spanish] = "misdeed")   129 **imports the argument**
signifies the plot   131 **counsel** a secret   136 **naught** naughty, lewd

HAMLET.   Is this a prologue, or the posy of a ring?   140
OPHELIA.   'Tis brief, my lord.
HAMLET.   As woman's love.

Enter Player KING *and* QUEEN.

PLAYER KING.

Full thirty times hath Phoebus' cart gone round
Neptune's salt wash, and Tellus' orbèd ground,
And thirty dozen moons with borrowed sheen   145
About the world have times twelve thirties been,
Since love our hearts, and Hymen did our hands
Unite commutual, in most sacred bands.

PLAYER QUEEN.

So many journeys may the sun and moon
Make us again count o'er ere love be done,   150
But woe is me, you are so sick of late,
So far from cheer, and from your former state,
That I distrust you: yet though I distrust,
Discomfort you, my lord, it nothing must.
For women fear too much, even as they love,   155
And women's fear and love hold quantity,
In neither aught, or in extremity:
Now what my love is, proof hath made you know,
And as my love is sized, my fear is so.
Where love is great, the littlest doubts are fear, 160
Where little fears grow great, great love grows there.

PLAYER KING.

Faith, I must leave thee love, and shortly too,
My operant powers their functions leave to do,
And thou shalt live in this fair world behind,
Honoured, beloved, and haply one as kind   165
For husband shalt thou—

PLAYER QUEEN.   O confound the rest:
Such love must needs be treason in my breast.
In second husband let me be accurst,
None wed the second, but who killed the first.

HAMLET.   [*Aside.*] That's wormwood, wormwood.   170

---

140 **posy** motto
(engraved in a ring)   143 **Phoebus' cart** chariot of the sun (the rhetoric is reminiscent of
older Elizabethan plays)   144 **wash** sea   **Tellus' . . . ground** the earth (Tellus was a
Roman earth goddess)   148 **commutual** mutually   153 **distrust you** am worried about
you   156 **quantity** proportion   157 **In neither . . . extremity** their love and fear are
either absent or excessive   158 **proof** experience   163 **operant** vital   **leave** cease   165
haply perhaps   166 **confound** may God destroy   170 **wormwood** bitter (like the

PLAYER QUEEN.

  The instances that second marriage move
  Are base respects of thrift, but none of love.
  A second time I kill my husband dead,
  When second husband kisses me in bed.

PLAYER KING.

  I do believe you think what now you speak,   175
  But what we do determine, oft we break:
  Purpose is but the slave to memory,
  Of violent birth but poor validity:
  Which now like fruit unripe sticks on the tree,
  But fall unshaken when they mellow be.   180
  Most necessary 'tis that we forget
  To pay ourselves what to ourselves is debt:
  What to ourselves in passion we propose,
  The passion ending, doth the purpose lose.
  The violence of either grief or joy   185
  Their own enactures with themselves destroy:
  Where joy most revels, grief doth most lament;
  Grief joys, joy grieves, on slender accident.
  This world is not for aye, nor 'tis not strange
  That even our loves should with our fortunes change: 190
  For 'tis a question left us yet to prove,
  Whether love lead fortune, or else fortune love.
  The great man down, you mark his favourite flies,
  The poor advanced, makes friends of enemies:
  And hitherto doth love on fortune tend,   195
  For who not needs, shall never lack a friend,
  And who in want a hollow friend doth try,
  Directly seasons him his enemy.
  But orderly to end where I begun,
  Our wills and fates do so contrary run,   200
  That our devices still are overthrown,
  Our thoughts are ours, their ends none of our own.
  So think thou wilt no second husband wed,
  But die thy thoughts when thy first lord is dead.

PLAYER QUEEN.

  Nor earth to me give food, nor heaven light, 205

herb) 171 **instances** causes **move** motivate 172 **respects** considerations **thrift**
profit 178 **validity** strength 181–2 **Most . . . debt** we are easy creditors to ourselves and
forget our former promises (debts) 186 **enactures** fulfillments 189 **aye** ever 192
fortune love fortune lead love 195 **tend** attend 197 **hollow** false 198 **seasons him**
sees him mature into 201 **devices still** plans always 205 **Nor . . . nor** neither . . .
nor

Sport and repose lock from me day and night,
To desperation turn my trust and hope,
An anchor's cheer in prison be my scope,
Each opposite that blanks the face of joy,
Meet what I would have well, and it destroy,   210
Both here and hence pursue me lasting strife,
If once a widow, ever I be wife.

HAMLET.   If she should break it now.

PLAYER KING.

'Tis deeply sworn: sweet, leave me here awhile,
My spirits grow dull, and fain I would beguile   215
The tedious day with sleep.   *Sleeps.*

PLAYER QUEEN.   Sleep rock thy brain,
And never come mischance between us twain.   *Exit.*

HAMLET.   Madam, how like you this play?

QUEEN.   The lady doth protest too much methinks.

HAMLET.   O but she'll keep her word.   220

KING.   Have you heard the argument? Is there no offence in't?

HAMLET.   No, no, they do but jest, poison in jest, no offence
           i'th'world.

KING.   What do you call the play?

HAMLET.   The Mouse-trap. Marry, how? Tropically: this play is the   225
           image of a murder done in Vienna: Gonzago is the duke's
           name, his wife Baptista, you shall see anon, 'tis a knavish
           piece of work, but what of that? Your majesty, and we
           that have free souls, it touches us not: let the galled jade
           winch, our withers are unwrung.   230

Enter LUCIANUS.

           This is one Lucianus, nephew to the king.

OPHELIA.   You are as good as a chorus, my lord.

HAMLET.   I could interpret between you and your love, if I could see
           the puppets dallying.

OPHELIA.   You are keen my lord, you are keen.   235

HAMLET.   It would cost you a groaning to take off mine edge.

OPHELIA.   Still better and worse.

---

208 **anchor** anchorite (hermit)   **cheer** food   209 **opposite** contrary
event   **blanks** pales   211 **here and hence** in this world and the next   215 **fain**
gladly   221 **argument** plot   **no offence** nothing offensive   222 **offence** crime   225
Tropically figuratively   226 **image** representation   229 **free** innocent   229–30 **galled
jade winch** chafed old horse wince (from its sores)   230 **withers are unwrung** (1) shoulders
are unchafed (2) consciences are clear   232 **chorus** actor who introduced the action   233
interpret explain the action (as if I were chorus to a puppet show)   **love** lover   234
dallying engaging in amorous play   235 **keen** (1) sharp (Ophelia's meaning) (2) sexually
excited (Hamlet's interpretation)   237 **better and worse** better wit but a worse meaning

HAMLET.   So you mistake your husbands. Begin, murderer. Pox,
           leave thy damnable faces and begin. Come, 'the croaking
           raven doth bellow for revenge.'   240
LUCIANUS. Thoughts black, hands apt, drugs fit, and time agreeing,
           Confederate season, else no creature seeing,
           Thou mixture rank, of midnight weeds collected,
           With Hecate's ban thrice blasted, thrice infected,
           Thy natural magic, and dire property,   245
           On wholesome life usurps immediately.

                                Pours the poison in his ears.

HAMLET.   A' poisons him i'th'garden for's estate, his name's Gon-
           zago, the story is extant, and written in very choice
           Italian, you shall see anon how the murderer gets the love
           of Gonzago's wife.   250
OPHELIA.   The king rises.
HAMLET.   What, frighted with false fire?
QUEEN.   How fares my lord?
POLONIUS. Give o'er the play.
KING.   Give me some light. Away!   255
ALL.   Lights, lights, lights!

                                Exeunt all but Hamlet and Horatio.

HAMLET.   Why, let the strucken deer go weep,
               The hart ungallèd play,
           For some must watch while some must sleep,
               Thus runs the world away.   260
           Would not this sir, and a forest of feathers, if the rest of my
           fortunes turn Turk with me, with two Provincial roses on
           my razed shoes, get me a fellowship in a cry of players?
HORATIO.   Half a share.
HAMLET.   A whole one, I.   265
           For thou dost know, O Damon dear,

(w. wordplay on "better" and "bitter")   238 **mistake** mis-take, not "for better or worse"   **Pox** a plague on it   239 **faces** exaggerated facial expressions, making faces   239–40 **Come . . . revenge** (parody of a line from an older play about Richard III)   242 **Confederate . . . seeing** no one seeing me except time, my confederate   243 **midnight** (best time for collecting magic herbs)   244 **Hecate** goddess of witchcraft   **ban** evil spell   246 **wholesome** healthy   252 **false fire** discharge of blanks (not gunpowder)   254 **o'er** up   257–8 **deer . . . play** (the belief that a wounded deer wept, abandoned by the others)   258 **ungalled** unhurt   259 **watch** stay awake   261 **this** i.e. sample (of my theatrical talent)   **feathers** plumes (worn by actors)   262 **turn Turk with** cruelly turn against   **Provincial roses** rosettes named for Provins, France   263 **razed** slashed, decorated with cutouts   **fellowship** partnership   **cry** pack, troupe (fr. hunting)   264 **share** division of profits among members of theatre producing company   266 **Damon** legendary ideal friend to Pythias

                            This realm dismantled was
                            Of Jove himself, and now reigns here
                            A very very—pajock.
HORATIO.   You might have rhymed.   270
HAMLET.   O good Horatio, I'll take the ghost's word for a thousand
             pound. Didst perceive?
HORATIO.   Very well my lord.
HAMLET.   Upon the talk of the poisoning?
HORATIO.   I did very well note him.   275

                  Enter ROSENCRANTZ *and* GUILDENSTERN.

HAMLET.   Ah ha, come, some music. Come, the recorders.
             For if the king like not the comedy,
             Why then belike he likes it not, perdy.
             Come, some music.
GUILDENSTERN.
             Good my lord, vouchsafe me a word with you.   280
HAMLET.   Sir, a whole history.
GUILDENSTERN.
             The king, sir—
HAMLET.   Ay sir, what of him?
GUILDENSTERN.
             Is in his retirement, marvellous distempered.
HAMLET.   With drink sir?   285
GUILDENSTERN.
             No my lord, with choler.
HAMLET.   Your wisdom should show itself more richer to signify
             this to the doctor: for, for me to put him to his purgation,
             would perhaps plunge him into more choler.
GUILDENSTERN.
             Good my lord, put your discourse into some frame, and 290
             start not so wildly from my affair.
HAMLET.   I am tame sir, pronounce.
GUILDENSTERN.
             The queen your mother, in most great affliction of spirit,
             hath sent me to you.
HAMLET.   You are welcome.   295

---

268 **Jove** (Hamlet's
father)   269 **pajock** peacock (associated with lechery)   270 **rhymed** (used "ass" instead of
"pajock")   276 **recorders** soft-toned woodwind instruments, similar to flutes   278 **perdy**
surely (corruption of *par dieu*)   280 **vouchsafe** please grant   284 **distempered** ill (Hamlet
deliberately interprets as "intoxicated")   286 **choler** (1) yellow bile (which caused bilious-
ness) (2) anger   288 **purgation** (1) purging of excessive bile (2) judicial investigation (3)
purgatory   290 **frame** structure   291 **start** (like a wild horse)   296 **breed** (1) species (2)

GUILDENSTERN.

> Nay good my lord, this courtesy is not of the right breed.
> If it shall please you to make me a wholesome answer, I
> will do your mother's commandment: if not, your pardon
> and my return shall be the end of my business.

HAMLET.   Sir I cannot.   300

ROSENCRANTZ.

> What, my lord?

HAMLET.   Make you a wholesome answer: my wit's diseased. But
> sir, such answer as I can make, you shall command, or
> rather as you say, my mother: therefore no more, but to
> the matter. My mother you say.   305

ROSENCRANTZ.

> Then thus she says, your behaviour hath struck her into
> amazement and admiration.

HAMLET.   O wonderful son that can so stonish a mother. But is there
> no sequel at the heels of this mother's admiration? Impart.

ROSENCRANTZ.

> She desires to speak with you in her closet ere you go to 310
> bed.

HAMLET.   We shall obey, were she ten times our mother. Have you
> any further trade with us?

ROSENCRANTZ.

> My lord, you once did love me.

HAMLET.   And do still, by these pickers and stealers.   315

ROSENCRANTZ.

> Good my lord, what is your cause of distemper? You do
> surely bar the door upon your own liberty, if you deny
> your griefs to your friend.

HAMLET.   Sir, I lack advancement.

ROSENCRANTZ.

> How can that be, when you have the voice of the king 320
> himself for your succession in Denmark?

HAMLET.   Ay sir, but 'while the grass grows'—the proverb is some-
> thing musty.

---

manners   297 **wholesome** reasonable   298 **pardon** permission to depart   302
wholesome healthy   **wit** understanding   307, 309 **admiration** wonder   310 **closet** private room   315 **pickers and stealers** hands (fr. catechism of the Church of England: "keep
my hands from picking and stealing")   317–8 **deny . . . friend** refuse to let your friend
know the cause of your suffering   320 **voice** vote   321 **succession** i.e. to the throne   322
while . . . grows (the proverb ends: "the horse starves")   322–3 **something musty** somewhat too old and trite (to finish)

Enter the PLAYERS *with recorders.*

O the recorders, let me see one. To withdraw with you,
why do you go about to recover the wind of me, as if you 325
would drive me into a toil?

GUILDENSTERN.

O my lord, if my duty be too bold, my love is too unmannerly.

HAMLET.   I do not well understand that. Will you play upon this
pipe?   330

GUILDENSTERN.

My lord I cannot.

HAMLET.   I pray you.

GUILDENSTERN.

Believe me. I cannot.

HAMLET.   I do beseech you.

GUILDENSTERN.

I know no touch of it my lord.   335

HAMLET.   It is as easy as lying; govern these ventages with your
fingers and thumb, give it breath with your mouth, and it
will discourse most eloquent music. Look you, these are
the stops.

GUILDENSTERN.

But these cannot I command to any utt'rance of harmony, 340
I have not the skill.

HAMLET.   Why look you now how unworthy a thing you make of
me: you would play upon me, you would seem to know
my stops, you would pluck out the heart of my mystery,
you would sound me from my lowest note to the top of my 345
compass: and there is much music, excellent voice in this
little organ, yet cannot you make it speak. 'Sblood, do you
think I am easier to be played on than a pipe? Call me what
instrument you will, though you can fret me, you cannot
play upon me.   350

Enter POLONIUS.

God bless you sir.

POLONIUS.   My lord, the queen would speak with you, and presently.

---

324 **withdraw** speak privately   325 **recover . . . me**
drive me towards the wind, as with a prey, to avoid its scenting the hunter (fr.
hunting)   326 **toil** snare   327–8 **is too unmannerly** makes me forget my good
manners   330 **pipe** recorder   335 **know . . . it** have no skill at fingering it ("haven't the
touch")   336 **ventages** holes, stops   346 **compass** range   347 **organ** musical
instrument   349 **fret** (1) irritate (2) play an instrument that has "frets" (bars to guide the

HAMLET.   Do you see yonder cloud that's almost in shape of a camel?
POLONIUS. By th'mass and 'tis, like a camel indeed.
HAMLET.   Methinks it is like a weasel.   355
POLONIUS. It is backed like a weasel.
HAMLET.   Or like a whale?
POLONIUS. Very like a whale.
HAMLET.   Then I will come to my mother by and by.
           [*Aside.*] They fool me to the top of my bent.   360
           I will come by and by.
POLONIUS. I will say so.   *Exit.*
HAMLET.   'By and by' is easily said.
           Leave me, friends.   [*Exeunt all but Hamlet.*]
           'Tis now the very witching time of night,   365
           When churchyards yawn, and hell itself breathes out
           Contagion to this world: now could I drink hot blood,
           And do such bitter business as the day
           Would quake to look on: soft, now to my mother—
           O heart, lose not thy nature, let not ever   370
           The soul of Nero enter this firm bosom,
           Let me be cruel, not unnatural.
           I will speak daggers to her, but use none:
           My tongue and soul in this be hypocrites,
           How in my words somever she be shent,   375
           To give them seals, never my soul consent.

                                                        Exit.

        [SCENE III.]

        Enter KING, ROSENCRANTZ, *and* GUILDENSTERN.

KING.   I like him not, nor stands it safe with us
           To let his madness range. Therefore prepare you,
           I your commission will forthwith dispatch,
           And he to England shall along with you:
           The terms of our estate may not endure   5

---

fingering)   352 **presently** immediately   359 **by and by** very soon   360 **fool me** force me
to play the fool   **top . . . bent** utmost limits (as a bow bent as far as it can be)   365
witching when witches cast their spells   366 **churchyards yawn** graves open and let out the
dead   367 **Contagion** (1) evil (2) diseases believed to be carried by night air   370 **nature**
natural affection   371 **Nero** (who killed his mother)   374 **My tongue . . . hypocrites** I
will speak cruelly but intend no harm   375 **shent** chastised   376 **give them seals** confirm
them with action (as a legal "deed" is confirmed with a "seal")

    III, iii a room in the castle   1 **him** (his actions)   2 **range** roam freely   3 **forthwith**
dispatch immediately have prepared   5 **terms** circumstances   **our estate** my royal
office

Hazard so near's as doth hourly grow
Out of his brows.

GUILDENSTERN.   We will ourselves provide:
Most holy and religious fear it is
To keep those many many bodies safe
That live and feed upon your majesty.   10

ROSENCRANTZ.

The single and peculiar life is bound
With all the strength and armour of the mind
To keep itself from noyance, but much more
That spirit, upon whose weal depends and rests
The lives of many; the cess of majesty   15
Dies not alone, but like a gulf doth draw
What's near it, with it. O 'tis a massy wheel
Fixed on the summit of the highest mount,
To whose huge spokes, ten thousand lesser things
Are mortised and adjoined, which when it falls,   20
Each small annexment, petty consequence,
Attends the boist'rous ruin. Never alone
Did the king sigh, but with a general groan.

KING.   Arm you I pray you, to this speedy voyage,
For we will fetters put about this fear,   25
Which now goes too free-footed.

ROSENCRANTZ.   We will haste us.

Exeunt Gent.

Enter POLONIUS.

POLONIUS. My lord, he's going to his mother's closet:
Behind the arras I'll convey myself
To hear the process. I'll warrant she'll tax him home,
And as you said, and wisely was it said,   30
'Tis meet that some more audience than a mother,
Since nature makes them partial, should o'erhear
The speech of vantage; fare you well my liege,
I'll call upon you ere you go to bed,
And tell you what I know.

KING.   Thanks, dear my lord.   35

---

7 **brows** effronteries   **provide** prepare   8 **fear** worry   11 **peculiar**
individual   13 **noyance** harm   14 **weal** well-being   15 **cess** cessation, death   16 **gulf**
whirlpool   17 **wheel** (cf. II, 2, 473 ff.)   20 **mortised** securely fitted   22 **Attends**
accompanies   22 **boist'rous** crashing   23 **general** affecting the general public   24 **Arm**
prepare   25 **fetters** irons on the ankles of prisoners   29 **the process** what proceeds   **tax**
him home take him to task   31 **meet** fitting   32 **nature** natural affection   33 **of vantage**

Exit [POLONIUS.]

O my offence is rank, it smells to heaven,
It hath the primal eldest curse upon't,
A brother's murder. Pray can I not,
Though inclination be as sharp as will:
My stronger guilt defeats my strong intent,   40
And like a man to double business bound,
I stand in pause where I shall first begin,
And both neglect; what if this cursèd hand
Were thicker than itself with brother's blood,
Is there not rain enough in the sweet heavens   45
To wash it white as snow? Whereto serves mercy
But to confront the visage of offence?
And what's in prayer but this two-fold force,
To be forestallèd ere we come to fall,
Or pardoned being down? Then I'll look up,   50
My fault is past. But O what form of prayer
Can serve my turn? 'Forgive me my foul murder':
That cannot be, since I am still possessed
Of those effects for which I did the murder:
My crown, mine own ambition, and my queen.   55
May one be pardoned and retain th'offence?
In the corrupted currents of this world,
Offence's gilded hand may shove by justice,
And oft 'tis seen the wicked prize itself
Buys out the law; but 'tis not so above,   60
There is no shuffling, there the action lies
In his true nature, and we ourselves compelled
Even to the teeth and forehead of our faults
To give in evidence. What then? What rests?
Try what repentance can. What can it not?   65
Yet what can it, when one can not repent?
O wretched state! O bosom black as death!
O limèd soul, that struggling to be free,

---

from an advantageous position   37 **primal . . . curse** curse of Cain (who murdered his brother)   39 **inclination . . . will** my desire to pray is as strong as my determination to do so   41 **to double . . . bound** obliged to do two things at once   43 **neglect** omit   47 **confront . . . offence** plead in man's behalf against sin (at the Last Judgment)   49 **forestalled** prevented   54 **effects** results   56 **offence** crime (because of retaining the gains for which the crime was committed)   57 **currents** ways   58 **gilded** offering gold   59–60 **wicked . . . law** fruits of the crime bribe the judge   61 **shuffling** evasion   61–62 **action . . . nature** (1) deed is seen in its true nature (2) legal action is sustained according to the truth   63 **to the teeth . . . faults** meeting our sins face to face   64 **give in evidence** testify against ourselves   **rests** remains   65 **can** can do   68–9 **limed . . . engaged** like a bird caught in lime (a sticky substance spread on twigs as a snare), the soul in its struggle to clear itself only becomes more entangled

Art more engaged; help, angels, make assay:
Bow stubborn knees, and heart with strings of steel,   70
Be soft as sinews of the new-born babe,
All may be well.   [*He kneels.*]

Enter HAMLET.

HAMLET. Now might I do it pat, now a' is a-praying,
And now I'll do't, [*Draws his sword.*] and so a' goes
          to heaven,
And so am I revenged: that would be scanned: 75
A villain kills my father, and for that,
I his sole son, do this same villain send
To heaven.
Why, this is hire and salary, not revenge.
A' took my father grossly, full of bread,   80
With all his crimes broad blown, as flush as May,
And how his audit stands who knows save heaven,
But in our circumstance and course of thought,
'Tis heavy with him: and am I then revenged
To take him in the purging of his soul,   85
When he is fit and seasoned for his passage?
No.   [*Sheathes his sword.*]
Up sword, and know thou a more horrid hent,
When he is drunk asleep, or in his rage,
Or in th'incestuous pleasure of his bed,   90
At game, a-swearing, or about some act
That has no relish of salvation in't,
Then trip him that his heels may kick at heaven,
And that his soul may be as damned and black
As hell whereto it goes; my mother stays,   95
This physic but prolongs thy sickly days.   *Exit.*
KING. [*Rises.*] My words fly up, my thoughts remain below,
Words without thoughts never to heaven go.   *Exit.*

---

69 **make
assay** I'll make an attempt   73 **pat** opportunely   75 **would be scanned** needs closer
examination   79 **hire and salary** as if he had been hired to kill my father and I were now
paying him his reward   80 **grossly** unpurified (by final rites)   **bread** self-indulgence (cf.
Ezek. XVI.49: "pride, fullness of bread, and abundance of idleness")   81 **crimes** sins   81
broad blown in full flower   **flush** lusty   82 **audit** account   83 **in our . . . thought** from
the evidence we have and our speculation on the subject   84 **heavy** grievous   85 **him**
Claudius   86 **seasoned** ready (prepared)   88 **horrid hent** horrible opportunity ("hint")
for seizure ("hent") by me   92 **relish** taste   96 **physic** (1) medicine (2) purgation of your
soul by prayer

[SCENE IV.]

Enter QUEEN *and* POLONIUS.

POLONIUS. A' will come straight, look you lay home to him,
Tell him his pranks have been too broad to bear with,
And that your grace hath screened and stood between
Much heat and him. I'll silence me even here:
Pray you be round with him.   5

HAMLET. [*Within.*] Mother, mother, mother.

QUEEN.   I'll war'nt you,
Fear me not. Withdraw, I hear him coming.

[*Polonius hides behind the arras.*]

Enter HAMLET.

HAMLET. Now mother, what's the matter?

QUEEN. Hamlet, thou hast thy father much offended.

HAMLET. Mother, you have my father much offended.   10

QUEEN. Come, come, you answer with an idle tongue.

HAMLET. Go, go, you question with a wicked tongue.

QUEEN. Why, how now Hamlet?

HAMLET.   What's the matter now?

QUEEN. Have you forgot me?

HAMLET.   No by the rood, not so,
You are the queen, your husband's brother's wife,   15
And would it were not so, you are my mother.

QUEEN. Nay, then I'll set those to you that can speak.

HAMLET. Come, come, and sit you down, you shall not budge,
You go not till I set you up a glass
Where you may see the inmost part of you.   20

QUEEN. What wilt thou do? Thou wilt not murder me?
Help, help, ho!

POLONIUS. [*Behind the arras.*] What ho! help, help, help!

HAMLET. How now, a rat? dead for a ducat, dead.

Kills Polonius [*through the arras.*]

POLONIUS. O I am slain!

QUEEN. O me, what hast thou done?

III, iv the Queen's private quarters   1 **lay home** thrust home; speak "home truths"   2
broad unrestrained   4 **heat** anger   **silence me** hide in silence   5 **round** outspoken,
straightforward   11 **idle** foolish   14 **rood** cross   17 **speak** i.e. to you as you should be
spoken to   19 **glass** looking glass   23 **for a ducat** I wager a ducat

HAMLET.	Nay I know not, 25

HAMLET.   Nay I know not,   25
     Is it the king?
QUEEN.   O what a rash and bloody deed is this!
HAMLET.   A bloody deed, almost as bad, good mother,
     As kill a king, and marry with his brother.
QUEEN.   As kill a king?
HAMLET.   Ay lady, it was my word.   30
     [*To Polonius.*] Thou wretched, rash, intruding
          fool, farewell,
     I took thee for thy better, take thy fortune,
     Thou find'st to be too busy is some danger.
     [*To the Queen.*]
     Leave wringing of your hands, peace, sit you down,
     And let me wring your heart, for so I shall   35
     If it be made of penetrable stuff,
     If damnèd custom have not brazed it so,
     That it be proof and bulwark against sense.
QUEEN.   What have I done, that thou dar'st wag thy tongue
     In noise so rude against me?
HAMLET.   Such an act   40
     That blurs the grace and blush of modesty,
     Calls virtue hypocrite, takes off the rose
     From the fair forehead of an innocent love
     And sets a blister there, makes marriage vows
     As false as dicers' oaths, O such a deed,   45
     As from the body of contraction plucks
     The very soul, and sweet religion makes
     A rhapsody of words; heaven's face does glow,
     Yea this solidity and compound mass
     With heated visage, as against the doom,   50
     Is thought-sick at the act.
QUEEN.   Ay me, what act,
     That roars so loud, and thunders in the index?
HAMLET.   Look here upon this picture, and on this,
     The counterfeit presentment of two brothers:
     See what a grace was seated on this brow,   55

---

32 **thy better** the king   33 **too busy** too much of a busybody   37 **custom** habit   **brazed** brass-plated (brazened)   38 **proof** armor   **sense** sensibility   42 **rose** (symbol of perfection and innocence)   43 **forehead** (where character was ascertained)   44 **blister there** (whores were punished by being branded on the forehead)   46 **body of contraction** marriage contract   47 **religion makes** makes of the religious ceremony of marriage   48 **rhapsody** (meaningless) mixture   48 **glow** blush   49 **solidity . . . mass** solid earth, compounded of the four elements   50 **against the doom** expecting Judgment Day   52 **index** (1) table of contents (2) prologue to an "act" of a play   54 **counterfeit presentment** painted

Hyperion's curls, the front of Jove himself,
An eye like Mars, to threaten and command,
A station like the herald Mercury,
New-lighted on a heaven-kissing hill,
A combination and a form indeed,   60
Where every god did seem to set his seal
To give the world assurance of a man.
This was your husband. Look you now what follows.
Here is your husband, like a mildewed ear,
Blasting his wholesome brother. Have you eyes?   65
Could you on this fair mountain leave to feed,
And batten on this moor? Ha! Have you eyes?
You cannot call it love, for at your age
The hey-day in the blood is tame, it's humble,
And waits upon the judgment, and what judgment   70
Would step from this to this? Sense sure you have
Else could you not have motion, but sure that sense
Is apoplexed, for madness would not err,
Nor sense to ecstasy was ne'er so thralled
But it reserved some quantity of choice   75
To serve in such a difference. What devil was't
That thus hath cozened you at hoodman-blind?
Eyes without feeling, feeling without sight,
Ears without hands or eyes, smelling sans all,
Or but a sickly part of one true sense   80
Could not so mope: O shame, where is thy blush?
Rebellious hell,
If thou canst mutine in a matron's bones,
To flaming youth let virtue be as wax
And melt in her own fire. Proclaim no shame   85
When the compulsive ardour gives the charge,
Since frost itself as actively doth burn,
And reason pandars will.

QUEEN.   O Hamlet, speak no more,
Thou turn'st my eyes into my very soul,

---

likeness   56 **Hyperion** Greek sun god   **front** forehead   58 **station** bearing   62 **assur-**
ance of assurance that here was (fr. law)   64 **ear** i.e. of grain   65 **Blasting**
blighting   **wholesome** healthy   66 **leave to feed** leave off feeding   67 **batten** gorge
yourself   **moor** (w. wordplay on "Moor" and "fair")   69 **hey-day in the blood** youthful
passion   71 **Sense** perception by the senses   72 **motion** impulse   73 **apoplexed**
paralyzed   74 **sense . . . thralled** sensibility was never so enslaved by madness   75
quantity of choice small amount of discrimination   76 **in . . . difference** where the
difference was so great   77 **cozened . . . blind** cheated you at blindman's buff   79 **sans**
all without the other senses   80 **Or but** or else even   81 **so mope** be so dull   86
compulsive compelling   **gives the charge** attacks   88 **panders will** pimps for lust

And there I see such black and grainèd spots   90
As will not leave their tinct.

HAMLET.   Nay, but to live
In the rank sweat of an enseamèd bed,
Stewed in corruption, honeying, and making love
Over the nasty sty.

QUEEN.   O speak to me no more,
These words like daggers enter in mine ears,   95
No more, sweet Hamlet.

HAMLET.   A murderer and a villain,
A slave that is not twentieth part the tithe
Of your precedent lord, a vice of kings,
A cutpurse of the empire and the rule,
That from a shelf the precious diadem stole   100
And put it in his pocket.

QUEEN.   No more.
HAMLET.   A king of shreds and patches—

Enter the GHOST *in his night-gown.*

Save me and hover o'er me with your wings,
You heavenly guards. What would your gracious figure?

QUEEN.   Alas, he's mad.   105
HAMLET.   Do you not come your tardy son to chide,
That lapsed in time and passion lets go by
Th'important acting of your dread command?
O say!

GHOST.   Do not forget: this visitation   110
Is but to whet thy almost blunted purpose.
But look, amazement on thy mother sits,
O step between her and her fighting soul,
Conceit in weakest bodies strongest works,
Speak to her Hamlet.

HAMLET.   How is it with you lady?   115
QUEEN.   Alas, how is't with you,
That you do bend your eye on vacancy,
And with th'incorporal air do hold discourse?

90
grained dyed in grain, unfading   91 **leave their tinct** lose their color   92 **enseamed** greasy ("seam"=lard)   97 **tithe** one-tenth part   98 **vice** buffoon (like the character of Vice in the morality plays)   99 **cutpurse** pickpocket   102 **s.d. night-gown** dressing gown   102 **of shreds and patches** like a ragged beggar   107 **lapsed . . . passion** having let time elapse and passion cool   108 **important** urgent   112 **amazement** distraction   114 **Conceit** imagination   117 **vacancy** (having been unfaithful to the king, she cannot see his ghost)   118 **incorporal** bodiless   119 **spirits** vital forces (believed to rise to the surface in

Forth at your eyes your spirits wildly peep,
And as the sleeping soldiers in th'alarm,   120
Your bedded hairs, like life in excrements,
Start up and stand an end. O gentle son,
Upon the heat and flame of thy distemper
Sprinkle cool patience. Whereon do you look?

HAMLET.   On him, on him, look you how pale he glares,   125
His form and cause conjoined, preaching to stones,
Would make them capable. Do not look upon me,
Lest with this piteous action you convert
My stern effects, then what I have to do
Will want true colour, tears perchance for blood.   130

QUEEN.   To whom do you speak this?

HAMLET.   Do you see nothing there?

QUEEN.   Nothing at all, yet all that is I see.

HAMLET.   Nor did you nothing hear?

QUEEN.   No, nothing but ourselves.

HAMLET.   Why look you there, look how it steals away,
My father in his habit as he lived,   135
Look where he goes, even now out at the portal.

Exit GHOST.

QUEEN.   This is the very coinage of your brain,
This bodiless creation ecstasy
Is very cunning in.

HAMLET.   Ecstasy?
My pulse as yours doth temperately keep time,   140
And makes as healthful music. It is not madness
That I have uttered; bring me to the test
And I the matter will re-word, which madness
Would gambol from. Mother, for love of grace,
Lay not that flattering unction to your soul,   145
That not your trespass but my madness speaks,
It will but skin and film the ulcerous place,
Whiles rank corruption mining all within,
Infects unseen. Confess yourself to heaven,
Repent what's past, avoid what is to come,   150

---

moments of excitement)   121 **bedded** lying flat   **excrements** outgrowths (of the
body)   122 **an** on   123 **distemper** mental upset   124 **patience** self-control   127
capable i.e. of feeling pity   128–9 **convert . . . effects** transform my outward signs of
sternness   130 **want** lack   **colour** (1) lit. (he will be pale with pity) (2) motivation   135
habit . . . lived clothing he wore when alive   138–9 **bodiless . . . cunning in** madness is
very skillful in seeing hallucinations   144 **gambol** leap, shy away (like a horse)   **grace**
God's grace   145 **unction** salve   148 **mining** undermining

And do not spread the compost on the weeds
To make them ranker. Forgive me this my virtue,
For in the fatness of these pursy times
Virtue itself of vice must pardon beg,
Yea curb and woo for leave to do him good.   155
QUEEN.   O Hamlet, thou hast cleft my heart in twain.
HAMLET.   O throw away the worser part of it,
And live the purer with the other half.
Good night, but go not to my uncle's bed,
Assume a virtue if you have it not.   160
That monster custom, who all sense doth eat
Of habits evil, is angel yet in this,
That to the use of actions fair and good,
He likewise gives a frock or livery
That aptly is put on. Refrain tonight,   165
And that shall lend a kind of easiness
To the next abstinence, the next more easy:
For use almost can change the stamp of nature,
And either . . . the devil, or throw him out
With wondrous potency: once more good night,   170
And when you are desirous to be blessed,
I'll blessing beg of you. For this same lord,
I do repent; but heaven hath pleased it so
To punish me with this, and this with me,
That I must be their scourge and minister.   175
I will bestow him and will answer well
The death I gave him; so again good night.
I must be cruel only to be kind;
This bad beings, and worse remains behind.
One word more, good lady.
QUEEN.   What shall I do?   180
HAMLET.   Not this by no means that I bid you do:
Let the bloat king tempt you again to bed,
Pinch wanton on your cheek, call you his mouse,
And let him for a pair of reechy kisses,

manure   152 **virtue** sermon on virtue   153 **fatness** grossness   **pursy** flabby   155
curb and woo bow and plead   **him** vice   160 **Assume** put on the guise of   161–2 **all
sense . . . evil** confuses the sense of right and wrong in a habitué   163, 168 **use**
habit   165 **aptly** readily   168 **stamp** form   169 **either . . . the** (word omitted, for
which "tame," "curb," and "quell" have been suggested; Q3: "master")   172 **lord**
Polonius   175 **their . . . minister** heaven's punishment and agent of retribution   176
bestow stow away   **answer well** assume full responsibility for; make reparation for   179
bad . . . behind is a bad beginning to a worse end to come   181 **this** i.e. which is to
follow   182 **bloat** bloated with dissipation   184 **reechy** filthy   186 **ravel**
unravel   187 **essentially** really   190 **paddock, bat, gib** toad, bat, tomcat ("familiars" or

Or paddling in your neck with his damned fingers,　185
Make you to ravel all this matter out
That I essentially am not in madness,
But mad in craft. 'Twere good you let him know,
For who that's but a queen, fair, sober, wise,
Would from a paddock, from a bat, a gib,　190
Such dear concernings hide? who would do so?
No, in despite of sense and secrecy,
Unpeg the basket on the house's top,
Let the birds fly, and like the famous ape,
To try conclusions in the basket creep,　195
And break your own neck down.

QUEEN.　Be thou assured, if words be made of breath,
And breath of life, I have no life to breathe
What thou hast said to me.

HAMLET.　I must to England, you know that.

QUEEN.　　　　　　　　　　　　Alack,　200
I had forgot: 'tis so concluded on.

HAMLET.　There's letters sealed, and my two school-fellows,
Whom I will trust as I will adders fanged,
They bear the mandate, they must sweep my way
And marshal me to knavery: let it work,　205
For 'tis the sport to have the enginer
Hoist with his own petar, and't shall go hard
But I will delve one yard below their mines,
And blow them at the moon: O 'tis most sweet
When in one line two crafts directly meet.　210
This man shall set me packing,
I'll lug the guts into the neighbour room;
Mother good night indeed. This counsellor
Is now most still, most secret, and most grave,
Who was in life a foolish prating knave.　215
Come sir, to draw toward an end with you.
Good night mother.

Exit HAMLET *tugging in* POLONIUS.

demons in animal shape that attend on witches)　191 **dear concernings** matters concerning
one deeply　193–6 **Unpeg . . . down** (although the source of the story is unknown, it refers
to an ape that climbs to the top of a house and opens a basket of birds; when the birds fly
away, the ape crawls into the basket, tries to fly, and breaks his neck. The point is that if she
acts foolishly and gives away Hamlet's secret, she harms herself)　195 **try conclusions**
experiment　204–5 **sweep . . . knavery** (like the marshal who went before a splendid royal
procession, clearing the way with his staff, so Rosencrantz and Guildenstern clear Hamlet's
path, not to glory but to some unknown evil)　206 **enginer** maker of war engines　207
Hoist . . . petar blown up by his own bomb　210 **in one . . . meet** the digger of the mine
and the digger of the countermine meet halfway in their tunnels　211 **packing** (1) i.e. my
bags (2) rushing away (3) plotting　214 **grave** (w. obvious pun)　216 **to draw . . . you** to
finish our business

[Act Four]

[SCENE I.]

Enter KING *and* QUEEN *with*
ROSENCRANTZ *and* GUILDENSTERN.

KING.   There's matter in these sighs, these profound heaves,
You must translate, 'tis fit we understand them.
Where is your son?

QUEEN.   Bestow this place on us a little while.

Exeunt ROSENCRANTZ *and* GUILDENSTERN.

Ah mine own lord, what have I seen tonight!   5

KING.   What, Gertrude? How does Hamlet?

QUEEN.   Mad as the sea and wind when both contend
Which is the mightier, in his lawless fit,
Behind the arras hearing something stir,
Whips out his rapier, cries 'A rat, a rat,'   10
And in this brainish apprehension kills
The unseen good old man.

KING.   O heavy deed!
It had been so with us had we been there:
His liberty is full of threats to all,
To you yourself, to us, to every one.   15
Alas, how shall this bloody deed be answered?
It will be laid to us, whose providence
Should have kept short, restrained, and out of haunt
This mad young man; but so much was our love,
We would not understand what was most fit,   20
But like the owner of a foul disease,
To keep it from divulging, let it feed
Even on the pith of life: where is he gone?

QUEEN.   To draw apart the body he hath killed,
O'er whom his very madness, like some ore   25
Among a mineral of metals base,
Shows itself pure: a' weeps for what is done.

IV, i a room in the castle   1 **matter** meaning   2 **translate** interpret   4 **Bestow . . . us** leave us   11 **brainish apprehension** insane delusion   12 **heavy** wicked   13 **us** me (royal plural)   16 **answered** defended   17 **laid to us** blamed on me   17 **providence** foresight   18 **short** tethered by a short leash   18 **out of haunt** away from others   22 **divulging** being divulged   25–6 **ore . . . base** pure ore (such as gold) in a mine of base

KING.   O Gertrude, come away:
             The sun no sooner shall the mountains touch,
             But we will ship him hence, and this vile deed   30
             We must with all our majesty and skill
             Both countenance and excuse. Ho Guildenstern!

                         Enter ROSENCRANTZ *and* GUILDENSTERN.

             Friends both, go join you with some further aid:
             Hamlet in madness hath Polonius slain,
             And from his mother's closet hath he dragged him.   35
             Go seek him out, speak fair, and bring the body
             Into the chapel; I pray you haste in this.   *Exeunt Gent.*
             Come Gertrude, we'll call up our wisest friends,
             And let them know both what we mean to do
             And what's untimely done: [so haply slander,]   40
             Whose whisper o'er the world's diameter,
             As level as the cannon to his blank
             Transports his poisoned shot, may miss our name,
             And hit the woundless air. O come away,
             My soul is full of discord and dismay.   *Exeunt.* 45

             [SCENE II.]

             Enter HAMLET.

HAMLET.   Safely stowed.
             Gentlemen within: Hamlet, Lord Hamlet!
             But soft, what noise, who calls on Hamlet?
             O here they come.

                         Enter ROSENCRANTZ *and* GUILDENSTERN.

ROSENCRANTZ.
             What have you done my lord with the dead body?
HAMLET.   Compounded it with dust whereto 'tis kin.   5
ROSENCRANTZ.
             Tell us where 'tis that we may take it thence,
             And bear it to the chapel.
HAMLET.   Do not believe it.
ROSENCRANTZ.
             Believe what?

---

metal   32 **countenance** defend   36 **fair** courteously   42 **As level** with as straight
aim   42 **blank** target (lit. white bullseye at the target's center; fr. archery)   43 **his**
slander's   44 **woundless** invulnerable

HAMLET.   That I can keep your counsel and not mine own. Besides, 10
to be demanded of a sponge, what replication should be
made by the son of a king?

ROSENCRANTZ.
Take you me for a sponge, my lord?

HAMLET.   Ay sir, that soaks up the king's countenance, his rewards,
his authorities. But such officers do the king best service in 15
the end; he keeps them like an apple in the corner of his
jaw, first mouthed to be last swallowed: when he needs
what you have gleaned, it is but squeezing you, and
sponge, you shall be dry again.

ROSENCRANTZ.
I understand you not my lord.   20

HAMLET.   I am glad of it: a knavish speech sleeps in a foolish ear.

ROSENCRANTZ.
My lord, you must tell us where the body is, and go with
us to the king.

HAMLET.   The body is with the king, but the king is not with the
body. The king is a thing—   25

GUILDENSTERN.
A thing my lord?

HAMLET.   Of nothing, bring me to him. Hide fox, and all after.

Exeunt.

[SCENE III.]

Enter KING *and two or three.*

KING.   I have sent to seek him, and to find the body:
How dangerous is it that this man goes loose,
Yet must not we put the strong law on him,
He's loved of the distracted multitude,
Who like not in their judgment, but their eyes,   5
And where 'tis so, th'offender's scourge is weighed
But never the offence: to bear all smooth and even,
This sudden sending him away must seem
Deliberate pause: diseases desperate grown,

IV, ii another room in the castle   10–11 **keep . . . own** follow your advice and not keep
my own secret   10 **counsel** (1) advice (2) secret   11 **demanded of** questioned
by   **replication** reply to a charge (fr. law)   14 **countenance** favor   21 **sleeps in** means
nothing to   24 **king . . . king** Hamlet's father . . . Claudius   27 **Hide fox . . . after** (cry
in a children's game, like hide-and-seek)

IV, iii another room in the castle   4 **distracted multitude** confused mob   5 **in** according to   6 **scourge** punishment   7 **bear all** carry out everything   9 **Deliberate pause**

By desperate appliance are relieved,   10
Or not at all.

Enter ROSENCRANTZ *and all the rest.*

How now, what hath befallen?

ROSENCRANTZ.

Where the dead body is bestowed my lord,
We cannot get from him.

KING.   But where is he?

ROSENCRANTZ.

Without, my lord, guarded, to know your pleasure.

KING.   Bring him before us.

ROSENCRANTZ.   Ho, bring in the lord.   15

Enter HAMLET [*guarded*] *and* GUILDENSTERN.

KING.   Now Hamlet, where's Polonius?

HAMLET.   At supper.

KING.   At supper? where?

HAMLET.   Not where he eats, but where a' is eaten: a certain convocation of politic worms are e'en at him. Your worm is your 20
only emperor for diet, we fat all creatures else to fat us,
and we fat ourselves for maggots. Your fat king and your
lean beggar is but variable service, two dishes but to one
table, that's the end.

KING.   Alas, alas.   25

HAMLET.   A man may fish with the worm that hath eat of a king, and
eat of the fish that hath fed of that worm.

KING.   What dost thou mean by this?

HAMLET.   Nothing but to show you how a king may go a progress
through the guts of a beggar.   30

KING.   Where is Polonius?

HAMLET.   In heaven, send thither to see. If your messenger find him
not there, seek him i'th'other place yourself: but if indeed
you find him not within this month, you shall nose him as
you go up the stairs into the lobby.   35

KING.   [*To Attendants.*] Go seek him there.

HAMLET.   A' will stay till you come.   [*Exeunt.*]

KING.   Hamlet, this deed, for thine especial safety—

considered delay (not sudden action)   10 **appliance** remedy   14 **guarded** (Hamlet is
under guard until he boards the ship)   19 **convocation** assembly   20 **politic** (1) statesman-
like (2) crafty   **worms** (a possible reference to the Diet of Worms in 1521, where Luther
was condemned as a heretic)   **e'en** even now   23 **variable service** a variety of
courses   29 **go a progress** make a splendid royal journey from one part of the country to
another (as Queen Elizabeth often did)   39 **tender** cherish

Which we do tender, as we dearly grieve
For that which thou hast done—must send thee hence   40
With fiery quickness. Therefore prepare thyself,
The bark is ready, and the wind at help,
Th'associates tend, and every thing is bent
For England.

HAMLET.   For England.

KING.   Ay Hamlet.

HAMLET.   Good.

KING.   So is it if thou knew'st our purposes.   45

HAMLET. I see a cherub that sees them: but come, for England.
Farewell dear mother.

KING.   Thy loving father, Hamlet.

HAMLET. My mother: father and mother is man and wife, man and
wife is one flesh, and so my mother: come, for England.   50

KING.   [*To Rosencrantz and Guildenstern.*]   *Exit.*
Follow him at foot, tempt him with speed aboard,
Delay it not, I'll have him hence tonight.
Away, for every thing is sealed and done
That else leans on th'affair, pray you make haste.

                                        [*Exeunt.*]

And England, if my love thou hold'st at aught—   55
As my great power thereof may give thee sense,
Since yet thy cicatrice looks raw and red
After the Danish sword, and thy free awe
Pays homage to us—thou mayst not coldly set
Our sovereign process, which imports at full   60
By letters congruing to that effect,
The present death of Hamlet. Do it England,
For like the hectic in my blood he rages,
And thou must cure me; till I know 'tis done,
Howe'er my haps, my joys were ne'er begun.   *Exit.* 65

---

42 **at help** helpful   43 **tend**
wait, attend   **bent** in readiness   46 **cherub** (considered the watchmen of
heaven)   49–50 **father . . . mother** (though Hamlet continues to play mad, the explanation
has some "method" in it)   51 **at foot** at his heels   **tempt** coax   54 **leans on** relates
to   55 **England** King of England   **my love . . . aught** you place any value on my
favor   56 **sense** sense of the value   57 **cicatrice** scar   58–9 **free . . . homage** awe which
you, though free, still show by paying homage   59 **coldly set** lightly estimate   60 **process**
command   **imports** makes known   61 **congruing** congruent, agreeing   62 **present**
immediate   63 **hectic** fever   65 **haps** fortunes

[SCENE IV.]

Enter FORTINBRAS *with his army over the stage.*

FORTINBRAS.
          Go captain, from me greet the Danish king,
          Tell him that by his license, Fortinbras
          Craves the conveyance of a promised march
          Over his kingdom. You know the rendezvous:
          If that his majesty would aught with us,   5
          We shall express our duty in his eye,
          And let him know so.
CAPTAIN.   I will do't, my lord.
FORTINBRAS.
          Go softly on.   *Exit.*

Enter HAMLET, ROSENCRANTZ,
[GUILDENSTERN,] *etc.*

HAMLET.   Good sir whose powers are these?
CAPTAIN.   They are of Norway sir.   10
HAMLET.   How purposed sir I pray you?
CAPTAIN.   Against some part of Poland.
HAMLET.   Who commands them sir?
CAPTAIN.   The nephew to old Norway, Fortinbras.
HAMLET.   Goes it against the main of Poland sir,   15
          Or for some frontier?
CAPTAIN.   Truly to speak, and with no addition,
          We go to gain a little patch of ground
          That hath in it no profit but the name.
          To pay five ducats, five, I would not farm it;   20
          Nor will it yield to Norway or the Pole
          A ranker rate, should it be sold in fee.
HAMLET.   Why then the Polack never will defend it.
CAPTAIN.   Yes, it is already garrisoned.
HAMLET.   Two thousand souls, and twenty thousand ducats 25
          Will not debate the question of this straw:
          This is th'imposthume of much wealth and peace,

IV, iv a plain in Denmark   3 **conveyance of** escort for   6 **in his eye** face to face   8
softly slowly   9 **powers** troops   15 **main** body   19 **name** reputation to be gained (as
conqueror)   20 **pay** pay the annual rent of   22 **ranker** higher (as annual interest on the
total)   **in fee** outright   26 **debate . . . of** settle the dispute over   **straw** triviality   27
imposthume . . . peace swelling discontent (inner abscess) resulting from too much wealth
and peace

That inward breaks, and shows no cause without
Why the man dies. I humbly thank you sir.
CAPTAIN.   God bye you sir.   [*Exit.*]
ROSENCRANTZ.   Will't please you go my lord?   30
HAMLET.   I'll be with you straight, go a little before.

                                    [*Exeunt all but Hamlet.*]

How all occasions do inform against me,
And spur my dull revenge. What is a man
If his chief good and market of his time
Be but to sleep and feed? a beast, no more: 35
Sure he that made us with such large discourse,
Looking before and after, gave us not
That capability and god-like reason
To fust in us unused. Now whether it be
Bestial oblivion, or some craven scruple   40
Of thinking too precisely on th'event—
A thought which quartered hath but one part wisdom,
And ever three parts coward—I do not know
Why yet I live to say 'This thing's to do,'
Sith I have cause, and will, and strength, and means   45
To do't; examples gross as earth exhort me:
Witness this army of such mass and charge,
Led by a delicate and tender prince,
Whose spirit with divine ambition puffed,
Makes mouths at the invisible event,   50
Exposing what is mortal, and unsure,
To all that fortune, death, and danger dare,
Even for an egg-shell. Rightly to be great,
Is not to stir without great argument,
But greatly to find quarrel in a straw   55
When honour's at the stake. How stand I then
That have a father killed, a mother stained,
Excitements of my reason, and my blood,
And let all sleep, while to my shame I see
The imminent death of twenty thousand men,   60
That for a fantasy and trick of fame

---

32 **inform** take shape   34 **market** profit   36 **discourse** power of
reasoning   37 **Looking . . . after** seeing causes and effects; remembering the past and
projecting the future   39 **fust** grow moldy   40 **Bestial oblivion** forgetfulness, as a beast
forgets its parents   **craven** cowardly   41 **event** outcome   46 **gross** obvious   47
charge expense   48 **delicate and tender** gentle and young   50 **mouths** faces   **event**
outcome   53–6 **Rightly . . . stake** the truly great do not fight without just cause ("argument"), but it is nobly ("greatly") done to fight even for a trifle if honor is at stake   58

Go to their graves like beds, fight for a plot
Whereon the numbers cannot try the cause,
Which is not tomb enough and continent
To hide the slain. O from this time forth,   65
My thoughts be bloody, or be nothing worth.   *Exit.*

[SCENE V.]

Enter QUEEN, HORATIO, *and a Gentleman.*

QUEEN.   I will not speak with her.
GENTLEMAN.
          She is importunate, indeed distract,
          Her mood will needs be pitied.
QUEEN.   What would she have?
GENTLEMAN.
          She speaks much of her father, says she hears
          There's tricks i'th'world, and hems, and beats her heart, 5
          Spurns enviously at straws, speaks things in doubt
          That carry but half sense: her speech is nothing,
          Yet the unshapèd use of it doth move
          The hearers to collection; they aim at it,
          And botch the words up fit to their own thoughts,   10
          Which as her winks, and nods, and gestures yield them,
          Indeed would make one think there might be thought,
          Though nothing sure, yet much unhappily.
HORATIO.   'Twere good she were spoken with, for she may strew
          Dangerous conjectures in ill-breeding minds.   15
QUEEN.   Let her come in.   *Exit Gentleman.*
          [*Aside.*] To my sick soul, as sin's true nature is,
          Each toy seems prologue to some great amiss,
          So full of artless jealousy is guilt,
          It spills itself, in fearing to be spilt.   20

Enter OPHELIA, *distracted.*

Excitements incitements   **blood** emotions   61 **fantasy** illusion   **trick** trifle   63
Whereon . . . cause too small to accommodate all the troops fighting for it   64 **continent**
container
    IV, v a room in the castle (some editors begin the fourth act here, basing the act division on
Hamlet's departure and return)   2 **distract** insane   3 **will needs be** needs to be   5 **tricks**
deceits   **hems** coughs   6 **Spurns . . . straws** reacts maliciously to trifles, like kicking
viciously at straws   **in doubt** ambiguous   9 **collection** inference   **aim** guess   10
botch patch   12 **thought** i.e. behind her remarks   15 **ill-breeding** incubating evil   17
as sin's . . . is as is natural for the guilty   18 **toy** trifle   **amiss** disaster   19 **artless**
jealousy uncontrollable suspicion   20 **spills** destroys   20 s.d. **distracted** mad

OPHELIA.	Where is the beauteous majesty of Denmark?
QUEEN.	How now Ophelia?
OPHELIA.	[*Sings.*] How should I your true love know

          From another one?

          By his cockle hat and staff,   25

          And his sandal shoon.

QUEEN.	Alas sweet lady, what imports this song?
OPHELIA.	Say you? nay, pray you mark.

    [*Sings.*] He is dead and gone, lady,

          He is dead and gone,   30

          At his head a grass-green turf,

          At his heels a stone.

    O ho.

QUEEN.	Nay but Ophelia—
OPHELIA.	Pray you mark.

    [*Sings.*] White his shroud as the mountain snow—

Enter KING.

QUEEN.	Alas, look here my lord. 35
OPHELIA.	[*Sings.*] Larded all with sweet flowers,

          Which bewept to the ground did not go,

          With true-love showers.

KING.	How do you, pretty lady?
OPHELIA.	Well, God 'ild you. They say the owl was a baker's 40

daughter. Lord, we know what we are, but know not what
we may be. God be at your table.

KING.	Conceit upon her father.
OPHELIA.	Pray you let's have no words of this, but when they ask

you what it means, say you this: 45

    [*Sings.*] Tomorrow is Saint Valentine's day,

          All in the morning betime,

          And I a maid at your window

          To be your Valentine.

          Then up he rose, and donned his clo'es,   50

          And dupped the chamber door,

25

cockle hat and staff (marks of the pilgrim, the cockle shell symbolizing his journey to the shrine of St. James; the pilgrim was a common metaphor for the lover, as in *R&J*, I, 5, 95-109)   **26 shoon** shoes   **27 imports** signifies   **36 Larded** trimmed   **37 not** (a departure from the rhythm of the song, and possibly an allusion to her father's hasty burial)   40 **God 'ild** God yield (reward)   **40-1 owl . . . daughter** (in a medieval legend, a baker's daughter was turned into an owl because she gave Jesus short weight on a loaf of broad)   42 **God . . . table** (a blessing at dinner and a reference to the inhospitable baker's daughter)   **43 Conceit** thinking   **47 betime** early (because the first girl a man saw on Valentine's Day would be his true love)   **51 dupped** opened   **56 Gis** contraction of

    Let in the maid, that out a maid,
     Never departed more.

KING.   Pretty Ophelia.

OPHELIA.   Indeed, la, without an oath I'll make an end on't.   55
    [*Sings.*] By Gis and by Saint Charity,
     Alack and fie for shame,
    Young men will do't, if they come to't,
     By Cock they are to blame.
    Quoth she, Before you tumbled me,   60
     You promised me to wed.
  (He answers)
    So would I ha' done, by yonder sun,
     And thou hadst not come to my bed.

KING.   How long hath she been thus?   65

OPHELIA.   I hope all will be well. We must be patient, but I cannot
    choose but weep to think they would lay him i'th'cold
    ground. My brother shall know of it, and so I thank you
    for your good counsel. Come, my coach: good night
    ladies, good night. Sweet ladies, good night, good night. 70

KING.   Follow her close, give her good watch I pray you.

            [*Exit* HORATIO.]

  O this is the poison of deep grief, it springs
  All from her father's death, and now behold:
  O Gertrude, Gertrude,
  When sorrows come, they come not single spies,   75
  But in battalions: first her father slain,
  Next, your son gone, and he most violent author
  Of his own just remove, the people muddied,
  Thick and unwholesome in their thoughts and whispers
  For good Polonius' death: and we have done but greenly 80
  In hugger-mugger to inter him: poor Ophelia
  Divided from herself and her fair judgment,
  Without the which we are pictures or mere beasts,
  Last, and as much containing as all these,
  Her brother is in secret come from France,   85
  Feeds on his wonder, keeps himself in clouds,
  And wants not buzzers to infect his ear

"Jesus" 59 **Cock** (vulgarization of "God" in oaths) 75 **come not** come not as 78
remove removal **muddied** stirred up 80 **done but greenly** acted like amateurs 81
hugger-mugger secret haste 83 **pictures** imitations 84 **containing** i.e. cause for
sorrow 86 **Feeds . . . wonder** sustains himself by wondering about his father's
death **clouds** gloom, obscurity 87 **wants** lacks **buzzers** whispering
scandalmongers

                    With pestilent speeches of his father's death,
                    Wherein necessity, of matter beggared,
                    Will nothing stick our person to arraign   90
                    In ear and ear: O my dear Gertrude, this
                    Like to a murdering-piece in many places
                    Gives me superfluous death.   *A noise within.*
QUEEN.   Alack, what noise is this?
KING.   Attend!   *Enter a* MESSENGER.
                    Where are my Switzers? Let them guard the door.   95
                    What is the matter?
MESSENGER.   Save yourself, my lord.
                    The ocean, overpeering of his list,
                    Eats not the flats with more impiteous haste
                    Than young Laertes in a riotous head
                    O'erbears your officers: the rabble call him lord,   100
                    And as the world were now but to begin,
                    Antiquity forgot, custom not known,
                    The ratifiers and props of every word,
                    They cry 'Choose we, Laertes shall be king!'
                    Caps, hands, and tongues applaud it to the clouds,   105
                    'Laertes shall be king, Laertes king!'   *A noise within.*
QUEEN.   How cheerfully on the false trail they cry.
                    O this is counter, you false Danish dogs.
KING.   The doors are broke.

                    Enter LAERTES *with others.*

LAERTES.   Where is this king? Sirs, stand you all without.   110
DANES.   No, let's come in.
LAERTES.   I pray you give me leave.
DANES.   We will, we will.   [*They retire.*]
LAERTES.   I thank you, keep the door. O thou vile king,
                    Give me my father.
QUEEN.   Calmly, good Laertes.
LAERTES.   That drop of blood that's calm proclaims me bastard,   115
                    Cries cuckold to my father, brands the harlot
                    Even here between the chaste unsmirchèd brows
                    Of my true mother.

89–90 **Wherein . . . arraign** in which the tellers, lacking facts, will not
hesitate to accuse me   91 **In ear and ear** whispering from one ear to another   92
murdering-piece small cannon shooting shrapnel, to inflict numerous wounds   95
Switzers Swiss guards   97 **overpeering . . . list** rising above its usual limits   98 **flats**
lowlands   **impiteous** pitiless   99 **head** armed force   103 **word** promise   108 **counter**
following the scent backward (fr. hunting)   110 **without** outside   111 **leave** i.e. to enter
alone   116 **cuckold** betrayed husband   **brands** (so harlots were punished; cf. III, 4,

KING.   What is the cause Laertes,
          That thy rebellion looks so giant-like?
          Let him go Gertrude, do not fear our person,   120
          There's such divinity doth hedge a king,
          That treason can but peep to what it would,
          Acts little of his will. Tell me Laertes,
          Why thou art this incensed. Let him go Gertrude.
          Speak man.   125
LAERTES. Where is my father?
KING.   Dead.
QUEEN.   But not by him.
KING.   Let him demand his fill.
LAERTES. How came he dead? I'll not be juggled with.
          To hell allegiance, vows to the blackest devil,
          Conscience and grace, to the profoundest pit.   130
          I dare damnation: to this point I stand,
          That both the worlds I give to negligence,
          Let come what comes, only I'll be revenged
          Most throughly for my father.
KING.   Who shall stay you?
LAERTES. My will, not all the world's: 135
          And for my means, I'll husband them so well,
          They shall go far with little.
KING.   Good Laertes,
          If you desire to know the certainty
          Of your dear father, is't writ in your revenge,
          That swoopstake, you will draw both friend and foe,   140
          Winner and loser?
LAERTES. None but his enemies.
KING.   Will you know them then?
LAERTES. To his good friends thus wide I'll ope my arms,
          And like the kind life-rend'ring pelican,
          Repast them with my blood.
KING.   Why now you speak   145
          Like a good child, and a true gentleman.
          That I am guiltless of your father's death,
          And am most sensibly in grief for it,

---

44)   120 **fear** i.e. for   121 **divinity** divine protection   **hedge** enclose   122 **peep to**
strain to see (as if through or over a hedge)   123 **Acts** puts into action   **his**
treason's   129, 130 **to** go to   130 **grace** God's grace   131 **to** on   132 **both . . .
negligence** I care nothing for this world or the next   135 **world's** i.e. will   136 **means** (1)
methods (2) money   **husband** economize   140 **swoopstake** sweeping in all the stakes in a
game, both of winner and loser   144 **pelican** (the mother pelican was believed to nourish
her young with blood pecked from her own breast)   148 **sensibly** feelingly

It shall as level to your judgment 'pear
As day does to your eye.
A noise within: Let her come in.   150
LAERTES.   How now, what noise is that?

Enter OPHELIA.

O heat, dry up my brains, tears seven time salt,
Burn out the sense and virtue of mine eye!
By heaven, thy madness shall be paid with weight,
Till our scale turn the beam. O rose of May,   155
Dear maid, kind sister, sweet Ophelia:
O heavens, is't possible a young maid's wits
Should be as mortal as an old man's life?
Nature is fine in love, and where 'tis fine,
It sends some precious instance of itself   160
After the thing it loves.
OPHELIA.   [*Sings.*]
            They bore him barefaced on the bier,
            Hey non nonny, nonny, hey nonny:
            And in his grave rained many a tear—
Fare you well my dove.   165
LAERTES.   Hadst thou thy wits, and didst persuade revenge,
It could not move thus.
OPHELIA.   You must sing 'adown adown,' and you call him adown-a.
O how the wheel becomes it. It is the false steward that
stole his master's daughter.   170
LAERTES.   This nothing's more than matter.
OPHELIA.   There's rosemary, that's for remembrance, pray you love
remember: and there is pansies, that's for thoughts.
LAERTES.   A document in madness, thoughts and remembrance fit-
ted.   175
OPHELIA.   There's fennel for you, and columbines. There's rue for
you, and here's some for me, we may call it herb of grace
o'Sundays: O, you must wear your rue with a difference.

149 **level**
plain   153 **sense and virtue** feeling and power   154 **with weight** with equal
weight   155 **turn the beam** outweigh the other side ("beam"=balance bar)   159–61
Nature . . . loves filial love that is so refined and pure sends some precious token (her wits)
after the beloved dead   169 **wheel becomes it** refrain ("adown") suits the subject
(Polonius's fall)   **It** (the subject of the song she is singing [which is unknown])   171 **more
than matter** more eloquent than sane speech   172 **There's rosemary** (given to Laertes; she
may be distributing imaginary or real flowers, though not necessarily those she
mentions)   174 **document** lesson   **thoughts . . . fitted** thoughts of revenge matched with
remembrance of Polonius   176 **fennel, columbines** (given to the king; symbolizing flattery
and ingratitude, respectively)   **rue** (given to the queen; symbolizing sorrow or
repentance)   177 **herb of grace** (because it symbolizes repentance)   178 **with a**

There's a daisy, I would give you some violets, but they
withered all when my father died: they say a' made a good 180
end;
[*Sings.*] For bonny sweet Robin is all my joy.

LAERTES. Thought and affliction, passion, hell itself,
She turns to favour and to prettiness.

OPHELIA. [*Sings.*] And will a' not come again,   185
And will a' not come again?
No, no, he is dead,
Go to thy death-bed,
He never will come again.

His beard was as white as snow,   190
All flaxen was his poll,
He is gone, he is gone,
And we cast away moan,
God ha' mercy on his soul.

And of all Christian souls, I pray God. God bye you. 195

Exit OPHELIA.

LAERTES. Do you see this, O God?
KING.   Laertes, I must commune with your grief,
Or you deny me right: go but apart,
Make choice of whom your wisest friends you will,
And they shall hear and judge 'twixt you and me;   200
If by direct or by collateral hand
They find us touched, we will our kingdom give,
Our crown, our life, and all that we call ours
To you in satisfaction; but if not,
Be you content to lend your patience to us,   205
And we shall jointly labour with your soul
To give it due content.
LAERTES.   Le this be so.
His means of death, his obscure funeral,
No trophy, sword, nor hatchment o'er his bones,
No noble rite, nor formal ostentation,   210
Cry to be heard as 'twere from heaven to earth,

---

difference (1) for a different reason (Ophelia's is for sorrow and the queen's for repentance)
(2) "difference" = alteration of the coat of arms for a younger member of the family (fr.
heraldry)   179 **daisy** (symbolizing dissembling; she probably keeps it)   **violets** (symbolizing faithfulness)   182 **For . . . joy** (line from an old ballad)   183 **Thought**
despondency   **passion** suffering   184 **favour** beauty   **prettiness** aptness   191 **poll**
head   201 **collateral** indirect   202 **touched** tainted with guilt   209 **trophy**
memorial   **hatchment** tablet displaying coat of arms   210 **ostentation** ceremony   211
Cry cry out

That I must call't in question.

KING.   So you shall,
And where th'offence is, let the great axe fall.
I pray you go with me.   *Exeunt.*

[SCENE VI.]

Enter HORATIO *and others.*

HORATIO.   What are they that would speak with me?
GENTLEMAN.

Seafaring men sir, they say they have letters for you.
HORATIO.   Let them come in.   [*Exit Attendant.*]
I do not know from what part of the world
I should be greeted, if not from Lord Hamlet.   5

Enter SAILORS.

SAILOR.   God bless you sir.
HORATIO.   Let him bless thee too.
SAILOR.   A' shall sir, an't please him. There's a letter for you sir, it
came from th'ambassador that was bound for England, if
your name be Horatio, as I am let to know it is.   10
HORATIO.   [*Reads the letter.*] 'Horatio, when thou shalt have overlooked this, give these fellows some means to the king,
they have letters for him. Ere we were two days old at sea,
a pirate of very warlike appointment gave us chase. Finding ourselves too slow of sail, we put on a compelled   15
valour, and in the grapple I boarded them. On the instant
they got clear of our ship, so I alone became their prisoner.
They have dealt with me like thieves of mercy, but they
knew what they did. I am to do a good turn for them. Let
the king have the letters I have sent, and repair thou to me   20
with as much speed as thou wouldest fly death. I have
words to speak in thine ear will make thee dumb, yet are
they much too light for the bore of the matter. These good
fellows will bring thee where I am. Rosencrantz and
Guildenstern hold their course for England. Of them I   25
have much to tell thee. Farewell.
             He that thou knowest thine, Hamlet.'
Come, I will give you way for these your letters,
And do't the speedier that you may direct me
To him from whom you brought them.   *Exeunt.*   30

IV, vi another room in the castle   11 **overlooked** read over   14 **appointment**
equipment   16 **in the grapple** when the pirate ship hooked onto ours   18 **of mercy**
merciful   20 **repair** come   23 **bore** size (lit. gun caliber, which determines the size of the
missile)   28 **way** access (to the king)

[SCENE VII.]

Enter KING *and* LAERTES.

KING.   Now must your conscience my acquittance seal,
                And you must put me in your heart for friend,
                Sith you have heard and with a knowing ear,
                That he which hath your noble father slain
                Pursued my life.

LAERTES.   It well appears: but tell me   5
                Why you proceeded not against these feats
                So crimeful and so capital in nature,
                As by your safety, greatness, wisdom, all things else,
                You mainly were stirred up.

KING.   O for two special reasons,
                Which may to you perhaps seem much unsinewed,   10
                But yet to me they're strong. The queen his mother
                Lives almost by his looks, and for myself,
                My virtue or my plague, be it either which,
                She's so conjunctive to my life and soul,
                That as the star moves not but in his sphere,   15
                I could not but by her. The other motive,
                Why to a public count I might not go,
                Is the great love the general gender bear him,
                Who dipping all his faults in their affection,
                Would like the spring that turneth wood to stone, 20
                Convert his gyves to graces, so that my arrows,
                Too slightly timbered for so loud a wind,
                Would have reverted to my bow again,
                And not where I had aimed them.

LAERTES.   And so have I a noble father lost,   25
                A sister driven into desperate terms,
                Whose worth, if praises may go back again,
                Stood challenger on mount of all the age
                For her perfections. But my revenge will come.

IV, vii another room in the castle   1 **my acquittance seal** confirm my acquittal   6
proceeded not did not bring legal proceedings   9 **mainly . . . up** were strongly urged   10
much unsinewed very weak   14 **conjunctive** closely allied (like two adjoining
planets)   15 **in his sphere** (referring to the Ptolemaic belief that each planet, fixed in its own
sphere, revolved around the earth)   16 **motive** reason   17 **count** accounting, trial   18
general gender common people   20 **the spring . . . stone** (the baths of King's Newnham
in Warwickshire were described as being able to turn wood into stone)   21 **Convert . . .
graces** regard his fetters (had he been imprisoned) as honors   22 **slightly timbered**
light-shafted   22 **loud** rough   26 **desperate terms** a condition of madness   27 **go back**
i.e. before her madness   28–9 **challenger . . . perfections** like a challenger on horseback,
ready to defend against the world her claim to perfection

KING.   Break not your sleeps for that, you must not think   30
               That we are made of stuff so flat and dull,
               That we can let our beard be shook with danger,
               And think it pastime. You shortly shall hear more,
               I loved your father, and we love ourself,
               And that I hope will teach you to imagine—   35

                        Enter a MESSENGER *with letters.*

               How now. What news?
MESSENGER.   Letters my lord, from Hamlet.
               These to your majesty, this to the queen.
KING.   From Hamlet? Who brought them?
MESSENGER.
               Sailors my lord they say, I saw them not:
               They were given me by Claudio, he received them   40
               Of him that brought them.
KING.   Laertes you shall hear them:
               Leave us.   *Exit* [MESSENGER.]
               [*Reads.*] 'High and mighty, you shall know I am set naked
               on your kingdom. Tomorrow shall I beg leave to see your
               kingly eyes, when I shall, first asking your pardon there-   45
               unto, recount the occasion of my sudden and more strange
               return.   Hamlet.'
               What should this mean? Are all the rest come back?
               Or is it some abuse, and no such thing?
LAERTES.   Know you the hand?
KING.   'Tis Hamlet's character. 'Naked,'   50
               And in a postscript here he says 'alone.'
               Can you devise me?
LAERTES.   I am lost in it my lord, but let him come,
               It warms the very sickness in my heart
               That I shall live and tell him to his teeth,   55
               'Thus didest thou.'
KING.   If it be so Laertes—
               As how should it be so? how otherwise?—
               Will you be ruled by me?
LAERTES.   Ay my lord,
               So you will not o'errule me to a peace.

---

43 **naked** without
resources   44–5 **see . . . eyes** appear in your royal presence   45 **pardon**
permission   49 **abuse** deception   50 **character** handwriting   52 **devise me** explain
it   53 **lost in** at a loss regarding   57 **As how . . .?** How could it be (that Hamlet has
returned)? How could it be otherwise (as I have his letter)?   61 **checking at** altering the

KING.	To thine own peace: if he be now returned,	60
	As checking at his voyage, and that he means	
	No more to undertake it, I will work him	
	To an exploit, now ripe in my device,	
	Under the which he shall not choose but fall:	
	And for his death no wind of blame shall breathe,	65
	But even his mother shall uncharge the practice,	
	And call it accident.	
LAERTES.	My lord, I will be ruled,	
	The rather if you could devise it so	
	That I might be the organ.	
KING.	It falls right.	
	You have been talked of since your travel much,	70
	And that in Hamlet's hearing, for a quality	
	Wherein they say you shine: your sum of parts	
	Did not together pluck such envy from him	
	As did that one, and that in my regard	
	Of the unworthiest siege.	
LAERTES.	What part is that my lord?	75
KING.	A very riband in the cap of youth,	
	Yet needful too, for youth no less becomes	
	The light and careless livery that it wears,	
	Than settled age his sables and his weeds	
	Importing health and graveness; two months since,	80
	Here was a gentleman of Normandy—	
	I have seen myself, and served against the French,	
	And they can well on horseback—but this gallant	
	Had witchcraft in't, he grew unto his seat,	
	And to such wondrous doing brought his horse,	85
	As had he been incorpsed and demi-natured	
	With the brave beast. So far he topped my thought,	
	That I in forgery of shapes and tricks	
	Come short of what he did.	
LAERTES.	A Norman was't?	
KING.	A Norman.	90
LAERTES.	Upon my life, Lamord.	

---

course of (fr. falconry: when the falcon forsakes one quarry for another)   63 **ripe in my device** already planned by me   66 **uncharge the practice** acquit the plot (of treachery)   69 **organ** instrument   72 **your sum of parts** all your accomplishments   75 **siege** rank   76 **very riband** mere decoration   77 **becomes** befits   78 **careless** carefree   **livery** clothing (denoting rank or occupation)   79 **sables** fur-trimmed gowns   **weeds** garments   80 **health** prosperity   **since** ago   83 **can** can do   86 **incorpsed . . . natured** made into one body, sharing half its nature   87 **brave** splendid   88 **in forgery of** imagining

KING.   The very same.
LAERTES.   I know him well, he is the brooch indeed
            And gem of all the nation.
KING.   He made confession of you,
            And gave you such a masterly report   95
            For art and exercise in your defence,
            And for your rapier most especial,
            That he cried out 'twould be a sight indeed
            If one could match you; the scrimers of their nation
            He swore had neither motion, guard, nor eye,   100
            If you opposed them; sir this report of his
            Did Hamlet so envenom with his envy,
            That he could nothing do but wish and beg
            Your sudden coming o'er to play with him.
            Now out of this—
LAERTES.   What out of this, my lord?   105
KING.   Laertes, was your father dear to you?
            Or are you like the painting of a sorrow,
            A face without a heart?
LAERTES.   Why ask you this?
KING.   Not that I think you did not love your father,
            But that I know love is begun by time,   110
            And that I see in passages of proof,
            Time qualifies the spark and fire of it:
            There lives within the very flame of love
            A kind of wick or snuff that will abate it,
            And nothing is at a like goodness still,   115
            For goodness growing to a plurisy,
            Dies in his own too-much. That we would do
            We should do when we would: for this 'would' changes,
            And hath abatements and delays as many
            As there are tongues, are hands, are accidents,   120
            And then this 'should' is like a spendthrift sigh,
            That hurts by easing; but to the quick of th'ulcer:
            Hamlet comes back, what would you undertake
            To show yourself in deed your father's son
            More than in words?

94 **confession** report   95–6 **gave you . . . defence** reported you
such a master of (fencing) theory and practice   99 **scrimers** fencers   100 **motion**
movements   102 **envenom** poison   111 **passages of proof** examples drawn from
experience   112 **qualifies** weakens   114 **snuff . . . it** charred end of the wick that will
diminish the flame   115 **still** always   116 **plurisy** excess   117 **That** what   118 **'would'**
will to act   121 **'should'** reminder of one's duty   121–2 **spendthrift . . . easing** a sigh
which, though giving temporary relief, wastes life, as each sigh draws a drop of blood away
from the heart (a common Elizabethan belief)   122 **quick** most sensitive spot   126

LAERTES.	To cut his throat i'th'church. 125
KING.	No place indeed should murder sanctuarize,

KING.   No place indeed should murder sanctuarize,
           Revenge should have no bounds: but good Laertes,
           Will you do this, keep close within your chamber:
           Hamlet returned shall know you are come home,
           We'll put on those shall praise your excellence,   130
           And set a double varnish on the fame
           The Frenchman gave you, bring you in fine together,
           And wager on your heads; he being remiss,
           Most generous, and free from all contriving,
           Will not peruse the foils, so that with ease,   135
           Or with a little shuffling, you may choose
           A sword unbated, and in a pass of practice
           Requite him for your father.

LAERTES.   I will do't,
           And for the purpose, I'll anoint my sword.
           I bought an unction of a mountebank   140
           So mortal, that but dip a knife in it,
           Where it draws blood, no cataplasm so rare,
           Collected from all simples that have virtue
           Under the moon, can save the thing from death
           That is but scratched withal: I'll touch my point   145
           With this contagion, that if I gall him slightly,
           It may be death.

KING.   Let's further think of this,
           Weigh what convenience both of time and means
           May fit us to our shape; if this should fail,
           And that our drift look through our bad performance,   150
           'Twere better not assayed; therefore this project
           Should have a back or second that might hold
           If this did blast in proof; soft, let me see,
           We'll make a solemn wager on your cunnings—
           I ha't: 155
           When in your motion you are hot and dry,
           As make your bouts more violent to that end,
           And that he calls for drink, I'll have prepared him

---

murder sanctuarize give sanctuary to murder   130 **put on** incite   132 **in fine**
finally   133 **remiss** easy-going   137 **unbated** not blunted (the edges and points were
blunted for fencing)   **pass of practice** (1) match for exercise (2) treacherous thrust   140
unction ointment   **mountebank** quack doctor, medicine man   141 **mortal** deadly   142
cataplasm poultice   143 **simples** herbs   143 **virtue** power (of healing)   144 **Under the
moon** (when herbs were supposed to be collected, to be most effective)   146 **gall**
scratch   149 **shape** plan   150 **drift** aim   150 **look through** be exposed by   153 **blast
in proof** fail when tested (as a bursting cannon)   154 **cunnings** skills   156 **motion** regu-
lated movements (fr. fencing)   157 **As make** as be sure to make

A chalice for the nonce, whereon but sipping,
If he by chance escape your venomed stuck,   160
Our purpose may hold there; but stay, what noise?

Enter QUEEN.

How, sweet queen?
QUEEN.   One woe doth tread upon another's heel,
So fast they follow; your sister's drowned, Laertes.
LAERTES.   Drowned! O where?   165
QUEEN.   There is a willow grows aslant a brook,
That shows his hoar leaves in the glassy stream,
There with fantastic garlands did she make
Of crow-flowers, nettles, daisies, and long purples,
That liberal shepherds give a grosser name,   170
But our cold maids do dead men's fingers call them.
There on the pendent boughs her coronet weeds
Clamb'ring to hang, an envious sliver broke,
When down her weedy trophies and herself
Fell in the weeping brook: her clothes spread wide,   175
And mermaid-like awhile they bore her up,
Which time she chanted snatches of old tunes,
As one incapable of her own distress,
Or like a creature native and indued
Unto that element: but long it could not be   180
Till that her garments, heavy with their drink,
Pulled the poor wretch from her melodious lay
To muddy death.
LAERTES.   Alas, then she is drowned?
QUEEN.   Drowned, drowned.
LAERTES.   Too much of water hast thou, poor Ophelia,   185
And therefore I forbid my tears; but yet
It is our trick, nature her custom holds,
Let shame say what it will; when these are gone,
The woman will be out. Adieu my lord,
I have a speech o' fire that fain would blaze,   190
But that this folly douts it.   *Exit.*

---

159 **nonce**
occasion   160 **stuck** thrust   167 **hoar** grey (on the underside)   169 **crowflowers**
buttercups   169 **long purples** spikelike early orchid   170 **liberal** libertine   170 **grosser**
coarser   171 **cold** chaste   172 **coronet weeds** garland of weeds   173 **envious sliver**
malicious branch   178 **incapable of** unable to understand   179–80 **indued Unto** endowed by nature to exist in   187 **trick** natural trait   188 **these** i.e. tears   189 **woman**

KING.   Let's follow, Gertrude,
How much I had to do to calm his rage;
Now fear I this will give it start again,
Therefore let's follow.   *Exeunt.*

[Act Five]

[SCENE I.]

Enter two CLOWNS.

1. CLOWN. Is she to be buried in Christian burial, when she wilfully
seeks her own salvation?
2. CLOWN. I tell thee she is, therefore make her grave straight. The
crowner hath sat on her, and finds it Christian burial.
1. CLOWN. How can that be, unless she drowned herself in her own   5
defence?
2 CLOWN. Why, 'tis found so.
1. CLOWN. It must be 'se offendendo,' it cannot be else: for here lies
the point; if I drown myself wittingly, it argues an act, and
an act hath three branches, it is to act, to do, and to   10
perform; argal, she drowned herself wittingly.
2. CLOWN. Nay, but hear you, goodman delver.
1. CLOWN. Give me leave: here lies the water, good. Here stands the
man, good. If the man go to this water and drown himself,
it is, will he nill he, he goes, mark you that. But if the   15
water come to him, and drown him, he drowns not himself. Argal, he that is not guilty of his own death, shortens
not his own life.
2. CLOWN. But is this law?
1. CLOWN. Ay marry is't, crowner's quest law.   20
2. CLOWN. Will you ha' the truth on't? If this had not been a gentlewoman, she would have been buried out o' Christian
burial.

. . . **out** womanly qualities (which arouse tears) will be out of me   191 **this** . . . **it** these tears
put it out
V, i a churchyard s.d. **Clowns** rustics   1 **Christian burial** consecrated ground within a
churchyard (where suicides were not allowed burial)   3 **straight** straightway   4 **crowner**
. . . **her** coroner has ruled on her case   5–6 **her own defence** (as self-defense justifies
homicide, so may it justify suicide)   8 '**se offendendo**' (he means "*se defendendo*," in
self-defense)   11 **argal** (corruption of "ergo" = therefore)   15 **will he nill he** will he or will
he not (willy nilly)   20 **quest** inquest

1. CLOWN. Why there thou say'st, and the more pity that great folk
should have countenance in this world to drown or hang   25
themselves more than their even-Christen. Come, my
spade; there is no ancient gentlemen but gardeners, ditch-
ers and grave-makers; they hold up Adam's profession.

2. CLOWN. Was he a gentleman?

1. CLOWN. A' was the first that ever bore arms.   30

2. CLOWN. Why, he had none.

1. CLOWN. What, art a heathen? How dost thou understand the
Scripture? The Scripture says Adam digged; could he dig
without arms? I'll put another question to thee; if thou
answerest me not to the purpose, confess thyself—   35

2. CLOWN. Go to.

1. CLOWN. What is he that builds stronger than either the mason, the
shipwright, or the carpenter?

2. CLOWN. The gallows-maker, for that frame outlives a thousand
tenants.   40

1. CLOWN. I like thy wit well in good faith, the gallows does well, but
how does it well? It does well to those that do ill. Now
thou dost ill to say the gallows is built stronger than the
church. Argal, the gallows may do well to thee. To't
again, come.   45

2. CLOWN. 'Who builds stronger than a mason, a shipwright, or a
carpenter?'

1. CLOWN. Ay, tell me that, and unyoke.

2. CLOWN. Marry, now I can tell.

1. CLOWN. To't.   50

2. CLOWN. Mass, I cannot tell.

1. CLOWN. Cudgel thy brains no more about it, for your dull ass will
not mend his pace with beating, and when you are asked
this question next, say 'a grave-maker:' the houses he
makes lasts till doomsday. Go get thee to Yaughan, and   55
fetch me a stoup of liquor.

[*Exit* 2. CLOWN.]

Enter HAMLET *and* HORATIO *afar off.*

1. CLOWN. *(Sings.)*

In youth when I did love, did love,

---

25 **countenance** privilege   26 **even-Christen**
fellow Christian   30 **arms** (w. pun on "coat of arms," which a gentleman had)   35 **confess**
thyself i.e. "and be hanged" (well-known saying)   39 **frame** (1) framework of the gallows
(2) builder's framework   41 **does well** (1) is a good answer (2) does good   44 **to thee** i.e. by
hanging you   48 **unyoke** unharness (your wits, after this exertion)   55 **Yaughan** Yohan,

> Methought it was very sweet,
> To contract oh the time for a my behove,
> O methought there a was nothing a meet.   60

HAMLET. Has this fellow no feeling of his business, that a'sings in grave-making?

HORATIO. Custom hath made it in him a property of easiness.

HAMLET. 'Tis e'en so, the hand of little employment hath the daintier sense.   65

1. CLOWN. *(Sings.)*

> But age with his stealing steps
> Hath clawed me in his clutch,
> And hath shipped me intil the land,
> As if I had never been such.

> [*Throws up a skull.*]

HAMLET. That skull had a tongue in it, and could sing once: how the   70 knave jowls it to the ground, as if 'twere Cain's jaw-bone, that did the first murder. This might be the pate of a politician, which this ass now o'erreaches; one that would circumvent God, might it not?

HORATIO. It might my lord.   75

HAMLET. Or of a courtier, which could say 'Good morrow sweet lord, how dost thou good lord?' This might be my lord such-a-one, that praised my lord such-a-one's horse, when a' meant to beg it, might it not?

HORATIO. It might my lord.   80

HAMLET. Why e'en so, and now my Lady Worm's, chopless, and knocked about the mazzard with a sexton's spade; here's fine revolution and we had the trick to see't. Did these bones cost no more the breeding, but to play at loggets with them? Mine ache to think on't.   85

1. CLOWN. *(Sings.)*

> A pick-axe and a spade, a spade,
> For and a shrouding sheet,
> O a pit of clay for to be made

John (possibly a local taverner)   56 **stoup** drinking vessel   57–60 **In youth . . . meet** (the song is a garbled version of "The Aged Lover Renounceth Love" by Vaux, printed in *Tottel's Miscellany*)   59 **contract** shorten   **a, oh** (he grunts as he works)   **behove** benefit   60 **meet** suitable   63 **Custom . . . easiness** being accustomed to it has made him indifferent   65 **daintier sense** finer sensibility (being uncalloused)   68 **intil** into   71 **jowls** casts (with obvious pun)   **Cain's jawbone** the jawbone of an ass with which Cain murdered Abel (the third reference to Cain in the play)   73 **politician** schemer   **o'erreaches** (1) reaches over (2) gets the better of   74 **would circumvent** tried to outwit   81 **chopless** lacking the lower jaw   82 **mazzard** head   83 **trick** knack   84 **play at loggets** game where small pieces of wood were thrown at fixed stakes

For such a guest is meet.

[Throws up another skull.]

HAMLET.   There's another: why may not that be the skull of a 90
lawyer? Where be his quiddities now, his quillets, his
cases, his tenures, and his tricks? Why does he suffer this
rude knave now to knock him about the sconce with a
dirty shovel, and will not tell him of his action of battery?
Hum, this fellow might be in's time a great buyer of land, 95
with his statutes, his recognizances, his fines, his double
vouchers, his recoveries: is this the fine of his fines, and
the recovery of his recoveries, to have his fine pate full of
fine dirt? Will his vouchers vouch him no more of his
purchases, and double ones too, than the length and 100
breadth of a pair of indentures? The very conveyances of
his lands will scarcely lie in this box, and must th'inheritor
himself have no more, ha?

HORATIO.   Not a jot more my lord.

HAMLET.   Is not parchment made of sheep-skins?   105

HORATIO.   Ay my lord, and of calves'-skins too.

HAMLET.   They are sheep and calves which seek out assurance in
that. I will speak to this fellow. Whose grave's this, sirrah?

1. CLOWN.   Mine sir:

[Sings.]   O a pit of clay for to be made   110
For such a guest is meet.

HAMLET.   I think it be thine indeed, for thou liest in't.

1. CLOWN.   You lie out on't sir, and therefore 'tis not yours; for my
part I do not lie in't, and yet it is mine.

HAMLET.   Thou dost lie in't, to be in't and say it is thine: 'tis for the 115
dead, not for the quick, therefore thou liest.

1. CLOWN.   'Tis a quick lie sir, 'twill away again from me to you.

HAMLET.   What man dost thou dig it for?

1. CLOWN.   For no man sir.

HAMLET.   What woman then?   120

1. CLOWN.   For none neither.

HAMLET.   Who is to be buried in't?

1. CLOWN.   One that was a woman sir, but rest her soul she's dead.

---

89 **meet**
fitting   91 **quiddities** subtle definitions   **quillets** minute distinctions   92 **tenures**
property holdings   93 **sconce** head   96 **statutes** mortgages   **recognizances** promissory
bonds   **fines, recoveries** legal processes for transferring real estate   97 **vouchers** persons
who vouched for a title to real estate   97 **fine** end   98 **recovery** attainment   100–1
length . . . indentures contracts in duplicate, which spread out, would just cover his
grave   101 **conveyances** deeds   102 **box** the grave   **inheritor** owner   107 **assurance**
(1) security (2) transfer of land   113 **on** of   116 **quick** living   124 **absolute** precise   **by**

HAMLET.   How absolute the knave is, we must speak by the card, or
           equivocation will undo us. By the Lord, Horatio, this 125
           three years I have took note of it, the age is grown so
           picked, that the toe of the peasant comes so near the heel of
           the courtier, he galls his kibe. How long hast thou been
           grave-maker?
1. CLOWN. Of all the days i'th 'year I came to't that day that our last 130
           king Hamlet overcame Fortinbras.
HAMLET.   How long is that since?
1. CLOWN. Cannot you tell that? Every fool can tell that. It was the
           very day that young Hamlet was born: he that is mad and
           sent into England.   135
HAMLET.   Ay marry, why was he sent into England?
1. CLOWN. Why because a' was mad: a' shall recover his wits there, or
           if a' do not, 'tis no great matter there.
HAMLET.   Why?
1. CLOWN. 'Twill not be seen in him there, there the men are as mad 140
           as he.
HAMLET.   How came he mad?
1. CLOWN. Very strangely they say.
HAMLET.   How strangely?
1. CLOWN. Faith, e'en with losing his wits.   145
HAMLET.   Upon what ground?
1. CLOWN. Why here in Denmark: I have been sexton here man and
           boy thirty years.
HAMLET.   How long will a man lie i'th'earth ere he rot?
1. CLOWN. Faith, if a' be not rotten before a' die, as we have many 150
           pocky corses nowadays that will scarce hold the laying in,
           a' will last you some eight year, or nine year. A tanner will
           last you nine year.
HAMLET.   Why he more than another?
1. CLOWN. Why sir, his hide is so tanned with his trade, that a' will 155
           keep out water a great while; and your water is a sore
           decayer of your whoreson dead body. Here's a skull now:
           this skull hath lien you i'th'earth three-and-twenty years.
HAMLET.   Whose was it?
1. CLOWN. A whoreson mad fellow's it was, whose do you think it 160
           was?
HAMLET.   Nay, I know not.

---

the card exactly to the point ("card" = card on which the sailor's compass points are
marked)   125 equivocation ambiguity   127 picked fastidious ("picky")   128 galls his
kibe chafes the chilblain on the courtier's heel   151 pocky rotten (with venereal
disease)   156 sore grievous

1. CLOWN.   A pestilence on him for a mad rogue, a' poured a flagon of
           Rhenish on my head once; this same skull sir, was sir,
           Yorick's skull, the king's jester.   165

HAMLET.   This?

1. CLOWN.   E'en that.

HAMLET.   Let me see. [*Takes the skull.*] Alas poor Yorick, I knew him
           Horatio, a fellow of infinite jest, of most excellent fancy,
           he hath borne me on his back a thousand times: and now   170
           how abhorred in my imagination it is: my gorge rises at it.
           Here hung those lips that I have kissed I know not how
           oft. Where be your gibes now? your gambols, your songs,
           your flashes of merriment, that were wont to set the table
           on a roar? not one now to mock your own grinning? quite   175
           chop-fallen? Now get you to my lady's chamber, and tell
           her, let her paint an inch thick, to this favour she must
           come. Make her laugh at that. Prithee Horatio, tell me one
           thing.

HORATIO.   What's that, my lord?   180

HAMLET.   Dost thou think Alexander looked o' this fashion
           i'th'earth?

HORATIO.   E'en so.

HAMLET.   And smelt so? pah.   [*Puts down the skull.*]

HORATIO.   E'en so my lord.   185

HAMLET.   To what base uses we may return, Horatio. Why may not
           imagination trace the noble dust of Alexander, till a'find it
           stopping a bung-hole?

HORATIO.   'Twere to consider too curiously, to consider so.

HAMLET.   No faith, not a jot, but to follow him thither with modesty 190
           enough, and likelihood to lead it; as thus: Alexander died,
           Alexander was buried, Alexander returneth to dust, the
           dust is earth, of earth we make loam, and why of that loam
           whereto he was converted, might they not stop a beer-
           barrel?   195
               Imperious Cæsar, dead and turned to clay,
               Might stop a hole to keep the wind away.
               O that that earth which kept the world in awe,
               Should patch a wall t'expel the winter's flaw.
           But soft, but soft awhile, here comes the king,   200

---

164 **Rhenish** Rhine wine   169 **fancy** imagination   175
on a roar roaring with laughter   176 **chopfallen** (1) lacking a lower jaw (2) dejected, "down
in the mouth"   177 **favour** appearance   186 **base** vile   188 **bung-hole** hole in a
cask   189 **curiously** minutely   190 **modesty** moderation   193 **loam** a clay mixture used
as plaster   199 **flaw** windy gusts   202 **maimed** abbreviated   204 **Fordo it** destroy

The queen, the courtiers.

> *Enter* KING, QUEEN, LAERTES, [*Doctor of*
> *Divinity*], *and a coffin, with Lords atten-*
> *dant.*

                   Who is this they follow?
And with such maimèd rites? This doth betoken
The corse they follow did with desp'rate hand
Fordo it own life; 'twas of some estate.
Couch we awhile, and mark.   [*They retire.*] 205

LAERTES. What ceremony else?

HAMLET.   That is Laertes,
A very noble youth: mark.

LAERTES. What ceremony else?

DOCTOR. Her obsequies have been as far enlarged
As we have warranty: her death was doubtful,   210
And but that great command o'ersways the order,
She should in ground unsanctified have lodged
Till the last trumpet: for charitable prayers,
Shards, flints and pebbles should be thrown on her:
Yet here she is allowed her virgin crants,   215
Her maiden strewments, and the bringing home
Of bell and burial.

LAERTES. Must there no more be done?

DOCTOR.   No more be done:
We should profane the service of the dead,
To sing sage requiem and such rest to her   220
As to peace-parted souls.

LAERTES.   Lay her i'th'earth,
And from her fair and unpolluted flesh
May violets spring: I tell thee churlish priest,
A minist'ring angel shall my sister be,
When thou liest howling.

HAMLET.   What, the fair Ophelia?   225

QUEEN. [*Scattering flowers.*] Sweets to the sweet, farewell.
I hoped thou shouldst have been my Hamlet's wife:
I thought thy bride-bed to have decked, sweet maid,
And not have strewed thy grave.

---

its   **estate** social rank   205 **Couch** hide   208 **else** in addition   210 **doubtful**
suspicious   214 **Shards** bits of broken pottery   215 **crants** garland   216 **strewments**
flowers strewn on the grave   216–17 **bringing home Of** laying to rest with   220 **sage**
requiem solemn dirge   221 **peace-parted souls** those whose souls have departed in
peace   225 **howling** i.e. in hell

LAERTES.   O treble woe
              Fall ten times treble on that cursèd head   230
              Whose wicked deed thy most ingenious sense
              Deprived thee of. Hold off the earth awhile,
              Till I have caught her once more in mine arms;
                                              Leaps in the grave.
              Now pile your dust upon the quick and dead,
              Till of this flat a mountain you have made   235
              T'o'ertop old Pelion, or the skyish head
              Of blue Olympus.

HAMLET.   [*Comes forward.*]   What is he whose grief
              Bears such an emphasis? whose phrase of sorrow
              Conjures the wand'ring stars, and makes them stand
              Like wonder-wounded hearers? This is I,   240
              Hamlet the Dane.   *Hamlet leaps in after Laertes.*

LAERTES.   [*Grapples with him.*]   The devil take thy soul.

HAMLET.   Thou pray'st not well,
              I prithee take thy fingers from my throat,
              For though I am not splenitive and rash,
              Yet have I in me something dangerous,   245
              Which let thy wiseness fear; hold off thy hand.

KING.   Pluck them asunder.

QUEEN.   Hamlet, Hamlet!

ALL.   Gentlemen!

HORATIO.   Good my lord, be quiet.

              [*Attendants part them, and they come out of
                  the grave.*]

HAMLET.   Why, I will fight with him upon this theme
              Until my eyelids will no longer wag.   250

QUEEN.   O my son, what theme?

HAMLET.   I loved Ophelia, forty thousand brothers
              Could not with all their quantity of love
              Make up my sum. What wilt thou do for her?

KING.   O he is mad, Laertes.   255

QUEEN.   For love of God, forbear him.

HAMLET.   'Swounds, show me what thou't do:
              Woo't weep? woo't fight? woo't fast? woo't tear thyself?

---

231 **most ingenious sense** mind   234 **quick** live   236
Pelion mountain in Thessaly (on which the Titans placed Mt. Ossa, to scale Mt. Olympus
and reach the gods [Vergil])   239 **Conjures . . . stars** casts a spell over the planets   241
Dane (rightful) King of Denmark   244 **splenitive** quick-tempered (anger was thought to
originate in the spleen)   256 **forbear** be patient with   257 **'Swounds** corruption of "God's

Woo't drink up eisel? eat a crocodile?
I'll do't. Dost thou come here to whine?   260
To outface me with leaping in her grave?
Be buried quick with her, and so will I.
And if thou prate of mountains, let them throw
Millions of acres on us, till our ground,
Singeing his pate against the burning zone,   265
Make Ossa like a wart. Nay, and thou'lt mouth,
I'll rant as well as thou.

QUEEN.   This is mere madness,
And thus awhile the fit will work on him:
Anon as patient as the female dove
When that her golden couplets are disclosed,   270
His silence will sit drooping.

HAMLET.   Hear you sir,
What is the reason that you use me thus?
I loved you ever; but it is no matter,
Let Hercules himself do what he may,
The cat will mew, and dog will have his day.   275

                               Exit HAMLET.

KING.   I pray thee good Horatio, wait upon him.

                               [HORATIO *follows.*]

[*Aside to Laertes.*] Strengthen your patience in our last
        night's speech,
We'll put the matter to the present push—
Good Gertrude, set some watch over your son—
This grave shall have a living monument: 280
An hour of quiet shortly shall we see,
Till then, in patience our proceeding be.   *Exeunt.*

[SCENE II.]

Enter HAMLET *and* HORATIO.

HAMLET.   So much for this sir, now shall you see the other;
          You do remember all the circumstance.

wounds"   258 **Woo't** contraction of "wilt thou"   **fast, tear** (exaggerated signs of
mourning)   259 **eisel** vinegar (thought to reduce anger and encourage
melancholy)   **crocodile** (associated with hypocritical tears)   265 **burning zone** zone in
the celestial sphere between the tropics of Cancer and Capricorn   266 **Ossa** (see above, 1.
236 n.)   267 **mere** absolute   270 **golden couplets** fuzzy yellow twin fledglings   278
present push immediate test   280 **living monument** (1) lasting tombstone (2) living sacrifice (Hamlet) to memorialize it
   V, ii a hall in the castle   1 **this** this part of the story

HORATIO. Remember it my lord!

HAMLET.   Sir, in my heart there was a kind of fighting
          That would not let me sleep; methought I lay   5
          Worse than the mutines in the bilboes. Rashly—
          And praised be rashness for it: let us know,
          Our indiscretion sometime serves us well
          When our deep plots do pall, and that should learn us
          There's a divinity that shapes our ends,   10
          Rough-hew them how we will—

HORATIO.   That is most certain.

HAMLET.   Up from my cabin,
          My sea-gown scarfed about me, in the dark
          Groped I to find out them, had my desire,
          Fingered their packet, and in fine withdrew   15
          To mine own room again, making so bold,
          My fears forgetting manners, to unseal
          Their grand commission; where I found, Horatio—
          Ah royal knavery—an exact command,
          Larded with many several sorts of reasons,   20
          Importing Denmark's health, and England's too,
          With ho, such bugs and goblins in my life,
          That on the supervise, no leisure bated,
          No, not to stay the grinding of the axe,
          My head should be struck off.

HORATIO.   Is't possible?   25

HAMLET.   Here's the commission, read it at more leisure.
          But wilt thou hear now how I did proceed?

HORATIO. I beseech you.

HAMLET.   Being thus be-netted round with villainies,
          Ere I could make a prologue to my brains,   30
          They had begun the play. I sat me down,
          Devised a new commission, wrote it fair—
          I once did hold it, as our statists do,
          A baseness to write fair, and laboured much
          How to forget that learning, but sir now   35

---

6 **mutines . . . bilboes** mutineers
in shackles   6 **Rashly** impulsively   7 **know** recognize   8 **indiscretion** impulse   9 **pall**
fail   13 **sea-gown** short-sleeved knee-length gown worn by seamen   15 **Fingered** got my
fingers on   15 **in fine** to finish   20 **Larded** embellished   21 **health** welfare   22 **bugs**
. . . **life** imaginary evils attributed to me, like imaginary goblins ("bugs") meant to frighten
children   23 **supervise** looking over (the commission)   **leisure bated** delay
excepted   24 **stay** await   29 **be-netted** trapped   30–1 **Ere . . . play** before I could
outline the action in my mind, my brains started to play their part   32 **fair** with professional skill (like a paid copyist)   33 **statists** statesmen   34 **baseness** mark of humble

It did me yeoman's service: wilt thou know
Th'effect of what I wrote?

HORATIO.   Ay, good my lord.

HAMLET.   An earnest conjuration from the king,
As England was his faithful tributary,
As love between them like the palm might flourish,   40
As peace should still her wheaten garland wear
And stand a comma 'tween their amities,
And many such like 'as'es' of great charge,
That on the view and know of these contents,
Without debatement further, more or less,   45
He should those bearers put to sudden death,
Not shriving time allowed.

HORATIO.   How was this sealed?

HAMLET.   Why even in that was heaven ordinant,
I had my father's signet in my purse,
Which was the model of that Danish seal: 50
Folded the writ up in the form of th'other,
Subscribed it, gave't th'impression, placed it safely,
The changeling never known: now the next day
Was our sea-fight, and what to this was sequent
Thou knowest already.   55

HORATIO.   So Guildenstern and Rosencrantz go to't.

HAMLET.   Why man, they did make love to this employment,
They are not near my conscience, their defeat
Does by their own insinuation grow:
'Tis dangerous when the baser nature comes   60
Between the pass and fell incensed points
Of mighty opposites.

HORATIO.   Why, what a king is this!

HAMLET.   Does it not, think thee, stand me now upon—
He that hath killed my king, and whored my mother,
Popped in between th'election and my hopes,   65
Thrown out his angle for my proper life,

---

status   36 **yeoman's** (in the sense of "faithful")   38 **conjuration** entreaty (he parodies the rhetoric of such documents)   42 **comma** connection   43 **'as'es'** (1) the "as" clauses in the commission (2) asses   **charge** (1) weight (in the clauses) (2) burdens (on the asses)   45 **debatement** discussion   46 **sudden** instant   47 **shriving time** time for confession and absolution   48 **was heaven ordinant** it was divinely ordained   49 **signet** seal   50 **model** replica   52 **Subscribed** signed   **impression** i.e. of the seal   53 **changeling** substitute (baby imp left when an infant was spirited away)   54 **sequent** subsequent   56 **to't** to their deaths   57 **did . . . employment** asked for it (Folio line; not in Q2)   59 **insinuation** intrusion   60 **baser** lower-ranking   61 **pass** thrust (fr. fencing)   **fell** fierce   63 **stand . . . upon** become incumbent upon me now   65 **election** (the Danish king was so chosen)   66 **angle** fishing hook   **proper** very own

And with such cozenage—is't not perfect conscience
To quit him with this arm? And is't not to be damned,
To let this canker of our nature come
In further evil?   70

HORATIO.   It must be shortly known to him from England
What is the issue of the business there.

HAMLET.   It will be short, the interim is mine,
And a man's life's no more than to say 'One.'
But I am very sorry good Horatio,   75
That to Laertes I forgot myself;
For by the image of my cause, I see
The portraiture of his; I'll court his favours:
But sure the bravery of his grief did put me
Into a towering passion.

HORATIO.   Peace, who comes here?   80

Enter young OSRIC.

OSRIC.   Your lordship is right welcome back to Denmark.

HAMLET.   I humbly thank you sir. [*Aside to Horatio.*] Dost know this
water-fly?

HORATIO.   No my good lord.

HAMLET.   Thy state is the more gracious, for 'tis a vice to know him: 85
he hath much land, and fertile: let a beast be lord of beasts,
and his crib shall stand at the king's mess; 'tis a chough,
but as I say, spacious in the possession of dirt.

OSRIC.   Sweet lord, if your lordship were at leisure, I should
impart a thing to you from his majesty.   90

HAMLET.   I will receive it sir, with all diligence of spirit; put your
bonnet to his right use, 'tis for the head.

OSRIC.   I thank your lordship, it is very hot.

HAMLET.   No, believe me, 'tis very cold, the wind is northerly.

OSRIC.   It is indifferent cold my lord indeed.   95

HAMLET.   But yet methinks it is very sultry and hot for my complexion.

OSRIC.   Exceedingly, my lord, it is very sultry, as 'twere, I cannot

---

67 **cozenage** deception   68 **quit**
repay, requite   69 **canker of our nature** cancer of humanity   70 **In** into   72 **issue**
outcome   74 **to say "One"** to score one hit in fencing (cf. below, l. 263)   77–8 **by the
image . . . his** in the depiction of my situation, I see the reflection of his   79 **bravery**
ostentation   83 **water-fly** insect which skips on the water's surface ("emblem of a busy
trifler:" Johnson)   85 **gracious** favorable   86–7 **let a beast . . . mess** an ass who owns
enough property can eat with the king   87 **chough** chattering bird, jackdaw   92 **bonnet**
hat   **head** (Osric has removed his hat as a sign of respect)   95 **indifferent**
reasonably   96 **complexion** temperament   103 **for my ease** for my own comfort (com-

tell how: but my lord, his majesty bade me signify to you
that a' has laid a great wager on your head. Sir, this is the 100
matter—

HAMLET.   [*Moves him to put on his hat.*]   I beseech you remember—

OSRIC.   Nay good my lord, for mine ease, in good faith. Sir, here
            is newly come to court Laertes, believe me, an absolute
            gentleman, full of most excellent differences, of very soft 105
            society, and great showing: indeed to speak feelingly of
            him, he is the card or calendar of gentry: for you shall find
            in him the continent of what part a gentleman would see.

HAMLET.   Sir, his definement suffers no perdition in you, though I
            know to divide him inventorially would dozy 110
            th'arithmetic of memory, and yet but yaw neither, in
            respect of his quick sail, but in the verity of extolment, I
            take him to be a soul of great article, and his infusion of
            such dearth and rareness, as to make true diction of him,
            his semblable is his mirror, and who else would trace him, 115
            his umbrage, nothing more.

OSRIC.   Your lordship speaks most infallibly of him.

HAMLET.   The concernancy sir? why do we wrap the gentleman in
            our more rawer breath?

OSRIC.   Sir?   120

HORATIO.   Is't not possible to understand in another tongue? You
            will do't sir, really.

HAMLET.   What imports the nomination of this gentleman?

OSRIC.   Of Laertes?

HORATIO.   His purse is empty already, all's golden words are spent. 125

HAMLET.   Of him, sir.

---

mon expression of politeness)   103–134 **Sir . . . he's unfellowed** (probably cut in production, as it is omitted in Folio, which substitutes: "Sir, you are not ignorant of what excellence
Laertes is at his weapon")   104 **absolute** perfect   105 **differences**
accomplishments   105–6 **soft society** refined manners   **showing** appearance   106
feelingly discerningly   107 **card or calendar** chart (shipman's compass card) or
almanac   **gentry** courtesy   108 **continent . . . see** (continuing the marine metaphor of
"card"=compass card) (1) geographical continent whose foreign parts a gentleman traveler
should see (2) all the qualities a gentleman would look for   109–16 **Sir . . . more** (Hamlet
outdoes Osric in the affected speech seemingly fashionable at the court of Elsinore)   109
definement description   **perdition** loss   110 **divide him inventorially** make a catalog or
take inventory (of his virtues)   110 **dozy** dizzy   111–12 **yaw . . . sail** (1) moving in an
unsteady course (as another boat would do, trying to catch up with Laertes' "quick sail") (2)
staggering to one trying to list his accomplishments   112 **in . . . extolment** to praise him
truthfully   113 **article** scope   **infusion** essence   114 **dearth** scarcity   114–16 **as to
make . . . more** to describe him truly I would have to employ his mirror to depict his only
equal—himself, and who would follow him is only a shadow   115 **semblable**
equal   **trace** (1) describe (2) follow   116 **umbrage** shadow   118 **concernancy**
relevance   119 **rawer breath** crude speech   121 **Is't not . . . tongue** cannot Osric understand his own way of speaking when used by another?   123 **nomination** naming

OSRIC.	I know you are not ignorant—
HAMLET.	I would you did sir, yet in faith if you did, it would not much approve me. Well, sir.
OSRIC.	You are not ignorant of what excellence Laertes is— 130
HAMLET.	I dare not confess that, lest I should compare with him in excellence, but to know a man well were to know himself.
OSRIC.	I mean sir for his weapon, but in the imputation laid on him by them in his meed, he's unfellowed.
HAMLET.	What's his weapon? 135
OSRIC.	Rapier and dagger.
HAMLET.	That's two of his weapons—but well.
OSRIC.	The king sir, hath wagered with him six Barbary horses, against which he has impawned, as I take it, six French rapiers and poniards, with their assigns, as girdle, han- 140 gers, and so. Three of the carriages in faith are very dear to fancy, very responsive to the hilts, most delicate carriages, and of very liberal conceit.
HAMLET.	What call you the carriages?
HORATIO.	I knew you must be edified by the margent ere you had 145 done.
OSRIC.	The carriages sir, are the hangers.
HAMLET.	The phrase would be more germane to the matter, if we could carry a cannon by our sides: I would it might be hangers till then, but on: six Barbary horses against six 150 French swords, their assigns, and three liberal-conceited carriages—that's the French bet against the Danish. Why is this all 'impawned' as you call it?
OSRIC.	The king sir, hath laid sir, that in a dozen passes between yourself and him, he shall not exceed you three hits; he 155 hath laid on twelve for nine, and it would come to im-mediate trial, if your lordship would vouchsafe the an-swer.
HAMLET.	How if I answer no?
OSRIC.	I mean my lord, the opposition of your person in trial. 160

128–9
if you did . . . me if you found me to be "not ignorant," it would prove little (as you are no judge of ignorance)   131 **compare with** vie with   132 **to know . . . himself** to know a man well, one must first know oneself   133 **imputation** repute   134 **meed** worth   **unfellowed** unequalled   136 **Rapier and dagger** sword and dagger (to fend off blows)   139 **impawned** staked   140 **poniards** daggers   **assigns** accessories   140 **gir-dle, hangers** belt, straps attached thereto, from which swords were hung   141 **carriages** hangers   142 **dear to fancy** rare in design   143 **liberal conceit** elaborate conception   145 **margent** marginal note   149 **cannon** (referring to the "carriage" on which a cannon is transported)   154–5 **laid . . . three hits** wagered that in twelve bouts Laertes must win three more than Hamlet   155–6 **he . . . nine** Laertes has stipulated

HAMLET.	Sir, I will walk here in the hall; if it please his majesty, it is the breathing time of day with me; let the foils be brought, the gentleman willing, and the king hold his purpose, I will win for him an I can, if not, I will gain nothing but my shame and the odd hits.
OSRIC.	Shall I re-deliver you e'en so?
HAMLET.	To this effect sir, after what flourish your nature will.
OSRIC.	I commend my duty to your lordship.
HAMLET.	Yours, yours. [*Exit* OSRIC.]
	He does well to commend it himself, there are no tongues else for's turn.
HORATIO.	This lapwing runs away with the shell on his head.
HAMLET.	A' did comply sir, with his dug before a' sucked it: thus has he—and many more of the same bevy that I know the drossy age dotes on—only got the tune of the time, and out of an habit of encounter, a kind of yeasty collection, which carries them through and through the most fond and winnowed opinions; and do but blow them to their trial, the bubbles are out.

Enter a LORD.

LORD.	My lord, his majesty commended him to you by young Osric, who brings back to him that you attend him in the hall. He sends to know if your pleasure hold to play with Laertes, or that you will take longer time.
HAMLET.	I am constant to my purposes, they follow the king's pleasure, if his fitness speaks, mine is ready: now or whensoever, provided I be so able as now.
LORD.	The king, and queen, and all are coming down.
HAMLET.	In happy time.
LORD.	The queen desires you to use some gentle entertainment to Laertes, before you fall to play.
HAMLET.	She well instructs me. [*Exit* LORD.]
HORATIO.	You will lose this wager, my lord.

165

170

175

180

185

190

---

twelve bouts instead of the usual nine   157 **answer** acceptance of the challenge (Hamlet interprets as "reply")   162 **breathing time** exercise period   166 **re-deliver you** take back your answer   167 **after . . . will** embellished as you wish   168 **commend** offer (Hamlet interprets as "praise")   170–1 **no tongues . . . turn** no others who would   172 **lapwing** (reported to be so precocious that it ran as soon as hatched)   173 **comply** observe the formalities of courtesy   **dug** mother's breast   175 **drossy** frivolous   176 **habit of encounter** habitual association (with others as frivolous)   176 **yeasty collection** frothy assortment of phrases (metaphor from fermenting barley)   177–8 **fond and winnowed** trivial and considered   178–9 **blow . . . out** blow on them to test them and they are gone   185 **his fitness speaks** it agrees with his convenience   189 **gentle entertainment** friendly treatment

HAMLET.   I do not think so, since he went into France, I have been in
continual practice, I shall win at the odds; but thou
wouldst not think how ill all's here about my heart: but it 195
is no matter.

HORATIO.   Nay good my lord—

HAMLET.   It is but foolery, but it is such a kind of gaingiving as
would perhaps trouble a woman.

HORATIO.   If your mind dislike any thing, obey it. I will forestall their 200
repair hither, and say you are not fit.

HAMLET.   Not a whit, we defy augury; there is special providence
in the fall of a sparrow. If it be now, 'tis not to come:
if it be not to come, it will be now; if it be not now,
yet it will come—the readiness is all. Since no man has 205
aught of what he leaves, what is't to leave betimes? let
be.

        *A table prepared. Trumpets, Drums, and
officers with cushions. Enter* KING, QUEEN,
and all the state, [OSRIC], *foils, daggers, and*
LAERTES.

KING.   Come Hamlet, come and take this hand from me.
[Puts Laertes' hand into Hamlet's.]

HAMLET.   Give me your pardon sir, I have done you wrong,
But pardon't as you are a gentleman.   210
This presence knows, and you must needs have heard,
How I am punished with a sore distraction.
What I have done
That might your nature, honour, and exception
Roughly awake, I here proclaim was madness: 215
Was't Hamlet wronged Laertes? never Hamlet.
If Hamlet from himself be ta'en away,
And when he's not himself, does wrong Laertes,
Then Hamlet does it not, Hamlet denies it:
Who does it then? his madness. If't be so,   220
Hamlet is of the faction that is wronged,
His madness is poor Hamlet's enemy.
Sir, in this audience,

---

198 **gaingiving** misgiving   201 **repair** coming   202 **augury**
omens   202–3 **special . . . sparrow** ("Are not two sparrows sold for a farthing? and one of
them shall not fall on the ground without your Father": Matt. X.29)   205 **all** all that
matters   206 **betimes** early (before one's time)   212 **sore distraction** grievous
madness   214   **nature**   filial   affection   **honour**   reputation   **exception**

Let my disclaiming from a purposed evil,
Free me so far in your most generous thoughts,   225
That I have shot my arrow o'er the house
And hurt my brother.

LAERTES.   I am satisfied in nature,
Whose motive in this case should stir me most
To my revenge, but in my terms of honour
I stand aloof, and will no reconcilement,   230
Till by some elder masters of known honour
I have a voice and precedent of peace
To keep my name ungored: but till that time,
I do receive your offered love, like love,
And will not wrong it.

HAMLET.   I embrace it freely,   235
And will this brother's wager frankly play.
Give us the foils: come on.

LAERTES.   Come, one for me.

HAMLET.   I'll be your foil Laertes, in mine ignorance
Your skill shall like a star i'th' darkest night
Stick fiery off indeed.

LAERTES.   You mock me sir.   240

HAMLET.   No, by this hand.

KING.   Give them the foils young Osric. Cousin Hamlet,
You know the wager.

HAMLET.   Very well my lord.
Your grace has laid the odds o'th'weaker side.

KING.   I do not fear it, I have seen you both,   245
But since he is bettered, we have therefore odds.

LAERTES.   This is too heavy: let me see another.

HAMLET.   This likes me well, these foils have all a length?

OSRIC.   Ay my good lord.   *Prepare to play.*

KING.   Set me the stoups of wine upon that table: 250
If Hamlet give the first or second hit,
Or quit in answer of the third exchange,
Let all the battlements their ordnance fire.

---

disapproval   226–7 **That I have ... brother** (that it was accidental, not
"purposed")   227 **in nature** with regard to filial affection and duty   229 **in . . . honour**
with regard to my reputation   231 **masters** experts   232 **voice and precedent** opinion
based on precedent   **of peace** for reconcilement   233 **name ungored** reputation
uninjured   236 **frankly** freely   238 **foil** (1) the blunted sword with which they fence (2)
leaf of metal set under a jewel to make it shine more brilliantly   240 **Stick firey off** show in
shining contrast   242 **Cousin** kinsman   246 **bettered** either (a) judged to be better, or (b)
better trained   247 **another** (the unbated and poisoned sword)   248 **likes** pleases   **all a**
all the same   250 **stoups** goblets   252 **quit in answer of** score a draw in

The king shall drink to Hamlet's better breath,
And in the cup an union shall he throw,   255
Richer than that which four successive kings
In Denmark's crown have worn: give me the cups,
And let the kettle to the trumpet speak,
The trumpet to the cannoneer without,
The cannons to the heavens, the heaven to earth,   260
'Now the king drinks to Hamlet.' Come begin.
And you the judges bear a wary eye.

Trumpets the while.

HAMLET.   Come on sir.
LAERTES.   Come my lord.

They play.

HAMLET.   One.
LAERTES.   No.
HAMLET.   Judgment.
OSRIC.   A hit, a very palpable hit.

Flourish. Drum, trumpets and shot.
A piece goes off.

LAERTES.   Well, again.
KING.   Stay, give me drink. Hamlet, this pearl is thine.   265
Here's to thy health: give him the cup.
HAMLET.   I'll play this bout first, set it by a while.
Come.

[They play.]

Another hit. What say you?
LAERTES.   A touch, a touch, I do confess't.
KING.   Our son shall win.
QUEEN.   He's fat and scant of breath.   270
Here Hamlet, take my napkin, rub thy brows.

[She takes Hamlet's cup.]

The queen carouses to thy fortune, Hamlet.
HAMLET.   Good madam.
KING.   Gertrude, do not drink.
QUEEN.   I will my lord, I pray you pardon me.
KING.   [*Aside.*] It is the poisoned cup, it is too late.   275
HAMLET.   I dare not drink yet madam: by and by.
QUEEN.   Come, let me wipe thy face.
LAERTES.   [*To the King.*] My lord, I'll hit him now.

---

255 **union** large
pearl   258 **kettle** kettle drum   264 **s.d. piece** i.e. of ordnance   270 **fat** sweating (sweat
was thought to be melted body fat)   271 **napkin** handkerchief   272 **carouses** drinks (a full

KING.   I do not think't.

LAERTES.   [*Aside.*] And yet 'tis almost 'gainst my conscience.

HAMLET.   Come for the third Laertes, you do but dally,   280
               I pray you pass with your best violence,
               I am afeard you make a wanton of me.

LAERTES.   Say you so? Come on.
                                           Play.

OSRIC.   Nothing neither way.   [*They break off.*]

LAERTES.   Have at you now.   [*Wounds Hamlet.*]
                   In scuffling they change rapiers.

KING.   Part them, they are incensed.   285

HAMLET.   Nay, come again.   [*The Queen falls.*]

OSRIC.   Look to the queen there, ho!

                   [*Hamlet wounds Laertes.*]

HORATIO.   They bleed on both sides. How is it, my lord?

OSRIC.   How is't, Laertes?

LAERTES.   Why as a woodcock to my own springe, Osric,
               I am justly killed with mine own treachery.   290

HAMLET.   How does the queen?

KING.   She sounds to see them bleed.

QUEEN.   No, no, the drink, the drink, O my dear Hamlet,
               The drink, the drink, I am poisoned.   [*Dies.*]

HAMLET.   O villainy! ho! let the door be locked,
               Treachery, seek it out!   295

LAERTES.   It is here Hamlet. Hamlet, thou art slain,
               No medicine in the world can do thee good,
               In thee there is not half an hour of life,
               The treacherous instrument is in thy hand,
               Unbated and envenomed. The foul practice   300
               Hath turned itself on me, lo, here I lie
               Never to rise again: thy mother's poisoned:
               I can no more: the king, the king's to blame.

HAMLET.   The point envenomed too:
               Then venom, to thy work.   *Hurts the King.* 305

ALL.   Treason! treason!

KING.   O yet defend me friends, I am but hurt.

HAMLET.   Here, thou incestuous, murderous, damnèd Dane,

---

draught)   281 **pass** thrust   282 **make a wanton of me** are indulging me like a spoiled child   284 **Nothing neither way** a draw   285 **Have . . . now** (the bout is over when Laertes attacks Hamlet and catches him off guard)   289 **woodcock** snipe-like bird (believed to be foolish and therefore easily trapped)   **springe** trap   291 **sounds** swoons   300 **Unbated** not blunted   **practice** plot   307 **but hurt** only wounded

Drink off this potion: is thy union here?
Follow my mother. *King dies.*

LAERTES. He is justly served, 310
It is a poison tempered by himself:
Exchange forgiveness with me, noble Hamlet,
Mine and my father's death come not upon thee,
Nor thine on me. *Dies.*

HAMLET. Heaven make thee free of it, I follow thee. 315
I am dead, Horatio; wretched queen, adieu.
You that look pale, and tremble at this chance,
That are but mutes, or audience to this act,
Had I but time, as this fell sergeant Death
Is strict in his arrest, O I could tell you— 320
But let it be; Horatio, I am dead,
Thou livest, report me and my cause aright
To the unsatisfied.

HORATIO. Never believe it;
I am more an antique Roman than a Dane:
Here's yet some liquor left.

HAMLET. As thou'rt a man, 325
Give me the cup, let go, by heaven I'll ha't.
O God, Horatio, what a wounded name,
Things standing thus unknown, shall live behind me.
If thou didst ever hold me in thy heart,
Absènt thee from felicity awhile, 330
And in this harsh world draw thy breath in pain
To tell my story. *A march afar off, and shot within.*
What warlike noise is this?

OSRIC. Young Fortinbras with conquest come from Poland,
To th'ambassadors of England gives
This warlike volley.

HAMLET. O I die Horatio, 335
The potent poison quite o'er-crows my spirit,
I cannot live to hear the news from England,
But I do prophesy th'election lights
On Fortinbras, he has my dying voice,
So tell him, with th'occurrents more and less 340

---

309 **union** (1) pearl
(2) union with Gertrude in death   311 **tempered** mixed   313 **come. . . thee** are not to be
blamed on you   315 **free** guiltless   318 **mutes** actors without speaking parts   319 **fell
sergeant** cruel sheriff's officer (who summoned one to court)   323 **unsatisfied**
uninformed   324 **antique Roman** ancient Roman (who considered suicide
honorable)   336 **o'er-crows** overpowers, conquers (fr. cockfighting)   **spirit** vital
force   338 **election** (for King of Denmark)   339 **voice** vote   340 **occurrents**

        Which have solicited—the rest is silence.   *Dies.*

HORATIO.   Now cracks a noble heart: good night sweet prince,
        And flights of angels sing thee to thy rest.
        Why does the drum come hither?

                 Enter FORTINBRAS *and English*
                 Ambassadors, with drum, colours,
                 and attendants.

FORTINBRAS.
        Where is this sight?

HORATIO.   What is it you would see? 345
        If aught of woe, or wonder, cease your search.

FORTINBRAS.
        This quarry cries on havoc. O proud death,
        What feast is toward in thine eternal cell,
        That thou so many princes at a shot
        So bloodily hast struck?

AMBASSADOR.   The sight is dismal,   350
        And our affairs from England come too late;
        The ears are senseless that should give us hearing,
        To tell him his commandment is fulfilled,
        That Rosencrantz and Guildenstern are dead:
        Where should we have our thanks?

HORATIO.   Not from his mouth,355
        Had it th'ability of life to thank you;
        He never gave commandment for their death;
        But since so jump upon this bloody question,
        You from the Polack wars, and you from England
        Are here arrived, give order that these bodies   360
        High on a stage be placèd to the view,
        And let me speak to th'yet unknowing world
        How these things came about; so shall you hear
        Of carnal, bloody and unnatural acts,
        Of accidental judgments, casual slaughters,   365
        Of deaths put on by cunning and forced cause,
        And in this upshot, purposes mistook,

---

occurrences   **more and less** great and small   341 **solicited** incited me   347 **quarry . . .**
havoc heap of dead bodies proclaims slaughter done here (fr. warfare: "cry havoc"=signal to
ravage)   348 **toward** in preparation   352 **ears** (of Claudius)   358 **jump**
opportunely   **question** matter   364 **carnal . . . unnatural acts** adultery, murder, and
incest (by Claudius)   365 **judgments** deaths that will bring the deceased to judgment (of
Ophelia and Gertrude)   **casual** unpremediated (as Polonius's)   366 **deaths** (of Rosencrantz and Guildenstern)   **put on** prompted by   **forced cause** being forced to act in
self-defense   367–8 **purposes . . . heads** plots gone wrong and destroying their inventors

Fall'n on th'inventors' heads: all this can I
Truly deliver.

FORTINBRAS.   Let us haste to hear it,
And call the noblest to the audience.   370
For me, with sorrow I embrace my fortune;
I have some rights of memory in this kingdom,
Which now to claim my vantage doth invite me.

HORATIO.   Of that I shall have also cause to speak,
And from his mouth whose voice will draw on more: 375
But let this same be presently performed,
Even while men's minds are wild, lest more mischance
On plots and errors happen.

FORTINBRAS.   Let four captains
Bear Hamlet like a soldier to the stage,
For he was likely, had he been put on,   380
To have proved most royal; and for his passage,
The soldiers' music and the rite of war
Speak loudly for him:
Take up the bodies, such a sight as this,
Becomes the field, but here shows much amiss.   385
Go bid the soldiers shoot.

Exeunt marching: after the which a peal
of ordnance are shot off.

FINIS.

(Laertes and the king)   372 **of memory** remembered   373 **vantage** advantageous
position   375 **draw on more** influence more (votes)   376 **this same** this telling of the
story   **presently** immediately   377 **wild** upset   378 **On** on top of   380 **put on** i.e. the
throne   381 **passage** i.e. to the next world

Textual Notes

I, i   63 **sledded Polacks** Malone em.; Q2: "sleaded pollax"; F: "sledded Pollax"   65 **jump** Q2; F: "iust"   93 **co-mart** Q2; F: "Cov'nant"   98 **lawless** Q2; F: "Landlesse"   108–25 Q2; F omits   116–17 line probably missing between these two   127 **s.d.** Q2: "It spreads his armes"

     I, ii   38 **delated** Q2; F: "dilated" [detailed]   129 **sullied** Q2: "sallied", which also meant "tainted"; F: "solid"   149 **even she** F; not in Q2   175 **to drink deep** F; Q2: "for to drinke"   198 **waste** Q2, F; Q1: "vast"   237 **very like** F; not in Q2, which does not repeat

     I, iii   21 **sanctity** F; Q2: "safety"   65 **comrade** F; Q2: "courage"=young blood   109 **Running** Collier em.; Q2: "Wrong"; F: "Roaming"   130 **bonds** Q2, F; Theobald emends "bawds"

     I, iv   17–38 omitted in F, possibly because the wife of James I was a Dane   36 **evil** Keightley em.; Q2: "eale"   37 **of a doubt** Steevens emends to "often dout" [put out]; Tannenbaum to "oft adulter"   49 **interred** Q2; F: "enurn'd"

     I, v   20 **fretful** F; Q2: "fearful"   33 **rots** F; Q2: "rootes"   62 **hebona** Q2; F: "Hebenon"   95 **stiffly** F; Q2: "swiftly"   132 **Look you** F; Q2 omits

     II, i   38 **warrant** F; Q2: "wit"   39 **sullies** F; Q2: "sallies" (cf.I,ii, 129)

     II, ii   12 **haviour** Q2; F: "humour"=disposition   73 **threescore** Q2; F: "three"   137 **winking** F; Q2: "working"   146 **repelled** Q2; F: "repulsed"   227 **cap** F; Q2: "lap"   236–64 **Let me . . . attended** F; not in Q2   350 **'Sblood** Q2; F omits blasphemy, censored by an act of 1606   422 **affection** Q2; F: "affectation"   550 **'swounds** F omits   556 **O vengeance!** F; not in Q2   558 **father** Q4; Q2, F omit   562 **scullion** F; Q2: "stallion"=prostitute of either sex

     III, i   1 **conference** Q2; F: "circumstance"   46 **loneliness** F; Q2: "lowlines"   48 **sugar** Q2; F: "surge"   72 **disprized** F; Q2: "despiz'd"   86 **pitch** Q2; F: "pith"=importance   87 **awry** Q2; F: "away"   152 **expectancy** F; Q2: "expectation"

     III, ii   64 **co-mingled** F; Q2: "comedled"   126 **s.d. condole** Q2; F: "lament"   **harsh** Q2; F: "loath and unwilling"   155 **For . . . love** Q2; it may be a first draft of line 156, as there is no rhyming line

     III, iii   15 **cess** Q2; F: "cease"   17 **O 'tis** Wilson em.; Q2: "or it is"   25 **about** Q2; F: "upon"   79 **hire and salary** F; Q2: "base and silly"

     III, iv   50 **heated** Q2; F: "tristfull"   90 **grained** F; Q2: "greeved"   102 **s.d.** Q1; not in Q2, F   162 **evil** Theobald em.; Q2: "devill"   179 **This** Q2; F: "Thus"

     IV, i   40 **so haply slander** Capell em. fr. Theobald, for half-line omitted in Q2 and F

     IV, ii   16 **apple** Q2; F: "ape"   27 **Hide fox . . . after** F; not in Q2

     IV, v   9 **aim** F; Q2: "yawne"   37 **ground** Q2; F: "grave"   73 **and now behold** Q2; not in F   86 **Feeds on his** Q2: "Feeds on this"; F: "keepes on his"   159–61 **Nature . . . loves** F; Q2 omits   208 **funeral** Q2; F: "buriall"

     IV, vii   8 **greatness** Q2; F omits   52 **devise** Q2; F: "advise"   87 **topped** Q2; F: "past"   158 **prepared** F; Q2: "prefard"=proferred   166 **aslant** F; Q2: "ascaunt"=sidewise   177 **tunes** F, Q1; Q2: "laudes"=hymns   191 **drowns** Q2; F: "doubts", em. by Knight to "douts"=extinguishes

     V, i   67 **clawed** Q2; F: "caught"   79 **meant** F; Q2: "went"   102 **scarcely** Q2; F: "hardly"   147 **sexton** F; Q2: "sixteene"   158 **three-and-twenty** Q2, F; Q1: "this dozen"   175 **grinning** Q2; F: "Jeering"   201 **s.d. Doctor of Divinity** Wilson fr. Q2 speech heads   220 **sage** F; Q2: "a"   241 **s.d.** Q1

     V, ii   57 **Why . . . employment** F; Q2 omits   68–80 **To . . . here** F; not in Q2   78 **court** Rowe em.; F: "count"   103–34 **Sir . . . unfellowed** Q2; F omits and reads: "Sir, you are not ignorant of what excellence Laertes is at/ his weapon"   174 **bevy** Q2; F: "breede"   176 **out of an** Q2; F: "outward"   **yeasty** Q2; F: "histy"   177–8 **fond and winnowed** F; Q2: "prophane and trennowed"   205 **has** F; Q: "of";   206 **what is't** F; Q: "knowes what ist"   246 **bettered** F; Q: "better"   327 **God** Q2; F: "good"